I0869328

Texas Place Names

NUMBER TWENTY-TWO

Clifton and Shirley Caldwell Texas Heritage Series

Texas Place Names

EDWARD CALLARY
WITH JEAN K. CALLARY

University of Texas Press, Austin

Publication of this work was made possible in part by support from Clifton and Shirley Caldwell and a challenge grant from the National Endowment for the Humanities.

Printed in the United States of America
First edition, 2020

♾ The paper used in this book meets the minimum requirements of ANSI/NISO Z39.48-1992 (R1997) (Permanence of Paper).

Library of Congress Cataloging-in-Publication Data

Names: Callary, Edward, author. | Callary, Jean K., author.
Title: Texas place names / Edward Callary, Jean K. Callary.
Description: First edition. | Austin : University of Texas Press, 2020. | Includes bibliographical references and index.
Identifiers: LCCN 2019030203
ISBN 978-1-4773-2064-8 (paperback)
ISBN 978-1-4773-2065-5 (library e-book)
ISBN 978-1-4773-2066-2 (non-library e-book)
Subjects: LCSH: Names, Geographical—Texas. | Texas—History.
Classification: LCC F384 .C35 2020 | DDC 976.4—dc23
LC record available at https://lccn.loc.gov/2019030203

DOI:10.7560/320648

Dedicated to the memory of Fred Tarpley:
"Mister Texas Names"

Contents

INTRODUCTION

This is a book about the place names of Texas—where they came from and how they were created. We all have a natural interest in place names, especially odd and unusual names, of which Texas has its share—Bug Tussel, Ding Dong, Telephone, Uncertain—but remarkable names are only a fraction of the thousands of names that make up the Texas "namescape."

Place names don't just happen: They have a reason and a purpose. Texas place names tell stories about the people, places, and events that contributed to Texas history and its constantly changing culture. Consider Hanna Strobridge: It's late in 1882 and she's been reading a Jules Verne novel in which Marfa Strogoff is a central character. Given the opportunity to recommend a name for a new Texas town, she offered Marfa, and so it is today. In 1870 Ossamus Hitch Methvin climbed to the top of Rock Hill in Gregg County and was so impressed by the "long view" across the prairie that he named the railroad town Longview. In 1936 Dion McDonald opened a store in Delta County; contrary to his wishes the store, and later the community, became known as Jot 'Em Down after the fictional store kept by Lum and Abner on their popular radio show. In 1901 a new town was named Dalhart because it straddled the Dallam-Hartley county line, and in 2005 the town of Clark, north of Fort Worth, changed its name to Dish after Dish Network, offered free satellite TV service to all residents for ten years.

Texas is a big state, really big—over 270,000 square miles—and needs many names for simple geolocation, for getting from one place to another. How many

Texas place names are there? That depends on what you count, and when. Places may have had several names over time. They may change their names for reasons that are cultural (San Angela became San Angelo), historical (Waterloo became Austin), or strictly personal (Pease became Margaret in honor of the postmaster's four-year-old daughter). Sometimes a town leaves a state (Booker moved south from Oklahoma to be close to a railroad line; most of Texhoma left Texas when the Oklahoma state line moved south), or even a country (Brownsville was no longer in Mexico after the 1848 Treaty of Guadalupe Hidalgo).

Then, too, Texas has its share of ghost towns. As the last residents move on, maps age and are consigned to archives, and the names of once flourishing places disappear from public view and private memory. Offsetting the loss of names, Texas, like most states, gains new names daily. There is constant naming or renaming of schools, parks, streets, and newly populated places—especially residential tracts with names that are part pastoral lifestyle and part oxymoron—Westlake Hills (Austin), The Falls at Dry Creek (Houston), Wolf Ranch (Georgetown).

The best estimate we have of the number of Texas names is from GNIS, the Geographic Names Information System, the nation's digital gazetteer. As of early 2019, GNIS listed more than 115,000 Texas names. The greatest share, nearly 14,000, named churches; the least, a pair of tunnels (Baytown Tunnel in Harris County and the Quitaque Railway Tunnel in Floyd County) and a single crater (Odessa Meteor Crater in Ector County).

The Data

From the GNIS list we took the 10,188 names of Populated Places, added the names of the 254 Texas counties, added the names of cities and towns found in the 2019–2020 *Texas Almanac* that were not in GNIS, and spent the next three years tracking down place name origins in county and state histories; county, state, and community archives; theses and dissertations; historical society publications; church histories; personal diaries; local interviews; and websites beyond number—wherever reliable information on the sources of the names could be found. Several resources were especially valuable. *The Handbook of Texas Online* has been a constant and indispensable companion. However, because the *Handbook*, like all sources, is fallible, whenever possible the entries in this book have been verified from primary sources such as census records; birth, death, and marriage records; land survey records; property sale and tax records; cemetery inscriptions; and obituary notices.

In addition to the *Handbook*, we are indebted to the library of the Dolph Briscoe Center for American History at the University of Texas, Austin. The extensive Briscoe collection and the help we received from the Briscoe's knowledgeable and personable staff, notably Catherine Best, are especially appreciated. Also of great value was the Fred Tarpley collection at the Gee Library, Texas A&M University–Commerce, and the help of archivist Michael Barera. Fred Tarpley, a student at what was then East Texas State Teachers College and a career faculty member at Texas A&M–Commerce,

was a master folklorist and an indefatigable collector of names, especially the names of northeast Texas. His books, field records, manuscripts, and clippings enlighten many of the entries in this book.

Pronunciation Guide

A broad transcription guide indicates local pronunciation where it might not be obvious from the spelling (Cuevitas [kwuh VEET uhs], DeKalb [dee KAB]). Residents of Wied live in the town of "weed"; Gruene is "green"; and if you don't want to be spotted as an outsider, when in Elgin remember to say [EL gin] (as in "begin"), not [EL jin].

Organization of the Entries

The content of entries varies according to the available information, but each entry begins with the place name followed by either the local pronunciation (if different from what the spelling would suggest) and the county of location (in parentheses). Some descriptions are brief—the name of an early settler or the first post office; others offer historical or cultural information if it adds to the source of the name or the circumstances surrounding its adoption. Post office information follows. Texas counties are included in the alphabetical entries, and precede identical place names.

Some examples:

NADA [NAY duh] (Colorado) Organized about 1890 by Czechs and Germans from the area around Frelsburg. Named from Czech *naděje*, "hope." PO 17 Apr 1894, PM William Engbrock.

NAT (Nacogdoches) Nathaniel (Nat) Jarrell was a dry goods salesman and the first postmaster 12 Apr 1895.

NATALIA (Medina) The Medina Irrigation Company founded Natalia in 1912, named for Natalie Pearson, daughter of engineer Frederick Stark Pearson who built the dam that created Medina Lake in 1913. PO 19 Mar 1913, PM Thomas Ragsdale. See Pearson.

ZAPATA [zuh PAHT uh] (County) Created and organized 1858. Named for Antonio Zapata (c. 1800–1840), a pioneer rancher and military leader who fought against Santa Anna and the Mexican Centralist government in the 1830s.

* Names in small capital letters have their own entries.
* "See" indicates entries in which additional information regarding the community, the founder, the namer, or the namesake can be found.
* PO is the abbreviation for post office; PM is the abbreviation for postmaster.

Sources of the Names

SPANISH

Spanish has had an enormous influence on Texas names from the 16th century when Cabeza de Vaca named an island off the Texas coast Isla de Malhado, the "island of misfortune," to the present day, when developers open new subdivisions such as La Cima, a residential community in San

Marcos, and Vista Verde in Wimberly. There are more than two hundred names of Spanish origin in this book: A to Z (almost), they include Amarillo, Bosque, Charco, Dinero, Elmaton, Frio, Ganado, Hondo, El Indio, Jardin, Lagarto, Malvado, Nueces, Olmito, Penitas, Quemado, Realitos, Sandia, Tornillo, Val Verde, Ysleta, and Zavala.

POST OFFICES

For small settlements, the opening of a post office was an important event: the date often suggests the time when a cluster of buildings and a few citizens began to organize into a recognizable town, and also when the name, which may have been current for years, became at least somewhat official. The first postmaster was an important figure in the community and was often responsible for choosing the name of the office, which frequently became the name of the town. Since this is a book about names and not about postal history, we have generally omitted information on postmasters who followed the first postmaster of record and dates when the office may have closed unless these are important for understanding the name. For readers who are interested in more detailed post office information we recommend *Texas Post Offices by County*, by John J. Germann and Myron R. Janzen.

NATIVE AMERICANS

A few names, such as Navasota and Mobeetie, were taken directly from local Native American languages, but most Texas names that we think of as "Native American" were not used by Texas natives in the way place names are used today. Many were brought to Texas by Spanish explorers and settlers. A dozen or more are from Nahuatl (Aztec), taken into Spanish in Mexico, brought to Texas, and applied to local land features—names such as Comal, Mesquite, Helotes, and Anaqua. Others were transferred from Muskogean languages used as place names in southeastern states, especially Mississippi and Alabama—names such as Panola, Cusseta, and Opelika. More recently, Texas counties and towns were named in honor of local Native American leaders such as Quanah, Nocona, and Katemcy; others recognize Native American tribes resident in Texas, such as Badias, Tawakoni, and Wichita.

TRANSFERS

The names of former homes are powerful reminders of the lives settlers left behind. Memories may be preserved, at least for a generation or two, by applying an old name to a new home. German Settlers in Texas brought with them the names Dresden, Muenster, Nordheim, Oldenburg, and Hanover; Czech settlers brought Hranice, Vsetin, Hostyn, and Roznov. The "old country" may be less than an ocean away, but the sentiments are still the same: Settlers from Alabama brought the names Arcola, Dothan, and Huntsville; Mississippians brought Carthage, Como, and Oxford; Tennesseans brought Bedford, Lebanon, and Gallatin; Kentuckians brought Lancaster, Paducah, and Waterloo; Californians brought Chico and Pasadena; and Illinoisans brought Tuscola and Mahomet. Other names applied to new locations were chosen for their importance to the namers. Thus, Paris and Jeddo were named not by former Parisians or Japanese but by people who were taken by the name and by the cultures of France and Japan.

COMMEMORATIVE NAMES

A striking Texas naming tradition of the 19th century was commemoration: naming a town or county for a notable person, a military or political leader, or someone of importance to the community or to the namer. Texas counties and towns are named for American presidents George Washington, Thomas Jefferson, and James K. Polk; for the four presidents of the Republic of Texas, David Burnet, Sam Houston, Mirabeau Buonaparte Lamar, and Anson Jones; for Texas governors including James Pinckney Henderson, Jim Hogg, Sul Ross, and James Allred; for Texas historical figures such as Richard Andrews (the first soldier killed in the Texas Revolution), Alamo defenders Jim Bowie, George Cottle, David "Davy" Crockett, and William King (at age fifteen the youngest Texan to die at the Alamo); and for history-making ranchers such as Charles Goodnight and Oliver Loving, founders of the Goodnight-Loving Trail, which lives on in books, movies, and visitors' guides.

Beginning in 1850, when the first Texas railroad, the Buffalo Bayou, Brazos & Colorado Railway, was chartered, railroads have been a major influence on Texas naming, and most of the railroad names were commemorative. The San Antonio & Aransas Pass Railway named BenArnold for a sheriff, Edcouch for a banker, Edgar for an early settler, and Yoakum for a railroad traffic manager. The Texas Central Railway named Allen for a former Texas attorney general, Angus for a terminal agent, Burton for a carpenter, and Paige for a surveyor. The Santa Fe Railroad named Slaton for a chief engineer, Bradshaw for a landowner, Ballinger for a Galveston attorney and railroad investor, and Higgins for a financier. Railroad names and names of notable Texans aside, by far the most commemorative names, numbering in the hundreds, were given by the pioneers and settlers who established the first towns and post offices, which they named for themselves, a family member, or a local person of importance (often an early settler, the town physician, or a large landowner).

COMPRESSION AND BLENDING

Two or more words—usually names—may be compressed into one: Temple Doswell Smith established the First Bank of Fredericksburg in 1887 and became known as "banker Smith." The town of Bankersmith was named in his honor. Similarly, Maud Lowe O'Connor gave her name to the town of Maudlowe and Tom Ball gave his name to Tomball.

Blending is a kind of compression in which names are shortened and joined into a single word. Balmorhea is named for Ernest *Bal*com, Hugh *Mor*row, and John *Rhea*; Dalworthington Gardens for *Dal*las, Fort *Worth*, and Arl*ington*. South Texas land developers William *Har*ding and Samuel Lamar *Gill* were especially fond of blends. In the 1910s they founded Hargill, later named for themselves; in 1921 they founded Willamar, also named for themselves; and in 1924 they founded Lasara, named for their wives, *La*ura Harding and *Sara*h Gill.

Suffixing

A place name may be created by adding a suffix to an existing name or common noun. By far the most common suffix in Texas is "–ville": Pflugerville for Henry Pfluger, Coletoville for Coleto Creek, Pumpville for a railroad pumping station. Other frequent Texas name suffixes include:

CITY Custer City for George Armstrong Custer, Gun Barrel City for Gun Barrel Lane (Texas Hwy. 198)

-TOWN Stairtown for Oscar Stair, Smeltertown for the local copper smelter

-TON Belton for Bell County, Princeton for Prince Dowlen

-DALE Sisterdale for Sister Creeks, Tivydale for Joseph Tivy

-IA Flatonia for Friedrich Flato, Blanconia for Blanco Creek

-BURG Pittsburg for William Harrison Pitts, Fredericksburg for Prince Frederick of Prussia

-BORO Brownsboro for Ransom and Jemima Brown, Woodsboro for Tobias DeCantillon Wood

-LAND Sharyland for developer John Shary, Pearland for the local pear orchards

MISTAKES

Intended names may be changed during the naming process. In the 19th and early 20th centuries the handwritten names on post office applications were particularly vulnerable to change; they may have become illegible or been misread or misinterpreted. The US Post Office Department (so called until 1971 when it became the US Postal Service) inadvertently, and at times arbitrarily, changed names that were accepted with a shrug by townspeople pleased to have a post office with any name at all. Through postal mistakes at one level or another Pulaski became Plaska, Arthur became Authon, Pivot became Divot, and Valdosta became Valdasta.

WORDPLAY AND CREATIVE NAMING

Creativity is a hallmark of Texas names and it would add many pages to this book to do justice to the imagination and playfulness of Texas namers. A few examples will have to suffice: About 1900 the citizens of a fledgling town in Nacogdoches County requested a post office named Lucas. When that name was rejected because Texas already had a Lucas post office, the resourceful people spelled Lucas backward and resubmitted the application; it was approved as Sacul, the name of the town today. In like manner Walker became Reklaw, Waco became Ocaw, and Sunset became Tesnus. Place name wordplay can be both clever and subtle. A site on the King Ranch was to be named for Jim Wells; when this name was rejected by the Post Office Department, the name was resubmitted as Norias, Spanish for "wells." In 1881 William Gentry applied for a Gentry post office in Fannin County. When that name was rejected, Gentry resubmitted the requested name as Nobility, a clever synonym for Gentry.

POPULAR ETYMOLOGY

When the spelling of a name is unusual or when its origin is unknown, the name is often respelled in a more familiar form or people invent plausible stories to explain its origin. The family name of sheep rancher William Keliehor was respelled Keler when the post office application was submitted as Keelersville in 1895. Similarly, Wantz was respelled Vance to reflect the German pronunciation.

Consider Poetry, a town in Kaufman County. The origin of the name is uncertain, but several popular etymologies have been created that contribute to the folklore of Texas names. According to one, a peddler passing through came upon a ragged boy and an even more ragged dog and remarked, "Now that's a poor Tray if I ever saw one." Over time "poor Tray" became Poetry. According to another, a live oak tree in the town square became a meeting place where local writers read their poems. The "Poet's tree" became Poetry.

According to a well-traveled popular etymology, Nogalus Prairie in Trinity County was named from an incident in which horse thieves had to be hanged from a tree because no real gallows were available. The community became known as the town of No Gallows, which became Nogalus. The name, in fact, is from Spanish *nogal* "walnut." Names like Black Ankle, Oatmeal, and Point Blank lend themselves to fanciful explanations. You will find many such in this book—start with Laredo, it's got Texas written all over it.

PRONUNCIATION GUIDE

SYMBOL	AS IN	TEXAS PLACE NAMES
a	cat	DeKalb [dee KAB], Latium [LACH uhm]
ah	hot	Olney [AHL nee], Chillicothe [chil uh KAH thee]
ahr	are	Marquez [mahr KAY], Kennard [kuh NAHRD]
aw	raw	Van Alstyne [van AWL steen], Losoya [luh SAW yuh]
ay	say	Sagerton [SAY ger tuhn], Ganado [guh NAY do]
ch	itch	Weesatche [WEE sach], Zabcikville [ZAHB chik vil]
e	bet	Ysleta [is LET uh], Tenaha [TEN uh hah]
ee	me	Carmine [kar MEEN], Chireno [shuh REE no]
ehr	hair	Arah [EHR uh], Cuero [KWEHR o]
er	herd	Muellersville [MIL erz vil], Murchison [MERK i suhn]
eye	nice	Iatan [EYE tan], Celina [suh LEYE nuh]
g	go	Gholson [GOL suhn], Elgin [EL gin]
i	hit	Burnet [BUHR nit], Nix [NIKS]
ihr	ear	Brashear [bruh SHIHR], Lanier [luh NIHR]
j	edge	Giles [JEYELZ], Avinger [A vin jer]
kw	quick	Cuero [KWEHR o], Anaqua [uh NAH kwuh]
ng	finger	Mingus [MING guhs], Blanco [BLANG ko]
o	toe	Culleoka [kuhl ee O kuh], Howth [HOWTH]

oo	boot	Blewett [BLOO it], Cotulla [kuh TOO luh]
or	tour	Orozimbo [or uh ZIM bo], Missouri City[muh ZOR uh]
ow	how	Crowley [KROW lee], Lindenau [LIN duh now]
oy	toy	La Joya [luh HOY yuh], Etoile [ee TOYL]
sh	shot	Kosciusko [kuh SHOOS ko], Schroeder [SHRAY der]
th	bath	Goldthwaite [GOL thwayt], Theon [THEE ahn]
u	foot	Hood [HUD], Hooks [HUKS]
uh	cut	Annona [uh NO nuh], Upton [UHP tuhn]
yoo	cute	Buda [BYOO duh], Neuville [NYOO vil]

Texas Place Names

Texas Towns & Counties

A

ABBOTT (Hill) Abbott was founded on the line of the Missouri–Kansas–Texas Railroad (aka The KATY) in 1881 and named for Joseph Abbott, Hill County lawyer and district judge. Abbott served in the Texas Legislature in the early 1870s and was a five-term US Congressman in the 1890s. PO 14 June 1882, PM Winston Treadwell.

ABERDEEN (Collingsworth) Founded in 1889 as headquarters of the Rocking Chair Ranch. Named for Scottish politician John Hamilton-Gordon, 1st Marquess of Aberdeen and Temair, known at the time as the Earl of Aberdeen. Hamilton-Gordon and his father-in-law, the 1st Baron Tweedmouth, were major investors in the Rocking Chair and other Texas ranches. PO 28 Dec 1889, PM Henry J. Nesper. See Wellington.

ABERFOYLE (Hunt) Farmer Macon A. Lucky proposed the name for the Aberfoyle textile mills of Belmont, NC, his former home. PO 3 June 1884, PM John R. King.

ABERNATHY (Hale, Lubbock) Named for Monroe G. Abernathy, surveyor for the Santa Fe Railroad and treasurer of the South Plains Investment Company that laid out the town in 1909. When the railroad bypassed Bartonsite, a number of businesses moved southeast and joined Abernathy at trackside. PO 13 Jan 1910, PM James Anderson.

ABILENE [AB uh leen] (Jones, Taylor) Abilene was founded in 1880, anticipating construction of the Texas & Pacific Railway. Rancher Claiborne Walker Merchant, known as the "Father of Abilene," owned much of the townsite and chose the name for the cattle town of Abilene, KS, itself named from the Biblical Abilene, taken to mean "meadow, grassy plain." PO 14 Feb 1881, PM Henry Montgomery.

ABINGTON (Childress) Probably named for William H. Abington who was born in Childress in 1921 and represented Tarrant County in the Texas Legislature 1949–1953.

ABLES SPRINGS (Kaufman) Founded about 1878 when James and Eliza Abels donated land to the Methodist Episcopal Church in honor of James Abels's father, Ezekiel, the first site owner.

ABNER (Kaufman) Abner Johnson, slave holder, founder of Sunnyside Plantation, and sheriff of Chicot County, Arkansas Territory from the 1820s, became a Kaufman County landowner in 1849. The Johnson's Point PO opened 13 June 1871 and was changed to Terrell 23 Sept 1873. Abner Johnson's son, William Oscar, opened the Abner PO 3 Sept 1885.

ABRAM (Hidalgo) Named for Abraham (Abram) Dillard, a Texas Ranger, county sheriff, and tax collector; considered the first Anglo settler in the area then known as *Ojo de Agua* "waterhole." PO 25 May 1901, PM Francisca Hawkins.

ACADEMY (Bell) See Little River.

ACALA [uh KAY luh] (Hudspeth) Named for Acala cotton, the long-staple cotton found growing wild near Acala, Mexico, in the early 20th century. Acala, Chiapas, Mexico, was named from Nahuatl (Aztec) "place of boats." PO 19 Nov 1925, PM Julia A. Vaughan.

ACAMPO [uh KAM po] (Shackelford) From Spanish *acampar* "to camp." The site was likely named for the community of boxcars in which workers "camped" while building the Missouri–Kansas–Texas Railroad.

ACE (Polk) Smith's Field or Smithfield, named for early settler Robert Smith, was renamed 29 Jan 1915 when Asa Caswell Emanuel, known from his initials as Ace, opened the post office. His son, Asa Harvey Emanuel, was the second PM in 1916.

ACKERLY (Dawson, Martin) Paul Ackerly, a New York and Atlanta textile and wool merchant, was hired in 1923 to divide the Slaughter Ranch into residential and farming tracts. PO Feb 1924, PM Willis Wilson.

ACME (Hardeman) About 1890 the Lone Star Plaster Company began mining the local gypsum deposits. According to local historian Paul Jones, the name likely refers to the cement and plaster products that were known as "Acme goods" because of their quality and desirability. PO 17 June 1898, PM Thomas Flynn.

ACTON (Hood) By one local story, shopkeeper Clarence Hollis chose the name for his first sweetheart whose family name was Acton; by another, Acton is an adaptation of Oak Town, for the many oak trees in the area. Acton, however, is a popular place name, occurring in more than a dozen states and Acton, TX, is more likely a transfer, perhaps from Acton, AL, or Acton, GA, themselves transfers from Actons in New England, in turn transfers from the first Acton in Cheshire, England. PO 13 Aug 1861, PM Miles Hensley.

ACUFF [AY kuhf] (Lubbock) Named for brothers Michael and Thomas Acuff, born in Tennessee, landowners and developers who arrived in the area in the 1890s. PO 2 May 1903, PM Terrell B. Williamson.

ACWORTH (Red River) Named by James H. Cox for his former home, Acworth, Cobb County, GA, which was named for Acworth, Sullivan County, NH, itself named for Sir Jacob Acworth, 18th century surveyor for the British Royal Navy. PO 10 May 1902, PM Frank H. Clark.

ADDICKS (Harris) Founded by German immigrants in the early 1850s and named for Johann Heinrich Eidecks (Henry Addicks) who emigrated from Oldenburg, Germany in the early 1850s. PO 23 Sept 1884, PM William Schulz.

ADDIELOU [ad ee LOO] (Red River) Samuel H. Patterson established the PO 23 Sept 1916 and named the office for Addie Lou Walker of Kanawha.

ADDISON (Dallas) About 1890 the St. Louis, Arkansas & Texas Railway established Noell Junction, a coaling station named for site owner Sidney Noell. The name was changed when James Adkins opened the Addison PO 19 Feb 1904, named for Addison Wilkerson Robertson who relocated from Sulphur Rock, AR, in the late 1860s.

ADDRAN [A dran] (Hopkins) In the early 1870s, brothers *Add*ison and *Ran*dolph Clark founded the AddRan Male and Female College in Fort Worth, a preparatory school and predecessor of Texas Christian University. PO 8 Dec 1890, PM Henry G. Ewing.

ADELL (Parker) Founded about 1889 when John R. Fondren opened a general store. The next year, when merchant Alex Sanger was asked to choose a name for the post office, he reportedly replied "name it for my daughter Adell, the prettiest girl in Dallas." PO 19 Sept 1890, PM Bentley Barton. See Advance.

ADINA [uh DEE nuh] (Lee) About 1890 Robert (Richard) Leonidas Cain donated land for a school and a cemetery. When Edward L. Sorelle established the PO 6 Sept 1895, Cain suggested the name Adina, apparently for the heroine of Henry James's serialized novel *Adina*, published in the 1870s.

ADKINS (Bexar) William Adkins Jones, a cotton ginner and merchant, donated land for a station on the Galveston, Harrisburg & San Antonio Railway in the mid-1880s. Jones opened the Adkins PO 1 Apr 1896.

ADRIAN (Oldham) Founded in the early 1900s when the Chicago, Rock Island & Gulf Railway surveyed the area. Apparently named for Adrian Cullen, a local landowner about whom little is known. PO 2 Dec 1908, PM Frederick Ritterspach.

ADSUL [AD suhl] (Newton) In 1906 George *Ad*ams, Jr. and Thomas B. *Sul*livan organized the Adsul Lumber Company. PO 6 Mar 1907, PM James K. Sullivan.

ADVANCE (Parker) Merchant Bentley Ballard Barton, a founder of BARTONVILLE in the early 1880s, moved to ADELL where he opened the post office in 1890, and to the site of Advance where he kept a general store and was the first postmaster 7 May 1894. Barton's reasons for choosing the name are unknown.

ADY [AY dee] (Potter) Established in 1887 as a switch on the Fort Worth & Denver City Railway, named for George Ady of Denver, general passenger agent of the FW&DC.

AFTON (Dickens) The local account is that schoolteacher Myra Kelly chose the name for a nearby stream that brought to mind the song "Flow Gently, Sweet Afton," based upon Robert Burns's poem of the same name. PO 24 Apr 1900, PM James Jones.

AGNES (Parker, Wise) First known as Barnard's Store for the general store opened by Brazilla and Malisse Barnard in the mid-1870s. The name was changed when Abner Wilson established the Agnes post office 7 July 1879 named for Agnes Mull, two-year-old daughter of pioneering physician William F. Mull.

AGUA DULCE [ah wuh DOOL see] (Nueces) Named from Agua Dulce (Spanish "sweet water") Creek. PO 12 Aug 1908, PM James Petray.

AGUA NUEVA [ah wuh noo AY vuh] (Jim Hogg) *Agua Nueva de Abajo* "lower new water," the name of a tract of land granted to Juan Ramírez in the 1850s, shortened when Sixto Garcia opened the PO 10 June 1910.

AGUILARES [ah guh LAHR uhs] (Webb) Named about 1880, reportedly for Francisco,

José, Librado, Locario, and Próspero Aguilar, 1870s settlers. PO 20 Oct 1890, PM Herbert A. Grantham.

AIKEN [AY kin] (Floyd) Formerly known as Floco, from *Flo*yd *Co*unty. Formally named in 1922 for townsite owners Frank and Ziddie Aiken. PO 18 Oct 1915 as Floco; changed to Aiken 22 Sept 1922, PM Robert E. Jones.

AIKIN GROVE [AY kin grov] (Red River) Named for an Aikin family. Alexander Aikin from Mississippi began farming in the area about 1890. Alexander Mack Aikin, Jr., who was born in Aikin Grove, was Texas's longest-serving legislator as a member of the Texas House or Senate from 1933 through 1979.

ALAMO (Hidalgo) In 1909 John Beamer, founder of the Alamo Land and Sugar Company, bought Ebenezer Station and contracted with the Alamo Townsite Company to lay out the town of Alamo and promote the sale of residential and business lots. Alamo was possibly named from the Alamo Mission in San Antonio; however, according to local histories, from the 18th century the area was known as *Agostadero de Alamo* "cottonwood pasture," from which the town's organizers likely took the name, influenced by the Alamo Mission. The Forum PO, opened 29 Aug 1919, was changed to Alamo 30 Oct 1919, PM Lewis E. Wigton.

ALANREED (Gray) Alanreed, also known as Gouge Eye for a barroom brawl in which "eye balls were gouged out," was laid out by the Choctaw, Oklahoma & Texas Railroad in 1901. The town was reportedly named for the Allan & Reed construction firm. PO 20 Mar 1886 as Eldridge; changed to Alanreed 7 Feb 1902, PM Robert Y. Mangum.

ALAZAN [al uh ZAHN] (Nacogdoches) Named from Alazan (Spanish "sorrel, chestnut colored") Creek, likely named for the color of the water. PO 14 May 1901, PM John N. Rogers.

ALBA [AL buh] (Wood) Alba was founded about 1880 when the Missouri–Kansas–Texas Railroad built through the area. By one local account Alba was named for a relative of a KATY official; by another the town was intended for Anglo settlers only and was named from Latin *alba* "white." However, Alba was reportedly known as Albia which suggests a transfer from Albia, KY, or from the railroad town of Albia, IA. PO 4 Oct 1881, PM Henry R. Thrasher.

ALBANY (Shackelford) Named in 1875 by William Cruger, Shackelford county sheriff and contractor for the Texas Central Railway, for his former home, Albany, GA, named in 1836 for Albany, NY, itself named for James, Duke of York, Albany and Ulster, later King James II. PO 1 Aug 1876, PM Henry C. Jacobs.

ALBERT (Gillespie) Albert was first known as Martinsburg, founded in the late 1870s by settlers from Fredericksburg, TX. The town was formally named 24 May 1892 when Wilhelmina Sophie "Minnie" Luckenbach opened the PO that she named for her husband, Carl Albert Luckenbach. See Luckenbach.

ALEDO [uh LEE do] (Parker) Littleberry Rudolph Fawks established the Parker PO 14 June

1880. Two years later the name was changed to Aledo, apparently suggested by an official of the Texas & Pacific Railway for Aledo, IL. PO 25 May 1882 as Aledo, PM Eli J. McConnell.

ALEMAN [AYL muhn] (Hamilton) In the early 20th century the community was known as Piggtown for saloon keeper Mack Pigg and landowner Jackson Pigg, which gave rise to a number of colorful comments and descriptions of the town. Later renamed Aleman (Spanish "German"), which was often used by Mexican workers to refer to the largely German population. PO 20 Apr 1914, PM Gideon P. Toland.

ALEXANDER (Erath) Probably named for Alexander Hutchison who built the Texas Central Railway station in 1881. The Harpers Mill PO, established 21 Aug 1876; changed to Alexander 17 May 1881, PM John D. St. Clair.

ALFRED (Jim Wells) Founded in 1888 as Driscoll, named for rancher Robert Driscoll. The Driscoll PO, established 17 Jan 1890 by PM Thomas Charles Wright, was changed to Alfred 20 June 1905, named for Alfred Wright, son of Thomas Charles Wright.

ALGERITA [al juh REET uh] (San Saba) Charles C. Yarborough opened the Algerita PO in his general store 19 Aug 1885. The name was chosen by Yarborough or by Fred H. Wigzell, the second PM, for the Algerita shrub (*Mahonia trifoliolata*), also known as Currant-of-Texas, native to much of the Southwest.

ALGOA [al GO uh] (Galveston) Algoa was founded by the Leon and H. Blum (Bloom) Land Company of Galveston and named in honor of the October 1896 arrival of the Algoa, a British vessel and the largest cargo ship in the world at the time. The ship channel was deepened for the occasion and the Algoa was reportedly welcomed with a 100-gun salute. The celebrated ship was named from Algoa Bay, Portuguese for "lagoon bay," in South Africa. PO 14 Oct 1897, PM Louis Loeb. See Blum.

ALICE (Jim Wells) The San Antonio & Aransas Pass Railway established Bandana Station in the early 1880s. When the application for a post office to be named Kleberg for King Ranch manager Robert Justus Kleberg was denied, the request was resubmitted as Alice, for Alice Gertrudis King, daughter of King Ranch owners Richard and Henrietta King and wife of Robert Justus Kleberg. She was named in part for the *Rincón de Santa Gertrudis* and *Santa Gertrudis de la Garza* land grants of the early 1800s that were purchased in the early 1850s by Richard King and incorporated into the King Ranch. PO 22 Aug 1888, PM Frederick Nayer. See Kleberg, see King.

ALIEF [AY leef] (Harris) Platted as Dairy in 1894, the name was changed the next year for Alief Ozella (Ozelda) Magee who opened the PO 16 Aug 1895. Now part of greater Houston.

ALLAMOORE (Hudspeth) Named for Allie (Alla) Roberta Moore who opened the PO 9 Apr 1888.

ALLEN (Collin) Founded in 1872 with construction of the Texas Central Railway. Named for Ebenezer Allen, the last Attorney General of the Republic of Texas and business manager of the Galveston & Red River Railroad which became the Texas Central in 1856. PO 10 Jan 1876, PM James Franklin.

ALLEN'S POINT (Fannin) Wilson Bruce Allen brought his mother and siblings to Texas from Haywood County, TN, and established a sugarcane plantation on Honey Grove Creek in 1837.

ALLENDALE (Wichita) Founded in 1889 by Elbert J. *Allen* and Baltis *Dale* Hinkle. PO 6 Feb 1891 as Huff, PM Elbert J. Allen; changed to Allendale 15 Apr 1892, PM John B. Burton.

ALLENFARM (Brazos) Several local accounts claim the namesake is Robert A. Allen, a local plantation owner. However, his name appears on no known land records, leading the editors of the 1986 *Brazos County History* to devote a section of the Allenfarm entry to "the mystery of how the community got its name" (37). Adding to the mystery is the naming and renaming of the post office, which was established as Allenfarm by Augustus May Henslee 19 Jan 1885. The name was changed to Alligator in August 1888; changed back to Allenfarm in October 1888; changed to Ella in March 1890; changed again to Allenfarm in October 1893.

ALLENHURST (Matagorda) Founded about 1905 with construction of the St. Louis, Brownsville & Mexico Railway. Allenhurst is a blend of *Allen*town, for Allentown, PA, birthplace of Jeff N. Miller, vice president and general manager of the StLB&M, with *hurst*, German for "woods," added for effect. See Cranell.

ALLEYTON (Colorado) Named in the 1850s for Abraham, William, Rawson, and Thomas Alley, relatives from Missouri who settled in Texas in the early 1820s. PO 29 June 1860, PM Leander Cunningham.

ALLISON (Hood) Likely named for John Allison and his son James who bought Clarence Hollis's store in the late 1850s.

ALLISON (Wheeler) Founded as a Panhandle & Santa Fe Railway station in 1929. Named for Robert H. Allison, general manager of the Santa Fe Western Railway lines. In the early 1930s, Allison absorbed Zyback, its northern neighbor. PO 5 Oct 1929, PM James Robert Blair.

ALLISON (Wise) Waxahachie and Dallas land speculators founded Allison about 1910 on rumors that a railroad would be built between Decatur and Denton. The town was platted and named for Elisha Montgomery Allison, a recently elected county judge. Unfortunately, the rail line did not materialize and little is left of Allison.

ALLMON (Floyd) Named for William R. and Etta M. Allmon (originally Almond), farmers who settled in the area in the early 1900s.

ALLRED [AWL red, AHL red] (Yoakum) Founded by Walter E. Young in 1937. Named for James Allred, 33rd Governor of Texas (1935–1939). PO 15 June 1938, PM Ethel V. Myrick.

ALMA [AHL muh] (Ellis) Named in the 1870s for Alma Hartridge Hemming, daughter of Brenham banker Charles Cornelius Hemming. In 1896 Charles Hemming, a native Floridian, donated money for a Confederate memorial in St. James Park in Jacksonville, FL. The park was renamed in his honor in 1898. PO 3 Aug 1881, PM John Dixon.

ALMEDA [al MEED uh] (Harris) Named for Almeda King, daughter of Willis Percival King, a pioneering Missouri physician and surgeon for the Missouri Pacific Railroad. King promoted the area in the early 1880s. PO 29 Apr 1893, PM James W. Hicks.

ALPINE (Brewster) Formerly known as Osborne, likely named for an official or employee of the Texas & New Orleans Railroad that established a station there in the early 1880s. Several years later the railroad changed the name to Murphyville for site owner Thomas Murphy; that name was replaced by Alpine in 1888. Several tales are told about the naming of Alpine. By one, Clarence Way, the Brewster County Clerk, and a young lady were buggy riding and she remarked that the landscape reminded her of the beauty of the Swiss Alps and how nice it would be to live in Alpine. The second story (more reliable but much less romantic) tells of a meeting where people were discussing a new name for the town and local merchant Walter Garnett opened a copy of the post office guide and the name Alpine, AL, "glared up at him from the page." He proposed Alpine and that name was acceptable to all. PO 14 Dec 1883 as Murphyville; changed to Alpine 3 Feb 1888, PM James Darling.

ALSDORF [ALZ dorf] (Ellis) Alsdorf was organized in the 1880s when the Texas & New Orleans Railroad established Faulkner Station, named for Alsdorf Faulkner, general passenger agent of the T&NO. PO 9 Sept 1895 as Alsdorf, PM Charles Parker.

ALTAIR [AL tehr] (Colorado) Altair was founded in 1890 with construction of the Texas & New Orleans Railroad. Probably named for Altair, the brightest star in the Aquila Constellation. PO 4 Oct 1888 as Stafford's Ranch, PM John Stafford; changed to Altair 1 Jan 1891, PM John S. West.

ALTO (Cherokee) In the late 1840s merchant and hotelier Robert Mitchell founded Branchtown; renamed Alto (Spanish "high") in 1850 by plantation owners Henry and Helena Berryman. The site was believed to be the highest point between the Neches and Angelina rivers. PO 12 Dec 1850 as Branchtown; changed to Fort Lacey 27 May 1851; changed to Alto 30 June 1852, PM James W. Collier.

ALTOGA [al TO guh] (Collin) The town's motto, "All Together," was suggested by Aaron W. Owensby, an early settler from North Carolina. When All Together as a PO name was rejected by the Post Office Department, the application was resubmitted with All Together compressed to Altoga. PO 4 Jan 1889, PM James Moreland. This is the only Altoga in the US.

ALTUDA (Brewster) Altuda is an adaptation of Spanish *altura* "height, elevation," probably influenced by English "altitude." The town was named from one of the nearby hills or from the perception that this was the highest point on the Southern Pacific Railroad line. This is the only Altuda in the US.

ALUM (Wilson) Named around 1900 from Alum Creek, noted for its unappealing, alum-tainted water. PO 25 Jan 1905, PM Gus Burris.

ALVARADO [al vuh RAY do] (Johnson) Platted as Pittsburgh about 1850 by site owner William Balch. Abraham Hood Onstott (Onstoot), the first sheriff of Johnson County, suggested the name change for Alvarado, the naval base in Vera Cruz where he had taken part in an 1847 military operation during the Mexican War. PO 29 Aug 1854, PM John Waddell.

ALVIN (Brazoria) From about 1870 the flag station on the Gulf Coast & Santa Fe Railway was known as Morgan for Alvin Morgan who supervised the loading and transporting of cattle for the GC&SF. The 1880 PO application requesting the name Morgan was rejected and resubmitted as Alvin. PO 12 Apr 1881, PM Alvin Morgan.

ALVORD [AL verd] (Wise) Alvord, settled about 1880 as Nina, was renamed in 1882 for Everett M. Alvord, trainmaster and superintendent of telegraph for the Fort Worth & Denver Railway that was building through Wise County at the time. PO 18 Dec 1882, PM Shem Hatchett.

AMANDA (Kinney) Named for Amanda Jane Dignowity, wife of Anthony Dignowity who emigrated from Bohemia in 1832 and became a notable San Antonio doctor and businessman. The Dignowitys founded the Dignowity Hill section of San Antonio in the 1850s. PO 30 June 1884 as Olds, PM David Olds; changed to Amanda 13 Mar 1888, PM Oscar E. Flato. See Standart.

AMARGOSA (Jim Wells) Named from the Amargosa Ranch, in turn named from Amargosa (Spanish "bitter") Creek.

AMARILLO [am uh RIL o, am uh RIL uh] (Potter, Randall) Founded in the late 1870s on the anticipated route of the Fort Worth & Denver City Railway. James T. Berry, a founder of Abilene, laid out the community as Oneida. By November 1887 the name had been changed to Amarillo (Spanish "yellow"), named from Amarillo Lake, a playa reportedly named for the proliferation of yellow flowers along its banks in springtime or for the yellow soil around the lake. PO 23 Nov 1887, PM Robert McKenzie Moore.

AMBIA [AM bee uh] (Lamar) According to local legend Ambia is an altered form of Amber, named from the amber streams of tobacco juice aimed at spittoons (and occasionally hitting their target) in John Boyd's general store. PO 17 June 1886, PM George O'Daniel.

AMBROSE (Grayson) Ambrose Bible came to Texas from Tennessee in the early 1880s and donated land for the townsite, a railroad station, and a school. Ambrose Bible is often confused with Ambrose White, the namesake of WHITESBORO. PO 11 Sept 1902, PM James Moor.

AMES [AYMZ] (Liberty) Although local accounts claim the namesake is a section foreman on the Texas & New Orleans Railroad, the community was most likely named for Oakes Ames, a Boston financier and major underwriter of the Union Pacific Railroad. When bondholders of the T&NO went unpaid in 1871 the section of the line between

Liberty and Orange was sold to a consortium that included Oakes Ames. Ames, IA, was named in his honor in 1865.

AMHERST [AM herst] (Lamb) In 1913 the Pecos & Northern Texas Railway established Amherst Station, reportedly named for Amherst, MA, on William Ewing Halsell's Mashed O Ranch. A decade later the Halsell Land Company established the town of Amherst, named from the P&NT station. PO 3 Dec 1923, PM Hurlburt Slate. See Earth.

AMMANNSVILLE [AM uhnz vil] (Fayette) Named for Andreas Ammann who emigrated from Switzerland in the 1840s. Ammann and Heinrich Kreische, both stonemasons, built the second Fayette County jail in the early 1850s. PO 7 July 1879, PM Henry Holste.

AMPHION [AM fee uhn] (Atascosa) Perhaps the namer was familiar with Greek mythology and the story of Amphion, a great singer and son of Zeus, or had visited the Amphion resort in southeast France. PO 27 Aug 1886, PM John W. Hunt. This is the only Amphion in the US.

ANACUA (Starr) See Anaqua.

ANADARKO [an uh DAR ko] (Rusk) Anadarko was founded in the 1840s by Julien Devereux, a planter and state legislator who took the name from Anadarko Creek, named for the Anadarko, a Native American Caddoan group who lived in Texas until the middle of the 19th century. Today many of their descendants live in Anadarko, Caddo County, OK. Anadarko is a Caddoan place name meaning "where there are bumblebees." PO Nov 1849, PM William Barry.

ANAHUAC [AN uh wak] (Chambers) Anahuac, from Nahuatl "near the water," an Aztec reference to the Valley of Mexico, was apparently named by José Manuel de Mier y Terán in the early 1830s when he was commandant general of the Eastern Interior Provinces that included Texas and Coahuila. Thomas Chambers, the namesake of Chambers County and a resident of Anahuac, changed the name to Chambersia in honor of himself. PO May 1838 as Anahuac, PM Charles Willcox; changed to Chambersia 15 Aug 1846; changed back to Anahuac 11 Apr 1849.

ANAQUA [uh NAH kwuh] (Victoria) Spanish from Nahuatl (Aztec), usually translated as "paper tree." The local *anaqua* (*anacua*) trees were themselves named from the Anaqua people who were established in the area by the mid-16th century. The trees, also known as knockaway and sandpaper trees, are common to eastern Mexico and southern Texas. PO 10 Jan 1852, PM Alexander Cromwell.

ANARENE [AN uh reen] (Archer) Founded in 1908 on the line of the Wichita Falls & Southern Railroad. PO 6 Mar 1909, PM Charles Graham who chose the name for his wife, *Anna* Law*rene* Keene Graham, not Annie Lawrence Graham or Anna Laurene Graham, as often reported.

ANCHOR (Brazoria) In the mid-1890s Jacob Whistler opened a hotel at what was then called Fruitland. He changed the name in 1897 for his former home, Anchor, McLean County, IL, itself named from the popular hymn "My Soul is Anchored in the Cross." PO 28 Apr 1897, PM George W. Ritchey.

ANCHORAGE (Atascosa) The local story is that Thomas Whittet, a longtime seaman, chose the name because he had at last found a place to "anchor" his life. The PO opened at the height of the Alaska Gold Rush in Anchorage which may have influenced the choice of this name. PO 2 Jan 1889, PM Thomas Whittet.

ANDER (Goliad) Founded by German settlers in the 1850s as Hanover, named for Hanover, Germany. The name was changed in 1900 in honor of local Lutheran pastor Theodore Ander. PO 1 June 1900, PM Ferdinand Albrecht.

ANDERSON (County) Created and organized 1846. Named for Kenneth Lewis Anderson (1805–1845), lawyer, statesman, and politician. Anderson, a close friend and advisor to Sam Houston, was the fourth and last Vice President of the Republic of Texas (1844–1845).

ANDERSON (Grimes) About 1835 English merchant and real estate speculator Henry Fanthorp established Fanthorp's Inn. The town that grew around the inn was known as Alta Mira (Spanish "high look") until 1846 when the name was changed to Anderson in honor of Kenneth Lewis Anderson who died at Fanthorp's Inn in July 1845. PO 1836 as Allcorn's; changed to Fanthorp 22 May 1846; changed to Anderson 9 Apr 1849, PM John B. Harris. See Anderson County.

ANDICE [AN dis] (Williamson) Formerly known as Berry's Creek from the PO established by Andrew Jackson in October 1876. That office was discontinued in December 1879. The community was without a post office until 28 Nov 1899 when shopkeeper William Isaac Newton opened an office named for his newborn son, Audice. The application was misread as Andice.

ANDREWS (County) Created 1876, organized 1910. Named for Richard Andrews (1797–1835). Andrews worked his way from Georgia to Texas in 1827. He joined the Texas Army, was wounded at Gonzales and killed at the Battle of Concepción in October 1835. Andrews is the first soldier known to have died in the Texas Revolution.

ANDREWS (Andrews) Established about 1908 and named from Andrews County. PO 20 Jan 1909, PM Thomas M. White.

ANGEL CITY (Goliad) Little remains of Angel City except a legend of how it got its name: Two young girls, both dressed in white, came to where a water well was being drilled. As they were leaving one crew member remarked, "They look just like angels."

ANGELINA [an juh LEE nuh] (County) Created and organized 1846. Named from the Angelina River, known as the *Pascua del Espiritu Santo* "Pentecost" until the late 17th century when it was named for a young Hasinai (Caddo) woman who studied at the mission and was known by Franciscan priests as Angelina, the "Little Angel." She was an interpreter and guide for a number of Spanish expeditions and for several missions along the Rio Grande and in East Texas. Her Hasinai name is unknown.

ANGLETON (Brazoria) In 1891 Lewis Bryan and Faustino Kiber donated half of the townsite to the Velasco Terminal Railway and laid out the community named for VTR general manager George Washington Angle. PO 16 May 1892, PM Rufus C. Hancock.

ANGUS (Navarro) Named for Alexander Angus, born in Bristol, England and raised in Houston. Angus was terminal agent for the Houston & Texas Central Railway that established Angus Station in 1871. PO 29 May 1877, PM John B. Jones.

ANHALT [AN hahlt] (Comal) A popular etymology claims the name is from German *anhalten* "to stop," signifying a resting place for German settlers who began to arrive in the late 1850s. Rather, the community was named for Anhalt, the former state in central Germany, now part of Saxony-Anhalt. PO 24 Nov 1879, PM Louis Krause.

ANNA (Collin) Named for Anna Elizabeth Quinlan, daughter of George Austin Quinlan, vice president of the Houston & Texas Central Railway that built through the area in the early 1870s. PO 29 May 1883, PM William Barnett. See Quinlan.

ANNAVILLE (Nueces) Founded in the late 1930s by Leo Stewart, a Corpus Christi chiropractor who named the town for his wife Annie, also a chiropractor. The Stewarts divorced soon thereafter. Annaville was annexed by Corpus Christi in the 1960s.

ANNETTA (Parker) Alexander Frazer opened the PO in his general store 8 Aug 1876; named for his four-year-old daughter, Anneta.

ANNONA [uh NO nuh] (Red River) The Missouri Pacific Railroad established Walker Station in 1874, named for George W. Walker from Illinois, who opened a general store in the mid-1860s. The Savannah PO, opened in May 1846, was changed to Walker Station by George Walker in March 1874. The Annona PO was kept by merchant Oliver English from its opening in March 1872 until its closing in June 1887. In April 1884 the Walker Station office was changed to Annona. The source of the name is uncertain. By a popular etymology Annona is a blend of Ann and Ona, two local girls; in several local stories, Annona is a beautiful Indian princess. The town may be named for the Annona, a flowering plant of the pawpaw family native to extreme southern Texas.

ANSON (Jones) Founded about 1880 as Jones City, named from Jones County. In 1882 the community was formally named for Anson Jones, the last President of the Republic of Texas. PO 4 Apr 1881, PM William M. Bowyer. See Jones County.

ANTHONY (El Paso) Reportedly named for a chapel dedicated to St. Anthony of Padua. The area became known as La Tuna, named for the edible pads of the local prickly pear cactus, when the Federal Correctional Institution at La Tuna opened in 1932. The La Tuna PO was established 18 June 1932, PM James C. Lynch; discontinued 5 Nov 1965. The Anthony PO was established 2 Nov 1981, PM Raymond A. Evans.

ANTIOCH (Cass) Named in the 1880s from the local Antioch Church, itself probably named for an Antioch further east. The name is from the Biblical Antioch, the place where Jesus's disciples were first called Christians. There are more than a thousand Antioch churches in the US. PO 7 June 1888 as Anti, PM Auswell Sargeant Griffin.

ANTIOCH (Delta) Founded in 1890 and named from the local Antioch Baptist Church, apparently named from the Antioch Cemetery established about 1850, itself named from an eastern Antioch or directly from the Biblical Antioch.

ANTON [ANT uhn] (Hockley) About 1925 the Pecos & Northern Texas Railway platted a townsite at the Danforth Switch, part of the Spade Ranch. The town was formally named for James Frederick Anton, superintendent of the Santa Fe Railroad system, of which the P&NT was a subsidiary. PO 30 Apr 1925, PM John C. Arnett.

APOLONIA (Grimes) Named in the mid-1830s by Polish Catholic settlers for Saint Apollonia, 3rd century Christian martyr and patron saint of dentists because her torture included having her teeth violently broken or pulled. PO 14 Aug 1889, PM Frances Lowery.

APPELT HILL [AP uhlt] (Lavaca) Named from the Appelt Farm owned by Franz "Frank" Appelt who emigrated from Germany in the early 1850s.

APPLE SPRINGS (Trinity) Originally May Apple Springs. The name was shortened when the PO was established 23 June 1884, PM Young W. Randolph.

APPLEBY (Nacogdoches) Named for James Appleby, general auditor for the Houston East & West Texas Railway when the railroad built through the area in the early 1880s. PO 14 Aug 1889, PM William T. Skeeters.

AQUILLA [uh KWIL uh] (Hill) In the 1850s Presbyterian minister John Patton established a gristmill in what became known as Patton's Mill or, informally, Mud Town, because of the poor condition of its streets after a rain. PO 12 Dec 1859 as Aquilla, PM Claiborne Terry. Named from Aquilla Creek, likely named for early settler Aquilla Jones.

ARAH [EHR uh] (Scurry) PO 9 Oct 1907, PM Eugene Gray who chose the name for Arah Gray, his two-year-old daughter.

ARANSAS [uh RAN zuhs] (County) Created and organized 1871. Named from the Aransas River. Aransas is a shortened form of *Río Nuestra Señora de Aránzazu* "River of Our Lady of Aranzazu." The name, in use by Spanish explorers by the middle of the 18th century, was a transfer from the Franciscan sanctuary of Our Lady of Aranzazu (Arantzazu) in northern Spain where the Virgin Mary is said to have appeared to a shepherd in the 15th century. From Basque *Arantzazu* "place of hawthorns."

ARANSAS PASS (San Patricio) First known as Aransas Harbor, the name was changed in 1892 with completion of the Aransas Harbor Terminal Railroad that connected the town and the shipping station. The Rockport PO, opened in May 1868, was changed to Aransas Pass in Dec 1889 and back to Rockport in Dec 1891. The Aransas Harbor PO, opened Aug 1890, was changed to Aransas Pass Aug 1892, PM Charles T. Black.

ARBALA [ahr BAY luh] (Hopkins) Perhaps a misspelling of Arbela, a transfer from Arbela, Scotland County, MO, itself named for Arbela, the ancient city in Mesopotamia, now Arbil, Iraq. PO 25 Feb 1899, PM Christopher Columbus Harper.

ARCADIA (Galveston) Founded in 1890 by banker and merchant Henry J. Runge who named the town for Arcadia, Bienville Parish, LA, itself named for the Arcadia district of ancient Greece, considered a land of pleasant living. Arcadia is now part of SANTA FE. PO 14 Apr 1891, PM George W. Judson. See Runge, see Santa Fe.

ARCHER (County) Created 1858, organized 1890. Named for Branch Tanner Archer (1790–1856), a leading political figure in the Republic of Texas serving in the First Texas Congress and as Secretary of War under President Mirabeau Lamar.

ARCHER CITY (Archer) Archer City, named from Archer County, was designated the county seat when Archer County was created in 1858 but the townsite was not surveyed until 1876. PO 24 June 1878, PM Capers Burnette Hutto.

ARCOLA [ahr KO luh] (Fort Bend) Arcola is a transfer name from Arcola, now a ghost town in Hale County, AL, itself named for Arcola (Arcole) in northern Italy where a French army defeated Austrian forces in 1796. The name was brought to Texas by Jonathan Dawson Waters who established the Arcola Plantation in the 1840s. PO 22 Feb 1869, PM William Dering.

ARDEN (Irion) John Arden introduced sheep ranching to the area, bringing the first flock from California in the late 1870s. Arden was Tom Green County commissioner before the creation of Irion County. PO 5 Sept 1890, PM William P. Moore.

ARGENTA (Live Oak) Founded by Edward and James Bomer, brothers from Arkansas who began farming in the area in the early 20th century. Argenta (Spanish "silver") is probably a transfer from Argenta, AR (now North Little Rock), itself named for the local silver mines. PO 27 May 1907 as Ego; changed to Argenta 1 Jan 1911, PM James M. Bomer.

ARGO (Titus) Founded in the 1870s by John Rountree, Millard Wilhite, and John Arnold. By a local story Arnold honored his dead childhood sweetheart by naming the community for her. Just as likely Argo is a transfer from an Argo in Alabama, Kentucky, or Missouri. PO 3 Sept 1885, PM James S. Rountree.

ARGYLE (Denton) First known as Pilot Knob from a nearby prominence used as a landmark by early travelers and settlers. In 1881 the Texas & Pacific Railway established Argyle Station, named by either a railroad official or by Pilot Knob physician Daniel McIntyre Stewart for his ancestral home, Argyle, Scotland. PO 24 July 1878 as Pilot Knob; changed to Argyl 28 Nov 1881, PM Herman R. Fehleison.

ARIOLA [ahr ee O luh] (Hardin) Known as Buzzard Roost until the 1880s when the East Texas Railroad established Sharon Station and George Washington Hooks built a lumber mill. PO 6 Nov 1888 as Hooks Switch, PM George W. Hooks; changed to Ariola 21 Feb 1901, PM Sherwood Burch who chose the name for Eduardo and Francisco Ariola, the original land grantees.

ARISPE (Hudspeth) Arispe, founded about 1885, is a transfer from Arizpe [*sic*], Sonora, Mexico, itself founded in the mid-17th century, named from Basque "under the oaks." The town was served by the La Valley PO, opened 24 Nov 1909, PM Alice Auten.

ARLIE (Childress) Named for Arlington (Arlie) Roberta Griffith around the time of her marriage to inventor Ulysses S. Weddington in the early 1880s. PO 18 June 1888, PM James Alexander.

ARLINGTON (Tarrant) Laid out in 1876 by the Texas & Pacific Railway as Hayter, named for Presbyterian minister Andrew S. Hayter who surveyed the townsite for the T&P. Renamed for Robert E. Lee's Arlington House in Arlington County, VA. PO 29 July 1875 as Hayter; changed to Arlington 22 Jan 1877, PM Solomon S. Daniel.

ARMSTRONG (County) Created 1876, organized 1890. The namesake is unknown; the county is assumed to have been named for an early settler or pioneer family named Armstrong.

ARMSTRONG (Bell) Founded about 1900. Named about 1916 when the Armstrong School District was created on land donated by real estate agent Charles I. Armstrong.

ARMSTRONG (Kenedy) Named in honor of John Barclay Armstrong, renowned Texas Ranger and US Marshal. PO 28 Nov 1904 as Katherine, PM John B. Armstrong who chose the name for his daughter, Julia Katherine; changed to Armstrong shortly after he died in 1913.

ARNECKEVILLE [AHR nuh kee vil] (DeWitt) Andreas Christoph Heinrich Arnecke and Ursala Barbara Arnecke emigrated from Germany and established the first general store in the 1850s. PO 3 June 1872, PM Heinrich (Henry) Arnecke.

ARNETT (Hockley) Named for the extended family of rancher Cullen Curlee (C.C.) Arnett. David Nathan Arnett, son of C.C., was foreman of the Renderbrook Ranch for several decades in the late 19th and early 20th centuries.

ARNEY (Castro) Named for the James Arney family who settled in the area about 1900. PO 9 Aug 1902, PM William Robinson.

ARP (Smith) Known as Jarvis Switch after the International–Great Northern Railroad built through the area in the early 1870s. PO 19 Apr 1898 as Strawberry, PM Charles P. Orr who changed the name the following year to Arp. Orr, a native Georgian, chose the name for Bill Arp, the pen name of Charles Henry Smith, a homespun Southern humorist who wrote a weekly column for the *Atlanta Constitution* in the decades following the Civil War. The towns of Arp and Bill Arp, GA, are also named in his honor, and probably Arp, TN, as well.

ART (Mason) Known as Upper Willow Creek and as Plehweville for Otto Plehwe who opened the Plehwe PO March 1886. In 1920 Plehweville, with its difficult spelling, was changed to Art, a shortening and adaptation of Dechert (Deckart), for then postmaster Eli Dechert.

ARTHUR CITY (Lamar) Founded in 1886 with construction of the St. Louis–San Francisco Railway on land donated by plantation owner Captain James G.C. Arthur. PO 28 Aug 1886, PM John Arthur.

ASA [AY suh] (McLennan) Named by the Texas & New Orleans Railroad for Asa Warner, a Waco businessman and plantation owner of the 1910s and 1920s.

ASH (Houston) Founded in the early 1870s by farmer and Houston County native James Benjamin Ash. PO 21 Aug 1890, PM Charles L. Vickers.

ASHBY (Matagorda) William E. Moore who opened the PO 16 July 1890 named the office in honor of his Civil War commander, Henry Marshall Ashby.

ASHERTON (Dimmit) Asher Richardson, a wool merchant and entrepreneur who moved to Texas from southern Maryland in the 1870s, founded the Asherton Land and Irrigation Company that laid out the town in the 1900s. PO 13 Jan 1909, PM Edward Armstrong.

ASHTOLA [ash TOL uh] (Donley) Possibly a transfer from Ashtola, Somerset County, PA, the only other Ashtola in the US. PO 20 Mar 1906 as Southard; discontinued and reestablished as Ashtola 22 May 1916, PM Granville Shaw. The local story is that Shaw submitted the name of Ashtola along with that of Poovieville for landowner William A. Poovie. Without comment the Post Office Department approved the office as Ashtola.

ASPERMONT (Stonewall) Founded in 1889 by site owner Alphonse L. Rhomberg, son of Joseph Rhomberg, a builder of the Austin & Northwestern Railroad and a major figure in the development of Davenport, IA. Aspermont is Latin, literally "rough hill"; Rhomberg is German, literally "rough hill." Generations back the family name Aspermont may have been changed to Rhomberg for political or social reasons and in 1889 Alphonse Rhomberg or a close friend thought it would be clever to name the new town Aspermont, Rhomberg in disguise. PO 19 Sept 1889, PM David L. Flynt.

ATASCOSA [at uhs KO suh] (County) Created and organized 1856. Named from the Atascosa River, whose two branches join in northwestern Atascosa County and flow for nearly one hundred miles before emptying into the Frio River north of Three Rivers in Live Oak County. The name Atascosa (Spanish "boggy") described patches of the landscape along the river that were in use from at least the 1780s when the first permanent settlers arrived from Mexico.

ATASCOSA [at uhs KO suh] (Bexar) Settled in the late 1860s and named from the Atascosa River. PO 5 Sept 1872, PM Benjamin Andrews.

ATER [AYT er] (Coryell) Named for Josiah "Joe" Ater, who opened the PO in his general store 20 May 1899. The area was formerly known as Sardis, a transfer name from Sardis, MS, itself named for the Biblical Sardis.

ATHENS (Henderson) Named in the late 1840s by Dulcina Holland or other settlers for their former home, Athens, AL, itself named for Athens, Greece. PO 15 June 1848 as Alfred, PM Alfred Mallard; changed to Athens 24 Dec 1850, PM Eli L. Smith.

ATLANTA (Cass) Founded about 1870 when the Texas & Pacific Railway was laying tracks between Texarkana and Jefferson. The name was chosen by native Georgians Martha and Jesse Dodd for Atlanta, GA. PO 13 Nov 1871, PM George H. Salmon.

ATLAS (Lamar) Named by Edward Howland Robinson Green, owner of the Texas Midland Railroad, apparently for Atlas of Greek mythology who carried the world on his shoulders. PO 13 Feb 1884, PM James Price. See Cash, see Howland, see Jiba.

ATTOYAC [AT uh yak] (Nacogdoches) Laid out in 1836; named from Attoyac Bayou, itself named from Atoyac [*sic*], Jalisco, Mexico. From Nahuatl (Aztec) "near the river." PO 1 Dec 1907, PM August Stephens. Atoy in eastern Cherokee County is a variant.

ATWELL (Callahan) Named for William Hawley Atwell, a Dallas lawyer and US attorney for the Northern District of Texas in the late 1890s and early 1900s. PO 28 Feb 1899, PM John W. Clark.

AUBREY (Denton) Aubrey grew around a Texas & Pacific Railway station established in the early 1880s on land donated by Lemuel Edwards, an early settler in 1867. The local account is that the Aubrey slip was drawn from suggested names tossed into a hat. PO 27 June 1881, PM James A. Wood.

AUDELIA (Dallas) Possibly named for Ardelia Chenault, daughter of Wesley and Elizabeth Chenault. In the 1850s Wesley Chenault operated a sawmill and grist mill on White Rock Creek and became the owner of a number of building lots in what is now downtown Dallas. Probably named for Ardelia Jackson, daughter of James and Diana Jackson, who farmed in the area from the late 1840s. The spelling was changed either intentionally or accidentally when Junius Rhoton established the PO 11 Oct 1899.

AUSTIN (County) An original Texas county created in 1836. Named for Stephen F. Austin (1793–1836), in Sam Houston's words, "The Father of Texas." In the early 1820s Austin's father, Moses, was given a contract by the Spanish government to bring American settlers to Texas, but he died before his colony could be established. Stephen continued his father's work and by late 1825 he had brought the first families, part of the Old Three Hundred, to the first Austin Colony in southeast Texas.

AUSTIN (Travis) Having a major city in Texas named Austinia was a dream of Moses Austin but the only Austinia to materialize was a small settlement on Galveston Bay, managed by Emily Austin, Stephen F. Austin's sister. The site is now known as Texas City. In 1838 George Sutherland, a member of the Second Congress of the

Republic of Texas, proposed a site on the Colorado River for the new capitol of Texas. Thomas Jones Hardeman (see Hardeman County), also serving in the legislature, proposed the name Austin in honor of Stephen F. Austin. Known briefly as Waterloo, present Austin includes the former community of Montopolis "city on a hill," settled in the late 1830s. Austin formally annexed Montopolis in the early 1950s. PO 14 Jan 1897 as Montopolis, discontinued 10 Dec 1902. PO 22 May 1846 as Austin, PM John D. McLeod.

AUSTONIO (Houston) Formerly known as Pearville, reportedly for the bumper crops of pears that made the production of illegal whiskey possible. The name was changed about 1930 through a naming contest with a prize of $10. Ruth Tucker is credited with suggesting the name, a blend of Austin and San Antonio. PO 2 May 1932, PM Dudley Hester.

AUSTWELL [AWS wel] (Calhoun, Refugio) Austwell was founded in 1911 by the Refugio Land and Irrigation Company, organized by Preston *Aust*in and his business partner Jesse McDo*well*, the founders of TIVOLI. PO 26 Oct 1912, PM Edward R. Willenberg.

AUTHON (Parker) In 1882, John Pennington applied for a post office to be named for his three-year-old son Arthur. Through misreading or poor handwriting, the application was approved as Authon.

AVALON (Ellis) In 1860 William and Robert John (John[s], brothers from MO, began farming in the area. William John reportedly named the community for the Johns's family home, Avalon, TN. PO 3 Aug 1881, PM Patrick Alderman.

AVANT PRAIRIE [uh VAHNT] (Freestone) Formerly known as Durham for Durham Avant, a surveyor, Texas Ranger, and Athens hotelier in the 1850s. PO 22 Jan 1853 as Avant, PM James W. Brewer.

AVERY [AY vree] (Red River) Avery was first known as Douglas, named from Douglas Station, established by the Texas & Pacific Railway in the early 1870s and named for James P. Douglas, organizer of the Tyler Tap Railroad that connected with the T&P at Big Sandy. The name was changed to Avery for Ed Avery, the first station agent. PO 15 June 1881 as Isaca, an apparent misspelling or misreading of Isaac, for PM Isaac Bradford; changed to Avery 14 Feb 1902.

AVINGER [A vin jer] (Cass) In 1876 when the East Line & Red River Railroad laid tracks north of Hickory Hill, founded in the early 1840s, many Hickory Hill businesses and homes were moved to trackside. The station was named for the site owner, Dr. Hamilton J. Avinger, a horseback physician from 1855 and a Texas State Senator in the early 1870s. PO 17 May 1848 as Hickory Hill; changed to Avinger 25 Oct 1877, PM David L. Hendricks.

AVOCA [uh VO kuh] (Jones) In 1893 James Pendley applied for the Avoca PO, probably named for Avoca, AR. Through illegibility or misreading the office was approved as Avo. When the Texas Central Railway bypassed Avo in 1900 the new town that grew beside the tracks was called Avoca, a return to

Pendley's original intention. PO 29 Sept 1893 as Avo, PM James M. Pendley; changed to Avoca 26 Mar 1900, PM John Crump. See Voca.

AVONDALE (Tarrant) Founded in 1882 with construction of the Fort Worth & Denver City Railway. Avondale is a popular place name, occurring in more than half the states. Avondale, TX, is probably a transfer, likely from an Avondale in Alabama, Georgia, or Tennessee. PO 13 Nov 1890, PM Helen C. Larmon.

AXTELL [AKS tuhl] (McLennan) Named for Daniel Benton Axtell, the engineer in charge of building the Texas & St. Louis Railway from Corsicana to Waco in the early 1880s. PO 29 June 1882, PM Edward P. Rino.

AZLE [AY zuhl] (Parker, Tarrant) In the early 1880s pioneer physician James Azle Steward (Stewart) donated land for the townsite. PO 5 Sept 1881 as O'Bar, named for rancher William O'Bar; changed to Azle 6 Nov 1883, PM Joseph L. Fowler.

B

BABY HEAD (Llano) The town, now little more than a cemetery, was named from Baby Head Mountain. Several local stories are told to explain the name; all have to do with the death and mutilation of a child on the mountain. The most often told is that a group of marauding Indians kidnapped a settler's baby and set out to cross the mountain. Realizing that they were being pursued and the child was slowing them down, they killed her (in the stories the baby is usually a girl) and left her head on a pole. From this grisly incident the mountain was named supposedly sometime in the mid-1850s. PO 21 Mar 1879, PM Whelby Walling.

BACK (Gray) Rancher John David Back arrived in the area in the early 1900s and became a town promoter and community benefactor, donating land for the Back School. PO 11 Oct 1899 as Northfork, PM John J. Simpkins. Also known as Pumpkin Ridge.

BACLIFF [BAY klif] (Galveston) Founded in 1910 as Clifton-by-the-Sea, later altered to Bay Cliff, then to Bacliff when the PO was established 1 Dec 1948, PM Leroy Lockwood.

BACON (Wichita) Named for Otis T. Bacon, the first mayor of Wichita Falls in 1889 and a director of the Wichita Falls & Oklahoma Railway. PO 21 Sept 1910, PM Fred H. Evert.

BADER (Medina) Joseph Bader, born in Wittelsheim, Haut Rhin, Alsace, France, emigrated in 1844 and established the Bader Hotel, from which the community took its name about 1860.

BAGDAD (Williamson) See Leander.

BAGWELL (Red River) Founded about 1878 with construction of the Texas & Pacific Railway. Named for Miles (or Milas) Bagwell who had established a tannery and a blacksmith shop in the 1840s. PO 7 Oct 1856 as Robbinsville; changed to Baywell 1 Nov 1876 (the misspelling was corrected two weeks later).

BAILEY (County) Created 1876, organized 1917. Named for Peter James Bailey (1812–1836), a Kentucky lawyer who came to Texas in January 1836 and died at the Alamo two months later.

BAILEY (Fannin) About 1860 Joseph (or Josiah) Bailey brought his family from Georgia to Texas where he became an influential farmer, shopkeeper, doctor, and druggist. Bailey donated land for the St. Louis Southwestern Railway (Cotton Belt) in 1885. PO 25 July 1884 as Portland; changed to Bailey 9 Aug 1887, PM Josiah S. Bailey.

BAILEY'S PRAIRIE (Brazoria) James Britton Bailey settled in southeast Texas in 1818 and established a sugar plantation in the early 1820s, several years before he became one of Stephen F. Austin's Old Three Hundred. Also spelled Baileys Prairie.

BAINVILLE (Karnes) Named for Judson L. Bain, a merchant and cotton farmer who relocated from Alabama in the 1890s.

BAIRD (Callahan) According to local sources the town was named for Matthew Baird, variously said to be a surveyor, engineer, owner, or director of the Texas & Pacific Railway that built through Callahan County in the early 1880s. The namesake is more likely Matthew Baird of Philadelphia, an important figure in 19th century American railroading. PO 7 Feb 1881 as Baird; changed to Vickery 16 May 1881; changed back to Baird 27 Feb 1883, PM Phillip Schwartz.

BAKER (Parker) In the 1850s Charles and Mary Baker brought their family, including son Gaston Commodore Scott Baker, from North Carolina.

BAKERSFIELD (Pecos) Robert Walker and John Baker founded Bakersfield shortly after oil was discovered in 1929. Named for Baker's father, John Thomas Baker, a partner in the White-Baker Ranch. PO 26 Dec 1929, PM Jay Vernon Davis.

BALCONES HEIGHTS (Bexar) Founded in the late 1940s and named from the Balcones Escarpment, the geological fault zone that marks the western uplifted Edwards Plateau from the eastern downwarp of the Texas coastal plain. In Central Texas the Balcones Fault sharply defines the eastern edge of the Texas Hill Country.

BALDWIN (Harrison) Probably named for Dr. Jack Baldwin who established a medical practice in nearby Marshall about 1900. PO 13 June 1902, PM Charles Alonzo Pilant.

BALLINGER (Runnels) Founded as Hutchings City for banker John Henry Hutchings with construction of the Gulf, Colorado & Santa Fe Railway in 1866. Renamed for William Pitt Ballinger, a Galveston attorney and railroad investor. PO 1 June 1886, PM William A. Procter.

BALMORHEA [bal muh RAY] (Reeves) Balmorhea is a blend of the names of the town founders: Ernest D. *Bal*com, a southwest irrigation developer; Hugh R. *Mo*rrow, a partner in the Morrow-Thomas Hardware Company of Amarillo; and ranchers John and Joe *Rhea*. The blending of names was suggested by Billie Edwards, conductor of the train on which the founders were riding when they chose the name in 1907. PO 4 Aug 1908, PM William C. Kelley.

BAMMEL (Harris) Charles Bammel and his business partner Herman Kuehnle opened the Bammel and Kuehnle Merchandise store in 1915. PO 28 Feb 1916, PM Herman Kuehnle. Now part of Houston.

BANCROFT (Orange) Englishman Thomas Bancroft opened a sawmill and shingle mill along the Sabine River in the early 1870s. His son George was president of the Orange National Bank and mayor of Orange when Bancroft was platted in 1903.

BANDERA [ban DEHR uh] (County) Created and organized 1856.

BANDERA (Bandera) Named from the county, the town was designated the county seat and laid out the same year the county was created. Both county and town were named from Bandera Pass, the gap in the hills just south of the Kerr County line. The source of the name is Spanish *bandera* "banner, flag," but how the pass came by that name is uncertain. There are two oft-repeated accounts. By one, the pass was named in honor of a General Bandera, a Spanish officer who defeated Apache warriors in a pitched battle in the 1730s. By the other, the name resulted from a peace treaty between Apaches and Spanish soldiers, again in the 1730s, when a red flag was placed on the highest point of the pass to mark the boundary between Spanish and Apache territory. Early maps such as Stephen F. Austin's, circa 1830, label the pass *Puerta de la Bandera* "door of the flag," suggesting that the second account is more likely. See Peggy Tobin's article "Bandera Pass" in the *Handbook of Texas Online.*

BANGS (Brown) Samuel Bangs brought the first printing press to Texas in 1817. He was granted a site by Texas Governor James Pinckney Henderson in 1847. PO 6 Jan 1886 as Atchison; changed to Bangs 24 May 1886, PM James W. Atchison.

BANKERSMITH (Kendall) PO 28 Sept 1914, PM Rudolph Habenicht who chose the name for banker Temple Doswell Smith, "Banker Smith," who established the Bank of Fredericksburg in 1887.

BANQUETE [ban KET ee] (Nueces) Apparently named from a four-day party in 1832 held to celebrate completion of the road linking San Patricio, TX, with Matamoros, Mexico. PO 16 Sept 1859, PM John Williamson Moses.

BARBAROSA [bahr buh ROS uh] (Guadalupe) Founded by German settlers in the 1870s. Perhaps named for an immigrant named Barbarosa; perhaps named for Frederick Barbarossa, Holy Roman Emperor in the late 12th century. PO 6 July 1900, PM Nina E. Wolf.

BARCLAY [BAHRK lee] (Falls) William Anderson Barclay was a Texas entrepreneur who established ranches, railroads, banks, and stores from the mid-1870s. He was the first PM, 7 Nov 1881.

BARDWELL (Ellis) Native Ohioan John W. Bardwell established a cotton gin about 1880. PO 30 June 1893, PM Alfred Willis.

BARKER (Harris) Barker was laid out in 1895 with construction of the Missouri–Kansas–Texas Railroad (aka The KATY) and named for either Edwin Barker, keeper of the local general store and saloon and a contractor for the railroad or, more likely, for James Barker, general passenger agent and ticket agent for the KATY with offices in St. Louis. PO 31 Oct 1898, PM George T. Miller.

BARKSDALE (Edwards) Formerly known as Dixie for Camp Dixie, a Texas Ranger post of the 1850s. PO 20 Sept 1882 named for Lewis Barksdale who received a land grant for his service in the Texas Revolution, PM James Neel.

BARNHART (Irion) Founded about 1910 with construction of the Kansas City, Mexico & Orient Railway. Named for station agent William B. Barnhart. PO 24 Aug 1912, PM Clarence Luther.

BARRETT (Harris) Founded at the end of the Civil War by former slave Harrison Barrett who spent several years locating members of his dispersed family and moving them to Barrett's Settlement.

BARRY (Navarro) The community moved north from its original location when the Cotton Belt Railroad established a station in the late 1880s. The townsite was owned by Bryan Thomas Barry, an attorney and Dallas mayor for three terms in the late 19th and early 20th centuries. PO 24 May 1886, PM Owen Taylor.

BARSTOW (Ward) About 1890 George Eames Barstow, a Rhode Island industrialist, laid out the townsite. He later organized the Barstow Improvement Company and the Barstow Irrigation Company to develop irrigation projects fed by the Pecos River and to promote the sale of building lots. PO 3 Nov 1891, PM Minnie L. Cranson.

BARTLETT (Bell, Williamson) About 1880 site owners John Bartlett and Julius Pietzsch donated land for the townsite and for a Missouri–Kansas–Texas Railroad station. PO 5 Oct 1882, PM Thomas McKnight.

BARTON CREEK (Travis) This upscale residential and commercial community west of Austin was established in the early 1970s by an investment group that included John Connally, Texas Governor (1963–1969). Named from Barton Creek and Barton Springs, natural perpetual springs created by the Balcones Fault. The springs were named for William Barton, a member of Stephen F. Austin's Second Colony, who settled near the springs in the late 1830s.

BARTONVILLE (Denton) Bartonville, along with Shiloh and Waketon, was originally part of the Chinn's Chapel Settlement established by Elisha Chinn in the early 1850s. The town of Barton's Mills grew around a store and gristmill established by Bentley Ballard Barton in the early 1880s. PO 6 Jan 1886, PM Bentley B. Barton. See Advance.

BARWISE (Floyd) The town of Stringer, named for site owner James W. Stringer, was founded early in 1928 soon after construction of the Fort Worth & Denver City Railway. Stringer was renamed the following year for Joseph Hodson Barwise, an organizer of Wichita County and a Wichita Falls businessman.

BASCOM (Smith) Bishop Henry Bid(d)leman Bascom was a leader of the Methodist Episcopal Church South in the first half of the 19th century. The name was most likely suggested by Dr. Lazariah Smith who established the PO 3 July 1856.

BASSETT (Bowie) John Bassett was reportedly the first local landowner in the early 1850s. PO 1 June 1882, PM Gordentia Elgin Dalby.

BASTROP [BAS trahp] (County) Bastrop was one of the original 23 counties of the Texas Republic. On December 18, 1837 Sam Houston, President of the Republic of Texas, signed the act that created the town and county of Bastrop, both established as Mina in the late 1820s by Stephen F. Austin, probably named in honor of Martín Francisco Xavier Mina y Larra, a hero of the Mexican Revolution. The names of both the county and the seat were changed to Bastrop for Philip Hendrik Nering Bögel, a government official in the Netherlands who assumed the Spanish version of his name, Felipe Enrique Neri, and added the aristocratic title Baron de Bastrop.

BASTROP (Bastrop) The settlement known as Mina was renamed Bastrop when it became the governmental center of Bastrop County in 1837. By the mid-1790s Baron Bastrop was a businessman and colonizer in Spanish Louisiana (for whom the town of Bastrop in Morehouse Parish was later named). In the early 19th century he moved to Texas where he became an influential diplomat instrumental in securing permission for both Moses and Stephen F. Austin to establish Texas colonies. PO 1836 as Bastrop, PM John McGehee.

BATESVILLE (Zavala) In the 1860s Elijah Bates and sons Finis and Felix emigrated from Alabama and established Bates Ranch, which became a locus for the community of Bates Ditch, named for the irrigation canal that brought water to the Bates's farmland. When Bates Ditch became the county seat in the mid-1880s the name was changed to the more attractive Batesville. PO 16 Apr 1884, PM Melverda Downs.

BATH (Walker) Farmer James H. Bell brought his family from Alabama in 1852 and established the Bath PO 13 Dec 1887. Perhaps a transfer from Bath, Aiken County, SC.

BATSON (Hardin) Probably named for Eli and Martha Batson who began farming on what became known as Batson Prairie in the 1840s. PO 14 May 1891 as Otto, PM Richard Otto Middlebrook; discontinued 8 Aug 1898; reestablished as Batson 14 Feb 1902, PM William D. Daniel.

BATTLE (McLennan) Named for Nicholas William Battle, Waco district judge in the 1870s and community benefactor. PO 13 May 1886 as Battle Institute; changed to Battle 28 Mar 1890, PM Armstead L. Scott.

BAY CITY (Matagorda) Early in 1894 David Swickheimer, Guilford Magill, Nicholas Vogelsand, and Nicholas King, partners in the Bay City Town Company, founded the community named from Bay Prairie. PO 28 Feb 1872 as Elliott; changed to Bay City 27 Dec 1894, PM Joseph D. Moore.

BAYLOR (County) Created 1858, organized 1879. Named for Henry Weidner Baylor (1818–1853), born in Kentucky. Baylor settled in Texas about 1840 and established a medical practice at La Grange. He enlisted as a Texas Mounted Rifleman at the outbreak of the Mexican War in 1846 and became regimental surgeon. Henry Baylor was a nephew of Robert Emmett Bledsoe Baylor, a founder and the namesake of Baylor University in Waco.

BAYTOWN (Harris) Founded on the estate of William Scott who received a land grant from Stephen F. Austin in 1824. Named from Scott's Bay, now San Jacinto Bay. Modern Baytown includes the former communities of Goose Creek and Pelly, the latter named for site owner Fred Pelly.

BEASLEY (Fort Bend) Founded as Dyer about 1895 on the line of the Galveston, Harrisburg & San Antonio Railway. Ticket agent and Richmond banker Cecil Beasley proposed the name Dyer for his fiancée, Isabel Dyer. Because of an existing Dyer PO, John Cates opened the PO as Beasley 13 May 1898.

BEATTIE (Comanche) PO 19 July 1902, PM general store owner James W. Beattie.

BEAUMONT [BO mahnt] (Jefferson) In 1835 businessmen and land speculators Henry Millard, Joseph Pulsifer, and Thomas Huling founded Beaumont, named by Millard for the Beaumont family of Natchez, MS. Millard's wife was Mary Dewburleigh Barlace Warren Beaumont; his brothers-in-law were Franklin Beaumont, his business partner, and Jefferson Beaumont, a Natchez merchant whom some say is the namesake of Jefferson County. Millard moved to Texas about 1834 and the Beaumont brothers followed him in the early 1840s. Beaumont includes the earlier settlements of Tevis Bluff and Santa Anna. PO 1836, PM Joseph P. Pulsifer.

BEBE [BEE BEE] (Gonzales) The local naming story as told by Fred Tarpley (*1001 Texas Place Names*): "Just as the town was looking for a name, a salesman promoting Beebee Baking Powder plastered signs in the community, and the town became known as Bebe." PO 11 July 1894 as Stroman, named for merchant Govan Stroman; closed 7 Aug 1896; reestablished as Bebe 10 Aug 1900, PM Warren G. Blair.

BECKER (Kaufman) Named for William E. Becker, who emigrated from Snow Creek, Jefferson County, IL, in the 1860s. Becker opened the PO 13 Feb 1888.

BECKMAN (Bexar) Founded in the late 19th century and named for blacksmith and metal worker John Conrad Beckmann, born in Westphalia, Germany, and his son, Albert Felix Beckmann, a San Antonio architect of the 1880s. Also spelled Beckmann.

BECKVILLE (Panola) In the 1850s Matthew Beck built a store and tavern that served food and liquid refreshments to travelers on the Shreveport–Douglas Road. PO 8 Aug 1857, PM Joseph Sweeten.

BECTON (Lubbock) Named for community benefactors Abner and Cornelia Becton who moved to the area in 1898. PO 13 Mar 1918, PM Ellis H. Moody. Also known as Bledsoe for William E. Bledsoe, owner of the Three Circle Ranch.

BEDFORD (Tarrant) About 1870 Weldon Wiles Bobo and Mary Bobo opened a general store and founded Bedford, named for Bedford County, TN, Mary Bobo's birthplace. PO 26 Feb 1877, PM Weldon W. Bobo.

BEDIAS [BEE deyes] (Grimes) Named from Bedias Creek, itself named for the Bedia (Bedai), a Native American people with no known survivors and about whom little is known. By a local popular etymology Bedia was the name of a Native American leader who had "beady eyes." The area was first settled by Europeans in the mid-1830s and took the name Plasterville for plantation owner Thomas Pliny Plaster. PO 1845 as Bedi [*sic*], PM Thomas Plaster; closed 5 Nov 1866; reestablished as Bedias 24 Sept 1867, PM Paschal H. Wilkinson.

BEE (County) Created 1857, organized 1858. Named for Barnard Elliott Bee (1787–1854), a native South Carolinian. Bee held a number of offices in pre-Republic of Texas and in the Republic of Texas. He was Secretary of the Treasury and Secretary of State in David G. Burnet's ad interim cabinet, Secretary of War under Sam Houston, and Secretary of State under Mirabeau B. Lamar.

BEE CAVE (Travis) Named for the Mexican honeybees that swarmed in a cavern near what became known as Bee Cave Creek. PO 19 Apr 1870 as Bee Caves, PM Martin V. Lackey.

BEEVILLE (Bee) Founded in 1858 as Beeville-on-the-Medio, the Bee County seat on Medio Creek. The town moved to its present location on Poesta Creek the following year and for a short time in 1859 was known as Maryville. PO 31 Oct 1857 as Medio Hill; changed to Beeville 6 May 1859, PM Henderson Williams. See Bee County.

BELCHERVILLE (Montague) John and Alexander Belcher formed the Belcher Land and Cattle Company and platted the town of Belcher in the mid-1880s anticipating construction of the Gainesville, Henrietta & Western Railway. PO 27 Aug 1887, PM Henry P. Turner.

BELDING (Pecos) Horace Stevens and John Brooks platted the community in 1913 for the Davenport Irrigation and Land Associates Company. Named for Alvah Norton Belding, a New York financier and a director of the Kansas City, Mexico & Orient Railway.

BELFALLS (Bell, Falls) Named for the town's location on the Bell County–Falls County line. PO 28 May 1891, PM Isham H. Couey.

BELGRADE (Newton) William and Thomas McFarland, father and son from Indiana, laid out the town in 1837 and reportedly chose the name because, to their thinking, Belgrade, TX, lay on the Sabine River much as Belgrade, Serbia, lay on the Danube. PO 17 Dec 1849 as Biloxi; changed to Belgrade 1 Sept 1860, PM Thomas S. McFarland.

BELL (County) Created and organized 1850. Named for Peter Hansborough Bell (1812–1898), a native Virginian. Bell fought at the Battle of San Jacinto, was a Texas Ranger, won a badge of distinction during the Mexican War, was Governor of Texas (1849–1853), and represented Texas in the US Congress (1853–1857).

BELLAIRE (Harris) Founded about 1909 by the South End Land Company whose president, William Wright Baldwin, was vice president of the Chicago, Burlington & Quincy Railroad. Local lore claims that Bellaire "good air" was named from the cool Gulf breezes, but more likely the name is a transfer from Bellaire, Belmont County, OH, itself named by settlers from Bel Air [*sic*], Harford County, MD. PO 12 Mar 1859, PM Simon Hageman.

BELLEVUE (Clay) The local account is that a surveyor for the Fort Worth & Denver City Railway chose the name for Bellevue Hospital in New York City when the station was established about 1880. PO 17 Nov 1882, PM Charles Hale.

BELLMEAD (McLennan) Bellmead grew around a locomotive shop established by the Missouri–Kansas–Texas Railroad in 1924.

Perhaps named from Belle Meade Plantation in Davidson County, TN, now part of Nashville. PO 10 Apr 1937, PM Alvis L. Gilliam.

BELLS (Grayson) The local story is that the name came from the tolling of the bells of the many churches on Gospel Ridge. PO 12 June 1871 as Dugansville, named for early settler Daniel Dugan; changed to Bell's 8 Sept 1879, PM Edward S. Aston; changed to Bells 19 June 1893. The apostrophe suggests the office was named for one of the dozen or so Bell families in the area.

BELLVILLE (Austin) Bellville was founded in 1848 as the seat of Austin County, replacing San Felipe. The townsite was donated by namesakes Thomas and James Bell, brothers and early settlers in Stephen F. Austin's First Colony established December 1821. PO 1 Oct 1839 as Brazoria; changed to Bellville 3 July 1849, PM Benjamin Grenville.

BELMONT (Gonzales) In the 1850s and 1860s August Belmont was a New York diplomat and financier who invested heavily in Texas railroads, especially the Missouri–Kansas–Texas Railroad line. Belmont was a member of a well-known New York horse racing family for whom Belmont Park is named. PO 27 Jan 1849 as Belleville; changed to Belmont 1 Oct 1849, PM Thomas A. Gay.

BELOTT (Houston) Apparently named for Andrew J. Belott, an early settler in the 1860s. PO 20 Mar 1890, PM John N. Johnson.

BELTON (Bell) Originally Nolansville or Nolan Springs, apparently named for Philip Nolan, a late 18th century explorer and trader and the namesake of NOLANVILLE. The site was surveyed, designated the county seat, and formally named for Bell County in 1850. PO 4 Oct 1850 as Nolansville; changed to Belton 22 Apr 1852, PM William D. Eastland.

BEN ARNOLD (Milam) Named with construction of the San Antonio & Aransas Pass Railway in 1891 for Benjamin I. Arnold and his daughter, Bennie Mabel Arnold. Arnold was a sheriff of Milam County in the 1870s and mayor of CAMERON in the 1890s. PO 16 May 1892, PM Vincent Kahler. Also spelled Benarnold.

BEN BOLT (Jim Wells) Laid out in 1904 by Livingston Gideon Collins, an ALICE businessman and rancher. Collins was apparently inspired by "Ben Bolt and Sweet Alice," a maudlin poem and song from the 1840s, or by one of its many parodies. Sentiments aside, Collins decided that Ben Bolt would be a good name for a town just down the railroad line from Alice. PO 4 Dec 1906, PM Glenon Rover.

BEN FRANKLIN (Delta) Named for Benjamin Franklin Simmons, both Sr. and Jr., who emigrated from Giles County, TN, in the 1830s. PO 8 Sept 1853, PM Isaac Nelson.

BEN HUR (Limestone) According to local accounts, when names for the PO were solicited in 1895, Alfred Derden suggested Ben Hur for the popular 1880 novel by Lew Wallace, a Union general and Governor of New Mexico Territory (1878–1881). Ben Hur, then, is one of the few places in Texas associated with a Union Army officer. PO 3 May 1895, PM James E. Parker.

BEN WHEELER (Van Zandt) George Washington Clough came to the area from Virginia in the 1840s and in 1876 established the PO named for Benjamin Franklin Wheeler, regarded as the first person to bring mail to Van Zandt County.

BENAVIDES (Duval) About 1881 the Texas Mexican Railway established Benavides Station on the Rancho Palo Alto of Plácido Benavides. PO 19 May 1879 as Piedras Pintas "painted rocks"; changed to Benavides 18 Jan 1881, PM Jacob W. Toklas.

BENBROOK (Tarrant) James Benbrook, born in Indiana, began farming in the area in the 1870s. The Texas & Pacific Railway built through the area in 1876 and the town was named for Benbrook when PM Samuel Hamilton opened the PO 3 Aug 1880.

BENCHLEY (Robertson) Known as Staggers Point until 1869 when trustees of the Houston & Texas Central Railway laid out the town of Benchley, named for Henry W. Benchley, Lieutenant Governor of Massachusetts in the 1850s and an employee of the H&TC in the 1860s. PO 12 Apr 1882, PM Gabriel F. Thornhill.

BENJAMIN (Knox) Hilory Green Bedford, president of the Wichita and Brazos Stock Company that managed the L Bar Ranch, platted the community in 1885. Bedford opened the PO 17 Nov 1884, named for his brother and/or his father, both named Benjamin Coleman Bedford.

BENNETT (Parker) The town grew around George E. Bennett's Acme Pressed Brick Company that went into full production in 1891. In 1916 Bennett's son Walter became president of the renamed Acme Brick Company.

BENOIT (Runnels) Founded in 1886 as Norwood. The name was changed in March 1906 when William Tyson established the Benoit post office. Probably named for an early settler or family named Benoit.

BENONINE (Wheeler) Benjamin Harbert platted the town on the line of the Chicago, Rock Island & Gulf Railway in 1909. Named for the Benonine Oil and Gas Company of Amarillo. PO 6 Oct 1909, PM Clarence A. Webber.

BERCLAIR [ber KLAR] (Goliad) In 1889 the Goliad County line of the Gulf, Western Texas & Pacific Railway was surveyed by construction engineer Bernard Moore Temple, a major figure in Texas railroading and the namesake of TEMPLE in Bell County. Temple suggested the name for his birthplace, Berclair Plantation in Spotsylvania County, VA. PO 2 Dec 1889, PM Louis Brown.

BEREA [buh REE uh] (Marion) William McCutchen, president of the Texas Conference of Seventh Day Adventists, purchased the site in 1914. The name, like most of the dozen Bereas in the US, was probably chosen for its religious associations. Berea was the city in Macedonia where Paul spoke to an "open-minded" audience.

BERGHEIM [BERG heyem] (Kendall) Andreas Engel, who emigrated from Austria and opened a general store in 1883, chose the name for one of the Bergheims in Germany.

German for "mountain home." PO 17 May 1901; PM Andreas Engel.

BERGS MILL (Bexar) Named for Louis S. Berg, a San Antonio merchant and alderman in the early 1880s and later president of the Mobile, Jackson & Kansas City Railroad. PO 23 Mar 1887, PM William Braden.

BERLIN [BER luhn] (Washington) Named for Berlin, Germany, by German settlers who began arriving in the late 1840s. PO 26 Nov 1860, PM William Binding.

BERTRAM (Burnet) When the Austin & Northwestern Railroad built through the area in 1882 the community of South Gabriel, named for its location on the San Gabriel River, was moved to trackside and the name was changed to Bertram for Rudolph Bertram of Austin, the largest stockholder of the A&N. PO 29 Sept 1871 as South Gabriel; changed to Bertram 8 Dec 1882, PM Peter R. Weston.

BESSMAY (Jasper) Bessmay grew around the Kirby Lumber Company's sawmill and planer; named for mill owner John Kirby's daughter, Bessie May. PO 16 Sept 1903, PM George Rogers. See Kirbyville.

BEST (Reagan) Named for Tom Best, a British stockholder in the Orient of Texas Railroad, a subsidiary of the Kansas City, Mexico & Orient Railway that established Best Station in 1924. PO 26 Aug 1924, PM John R. Hodge.

BETHEL (Hopkins) Earlier known as Askew for brothers John and Richard Askew who settled in the area in the 1850s. Likely named from a local Bethel Church, of which there are about 200 in Texas.

BETTIE (Upshur) Named from the Bettie PO, established 12 Apr 1882 by Isaac Neri Anderson who named the office for his wife, Margaret Elizabeth Anderson, known as "Aunt Bettie."

BEXAR [BEHR] (County) An original Texas county, created 1836, that included nearly half of western Texas. Bexar was named from San Antonio de Béxar, one of several Spanish administrative districts of Texas. The name dates from at least 1718 when Martín de Alarcón, the Spanish governor of Texas, founded the San Antonio de Béxar Presidio and the Villa de Béxar, named for the dukes of Béxar (Béjar) in Salamanca, Spain, in particular for Baltasar de Zúñiga y Guzmán, Duke of Arión and Marquis of Valero, second son of the Duke of Bejar and Viceroy of New Spain 1716–1722.

BEYERSVILLE (Williamson) Known from the 1860s as Dacus. PO 15 Apr 1893 as Beyersville, PM German emigrant Gustav Beyer.

BIARDSTOWN [BAHRDZ tuhn] (Lamar) Brothers William Washington and John Gaines Biard came to Texas from Limestone County, AL, in 1848. Postal officials took Biard to be a misspelling of Baird and authorized the Baird PO 3 May 1880. The name was changed to Biard three weeks later and to Biardstown 27 Feb 1883, PM William A. Milling.

BIG LAKE (Reagan) The Kansas City, Mexico & Orient Railway established a shipping station about 1911, named from Big Lake, a thousand-acre playa south of the townsite. PO 13 Apr 1912, PM James D. Nairn.

BIG SANDY (Upshur) Named from Big Sandy Creek when the Texas & Pacific Railway built through the area in the early 1870s. PO 14 June 1875, PM Steven P. Kay.

BIG SPRING (Howard) From the 1870s Big Spring was an informal campground south of the present city, a collection of tents and lean-tos around the "big spring," that had been a source of water for Native Americans, buffalo, and wild horses for centuries. In 1880, the Texas & Pacific Railway established a station on Sulphur Draw that became the nucleus of the town of Big Spring. The PO was established by Joseph Anderson when Big Spring became the Howard County seat in 1882.

BIG SQUARE (Castro) The local account is that Marcus and Sarah Stiles, early 1900s settlers, arranged the houses of their extended family into the pattern of a big square. PO 12 Aug 1910, PM Otis Burton.

BIG WELLS (Dimmit) Dimmit County commissioner Sal Armstrong named the town about 1910 for the local artesian wells. PO 2 Feb 1911, PM Enos Simon.

BIGFOOT (Frio) Named for William Alexander Anderson "Bigfoot" Wallace, a legendary Texas folk hero and teller of tales. By local legend Wallace received his nickname from his efforts to bring to justice an imposing Waco Indian named Bigfoot who was stealing settlers' supplies. On one occasion Wallace was misidentified as the Waco and given the name Bigfoot amid fits of laughter. Wallace lived the last years of his life in the 1890s as an admired local figure near the town of Bigfoot. PO 7 Feb 1883, PM James Connelly.

BIROME [beye ROM] (Hill) Founded about 1910 as a shipping station on the International–Great Northern Railroad. Named for brothers Elisha *Bi*ckham Cartwright and Columbus Je*rome* Cartwright, owners of the Cartwright Ranch and sons of Robert Cartwright of Waco, a noted Texas historian of the late 19th century. PO 29 Aug 1912, PM Isaac C. Byerley.

BIRTHRIGHT (Hopkins) In 1867 Clayborn Edward Birthright brought his family from Missouri to Hopkins County and with his sons established a gristmill and general store. PO 10 July 1871, PM Edward McLaughlin.

BIRY (Medina) Biry is probably an adaptation of Bereig, from Jacob Bereig, one of the first French settlers in Henri Castro's Colony. His son, also Jacob Bereig (Biry) founded the community as Briar Branch about 1888. PO 26 Sept 1907 as Biry, PM Joseph Franger.

BISHOP (Nueces) Founded in 1910 by Frank Zion Bishop, a real estate agent of Corpus Christi and later of Dallas. PO 21 Sept 1910, PM Charles Jones.

BIVINS (Cass) Named for brothers Frank and James Bivins, sawmillers of northeast Texas from the late 1880s. PO 26 May 1881 as Hoxie, PM William F. Cobb; changed to Wayne 11 May 1883; changed to Bivens

20 Nov 1889; changed to Bivins 10 Nov 1894, PM Richard Cobb.

BIXBY (Cameron) Probably named for William K. Bixby, a St. Louis industrialist, philanthropist, and financier who held stock and served on the boards of several Texas railroads in the late 19th and early 20th centuries.

BLACK (Parmer) In 1898 the Pecos & Northern Texas Railway established a station named for site owner, rancher, and businessman Epenetus (several spellings) Bushrod Black. The E. B. Black House in Hereford, TX, is on the National Register of Historic Places. PO 26 Apr 1912, PM Joseph C. Baker.

BLACK ANKLE At least two Texas towns have been known as Black Ankle. In San Augustine County the local story, told tongue in cheek, is that a young woman on her way to a community dance, tore one of her silk stockings and concealed the hole by painting her bare ankle with soot. That same story is told about the origin of Black Ankle in Caldwell County, accompanied by a second account that the name refers to the heavy black soil that sticks to one's boots ankle high after a heavy rain.

BLACK HILL (Atascosa) John Temple established the Black Hill School in 1920. According to Temple, "There was a hill here that was called Loma Prieta. I didn't like that name for the school but I liked what it meant translated so that's what the county superintendent and I decided to call the school, Black Hill School" (Clover, 81).

BLACKJACK (Cherokee) In the 1840s Robert G. Stadler, a soldier in the Texas Revolution, and members of his family from South Carolina settled at the site they called Black Jack Grove, apparently named for the stands of Blackjack oaks (*Quercus Marilandica*).

BLACKLAND (Rockwall) Blackland was named for its location on the western edge of the Blackland Belt, the fertile prairie ecological region that runs from the Red River south to San Antonio. PO 25 Sept 1876, PM William Harvey.

BLACKWELL (Coke, Nolan) Known in the early 20th century as James or Jamestown. PO 4 June 1907 as Blackwell, PM David Hunt. Probably named for George S. Blackwell, a British stockholder in the Kansas City, Mexico & Orient Railway.

BLAIR (Taylor) When the Gulf, Colorado & Santa Fe Railway built through the area in 1910 the station took the name of the Blair School, itself named for community benefactor Walter (Watt) Blair. PO 9 May 1905 as Blair, PM Charlie B. Hill who chose the name for the school.

BLANCHARD (Polk) Founded about 1908 with construction of the Beaumont & Great Northern Railroad line between Onalaska and Livingston. Named by William Carlisle, owner of the sawmill at Onalaska, reportedly in honor of his brother-in-law, Ben Blanchard. PO 4 Aug 1908, PM Stephen Andress. See Onalaska.

BLANCO [BLANG ko] (County) Created and organized 1858. Pittsburgh, the first formal settlement in the area, was established by the Pittsburgh Land Company, organized by and named for John D. Pitts in the mid-1850s. The county was named from the Blanco (Spanish "white") River, itself probably named during the 1721 expedition of Marqués de Aguayo for the white limestone lining the river's banks and much of its bed.

BLANCO (Blanco) Founded shortly after Blanco County was created and named for the county. PO 26 Dec 1857 as New Pittsburgh; changed to Blanco 28 Sept 1858, PM Thomas Durham.

BLANCONIA [BLANG kon ee uh] (Bee) Blanconia has been known informally as Pull Tight, advice given to wagon drivers to keep tight reins when crossing Blanco Creek, and Dark Corner, supposedly for the abundance of large post oak trees which, according to some early riders, "blotted out the sun." Blanconia was formally named from Blanco Creek when Martin McGuill opened the PO in his general store 30 Jan 1888.

BLANDLAKE (San Augustine) In 1901 the Gulf, Colorado & Santa Fe Railway established a flag station called—appropriately—Stop. James Jefferson Bland from Muscogee County, GA, opened the Stop PO 9 May 1901 and changed the name to Blandlake 7 Dec 1903.

BLANKET (Brown) Traditionally the name comes from an incident in the early 1850s when Indians on a hunting expedition were caught in a thunderstorm and later spread their blankets on some bushes to dry. A group of surveyors came by, saw the drying blankets, and decided this would be a good name for the creek. PO 10 June 1875, PM Pinkney Anderson.

BLEAKWOOD (Newton) Thomas McFarland, who surveyed the site of Belgrade and San Augustine, established a plantation in the late 1840s, apparently named Cotland after his former plantation home in San Augustine County (perhaps a misspelling of Scotland, McFarland's ancestral home). The Cotland PO, with McFarland's son Samuel as the first PM, operated from 1850 until 1860. In 1867 the office was relocated and renamed Bleakwood, reportedly by T. L. McDonald, for his ancestral estate in Scotland.

BLEDSOE (Cochran) Founded in 1925 by the Atchison, Topeka & Santa Fe Railway. Named for Samuel T. Bledsoe, at the time general counsel and later president of the AT&SF. PO 7 June 1926, PM James Lackey.

BLEIBLERVILLE [BLEEB ler vil] (Austin) Rudolph Bleibler emigrated from Switzerland in the early 1880s, apparently changed his name to Robert Bleibler, opened a saloon and general store, and established the Bleiblerville PO 24 Nov 1891.

BLESSING (Matagorda) The area was first known as Deming's Bridge, named for PM Edwin Deming. In 1900 Jonathan Pierce led a campaign to change the name to Hawley for Congressman Robert Hawley. Not satisfied with this change, in 1903 Pierce donated land to the Galveston, Harrisburg & San Antonio Railway with the stipulation that the name of the town be changed to "Thank God" in gratitude for the railroad's arrival.

When this name was rejected, the PO application was resubmitted with the somewhat related name, Blessing.

BLEWETT [BLOO it] (Uvalde) Named about 1912 for John Blewett Smyth, a Beaumont lumberman and financier. PO 14 July 1928, PM William H. Smith.

BLODGETT (Titus) Formerly known as Liberty. PO 22 Sept 1903, PM John F. Blodgett.

BLOOMBURG (Cass) Founded in 1895 with construction of the Texarkana & Fort Smith Railway. The namesake is probably a railroad underwriter named Bloomburg, one of several Dutch investors in the T&FS. PO 17 Mar 1896, PM Wiley J. Easters. See Nederland.

BLOOMINGTON (Victoria) Founded in 1910 after construction of the St. Louis, Brownsville & Mexico Railway. Probably named by settlers from Bloomington, IL. PO 28 Aug 1907, PM Wilson M. Smith.

BLOSSOM (Lamar) Named from the flourish of wildflowers on Blossom Prairie. PO 12 May 184 as Blossom Prairie, PM George Wilson; changed to Blossom 29 Feb 1888, PM William H. Byrn.

BLOWOUT (Blanco) Blowout was founded in the mid-1850s; named from Blowout Spring and Blowout Cave. By local accounts the cave was home to thousands of bats and was named Blowout when a bolt of lightning struck the cave mouth causing an explosion of the gases that had built up from years of accumulating bat guano. PO 10 June 1875, PM Zebulon Rabb.

BLOX (Jasper) Edgar Daniel Bloxsom was chief statistician of the Kirby Lumber Company that founded the town as a lumber camp about 1919. In the early 1930s most of the town was physically moved some 20 miles northwest and renamed New Blox. PO 21 Nov 1919, PM Dora Wilson. See Kirbyville.

BLUEGROVE (Clay) The local account is that the community takes its name from a concentration of post oak trees that from a distance appear to be surrounded by an azure haze. PO 7 June 1888, PM Alonzo W. Flinn.

BLUETOWN (Cameron) Bluetown developed in the early 1940s as a marketing center for fruit and other crops grown in the Rio Grande Valley. The community prospered for a time but shrank and nearly disappeared until a colonia was established in the 1960s. By one account the name arose between the Bed and Blue forces from the war games of Fort Brown and Fort Ringgold. The community is now part of Bluetown-Iglesia Antigua.

BLUFFTON (Llano) William Davis, his son Edward, and Isaac Maxwell were early settlers in the mid-1850s. The trio named the town for their former home, Bluffton, Yell County, AR. PO 30 Jan 1873, PM John D. Brown.

BLUM [bluhm] (Hill) Founded in 1881 with construction of the Gulf, Colorado & Santa Fe Railway. Named for Leon Blum, a prominent Galveston importer and exporter, and a major stockholder in the GC&SF. Blum was instrumental in the founding of ALGOA. PO 17 Jan 1882, PM Asa Thames.

BLUNTZER (Nueces) Named for Nicholas and Teresa Bluntzer who emigrated from Bavaria in the 1840s as part of Henri Castro's Colony. PO 17 Apr 1894, PM Fred Bitterman.

BOBVILLE (Montgomery) See Dobbin.

BOERNE [BER nee] (Kendall) In 1849 German colonists from the Bettina commune in Llano County founded Tusculum, named for the estate of Roman orator Marcus Tullius Cicero. In the early 1850s Gustav Theissen platted Tusculum as Boerne, named for Karl Ludwig Börne (born Loeb Baruch), German intellectual, political writer, and satirist of the 1820s and 1830s. PO 18 June 1856, PM August Staffel.

BOGATA [buh GOT uh] (Red River) In 1881 James Horner, a Latin American history buff with a special interest in Simon Bolivar, applied for the Bogota PO, named for the capitol of Colombia, but the name was miswritten or misread and the PO was approved as Bogata.

BOIS D'ARC [BO DAHRK] (Rains) Founded in the 1890s and named for the bois d'arc trees (*Maclura pomifera*) native to East and Central Texas and used by early settlers for fenceposts and to create hedge rows to restrain livestock. The bois d'arc, French for "wood of the bow," was so named because the wood was prized for making bows by many groups of Native Americans. The fruit of the bois d'arc was often called osage oranges or horse apples because their color and shape were similar to that of fresh horse droppings.

BOLDTVILLE (Bexar) The area was known as Calaveras until 1919 when the Calaveras school was replaced by the new Boldtville school, built on land donated by blacksmith and school trustee Alfred F. Boldt. See Calaveras.

BOLES HOME (Hunt) William and Mary Boles founded Boles Home in 1923 as a refuge for orphans and abandoned children.

BOLING (Wharton) About 1900 land speculator Robert Edward Vineyard laid out the community as Bolling, named for his daughter, Mary Bolling Vineyard, who was named for her grandmother, Mary Rebecca Bolling. The name lost an "l" when Lloyd Travis established the Boling PO 24 Apr 1926.

BOLIVAR [BAHL uh ver] (Denton) Hiram Daily—doctor, preacher, and shopkeeper—founded New Prospect in 1859. A decade later farmer Ben Brown suggested the name be changed for his hometown, Bolivar, TN. Brown and Daily put the question to voters in 1861. Bolivar received the most votes, although some say the winning margin was created by the free whiskey Brown provided for undecided voters. PO 2 May 1872, PM Samuel McAdams.

BOMARTON [BO mer tuhn] (Baylor) William and Alameda Bomar from Tennessee settled in the area in the early 1900s. The town was named for the Bomars when the Wichita Valley Railway built through the area in 1906. PO 9 Nov 1905 as Worleys, PM King Worley; changed to Bomarton 19 Dec 1906, PM John T. McClure.

BON WIER (Newton) Bon Wier, founded as a Jasper & Eastern Railway station in 1905, was named for Benjamin Franklin *Bon*ner and Robert Withrow *Wier*, both associated with the Kirby Lumber Company at the time and subsequently vice president and president, respectively, of the R. W. Wier Lumber Company with headquarters at WIERGATE. PO 1 Dec 1906, PM John Gilchrist.

BONAMI (Jasper) Robert J. Cooper, a restaurateur and native Louisianan, suggested the name in the early 1900s, probably for Bon Ami, Beauregard Parish, LA. PO 8 Sept 1902, PM Charles A. Mixson. Also spelled Bon Ami (French "good friend").

BONANZA (Hopkins) As a place name, Bonanza, from Spanish "prosperity," was popularized by the Bonanza boom towns and Bonanza mines associated with the California gold fields and Nevada silver mines of the 19th century. Bonanza is a popular place name, occurring in about 20 states. Bonanza, TX, may be a transfer or may have been chosen for the good fortune that it suggests. PO 14 July 1879 as Fowler's Store; changed to Cold Hill 21 Feb 1883; changed to Bonanza 31 Jan 1898, PM Archibald R. Hunter.

BONHAM [BAHN uhm] (Fannin) In 1836 Bailey Inglish built a small blockhouse that became known as Fort Inglish and later as Bois D'Arc. The community that grew around Inglish's fort was formally named in 1844 in honor of James Butler Bonham, a major figure in the political and military affairs of Texas in 1835. A relative of William B. Travis, Bonham died with Travis at the Alamo. PO 1 Feb 1840 as Fort Inglish, PM Bailey Inglish; changed 1 Apr 1843 to Bois D'Arc, PM Roswell W. Lee; changed to Bonham 26 Feb 1844.

BONITA (Montague) From Spanish "pretty." Bonita Station was established by the Gainesville, Henrietta & Western Railway in 1886. By local tradition the name was suggested by a railroad engineer for his daughter, Bonita Hansen. PO 14 June 1880 as Duxbury; changed to Bonita 18 Feb 1887, PM Elijah W. Giles.

BONNERVILLE (Freestone) Brothers William Andrew and John Oliver Bonner, landowners from Alabama, operated a cotton gin and gristmill from the 1850s. PO 6 Apr 1880 as Bonner, PM William Bonner.

BONNEY (Brazoria) Named in the 1870s, probably for Joseph Bonney, reportedly a conductor on the Columbia Tap Railroad. PO 20 July 1889, PM Louis Wanner.

BONNIE VIEW (Refugio) Founded about 1908 on the Bonnie View Ranch, itself established about 1850 by John Howland Wood. According to local accounts, upon seeing the ranch land for the first time, Wood's wife, Nancy Clark, exclaimed, "This is a bonny view." See Woodsboro.

BONO (Johnson) Calvin Lafayette Jones and Benjamin Hardy Williamson donated land for the townsite in the early 1870s. Jones reportedly took the name from a Latin dictionary where *bono* was translated as "good" that he took to be an omen for the community. PO 11 Apr 1879, PM William Hunter.

BONUS (Wharton) William Eldridge, general manager of the Cotton Belt Railroad and William Dunovant, president of the CB, founded Bonus in the 1890s. When Alamo was rejected as a name for the PO, the application was resubmitted requesting the name Bonus. According to local accounts the name recognized the bonus given to the CB for early completion of the line. Rather, the office was named for Eldridge's farm known as "Bonus Plantation." PO 14 Feb 1896, PM Andrew C. Mersfelder.

BOOKER (Lipscomb) La Kemp, OK, was founded about 1909. A decade later, with construction of the Panhandle & Santa Fe Railway, the town was moved six miles south to Texas. Thomas C. Spearman, vice president of the Santa Fe Railroad and the namesake of SPEARMAN, chose the name for locating engineer, Benjamin Franklin Booker. PO 25 Sept 1919, PM Jesse Bell.

BOONSVILLE (Wise) Named in the 1870s from Boon's Creek, itself reportedly named for early settler Stephen Boon. PO 10 Jan 1878, PM Joseph Roth.

BOOTH (Fort Bend) Freeman Irby Booth, a Richmond, TX, merchant and mill operator, founded the community in the early 1890s. PO 21 Mar 1894, PM Frank Tevis.

BOOTLEG (Deaf Smith) By one local story, bootleg liquor was produced at the Moonshine Sheep Camp and sold to travelers on the road from La Plata to New Mexico; by another, creative land agents built a small, portable building that could pass for a school house that was moved from one place to another, leading prospective land buyers to believe there was an existing school on the site they were being shown. Because of its mobility the "school" was called the "bootleg school."

BORACHO (Culberson) According to a local legend the town was named from Spanish *borracho* "drunk" following an incident in the 1880s when two railroad crews were competing in a tracklaying contest. A crew from the Galveston, Harrisburg & San Antonio line laid more miles of track after they presented several kegs of whiskey to their Texas & Pacific Railway competitors who became too mellow to compete. However, *borracho* can mean "violet colored" and the community was more likely named from nearby Boracho Peak that can take on a purple hue at sunset. PO 7 Dec 1908, PM Mary Glenn.

BORDEN (County) Created 1876, organized 1891. Named for Gail Borden, Jr. (1801–1874), born in New York. After spending time in Indiana and Mississippi, Borden had a long, varied, and distinguished career in Texas. He arrived in Galveston in 1829, was a surveyor for Stephen F. Austin, founded the *Telegraph and Texas Register* newspaper in 1835, prepared the first topographical map of Texas, assisted in laying out the site of Houston in 1836, and in 1857 founded the Borden Company, best known for the production of condensed milk. Bordenville in Colorado County and Gail in Borden County are also named in his honor.

BORDEN (Colorado) Shortly after the end of the Civil War, Gail Borden, Jr., founder and namesake of the Borden Milk Company, established a meat packing plant and the company town of Bordenville on what was then known as Harvey's Creek. Borden's brother John opened the PO as Borden 19 Jan 1874.

BORDERSVILLE (Harris) When the sawmills at Humble closed in the 1920s, the predominately African American workers moved to the mill operated by Edgar Borders and established Bordersville. Houston annexed Bordersville in 1965.

BORGER [BOR ger, BAHR ger] (Hutchinson) Asa Phillip Borger, a banker and real estate promoter, founded several oil towns in Oklahoma and the Texas Panhandle in the late 1910s and 1920s, including Borger in 1926. PO 21 Apr 1926, PM Lawrence Brain.

BOSQUE [BAHS kee] (County) Created and organized 1854. Named from the Bosque River, the north branch of which flows through the heart of the county. Although some have suggested the river was named for Juan Bosquet, a French trader who lived with the Tawakoni in the 1770s, the name is from Spanish *bosque* "woods, forest." In American Spanish, *bosque* referred in particular to clumps of trees or underbrush along the banks of rivers and smaller streams. The Bosque River was likely named by a member of the Marqués de Aguayo Expedition of 1719. There are several dozen places named Bosque in the American Southwest, most are in Texas and New Mexico.

BOSQUEVILLE (McLennan) Laid out in 1858; named from the Bosque River. PO 14 Apr 1860, PM Cornelius P. Petit (Pettit).

BOSTON (Bowie) Boston, New Boston, and Old Boston are all named from the original Boston, established in 1842. A traditional account holds that the community was named for shopkeeper W. J. Boston, about whom little, if indeed anything factual, is known. Hal Simpson offers the simplest and most likely correct source of the name, gathered from interviews with local people and early settlers' accounts. According to Simpson, in the 1820s a trading post catering to travelers was established where the Choctaw Trail crossed the Old Spanish Trail. The innkeeper would ask travelers where they were from and so many were from the Boston, MA, area that he decided to call the town Boston. PO 21 Feb 1843, PM John A. McKinney.

BOTINES (Webb) Apparently named from Spanish *bootines*, "boots, socks."

BOVINA [bo VEE nuh] (Parmer) According to local accounts, livestock feed unloaded at the Pecos & Northern Texas Railway switch often spilled and attracted cattle that obstructed the tracks, delayed trains, and gave the site its first name, Bull Town. When it came time to apply for a post office Bull Town was thought to be unseemly and the name was changed to the more refined Bovina, from Latin *bos* "cow." This is one of five Bovinas in the US. PO 31 Jan 1899, PM William Lafayette Guy.

BOWIE (County) Created and organized 1840. Named for James "Jim" Bowie (1796–1836), born in Kentucky and raised in Louisiana. Bowie was a legendary knife fighter, hero of the Alamo, and namesake and promoter if not inventor of the famous Bowie fighting knife known as an "Arkansas Toothpick."

BOWIE [BO ee, BOO ee] (Montague) Named in 1882 for Alamo defender James "Jim" Bowie when the Fort Worth & Denver Railway was built through Montague County. PO 24 Aug 1882, PM James Independence Gillespie Cowan.

BOWMAN (Archer) Known from the early 1880s as Springtown, the name was changed about 1890 in honor of Thomas Bowman, Bishop of the Evangelical Association, elected to the Episcopacy in 1875. PO 2 Dec 1892, PM William H. Bachman. Accidental, I am sure, but the name Bowman is amusingly appropriate for a town in Archer County. PO 2 Dec 1890, PM William H. Bachman.

BOWSER (San Saba) Bowser Bend was established on Abel Bowser's farm and mill near the sharp south-north bend in the Colorado River. Because of persistent floods, the town relocated to its present site in the early 1890s. PO 9 June 1887 as Bowser Bend; discontinued 15 May 1893. PO 30 Dec 1892 as Bowser, PM Eliza Boyd Maxwell.

BOYCE (Ellis) William A. Boyce emigrated from Alabama in 1870 and donated land for a Southern Pacific Railroad station in 1878. PO 4 Dec 1883, PM Charles Weideman.

BOYNTON (Angelina) Named from the Boynton Lumber Company operated by Albert and Walter Boynton in the early 1900s.

BOYS RANCH (Oldham) Cal Farley, an Amarillo businessman and former professional wrestler, founded the Maverick Boys Ranch for homeless boys in 1939. PO 1 Sept 1952, PM John O. Nickles.

BOZ [BAHZ] (Ellis) George and Tennessee Cunningham began farming in the area in the 1850s. The town was named for their son, Bozillia (Barzillia) Cunningham, known as Boz. PO 7 Mar 1891, PM James H. Alexander.

BRACHFIELD [BRACH feeld] (Rusk) Known as Needmore because "it needed more of everything" until 1900 when Ella Irene Phillips established the Brachfield post office, named for Charles Brachfield, a Henderson lawyer and Texas State Senator (1903–1911).

BRACKEN (Comal) The town of Davenport, named for early settler James G. Davenport, was established about 1850 with construction of the International–Great Northern Railroad and renamed in the early 1880s for site owner William Bracken who had been part of a crew that surveyed the area in 1839. PO 26 Dec 1883, PM Charles Schmitz.

BRACKETTVILLE (Kinney) The town of Las Moras (Spanish "the mulberries"), a supply post for Fort Clark, was formally named for Oscar Bernadotte Brackett, a merchant from Syracuse, NY, who opened a general store in 1852. PO 5 Sept 1855 as Fort Clark; changed to Brackettville 5 May 1873, PM Lawrence Hagarty.

BRAD (Palo Pinto) Named for site owner Bradford Fitzgerald from Tennessee who began farming in the area in the early 1860s. PO 28 May 1901, PM John W. Keegan.

BRADFORD (Anderson) Merchant Powell Luke Bradford opened the PO in his dry goods store 26 May 1882.

BRADSHAW (Taylor) Founded about 1900 as Audra, named for Audra Sheppard, daughter of merchant Frank Sheppard. The town was moved several miles east to trackside when the Santa Fe Railroad established a station on land donated by Charles M. Bradshaw. PO 24 Jan 1900 as Audra; changed to Bradshaw 19 Nov 1909, PM Charles P. Bennett.

BRADY (McCulloch) Brady's Creek was named for Peter Rainsford Brady who surveyed McCulloch and San Saba counties in the late 1840s. When McCulloch County was organized in 1876 the seat was named Brady City from Brady's Creek. PO 8 Aug 1876, PM Rupert R. Claridge.

BRAGG (Hardin) Founded about 1900 on the line of the Gulf, Colorado & Santa Fe Railway. Named for Confederate General Braxton Bragg. PO 24 Sept 1904, PM Albert B. Marcontell.

BRANOM (Hopkins) Named for Mary Rue and David Merit Branom, area farmers from the 1880s.

BRASHEAR [bruh SHIHR] (Hopkins) George W. Mahoney, the namesake of MAHONEY and an agent for a Seattle land consortium, purchased and subdivided the Wise Ranch about 1898. Part of the ranch became the town of Brashear, named for surveyor Joseph Brashear. PO 15 June 1899, PM William Y. Crain.

BRAZORIA (County) Created 1836, organized 1837. Named from the community of Brazoria.

BRAZORIA (Brazoria) Laid out in 1828 by John Austin (apparently unrelated to Stephen F. Austin, the site grantee), who adapted the name from the Brazos River. In an 1829 letter John Austin wrote of "a new town we laid off on the Brazos river...called Brassoria—a name I gave it for the single reason that I know of no other like it in the world" (Creighton, 37). PO 22 May 1846, PM Stephen Westervelt.

BRAZOS [BRAH zuhs] (County) Created 1841 as Navasota County, named from the Navasota River. The name was changed early in 1842 at the request of James Head, Navasota County's newly elected representative to the Texas Legislature. Head suggested the name for the Brazos River which flows more than 800 miles across Texas from Stonewall County to Brazoria County where it empties into the Gulf of Mexico. Brazos is a shortening of *Los Brazos de Dios* "the arms of God." There are a number of legends explaining the name, most having to do with lost, exhausted men parched with thirst who stumble upon the river that welcomes them like the arms of God.

BRECKENRIDGE (Stephens) Pickettville was founded north of current Breckenridge in the early 1850s. In March 1862 Camp Breckenridge, named (with altered spelling) for US Senator from Kentucky John C. Breckinridge, was established nearby and Pickettville was abandoned. Breckenridge was formally laid out when Stephens County was organized in 1876. PO 15 Dec 1876, PM James A. McAmiss.

BREMOND (Robertson) In the late 1860s the Houston & Texas Central Railway established Bremond Station, named for Paul Bremond, president of the H&TC. PO 21 Apr 1863 as Bellona; changed to Bremond 17 Nov 1869, PM John W. Park.

BRENHAM (Washington) Known as Hickory Grove until 1843 when the name was changed for Richard Fox Brenham, a doctor with a practice in Austin. Brenham was appointed by Texas President Mirabeau Lamar as one of the civil commissioners of the Texan Santa Fe Expedition in 1841. He later joined the Somervell Expedition and died at Ciudad Mier in December 1842. PO 1837 as McGarrah's; changed to Brenham 18 May 1844, PM Joseph Ralston.

BRESLAU [BRES law] (Lavaca) Named for Breslau, Prussia (now Wrocław, Poland) in November 1880 when Henry H. Hoffman opened the Breslau PO. The name was likely suggested by Friedrich (Fritz) Ladewig (Ludwig) who emigrated from Prussia in the 1860s. Ladewig kept a general store, operated a cotton gin, and donated land for a number of civic projects. PO 9 Nov 1880, PM Henry H. Hoffman.

BREWSTER (County) Created and organized 1887. Named for Henry Percy Brewster (1816–1884), a native South Carolinian. Brewster joined the Texas Army in 1836 and was Sam Houston's personal secretary, Secretary of War for the Republic of Texas, and Texas Attorney General in the 1850s.

BRIARY (Milam) Named from Big Briary Creek, itself presumably named for the briars and thick vegetation along its course.

BRICE (Hall) Charles Rufus Brice was Hall County attorney in the 1890s and mayor of Carlsbad, NM, in the 1900s. PO 2 Mar 1899, PM William C. Smith.

BRIDGE CITY (Orange) Named for the Neches River bridge between Orange County and Port Arthur. Formerly known as Prairie View. PO 1 July 1846, PM James B. Scales.

BRIDGEPORT (Wise) Bridgeport was founded about 1860 when William H. Hunt formed a land company to build a toll bridge over the West Fork of the Trinity River. The wood bridge was replaced by an iron structure in the early 1870s and the community was formally named for the bridge when Samuel I. Gibbs established the PO 5 May 1873.

BRIGHT STAR (Rains) Founded in the 1860s and reportedly named from the Bright Star Baptist Church of Alba in Wood County.

BRINKER (Hopkins) Named for William Isaac and Elizabeth Drusilla Brinker who relocated from Shelby County, AL, and began farming in the area about 1870. PO 20 Feb 1901, PM Susan W. Coppedge. Formerly known as Richland.

BRISCOE (County) Created 1876, organized 1892. Named for Andrew Briscoe (1810–1849), born on his parents' plantation in Mississippi. Briscoe became a successful

Texas merchant in the early 1830s, fought in the Texas Revolution, and was appointed chief justice of Harrisburg by Sam Houston. Dolph Briscoe, Jr., a descendant of Andrew Briscoe, was Governor of Texas in the 1970s.

BRISCOE (Wheeler) In 1929 the Lone Star Townsite Company laid out Briscoe, named for Jerry B. Briscoe of Amarillo, division superintendent of the Atchison, Topeka & Santa Fe Railway. PO 28 July 1930, PM Ira Elmer Byars.

BRISTOL (Ellis) Joshua Brock, who arrived in the area in the 1840s, opened the Brocksville PO 22 Sept 1854. The office closed in September 1868 and was reopened 15 Aug 1872 as Bristol, the name reportedly suggested by Steven Mills, a maritime trader who had conducted business in Bristol, England.

BRITTON (Ellis) Founded as Hellandville for Hans Helland (Holland), engineer for the Houston & Texas Central Railway in the 1890s. Likely renamed for James Britton, a contractor for the Texas & New Orleans Railroad. PO 19 Jan 1895 as Hellandville; changed to Britton 13 Nov 1896, PM Garrette Maynard.

BROADWAY (Crosby) Reportedly named for the endless view of the prairie by Joseph "Uncle Shorty" Reynolds, a cattle driver on the Chisholm Trail in the 1880s and a shopkeeper in DICKENS and Broadway in the early 20th century.

BROCK (Parker) Farmer and carpenter John Henry Brock relocated from Georgia in the early 1870s. He and his business partner, Willie Brannon, established a cotton gin and gristmill about 1880. PO 23 Apr 1888, PM James Cherry.

BRONCO (Yoakum; Lea, NM) According to the local story, the name was suggested by a traveling salesman after seeing a cowboy riding a bucking horse. PO 21 Nov 1903, PM Herchel R. Field.

BRONSON (Sabine) Named in 1902 with construction of the Gulf, Beaumont & Great Northern Railroad for Samuel Bronson Cooper who served in the Texas Senate and seven terms in the US House beginning in 1893. PO 11 Oct 1902, PM Nathan Pratt.

BRONTE [BRAHNT] (Coke) Dr. Wesley Fletcher Key, a physician from Butts County, GA, founded Bronte in the early 1890s. Key chose the name for the British Bronte family of writers and artists that included Emily, Charlotte, Anne, and Branwell Bronte. PO 19 Sept 1890, PM George Kelly. Earlier known as Oso, (Spanish "bear"), and also as Bronco.

BROOKELAND (Sabine) Named from the post office established by John C. Brooke 26 July 1866.

BROOKESMITH (Brown) Brooke Smith, a Brownwood benefactor, was a founder of the Pecan Valley Bank and mayor of BROWNWOOD in 1886. PO 30 Jan 1903, PM William Carr.

BROOKS (County) Created 1911, organized 1912. Named for James Abijah Brooks (often identified as John Abijah Brooks) (1855–1944), born in Kentucky. Brooks was a legendary Texas Ranger, a county judge, and Texas State Representative from Starr County in the early 20th century where he was instrumental in creating the county named for him.

BROOKSHIRE (Waller) Nathan Brookshire received a section of land in Stephen F. Austin's Fifth Colony in the 1830s. He is best known for his participation in the Bird's Creek Indian Fight in 1839. PO 27 Oct 1878 as Leslie, PM Robert H. Leslie; changed to Brookshire 14 June 1893, PM Willie J. Cooper.

BROOKSTON (Lamar) Named about 1873 for site owner Arnold D. Brooks of Paris, TX. In the 1880 census Brooks's occupation is "gambler." PO 1 Dec 1873, PM Robert Mayo.

BROOME (Sterling) Founded in 1924 on the Panhandle & Santa Fe Railway line. Named for rancher Claude Aylmer Broome. PO 13 Apr 1912, PM Thomas W. Osteen.

BROWN (County) Created 1856, organized 1857. Named for Henry Stevenson Brown (1793–1834). Brown, a native Kentuckian, fought in the War of 1812, was a trader and Indian fighter in Texas from the mid-1820s, and participated in the Battle of Velasco in 1832.

BROWN (Martin) Named for Albert and Mary Brown who brought their family from Runnels County, TX, about 1905.

BROWNDELL (Jasper) Founded about 1903 by the Kirby Lumber Company. The "Brown" of Browndell is for John Wilcox Brown, president of the Maryland Trust Company and a financial backer of John Kirby's lumber enterprises; "dell" is an adaptation of Ellen for Brown's wife, Ellen Turner McFarland Brown. Earlier known as Weed. PO 14 Aug 1903, PM John P. Lynd. See Kirby.

BROWNFIELD (Terry) Named for Alfred Marion Brownfield who sold the townsite to land speculators William Gaines Hardin, Alfred Franklin Small, and his father, Marion Virgil Brownfield, who laid out the community in 1903. Named for Alfred Marion Brownfield who sold the townsite to his father, Marion Virgil Brownfield, and land speculators William Gaines Hardin and Alfred Franklin Small. PO 1 Apr 1903, PM Joseph R. Hill, the town's first hotelier.

BROWNING (Smith) In 1852 Isaiah Nicholas Browning moved from Alabama to Texas via Mississippi. About 1870 he established a cotton gin and gristmill and opened a general store. PO 16 June 1879 as Browning('s), PM William A. Owens.

BROWNSBORO (Caldwell) Named about 1860 for farmers Ransom and Jemima Brown who arrived in the area in the late 1840s.

BROWNSBORO (Henderson) Named for John "Red" Brown, who served in the first legislature of the State of Texas and was instrumental in the creation of Henderson County and ATHENS as the county seat. Brownsborough was organized shortly after Brown died in 1852. PO 12 May 1852 as Brownsborough, PM Beaufort W. Brown; changed to Brownsboro 8 Sept 1892.

BROWNSVILLE (Cameron) In March 1846, when war with Mexico was imminent, the US Army built Fort Texas on the Rio Grande opposite Matamoros, Mexico. General Zachary Taylor renamed the installation Fort Brown in honor of Major Jacob Brown, in command of Fort Texas until he was killed by Mexican artillery in early May 1846. In 1848 Charles Stillman, a trader and industrialist, with his business partner Samuel Belden, purchased the site and laid out the town of Brownsville, named from the fort. PO 3 Feb 1849, PM Reuben Clements.

BROWNWOOD (Brown) Founded and named in 1857 with the organization of Brown County. PO 23 Aug 1858, PM Henry C. Knight.

BRUCEVILLE-EDDY (Falls, McLennan) When the Missouri–Kansas–Texas Railroad built through the area in 1882, landowner Lucien Bruce donated land for the station that became the nucleus of the town of Bruce. About the same time, a mile south of Bruce, the Eddy post office was established and named for Everett B. Eddy, division superintendent of the railroad. The communities merged as the city of Bruceville-Eddy in 1974. PO 15 Mar 1887 as Bruceville, PM George W. Kincheloe. PO 7 July 1882 as Eddy, PM Frank K. Richardson.

BRUNDAGE (Dimmit) Named about 1909 for Spencer Brundage, founding partner of the Hurst and Brundage Company, a San Antonio land development firm. PO 24 Feb 1910, PM Etta Rudolph.

BRUNI [BROO nee] (Webb) Founded by Antonio Mateo Bruni, born in Emilia-Romagna, Italy. Bruni, a Laredo businessman, was a merchant, rancher, and local official, and a director of the Texas Mexican Railway. PO 24 Apr 1899 as Bruniville, PM Lodovico Moglia; changed to Bruni 16 Feb 1900.

BRUNSWICK (Cherokee) Apparently named by Edward Body for New Brunswick, Canada. Body was supervisor of the experimental farm established about 1903 by the Cherokee Orchard Company.

BRYAN (Brazos) In the late 1850s William Joel Bryan, son of James Bryan and Emily Austin, sister of Stephen F. Austin, donated land for a townsite and station for the Houston & Texas Central Railway. PO 22 May 1846 as Boonville; changed to Bryan 19 Dec 1866, PM Mercer Phelan.

BRYARLY (Red River) Founded about 1839 as Mound City, a steamboat landing on the Red River, by Rowland Thornton Bryarly. The name was changed when R. T. Bryarly's nephew, Joseph Lupton Bryarly, established the Bryarly PO 22 Apr 1892.

BRYSON (Jack) Earlier known as Mount Hecla, named from the PO established 28 May 1878 by Hamilton Millikin. The office was probably named for Mount Hecla, one of Iceland's more famous volcanoes, which had erupted spectacularly the month before. Milliken renamed the Hecla PO in 8 Apr 1884 in honor of early settler Henry Elam Bryson from Tennessee who built the first shelter in the 1870s in what became the town of Bryson.

BUCHANAN DAM [buhk HAN uhn] (Llano) In 1931 construction began on a dam to control floods on the Colorado River. The project created Lake Buchanan and the dam was dedicated in 1937, named in honor of James Paul Buchanan, US Representative (1913–1937).

BUCHEL [boo SHEL] (Wise) Named in the early 1890s for Cuero merchant and banker Otto Buchel who donated land for the Buchel school.

BUCKEYE (Matagorda) Founded in 1902 as the Buckeye Irrigation Farm by Ambrose Plotner and John Stoddard, both from Dayton, OH, the Buckeye State. PO 23 July 1907, PM Arthur H. Yerxa.

BUCKHOLTS (Milam) John Abel Buckholts, Milam County Representative in the Texas Legislature in the early 1860s, donated land for a station on the line of the Gulf, Colorado & Santa Fe Railway in 1881. PO 17 Jan 1882, PM William A. Hardin.

BUCKNER (Parker) James Monroe Buckner and his son William "were attempting to cross the Brazos on May 12, 1877, when a sudden headrise in the river swept William from the wagon. His father jumped into the swift water but before he could rescue the boy, they both drowned" (Parker Historical Commission, 187). PO 7 Jan 1884, PM John S. Morton.

BUDA [BYOO duh] (Hays) In 1881 the International–Great Northern Railroad established Dupree Station. By one local story the name Dupree is the result of a citizen pleading with railroad officials "Do, pray, give us a depot" that was misinterpreted and taken to be the name of the town. More likely the station was named for Levis J. DuPre, then editor of the *Austin Democratic Statesman*. By the end of 1887 the name Dupree had been replaced by Buda. A frequent explanation is that Buda is a popular etymology of Spanish *viuda* "widow," familiar to railroad workers since *viuda* was the name given to female cooks in the hotel dining room run by Sarah Carrington, wife of postmaster and hotelier Leonidas Carrington who changed the name of the Dupree PO to Buda. Other than tradition there is little support for this etymology and Carrington or another citizen most likely renamed the office for Buda, Hungary, on the west bank of the Danube River, which was in the news because of its 1873 merger with Pest on the east bank, creating modern Budapest. PO 24 Dec 1867 as Onion Creek; changed to Dupree 21 Mar 1881; changed to Buda 25 Aug 1887, PM Leonidas D. Carrington. For additional information, see Barry Popik's Buda.

BUG TUSSLE (Fannin) One of Texas's notable place names. As we would expect, there are a number of local stories explaining the name. By one, swarms of bugs disrupted an ice cream social; by another, after Sunday School picnics there was nothing to do but watch the bugs tussle among themselves. As Fred Tarpley so pointedly put it, whatever the origin of the name, "the area was a favorite gathering place for both bugs and Sunday School outings." (*1001 Texas Place Names*)

BULA [BYOO luh] (Bailey) In 1924 William Barnes Newsome, a Dallas banker, and his son Tom subdivided the Newsome Ranch and laid out the town of Beulahland, shortened to Bula, likely named for Beulah Carles, who kept the Muleshoe PO from April 1920 until April 1935. PO 29 May 1925, PM William H. Thorn.

BULLARD [BUL erd] (Cherokee, Smith) When the Kansas & Gulf Short Line Railroad extended its line from Tyler to Lufkin in 1883, the towns of Hewsville and Aetna moved to trackside and merged when Hewsville PM John H. Bullard changed the name of the office 13 Nov 1883.

BULVERDE (Comal) Named for Luciano Bulverde, a landowner from the 1830s.

BUNA [BYOO nuh] (Jasper) The site was originally known as Carrolla, named for Frank and Joseph Carroll who managed the Beaumont Lumber Company from the mid-1870s. Formally named in the late 1880s for Lillian Buena Corley, daughter of James Marion Corley, a business associate and probably a relative of the Carrolls. Buna may be a misreading or perhaps a family pronunciation of Buena. PO 28 Sept 1893, PM Joseph E. Carroll.

BUNAVISTA (Hutchinson) Bunavista was founded in 1942 as a factory town for employees of the Phillips Petroleum plant, manufacturer of Styrene-Butadiene Rubber (SBR), the synthetic rubber developed by German chemists in the 1930s. The name is apparently an acronym: BU from Butadiene and NA from Natrium (a former name for sodium) with "vista" added to associate the name with *buena vista* (Spanish "good view"). Bunavista is now part of BORGER.

BUNCOMBE [BUHNG kuhm] (Panola) A local tale is that the community was named when an Indian pointed to where he slept and announced, "me bunkum." More likely the name is a transfer, probably from Buncombe County, NC. PO 26 Oct 1891 as Buncomb, PM William J. Snow. Also spelled Bumcomb, Bunkom, Bunkum.

BUNGER (Young) Founded in 1872 by William Thomas Bunger who emigrated from Hardin County, KY, in the mid-1860s and became an early sheriff of Young County. PO 26 July 1909, PM John L. Castleman.

BURFORD (Marion) Named for Nathaniel Macon Burford, John Reagan's Dallas law partner, who was elected district attorney and district judge in the 1870s.

BURKBURNETT (Wichita) Jeremiah and Nancy Burnett brought their family to Texas from Missouri about 1859. Their son, rancher Samuel Burke Burnett, established the 6666 brand in the late 1860s and in the early 20th century sold a large tract to the Red River Land Company that laid out the townsite as Burkburnett about 1906. PO 18 Apr 1907, PM Maggie Weaver.

BURKE (Angelina) In 1882 the Houston East & West Texas Railway extended a line to a site known as Rhodes. The station was named for Edmund Burke, chief of the crew that surveyed the route of the HE&WT and the son of Houston merchant and railroad investor Andrew J. Burke. PO 25 June 1883 as Rhodes, PM Harris Rhodes; changed to Burke 23 Apr 1886, PM David M. Stovall.

BURKETT (Coleman) Named by PM William Burkett who established the post office 10 Aug 1889.

BURKEVILLE (Newton) Founded on Little Cow Creek by John R. Burke in 1844. Burke represented the district in the Texas House of Representatives in the early 1850s. PO 27 Oct 1847, PM John R. Burke.

BURLESON (County) Created and organized 1846. Named for Edward Burleson (1798–1851), born in Buncombe County, NC. Burleson arrived in Texas in 1830. He was a regimental commander at San Jacinto and an Indian fighter after the Texas Revolution. Burleson was Vice President of the Republic of Texas in 1841 and assisted in laying out the city of San Marcos in 1851. He is often confused with his son, also Edward Burleson, both of whom served in the Mexican War.

BURLESON (Johnson) Burleson was founded in 1882 with construction of the Missouri–Kansas–Texas Railroad on land owned by Henry C. Renfro, a Baptist minister, who chose the name in honor of Rufus Columbus Burleson, his professor at Baylor and president of the university 1851–1861 and 1886–1897. PO 17 Jan 1882, PM Samuel Williams.

BURLINGTON (Milam) From the 1870s the community was known as the Irish Settlement and later as Waterford for Waterford, Ireland. PO 24 June 1884 as Waterford; changed to Burlington 29 Nov 1889 by PM Timothy Gleason for his former home, Burlington, VT.

BURNELL (Karnes) Named for rancher and trail driver Pleasant Burnell Butler.

BURNET [BUHR nit] (County) Created 1852, organized 1854. Named for lawyer and politician David Gouverneur Burnet (1788–1870). Burnet was President of the provisional government of the Republic of Texas, March 17–October 22, 1836, thus he is often cited as the first President of the Republic. He served as Vice President of the Republic of Texas (1838–1841) in the administration of Mirabeau Buonaparte Lamar.

BURNET (Burnet) Founded in 1852 as Hamilton and the county seat, named for early settler John Hamilton. PO 30 Aug 1852 as Burnet, PM Logan Vandeveer.

BURR (Wharton) Burr Albert Harrison emigrated from Virginia about 1859 and became the proprietor and operator of sugar and gristmills on Caney Creek. PO 2 Mar 1899 as Kriegel, PM Charles Kriegel; changed to Burr 17 May 1910, PM Gerard A. Harrison.

BURRANTOWN (Houston) Named for John Milton and Nancy Ann Burran who relocated from Louisiana in the 1870s.

BURTON (Washington) Named for John M. Burton, a carpenter and farmer born in Georgia. Burton was instrumental in attracting a branch line of the Texas Central Railway in the early 1870s. PO 6 June 1870, PM Benjamin J. Arnold.

BUSHLAND [BUSH luhnd] (Potter) William Henry Bush, a Chicago businessman, was the Texas agent for the sale of barbed wire and son-in-law of the inventor of barbed wire, Joseph Glidden of DeKalb, IL. In 1908 Bush, part owner of the Frying Pan Ranch, donated land for the townsite and for the Chicago, Rock Island & Gulf Railway right of way. PO 14 Jan 1909, PM Charles Bush.

BUSTAMANTE (Zapata) Founded on the *Rancho Las Comitas*, land granted to Pedro José Bustamante in 1835. PO 16 Oct 1913, PM Sylvester J. Dilly.

BUTLER (Bastrop) Michael Butler emigrated from Limerick, Ireland, in 1866, manufactured bricks in Dallas, and founded the Elgin-Butler Brick Company in Austin. The town was named for Butler with construction of the Texas & New Orleans Railroad in 1871.

BUTLER (Freestone) Named in the mid-1850s by settlers from Butler County, AL. PO 7 Aug 1855 as West Point; changed to Butler 23 May 1856, PM John T. Gill.

BYERS (Clay) In the early 20th century George and Anthony Byers, farm implement and machinery dealers in Sherman, TX, and ranch owners in Clay County donated land for a station on the Wichita Falls & Oklahoma Railway line and laid out a town on a corner of their property. PO 8 Sept 1876 as Benvanue; changed to Byers 6 Sept 1904, PM Robert M. Harris.

BYRD (Ellis) Farmer Charles Byrd moved to Texas from Little Rock, AR, in the 1870s and donated land for the first school about 1880. PO 6 Sept 1894 as Byron, PM William Champ; discontinued 14 Sept 1905.

BYRDS (Brown) Martin H. Byrd (Bird) emigrated from Missouri about 1865, established the first general store in the area, and opened the PO 6 Nov 1877 as Byrd's Store; changed to Byrds 18 Mar 1896, PM Alfred Mills.

O

CACTUS (Moore) Cacti have long been associated with the Southwest and the name was a natural choice in 1942 when the Cactus Ordnance Works was organized to produce ammunition and explosives for the US military during World War. PO 1 Mar 1948, PM Leona G. Cleveland.

CADDO (Stephens) Founded in the 1870s on a site presumed to be a Caddo village or campground. The Caddo are a Native American people who inhabited the area for several hundred years until 1854 when they were removed first to the Brazos Reservation and then to Indian Territory. The name is a French shortening of Kadohadacho "true chief." PO 28 May 1877, PM Robert Caradine.

CADDO MILLS (Hunt) Named for the grist and lumber mills established by Isaac Johnson and Thomas King on Caddo Creek in the 1870s. PO 16 June 1879, PM Arthur B. Mason.

CADIZ [KAY deez] (Bee) Cadiz, a port city in southwestern Spain, came to the world's attention during the Peninsular War of the early 1800s. Shortly thereafter Cadiz was transferred to Trigg County, KY, and may have been transferred from KY to TX. Alternatively, Stephen Worly, a native Illinoisan, may have transferred the name from Cadiz in southern Illinois when he established the Cadiz PO 31 Oct 1892.

CAESAR (Bee) From the mid 1870s the area was known as Wolfe's Neighborhood, reportedly for early settler Peter Wolfe. According to local sources, the post office application included a number of possible names drawn from the Bible and postal authorities chose Caesar. PO 8 Dec 1903, PM Robert L. Peavy.

CAIN CITY (Gillespie) John C. Stinson, a San Antonio businessman, founded the town named for Charles Cain who was instrumental in attracting a station on the Fredericksburg & Northern Railway in 1913. F&N station agent Hugo A. Pahl established the PO 9 Jan 1915.

CALALLEN [KAL AL uhn] (Nueces) The Calvin Townsite Company, organized by *Cal*vin J. *Allen*, founded the community in 1910. Calallen was annexed by Corpus Christi in 1970. PO 25 Mar 1908, PM Ira Magee.

CALAVERAS [kal uh VER uhs] (Wilson) Named for Calaveras Creek which empties into the San Antonio River southwest of Calaveras. Spanish for "skulls," the place name Calaveras occurs in California, New Mexico, and Texas and refers to areas where remarkable numbers of skulls, often buffalo skulls, were found. PO 24 Mar 1882 as Wright, PM William P. Wright; changed to Calaveras 15 Dec 1882, PM William Frazier.

CALDWELL (County) Created and organized 1848. Named for Mathew Caldwell (1798–1842), a native Kentuckian who came to Texas by way of Missouri in 1831. Caldwell was a signer of the Texas Declaration of Independence in 1836 and a military leader in the 1840s, distinguishing himself in combat with Comanche and later Mexican forces.

CALDWELL (Burleson) Authorized by the Texas Legislature about 1840 and named for Mathew Caldwell. See Caldwell County.

CALF CREEK (McCulloch) The area was known as Deland for Edward and Narcis Deland who emigrated from Kansas in the late 1860s, and then as Tucker for the general store kept by Lum Tucker from about 1910. The town then took the name of Calf Creek, so named, according to legend, by cattle rustlers who found the creek's brushy banks a perfect cover for stolen livestock. PO 8 May 1906 as Deland; changed to Tucker 20 Mar 1909; changed to Calf Creek 11 May 1915, PM William W. Currie.

CALHOUN (County) Created and organized 1846. Named for John Caldwell Calhoun (1782–1850), born in South Carolina. Calhoun was US Vice President under John Quincy Adams and Andrew Jackson, and US Senator from South Carolina when Calhoun County was created. As Secretary of State in 1844 Calhoun was a strong supporter of Texas statehood.

CALL (Jasper, Newton) Named for Dennis Call, part owner of a sawmill established by 1895 by the Cow Creek Tram Company organized by Call and George Adams to transport timber to the Sabine River. PO 25 July 1896, PM Chauncey B. Shepard.

CALLAGHAN (Webb) Named from the Callaghan Ranch, a quarter of a million acres between San Antonio and Laredo, established by sheep rancher Charles Callaghan shortly after the close of the Civil War.

CALLAHAN (County) Created 1858, organized 1877. Named for James Hughes Callahan (1812–1856), a native Georgian. Callahan fought in the Texas Revolution and assisted in the establishment of SEGUIN.

CALLIHAM (McMullen) In the late 1910s Harvey Hiram McGuffey kept a general store in an oil boomtown that became known as Guffeyola. About 1920 McGuffey left the area and the town was renamed Calliham for rancher and site owner Joseph Calliham. PO 20 Aug 1923, PM John R. Elliott.

CALLISBURG (Cooke) Samuel Callis, from Tennessee by way of Arkansas and Missouri, established a blacksmith shop about 1870 and opened the PO as Callisburgh [*sic*] PO 26 May 1873.

CALVERT (Robertson) Robert Calvert and other cotton planters and investors laid out the community in 1868 with assurance that the Houston & Texas Central Railway would shortly be building through the area. PO 29 July 1868, PM Charles Moore.

CAMERON (County) Created and organized 1848. Named for Ewen (often reported as Ewing) Cameron who emigrated from Scotland in the 1830s. Cameron joined the Texas Revolutionary Army and played a major role in the battle of Mier and although he drew the white bean of life in the mortal lottery, he was shot and killed attempting to escape.

CAMERON (Milam) Named for Ewen Cameron in 1846, replacing Nashville as the Milam county seat. PO 8 Mar 1847, PM Albert Gallatin. See Cameron County.

CAMEY (Denton) In the early 1850s the St. Louis–San Francisco Railway established Camey Spur named for site owner William McKamy [*sic*]. PO 10 July 1913, PM Ernest Thomas.

CAMILLA (San Jacinto) Named for Camilla Gertrude Hardin Davis, descendant of a storied patriot family and wife of George W. Davis, a Galveston lawyer of the 1880s. PO 2 Dec 1895, PM William D. Phillips.

CAMP (County) Created and organized 1874. Named for John Lafayette Camp (1828–1891). Camp, from Alabama by way of Tennessee, emigrated to northeast Texas in 1849 and became one of the area's best known and most successful plantation owners and lawyers. He was elected to the Texas Senate in 1874 where he presented the petition to create Camp County.

CAMP VERDE (Kerr) The town was named for Camp Verde, a US Army post established in 1856 as headquarters for the 1850s "camel corps" experiment. The post was named from its location on Rio Verde (Verde Creek), from Spanish *verde* "green." PO 10 June 1858, PM Richard Meade.

CAMP WOOD (Real) The Uvalde Cedar Company founded Camp Wood as a company town in 1920, named from Camp Wood, a military outpost first established in 1857 and named in honor of Brevet Major George W. F. Wood who was stationed at a number of posts on the Texas frontier and died of yellow fever in 1854. PO 24 July 1879, PM George B. Johnson.

CAMPBELL (Hunt) Named for Thomas Mitchell Campbell, a Longview lawyer who was largely responsible for attracting a station on the East Line & Red River Railroad in 1880. Campbell would become the 24th Governor of Texas in 1907. PO 27 June 1881 as Oliverea; changed to Campbell 18 Sept 1882, PM Edwin Thomas.

CAMPBELLTON (Atascosa) Campbellton was founded in the 1860s by John Campbell, who emigrated from Donegal, Ireland, about 1850. Jourdan Campbell, son of John and Mary Campbell, was a founder of CHARLOTTE and JOURDANTON. PO 5 Aug 1879, PM John Campbell.

CAMPTI (Shelby) Named about 1880 by settlers from Campti, Natchitoches Parish, LA, itself apparently named for a Caddo leader of the mid-18th century, called by French explorers *Le Roi Campti* "King Campti," whose village was nearby. PO 23 Jan 1902, PM John Pierce.

CANADIAN (Hemphill) Canadian was founded about 1887 by Orville Howell Nelson's Finch, Lord & Nelson Townsite Company that laid out several prospective towns in preparation for stations on the Panhandle & Santa Fe Railway. The community was named from the Canadian River, itself named from a Caddo name for the Red River, altered by popular etymology to Spanish *Río Canadiano* and then to English Canadian. The river was earlier known as *Río Magdalena*, probably named by Juan de Oñate about 1600, perhaps in honor of his sister, Magdalena Mendoza de Salazar. PO 3 Aug 1887, PM Matthew Locke.

CANEY [KAY nee] (Matagorda) Named from Caney Creek. PO 22 May 1846, PM Thomas Dennis.

CANNON (Grayson) In 1852 Elijah Cannon brought his family and slaves from Pickens

County, SC, to the area where he became a wealthy planter, miller, and ginner. PO 27 June 1877, PM William Hoard.

CANTON (Van Zandt) Founded in the early 1850s by settlers from Old Canton (now Omen) in Smith County, itself named by postmaster Thomas N. Gregory in 1851. The source of the name is uncertain. By one account, Canton is an adaptation of "canton," a French term for a civil or geographical division; by another the name arose from a famous race where a horse named Canter bested another whose name is lost to history, the fate of those who come in second. More likely Canton, TX, is a transfer, perhaps from Canton, KY, or Canton, MO. PO 7 Apr 1852, PM George H. Fain.

CANUTILLO [kan yuh TEE o] (El Paso) In 1910 the Canutillo Townsite and Land Company laid out the community, named from the Canutillo land grant of 1823, itself probably named from the *canutillo* or erect ephedra, the shrub also known as Mormon Tea. PO 11 July 1911, PM Tillie Spivey.

CANYON (Randall) Rancher Lincoln Guy Conner laid out the townsite and established the Canyon post office in September 1889. Initially named Canyon City from Palo Duro (Spanish "hard wood") Canyon, the name was shortened to Canyon in 1910. See Paloduro.

CAPLEN (Galveston) Caplen, a resort town since the 1890s, was named for John Caplen who surveyed the site about 1909. PO 29 June 1897 as Rollover; changed to Caplen 27 June 1907, PM Raymond C. Bouse.

CAPS (Taylor) According to local lore, at a meeting to choose a name for the post office someone threw a cap into the air and declared, "let's call it caps." Perhaps, but more likely the namesake is a local Caps family, perhaps that of William J. Caps who began farming and ranching in the area in the 1860s. PM 16 Apr 1894, PM Catharin A. Miliken.

CARADAN (Mills) Named for site owners and town founders Samuel Losson (Lawson) *Cara*way and *Dan*iel Thornton Bush. PO 3 July 1899, PM Samuel Caraway.

CARANCAHUA [kuh RANG kuh wuh] (Jackson) Named from Carancahua Bay, itself named for the Carancahua (Karankawa) Native Americans, who have no known descendants. PO 15 July 1878, PM Leander Garrett. Also known as Freeport.

CARBON (Eastland) Named from the local mineral deposits. Street names in Carbon include Anthracite, Coal, and Cannel. PO 25 Jan 1882, PM Neill Haynes.

CARBONDALE (Bowie) Like most of the dozen or so Carbondales in the US, Carbondale, TX, was named for the local coal deposits. PO 19 July 1907, PM David J. Morgan.

CARDIFF (Waller) Named for the William Cardiff family who developed the local rice industry in the mid-20th century.

CAREY (Childress) Carey was founded in the early 1890s as Carey Station, named for Dan Carey, a construction foreman for the Fort Worth & Denver City Railway. PO 2 May 1892 as Carey Station, PM John W. Templar; discontinued 30 July 1895; reopened 7 July

1896 as Tallulah, PM Francis Collier who named the office for his daughter; changed to Carey 5 May 1898, PM Thomas R. Humes.

CARGRAY (Carson) Named in the early 1930s for its location on the Carson-Gray county line, probably by Stanley Marsh who, with several partners, established a refinery to produce gasoline from natural gas.

CARLISLE (Trinity) Named for farmer and miller John Layton Carlisle who established several gristmills in the area in the late 19th century. PO 12 May 1906, PM John W. Chessher.

CARLSBAD (Tom Green) The Concho Land Company laid out the town of Hughes on the Hughes Ranch in 1907. The local springs were claimed to have medicinal benefits and the community was promoted as a health resort. Renamed Carlsbad for the European spa Karlsbad (German "karl's bath"), now Karlovy Vary in the Czech Republic. Carlsbads in San Diego County, CA, and Eddy County, NM, are also named for the presumed healing powers of their waters. PO 27 July 1908, PM Edward C. Perry.

CARLTON (Hamilton) The Honey Creek PO opened 22 Mar 1875; changed to Carlton 11 Mar 1879 by site owner, physician, and first PM Francis Marion Carlton.

CARMINE [kar MEEN] (Fayette, Washington) Founded as Sylvan about 1884 by Benjamin Thigpen, a physician and station agent for the Houston & Texas Central Railway. Renamed for saddler and harness maker Isaac Newton Carmean, son of John and Sarah Carmean, early settlers from Ohio in the 1850s. PO 14 Jan 1886 as Carmean, PM Elizabeth Price; changed to Carmine 15 June 1892.

CARMONA (Polk) Founded in the 1850s on land granted to Juan Carmona in 1835. PO 16 Feb 1894, PM Ambrose B. Martindale.

CARO [KAH ro] (Nacogdoches) Organized in the early 1900s on a site granted to José Antonio Caro in 1835. PO 13 June 1904, PM Charles Rhodes.

CARRICITOS [kar uh SEE tos] (Cameron) A shortening of *Concepción de Carricitos*, the 1789 Spanish land grant to Eugenio and Bartolomé Fernández. PO 18 Nov 1908, PM Juan Alcala.

CARRIZO SPRINGS [kuh REE zuh SPRINGZ] (Dimmit) Levi English, a community benefactor who donated land for the Dimmit County seat, brought the first settlers to the area in 1865. As a place name, Carrizo (Spanish "reeds, canes"), occurs throughout the Spanish Southwest. Carrizozo, NM, is a variant. PO 21 Nov 1878, PM Samuel Kellogg.

CARROLLTON (Collin, Dallas, Denton) Carrollton is a transfer from Carrollton, Green County, IL, itself named for Carrollton, MD, home of namesake Charles Carroll, the last surviving signer of the Declaration of Independence. The name was brought to Texas about 1845, probably by David Myers, a Baptist minister, and his son John, the first Carrollton PM in 1878. Carrollton includes the former community of Trinity Mills.

CARSON (County) Created 1876, organized 1888. Named for Samuel Price Carson

(1798–1838). Carson, a US Representative from North Carolina in the 1820s, became friends with Davy Crockett. He came to Texas early in 1836, was a signatory to the Texas Declaration of Independence, and the first Secretary of State of the Republic of Texas.

CARTA VALLEY (Edwards) In the 1880s Stockman Richard Edward Carta settled in the valley that now bears his name. PO 1 Oct 1907, PM general store owner William Varga.

CARTER (Denton) Named for Wormley Carter, a Virginia native who moved to the area in 1846 and was Dallas County constable in the late 1850s. PO 16 May 1860, PM Peter W. Rozel.

CARTHAGE (Panola) Carthage was founded in 1848 as the permanent seat of Panola County, replacing Pulaski. The name was proposed for Carthage, MS, by either John Allison, an organizer of Panola County, or by Spearman Holland, a planter and Texas state legislator in the 1860s. Carthage, MS, is itself a transfer from Carthage, TN. PO 31 July 1849, PM William Powers. See Panola County.

CARTWRIGHT (Wood) Matthew Cartwright was president of the First National Bank of Terrell in the 1890s and an early mayor of Terrell. PO 19 Mar 1894, PM Elmore Wright.

CASA BLANCA (Jim Wells) In 1807 Jose de la Garza Montemayor received the *Casa Blanca* "white house" land grant from Spain. John L. Wade purchased the property and established the Casa Blanca Ranch. PO 13 Apr 1860, PO Walter L. Mann.

CASA PIEDRA [kah suh pee ED ruh] (Presidio) Spanish "stone house." Named for the house built from native materials by Feliciano Mata in the 1875. PO 24 Aug 1912, PM Conrado L. Vasquez.

CASH (Hunt) From the mid-1890s, Cash was known as Sylvia, named by Edward Howland Robinson Green, president and general manager of the Texas Midland Railroad, in honor of his younger sister, Harriet Sylvia Ann Howland Green Wilks. According to the local story the PO was to be named Money for PM John A. Money, but some leading citizens wanted a more elegant name, so the office was opened as Cash 3 Dec 1895. See Atlas, see Howland, see Jiba.

CASON (Morris) Founded as Snow Hill in the 1850s on the Morris-Titus county line. When the East Line & Red River Railroad built through the area in the late 1870s, many of the homes and businesses of Snow Hill were moved three miles south to trackside. Snow Hill was renamed for John Washington Cason, a Snow Hill merchant and the site owner. PO 5 May 1857 as Buchanan; changed to Snow Hill 21 Oct 1857; changed to Cason 14 Jan 1878, PM William M. Cason.

CASS (County) Created and organized 1846. Named for Lewis Cass (1782–1866), born in Detroit, MI. His political career extended for more than half a century. Between 1806 and 1860 he was Governor of Michigan Territory, Ambassador to France, Secretary of War, and Secretary of State. He was US Senator from Michigan when Cass County was created. Cass was a respected politician and more than a dozen US counties as well as numerous townships and communities were named in his honor. Cass County was renamed Davis in honor of Jefferson Davis in 1861, then changed back to Cass in 1871.

CASSIE (Burnet) Named for Cassie Friedsam, mother of Linda Lou Friedsam who sold the site on Lake Buchanan to developer Raymond Jones in the early 1850s.

CASSIN (Bexar) Founded about 1890 by William Cassin from Kilkenny, Ireland. Cassin was a rancher and Bexar County surveyor from the 1870s.

CASTELL (Llano) Castell was founded in 1847 by German settlers led by Emil von Kriewitz and named for Carl Frederick Christian, the Count of Castell-Castell in Bavaria and business manager of the Adelsverein, the German Emigration Society organized in the early 1840s to establish German colonies in Texas. PO 22 Aug 1872, PM Christian Schneider.

CASTOLON (Brewster) The first known settler, Cipriano Hernández, named the site Santa Elena about 1903. By the 1920s the US Army had established Campo Santa Helena. The town was named from Cerro Castellan (literally "ruler of a castle on a hill"), the thousand-foot prominence in Big Bend National Park. PO 29 Mar 1926, PM Richard W. Derrick.

CASTRO (County) Created 1876, organized 1891. Named for Texas colonizer Henri Castro (1786–1865), born in Landes, France. Castro, a banker, was instrumental in securing loans for the Republic of Texas. In the 1840s he became an empresario and brought several thousand settlers, many from Alsace, to Castro's Colony west of San Antonio.

CASTROVILLE (Medina) Founded in 1844 on land granted to Henri Castro in 1842. Many of Castro's early settlers were Alsatian farmers; thus, the town's nickname "Little Alsace." PO 12 Jan 1847, PM Joseph de Laroche. Henri Castro was PM in 1849. See Castro County.

CAT SPRING (Austin) In the 1830s Robert Kleberg, the namesake of Kleberg County, brought German settlers, primarily from Westphalia and Oldenburg, to the area. The local account is that the name arose when a member of the von Reoder family killed a mountain lion, a "cat," at a spring near the San Bernard River. PO 13 Dec 1853, PM Charles C. Amsler.

CATARINA (Dimmit) Founded about 1910 when the Asherton & Gulf Railway established Catarina Station, named from the Catarina Ranch. According to one local account the town was named for a woman named Catarina who was killed here by Indians; by another a ranch employee named Catarina died and was buried at the site. However, the name dates from at least the late 18th century when the area was known as *Aguaje de Santa Catarina* "waterhole of Saint Catherine" or, simply, Catarina. PO 16 Dec 1910, PM John Green.

CAVINESS (Lamar) Named for one or more Caviness families. Jesse B. Caviness from NC and Mary Cothran Caviness were established farmers by 1850. PO 5 Aug 1895, PM Samuel A. Whitten.

CAVITT (Coryell) Founded about 1882 by the Texas & St. Louis Railway. Named for landowner and surveyor Andrew Cavitt.

CAYOTE [KAY ot] (Bosque) Cayote grew around a general store kept from about 1866 by John Cox. The name was originally Coyote, probably for the local abundance of *canis latrans*. Through a transcription error the PO was established as Cayote 29 Dec 1879, PM Robert Y. Goodall.

CAYUGA [kay YOO guh] (Anderson) William Davenport established the PO 7 May 1894, named for Cayuga County, NY, his former home, itself named for the Cayuga, an Iroquoian people. The area was formerly known as Wildcat Bluff.

CEDAR PARK (Williamson) The area was first known as Running Brushy, for the spring that fed Cluck Creek, named for early settlers George and Harriet Cluck. With construction of the Austin & Northwestern Railroad in 1882 the name became Brueggerhoff for William Brueggerhoff, an Austin business leader with ties to the A&N. In 1887 George and Harriet Cluck's son Emmett, a local shopkeeper, changed the name to Cedar Park. PO 27 Feb 1874 as Running Brushy; discontinued and reestablished as Brueggerhoff 5 June 1882; changed to Cedar Park 25 Aug 1887, PM Wesley C. Isaacks.

CEE VEE (Cottle) Named from the CV Ranch and brand first registered by *C*laiborne *V*arner in 1850. The PO was opened by merchant William Newsom 22 Nov 1928.

CEGO [SEE go] (Falls) Formerly known as Pleasant Valley. Perhaps named for a family or individual named Cego. Perhaps a respelling of Sego, also a family name or a transfer from an existing Sego community. PO 23 Dec 1895, PM Aaron Turner Donelson.

CELESTE (Hunt) The Gulf, Colorado & Santa Fe Railway platted Celeste in 1886 and named the town for Celeste Willis, daughter of site owner Peter J. Willis, a Galveston merchant and business associate of George Sealy, owner of the GC&SF. PO 26 Nov 1886, PM Edward D. Croft. See Sealy.

CELINA [suh LEYE nuh] (Collin) John T. Mulkey opened the PO 28 Feb 1881, named for his former home, Celina, Clay County, TN.

CELOTEX [SEL uh teks] (Fisher) In 1945 the Celotex Corporation of America, makers of insulation, roofing, and building materials (asbestos being a primary component), bought the site known as Plasterco and changed the name to Celotex.

CENTER (Shelby) In 1866, Shelby County clerk Robert L. Parker and his associates unceremoniously moved the county records from Shelbyville to the new site, named, as local accounts claim, "because it's in the center of the county," as required by the state. PO 6 Apr 1848 as White Cottage; changed to Center 11 Oct 1866, PM Benjamin Harkness.

CENTER POINT (Kerr) In November 1859 Charles Ganahl established the Zanzenberg PO, named for his grandfather, Joseph Ganahl von Zanzenberg, an Austrian nobleman whose son, Johann Joseph, emigrated to America in the mid-1810s. The name of the office was changed to Centre Point in

September 1872 when George Harwell, the local physician, became postmaster. Harwell is reported to have chosen the name because the site was presumed to be halfway between Comfort and Kerrville and also halfway between Fredericksburg and Bandera. Spelling changed to Center Point 27 June 1882.

CENTERVILLE (Leon) Founded and named in 1850 in response to a Texas law that required all county seats to be located within five miles of the geographic center of the county in which they were located. PO 27 Dec 1850, PM William Johnston.

CENTRALIA (Trinity) Named for its perceived location midway between Apple Springs and Nogalus Prairie. PO 22 June 1874, PM William C. Thompson.

CESTOHOWA [ses tuh HO vuh] (Karnes) In 1873 some forty families from PANNA MARIA formed a new community that they named for Częstochowa, Poland, home of the Black Madonna of Częstochowa, a Christian icon. PO 20 Aug 1883, PM August Zaiontz.

CHALK (Cottle) Until the early 1900s the community was known as the Dutch Colony and as Richards Colony, founded on the Moon Ranch by site owner William Q. Richard(s). PO 1 Dec 1906 as Chalk, PM Oscar Brothers, named for ginner James M. Chalk who succeeded Brothers as PM in 1908.

CHAMBERS (County) Created and organized 1858. Named for Thomas Jefferson Chambers (1802–1865), born in Virginia. Chambers arrived in Texas in the late 1820s by way of Kentucky, Alabama, and Mexico. He was Surveyor General of Texas, Chief Justice of the Texas Supreme Court, and a founder of the Texas Philosophical Society in 1837. He retired to Anahuac and changed its name to Chambersia. See Anahuac.

CHAMBERSVILLE (Collin) In the mid-1860s Jacob Marion Bryan named the community for his wife Elizabeth Chambers and her family who had settled in Collin County in 1847. Bryan and his father-in-law Elisha Chambers donated land for a school, church, and cemetery in 1853. PO 6 Mar 1894, PM Jacob M. Bryan.

CHAMBLISS (Collin) Joseph J. Chambliss, a pioneering physician from Georgia, established a practice in the 1890s. PO 17 Nov 1898, PM James L. Davis.

CHANDLER (Henderson) Alphonso Chandler opened a general store in the 1860s and opened the Still Water PO 17 Apr 1873. When the Texas & St. Louis Railway established a station in 1880 the name was changed to Chandler 11 Oct 1880, PM William H. Whatley.

CHANEY (Eastland) Probably named for Leander and Nancy Cheaney (several spellings) who were established farmers by the mid-1870s. PO 15 Mar 1902 as Chauncey, PM Amos G. Chauncey; discontinued 15 May 1905.

CHANNING (Hartley) Founded as Rivers with construction of the Fort Worth & Denver City Railway in 1888, named for George Channing Rivers, paymaster of the FW&DC. When that name was rejected by the Post Office Department the application was resubmitted as Channing. PO 30 Jan 1891, PM Edward A. McKinnon.

CHAPMAN (Rusk) In the 1850s John Chapman settled on land granted to his relative Henry S. Chapman for his service in the Texas Revolution. PO 28 Apr 1894, PM Francis M. Bridges. Also known as Blossom Hill.

CHAPMAN RANCH (Nueces) In 1919 Philip Alexander Chapman and his son J. O. (John Ople), farmers and ranchers from Waxahachie, bought 34,000 acres of the King Ranch and established Nueces Farms that by 1925 was known as Chapman Ranch. PO 9 Jan 1926, PM Charles C. Simpson.

CHAPPEL (San Saba) In the late 1880s rancher and farmer Joab Harrell donated land to the Methodist Episcopal Church for a school and a church that became known as Harrell's Chapel. The name was misrecorded when Charles McCoury opened the Chappel PO 18 Oct 1897.

CHAPPELL HILL (Washington) In 1847 Mary Haller laid out the town named for her grandfather, Robert Wooding Chappell, an early settler and pioneer merchant in Milam County. PO 14 June 1847 as Jacksonville, PM Terrell Jackson; changed to Chappel [*sic*] Hill 2 Nov 1847, PM Jacob Haller; changed to Chapel Hill c. 1894; changed back to Chappel Hill 1 Nov 1953.

CHARCO (Goliad) Spanish "puddle, waterhole." The area was known to early travelers as a place where fresh water was usually available. PO 13 Dec 1855, PM William Hassell.

CHARLESTON (Delta) Charleston was named in the early 1850s, probably by settlers from Charleston, SC. The PO has made a remarkable journey; from Odd's Creek in May 1848, named for an Odd family; changed to Lake Creek in Nov 1848, named for a Lake family; changed to Charleston in Hopkins County in June 1857; changed to Charleston in Delta County in Feb 1886.

CHARLIE (Clay) Big Wichita Valley was founded by Henry Dunn who opened a general store in the 1870s. The Big Wichita Valley PO, established 19 May 1879 by PM Robert Worley, was changed to Charlie 19 June 1882 when PM Charlie Taylor became PM.

CHARLOTTE (Atascosa) Joseph Finney Edwards, president of the San Antonio, Rio Grande & Tampico Railroad, founded Charlotte on the Tobey Ranch in 1910. Edwards may have chosen the name for a relative or Charlotte may have been a daughter of Charles Franklin Simmons, a promoter of Atascosa and Live Oak counties. PO 6 Sept 1912, PM Wilbur M. Wilson.

CHATFIELD (Navarro) According to local accounts, about 1840 a peddler named Chatfield (sometimes identified as Champion Chatfield) decided to settle down and open a trading post on the San Antonio and Shreveport Trail. PO 28 Oct 1867 as Chatfield; PM William Pigg.

CHATT (Hill) Founded in the mid-1880s as Jessie, named for early settler and merchant Jessie McClure. When the

Missouri–Kansas–Texas Railroad built through the area in the 1890s, the town was renamed for chatt ballast, the crushed rock used to stabilize railroad beds.

CHEEK (Jefferson) Founded in 1906 by Galveston real estate agent James R. Cheek. PO 13 Feb 1906, PM Robert H. Hunter.

CHENEYBORO (Navarro) Francis Marion Cheney, Jr. was an entrepreneur and Corsicana benefactor in the late 19th and early 20th centuries. Cheney invested heavily in the Texas & Pacific Railway and owned several thousand acres near Cheneyboro.

CHEROKEE (County) Created and organized 1846. Named for the Cherokee, a native people from the Southeast who established villages in northeast Texas beginning in the early 19th century. They were forcibly removed to Indian Territory in 1839.

CHEROKEE (San Saba) Named from Cherokee Creek, earlier known as Mineral Creek. The name commemorates either a conflict between Cherokees and settlers or a Cherokee woman who married an early settler. PO 13 Aug 1861, PM John R. Williams.

CHESTER (Tyler) In 1883 the Trinity & Sabine Railway extended a line from Colmesneil that bypassed the town of Peach Tree Village. The trackside community was named from the Chester PO established 22 Aug 1876 by Arter Berry Green who apparently named the office for Chester A. Arthur, a rising star in the Republican Party at the time and later US President (1881–1885).

CHESTERVILLE (Colorado) William Chester laid out the town in 1894 for the Southern Texas Colonization Company. PO 31 July 1895, PM Alvina Chester.

CHICO (Wise) Named by James T. Brown for Chico, CA, his former home, itself named from Arroyo Chico "little stream." PO 12 Nov 1877, PM Theodore Merryman.

CHICOTA [chi KOT uh] (Lamar) Robert Wilkins Draper suggested the name for Checotah [*sic*], McIntosh County, OK, itself named for Samuel Checote, a Muskogee Creek leader who had commanded a regiment of Creek mounted volunteers in the Civil War. Checote, a Methodist Episcopal minister, was the principal Creek spokesman in the 1870s. PO 11 Nov 1879, PM Edgar Belvin.

CHILDRESS (County) Created 1876, organized 1887. Named for George Campbell Childress (1804–1841). Childress, a Tennessee lawyer, moved to Texas early in 1836, was the primary author of the Texas Declaration of Independence, and was appointed by President David Burnet to negotiate diplomatic recognition of the Republic of Texas with US President Andrew Jackson.

CHILDRESS (Childress) The town of Henry was renamed Childress, named from Childress County when the Fort Worth & Denver City Railway built through the area in 1887. PO 21 Feb 1887, PM Micajah Crenshaw.

CHILLICOTHE [chil uh KAH thee] (Hardeman) Grocer Ed Jones is generally credited with suggesting the name in the early 1880s for his former home, Chillicothe, MO, itself named for the first Chillicothe in Ross County, OH. Chillicothe is from a Miami/Illinois word that does not mean "big town where we live," as often claimed but was the name of a Shawnee clan. PO 17 Oct 1883, PM Charles E. Jones.

CHILTON (Falls) In 1876 Lysias Chilton and William DeBardeleben established a general store in which DeBardeleben opened a PO 2 May 1882, named for Chilton. The area was formerly known as Abney's Farm for early settler and local official Alexander Hamilton Abney.

CHINA (Jefferson) China Grove, named for the local chinaberry trees, was founded about 1860 on a Texas & New Orleans Railroad line. The name was shortened to China in 1893. About 1900 Beaumont real estate agents Charles Nash and Hal Land laid out Nashland east of China. In 1906 the T&NO moved business operations to Nashland and changed the name to China. PO 2 Oct 1893, PM Jerome T. Terry.

CHINA GROVE (Brazoria) In the 1830s, Warren DeWitt Clinton Hall, a Brazoria County lawyer, established China Grove Plantation, named from the chinaberry trees he planted along with cotton and figs. See Hall County.

CHINA SPRING (McLennan) Settled in the 1860s and named for one or more springs in a grove of chinaberry trees. PO 26 May 1873, PM Charles Eichelberger. Also spelled China Springs.

CHINATI [chuh NAHT ee] (Presidio) Named from the Chinati mountains, especially Chinati Peak that rises more than 7700 feet above sea level. The origin of the name is uncertain. Possible origins are Apache for "mountain pass" and Nahuatl (Aztec), through Spanish, for "blackbird." PO 18 May 1922, PM Darling T. Baldwin.

CHIRENO [shuh REE no] (Nacogdoches) About 1836 physician John Newton Fall purchased the townsite from the heirs of namesake José Antonio Chirino [*sic*] who was granted the land by Spain in 1792. PO 8 Nov 1843 as Marshall; changed 8 Jan 1880 to Chireno, PM Eliza Noble.

CHISHOLM (Rockwall) See McLendon-Chisholm.

CHISPA (Jeff Davis) Founded in 1882 with construction of the Southern Pacific Railroad. Named from Chispa Mountain, five miles north of the community. *Chispa* (Spanish "spark, lightning") usually refers to nuggets, especially gold nuggets. The application of the name to Chispa Mountain is unclear. PO 5 Dec 1895, PM Arthur Humphris.

CHITA [CHEET uh] (Trinity) Chita is a transfer from Chita, Attala County, MS, from Choctaw *chito* "big." PO 25 Apr 1895, PM William J. Dwire.

CHOATE (Karnes) Rancher and drover James Monroe Choate came to Texas from Tennessee by way of Mississippi in the mid-1850s. PO 23 Jan 1902, PM Thomas Rutledge.

CHOCOLATE BAYOU (Brazoria) About 1905 Angleton lawyers and brothers, William and Louis Rowan founded Rowanville, which became a ghost town about 1910 and was replatted as Chocolate Bayou, a popular etymology from the dark brown skin and chocolaty taste of the Chiltipiquin pepper, a local hot pepper related to cayenne, also known as the "Texas bird pepper." The name Chiltipiquin, from Nahuatl (Aztec) through Spanish, was popularly etymologized as chili pequin and, as chiltepin, became the official Texas state native pepper in 1996. PO 25 June 1909 as Rowanville; changed to Chocolate Bayou, 2 Apr 1911, PM Edward E. Murphree.

CHOICE (Shelby) By the early 1890s Eugene Alonzo and Henrietta Emma Fudge (who later changed their name to Cammack) had begun farming in the area. By one local story the Fudge/Cammacks chose the name about 1905, claiming that this was a "choice" place to live; by another, townspeople could not agree on a name so they sent a list to the Post Office Department which was promptly returned with instructions to "take your choice." PO 10 May 1904, PM Elijah Wilson.

CHRIESMAN [KRIS muhn] (Burleson) In the 1830s Alexander Thomson brought settlers to what was then called Yellow Prairie. After the Gulf, Colorado & Santa Fe Railway established a station in the early 1880s, the name was changed to honor Horatio Chriesman who had settled in Texas in 1822. Chriesman was a surveyor for Stephen F. Austin's Old Three Hundred and mayor of San Felipe in the early 1830s. PO 29 Aug 1881 as Yellow Prairie; discontinued and reestablished 13 Feb 1885 as Chriesman, PM Samuel M. Williams.

CHRISTINE (Atascosa) Charles Franklin Simmons, a San Antonio real estate developer and promoter, founded New Artesia, later known as Christine, about 1908. Christine is one of several towns reportedly named for daughters of Charles and Carrie Simmons, but daughter Christine is difficult to verify. The namesake may well be Christine Andrew, daughter of James and Rettie Andrew, born about 1910 when New Artesia was incorporated and renamed Christine. PO 11 Feb 1910, PM Joseph Wassenich. See Charlotte.

CHRISTOVAL [kris TO vuhl] (Tom Green) Christopher Columbus Doty, who kept a store on the South Concho River in the late 1880s, applied for a post office to be named *Cristóbal*, Spanish for "Christopher," but the application was returned as Christoval. PO 21 Jan 1889, PM Christopher C. Doty.

CIBOLO [suh BOL uh] (Guadalupe) Named from Cibolo Creek that forms the boundary between Guadalupe and Bexar counties. Settled shortly after the Civil War and organized around Charles Fromme's general store about 1880. *Cibolo*, American Spanish for "male buffalo," is a late 17th century adaptation from a Native American language. The local story is that the creek was so named because Indians stampeded buffalo over its high banks to their deaths below. The Cibolo Valley PO was established 4 June 1877; discontinued 31 Oct 1882 and reestablished 12 Dec 1883 as Cibolo by PM Charles Fromme.

CINCO RANCH (Fort Bend, Harris) In the mid-1980s the American General Insurance Company of Houston, with other investors, founded the Cinco Ranch Venture on the Cinco Ranch, itself established in the late 1930s by five business partners, thus the name Cinco (Spanish "five").

CIPRES [SEYE pruhs] (Hidalgo) Named for the cypress (Spanish *ciprés*) trees planted by Jacinta Hinojosa about 1910. PO 20 June 1913, PM Dorotea Garza.

CIRCLE (Lamb) Known as Punkin Center when Abe Winkle opened a general store in the late 1920s. Reportedly renamed for the curve in US Route 70.

CIRCLEVILLE (Williamson) Brothers James, Joseph, and William Eubank, artisans from KY, were early settlers in the mid-1850s. The Eubanks built their houses side by side in a semicircular pattern. PO 13 Mar 1857, PM James Eubank.

CISCO (Eastland) In 1881 the Houston & Central Texas Railway established Cisco Station, named by William H. Abrams, land commissioner of the H&CT, for New York financier and railroad underwriter John A. Cisco. PO 22 Apr 1878 as Red Gap, PM Cornelius G. Stephens; changed to Cisco 17 May 1881, PM William T. Caldwell.

CISTERN (Fayette) Ground water in the region was highly mineralized and farmers and ranchers relied on underground reservoirs called cisterns to catch and retain rainwater. PO 31 Mar 1858, PM Addison Kendall.

CITRUS CITY (Hidalgo) Iowa builder Howard Moffitt, known for his unusual architectural style, founded Citrus City in 1943 as a planned community where grapefruit and oranges would be the major agricultural products. The crops failed but the community endured.

CLAIREMONT (Kent) Alphonse Rhomberg, secretary and treasurer of the Austin & Northwestern Railroad, of which his father was part owner, named Clairemont in 1892, probably for Claire Becker, a Rhomberg family member. PO 31 Dec 1892, PM Loulah Posey. See Aspermont.

CLAIRETTE [kluh RET] (Erath) Founded about 1881 with construction of the Texas Central Railway. Apparently named for Clairette Soap, a popular brand of laundry soap in the late 19th century. PO 21 Dec 1892, PM Alwilda Johnson.

CLARA (Wichita) In 1870 Herman Specht left Germany for Galveston where he became a rancher and nurseryman specializing in exotic plants. Specht laid out the town in 1886, named for his wife, Clara. PO 3 June 1886, PM William Still.

CLARDY (Lamar) Likely named for the William and Allie Clardy family. The local story is that James Dunlap submitted a list of the names of six prominent area families from which the Post Office Department chose Clardy. PO 29 May 1899, PM James Dunlap.

CLARENDON (Donley) Methodist minister Lewis Henry Carhart founded Clarendon in 1878 as a "Christian Colony," free of liquor and other evils of the modern age. Some accounts claim that Carhart chose the name in honor of his wife, Clara Sully Carhart; rather Carhart named the Clarendon Land Investment and Agency Company of London, a consortium of British bankers, that sold the site to Carhart and his brother-in-law, Richard William Alexander Allen. PO 25 Sept 1878, PM John M. Recerd.

CLAREVILLE (Bee) Clareville was known as Lomita (Spanish "little hill") until the late 1880s when it was renamed for Henry and Mary Clare, their five sons, and three daughters. The Clares raised cattle from the mid-1870s and subdivided their ranch into building lots a decade later. PO 4 Dec 1896, PM John S. Bell.

CLARKSVILLE (Red River) Founded about 1834 by James Clark, postmaster and justice of the peace for Miller County, AR, until 1833 when he relocated to Sulphur Fork Prairie, TX. Clark was instrumental in ensuring that Red River County would be part of Texas rather than Arkansas. PO 22 May 1846, PM Alexander M. Crook.

CLARKSVILLE CITY (Gregg) Although settlement began in the 1840s, the town did not develop for a century and the opening of the East Texas oilfield in the 1930s. Named for peace officer George W. Clark. The name was changed to Clarksville City in 1956 after oil became the major industry.

CLAUDE (Armstrong) The local story is that the town was named for Claude Ayers, an engineer for the Fort Worth & Denver City Railway who drove the first train through the village in 1887. After his historic run, Ayers asked the name of the town and was told, "It ain't got no name." Ayers seized the moment and said, "Then why don't you name it Claude for me?" And they did. PO 5 June 1888, PM Elijah H. Trice.

CLAUENE [klaw EEN] (Hockley) Clauene is probably derived from catclaw (*uña de gato*), the bush commonly found in the area and so named because its thorns resemble cats' claws. Cat Claw Creek in San Saba County is from the same source. PO 9 Nov 1922, PM A. E. W. (Alexander Edmondson Williamson) White, called "Alphabet White," one of the first settlers of Clauene and a store owner from 1920. White was also a founder of IMPERIAL in Pecos County.

CLAWSON (Angelina) Formerly known as Bonnersville for the sawmill operated by Thomas R. Bonner. Named for Thomas W. Clawson who bought the Bonner mill about 1890. PO 13 June 1876 as Bonner's Mill; discontinued 11 Sept 1877; reopened as Clawson 26 Mar 1891, PM William M. Vinson.

CLAY (County) Created and organized 1857; organization rescinded 1862; organized 1873. Probably named for Henry Clay (1777–1852), US Senator from Kentucky, Speaker of the US House of Representatives, and Secretary of State. Clay was a popular politician and several dozen counties and townships are named in his honor as well as many communities, schools, and parks.

CLAY (Burleson) In the mid-1820s, after serving in the Kentucky Legislature, Nestor Clay settled near Independence. He was later joined by his brother, Tacitus, a mayor of Independence in the 1850s. Tacitus's son, Atreus McCreery Clay, donated land for a station on the Gulf, Colorado & Santa Fe Railway and is generally considered the town's namesake. PO 21 Oct 1884, PM Eliza M. Reynolds.

CLAYTON (Panola) The first known settler was Jacob Cariker who brought his family and slaves from North Carolina in 1845. By several accounts Clayton is an adaptation of Clayborne, one of Cariker's slaves, but more likely the name is a transfer from Clayton, Barbour County, AL, the home of a number of early settlers. PO 25 June 1874, PM Jesse W. Cariker.

CLAYTONVILLE (Fisher) Reuben M. Clayton and his business partners operated in southwest Fisher County from the early 1880s. PO 14 Mar 1891 as Claytonville, PM Reuben Clayton.

CLAYTONVILLE (Swisher) Named for and by Melvin Clayton who established a cotton gin and general store at the site in the mid-1950s.

CLEAR SPRINGS (Guadalupe) First known as Bernhardsville for Frank and Emily Bernhard. Frank Bernhard, who opened the Bernhardsville PO 22 June 1874, changed the name of the office to Clear Springs 22 Feb 1875.

CLEBURNE (Johnson) Founded about 1867 to replace Buchanan as the seat of Johnson County. Named for Patrick Ronayne Cleburne, an Irish-born Confederate Civil War General known as the "Stonewall of the West." Cleburne was killed at the 1864 Battle of Franklin in Tennessee. PO 19 Apr 1867 as Camp Henderson; changed to Cleburne 16 July 1867, PM George W. Ballard.

CLEGG (Live Oak) Named for George Austin Clegg, a well-known rancher and quarter horse breeder of the late 19th and early 20th centuries. PO 4 Nov 1913, PM Samuel A. Story.

CLEMVILLE (Matagorda) Probably named for Charles T. Clem who was instrumental in developing oilfields in the surrounding area in the early 20th century. Perhaps named for Annis W. Clem of Dallas who organized the Clem Oil Company about 1890 and the Clem Gravel Company soon thereafter. PO 5 May 1911, PM Walter F. Allen.

CLEO (Kimble) Founded about 1880 as Viejo (Spanish "old"), named from Viejo Creek. PO 11 Mar 1880 as Viejo; changed to Cleo 21 Aug 1920, PM Sam Pearson who named the office for his niece, Cleo Weston.

CLEVELAND (Liberty) Charles Lander Cleveland, a Galveston lawyer, federal judge, and Texas state legislator in the 1850s, donated land for a station on the Houston East & West Texas Railway in the late 1870s. Cleveland's relationship to William D. Cleveland, an original director of the HE&WT in 1875, if any, is unknown. PO 19 Feb 1880, PM Ephraim Jesse Crain.

CLICK (Llano) George and Temperance Click brought their family from Tennessee to Alabama and then to Texas in the mid-1830s. Their son Malachi was likely the first of the family to settle in Llano County. PO 17 May 1880, PM Benjamin Franklin Loe.

CLIFTON (Bosque) County judge William Sedberry suggested the name Cliff Town in the early 1850s for the local limestone outcroppings. Through popular etymology, Cliff Town became Clifton by the time Chester Dewey opened the Clifton PO 22 July 1859.

CLINE (Uvalde) Celeste Pingenot opened a general store in the early 1870s and established the Wallace PO 24 June 1878, named for his friend, legendary Texas Ranger William A. A. "Bigfoot" Wallace. The Wallace PO was discontinued 13 Aug 1879; reopened as Turkey Creek 7 Sept 1882, PM Archibald C. Hyde; changed to Cline 29 Jan 1883, named for August Cline, a clerk in Pingenot's store. See Bigfoot.

CLINT (El Paso) Thomas Collins opened the PO in his general store 20 Jan 1886, named for his wife, Mary Clinton Collins.

CLINTON (Hunt) Known as Massayville for site owner James Madison Massay until 1887 when the St. Louis Southwestern Railway (Cotton Belt) established Clinton Station, reportedly named for railroad official Charles Clinton. PO 28 July 1888, PM Dennis Newberry Massay (son of James).

CLOSE CITY (Garza) Charles W. Post, the founder and namesake of Post cereals, founded Post City as a model American wholesome community in the early 20th century. When it became necessary to move Post City to the present location of Post, the original site was renamed Close City for Post's son-in-law, Edward B. Close. See Post.

CLUTE (Brazoria) By the 1880s New Yorker Solomon Clute had laid out a community on the Eagle Island and Evergreen plantations. George Clute, probably Solomon's brother, became owner and the town was laid out as Clute City. PO 2 July 1942, PM Florence A. Coleman.

COAHOMA [kuh HO muh] (Howard) Earlier known as Signal or Signal Mountain from the prominence rising from the plain several miles to the south from which Indians are said to have sent smoke signals. A favorite story is that Coahoma is an "Indian" name meaning "a good place to live." Rather, Coahoma is a transfer from Coahoma County in northwest Mississippi named from Choctaw *kowi* "panther" and *homma* "red." PO 2 Feb 1892, PM James W. Shive.

COBB (Kaufman) Founded in the 1880s as a station on the Texas & Pacific Railway. Named for Cary Cobb, a Kaufman County commissioner and county judge. PO 10 July 1897, PM John B. Adams.

COBLE (Hockley) William Thomas Coble was a rancher, oilman and owner of the Turkey Track Ranch in the early decades of the 20th century.

COCHRAN (County) Created 1876, organized 1924. Named for Robert E. Cochran (1810–1836), born in New Hampshire and relative of James Cochran, namesake of COCHRAN. Cochran emigrated to Texas in 1835 and joined the Texas Revolutionary Army. Pvt. Cochran participated in the Siege of Bexar and died at the Alamo.

COCHRAN (Austin) James Cochran came to Texas from New Hampshire about 1832, sold supplies to the Texas Revolutionary Army, became a prosperous farmer and stockman, and represented Austin County in the Fourth Congress of the Republic of Texas. PO 9 May 1884, PM John Melton.

COCKRELL HILL (Dallas) Alexander Cockrell filed a claim on a section of land in Peters' Colony west of Dallas in 1847. Five years later he bought part of John Neely Bryan's claim that included a section that became the city of Dallas. He and his wife, Sarah Horton Cockrell, became leading Dallas-area landowners and entrepreneurs.

COESFIELD (Cooke) The PO was opened 23 Jan 1883 by PM Frank Liedtke who chose the name (with English spelling) for his birthplace, Coesfeld, Germany, now part of North Rhine-Westphalia.

COFFEEVILLE (Upshur) By local lore coffee was unavailable at any price during the early years of settlement and people were forced to grind corn, acorns, even okra into an acceptable if not desirable drink. The coffee drought ended when a wagonload of coffee beans arrived from Shreveport. The town was soon known as Coffeeville, the only place for many miles where real coffee could be found. More likely the town was named for an early settling Coffee family. PO 15 Mar 1852, PM Lucius McNairy.

COKE (County) Created and organized 1889. Named for Richard Coke (1829–1897), born in Virginia. Coke moved to Waco and opened a law office in 1850. He was the 15th Governor of Texas (1874–1876), and three-term US Senator (1877–1895).

COKE (Wood) Although several local accounts suggest the community was named for coke, a byproduct of coal refining, the namesake is surely Richard Coke, the 15th Governor of Texas (1874–1876). PO 6 Nov 1885, PM John D. Clough. See Coke County.

COLDSPRING (San Jacinto) Joseph K. Graves from Kentucky, opened the Coonskin PO 18 Jan 1847. Graves changed the name to Fireman's Hill 8 Mar 1847. When John Saunders became PM 30 Oct 1850, the name was changed to Cold Spring for the local spring water, described as cold and sweet.

COLEMAN (County) Created 1858, organized 1864. Named for Robert M. Coleman (1799–1837), a native Kentuckian who emigrated to Texas in 1831. Coleman was a Mina representative to the Convention of 1836 where he signed the Texas Declaration of Independence. He was aide-de-camp to Sam Houston at San Jacinto.

COLEMAN (Coleman) Founded in the summer of 1876 on land donated by Robert J. Clow, a Texas State Representative of the late 1850s. PO 7 Feb 1876, PM Marion M. Callan.

COLETOVILLE (Victoria) Named from Coleto Creek, a variant of COLITA. Coletoville was founded as Steiner's Settlement, named for Carl Steiner, who emigrated from Germany about 1850. PO 1 Apr 1875 as Colettoville, PM Louis Albrecht. See Colita.

COLFAX (Van Zandt) Martin Weaver moved to Texas from Indiana in the 1860s. PO 18 May 1870, PM Martin Weaver who chose the name in honor of Indiana politician Schuyler Colfax, US Vice President (1869–1873).

COLITA [kuh LEET uh] (Polk) Colita was a Coushatta (Koasati) Indian leader, born in Alabama, who lived near the Trinity River in Polk County in the early 19th century. Colita was highly regarded for his efforts to keep peace between Indians and settlers in the early years of the

Texas Republic. PO 9 Sept 1853, PM Samuel Rowe.

COLLEGE MOUND (Kaufman) According to a local story, early settlers in the 1840s dreamed of establishing a preparatory school on the nearby hill. The hope faded but not the name. PO 18 May 1850, PM John J. Beck.

COLLEGE STATION (Brazos) The name was a natural when the site was chosen as the home of the Agricultural and Mechanical College of Texas (now Texas A&M University) in 1871. PO 7 Feb 1877, PM Henry D. Parsons.

COLLEGEPORT (Matagorda) The Hurd Land Company laid out the site in 1908 and the following year established the Gulf Coast University of Industrial Arts, advertised as "a school for ambitious young men and women." PO 26 Aug 1909, PM Howard N. Sholl.

COLLEYVILLE (Tarrant) Named for physician Lilburn Howard Colley who moved to the area from Missouri and established a medical practice in the 1880s. Colleyville, now a Fort Worth suburb, includes the former communities of Bransford, Spring Garden, and Pleasant Glade. PO 1 Mar 1954, PM Tom Y. Stephens.

COLLIN (County) Created and organized 1846. Named for Collin McKinney (1766–1861). Born in New Jersey, McKinney lived in Virginia, Kentucky, Tennessee, and Arkansas before arriving in northeast Texas in 1830. At age 70 he was a delegate to the 1836 Constitutional Convention and a member of the committees that drafted the Texas Declaration of Independence and the Constitution of the Republic of Texas. When Collin County was created, McKinney had completed his third term in the Congress of the Republic of Texas. MCKINNEY, the seat of Collin County, is also named in his honor.

COLLINGSWORTH (County) Created 1876, organized 1890. Named for James Collinsworth (1806–1838). (His name was misspelled Collingsworth in the documents creating the county.) Collinsworth, a native of Davidson County, TN, established a law practice in Matagorda in the 1830s, was a member of the 1836 Constitutional Convention, a signer of the Texas Declaration of Independence, and the first Chief Justice of the Texas Supreme Court, serving from 1836 until his death.

COLLINSVILLE (Grayson) Shortly after the end of the Civil War Lodoweska Collins relocated from Michigan and organized what is generally regarded as the first free school in northeast Texas. PO 13 Nov 1872, PM Charles C. Collins, Lodoweska's son.

COLMESNEIL [KOL muhs neel] (Tyler) Founded about 1882 where the tracks of the Texas & New Orleans Railroad crossed those of the Trinity & Sabine Railway. William T. Colmesneil, a T&NO conductor, settled in the area in 1883. Colmesneil includes the former town of Ogden. PO 24 Oct 1882, PM Patrick Larkin.

COLOGNE [kuh LON] (Goliad) Founded in the late 1860s by former slaves as Perdido (Spanish "lost"), named from Perdido Creek. According to local accounts, the name was suggested ironically by William Young, the first postmaster in 1898. The town had become a center for cattle and hog slaughtering and the offal created uncommonly foul air. Young thought that naming the place for cologne, the perfume, would make for a sweeter-smelling community in one's mind if not in one's nose. PO 8 Apr 1898, PM William Madison Young.

COLONY (Fayette) John Young and a group of Mississippi cotton planters founded Mississippi Colony about 1880. PO 20 Mar 1884, PM Thomas J. Thomason who shortened the name.

COLORADO (County) An original Texas county created 1836, organized 1837. Named from the Colorado (Spanish "red") River that divides the county into northeast and southwest halves.

COLORADO CITY (Mitchell) Settled in the 1870s and named for the Colorado River when the Texas & Pacific Railway built through the area and the town was chosen as the seat of Mitchell County in 1881. PO 1 Apr 1836 as Crockett; changed to Colorado 18 Jan 1881, PM Aaron Dunn; changed to Colorado City 1 June 1939, PM Joseph Y. Fraser.

COLQUITT (Kaufman) Oscar Branch Colquitt was owner and publisher of the Pittsburg, TX, *Gazette* in the 1880s and the Terrell *Times-Star* in the 1890s. Colquitt was the 25th Governor of Texas (1911–1915). PO 9 Nov 1894, PM George Smith.

COLTHARP (Houston) Rev. Eli Strange Coltharp, a minister of the Missionary Baptist Church, opened a general store on Cochina Bayou in the late 1840s. PO 16 July 1857, PM Eli Coltharp.

COLTON (Travis) In June 1897 Frank Russell submitted an application for a post office requesting the name Cotton for the community's main crop, but the name was misread as Colton.

COLUMBIA, EAST AND WEST (Brazoria) In the early 1820s, Josiah Hughes Bell, one of Stephen F. Austin's Old Three Hundred, built a riverboat landing on the Brazos River, known first as Bell's Landing and later as Marion, now East Columbia. The towns were named from Columbia, a Latinized form of Columbus and a popular place name since the mid-1770s when it first appeared in Philip Freneau's patriotic poem, *American Liberty*. Columbia served as the first capital of the Republic of Texas from September to December 1836. PO 1836 as Columbia, PM David T. Fitchett; changed to East Columbia 16 Nov 1927, PM Alice O. Wright. PO as West Columbia 19 Dec 1905, PM Robert Faickney.

COLUMBUS (Colorado) Benjamin Beeson operated a ferry across the Colorado River in the 1820s, giving the community its first name, Beeson's Ferry. By the early 1830s, the village was known as Columbus, perhaps named by settlers from a Columbus in Mississippi, Georgia, Alabama, or Ohio. PO 23 June 1838, PM Rezin Byrne.

COMAL [KO mal] (County) Created and organized 1846. Named from the Comal River, known as the Little Guadalupe until the 1720s. Comal is from Nahuatl (Aztec) *comalli* "flat dish, cooking pan" through American Spanish.

COMANCHE (County) Created and organized 1856. Named for the Comanche, a branch of the Shoshone, who dominated North, Central, and West Texas in the 18th and much of the 19th centuries. *Comanche*, derived from a Ute word meaning "enemy, foreigner," was used by Spanish explorers from the early 18th century. The Comanche name for themselves was *Nermernuh* "the people."

COMANCHE (Comanche) Established in 1858 as the seat of Comanche County. PO 31 May 1860, PM James H. Tankersley.

COMBES (Cameron) About 1910 site owner and civic benefactor, James Henry Dishman named the community for the doctors Combe of Brownsville. Dr. Charles Combe established a medical practice in 1869; his son, Dr. Frederick Combe, was mayor of Brownsville in 1906. PO 23 Jan 1911, PM Edwin Templeton.

COMETA (Zavala) A prominence near Crystal City was known to early Spanish traders and travelers as *Loma de Cometas* "hill of the comets." In the mid-1880s Thomas Atlee Coleman, a former trail driver from Goliad, purchased a ranch whose brand was in the shape of a comet, a *cometa*, named from the nearby hill. PO 30 Oct 1905, PM Mollie Bell.

COMFORT (Kendall) Comfort was settled by German Freethinkers from New Braunfels in 1852 and formally laid out by Ernst Hermann Altgelt from Dusseldorf, Germany, who chose the name for its associations with peace and well-being. PO 12 July 1856, PM Theodore Goldbeck.

COMMERCE (Hunt) Settled in the mid-1850s in an area known as Cow Hill. By 1880 the name had become Commerce, largely through the business transactions of shopkeeper William Jernigan who told vendors to send their wares to "Commerce, Texas." The Ashland PO, opened 13 Jan 1873 by Josiah Jackson, was changed to Commerce 27 Dec 1880.

COMO (Hopkins) Known in the 1840s as Carroll('s) Prairie for pioneer settler Ferdinand Carroll. PO 7 Feb 1870 as Bacchus, PM Mary E. Miller; changed to Carroll's Prairie 16 May 1876; changed to Carroll Prairie 16 Nov 1892; changed to Como 24 Oct 1894, PM Henry Wood Clay who chose the name for Como, MS.

COMSTOCK (Val Verde) In the early 1880s the Galveston, Harrisburg & San Antonio Railway established Comstock Station, named for John B. Comstock, a dispatcher for the railroad. PO 12 June 1888, PM Thomas Aaron. The area was formerly known as Sotol, named for the tall, spiny shrub native to West Texas and Mexico, also known as Desert Spoon. The Sotol PO near Juno operated 5 May 1894–16 Oct 1895.

COMYN [ko MEEN] (Comanche) In 1881 the Texas Central Railway built through the area and established several stations named for railroad personnel or investors. According to local accounts the town was named for M. T. Comyn, a construction foreman for the TC; more likely the namesake is Daniel Comyn Moran of New York, a late 19th century railroad officer and director. Moran's father, Charles Moran, was a major stockholder and part owner of the TC. PO 27 May 1893 as Theny, PM William Matheny; changed to Comyn

1 Oct 1909, PM Benjamin F. Barnes. See Moran.

CONCAN [KAHN kan] (Uvalde) The town of Concan was named, seriously or facetiously, for *conquian*, "coon can" by popular etymology, a Mexican rummy-style card game with which it had become associated. The origin of the name *conquian* and the game itself is unknown. PO 4 Oct 1880, PM James A. Robinson.

CONCEPCION [kuhn sep see ON] (Duval) Named from *Santa Cruz de la Concepción*, a land grant to Francisco Cordente by the Spanish government in the early 19th century. SANTA CRUZ is named from the same grant. PO 6 Feb 1873, PM Rafael Salinas.

CONCHO (County) Created 1858, organized 1879. Named from the Concho River, itself named from Spanish *concha* "shell, shellfish" by 17th century explorers for the abundance of mussels and mussel shells. For a time, the river was known as the *Río de las Nueces* "river of nuts," for the local pecan trees.

CONCORD (Leon, Rusk) Concord is a popular place name, occurring in about a dozen Texas counties. Most are named for Concord churches or have naming stories emphasizing the harmonious relationships among the early settlers.

CONCRETE (DeWitt) Surveyed in 1846 by James Norman Smith who organized the first school in the early 1840s. Smith or an early resident chose the name for the adobe concrete blocks used in home construction. PO 22 Aug 1853, PM Joshua Kindred.

CONE (Crosby) James S. and Salina J. Cone brought their ten children from Cisco, TX, and began ranching in the area in 1900. PO 3 Sept 1901, PM Robert E. Chapman.

CONLEN (Dallam) James H. Conlen was vice-president, chief engineer, and general superintendent of the Chicago, Rock Island & Mexico Railway when the railroad built through Sherman, Dallam, and Hartley counties in the early 1900s. PO 23 Sept 1901, PM Alfred Wells.

CONNELL (Orange) Originally a siding on the Texas & New Orleans Railroad in the early 20th century, the town was named for Giles H. Connell, president and part owner of the Reese-Corriher Lumber Company that established a sawmill in 1913. PO 6 Nov 1913, PM Henry A. Corriher.

CONOLEY (Milam) In 1851 Malcolm Campbell Conoley, a Presbyterian minister from North Carolina, moved to Brazoria County and to Milam County where he established a church and school in 1869.

CONROE (Montgomery) Herbert Melville Hoxie, general superintendent of the International–Great Northern Railroad, proposed the name for Isaac Conroe, a Houston lumberman who established a sawmill near the line of the I-GN in the early 1880s. PO 4 Dec 1883, PM Isaac Conroe.

CONVERSE (Bexar) James Converse was senior construction engineer for the Galveston, Harrisburg & San Antonio Railway when the station was established in 1876. PO 12 Feb 1878, PM James Marmion.

COOKE (County) Created and organized 1848. Named for William Gordon Cooke (1808–1847), born in Virginia. Cooke was a distinguished military leader, serving in the Texas Army 1835–1841. He was Republic of Texas President Anson Jones's Secretary of War and the first Adjutant General of the State of Texas.

COOKVILLE (Titus) Andrew Barney Cook came to Texas from Georgia and opened the area's first general store in the late 1860s. PO 15 June 1870 as Clay Hill, PM David L. Hall; changed to Cookville 21 June 1880, PM Andrew B. Cook.

COOLIDGE (Limestone) Thomas Jefferson Coolidge was a Boston financier and a major stockholder in the Trinity & Brazos Valley Railway. When the T&BV built through the area in 1903 and bypassed the town of Armour, many Armour homes and businesses moved to trackside. PO 29 Jan 1883 as Armour; renamed Cooledge 14 Oct 1903, PM John M. Hill; changed to Coolidge 1 Jan 1931.

COOPER (Delta) Leroy Washington Cooper, Texas State Representative from Houston County, was chair of the Texas House Committee on Counties and Boundaries that created Delta County in 1870. The town of Cooper was founded and named in his honor, also in 1870. PO 7 Aug 1871, PM Thompson P. Pickins.

COPANO VILLAGE (Aransas) Copano, a Spanish port of entry on the northwest shore of Copano Bay from the 1720s, had become a ghost town by 1900. It was revived as Copano Village on the east shore of Copano Bay, a residential subdivision since about 1940. The town was named from the Copano (Copane), a local subtribe of the Karankawa.

COPEVILLE (Collin) John Miles Cope from Perry County, KY, began farming in the area about 1848. He established the Copeville PO 5 June 1878.

COPPELL [kuh PEL] (Dallas) Known as Gibbs for Barnett Gibbs, Texas State Senator and Lieutenant Governor in 1884. In the early 1890s the St. Louis, Arkansas & Texas Railway established Coppell Station, named for George A. Coppell, a New York banker and financier. PO 22 Dec 1887 as Gibbs; changed to Coppell 29 June 1892, PM William O. Harrison.

COPPERAS COVE [KAHP ruhs COV] (Coryell) Named for the ferrous sulfate content of some of the local wells. PO 25 Mar 1879 as Coperas Cove, PM Marsden Ogletree; changed to Copperas Cove 19 Dec 1901.

CORBET (Navarro) Corbet was organized as Cook's Schoolhouse about 1866. John N. Russell and his father, John S. Russell, the first two PMs, established the Corbet PO 15 May 1893 and most likely named it for James J. (Gentleman Jim) Corbett, a hero of the boxing world and internationally known since his defeat of John L. Sullivan several months earlier.

CORDELE [kor DEL] (Jackson) Founded in 1897 by the New York and Texas Land Company with offices in Palestine, TX, and New York City. PO 22 May 1897, PM Jesse W. Stapleton who chose the name for his former home, Cordele, GA, itself named for Cordelia Hawkins, daughter of the president of the Savannah, Americus & Montgomery Railway.

CORINTH [KOR inth] (Denton) The area was first known as Shiloh, apparently named by Thomas Ball who donated land for the Primitive Baptist Church in 1877. About 1880 officials of the Dallas & Wichita Railroad changed the name to Corinth, either a transfer from Alabama, Georgia, or Mississippi, themselves named for Corinth, Greece, or named in memory of the 1862 Civil War Siege of Corinth, MS. PO 29 Aug 1883, PM Charles E. Jones.

CORLENA (Dallam) Joseph F. Edwards, president of the San Antonio, Rio Grande & Tampico Railroad created Corlena in the early 1900s by blending the name of his mother-in-law, *Cor*inna Bradbury, with that of his baby daughter, *Lena*. PO 16 Nov 1907, PM Wyatt M. McFarlen. See Charlotte.

CORNETT [kor NET] (Cass) Formerly known as Troup for Troup County, GA, the home of a number of early settlers including George Cornett, for whom the community was formally named 21 Sept 1901 when O. C. (Osey) Porter established the Cornett PO. See Troup.

CORNUDAS (Hudspeth) Spanish "horns." Named in the 1930s from the Cornudas Mountains twelve miles to the north, themselves named for their horn-like rock formations, especially the peaks of Horned Mountain. PM 13 Jan 1938, Elzira J. Tinnin.

CORPUS CHRISTI (Nueces) The city of Corpus Christi was clearly named from Corpus Christi Bay, but the naming of the bay is uncertain. According to traditional accounts the name was given by the expedition of Alfonso Álvarez de Pineda who encountered the bay on the feast day of Corpus Christi "body of Christ" in the summer of 1519. There is little to support this story, however, and others have been given credit as well, including the French explorer René Robert Cavelier, the Sieur de La Salle. The first known recorded name of the bay appears in the report of Joaquín de Orobio y Basterra who explored the Texas Gulf Coast in 1746 and described the bay of *San Miguel Arcangel* "St. Michael the Archangel." The first reference to the bay as Corpus Christi was apparently by Diego Ortiz Parrilla in the mid-1760s. The first permanent settler in the present city was Henry Lawrence Kinney, a scoundrel and opportunist fleeing prosecution in Illinois for nonpayment of debts who established a saloon and emporium known as Kinney's Trading Post or Kinney's Rancho in 1839. General Zachary Taylor, on his way to the invasion of Mexico, established base camp at "Kinney's Rancho" in 1845 and by the time Taylor broke camp in 1846 Kinney's Rancho had become Corpus Christi. For a discussion of the complex and nuanced nature of place naming, with Corpus Christi as a primary example, see Rodman, "Rethinking Corpus Christi."

CORRIGAN (Polk) Corrigan developed in the early 1880s with construction of the Houston East & West Texas Railway. The town was reportedly named for Pat Corrigan, conductor of the first train through the area. PO 20 Mar 1882 as Corrigon, PM Joseph Kurth; changed to Corrigan 13 July 1883.

CORSICANA [kor suh KAN uh] (Navarro) Corsicana was organized in 1848 as the seat of Navarro County. José Antonio Navarro, for whom Navarro County is named, chose the name for the island of Corsica, his father's birthplace. PO 27 Jan 1849, PM Robert White. See Navarro County.

CORYELL (County) Created and organized 1854. Named from Coryell Creek that runs through Coryell County for some 30 miles before emptying into the Leon River west of Cavitt. The stream was named for James Coryell, a native Ohioan who held land in the area from the 1830s.

CORYELL CITY (Coryell) The area was known from the early 1850s as Rainey's Creek. The community became known as Coryell City after Coryell County was created in 1854. The Rainey's Creek PO operated intermittently from 1857 until 1874. The Coryell office was opened in Nov 1860, discontinued in Nov 1866, and replaced in Sept 1874 by the Rainey's Creek office, renamed Coryell.

COST (Gonzales) Cost was known from at least 1890 as Oso (Spanish "bear"). In 1897 Samuel Hindman applied for a post office in his general store and sought a name other than Oso. According to local lore, one bright citizen, not wanting to lose contact with the original name, suggested simply adding C at the beginning of Oso and changing the final O to T! The suggestion was met with cheers of approval. By another account William Muenzer submitted four names to the Post Office Department and the name chosen was Cost. PO 22 Sept 1897, PM Samuel C. Hindman.

COTTLE (County) Created 1876, organized 1892. Named for George Washington Cottle (1811–1836), born in Missouri. Cottle, a soldier of the Texas Revolution, fought in the October 2, 1835 Battle of Gonzales and is remembered as one of the Gonzales Immortal 32. On March 1, 1836 he entered the Alamo where he died five days later.

COTTON CENTER (Hale) The Cotton Center School opened in 1925 when the Anchor, Norfleet, and Bartonsite school districts consolidated. Cotton was the main cash crop of the area. PO 25 Sept 1935, PM Eunice Yates.

COTTON GIN (Freestone) Physician James Wills (Willis) established a mule-powered cotton gin, opened the first general store in the late 1840s, and was the first postmaster 17 Nov 1851.

COTTONDALE (Wise) The PO application in 1875 requested the name Cotton Valley in recognition of several remarkable cotton harvests; when this name was rejected the application was resubmitted as Cottondale. PO 17 Sept 1875, PM Arthur J. Gibson.

COTTONWOOD (Madison) Named from Cottonwood Creek, itself named for stands of cottonwood trees.

COTULLA [kuh TOO luh] (La Salle) Stock raiser Joseph Cotulla founded his namesake town when the International–Great Northern Railroad built through the area in 1881. PO 7 Nov 1881 as La Salle; changed to Cotulla 16 Aug 1883, PM John A. Kerr.

COUGHRAN [KOR uhn] (Atascosa) By the early 1910s, William Abraham "Abe"

Coughran had built a store, opened a bank, and organized a school. Coughran donated land for the San Antonio, Uvalde & Gulf Railroad station that was named in his honor in 1913. PO 13 Aug 1913, PM Rosalie Ormand, a relative of Coughran's wife, Pocahontas Janette Coughran.

COUNTY LINE (Nacogdoches) Located near the Nacogdoches–Cherokee county line.

COUPLAND [KOP luhnd] (Williamson) In 1887, as the Taylor, Bastrop & Houston Railway was building through the area, the Coupland City Company laid out the town named for site owner Theodore Van Buren Coupland. PO 28 Dec 1889, PM John Goetz.

COURTNEY (Grimes) Founded about 1860 with construction of the Houston & Texas Central Railway. Named for Courtney Ann Groce, wife of Leonard Waller Groce, oldest son of Jared E. Groce, one of the first settlers in Stephen F. Austin's Old Three Hundred and known as the "Father of Texas Agriculture." He is considered the first corn and cotton planter in the area. PO 7 Feb 1860, PM Daniel H. Carter.

COURTNEY (Martin) Named for community benefactor John E. Courtney who donated land for the Courtney School about 1907.

COVE (Chambers) Winfree's Cove, an indentation in the shoreline of Old River Lake, itself an arm of the Trinity River, was named for Absolom Jesse Winfree who settled in the area in the late 1820s. The name had been shortened by the time Allie Williams opened the Cove PO 29 June 1894.

COVINGTON (Hill) About 1850 James J. Gathings brought his family and thirty slaves to Hill County where he developed a large farming and ranching complex and laid out the town named for his wife, née Martha Wall Covington (for whose family the town of Covington, NC, was named). PO 11 July 1855, PM James J. Gathings.

COY CITY (Karnes) Rancher and soldier Trinidad Coy managed the *Rancho del Paso de la Conquista* near Coy City from the early 1850s. Coy served in the armed forces of the Republic of Mexico in the 1820s and early 1830s and those of the Republic of Texas in the late 1830s. PO 26 June 1930, PM Lurlene Coward.

COZY CORNER (Fayette) According to a local account two communities merged—The Prayer (apparently a local pronunciation of "The Prairie") and Post Oak. To avoid taking one name or the other, the new town took the name of Floyd Homer's Cozy Corner Cafe, opened in 1947.

CRABB (Fort Bend) About 1880 the Gulf, Colorado & Santa Fe Railway laid tracks on land owned by Eliza Jane Crabb, part of a grant to her first husband, Joseph Kuykendall, one of Stephen F. Austin's Old Three Hundred settlers. PO 28 Nov 1894, PM Sidney Johnson.

CRABBS PRAIRIE (Walker) Hillary and Rosanna Crabb settled in the area in the early 1840s. Hillary Crabb was a county judge and served in the 4th and 6th Texas Legislatures in the 1850s. He opened the Crabbs Prairie post office in May 1846. The office closed six months later.

CRAFT (Cherokee) Previously known as Independence, the town took the name of the Craft PO, opened 27 Oct 1891, PM Thomas J. Craft.

CRAFTON (Wise) George and Emily Craft laid out the town of Crafton in 1883. George Craft represented the district in the 20th Texas Legislature (1885–1887). PO 23 Apr 1878, PM James Elliott.

CRANDALL (Kaufman) Cornelius F. Crandall founded two towns, both of which he named for himself. In 1872 he donated the site of Crandall, IN, to the Southern Railroad and in 1880 he donated the site of Crandall, TX, to the Texas Trunk Line Railroad. Crandall established the PO 6 Dec 1881.

CRANE (County) Created 1887, organized 1927. Named for William Carey Crane (1816–1885). Crane, a Baptist minister, held pastorates in Mississippi in the 1840s, was president of several Southern colleges in the 1850s, moved to Houston in 1863, and assumed the presidency of Baylor University in January 1864, an office he held until his death.

CRANE (Crane) The town of Crane was largely undeveloped until oil was discovered in 1926 and Ollin Clumbers Kinnison, an El Paso oil speculator and real estate developer, laid out the townsite and opened an office to sell business and residential building lots. PO 9 Apr 1908 as Crane, named from the county, PM Walter R. Bates.

CRANELL (Refugio) Cranell is an adaptation and compression of Nellie Crane, wife of Jeff Miller, vice president and general manager of the St. Louis, Brownsville & Mexico Railway that built through the area in the mid-1900s. See Allenhurst.

CRANFILLS GAP (Bosque) Cranfills Gap, an opening in the hills separating Bosque and Hamilton counties, was named for George Eaton Cranfill (or Cranford), an early settler from Missouri in the 1850s. PO 21 May 1879, PM Samuel B. Cranford.

CRAWFORD (McLennan) William Nelson Crawford emigrated from Bledsoe County, TN, in the late 1840s. Crawford created a ford on the Middle Bosque River that was known as Crawford's Crossing or Tonk Crossing (from Tonk Creek, a shortening of Tonkawa, the Native American people that once lived in the area). Crawford is now known as the home of President George W. Bush. PO 7 Aug 1871, PM John Hamlin.

CREATH (Houston) Moffett Baskin Creath, born in Mississippi, established a general store and cotton gin in the late 1890s. PO 13 Feb 1904, PM William M. Robison.

CREECHVILLE (Ellis) Rosetta and Jesse Creech and their 12 children relocated from Illinois and began farming in the area in the 1880s. PO 2 Dec 1899, PM Sam Wilson.

CREEDMOOR (Travis) By a classic popular etymology Creedmoor reflected the religious creed of the citizens that was firmly moored to their hearts. PO 19 Jan 1880, PM Joseph Arthur Bailey.

CRESSON (Hood, Johnson, Parker) According to the local account, by 1850 the area was a rest stop on the stagecoach line and a popular camping site for wagon trains, several led by John Cresson. However, Shirley Smith's etymology is undoubtedly correct: Cresson, TX, was named for Cresson, Cambria County, PA, by Thomas Jackson, land agent for the Gulf, Colorado & Santa Fe Railway that joined the Fort Worth & Rio Grande Railway at Cresson in 1887. PO 30 Nov 1887, PM Campbell Tankersley.

CRISP (Ellis) Named for Charles Frederick Crisp of Georgia, Speaker of the US House of Representatives (1891–1895). PO 8 Jan 1892, PM John H. Anderson.

CROCKETT (County) Created 1875, organized 1891. Named for David "Davy" Crockett (1786–1836), born in North Carolina. Crockett was an explorer, US Congressman from Tennessee in the 1820s and 1830s, and an Alamo hero. Thanks to the 1955 Disney movie and song, Crockett became known as the "King of the Wild Frontier." He was famous for his aphorisms; the two most often attributed to him: "Make sure you're right, then go ahead" and "You can go to hell—I'm going to Texas."

CROCKETT (Houston) When Houston County was created in 1837, Elijah and Elizabeth Gossett donated land for the county seat and chose the name for Davy Crockett, reportedly the Gossett's neighbor when they lived in Tennessee. The Gossetts also chose the name of Houston County. PO 31 Mar 1838, PM J. H. Kirkhoffer (Kirchhoffer).

CROSBY (County) Created 1876, organized 1886. Named for Stephen Crosby (1808–1869), a native South Carolinian who came to Texas from Alabama in the 1840s and was Texas Land Commissioner in the 1850s and 1860s.

CROSBY (Harris) Crosby was probably named for Josiah F. Crosby, appointed receiver of the bankrupt Texas & New Orleans Railroad in 1869 and vice president when the T&NO was reorganized in 1875. PO 5 Feb 1877, PM Charles P. Karcher.

CROSBYTON (Crosby) Julian Bassett, a partner with Avery, John, Howard, and Prentiss Coonley in the CB (Coonley Brothers) Ranch and Livestock Company, founded Crosbyton in 1908, named from Crosby County. When the Crosbyton–Southplains Railroad established Crosbyton Station in 1910, the Crosby county seat was moved from Emma to Crosbyton. PO 29 May 1908, PM Julian Bassett.

CROSS CUT (Brown) James Bloodworth's general store was the nucleus of the community known as Cross Out, so named according to local legend because it was "across country and out of the way of usual travel." When Bloodworth applied for a Cross Out post office the application was misread and returned with the name Cross Cut. PO 9 Apr 1879, PM James M. Bloodworth.

CROSS PLAINS (Callahan) Cross Plains was organized when William M. Mattox opened the PO 25 July 1877, apparently named for the town's location where a stagecoach and military road crossed. The choice of the name is often attributed to a member of the McDermett (McDermitt) family.

CROW (Wood) PO 11 July 1906, PM John K. Rucker, a sawmill operator who apparently named the office for Walter W. Crow, a Kingston, LA, lumber inspector.

CROWELL [KROL] (Foard) Millard Thacker established the PO 29 May 1890, named for site owner George T. Crowell from Georgia who began farming in the area in the late 1880s.

CROWLEY [KROW lee] (Johnson, Tarrant) Formerly known as Deer Creek. Although local reports claim the namesake is S. H. Crowley, the town was named about 1881 for John H. Crowley of Galveston, road and transportation manager for the Gulf, Colorado & Santa Fe Railway. PO 7 July 1882, PM Jarrard T. Conn.

CROWN (Atascosa) Lagunillas (Spanish "little lakes") was founded about 1870 as a community for former slaves; renamed before 1900, probably for the Crown trademark and icon on a popular sewing machine. The Florence Sewing Machine Company of Florence, MA, introduced the Crown model about 1880. PO 14 June 1900, PM John W. Crouch.

CROWTHER (McMullen) Sam Crowther, born in England, arrived in San Antonio in 1883. Acting as agent for English investors he developed a townsite and railroad station between San Antonio and the Gulf coast. The project failed and Crowther moved on to San Angelo but not before he established the Crowther PO 18 Aug 1902.

CRYER CREEK (Navarro) According to Fred Tarpley, Cryer Creek was so named because the sound of the water swirling around the rocks reminded settlers of a woman crying. PO 24 Feb 1879 as Cryer Creek, PM Arthur William Stokes.

CRYSTAL CITY (Zavala) Land developers Carl Groos and Edwin Buckingham founded Crystal City in 1906 and were members of the first board of directors of the Crystal City & Uvalde Railroad in 1909. Local historians say the name was chosen for the "crystal clear" water from the local artesian wells. PO 19 Jan 1908, PM Andrew D. Jackson.

CRYSTAL FALLS (Stephens) A tributary of the Clear Fork of the Brazos River was apparently called Paint Creek by explorers and early settlers, reportedly a translation of Comanche *qua ho no*. Crystal Falls was named for a small, clear waterfall on the tributary or on Clear Fork itself. PO 30 Oct 1877, PM Joseph Reavis.

CUERO [KWEHR o] (DeWitt) Gustave Schleicher, the namesake of Schleicher County, founded Cuero with construction of the Gulf, Western Texas & Pacific Railway in 1872. Named from Cuero Creek, from Spanish *Arroyo del Cuero* "hide creek," a translation of a Native American name for the site where buffalo were butchered and the hides were tanned. PO 25 Mar 1840 as Quiro, PM George Blair.

CUEVITAS [kwuh VEET uhs] (Jim Hogg) Spanish "caverns." Founded about 1890 by members of the Guerra family led by Francisco Guerra. PO 8 Aug 1892 as Old San Antonio; changed to Cuevitas 26 July 1894, PM Encarnacion Salinas.

CULBERSON (County) Created 1911, organized 1912. Named for David Browning Culberson (1830–1900), born in Georgia. Culberson moved to Texas in 1856 and established a law practice in Upshur County. He served in the Texas Legislature in the late 1850s, was a state senator in 1873, and a ten-term US Congressman 1875–1897. His son, Charles Culberson, was Governor of Texas 1895–1899.

CULLEOKA [kuhl ee O kuh, occasionally kuhl ee O kee] (Collin) John T. Branch opened a general store near McKinney about 1885. He proposed the name for his former home, Culleoka, Maury County, TN, itself named from Choctaw *kali-oka* "spring water." PO 29 May 1893, PM John Morrow.

CUMBY (Hopkins) After the East Line & Red River Railroad built through the area in the 1880s, David B. Culberson suggested the name to honor Robert H. Cumby, a Rusk County plantation owner with whom he had served in the Texas Legislature. PO 9 Feb 1848 as Black Jack Grove; changed to Theodocia 2 Feb 1857; changed back to Black Jack Grove 3 May 1858; changed to Cumby 27 Mar 1896, PM Robert N. Holderness.

CUNDIFF (Jack) Walker Moore and William Cundiff, land speculators from Chico, TX, laid out the town in 1892. PO 14 Sept 1886 as Marmaduke, named for Marmaduke Norfleet Price, a Wise County landowner; changed to Cundiff 20 Jan 1891, PM Allen B. Flowers.

CUNEY (Cherokee) Settled in the late 1860s by freed slaves and named Andy for Andrew Bragg, one of the first landowners. About 1915 Henry Lee Price of Palestine laid out the town named for his son, Wright Cuney Price, who was named for Norris Wright Cuney of Galveston, a leading African American politician and advocate in the last decades of the 19th century. PO 26 Nov 1917, PM Lillie Hall.

CUNNINGHAM (Lamar) The Samuel and Victoria Cunningham family from Marshall County, TN, began farming in the area in the 1890s. PO 31 Aug 1912, PM Tilman Crafton.

CURTIS (Jasper) Settled by the Adam Byerly family from North Carolina in the early 1830s and known as Byerly's Gin until Adam Byerly, grandnephew of the first settler, became PO 1 May 1945 and named the office for his son, Curtis.

CUSHING (Nacogdoches) Founded in 1902 following the announcement that the Texas & New Orleans Railroad would be building through the area. Named for Edward Benjamin Cushing, assistant general manager of the T&NO. Cushing was later chair of the Texas A&M Board of Regents and is the namesake of Cushing Memorial Library on the College Station campus. PO 9 Dec 1902, PM De Calve Baines.

CUSSETA (Cass) The Cusseta Mountains (three peaks to the northwest) and the town of Cusseta are named either for Cusseta, Chambers County, AL, or Cusseta, Chattahoochee County, GA. *Cusseta* is from Muskogee with the probable meaning "trading place." The Cusseta people were members of the Creek Confederacy. PO 18 June 1856, PM John Heard.

CUSTER CITY (Cooke) Custer City was first known as Centennial City, named in 1876, the nation's 100th anniversary and the year Robert Jones and his son Jim established a cotton gin and gristmill. James Barrington opened the Custer City PO 19 Nov 1877. Although several accounts claim the office was named for a famous trotting horse named Custer, the namesake is George Armstrong Custer, a national hero even though his 7th Cavalry had been destroyed in a battle with Sioux and other Native American warriors the year before. As an army officer Custer spent time in Texas after the Civil War and was quite popular. After his defeat at the Little Big Horn, the Texas Legislature passed a "resolution of condolence" that begins "Whereas General G. A. Custer has endeared himself to the people of the frontier of Texas. . . ."

CUT AND SHOOT (Montgomery) One of the more colorful and most widely known of Texas place names, Cut and Shoot has inspired a number of naming stories. According to one related by Robin Navarro Montgomery, the name arose from a dispute over church services in the summer of 1912. Some religious groups were welcome to conduct services in the community chapel and others were not. Things came to a head one July morning when one group, determined to enter the building, was met by another, equally determined to keep them out. Tensions rose and when weapons were drawn, a young boy darted off exclaiming "I'm going to cut around the corner and shoot through the bushes." Legal proceedings followed and one witness, when asked where the scuffle had occurred, is said to have replied "where they had the cuttin' and shootin' scrape." By another account a local preacher was accused of becoming too friendly with women of the congregation and men ran from the church "to their wagons and buggies to get knives and rifles to cut and shoot." Churches must have been dangerous places in those days since a third account traces the name to an argument that arose over the design of a new church steeple.

CUTHAND (Red River) Cuthand was named from the PO established 11 Jan 1867 by Cornelius Crenshaw, itself named from Cuthand Creek. The source of the name is uncertain. Some say the name honors a Chief Cuthand who brought warring tribes together; others claim a cowboy's hand was severely cut in a knife fight and still others say the namesake is a "famous" Delaware Indian leader who lost part of his hand at the battle of Tippecanoe in 1811. To the first story is often added the claim that General Thomas Rusk, the namesake of Rusk County, was a friend of Chief Cuthand and named the stream in his honor.

CUYLER [KEYE ler] (Carson) Cuyler was part of the school district organized about 1910 and named for Cornelius Cornelissen Cuyler of New York who invested heavily in the White Deer Lands. See White Deer.

CYCLONE (Bell) According to a local tale, Charles McCall held a meeting to decide on a name for the PO and someone said, "Call it cyclone because it would take a cyclone to get this bunch together!" McCall submitted the name and opened the Cyclone PO 20 Jan 1886.

D

DACOSTA [duh KAHST uh] (Victoria) Founded in 1860 with construction of the San Antonio & Mexican Gulf Railroad. Named for Alfred DaCosta, a steamship captain based at Indianola and an agent for the Morgan Steamship Company. PO 2 Jan 1903, PM Benjamin Ulysses Fox.

DACUS [DAK uhs] (Montgomery) Judson Berry Dacus was Montgomery County treasurer from 1886 until his death in 1892. PO 8 Jan 1889, PM E. Eddings Ann Moore Goodin.

DAFFAN [DAF uhn] (Travis) Daffan was organized about 1900; named for Lawrence Aylett Daffan, division superintendent of the Texas Central Railway. His daughter, Katie Daffan, was a noted writer of Texas and women's history in the early 20th century.

DAINGERFIELD (Morris) Named about 1840 from Daingerfield Spring, itself named for London Daingerfield, a semi-legendary settler and Indian fighter of the 1820s or 1830s. Reportedly, when Daingerfield destroyed an Indian village at the spring, the Indians retaliated and killed his entire family. PO 7 Nov 1841, PM John N. King.

DAISETTA [duh ZET uh] (Liberty) Storekeeper James Newton Farris is generally credited with coining Daisetta by combining the names of Daisy Barrett and Etta White. PO 3 Mar 1921, PM Joseph White.

DALBY SPRINGS (Bowie) The springs were promoted for their medicinal properties from at least the 1850s. The water was claimed to "cure anything that ails you." Named for Warren Dalby, his three brothers, and other members of the Dalby family who came to the area from Tennessee in the late 1830s. PO 16 May 1860 as Dalby's Springs, PM Joseph Gordentia Dalby, Warren Dalby's son; discontinued 5 Nov 1866; reopened 8 Feb 1877 as Dalby Springs, PM J. M. Burroughs.

DALE (Caldwell) Apparently named for the dale (valley) in which the town is located. PO 2 June 1880, PM James S. Medaris.

DALHART (Dallam, Hartley) Early in 1901 real estate agent William Blair and physician Charles Thornton, both of Channing, founded a town where the lines of the Fort Worth & Denver City and Chicago, Rock Island & Mexico railroads crossed. The intersection was known as Twist or Twist Junction and later as Denrock for "Denver City" and "Rock Island." The Post Office Department rejected the name Denrock but approved Dalhart, a blend of *Dal*lam and *Hart*ley counties. The name was probably chosen by Ora D. Atkinson, a founder of the Dalhart Town Company that was organized later in 1901 to promote the town and sell building lots. PO 29 Apr 1901, PM William Scarborough.

DALLAM (County) Created 1876, organized 1891. Named for James Wilmer Dallam (1818–1847), lawyer and editor, born in Baltimore, MD. Dallam moved to Texas in 1839 and became a noted compiler of Texas laws and the author of several works of romantic fiction based upon events in Texas history.

DALLARDSVILLE (Polk) Named for John J. Dallard (Dollard), a merchant, teacher, and farmer who opened the Dallard PO 4 June 1877.

DALLAS (County) Dallas County and Polk County were created by the Texas Legislature on the same day, March 30, 1846, and named for sitting President James K. Polk and Vice President George Mifflin Dallas whose platform in the election of 1844 included statehood for Texas.

DALLAS (Dallas) The namesake of the city of Dallas is uncertain. Known as Dallas as early as 1842 when George Mifflin Dallas (see Dallas County) was in private legal practice in Philadelphia, hardly a recommendation for the name of a Texas town. Early evidence regarding the name is a comment (second hand at that) attributed to John Neely Bryan, the founder of Dallas, who is said to have remarked that he chose the name "for my friend Dallas," but the particular Dallas he had in mind remains elusive. Other namesakes that have been proposed include Alexander James Dallas, brother of George Mifflin Dallas and commander of the US West Indies Fleet stationed in Pensacola, FL, in the 1840s; and Joseph Dallas about whom little is known except that he settled in the area in the early 1840s. PO 22 May 1846, PM John Neely Bryan. Etymologist Barry Popik discusses the naming of the city of Dallas at www.barrypopik.com/index.php/new_york_city/entry/dallas_summary.

DALWORTHINGTON GARDENS (Tarrant) Founded in 1934 as a "subsistence homestead" through the National Industrial Recovery Act of 1933. Residents were expected to engage in subsistence farming and work at industrial jobs part time. The name was blended from the three cities that expressed an interest in the program: *Dal*las, Fort *Worth*, and Arl*ington*.

DAMON (Brazoria) Named from Damon's Mound, a 150-foot limestone elevation west of the community named for Samuel Damon, a carpenter who came to Texas from Massachusetts about 1830. After his service in the Texas Revolution, he operated a sawmill and brick factory near the site of Damon. PO 2 May 1888 as Damon's Mound, PM Hampton L. Bryan; changed to Damon 16 May 1895, PM Asa L. Woodward.

DANBURY (Brazoria) Named in 1905 by officials of the St. Louis, Brownsville & Mexico Railway, probably for Dan (Daniel C.) Miller, father of Jeff N. Miller, vice president and general manager of the StLB&M; possibly for Dan (Daniel J.) Moller whose ranch reportedly abutted the railroad tracks. Perhaps named for both. PO 22 Apr 1909, PM Thomas Boring.

DANCIGER [DAN si ger] (Brazoria) The Danciger Oil & Refinery Co., founded by Jack Danciger and producers of Road Runner gasoline, began drilling in the Pledger Dome oil field in the early 1930s. PM 3 Nov 1934, Oliver Lloyd Hodge.

DANEVANG [DAN uh vang] (Wharton) Danevang "Danish field" was founded in 1894 when the *Dansk Folkesamfund* "Danish People's Society," supported by the Danish Evangelical Lutheran Church, acquired some 25,000 acres for a colony where Danish language and culture would be preserved and perpetuated. PO 23 July 1895, PM Herman Peter Hermansen.

DANNER (Fannin) Wylie Lee Danner from North Carolina began farming in the area in the 1890s and established the PO 16 Feb 1901.

DANVILLE (Gregg) Danville is likely a transfer from Danville, KY, home state of Stephen Slade Barnett who represented Sabine County in the Fifth Congress of the Republic of Texas in the 1840s and was a co-founder of Danville about 1848. PO 19 July 1850 as Rabbit Creek; changed to New Danville 3 Apr 1852, PM John W. Wilson; discontinued 3 Feb 1873.

DARCO (Harrison) In 1921 the Atlas Powder Company and the Darco Corporation of Wilmington, DE, established an activated carbon plant in Marshall, TX. PO 16 Sept 1952, Velma M. Dixon.

DARROUZETT [dar uh ZET] (Lipscomb) Laid out in 1918 as Opal, named for Opal Lourwood, infant daughter of Charles and Lillie Lourwood and regarded as the first white child born in the vicinity. When the Panhandle & Santa Fe Railway established a station in 1919, the name was changed for John Darrouzett, a Galveston lawyer working for the P&SF. PO 5 Apr 1918 as Lourwood; changed to Darrouzett 16 July 1919, PM William L. Allen.

DAVILLA [duh VIL uh] (Milam) Named from the land grant awarded to Miguel Davila [*sic*] in 1833. The community was laid out in the 1860s and lots were sold with the provision that alcohol was strictly forbidden. PO 23 Aug 1871, PM Robert M. Wiley.

DAVIS (Atascosa) About 1914 the San Antonio, Uvalde & Gulf Railroad established Davis Switch on land donated by Matt and Olive Davis.

DAVISVILLE (Angelina) James Bonham McConnico, a Lufkin real estate agent and stockbroker, laid out the town in the early 1900s, named for his wife, Sarah Davis McConnico. PO 8 Apr 1908, PM William G. Harrington.

DAWN (Deaf Smith) In the late 1880s James Parrish bought the site and opened a general store. According to local tradition when Parrish relocated his family from Denton he remarked, "This is the dawn of a new day." PO 2 Dec 1889, PM Leander D. Parrish.

DAWSON (County) Created 1876, organized 1905. Named for Nicholas Mosby Dawson (1808–1842), born in Kentucky. Dawson came to Texas in 1834. He served in several Indian campaigns and fought in the Battle of San Jacinto. He is remembered for what is known as the Dawson Massacre of September 1842 in which all but two of the fifty-three men he was leading to join the battle at Salado Creek were killed or captured by Mexican forces.

DAWSON (Navarro) Named for rancher Britton Dawson and his sons David and Henry who donated land for a station on the Cotton Belt Railroad in 1881. PO 26 Jan 1882, PM Jerry Johnson.

DAYTON (Liberty) When the Texas & New Orleans Railroad built through the area about 1870 the flag stop was called Day's Town, named for Isiah Cates Day, a stock raiser from Tennessee. The town formally became Dayton when William Simpson established the Dayton PO 15 Jan 1877.

DE LEON [DEE lee AHN] (Comanche) Founded in 1881 by the Texas Central Railway. Named from the Leon River northeast of the community, itself named for Alonso de León, Spanish explorer and governor of Coahuila in the 1680s. PO 29 Aug 1881, PM Frank E. Bonipart.

DEADWOOD (Panola) In 1837 John William Adam LaGrone and Christeena Clementine LaGrone migrated from Newberry County, SC, by way of Perry County, AL, to the area known as Linus. According to the local story, several towns were competing for the PO when one citizen noticed an advantage and called out "We've got the deadwood on them now." (Deadwood was a western word of the 19th century meaning "advantage" or "upper hand"). PO 9 Feb 1882, PM William P. Potts.

DEAF SMITH (County) Created 1876, organized 1890. Named for Erastus Smith (1787–1837), born in New York state. Known for most of his life as "Deaf Smith" or "*El Sordo*" after a childhood illness that deprived him of much of his hearing. Smith settled near San Antonio in the early 1820s. He is best known as an intelligence officer of the Texas Revolution and courier for William B. Travis and Sam Houston. Smith's personal name is often pronounced [DEEF]; the county name is generally [DEF].

DEAL (Carson) Deal is a phonetic spelling of Deahl, for site owner George Washington Deahl, president or director of banks in Dodsonville, Wellington, Panhandle, and Childress. The town was established about 1925 as a flag stop on the Chicago, Rock Island & Gulf Railway. PO 11 Nov 1926, PM Sammie Peck.

DEAN (Clay) In the early 20th century the community developed around a shipping station on the Wichita Falls & Oklahoma Railway named for early settler and rancher Calloway Dean. Also known as Dean Dale.

DEANVILLE (Burleson) James and Josephine Dean settled in the area in the 1860s and opened a general store on a branch of the Chisholm Trail in the early 1870s. PO 27 June 1877, PM Judson Womble.

DEBERRY (Panola) Named for Alfred Wesley DeBerry, a Carthage lawyer, state legislator, and Texas Secretary of State under Governor Richard Coke in the mid-1870s. PO 22 June 1874, PM Daniel Rogers. Also known as Evergreen.

DECATUR (Wise) The legislation that created Wise county in 1856 directed that the seat be named Taylorsville in honor of General Zachary Taylor, an American hero of the Mexican War. Absolom Bishop, a member of the Texas State Legislature, disapproved of many of Taylor's Whig party policies and maneuvered to have the name changed for Commodore Stephen Decatur, a naval commander in the War of 1812 and the war against the Barbary Pirates in 1815. PO 5 May 1857 as Decatur, PM Daniel Howell; changed to Taylorsville 23 Sept 1857; changed back to Decatur 3 Sept 1858.

DECORDOVA (Hood) DeCordova takes its name from the DeCordova Bend of the Brazos River, itself named for Jacob de Cordova, a land agent, cartographer, author and Texas promoter. De Cordova assisted in the platting of Waco in 1848.

DEKALB [dee KAB] (Bowie) Named for Johann Kalb, born in Germany in 1721, who called himself Jean de Kalb when he joined the French infantry and Baron de Kalb when he served with George Washington at Valley Forge. A hero of the Revolutionary War, more than a dozen states have towns or counties named in his honor. The local story is that Davy Crockett passed through the community on his way to San Antonio in the winter of 1835 and asked its name. When told it had no name, he suggested they "name it for the Baron DeKalb." Alternatively, the name may have been brought to Texas by settlers from DeKalb, AL, or DeKalb, GA. PO 27 Feb 1839, PM Hiram A. Allen.

DEL RIO (Val Verde) According to the local account, in the mid-1630s Spanish explorers came to a stream they called *San Felipe del Río*, now San Felipe Creek, on the feast day of Saint Philip. Present Del Rio grew around a system of irrigation canals constructed by the San Felipe Agricultural, Manufacturing and Irrigation Company in the late 1860s. PO 26 Feb 1872, PM Felix Taylor.

DEL VALLE [del VAL ee] (Travis) Del Valle was established in the mid-1870s and named for the land grant of Santiago Del Valle, a member of the Mexican legislature and president of the congress of the state of Coahuila and Texas in the 1820s and 1830s. PO 5 June 1878, PM William M. Givens.

DELHI (Caldwell) According to local lore Delhi was the name (or stage name) of a traveling salesman of patent medicines who put on a show as he promoted his potions guaranteed to cure all afflictions and infirmities. PO 7 July 1873, PM John Reid.

DELL CITY (Hudspeth) Founded about 1847 shortly after the Bone Spring–Victorio Aquifer was discovered. The name was apparently taken from the word *dell* "valley" with an assist from the song "farmer in the dell," since the newly discovered ground water made irrigation and farming possible. "City" was a hopeful, optimistic addition to the name. PO 1 May 1849, PM Dallas H. Thompson.

DELMITA (Starr) Merchant Nicéforo Peña founded the town as Zaragosa in 1919. According to the local account, when Peña decided to change the name he wrote each letter of the alphabet on a slip of paper, dropped them into a box, mixed them and asked each of his seven sons to draw a letter. After several rounds, the seven letters drawn could be arranged to spell Delmita. PO 12 Sept 1925 as Zaragoza, PM Nicéforo C. Peña; changed to Delmita 1 May 1931.

DELTA (County) Created and organized 1870. Apparently named from its shape, roughly that of a horizontal delta, the fourth letter of the Greek alphabet.

DELWIN (Cottle) Ranchers Thomas and Ora Drummond of Paducah named the town for their son Delwin (Delwyn), born in 1912. PO 24 Mar 1916, PM Edward Burkhead.

DEMI-JOHN (Brazoria) Presumably named from the bend in Bastrop Bayou shaped like a demijohn, a large bulb-shaped bottle with a short narrow neck. Demijohn Bend in Comal County is claimed to have taken its name from a similar source, a demijohn-shaped bend in the Guadalupe River.

DENHAWKEN (Wilson) Denhawken was founded in the late 1890s with construction of the San Antonio & Gulf Railroad on land donated by Davis *Den*mark, William Lafayette *Hawk*, and Charles Steenk*en*.

DENISON (Grayson) William Munson, a Sherman lawyer and businessman, and Robert Stevens, general manager of the Missouri–Kansas–Texas Railroad (aka The KATY), founded and named Denison for George Denison, vice president of the KATY that built through the area in the early 1870s. PO 7 Oct 1872 as Denison City; changed to Denison 1 Apr 1886, PM Leonidas Maughs.

DENNIS (Parker) Nathan M. Dennis emigrated from Boston, MA, in the early 1890s, founded the town of Dennis, and was the first postmaster in May 1895.

DENTON (County) Created and organized 1846. Named for John B. Denton (1806–1841), born in Tennessee. Denton was a circuit riding Methodist minister in Arkansas and Missouri in the late 1820s and 1830s, and in the 1840s a militia officer under Edward Tarrant's command. He was killed in May 1841 fighting Cherokees and Caddos at the battle of Village Creek in what is now Tarrant County.

DENTON (Denton) Founded in 1857 as the Denton County seat following seats at Pinkneyville and Abbott. PO 17 Sept 1857, PM James Smoot.

DENVER CITY (Yoakum) Ben Eggink, drilling superintendent for the Denver Producing and Refining Company that was developing the Wasson oil field, founded the community as Denver in 1939. "City" was added to distinguish the town from Denver, CO and to suggest population growth and a bright future. PO 23 Mar 1938 as Wasson; discontinued, reopened and changed to Denver City 1 Apr 1939.

DENWORTH (Gray) Founded in 1919 as a station on the line of the Fort *Worth* & *Den*ver Railway. PO 7 Sept 1933, PM Ina Wall Marshall.

DEPORT (Lamar) Founded as Deeville, named for farmer Dee Thompson who emigrated from Tennessee in the early 1880s. As told by Fred Tarpley the name change from Deeville to Deport came about because "inhabitants persisted in associating [Deeville] with 'devil.' The exasperated Thompson family changed the name to Deport." (*Place Names of Northeast Texas*) PO 21 Nov 1883 as Deport, PM Millard C. Nobles.

DERBY (Frio) When the International–Great Northern Rail road built through the area in 1882 Edward Congdon established the Lenore post office. In December 1883, John Bennett, a British engineer for the IG-N became the Lenore postmaster and changed the name to Otley, the West Yorkshire home of his wife, Clara. In 1884 Bennett changed the name of the office again, this time for his birthplace, Derby, England.

DERDEN (Hill) Daniel Ball opened the Yaterville PO 12 Jan 1880, probably named for farmers William and Fannie Yater. Ball changed the PO to Derden 12 Apr 1881 for David Derden, clerk of the district court in Hillsboro, and his wife, Texanna.

DERMOTT (Scurry) By 1880 Peter Scott McDermott had emigrated from Pennsylvania and opened a general store in what became the town of McDermott. The name was shortened to Dermott when Peter McDermott's father-in-law, William H. H. Smith, established the post office 2 Dec 1902.

DESDEMONA (Eastland) Named for Amanda Desdemona Wynn, teenage daughter of Justice of the Peace John Jay Wynn and Frances Wynn. PO 25 July 1877 as Desdimonia, PM James R. Carpenter; changed to Desdemona 16 Dec 1901.

DESOTO (Dallas) Dr. Thomas Hernando DeSoto Stuart (Stewart), a native Georgian, established a medical practice about 1870. He may or may not have been a descendant of Hernando de Soto, the Spanish explorer who died in today's Arkansas in 1582. PO 2 Apr 1884, PM Jacob Rinehart.

DESSAU (Travis) Named by settlers from Dassau in east central Germany. The Dessau Dance Hall was a local fixture from 1876. PO 2 Dec 1886, PM William S. Lee.

DETROIT (Red River) Detroit grew around the Texas & Pacific Railway station established in the 1870s. PO 1 Nov 1876 as Bennett, PM Josiah Joplin; changed to Detroit 18 June 1887 at the suggestion of T&P station agent James M. Stephens for his birthplace, Detroit, MI.

DEVERS (Liberty) Philip Peyton Dever, born in KY, and his sons John and Thomas moved to what is now Liberty County in the mid-1820s and received a land grant from the Mexican government in 1830. PO 28 Sept 1874 as Dever's Woods, PM Jacob L. Holland; changed to Devers 14 June 1892.

DEVINE (Medina) The International–Great Northern Railroad named the station in 1881 in honor of Thomas Jefferson Devine, attorney for the I-GN. Devine was the first president of the Texas Bar Association and a justice of the Texas Supreme Court in the late 1880s. PO 17 Apr 1878 as Francisco; changed to Devine 29 Sept 1881, PM John L. Nix.

DEW (Freestone) Settled in the 1850s, the site became known as Sunshine, named from the Sunshine Methodist Church. According to a local account the PO application called for the name Drew but was misread by post office officials as Dew. PO 30 Dec 1885, PM Jacob Bishop Asbury Folk.

DEWALT (Fort Bend) In the late 1840s Thomas Waters Dewalt established the Dewalt Sugar Plantation that was divided into building lots and small farms at the end of the Civil War. PO 9 Apr 1898, PM Charles Jackson. Dewalt is now part of Missouri City.

DEWEES (Wilson) In 1849 Thomas Dewees and his brother John moved from northern Illinois and settled near Bastrop. After the Civil War they located in Wilson County where they became ranchers and drovers, driving cattle herds to Kansas railheads. PO 9 July 1906, PM William N. Robinson.

DEWEYVILLE (Newton) The Sabine Tram Company founded Deweyville in 1898, named in honor of Admiral George Dewey whose fleet had recently defeated the Spanish Armada at Manila Bay in the Philippines, a naval battle that made Dewey a national hero. PO 22 May 1900, PM Charles Smith.

DEWITT (County) Created and organized 1846. Named for empresario Green DeWitt (1787–1835), born in Kentucky. After initially rejecting his petition to establish a colony next to that of Stephen F. Austin, in 1825 the Mexican government gave DeWitt permission to settle some 400 Anglo-Americans.

DEWVILLE (Gonzales) Brothers John and Thomas Dew from Mississippi established farms and operated a cotton gin from about 1900. PO 28 June 1894, PM John F. Dew.

DEXTER (Cooke) Dexter is named for a famous trotting horse of the mid-and late 1860s owned by Robert Bonner, publisher of the *New York Ledger*. Dexter set a number of world racing records and in 1866 he and his trainer made an extended tour of the western states and in the process gave his name to Dexter, KS, and to Dexter, TX. PO 31 Mar 1873, PM James Schall.

D'HANIS [duh HAN uhs] (Medina) Alsatian farmers were attracted to the area by Empresario Henri Castro who named the community for William D'Hanis, a manager and promoter of the Castro Colony with an office in Antwerp. PO 24 June 1854, PM Henry Joseph Richarz. See Castro County.

DIAL (Fannin) The first settlement in the area was known as Lyday's Fort, a small blockhouse established in the mid-1830s by Isaac Lyday. In the 1850s William and Mary Dial relocated from Bledsoe County, TN. The town was named for their son James, a community benefactor and the third PM in 1893. PO 24 May 1880, PM Thomas Baker.

DIAL (Hutchinson) The Gulf Oil Company drilled several wells on the Dial Ranch and founded the town of Gulf Dial in the mid-1920s. PO 1 Sept 1939 as Dial, PM Pauline Pike.

DIALVILLE (Cherokee) At the end of the Civil War after serving with the 5th Alabama Infantry, John J. Dial joined a wagon train headed for Texas. He opened a general store in the 1880s and was the first PM 14 Dec 1885.

DIBOLL [DEYE bawl] (Angelina) In 1894 Thomas Lewis Latane Temple founded the Southern Pine Lumber Company on land previously owned by John C. Diboll. PO 25 May 1897, PM William P. Rutland, the namesake of RUTLAND.

DICEY (Parker) First known as Power, named from the PO established in April 1888 by James C. Power. That office was discontinued in 1890 and in 1891 Cynthia McDowell opened the Dicey office, named for Hanna Deborah Dicey Puryear, wife of farmer William Gholson Puryear.

DICKENS (County) Created 1876, organized 1891. Named for an Alamo defender whose full name is uncertain. Fred Arrington, in his *History of Dickens County*, says only that the county was "named in honor of J. Dickens. Rank: Private, native of England. He died in the siege of the Alamo." At least one roll of Alamo defenders lists a Sgt. James R. Dimpkins, born in England, whose name has also been recorded as Demkins and Dimkins, of which Dickens may be a misreading or a popular etymology.

DICKENS (Dickens) Named for the county, Dickens was settled in the 1880s and in 1892 replaced Espuela as the county seat. PO 20 Aug 1883, PM James H. Parrish.

DICKINSON (Galveston) John Dickinson, one of Stephen F. Austin's Old Three Hundred, was the original site owner in the mid-1820s. He left the area soon thereafter. PO 2 Nov 1857, PM William G. Nelson.

DICKWORSHAM (Clay) William Benjamin Worsham, known as "Uncle Dick Worsham," was a cattle drover, rancher, and banker who established the Worsham Bank in Henrietta in 1898. He is often credited with coining the derisive term "nester" to refer to farmers, claiming that farmhouses looked like birds' nests.

DIES [DEYEZ] (Tyler) Martin Dies, Jr. served in the US Congress from the early 1930s through the 1950s. The Martin Dies, Jr. State Park was named in his honor in 1965. Dies's father, also Martin Dies, served in the US Congress 1909–1919. PO 1 Sept 1931, PM Hill Dee Fortenberry.

DIKE (Hopkins) Samuel "Bud" Sheppard suggested the name for his hometown, Dike, Grundy County, IA. PO 23 Oct 1890, PM Isaac Rhodes. Also known as Union Valley.

DILLEY (Frio) Known as Darlington (Darlington Street in Dilly perpetuates the name) until the early 1880s when the International–Great Northern Railroad established Ford Station. Alex Meerscheidt of San Antonio purchased the site and laid out the town named for George M. Dilley, an agent for the I-GN. PO 13 Feb 1885 as Dilley; changed to Darlington 13 July 1891; changed back to Dilley 24 May 1892, PM Gilbert M. Williams.

DILWORTH (Gonzales) In 1887 a San Antonio & Aransas Pass Railway station was named for George N. Dilworth, founder of the Dilworth Bank and instrumental in attracting the SA&AP. PO 30 June 1892, PM Johanna Moren.

DIME BOX (Lee) The local account is that patrons would leave a letter and ten cents in a box at the Brown's Mills PO. This box became known as the "dime box." The Brown's Mills PO closed in 1883 and at a meeting to choose a name for a replacement, Dr. Richard Womack of Lexington reportedly suggested Dime Box and that name was accepted "enthusiastically." PO 6 June 1877 as Brown's Mills, PM Joseph Brown; discontinued 12 Oct 1883; reopened 16 May 1884 as Dime Box, PM Andrew M. Farmer.

DIMMIT (County) Created 1858, organized 1880. Named for Philip Dimmitt (1801–1841), born in Kentucky. Dimmitt was a prominent merchant in the 1820s and 1830s and a leading figure of the Texas Revolution, noted for his participation in the Goliad Campaign and for his support of the 1835 Goliad Declaration of Independence. The name was misspelled when the county was created. See Carrizo Springs.

DIMMITT (Castro) Hilory Green Bedford, organizer of the Bedford Town and Land Company, laid out the community in 1890, named by Bedford for his Civil War companion, William Currens Dimmitt, a Methodist revival minister with a congregation in Sherman. PO 10 Jan 1891, PM Thaddeus Belsher.

DIMPLE (Red River) In the late 1890s, William W. Crockett, a Clarksville farmer and photographer, opened a general store in what was then known as Cravens. On 30 Mar 1901 William Crockett's brother Samuel changed the name of the Cravens PO to Dimple in honor of William and Katy Crockett's daughter Dimple Dee Crockett who died at age two in October 1900.

DINERO [duh NEHR o] (Live Oak) Barlow's Ferry was renamed Dinero in the early 1870s. No one knows who chose the name or why but there are several local legends. By one, there are lost mines or buried treasure in the area; by another, Spanish silver miners were murdered by Indians for their *dinero* (Spanish "money"); and by another, Mexican soldiers, hastily retreating after the loss at San Jacinto, buried the payroll treasury somewhere in the area, giving rise to the legend of Santa Anna's gold. PO 4 Nov 1885, PM Robert W. Johnson.

DING DONG (Bell) Surely one of Texas's more notable names and quite appropriate for a town in Bell County. According to the local story, in the early 1920s Isaac Bertram Bell and his cousin Zoilus Ozzias Bell, a music teacher, opened a general store and asked a painter named Hoover to create a sign for their business. Hoover obliged by creating a work of art that included pictures of bells on either side—one bell labeled I. B. and the other Z. O. with the words "Ding Dong" between the two and so spaced that one shopkeeper was taken to be Ding and the other Dong.

DINGERVILLE (Madison) According to local lore this tiny community got its name about 1905 from the phrase "That's a dinger" (a shortening of "That's a humdinger," a favorite expression of farmer Allen Lasswell).

DINSMORE (Wharton) About 1910 Edward W. Roberts founded Roberts as a community for African Americans. That name never caught on and by 1920 had been replaced by Dinsmore for John Dinsmore, the original site owner.

DIRECT (Lamar) The local story is that the town was named by an evangelist who told the people they were going "direct" to hell for allowing Indians to cross the Red River "direct" for whiskey. PO 3 Sept 1887, PM Dora Lambeth.

DISH (Denton) Landis Clark founded the town as Clark in June 2000. Five years later Clark changed the name to Dish after the Dish Network offered free basic satellite TV to all residents for 10 years.

DITTLINGER [DIT ling er] (Comal) The Dittlinger Lime Company, owned by Hippolyt Dittlinger, established a flour mill in the late 1880s and founded Dittlinger about 1907 as a company town with housing and services for employees. One of Dittlinger's signature products was a wheat flour called Comal Lily.

DITTO (Atascosa) Ephraim Forest opened the Mottamosa post office in July 1866. That office was discontinued in 1875 and reopened by William Gates as Gates Valley in 1876. That office was discontinued in 1880 and the following year George F. Atkins petitioned to reopen the Gates Valley office, but instead of writing "Gates Valley" as the intended name, he simply wrote (the mark meaning ditto), thinking this would be interpreted by the Post Office Department as what went before—Gates Valley. Instead, post office officials, being very literary (and very literal) people, took this as Atkins's shortcut for "ditto." Rather than resubmitting the application Atkins chose to become master of the Ditto PO.

DIVOT (Frio) Divot was first known as Leona (Spanish "female lion"), named from the Leona River, and later as Kingsville for the store kept by Jesse King from about 1908. In 1912 when King applied for a Pivot post office the name was misread and the office was approved as Divot.

DIX (Martin) Dix, a stop on the Texas & Pacific Railway, was probably named for John A. Dix, president of the Union Pacific Railroad in the early 1860s.

DIXIE (Grayson) Confederate veterans settled in the area shortly after the end of the Civil War and named the town for the Southern states.

DIXON (Hunt) Dixon Allen moved to Texas from South Carolina via Kentucky in 1845. Allen established the Dixon PO 31 Aug 1881 and donated land for the Missouri–Kansas–Texas Railroad about 1882.

DOANS (Wilbarger) Ohioans Jonathan Doan and his nephew Corwin Doan opened a trading post in 1878 near the Red River crossing where cattle were driven from South Texas to the railhead at Dodge City, KS. PO 13 Nov 1879, PM Corwin F. Doan.

DOBBIN (Montgomery) The Central & Montgomery Railway built through the area in the late 1870s and brought with it the communities of Bobbin and Bobville, one mile apart. Both towns were apparently named for the same Robert or Bob, perhaps a railroad employee. James Stinson opened the Bobbin PO 2 June 1880; for unknown reasons the name was changed to Dobbin 1 Oct 1909. The Bobville PO opened 28 Apr 1911 and closed 15 July 1919, the mail going to Dobbin.

DOBROWOLSKI [do bruh WAHL skee] (Atascosa) PO 12 June 1920, PM Samuel G. Cross who named the office for Alec Dobrowolski, a real estate developer who subdivided the site and sold building lots in the 1920s.

DODD CITY (Fannin) Edward and Elizabeth Dodd from Kentucky established a general store and hotel about 1840. PO 10 Nov 1848 as Licke, PM Edmund Hall Dodd; discontinued and reestablished as Dodd 3 Nov 1873; changed to Dodd City 13 Feb 1902, PM Henry H. Morris.

DODGE (Walker) By a local popular etymology the town was named when the Houston & Great Northern Railroad "dodged" Huntsville. Rather, the H&GN station was named for William Earle Dodge, a co-founder of the Phelps Dodge Corporation that built much of the H&GN line. PO 1 July 1872 as Dodge Station, PM Russell Roark.

DODSON (Collingsworth) Frank Kell, part owner of the Wichita Falls & Northwestern Railway, named a station in 1910 for Elmore Dodson, a local rancher who donated several hundred acres for the railroad right of way. PO 3 Dec 1910 as Dodsonville, PM Thomas McDowell; changed to Dodson 1 July 1937.

DONLEY (County) Created 1876, organized 1882. Named for Stockton P. Donley (1821–1871), born in Missouri. Donley moved to Texas in 1846. He became a prominent Tyler lawyer, a district attorney, and a justice of the Texas Supreme Court in 1866.

DONNA (Hidalgo) In 1907 Uriah Lott, president of the St. Louis, Brownsville & Mexico Railway, named the station for Donna Hooks Fletcher, daughter of Thomas J. Hooks, businessman and site owner. She opened the Donna PO 1 June 1908.

DON-TOL (Wharton) Shortly after the Civil War William Toliver Taylor and his brother Solomon Tyre Taylor began farming near Wharton. Mexican workers referred to William Toliver Taylor as *Don* (Spanish "lord") Tol.

DOOLE [DOO lee] (McCulloch) The town of Gansel, named for local engineer George V. Gansel, developed around the Crossroads School about 1908. The name was changed in 1912 for David Doole, Jr., the postmaster at Brady. PO 2 Jan 1912, PM Logan L. Deen.

DORCHESTER (Grayson) Named for Chester B. Dorchester, a cashier of the Merchants & Planters National Bank of Sherman. PO 2 Sept 1896, PM George Voelkle.

DOSS (Gillespie) Formerly known as Lange or Lange's Mill for the family of miller William Lange. Renamed for John Doss who operated a gristmill from about 1850, and his brother Thomas, the postmaster at Fredericksburg. PO 21 Jan 1907, PM Tolbert Garrett.

DOTHAN [DOTH un] (Eastland) Named for Dothan, Houston County, AL, itself named for the Biblical Dothan. The name was probably proposed by Jacob and Minerva Dunaway who began farming in the area in the early 1890s. PO 22 Nov 1902, PM Charlie M. McClelan.

DOUCETTE (Tyler) About 1891 Peter A. Doucette, a Canada-born lumber trader, and William McCready, a Canada-born mill operator, bought Alva Carroll's sawmill and laid out the community named for Doucette. PO 31 May 1893, PM William McCready.

DOUGHERTY (Floyd) Francis (Frank) Dougherty was a Texas State Representative in the mid-1850s and also in the early 1880s. He was a promoter of Texas railroads and a community benefactor. PO 29 Oct 1928, PM Grace Garner.

DOUGHERTY [DAHRT ee] (Rains) Founded by James W. Dougherty, a farmer and tanner who brought his family to Texas from Kentucky in the 1840s. His son, Robert Newberry Daugherty [*sic*], was a community benefactor. The spelling has alternated, at times with acrimonious debate, between the supporters of Daugherty and those of Dougherty.

DOUGLASS (Nacogdoches) About 1836 Michael Costley founded Douglass, named for Kelsey Harris Douglass, a local dry goods merchant who represented Nacogdoches in the Second Congress of the Republic of Texas (1837–1838). PO 26 June 1839, PM P. H. Pearson.

DOUGLASSVILLE (Cass) Named for site owner John C. Douglass, a native Georgian who bought land in the area in 1855. PO 8 July 1854, PM James Chappell.

DOURO (Ector) Douro was founded with construction of the Texas & Pacific Railway in 1881, apparently named from Spanish *duro* "hard" for the mineralized caliche soil that underlay the roadbed.

DOWNING (Comanche) The local account is that the name was to have been Dawning for the stunning sunrises and for the town's growth potential, but Dawning was misread by the Post Office Department as Downing. Just as likely, the namesake was one of the several Downing families farming in the area in November 1888 when William Davidson established the Downing PO.

DOWNSVILLE (McLennan) William Wood Downs brought his family and fifty slaves from Alabama to the Waco area in 1854. With emancipation he granted each formerly enslaved family a dwelling and a plot of land. The community was named for Downs in the 1880s. PO 28 Apr 1890 as Price; changed to Downsville 12 Sept 1890, PM William P. Sparks.

DOYLE (Limestone) Doyle was founded as Shady Grove when the Houston & Texas Central Railway built through the area in the early 1870s. Shady Grove was renamed in 1903 for William Elliott Doyle, mayor of Mexia and later a Texas State Senator. PO 8 June 1903, PM Joseph B. Dixon.

DRAPER (Denton) In the early 1970s, in order to bypass Denton County's liquor laws, Geneva and James Helton founded and incorporated the community of Corral City, consisting of little more than a liquor store. In October 2016 the town was renamed for Mayor James Eddie Draper.

DRASCO (Runnels) First known as County Line for the proximity of the Taylor-Runnels county line. According to Runnels County historian Charlsie Poe, Drasco is an initialism created from the first letters of the names of six prominent citizens when the post office was established by Robert Kerr 16 Dec 1904.

DRAW (Lynn) Named from Mooar's Draw, the dry creek bed northeast of the town named for brothers John and Josiah Mooar, buffalo hunters of the 1870s. PO 16 Jan 1906, PM Della B. Glass.

DRESDEN (Navarro) Named for Dresden, Germany, perhaps the ancestral home of rancher and site owner Jacob Hartzell. PO 29 Oct 1844 as Melrose; changed to Melton's 22 May 1846, PM Ethan Melton; changed to Dresden 4 Oct 1852, PM William B. McCabe.

DREYER (Gonzales) Henry Dreyer was brought to Texas from Prussia as a child in 1842. By the 1890s he was owner of a gristmill and a large farm on the Guadalupe River. PO 17 July 1897 as Dryer, PM Charles G. Devot. Also known as Dryer.

DRIPPING SPRINGS (Hays) The name was apparently chosen in the mid-1850s by Indiana "Nannie" Moss for the Glen Ross springs that dripped from overhead limestone formations. The Milk House Branch Spring is often mentioned as the primary source of the name. PO 5 June 1857, PM John Moss.

DRISCOLL (Nueces) The St. Louis, Brownsville & Mexico Railway established a station on the ranch of Robert Driscoll, Sr. and Jr., in 1904. The younger Driscoll was a leader in Corpus Christi business and philanthropic endeavors in the first decades of the 20th century. ROBSTOWN is also named for the Robert Driscolls. PO 5 Oct 1910, PM Burr Westbrook.

DROP (Denton) Drop has generated its share of popular etymologies. By one, the town was so inconsequential it was just a drop in the bucket; by another, when Europeans settled in the area the Indians were constantly on the move and would "drop by" and then leave; and by still another, the application for a PO asked for the name Dewdrop and when that name was rejected, the application was resubmitted with the name shortened to Drop. PO 6 Jan 1886, PM John Haynes.

DRYDEN (Terrell) Eugene E. Dryden was chief engineer for the Galveston, Harrisburg & San Antonio Railway that built through the area in 1882. PO 2 July 1884 as Thurst; changed to Dryden 12 Dec 1888, PM Warner W. Simonds.

DUBINA (Fayette) Dubina, founded about 1867, is generally regarded as the first permanent Czech settlement in Texas. Formerly known as Navidad, the community was renamed for Dubina in the western Czech Republic by Augustine Haidušek, a lawyer, mayor of La Grange in 1875, and state legislator in the early 1880s. PO 3 Mar 1885, PM Joseph Peter.

DUBLIN (Erath) Dublin was founded in the mid-1850s and named in the early 1860s by Alexander Dobkins. When the Texas Central Railway established a station south of Mount Airy in 1881, Dublin and Mount Airy moved to trackside. Dublin may be a popular etymology of "double in," meaning to shelter together when in danger of Indian raids, as the early spelling Doublin suggests, or it may be a compression of "double log cabin," two log rooms connected by a covered walkway. It may, of course, be a transfer from Dublin, Ireland, or from one of the Dublins in eastern states. PO 14 June 1875, PM Franklin Oldham.

DUDLEY (Callahan) Named for Nicholas and Fannie Dudley who opened a general store in the 1880s. PO 27 Apr 1893, PM Nicholas M. Dudley.

DUFFAU [DUHF o] (Erath) Duffo, the name (or nickname) of a local Indian has been proposed as the namesake, but the town is more likely named for Francis T. Duffau, a Milam county clerk of the late 1840s and Austin city recorder in the 1850s. PO 13 Feb 1860, PM James Leech.

DUMAS [DOO muhs] (Moore) Louis Dumas, a Sherman businessman and real estate investor, organized the Panhandle Townsite Company that laid out the town in 1891. PO 27 June 1891, PM James Wilson.

DUMONT (King) Named for Auguste Alford Dumont of Paducah, a community benefactor and promoter. PO 17 Feb 1894, PM Nannie Sayers.

DUNCANVILLE (Dallas) Crawford Trees is the first known settler, arriving from Illinois in 1845. In 1881 the Chicago, Texas & Mexican Railroad built through the area and established Duncan Switch, named for financial director J. Duncan Smith. PO 2 Oct 1882, PM Charles P. Nance.

DUNDEE (Archer) Morgan Jones, a director of the Wichita Valley Railway and a giant of Texas railroading in the late 19th and early 20th centuries, chose the name about 1889, probably for Dundee, Scotland. PO 24 Jan 1890 as Souleman; changed to Dundee 30 June 1890, PM Amanda W. Giddens.

DUNLAP (Cottle) About 1905 Doss Swearingen, the namesake of SWEARINGEN, sold part of the OX Ranch to Julius Abbott and Weyman B. Dunlap, president of the Gulf National Bank of Beaumont. PO 21 Mar 1908, PM Emma Landers.

DUNLAP (Travis) About 1858 William Dunlap Hunter left South Carolina and established a plantation on the Colorado River east of Austin. He was the first postmaster 2 Oct 1886.

DUNLAY (Medina) About 1880 a town called Enterprise developed around a station on the Galveston, Harrisburg & San Antonio Railway; renamed in the mid-1890s, reportedly for Jerry Dunlay, a conductor on the GH&SA. PO 3 Mar 1890 as Enterprise; changed to Dunlay 11 May 1895, PM Norval S. Murray.

DUNN (Scurry) Dunn was founded on the line of the Texas & Pacific Railway by Alonzo T. Dunn and Will Richardson in the late 1880s. PO 19 Sept 1890, PM Alonzo T. Dunn.

DURANGO (Falls) A local story, usually told tongue in cheek, is that the name Durango originated when an inebriated cowboy thought he was in Durango, Mexico. The town probably was named for Durango, Mexico, but under different circumstances. The West Falls PO, established 29 Sept 1871, was changed to Durango 8 Jan 1883 by PM Sylvester J. Crump.

DUSTER (Comanche) Fred Tarpley recounts the local popular etymology: "Citizens met to choose a name. When inspiration was slow in coming, one of [them] picked up a sheet of paper covered with dust and said, 'Let's call her *Duster*.'" (*1001 Texas Place Names*) PO 28 Apr 1891, PM Isaac Tinney.

DUVAL [DOO VAWL] (County) Created 1858, organized 1876. Named for Burr Harrison Duval (1809–1836), born in Kentucky. Duval organized and led the Kentucky Mustangs in the Texas War of Independence. He and his brother, John Crittenden Duval, were with Fannin at Goliad. John escaped but Burr was among those who died in the March 1836 Goliad Massacre.

EAGLE PASS (Maverick) Eagle Pass grew around Fort Duncan, established on the Rio Grande several miles upstream from the original *El Paso del Águila* "eagle pass." PO 27 Jan 1851 as Fort Duncan; changed to Eagle Pass 24 Nov 1852, PM Richard Meade.

EARLY (Brown) Early was considered part of BROWNWOOD until the late 1920s when the school district was organized and named for Walter Urie Early, a Brownwood attorney who donated land for the first schoolhouse.

EARLYWINE (Washington) Named for John W. Earlywine who emigrated from Kentucky in the early 1870s. Earlywine was postmaster of the Wren post office northeast of Brenham from March 1878 until the office closed January 1883.

EARTH (Lamb) Earth was founded in 1924 by the Halsell Land Company. The source of the name is uncertain. According to one local story, when the PO application was being prepared there was a terrible dust storm and the earth seemed to be moving, so Earth was placed on the application. According to another the soil around the town was so fertile that it was called Good Earth, which was shortened to Earth. Most appropriate is the claim of an early settler, "There were no trees in sight. All you could see was earth." PO 8 June 1925, PM Frank Hyatt.

EAST BERNARD (Wharton) The Galveston, Harrisburg & San Antonio Railway was established in 1859 on the east bank of the San Bernard River (thus the name) but is now on the west bank. The Bernard Station PO operated 3 Aug 1866–20 May 1872. PO 1 July 1874 as East Bernard, PM Uriah G. Cooper.

EAST COLUMBIA (Brazoria) See Columbia.

EASTER (Castro) William and Prudence Easter moved from Hill County and began farming in the area in the 1870s.

EASTERLY (Robertson) Moses and Mary Easterly brought their family from Tennessee in the 1870s. Their son Daniel was postmaster of the Acorn PO in 1887. That office was changed to Lake in 1890. Daniel Easterly opened the Easterly office 6 June 1894.

EASTLAND (County) Created 1858, organized 1873. Named for William Mosby Eastland (1806–1843), born in Kentucky. Eastland moved to Texas in 1834 and was a career Texas soldier. He fought with Sam Houston at San Jacinto, joined the Texas Rangers, and died as a member of the Mier Expedition after drawing a black bean of death.

EASTLAND (Eastland) Founded in 1875 and named from the county. PO 27 Feb 1874 as McGue Springs; changed to Eastland 31 Jan 1876, PM Henry K. Martin.

EBONY (Mills) Victoria Griffin opened the Ebony PO Jan 1891, reportedly named for mail carrier and ranch hand Ebony Shaw.

ECHO (Coleman) The town took the name of the Echo Ranch established by William Dibrell in the 1880s. The ranch was reportedly named for the echoes from the cliffs on Jim Ned Creek. PO 2 Dec 1910, PM Martha Jones.

ECKERT (Gillespie) The area was first known as Nebo, named from the Nebo Mountain north of the town. PO 24 Feb 1904, PM

Wilhelm (William) Rudolph Eckert, general store owner.

ECLETO [uh KLEET o] (Karnes) Named from Dry Ecleto Creek. Ecleto is likely from a Native American language, Hispanicized as El Cleto and Americanized as Ecleto. PO 17 Apr 1852 as Cleto; changed to Ecleto 25 Apr 1854, PM Braxton W. Gillock; changed to Riddleville 9 June 1871; changed to Gillett 20 Sept 1905. PO 8 Dec 1921 as Ecleto, PM Walter G. Riedel. See Gillett.

ECTOR (County) Created 1887, organized 1891. Named for Mathew Duncan Ector (1822–1879), born in Georgia. Ector established a law practice in Henderson, TX, in the early 1850s. After the Civil War, during which he rose to the rank of Brigadier General, Ector returned to his law practice, served as district judge, and was a justice on the Texas Court of Appeals in 1875.

ECTOR (Fannin) Martha and Hickman Owens, who began farming in the area in the 1860s, suggested the name for their son George Ector Owens, born in 1880. PO 19 Mar 1886, PM Robert Phillips.

EDCOUCH (Hidalgo) Founded in 1927 as a station on the San Antonio & Aransas Pass Railway. Named for businessman and banker Edmund C. Couch. Along with his brothers, Daniel and Riley, Ed Couch was instrumental in founding WESLACO. PO 18 Mar 1927, PM Carrie Netz.

EDDY (McLennan) See Bruceville-Eddy.

EDEN (Concho) Frederick Ede emigrated from England in the 1870s, became a sheep rancher, and donated land for the townsite. Ede, the first PM, requested the name Ede or Eden; the petition was approved as Eden. PO 6 Nov 1883.

EDGAR (DeWitt) The area was informally known as Grassbur for the grassbur (sandbur) weed until 1887 when the San Antonio & Aransas Pass Railway established Edgar Station, named for James and Selah Edgar who relocated from TN in 1853. The site had been granted to their son Joseph for his service in the Texas Revolution. PO 1 June 1887 as Grassbur; changed to Edgar 30 Jan 1888, PM Thomas M. Dodd.

EDGE (Brazos) Brothers John and William Edge emigrated from Georgia and opened a general store in the 1870s. John Edge was a local physician. PO 14 Sept 1894, PM William Harrison Edge. The former communities of Concord, Liberty, and Payne's Prairie are now part of Edge.

EDHUBE (Fannin) James Benton applied for the Benton PO in 1894. When the application was rejected, Benton confected Edhube from the name of his father, early settler *Ed*mond *Hu*ston *Be*nton. PO 10 May 1894.

EDINBURG [ED uhn berg] (Hidalgo) About 1850 near present Hidalgo, John Young, a Brownsville merchant, laid out Edinburgh, named for his birthplace, Edinburgh, Scotland. Edinburgh was renamed Hidalgo for the county about 1885. In 1908 Hidalgo County sheriff John Closner, county judge Dennis Bangs Chapin, and several others laid out the town of Chapin. After Dennis Chapin became involved in a murder investigation the name of Chapin was changed to Edinburg. PO 5 Feb 1850 as Edinburgh, PM John Conway; changed to Hidalgo 19 Jan 1876. PO 3 Dec 1908 as Chapin, PM William D. Day; changed to Edinburg 1 Apr 1911.

EDMONSON (Hale) The Fort Worth & Denver Railway built through the area in 1929 and established a switch on land owned by William W. Edmonson. PO 8 Dec 1890 as Wadsworth; changed to Running Water 26 Jan 1891; changed to Edmonson 1 Feb 1937, PM Lillian Fortenberry.

EDNA (Jackson) In 1882 the New York, Texas & Mexican Railway extended a line between Rosenburg and Victoria. The station was named for Edna Telfener, daughter of Italian Count Joseph Telfener, officer and major financier of the NYT&M. Texana, which had been bypassed by the railroad, was replaced as the county seat by Edna in 1883. PO 12 Dec 1882 as Ednaville; changed to Edna 1 Apr 1886, PM George F. Horton. See Telferner [*sic*].

EDOM [EED uhm] (Van Zandt) Perhaps named from the Biblical Edom, the city founded by Esau. However, according to a local story, before it was named Edom the town was noted for its rowdiness and drunken behavior, so much so that a traveler exclaimed, "This place is more wicked than Sodom" and Sodom, with a few spelling modifications, became Edom. PO 8 May 1855, PM David O. Roark (O'Roark).

EDROY (San Patricio) The San Antonio, Uvalde & Gulf Railroad station established in 1913 was named for site owners and land developers *Ed*ward Cubage and *Roy* Miller. PO 22 Oct 1914, PM Andrew Brandt.

EDWARDS (County) Created 1858, organized 1883. Named for Haden (Hayden) Edwards (1771–1849), born in Virginia. Edwards was a Mississippi plantation owner before he moved to Texas and became a business associate and financial backer of Stephen F. Austin. Edwards worked with Austin in negotiations with the Mexican government that eventually allowed empresarios to settle American colonists in Texas.

EGYPT (Wharton) According to a Texas historical marker, the area received its name in 1827 when local farmers in the area, like their Biblical namesakes, brought wagonloads of corn and grain to their starving neighbors in surrounding areas suffering from drought and crop failures. The present town of Egypt was founded in the mid-1830s on Egypt Plantation, established by planter William J. E. Heard. There are at least three places called Egypt in Texas and several dozen in the US; all have similar naming stories. PO 17 Feb 1837, PM Eli Mercer.

EL CALABOZ (Cameron) El Calaboz is a colonia established in the late 1940s and named from Spanish *calabozo* "jail." The reason for the name is unknown.

EL CAMINO ANGOSTO (Cameron) Near San Benito, El Camino Angosto was settled in the late 20th century. The source of the name (Spanish "the narrow road") is uncertain but may be related to the Biblical narrow road that leads to salvation.

EL CAMPO (Wharton) In the early 1880s the New York, Texas & Mexican Railway established Prairie Switch, a railroad work site that became known as El Campo "the camp." PO 17 Mar 1890, PM Christian Bruns.

EL CENIZO [EL suh NEE zo] (Webb) Apparently named from the Cenizo (Seniso and other spellings), a native group of the Coahuiltecan culture that inhabited parts of the eastern Rio Grande Valley at the turn of the 18th century.

EL INDIO (Maverick) About 1850 William Cazneau, instrumental in organizing EAGLE PASS, founded El Indio (Spanish "the Indian") on the Indio Ranch, itself named from Indio Creek. The reasons for the name are unclear. PO 28 June 1880 as Indio, PM Charles S. Murphy; discontinued 3 Apr 1884; reopened as El Indio 18 Apr 1939, PM Joseph Henry Ulery.

EL OSO (Karnes) Spanish "the bear." Probably founded in the 1920s. The reason for the name is unknown.

EL PASO (County) Created 1849, organized 1850. Named *El Paso del Norte* "the Pass of the North" by Spanish explorers of the 1580s for the valley that provided a route through the mountains. The first county seat, SAN ELIZARIO, moved to El Paso in 1883.

EL PASO (El Paso) In 1859 Anson Mills surveyed a settlement known as Franklin or Smithsville that he formally named El Paso for El Paso County. PO 26 July 1852, PM Jarvis Hubbell.

EL SAUZ [EL sows] (Starr) Spanish "the weeping willows." Named from El Sauz Creek, now known as Los Olmos "the elms" Creek. PO 27 Apr 1928, PM Leandro Resendez.

EL TORO (Jackson) The source of the name is uncertain. By one popular etymology the name El Toro, Spanish for "the bull," was cleverly chosen because of its proximity to nearby Lavaca River, named from Spanish "the cow." PO 11 Jan 1899 as Eltoro, PM Joseph W. Draper.

EL VENADITO (Cameron) Spanish "little deer." Naming circumstances are unknown.

ELBERT (Throckmorton) Probably named for farmer and merchant John Elbert Keeter, son of Thomas and Stella Mae Keeter. PO 2 July 1898, PM Thaddeus S. Williams.

ELBERTA (Smith) When the International–Great Northern Railroad built through the area in the mid-1870s the station was named for Elberta peaches, many of which were shipped from the I-GN platform. The Elberta peach had only recently been developed by Samuel Rumph of Georgia who chose the name to honor his wife, Clara Elberta Moore.

ELDERVILLE (Gregg) Named for mule and horse trader Henry Trip Elder. PO 23 Feb 1876 as Iron Bridge; changed to Elderville 7 Jan 1888, PM George A. Erwin.

ELDORADO [el duh RAY do] (Schleicher) Verand—a blend of *Ver*mont and the name of a site owner, probably Sam Holl*and*—was established on the Vermont Ranch (named by investors from Windsor, VT) about 1890. In 1895 Whitaker Silliman laid out Eldorado five miles south of Verand and offered free building lots to anyone who would move to his site. The reasons for Silliman's choice of the name are unknown but the associations of Eldorado with wealth, especially mineral wealth, make it an attractive place name. PO 4 June 1892 as Verand; discontinued 15 Apr 1895; reestablished as Eldorado 20 July 1895, PM Willie Louis Gray.

ELDRIDGE (Colorado) Named for William T. Eldridge, a founder and director of the Cane Belt Railroad that built through the area in the early 1900s. PO 27 Feb 1906, PM Ernst Faber.

ELECTRA (Wichita) In the late 1880s the site was a shipping point for Dan Waggoner's cattle on the Fort Worth & Denver City Railway. The PO was opened 13 June 1893 by William T. Waggoner (Dan's son) who chose the name for his daughter, Electra. See Thrift.

ELECTRIC CITY (Hutchinson) The Panhandle Power and Light Company provided electricity to the local oilfields and founded Electric City in 1926. PO 2 June 1927, PM Nadine Woody.

ELGIN [EL gin] (Bastrop) Perryville, founded by Perry Young in the mid-1830s, was also known as Hog Eye, named, by one local account, from a villager who had a particular way of squinting that gave his eyes the shape of pig's eyes. When the Houston & Texas Central Railway established the Glasscock flag station in 1871 many of the businesses of Perryville moved to track-side and in 1872 the site was platted as Elgin, named for Robert Morris Elgin, land commissioner and surveyor for the H&TC. A local joke that plays cleverly on the pronunciation is that Elgin is a disguised version of "Hell Again," a name that originated when dismayed townspeople disrupted unwanted passenger trains by vandalizing the tracks and the station. This resulted in the warning to passengers that they were "going to Hell Again." PO 13 May 1873, PM Edward Smithwick. See Georgetown, see Glasscock County.

ELI (Hall) PO 29 June 1906, PM Joseph Brown who chose the name for local farmer Eli Melton Dennis who later opened a grocery store in Memphis, TX. The Eli PO, opened 29 June 1906, was discontinued in 1913 and reopened as Elite (perhaps by adding -te to Eli) 17 Nov 1915.

ELIASVILLE (Young) Shoemaker Elias DeLong lost his business in Georgia during the Civil War. He came to Young County in 1865 and opened a general store. PO 16 June 1879, PM Henry Howard.

ELIZABETHTOWN (Denton) In the early 1850s Peter Harmonson, an early settler and the first sheriff of Denton County, founded Elizabethtown named from Elizabeth Creek, itself named for Sarah Elizabeth Denton, daughter of John Denton, the namesake of Denton County. PO 19 Dec 1870 as Elizabeth, PM John W. Eatman.

ELLEN (Hale) Named for Almeda Ellafair Lavender White, wife of Edwin Miller

White, the founder of PETERSBURG. PO 20 May 1904, PM Carl Richardson.

ELLINGER [EL ing er, EL in jer] (Fayette) Farmer Andreas Ondry is generally credited with suggesting the name in honor of Joseph Ehlinger (Ellinger). Born in France, Ehlinger moved from New Orleans to Texas in 1835 and was granted a section of land for his participation in the Battle of San Jacinto. PO 23 Oct 1877, PM Fritz Hotmann.

ELLIOTT (Wilbarger) Known as Waggoner's Colony for rancher and businessman Dan Waggoner until 1907 when the town was named in honor of Sarah Elizabeth Elliott, regarded as the first local teacher. Also known informally as Bugscuffle. See Electra, see Thrift.

ELLIS (County) Created 1849, organized 1850. Named for Richard Ellis (1781–1846), born in Virginia. Ellis became an Alabama lawyer, then brought his family and several dozen slaves to what is now Bowie County where he established a large plantation in 1834. He is best known as president of the 1836 Constitutional Convention that declared Texas independence. The county name was probably proposed by Edward Tarrant, the namesake of Tarrant County and Ellis's friend and colleague.

ELM MOTT (McLennan) "Mott" is a Texas word for a clump of trees, especially one on an otherwise open plain. PO 8 Nov 1872, PM William Griffin. Formerly known as Geneva.

ELMATON [EL MAYT uhn] (Matagorda) Spanish *el matón* "the bully, the killer." The town of Elmaton was apparently named in the early 20th century by crews building the Missouri Pacific Railroad. The reasons for the name are unknown but Elmaton has generated a number of local stories. By one, during a drinking bout an argument arose and a man was killed. His assailant was labeled "El Maton." By another a man was killed when he caught his foot on a rail and was run over by a handcart; thereafter handcarts were called "el matons." By still another the location was the site of feed lots and a slaughterhouse where cattle were killed for their hides and tallow. The man whose job it was to kill the animals was called "El Maton." PO 23 Nov 1915, PM Boyd I. Horn.

ELMENDORF (Bexar) Henry Elmendorf was a director of the San Antonio & Aransas Pass Railway and mayor of San Antonio in the mid-1890s. PO 1 May 1886, PM William Kroeger.

ELMINA (Walker) Elmina was founded in the early 20th century when the Walker Lumber Company bought and expanded a sawmill established by Clarence Oliphant about 1870. Elmina is apparently an adaptation of El Mina, named from the El Mina Masonic Temple in Galveston. PO 17 Apr 1903, PM George M. Seaman.

ELMO (Kaufman) Elmo Scott surveyed and routed the Texas & Pacific Railway through Kaufman County in the early 1870s. PO 22 Aug 1873, PM Hugh B. McCockle.

ELMONT (Grayson) Harry Campbell opened a tavern and general store at a site called Crossroads about 1847. Campbell changed the name for Elmont, Nassau County, NY, one of his former homes. PO 16 June 1884, PM William A. Rexroat.

ELSA (Hidalgo) Elsa was founded in 1927 with construction of the Southern Pacific Railroad. Named by site owner William George for his wife Elsie, known as Elsa. PO 5 Apr 1927, PM Samuel Kelly.

ELYSIAN FIELDS (Harrison) The original community (Old Elysian Fields), a mile east of the present site, grew around a general store kept by Edward Smith from the 1830s. The local story is that Smith spoke in such glowing terms of the beauty of the area that a friend remarked, "You must have found the Elysian Fields." PO 7 Jan 1839, PM Edward Smith.

EMBERSON (Lamar) John Eldridge Emberson explored the area in 1816, fought in the Texas Revolution, was a captain in the Texas Rangers, and died a wealthy rancher in 1860. PO 23 Sept 1878, PM James Norvell.

EMBLEM (Hopkins) Emblem was founded about 1876, probably by merchant George Dallas Kennemur. According to Fred Tarpley, the "emblem" that provided the name was a grocery store sign showing an eagle and advertising a soft drink. Informally known as "Soon Over." As one wag reportedly put it, "this town has so few possibilities, it will be 'soon over'." PO 15 June 1892, PM Thomas J. Ross.

EMHOUSE (Navarro) When the Trinity & Brazos Valley Railway began construction in the area in the mid-1900s, the station was named for *E*dward *M*andell *House*, a native Houstonian and a founder of the T&BV in 1902. House was a diplomat, politician, and advisor to President Woodrow Wilson in the 1910s. PO 18 Nov 1908, PM George Owen.

EMINENCE (Chambers) PO 25 July 1898, PM Mary J. Silva. One can only speculate that the name was chosen in the hope if not expectation that the town would rise to a position of importance and prestige. PO 25 July 1898, PM Mary J. Silva.

EMMAUS (Cherokee) Named from the Emmaus Baptist Church of Christ, organized in 1877. Emmaus is a Biblical name from the New Testament; the risen Jesus appeared to two of his disciples while they were walking on the road to Emmaus. Also New Emmaus.

EMORY (Rains) Founded as Springville in the 1840s. The name was changed in 1870 when Rains County was created. Both the county and Emory, the county seat, were named for state legislator Emory Rains. PO 19 Dec 1870, PM Daniel R. Chambers. See Rains County.

ENCINAL [en suh NAHL] (La Salle) In 1856 the Texas Legislature authorized the creation of Encinal County with Encinal (Spanish "oak grove") as the county seat. Encinal County was never organized and most of the proposed territory became part of Webb County in 1899. The town of Ancaster, probably named for Ancaster, England, was founded by 1880 and annexed by Encinal by 1883. PO 19 Feb 1880 as Ancaster; changed to Encinal 25 Apr 1883, PM Henry Spohn.

ENCINO [en SEE no] (Brooks) From Spanish *encina* "live oak." Founded in the early 1900s on the site of *La Encantada y Encina del Pozo*, a Mexican land grant of the 1830s that combined the names of two adjoining grants, *La Encantada* "the place that delights, enchants" and *Encina del Pozo* "the live oak in a hole or well." PO 11 July 1914, PM Jessie E. Coward.

ENERGY (Comanche) Energy grew around a general store established by brothers Charles and William Baxter about 1895. According to the local story the Baxters chose the name to reflect the energy of the townspeople. PO 23 Nov 1897, PM John P. Moore.

ENGLE (Fayette) Perhaps named for Alphonso M. Engle of Houston, an engineer for the Galveston, Harrisburg & San Antonio Railway that established the flag stop in the late 1870s. PO 24 Dec 1888, PM Adolph G. Merseburger.

ENGLISH (Red River) The site was purchased in the 1840s by Oliver English and his uncle Simeon English who settled several families on cotton plantations in the early 1850s. PO 3 June 1890, PM Thomas W. Anderson.

ENLOE (Delta) The Texas Midland Railroad established a station on land donated by John A. Enloe in 1897. PO 12 July 1897, PM Jerry High.

ENNIS (Ellis) Named for Cornelius Ennis, mayor of Houston in the 1850s and incorporator, director, and general superintendent of the Houston & Texas Central Railway that reached the site in 1871. PO 2 Oct 1872, PM John M. Dixon.

ENOCH (Upshur) Enoch was a Mormon collectivist community established about 1912 and governed by the Order of Enoch. The name comes from Mormon scripture where Enoch is described as a city of the virtuous and pure-hearted.

ENON (Upshur) Enon was named from the Enon Baptist Church, organized in 1848 and considered one of the oldest churches in Upshur County. Enon (Aenon), the Biblical site of John's baptisms, is a popular name for churches with more than one hundred in the US; one of these may have given its name to Texas's Enon Baptist Church.

EOLIAN [ee OL ee uhn] (Stephens) The community coalesced around the Eolian post office established by William Clement in February 1880. The name was apparently chosen by someone at the Post Office Department. Eolian is ultimately from Aeolus, the Greek god of winds.

EPWORTH (Hale) Epworth was founded by Horatio Graves, a Methodist minister from northern New York state, who chose the name for Epworth, England, birthplace of John Wesley, the founder of Methodism. Graves established the PO 3 June 1884. See Hale Center.

ERA (Cooke) Allen and Mary Hargrove began farming in the area in the early 1870s. The town was organized in the late 1870s and named for their daughter Era (often miswritten as Eva), born in 1875. PM 10 Apr 1879, PM Levi Jones.

ERATH [EE rath] (County) Created and organized 1856. Named for George Bernard

Erath (1813–1891), born in Vienna, Austria. Erath emigrated to Texas in 1833, fought in the Texas Revolution, and served in several Republic of Texas legislatures. A well-known surveyor, Erath platted the towns of Caldwell, Erath, Stephenville, and Waco.

ERATH (Erath) Founded about 1855 by George Erath, Erath County namesake, and Neil McLennan, the namesake of McLennan County. Erath was absorbed by Waco in the 1980s. PO 21 Mar 1896, PM William E. Allen.

ESCOBARES [es ko BAHR uhs] (Starr) Based upon Spanish *escoba* "broom." Escobares likely referred to the sorghum variety known as broomcorn used to make brooms and brushes. Escobas in Zapata County is a variant. PO 13 Feb 1901, PM Emilio Naranjo.

ESCOBAS [es KOB uhs] (Zapata) Escobas (Spanish "brooms") was probably named for the local carrizo fronds often bound together and used as brooms. The name was shortened from Laguna de Escobas about 1930 with the oil boom. Escobares in Starr County is a variant. PO 21 Feb 1936, PM Hortensia Rangel. See Carrizo Springs.

ESKOTA [es KOT uh] (Fisher, Nolan) Founded about 1880 as a shipping point on the Texas & Pacific Railway. Named for Eskota, Yancey County, NC. Eskota is likely a Native American or Native American-inspired name of unknown origin. According to a local story the T&P inadvertently interchanged the "Eskota" and "Trent" station markers, so Eskota is where Trent should be and vice versa. PO 17 July 1888, PM William V. George.

ESPERANZA (Hudspeth) Named from the Esperanza farm (Spanish "hope"). PO 4 June 1935, PM Bessie Greene McCoy.

ESPERANZA (Montgomery) Esperanza (Spanish "hope") was founded by William Spiller who oversaw a tobacco and cotton plantation from the late 1870s. PO 10 Apr 1893 as Ada, named for Ada Lester; changed to Esperanza 15 Dec 1899, PM Joseph M. Westmoreland.

ESPEY (Atascosa) Named in 1918 by Julius and Adeline Espey from the Espey Silica Sand Company.

ESSEVILLE [ES uh vil] (Live Oak) Probably named for Willie and Mary Esse who established a general store and cotton gin in the early 1930s. Esseville in Atascosa County existed for several decades in the middle of the 20th century and was named for a different Esse family.

ESTACADO [es tuh KAHD o] (Crosby) In 1879 Paris Cox founded a Quaker colony named Maryetta for his wife Mary Ferguson Cox. The name was changed when George W. Singer established the Estacaddo [*sic*] PO 13 Oct 1881, a shortening of *Llano Estacado*, the "staked" or "palisaded" plains. See Llano County.

ESTELLE (Dallas) Jefferson and Frances Estill from Salem, TN, settled on Grapevine Prairie in 1855. PO 16 July 1857 as Estill's Station, PM Jefferson Estill; discontinued and reestablished as Estelles 14 June 1881; PM Milton A. Beall; changed to Estelle 21 Aug 1882, PM Henry Burgoon. (The spellings Estill and Estell alternate in early records.)

ESTELLINE (Hall) Founded by Elam Wright in the early 1890s. The PO was established 16 May 1892 by David Wright, Elam's brother, who named the office for Estelline Rose Deshields, daughter of David and Eunice Deshields who spent several years in the area on their way from Iowa to California.

ETHOLEN (Hudspeth) Named from the cluster of nearby buttes called the Etholen Knobs. The origin of the name is unknown. Etholen (Etolen) is a Finnish family name and early Finnish settlers or travelers may have given their name to the knobs (prominent rounded hills) that were reference points for travelers.

ETOILE [ee TOYL] (Nacogdoches) The site was known from at least the 1870s as Macedonia, named from the Macedonia Church and Macedonia Springs. The name was changed in January 1886 by Joseph Fisher, the first PM, part owner of the Fisher and Crown general store. Fisher's reasons for choosing Etoile, French for "star," are unknown but may have to do with Texas's nickname, the "Lone Star State."

ETTER (Moore) Founded in 1930 on the line of the North Plains & Santa Fe Railway and named for William Kirby Etter, general manager of the Santa Fe system. PO 7 Sept 1931, PM John Hulon Collier.

EULESS [YOO luhs] (Tarrant) In the mid-1860s Elisha Adam Euless relocated from Bedford, TN. Euless was precinct constable and Tarrant County sheriff in the 1890s. PO 3 Mar 1886, PM Cyrus Snow.

EULOGY (Bosque) Charles Walker Smith, a Disciples of Christ minister, founded the town and opened a general store about 1885. There was considerable sentiment for naming the post office after William Burley "Uncle Billy" Smith who clerked for his son. According to the local account, when a name for the PO was being considered, someone remarked it was a shame there was already a Smithville post office in Texas because the community "certainly did eulogize that ole man." From there it was a short step to naming the PO Eulogy 13 Nov 1885, PM Charley Walker Smith.

EUNICE (Leon) Eunice was founded about 1880 by John Morrison as Morrison's Chapel. The name was changed by Charles Jeff Hogan who opened the post office 20 July 1907, named for his two-year-old daughter, Eunice.

EUSTACE (Henderson) Known informally as Moseley for site owner William Lee Moseley and as Jolo for blacksmith Joseph Pickle, Eustace was formally named for William Tomlin Eustace, an Athens lawyer and hotelier. PO 9 Mar 1900 as Jolo; changed to Eustace 30 Apr 1900, PM John W. Moore.

EVADALE (Jasper) Known as Richardson's Bluff and also as Ford's Bluff until about 1904 when East Texas lumber baron John Henry Kirby established a railroad line and sawmill and formally named the site for Miss Eva Dale, a music teacher at the

Southeast Texas Male and Female College in Jasper. PO 6 May 1904, PM Frank K. Dornak. See Kirby.

EVANT [ee VAHNT] (Coryell, Hamilton) Evant (Evan) Brooks, a banker and local official who brought his family to the area from Alabama in the late 1870s, laid out the town of Evant about 1881. PO 23 Feb 1876 as Cove; changed to Evant 29 Jan 1885, PM Andrew J. Hunter.

EVERMAN [EVER muhn] (Tarrant) Known as Enon until 1904 when the name was changed for John W. Everman, general manager of the Texas & Pacific Railway. PO 17 Mar 1905, PM Jacob E. Dickeson.

EWELDER [EE welder] (San Patricio) John James Welder, rancher, president of the Bank of Victoria, and part owner of the San Antonio & Aransas Pass Railway, married Eliza Hughes in 1883 and she became the namesake for the town about 1890.

EWING [YOO ing] (Angelina) James A. Ewing was a major stockholder in the Bohlssen Manufacturing Company, the primary employer of the area. Ewing was a member of the family that owned the extensive Ewing plantation near Seguin. PO 30 Oct 1920, PM John W. Bohlssen.

EXELL [EKS uhl] (Moore) The town took its name from the Exell (Excell) Helium Plant, established in the early 1940s to produce helium for observation balloons in the early years of World War II. In addition to the positive association of the word, Exell is the pronunciation—reversed—of the name of the LX Ranch, one of the Texas Panhandle's iconic spreads, established in the late 1870s.

EYLAU (Bowie) Eylau was founded about 1840 by Collin (Cullin) Akin. The town may have been named for Eylau, formerly in Prussia, now in Russia and known as Bagrationovsk. Eylau was the site of a bloody but inconclusive battle between Napoléon's Grande Armée and the Imperial Russian Army in February 1807. PO 10 Feb 1885, PM Jay N. Faust.

EZZELL [ee ZEL] (Lavaca) Ira Ezzell from Missouri, was an early settler in the 1860s, he was joined by his brother Samuel. PO 23 Jan 1883, PM Ira Ezzell.

F

FABENS [FAY bunz] (El Paso) Fabens was founded in the early 1900s with construction of the Galveston, Harrisburg & San Antonio Railway, part of the Southern Pacific network; named for George Fabens, assistant land commissioner for the SP. PO 26 Dec 1906, PM Eugenio Pérez.

FAIR PLAY (Panola) Fair Play grew around John Allison's general store, established about 1848. According to local tradition, the name was a natural result of the fair rates and hospitality shown travelers who bought provisions at Allison's store and stayed at his guesthouse. There are about a dozen places in the US named Fair Play; most are named either for merchants' fair prices or for acts of kindness. PO 22 Mar 1851, PM Joshua Gill.

FAIRBANKS (Harris) John Joseph Fairbanks, a Denison real estate developer, founded Fairbanks in the mid-1880s. Fairbanks had earlier founded Colony in Anderson County, KS. PO 9 Oct 1876 as Gum Island; changed to Fairbanks 22 Oct 1895, PM Charles S. Wright.

FAIRCHILDS (Fort Bend) In 1890 Theo Aderholz, Charles Blohm, and August Bede founded a German settlement named for its location on Fairchilds Creek, itself named for Philo Fairchild who came to the area from New York state in the 1820s. PO 9 Feb 1912, PM Frank Fojt.

FAIRFIELD (Freestone) Mound Prairie was renamed Fairfield when the site was chosen for the county seat in 1850. Martha O. Bragg, wife of the first PM, Dunbar Bragg, who opened the office 17 Nov 1851, probably chose the name for Fairfield, Alabama, the home state of her family and a number of early settlers.

FAIRLIE (Hunt) Named for Fairly [*sic*] Webster Lee, son of farmers Albert and Mary Jane Lee. PO 1 Nov 1887 as Hinckley; changed to Fairlie 29 Sept 1892, PO Jesse S. Kelly.

FAIRVIEW (Howard) Reportedly so named by farmer Luther Lawrence because he could "see all the way to Big Spring."

FAIRY (Hamilton) Named in 1884 for petite Fairy Fort (said to weigh 40 pounds and stand about 3 feet tall), daughter of Battle Fort, who moved to the area from Mississippi in the 1870s. A Confederate officer, Battle Fort was named for the family of his mother, Martha Williams Battle. PO 17 Mar 1884, PM Leander J. Patterson.

FALCON (Zapata) The original Falcon settlement was founded near modern Falcón State Park, 2.5 miles SW of the present site, on a Spanish land grant issued in the mid-1700s. The community became known as *Ramireño de Abajo* (the "lower" Ramireño settlement, distinct from *Ramireño de Arriba*, the "upper" settlement). PO 18 July 1911, PM Daniel Yzaguirre. Named for Doña María Margarita de la Garza Falcón, daughter of Don José de la Garza and Doña Cándida Francisca Guerra, founders of Matamoros. See Ramireno.

FALFURRIAS [fal FYOO ree uhs] (Brooks) Edward Lasater, a major figure in the development of South Texas, founded Falfurrias about 1904 when the San Antonio

& Aransas Pass Railway built through the area. The town was named from the Falfurrias Ranch established by Lasater a decade earlier on a site called *La Mota de Falfurrias* "the Falfurrias grove of trees." The first use of the name Falfurrias is unknown, as is its meaning. Many sources have been proposed ranging from Spanish *falda* "skirt" through French *farfouilleur* "searcher" to "hoax" and even "bum." The origin of the name never concerned Lasater. On many occasions he made clear that for him Falfurrias was a Lipan Apache word meaning "the Land of Heart's Delight." PO 13 Dec 1898, PM Jose Trevino. See Dale Lasater's article, "Falfurrias" in the *Handbook of Texas Online*.

FALLS (County) Created and organized 1850. Named for the falls on the Brazos River near MARLIN.

FALLS CITY (Karnes) In 1886 the San Antonio & Aransas Pass Railway established Brackenridge Station, named for San Antonio businessman, banker, and railroad investor George Brackenridge. PO 11 Feb 1887 as Skiles; changed to Falls City 28 Nov 1893, PM Elias Crow who chose the name for the falls on the San Antonio River.

FAMULINER (Cochran) Named for rancher George W. Famuliner who moved to Texas from Cass County, MO, in the 1930s.

FANNETT (Jefferson) Founded by John Belizaire Fannett and Joseph Dugat who opened a general store on the line of the Gulf & Interstate Railway about 1895. The Taylor's Bayou PO was changed to Fannett 8 Sept 1899, PM Joseph Dugat.

FANNIN (County) Created 1837, organized 1838. Named for James Walker Fannin (1804–1836), born in Georgia. He is best remembered as a military leader at the March 19–20, 1836 Battle of Coleto Creek shortly after the fall of the Alamo. On March 27, 1836 Fannin and more than 300 survivors of Coleto Creek were executed in the Goliad Massacre. These killings led to the second imperative of the rallying cry of the Texas Revolution: Remember the Alamo! Remember Goliad! Fannin County, GA, is also named for James Fannin.

FANNIN (Goliad) Fannin was founded in 1852 on Perdido (Spanish "lost") Creek near the site of James Fannin's defeat by José de Urrea's Mexican forces at the Battle of Coleto Creek. The Fanning's Defeat PO operated 12 May 1852–17 Sept 1856. PO 25 Feb 1873 as Perdido; changed to Fannin 17 Mar 1890, PM Benson Goff. See Fannin County.

FARMER (Young) Informally known as Brush or Brushy for nearby Brushy Creek, the community was formally named in 1878 for William H. Farmer who opened the PO in his general store 7 Aug 1878.

FARNSWORTH (Ochiltree) Farnsworth was organized in 1919 with construction of the Panhandle & Santa Fe Railway and named for Hiram Warner Farnsworth, a leading figure in the governmental and educational affairs of Topeka, KS, and a director of the Atchison, Topeka & Santa Fe Railway, of which the P&SF was a subsidiary. PO 20 June 1905 as Nogal (Spanish "walnut"); changed to Rogerstown 7 Nov 1905; changed to Farnsworth 14 Jan 1920, PM Bird L. Rogers.

FARRAR (Limestone) Limestone County lawyer Lochlin Johnson Farrar represented the district in the Texas House and Senate in the 1870s and 1880s and was instrumental in establishing the PO 6 Mar 1883, PM John Bishop.

FARRSVILLE (Newton) Farr's Mill was named for the sawmill, gristmill, and cotton gin established on the plantation owned by Alfred Farr who brought his family and at least 80 slaves from Mississippi in the late 1830s. PO 8 Nov 1875, PM Benjamin Powell.

FARWELL (Parmer) Farwell was surveyed in 1905 as the seat of Parmer County, replacing Parmerton. Named for brothers John and Charles Farwell, directors of the Capitol Freehold Land and Investment Company. In the 1880s they oversaw establishment of the three million acre XIT Ranch that was found in portions of ten counties in the Texas Panhandle. PO 26 Dec 1906, PM Minnie Burton.

FASHING (Atascosa) According to the local story, the post office application requested the name Fashion, the brand name of a popular plug tobacco sold in his store, but the approved petition was returned as Fashing, either through misreading or clerical error, and the postmaster chose to accept the name rather than resubmit the application. PO 5 June 1920, PM Albert Schroeder.

FATE (Rockwall) Fate, a shortened form of Lafayette, was named for early settler and Rockwall county sheriff William Lafayette Brown, known by friends as Fate Brown. PO 13 July 1880, PM Harvey P. White.

FAUGHT (Lamar) Named about 1870 for physician Robert H. Faught from Mississippi. Faught was the first PM 18 Apr 1893.

FAULKNER (Lamar) Faulkner was apparently named about 1900 for merchant Ira Faulkner. The town is often confused with that of nearby Pin Hook.

FAWIL (Newton) The local story is that one Fonzo (or Fauzo) A. Wilson intended to write "F A Wilson" on a sign identifying his sawmill but the board was too short to accommodate any lettering beyond "F A Wil." Newcomers took "Fawil" to be the name of the town and Fawil became official when the Jasper & Eastern Railway established Fawil Station in the early 20th century.

FAYETTE (County) Created 1837, organized 1838. Named for the Marquis de Lafayette (1757–1834), the French noble who served with distinction in the American Revolution. Some two hundred US towns, townships, and counties are named directly for him and another forty or so are named for La Grange, his French estate. See La Grange.

FAYETTEVILLE (Fayette) Site owner Philip J. Shaver founded Fayetteville in 1847, named for his former home, Fayetteville, TN, which was named by settlers from Fayetteville, NC, named for Gilbert du Motier, the Marquis de Lafayette, for whom Fayette County, TX, was also named. PO 30 Oct 1850, PM Sylvester Munger.

FAYSVILLE (Hidalgo) Named for Fay Devine, wife of Patrick Devine, the civil engineer who laid out the townsite about 1920. PO 8 June 1932, PM Merrill A. Neel.

FEDOR (Lee) Named for Fedor Soder who emigrated from Magdeburg, Germany, in the 1850s and opened a store in SERBIN where he was the second postmaster in 1875. Soder donated land for a school and cemetery at Gloyna, now a ghost town, and was a shopkeeper at PAIGE. PO 22 Nov 1880, PM C. August Polnick. Earlier known as Long Prairie, Moab, and West Yegua.

FENTRESS (Caldwell) James Fentress, a physician from Tennessee by way of Kentucky, arrived in Texas about 1840. The community of Riverside, named for its location on the San Marcos River, was renamed in his honor about 1890. James Fentress was a member of the Fentress family for whom Fentress County, TN, is named. PO 6 June 1893, PM Archibald Harwood.

FERRIS (Ellis) Ferris was named in the 1870s for Royal Andrew Ferris, a banker who financed much of the Waxahachie Tap Railroad (later a part of the Houston & Texas Central system) and perhaps for his father, banker and lawyer Justus Wesley Ferris. as well. PO 22 June 1874, PM Jackson Straw.

FETZER (Waller) Named for Laura Fetzer, about whom little is known. She was probably associated with the Fetzer sawmill that operated in the early 1910s. As the Texas Forestry Museum so succinctly put it, "Miss Laura Fetzer encouraged lumbering and disappeared mysteriously one day after boarding a Ft. Worth-bound train." PO 18 June 1913, PM Fred Gibson.

FIELDS STORE (Waller) Caroline and Drury Holland Field settled in the area and opened a general store in the late 1840s. PO 1 July 1874, PM Isaac N. Jones.

FIELDTON (Lamb) According to a local account Jess Mitchell, editor of the *Lamb County Leader* newspaper and the townsite owner, thought the name was appropriate because Fieldton was halfway between Little*field* and Ol*ton*. PO 6 Dec 1930, PM William Fewell.

FIFE (McCulloch) Robert K. Finlay's mother, Agnes Blythe Finlay, chose the name about 1880 for their ancestral home, Fife, Scotland. PO 11 Sept 1902, PM Abraham Long.

FIFTH STREET (Fort Bend) This Houston bedroom community, named in the 1970s, straddles Fifth Street between Houston and Missouri City.

FILES VALLEY (Hill) Previously known as Eureka Valley, the name was changed in 1879 for David and Sarah Ann Files, the first permanent settlers in 1846. PO 31 Mar 1880 as Files, PM John S. Bounds.

FINCASTLE (Henderson) Daniel McRae, the first PM 6 Mar 1855, chose the name for Fincastle, Scotland, his ancestral home.

FISCHER (Comal) In the early 1850s Herman Fischer opened a trading post on the San Antonio–Blanco Road that became known as Fischer's Store. He established the first PO 24 July 1876.

FISHER (County) Created 1876, organized 1886. Named for Samuel Rhoads Fisher

(1794–1839), born in Pennsylvania. Fisher emigrated to Texas in 1830 and settled at Matagorda. In 1836 he signed the Texas Declaration of Independence and was named Secretary of the Texas Navy by President Sam Houston. He was removed from office by the Senate of the Republic of Texas in 1837.

FISK (Coleman) Bradley Allen Fiske [*sic*] was a US Navy Admiral who served in the Spanish-American War and was an important naval innovator and inventor. His ordnance rangefinder that became operational in 1895 had a significant effect on naval warfare. PO 9 Feb 1906, PM Thomas Stafford.

FLAGG (Castro) In 1904 businessman, rancher, banker, and lumberman Cornelius T. Herring bought the Seven-Up Ranch and changed the name to the Flag (Flagg) Ranch that he operated for several decades before subdividing and selling the property as farm tracts. PO 19 Nov 1925 as Flagg, PM Eva McEntire.

FLAT (Coryell) A shortening of Mesquite Flat from the local landscape and the first name of the area. PO 16 Sept 1897, PM Jesse Burgess.

FLATONIA (Fayette) Old Flatonia was settled in the 1840s by German immigrants, including the family of Flatonia's namesake, Friedrich Wilhelm Flato, a sailing master from Bremen, Germany. When the Galveston, Harrisburg & San Antonio Railway built through the area in the early 1870s much of Old Flatonia was moved a mile northwest to trackside. PO 21 Mar 1870, PM Alfred Wychetzky.

FLETCHER (Hardin) Founded about 1894 with construction of the Gulf, Beaumont & Kansas City Railway. Probably named for William Andrew Fletcher of Beaumont who owned several sawmills and shingle mills in Hardin and Jefferson counties. PO 7 Apr 1909 as Lumberton; changed to Fletcher 20 Apr 1914, PM Wiley J. Bracken.

FLINT (Smith) In 1887 Charles Brown applied for the Flynt PO, named for local landowner Robert P. Flynt, but the name was respelled and the office approved as Flint, 3 Nov 1887.

FLO (Leon) Reportedly named for David Haskins's faithful dog Flo. PO 6 Feb 1885 as Oden; changed to Flo when Haskins became PM 14 Jan 1892.

FLOMOT [FLO maht] (Motley) The town was named for its location on the *Flo*yd-*Mot*ley county line. PO 27 Jan 1902, PM Nelson R. Welch.

FLORENCE (Williamson) Florence was known informally as Limp Rag until the early 1850s when the name became Brooksville for Elisha and Sarah Florence Lashbrooks who began farming in the area in 1848. John Atkinson opened the Florence PO 25 Nov 1857, named for Sarah Florence Lashbrooks.

FLORESVILLE (Wilson) The first settlers were from the Canary Islands in the 18th century. Their descendants included the town's namesakes, Jose María Flores and Francisco Flores de Abrego, who built a hacienda and operated a ranch northwest of the present town by 1830. PO 20 Sept 1858 as Lodi; changed to Floresville 8 May 1872, PM Adam C. Staudt.

FLOREY (Andrews) Named for Albert J. Florey, a local rancher, merchant, and businessman. Informally known as Smackover. PO 18 Jan 1909, PM Lee N. Smith.

FLOWELLA (Brooks) San Antonio real estate agents and land developers Ernest Burton and Albert Danforth founded Flowella in 1909. The name apparently was coined to reflect the presence of a "flowing well" projected as the centerpiece of the town square. PO 8 Dec 1910, PM Roy M. Calahan.

FLOWER GROVE (Martin) Named for Hardy James Flowers who began farming in the area in the early 20th century.

FLOY (Fayette) Floy Siding was established by the Southern Pacific Railroad in 1900 and named for Floy Frances Arnim, newborn daughter of merchant Edward Alexander Arnim.

FLOYD (County) Created 1876, organized 1890. Named for Dolphin Ward Floyd (1804–1836), born in North Carolina. Floyd moved to Texas and was an established farmer in the Gonzales area by the early 1830s. He joined the Gonzales Rangers and was part of a relief force that reached the Alamo March 1, 1836. He died five days later.

FLOYDADA [floy DAYD uh] (Floyd) Founded in 1890 as Floyd City on a parcel of land donated by James B. and Caroline B. Price of Jefferson City, MO. The name was changed to Floydada, a blend of the county name, *Floyd*, and *ada*, for Ada Catherine Bear, niece of Caroline Price, when James Henderson opened the PO 4 Aug 1890.

FLUVANNA [floo VAN uh] (Scurry) Abilene real estate agent James M. Cunningham founded Fluvanna in 1908 on news that the Roscoe, Snyder & Pacific Railway would be establishing a terminal. The name was suggested by the townsite surveyor, Pleasant Telford, for his former home, Fluvanna County, VA. PO 26 June 1899 as Light; changed to Fluvanna 7 Jan 1908, PM Edward A. Boles.

FLYNN (Leon) Flynn was known informally as Bug Scuffle, reportedly named from the Bug Scuffle Saloon, known for its rowdy clientele and free-flowing homebrewed whiskey. The name was changed 1 Feb 1909 when PM James M. Reed changed the Connor PO to Flynn, named for John J. Flynn, general manager of the Trinity & Brazos Valley Railway.

FOARD (County) Created and organized 1891. Named for Robert Levi Foard (1831–1898), born in western Maryland. Foard, a Princeton-educated lawyer, moved to Texas in 1852 and established a law office at Columbus. He rose to the rank of major during the Civil War with orders to guard the Texas gulf coast. In 1891 Marcus Townsend, Foard's law partner and a Texas State Senator, proposed that a county be created and named for Robert Foard.

FOARD CITY (Foard) Named from Foard County shortly after the Kansas City, Mexico

& Orient Railway laid tracks through the area in 1908. PO 30 Oct 1909, PM Frank Edwards.

FODICE [FO duhs] (Houston) A local popular etymology claims that the name arose when a gambler called out "fo dice" after making his point of four. More likely Fodice is a phonetic spelling of Fordyce, perhaps a transfer from Fordyce, AR, or named for SAM FORDYCE. PO 13 May 1902, PM William Wiley.

FOLLETT (Lipscomb) Follett was founded in Beaver County, OK, in the early 1890s as Ivanhoe. The town moved south to Texas and was renamed at the suggestion of Thomas C. Spearman, namesake of SPEARMAN, for Horace Follett, a locating engineer for the Santa Fe Railroad. PO 12 Feb 1918, PM May S. Johnson.

FOOT (Collin) Gerard (or Gerald) Alexander Foote established a medical practice and drug store in the early 1850s. Foote was a surgeon in the Confederate Army, a member of the Texas Legislature and president of the Collin County Bank in the 1880s. PO 16 Jan 1901, PM John W. Cox.

FORDTRAN (Victoria) Founded by Eugene Henry Fordtran, a Galveston merchant and real estate agent. PO 29 Dec 1898, PM Sophia E. Cook.

FORNEY (Kaufman) Known as Brooklyn until the early 1870s when the Texas & Pacific Railway built through the area and named the station for John Wein Forney of Philadelphia, a director of the T&P. PO 29 Dec 1873, PM Erastus P. Shands.

FORRESTON (Ellis) Hardeman Carr Forrest, known as Captain Forrest for his elected rank during the Civil War, came to Texas from Tennessee in the mid-1850s, opened a general store, and donated land for a station on the Missouri–Kansas–Texas Railroad about 1890. PO 26 Sept 1844 as Chambers' Creek; changed to Forreston 28 Mar 1891, PM Carr Forrest.

FORSAN (Howard) George Clayton Stewart, a Big Spring rancher, donated land for the townsite in 1929. Forsan is a modification of "four sands" for the four local oil sands. PO 30 Jan 1929, PM Gladys Arnold.

FORT BEND (County) Created 1837, organized 1838. A group of Stephen F. Austin's colonists built a log cabin and a small blockhouse on a bend of the Brazos River in the early 1820s. The structure and the surrounding area became known as Fort Bend.

FORT CHADBOURNE (Coke) Fort Chadbourne was established October 1852, named in honor of Lieutenant Theodore L. Chadbourne, a West Point graduate who, in his early 20s, was killed at the May 9, 1846 Battle of Resaca de la Palma, one of the first engagements of the Mexican War. The post was abandoned in 1868. PO 28 Jan 1859, PM George Leigh.

FORT DAVIS (Jeff Davis) The town grew around Fort Davis, a military post established in 1854 to protect travelers and commerce on the San Antonio–El Paso Road. The fort was named for US Secretary of War Jefferson Davis, the namesake of Jeff Davis County. PO 19 May 1855, PM Thomas G. Pitcher.

FORT GRIFFIN (Shackelford) The community grew around a military outpost founded as Camp Wilson on the Clear Fork of the Brazos River in 1867. The fort was renamed for Major General Charles Griffin, a Union General in the Civil War and commander of the Department of Texas during Reconstruction. PO 17 Mar 1860, PM John C. Simpson.

FORT HANCOCK (Hudspeth) In 1881 the US military established Camp Rice; the facility was renamed Fort Hancock in 1886 in honor of the recently deceased General Winfield Scott Hancock, a veteran of the Mexican War and Civil War. PO 15 Apr 1884 as Camp Rice; changed to Fort Hancock 10 June 1886, PM Albert J. Warren.

FORT HOOD (Hood) Formerly Camp Hood and located within the town of Killeen. Built September 1942 and named for John Bell Hood, commander of the Texas Brigade during the Civil War.

FORT INGE (Uvalde) Fort Inge, established in 1849 to protect travelers on the San Antonio–El Paso Road, was known as Camp Leona, named from the Leona River, until 1849 when the name was changed in honor of Zebulon Montgomery Pike Inge who was killed in 1846 in one of the first engagements of the War with Mexico. PO 22 Aug 1853, PM Clement W. Howard.

FORT MCKAVETT (Menard) Fort McKavett was established by the US Army in 1868 and named for Henry McKavett, an army officer killed in 1846 in the Battle of Monterrey during the Mexican War. PO 26 Aug 1854, PM William H. Doak.

FORT QUITMAN (Hudspeth) Established in 1858 and named for Mexican War General John A. Quitman. The fort was decommissioned in 1882. PO 8 Nov 1858, PM Bartholomew J. DeWitt. See Quitman.

FORT SPUNKY (Hood) About 1850 George Barnard established a trading post on the Brazos River near George's Creek, named in his honor. The local story is that the community became known as Fort Spunky reportedly because of the regular fist fights at Barnard's establishment. PO 13 July 1886, PM Thomas Walsh.

FORT STOCKTON (Pecos) In 1858 Peter Gallagher laid out the town of Saint Gall, named for the late 6th century Irish patron saint of chickens, geese, and birds of the air. In 1881 Saint Gall was renamed Fort Stockton for the nearby US Army post established in 1852 as Camp Stockton. PO 9 Sept 1872 as Camp Stockton; changed to Fort Stockton 14 Jan 1879, PM Joseph Friedlander.

FORT WORTH (Tarrant) Named for career soldier William Jenkins Worth who served in the War of 1812 in which he was wounded and permanently crippled. He served under Winfield Scott in the Blackhawk War of 1832 and again under Scott in the War with Mexico where he commanded the troops that captured Chapultepec Castle in 1847. After the war he was commander of the Department of Texas. In June 1849 Major Ripley Arnold established a military outpost called Camp Worth where the branches of the Trinity River join. The post was officially named Fort Worth several months later. Julian Field, a namesake of MANSFIELD, was the first postmaster 28 Feb 1856.

FOSTER (Fort Bend) Randolph and Isaac Foster, brothers from Mississippi and sons of John Foster, probably the original recipient of the land grant, operated a rice and sugarcane plantation from the 1820s. PO 18 July 1882, PM Henry Bullwinkel.

FOSTORIA (Montgomery) Fostoria was founded as Clinesburg, named for Brazil, Milton, and Jesse Cline, owners of the Cline Brothers sawmill in Walker County. Renamed for John McCullough Foster, founder of the Foster Lumber Company that operated a sawmill in Montgomery County from the mid-1890s. PO 1 July 1896 as Clinesburg, PM John McCullough Foster; changed to Fostoria 22 Jan 1906, PM Ebbie C. Smith.

FOUKE (Wood) The George W. Fouke Lumber Company, with headquarters at Hawkins, established a sawmill at the site. Fouke, AR, and Fouke, MS, are also named for the George Fouke Lumber Company.

FOUR WAY (Moore) Reportedly so named because there were four ways out of the town: north or south on US 287/87; east or west on state road 354. Established in the late 1920s.

FOWLERTON (La Salle) James, Charles, and Ernie Fowler, owners of the Fowler Brothers Land Company of San Antonio, founded Fowlerton about 1910 on the former Dull Ranch. PO 17 Oct 1911, PM Ruth Fowler.

FRAME SWITCH (Williamson) In the early 1880s Solomon Yakey of Ohio and David Frame bought the site. About 1885 Frame and Yakey, now married to Frame's daughter, Harriet, established the town named for the switch on the International–Great Northern Railroad.

FRANCITAS (Jackson) Spanish "little France." Named for the cluster of French families who settled in the area in the late 1800s. PO 26 Jan 1911, PM Charles Hardy.

FRANKEL CITY (Andrews) Previously Fullerton, named for the Fullerton Oil Company of Fullerton, CA, that drilled its first local oil well in 1941; renamed in the mid-1940s for the Frankel Brothers Oil Company. PO 1 Oct 1948 as Fullerton; changed to Frankel City PO 1 Apr 1956, PM Grace Wilmont Blanchard.

FRANKELL (Stephens) Frank Kell, an entrepreneur instrumental in the development of Wichita Falls in the early 20th century, was an incorporator of the Wichita Falls & Southern Railroad in 1920. PO 7 July 1920, PM Chester C. Shafer.

FRANKLIN (County) Created and organized 1875. Although there are no official sources it is generally agreed that the namesake is Benjamin Cromwell Franklin (1805–1873), a Georgia lawyer who fought at San Jacinto, was appointed judge of the Brazoria district by Sam Houston in 1836, and was elected to several terms in the Texas Legislature in the 1850s and 1860s.

FRANKLIN (Robertson) Francis "Frank" Slauter (Slaughter) from Nashville, TN, was granted land that included the townsite in the 1830s. He was the first chief justice of Robertson County in the 1840s. PO 19 Aug 1838 as Franklin, PM Harrison

Own; discontinued 20 Oct 1851; reestablished 26 Jan 1880 as Volney; changed back to Franklin 26 Apr 1880, PM Elias Reynolds.

FRANKSTON (Anderson) Ayers Station was established about 1900 by the Texas & New Orleans Railroad, named for local physician William Ayers. In 1902 the name was changed to Frankston for Frankie Miller, daughter of Sam and May Miller, who donated land for the townsite. PO 16 Nov 1901 as Ayers; changed to Frankston 11 June 1902, PM Samuel E. Beard.

FREDERICKSBURG (Gillespie) Founded in 1846 by Otfried Hans Freiherr von Meusebach (later known as John O. Meusebach), commissioner general of the Adelsverein, "society of nobles," officially known as the *Verein zum Schutze deutscher Einwanderer in Texas* "Society for the Protection of German Immigrants in Texas"; generally known as the German Emigration Company, organized in 1842 to promote and facilitate German emigration to Texas. Meusebach named the future city for Adelsverein member Prince Frederick of Prussia. PO 7 Dec 1848 as Fredericksburgh, PM Theodore Specht; spelling changed to Fredericksburg 6 Feb 1894.

FREDONIA [fruh DON yuh] (Mason) Samuel Parker and William Lawrence Hays, brothers from Georgia, began farming in the 1870s. Samuel Hays opened the Deerton PO 17 Mar 1879. The name was changed 8 June 1880, reportedly at the suggestion of William Hays, who said he had no reason other than he "liked the name."

FREEPORT (Brazoria) Freeport was established in 1912 by the Texas Freeport Sulphur Company, organized to mine what was thought to be one of the largest sulphur deposits in the world. PO 4 Apr 1898, PM Lizzie Bullington. In 1957 Freeport annexed the town of VELASCO.

FREER (Duval) The area was known informally as *Las Hermanitas* "the little sisters," named from the nearby hills. Formally named for Charles and Minnie Freer who began farming in the area in the 1910s. PO 21 July 1927, PM Minnie Freer.

FREESTONE (County) Created 1850, organized 1851. Named for the local deposits of lignite or freestone coal. The boundary between Freestone and Limestone counties is roughly that of the deposits of lignite and limestone, the latter being characteristic of Limestone County from which Freestone County was later created.

FREESTONE (Freestone) Previously Bonds Prairie. The town of Freestone was named for the county in 1906 by Mary Alvaretta Beene. PO 6 Nov 1906, PM Frank Savage.

FREIHEIT [FREE HEYET] (Comal) Alonzo Nolte opened a general store and saloon about 1905 and later organized the Freiheit Bowling Club named from German *freiheit* "freedom, liberty," from which the community was named.

FRELSBURG (Colorado) William Frels emigrated from Germany in the early 1830s, fought in the Texas Revolution, and became a successful businessman and landowner. He donated land for the town, a school, and a cemetery and was the first PM 22 Sept 1847.

FRENSTAT (Burleson) Moravian settlers founded Frenstat in the mid-1880s, named for Frenstat (Frenštát pod Radhoštěm), now in the eastern Czech Republic. PO 7 Mar 1891, PM Frank Susilla.

FRESNO (Fort Bend) Fresno (Spanish "ash tree") was possibly named for the Fresno Scraper, a tool invented in Fresno, CA, used in constructing irrigation canals and drainage ditches; but was more likely named directly for the CA city. PO 31 May 1910, PM Frank Keir.

FREYBURG (Fayette) Founded in the late 1860s and named for Freyburg in eastern Germany. PO 11 Sept 1889, PM Adolph Kauffman.

FRIDAY (Trinity) Ellis Prairie was named for Benjamin B. Ellis, one of the commissioners appointed to organize Trinity County in 1850. The name was changed when the Friday post office was established in the summer of 1903 by PM James F. Friday.

FRIENDSHIP Friendship has been the name of Texas communities in more than a dozen counties. Often the naming stories recall the friendship among early settlers or the name was chosen to encourage good relationships. The names of some may have been chosen from "Friendship," the Texas motto official since 1930 but well known for decades before.

FRIENDSWOOD (Galveston) The Religious Society of Friends founded a Quaker colony in 1895. PO 15 Dec 1899, PM Flora E. Knode.

FRIO (County) Created 1858, organized 1871. Named from the *Frio* (Spanish "cold") River that runs southeast across Uvalde and Frio counties for 200 miles and joins the Nueces south of Three Rivers. The river was first mentioned in 1689 by Alonso de León who wrote, "We came upon a river to which we gave the name *Río Sarco*, because its water was blue."

FRIO (Frio) Once known as Frio City. Founded in 1871 and named for the county. PO 26 Aug 1872, PM James M. Elledge.

FRIONA [free O nuh] (Parmer) Friona, an adaptation of Spanish *frío* "cold," was named from Frio Draw. In the early 1900s the Capitol Syndicate founded the town of Frio on the line of the Pecos & Northern Texas Railway that had earlier established a shipping point on part of the XIT ranch. The name was modified to Friona when the post office was opened 16 Mar 1907 by Sarah D. Olson.

FRISCO (Collin, Denton) The first town in the area was Erudia, named from William Allen's 1890 book, *Erudia: Foreign Missionary to Our World*, in which Allen, the Methodist minister, decried the sinfulness of the time and pointed the way to peace and salvation. The name was changed in 1902 when the St. Louis, San Francisco & Texas Railway (the Frisco Line) established a station. PO 17 June 1895 as Erudia; changed to Frisco 24 Apr 1902, PM Thomas Duncan.

FRITCH (Hutchinson) Louis C. Fritch, vice president of the Chicago, Rock Island & Pacific Railway, was instrumental in selecting the railroad right of way, establishing the station, laying out the community, and naming its streets. PO 10 Mar 1928, PM John Hardin.

FROGNOT (Collin) One of Texas's notable names, Frognot has generated a number of creative etymologies. By one, the name arose from boys habitually bringing frogs and toads to school to scare the girls; when these were discovered the teacher admonished the boys, "frogs are not to be brought to school." By another there was a plague of frogs of Biblical proportions and the people went on a frog hunting campaign that reduced the frog population to zero; thus, the name Frognot. This is the only Frognot in the US.

FRONTON [frahn TON] (Starr) Fronton was founded in the late 18th century as the Spanish mission of *San Francisco de las Playas* and renamed from Spanish *frontón* "wall" from the rock wall on the Rio Grande. PO 16 June 1948, PM Velia Ramirez.

FROST (Navarro) Samuel R. Frost was a Navarro County judge, state representative in the 1880s, and attorney for the St. Louis Southwestern Railway (Cotton Belt) in 1881 when the St.LS built through the area. PO 18 Mar 1887, PM William Chesnut.

FRUITVALE (Van Zandt) In the 1880s Nathaniel Sykes Wheeler promoted local fruit nurseries and orchards. PO 15 June 1899 as Riley; changed to Speed 6 Jan 1900; changed to Fruitvale 21 May 1903, PM Eli H. Whitten. See Ben Wheeler.

FRY (Brown) The Rex-Tex Oil Company's first well began producing in 1926 on the ranch owned by James H. Fry. PO 5 May 1927, PM Athel J. Curry.

FRYDEK [FREYE dek] (Austin) Founded by Czech settlers in 1895 and named for Frydek, Silesia, Czech Republic, now joined with Mistek and known as Frýdek-Místek. PO 22 June 1901, PM Agnes F. Wojtek.

FULBRIGHT (Red River) David Ful(l)bright opened a general store in the 1840s and was later the first Red River County judge. PO 6 Sept 1882, PM John Hardin. Also known as Possum Trot.

FULDA (Baylor) Named by German settlers for Fulda, Hesse, Germany. PO 29 June 1892 as Bellah, named for Sam Bellah; changed to Fulda 2 Jan 1896, PM Antonia Flusche.

FULSHEAR [FUHL sher] (Fort Bend) Churchill Fulshear, born in France, was one of Stephen F. Austin's Old Three Hundred settlers. From 1824 he and his sons Benjamin, Churchill, and Graves farmed, ran cattle, and operated a cotton gin and gristmill. The town was laid out on the Fulshears' property shortly after the San Antonio & Aransas Pass Railway was granted a right of way in the late 1880s. PO 30 Sept 1880, PM Julius Wimberly.

FULTON (Aransas) Founded in 1866; named for George W. Fulton, a founder of the Coleman, Mathis, Fulton Cattle Company and the Coleman-Fulton Pasture Company in 1871. PO 4 Nov 1869, PM Charles M. Holden.

FURRH (Panola) John and Jane Furrh settled near Elysian Fields about 1858. John Furrh began operating a sawmill and grist mill in the 1860s and by the mid-1880s he and his son James were keeping a general store in what is now Furrh. PO 18 Apr 1898, PM Lucy C. Holt, daughter of John and Jane Furrh.

E

GADSTON (Lamar) The spelling was originally Gadsden and the community was probably named by settlers from Gadsden, AL, itself named for James Gadsden who negotiated the Gadsden Purchase that resolved territorial issues between Mexico and the US in the early 1850s. PO 7 Mar 1891 as Gadsden, PM William Y. Harmon.

GAGEBY (Hemphill, Wheeler) Gageby, also known as Nubbin Ridge, was named from Gageby Creek, itself named for James Harrison Gageby, an army officer who waged war against Indians in the late 1860s. PO 3 Feb 1910, PM Alonzo Q. Hennington.

GAIL (Borden) Gail was established in 1901 to supply local ranchers and farmers. The town was named for Gail Borden, founder of the Borden Corporation, manufacturer of condensed milk and the namesake of Borden County. PO 19 Feb 1891 as Gale, PM John I. Wilbourn; changed to Gail 25 Apr 1891.

GAINES (County) Created 1876, organized 1905. Named for James Taylor Gaines (1776–1856), a cousin of Edmund Pendleton Gaines for whom GAINESVILLE was named. Gaines, a native Virginian, was a member of the committee that drafted the Texas Declaration of Independence and the Constitution of the Republic of Texas. In 1850, after serving in three early congresses of the Texas Republic, Gaines left Texas to join the rush to the California gold fields and spent his remaining years in California.

GAINESVILLE (Cooke) Founded in 1850. Named for General Edmund Pendleton Gaines, a distinguished army officer who served during the War of 1812, the Seminole Wars, and the Black Hawk War of 1832. Gaines was a popular officer and a number of places have been named in his honor including Gainesvilles in Florida, New York, and Georgia, as well as Texas. PO 31 Oct 1851, PM Stephen Brown. See Gaines County.

GALENA PARK (Harris) Isaac Patterson founded a settlement about 1837 that he called Clinton for his former home in New York state. In 1935 the name was changed to Galena Park for the Galena Signal Oil Company of Texas, one of the first oil refineries in the area, later bought by Texaco. Galena Park is now firmly within the city of Houston. PO 12 Aug 1931, PM Fox H. Hollis.

GALLATIN [GAL uh tuhn] (Cherokee) John and Sophia Chandler, brother and sister and the site owners, founded Gallatin in 1902 with construction of the Texas & New Orleans Railroad. Charles Martin, a lawyer and friend of the Chandlers, suggested the name for his former home, Gallatin, TN, itself named for Albert Gallatin, Secretary of the Treasury in the early 19th century and later minister to France and the United Kingdom. Gallatin was a popular politician and about a dozen US places have been named in his honor. PO 30 Apr 1903, PM William Logue.

GALLE [GAL ee] (Guadalupe) In the early 1880s Friedrich (Frederick) Galle, born in Prussia, built one of the first houses in the town that was later named for his family. PO 24 May 1909, PM Walter Schulze.

GALVESTON (County) Created 1838, organized 1839. Named from the community.

GALVESTON [GAL vuhs tuhn] (Galveston) In 1785, Bernardo de Gálvez, a hero of the American Revolution and Viceroy of New Spain, sent master mariner and cartographer José Antonio de Evia to survey and map the Gulf Coast. Evia named the largest bay *Bahía de Galvezton* in honor of his patron. Mexico established the Port of Galveston in 1825 and the town that has become the city of Galveston was founded in the mid-1830s by Michel Branamour Menard, a French-Canadian Indian trader, and his business associates. Menard Creek in Liberty County, where Menard built a sawmill and gristmill in the early 1830s, is named in his honor. PO 8 Apr 1846, PM Robert Johnson. For details see David McComb, *Galveston: A History*. See Menard County.

GANADO [guh NAY do] (Jackson) In the early 1880s the Galveston, Harrisburg & San Antonio Railway established a station in what was known as the Mustang Settlement. The local account is that cattle were so plentiful a railroad official named the station Ganado (Spanish "herd"). PO 20 Feb 1883, PM Wilson Brown.

GARDEN CITY (Glasscock) The PO application requested the name Gardner City, named for Dora Gardner, the second PM. The application was apparently misread as Garden and the PO was approved as Garden City. PO 28 July 1886, PM Amanda Hines.

GARDENDALE (La Salle) Founded about 1908 and named for its location in the Winter Garden Region of southwest Texas where vegetables are grown the year around. PO 27 Apr 1909, PM Laura Mack.

GARFIELD (DeWitt) Named about 1881 in honor of US President James A. Garfield.

GARFIELD (Travis) Named for President James A. Garfield who was assassinated six months before the post office was established by Edward Rousseau 7 Nov 1881.

GARLAND (Dallas) Duck Creek, the first community in the area, was settled in the early 1840s. In 1886 the Gulf, Colorado & Santa Fe Railway established Embree Station east of Duck Creek, named for Kelly Embree, a Dallas physician and former Duck Creek postmaster. When friction arose over the renaming, US Representative Joseph Abbott suggested the post office be moved to a site between Duck Creek and Embree and be renamed for Augustus Hill Garland, US Attorney General. PO 20 July 1848 as Duck Creek, PM Henry K. Vollentine; discontinued 5 Nov 1866; reopened 12 Nov 1877, PM Emily Strother; changed to Embree 1 Feb 1887, PM Jefferson D. Robinson; changed to Garland 31 Dec 1887.

GARNER (Parker) Garner, a shortening of Bumgarner, was named for Absolom Bumgarner who opened the Garner PO 26 Dec 1890.

GARRETT (Ellis) William Garrett, a San Augustine plantation owner, bought the site in 1875. It is unlikely that he ever lived there. PO 28 Mar 1882 as Guide, PM Harris T. Kennedy; changed to Garrett 2 Apr 1894, PM Thomas H. Campbell.

GARRETTS BLUFF (Lamar) Jesse Garrett began ferry service across the Red River in the 1860s and established the PO 28 Aug 1873.

GARRISON (Nacogdoches) In the mid-1880s lumberman James H. Garrison donated land for a right of way to the Houston East & West Texas Railway. The station was named in his honor in 1886. PO 12 Apr 1871 as Wonders, PM Susan Fears; changed to Garrison 30 Nov 1885, PM Henry D. Garrison.

GARWOOD (Colorado) Garwood was known as Red Bluff until the 1900s when Marcus Townsend built an irrigation system to facilitate local rice cultivation. Townsend named the community for Hiram Garwood, a Houston attorney with whom he had served in the Texas Legislature in the late 1880s. PO 26 Apr 1901, PM Nelle Griffith.

GARY (Panola) Gary was founded in 1898 when the Marshall, Timpson & Sabine Pass Railway extended a line to Carthage. Land for the station was donated by Thomas Smith Garrison, a Timpson businessman who chose the name for his seven-year-old grandson, Gary Bonner Sanford. PO 13 June 1883, PM James Thomas; changed to Gary 9 Mar 1899, PM Andrew T. Davis.

GARZA (County) Created 1876, organized 1907. Named for the Garza family, the best-known being José Antonio de la Garza of San Antonio, one of the largest landowners in Bexar County in the early 19th century. Garza was the first person to legally coin money in Texas. His mintings of the 1810s included coins with a single star, perhaps a reflection of or inspiration for Texas as the Lone Star State.

GASOLINE (Briscoe) About 1906 a gasoline powered cotton gin, then a great novelty, was such a feature of the community that gin operator Milton Tomson named the PO Gasoline when he opened the office 1 Oct 1907.

GASTONIA (Kaufman) Gastonia was founded in the late 1800s and likely named for William H. Gaston, a founder of the first permanent bank of Dallas and a Dallas merchant, real estate broker, benefactor, and promoter.

GATESVILLE (Coryell) Fort Gates was a US military installation established in 1849 and named for Collinson Reed Gates who distinguished himself in the Mexican War engagements of Resaca de la Palma and Palo Alto in 1846. The town of Gatesville, named from nearby Fort Gates and the county seat, was founded in 1854 with the creation of Coryell County. PO 16 Mar 1854 as Gates, PM James Newton.

GAUSE [gawz] (Milam) In 1873 the International–Great Northern Railroad laid out the town named for site owner and stock raiser William James Gause. PO 24 June 1874, PM James S. Reynolds.

GAY HILL (Fayette) Named for James Gay, a plantation owner and brother of Thomas Gay, for whom Gay Hill in Washington County is named.

GAY HILL (Washington) Named from the Gay-Hill general store, established in the late 1830s by Thomas Gay and William Carroll Andrew Jackson Hill (who mercifully went by W. C. J. Hill). PO 1 May 1850, PM Francis Thompson.

GEM [JEM] (Hemphill) In 1909 the Moody Land Company laid out the town named for

Gem Hibbard Moody, wife of rancher and site owner Thomas F. Moody. PO 19 June 1909, PM Robert K. Rhea.

GENOA [juh NO uh] (Harris) Founded in 1892 by Galveston banker John H. Burnett, who claimed the climate of the area reminded him of Genoa, Italy. Genoa was annexed by Houston in the 1960s. PO 27 July 1892, PM Abel Preston.

GENTRY (Potter) Probably named by William H. Bush, the namesake of BUSHLAND for the family of his second wife, Ruth Russell Gentry.

GENTRYS MILL (Hamilton) In 1875 Frederick Browder Gentry established a gristmill on land granted for his service in the Texas Revolution. PO 22 Aug 1876, PM Samuel D. Terry.

GEORGE (Madison) George R. Donaho established the George PO in his general store 20 Apr 1903.

GEORGE WEST (Live Oak) Livestock breeder and trail driver George Washington West operated a ranch in Live Oak County from the early 1900s. In the early 1910s West donated land for the townsite and the right of way to the San Antonio, Uvalde & Gulf Railroad. PO 14 Nov 1914, PM Chauncy Zachariah Canfield.

GEORGES CREEK (Somervell) Named from Georges Creek, itself named for George Barnard, an Indian trader along the Brazos River in the 1840s and 1850s. PO 21 Aug 1876, PM James Chambers. See Glen Rose.

GEORGETOWN (Williamson) In 1832 George Washington Glasscock was a company commander in the Black Hawk War in Illinois. (Abraham Lincoln was a private in Lieutenant Glasscock's company.) At the end of the war Glasscock moved to Texas where he was instrumental in organizing Williamson County. Glasscock and his business partner, Thomas B. Huling, donated land for the county seat which was named in Glasscock's honor in 1848. PO Nov 1847 as Brushy; changed to Georgetown 27 July 1848, PM Francis M. Nash. See Glasscock County.

GERMANIA [jer MAYN ee uh] (Midland) Founded by the Texas & Pacific Railway in 1883 and named by settlers of German descent. During the First World War, citizens temporarily changed the name to Paul to show their patriotism and to avoid the prejudice directed toward those living in towns with "German" names. PO 21 Jan 1885, PM Frederick Nordheimer. This is one of a dozen Germanias in the US.

GERONIMO [juh RAHN uh mo] (Guadalupe) José Antonio Navarro operated the San Gerónimo Ranch east of San Antonio, named for San Gerónimo (Saint Jerome), the late 4th and early 5th century priest and theologian who translated the Bible into Latin, the "Vulgate." Navarro owned the ranch from about 1824, five years before Geronimo, the Apache leader, was born. PO 20 Nov 1889, PM Edgard Von Boeckmann.

GETHSEMANE (Marion) Probably founded in the late 1860s; named from the Gethsemane United Methodist church, itself likely named from one of 300 Gethsemane churches in the US.

GHOLSON [GOL suhn] (McLennan) Gholson was known as Sardis from the 1840s until 1858 when Thomas J. Rhodes opened the Gholson PO named for brothers Samuel Sullivan and Benjamin Franklin Gholson, and their father, Albert Gholson, who joined Robertson's Colony in the 1830s.

GIBTOWN (Jack) Known as New Hope City until 28 Feb 1883 when Burdett L. Gibbins opened the Gibtown PO in his general store.

GIDDINGS (Lee) Giddings was founded in 1871 with construction of the Houston & Texas Central Railway. Three Giddings brothers have figured in Texas history and all three have some claim to be the namesake of Giddings: Dewitt Clinton Giddings, a Brenham lawyer and construction superintendent of the Washington County H&TC railroad; Giles Albert Giddings, mortally wounded at the Battle of San Jacinto; and Jabez Deming Giddings, a lawyer, stockholder, and director of the H&TC. Of the three, J. D. Giddings, for his association with the H&TC, is the most likely. PO 27 June 1871, PM Gottlieb Pauli.

GILCHRIST [GIL krist] (Galveston) Gibb Gilchrist, a construction engineer for the Santa Fe Railroad, rebuilt the line between Port Bolivar and High Island after the 1915 Galveston hurricane. Gilchrist was president of Texas A&M University in the 1940s. PO 16 Sept 1950, PM Obie Andrews.

GILES [JEYELZ] (Donley) Reportedly named for Giles Flippin, an early stock raiser and a deputy marshal who was killed in a shootout about 1890. PO 9 Nov 1888, PM Glenn Willingham.

GILL (Harrison) PO 14 Apr 1894, PM Miles Stephens who chose the name for a ferryboatman named Gill.

GILLESPIE [guh LES pee] (County) Created and organized 1848. Named for Robert Addison Gillespie (1815–1846), born in Blount County, TN. Gillespie moved to Texas in 1837. He and his brothers James and Matthew became well-to-do merchants and dealers in real estate. Robert Gillespie joined the First Regiment of Texas Mounted Riflemen at the outbreak of the Mexican War and was mortally wounded at the Battle of Monterrey in September 1846.

GILLETT [juh LET] (Karnes) The post office application requested the name Riedelville for local miller and ginner Carl Edward Riedel, but through popular etymology the office was approved as Riddleville, later changed to Gillett for Edwin G. Gillett of Runge. The Ecleto PO was changed to Riddleville 9 June 1871; changed to Gillett 20 Sept 1905, PM Loula Fore. See Ecleto.

GILMER (Upshur) Thomas W. Gilmer, US Secretary of the Navy, was killed in the explosion of an experimental gun on a ship in the Potomac River in late February 1844, the same blast that killed US Secretary of State Abel P. Upshur, the namesake of Upshur County. PO 8 Mar 1847, PM Jonathan Betsell.

GILPIN (Dickens) William Gilpin was a county judge and superintendent of schools of Motley County in the 1890s. He established the Gilpin PO in Motley County 17 May 1892; discontinued 31 Oct 1894. Gilpin opened the Poet PO in Dickens County 13 Nov 1908; changed to Gilpin 1 Jan 1910.

GINGER (Rains) Founded in the 1880s with construction of the Missouri–Kansas–Texas Railroad. Reportedly named for the unusual color of the local clay and the bricks made from it. PO 1 May 1909, PM Walter B. Fraser.

GINSITE (Cottle) Founded in 1901 as Willett, named for the Willett Milling Company of Paducah that produced commercial livestock feeds in the early 1900s. PO 6 May 1901 as Willett; changed to Ginsite for the location of the Willett Cotton Gin 11 Feb 1908, PM Jesse Dulaney.

GIRARD [juh RAHRD] (Kent) In 1909 Swante Magnus Swenson, owner of the Swenson Land and Cattle Company, donated land for a station on the line of the Stamford & Northwestern Railroad. The traditional account is that the namesake is a Swenson Company bookkeeper named Girard, but most likely the community was named for the Girard Trust Company of Philadelphia, founded and named for financier and philanthropist Stephen Girard. Swenson and the Girard Trust were partners in the Spur Ranch on which the town of Girard was sited. PO 24 Dec 1909, PM Ferd Woody. See Spur.

GIRLSTOWN (Cochran) Girlstown originated as a refuge for homeless girls in Buffalo Gap; it moved to its present location in 1939. In 1987 Girlstown merged with Cal Farley's Boys Ranch. See Boys Ranch.

GIRVIN (Pecos) Settlement began in the 1890s but the town did not develop until the Kansas City, Mexico & Orient Railway established a station on John Girvin's ranch in 1912. PO 31 Jan 1913, PM Ezekiel P. Kenney.

GIST [GIST] (Jasper) Site owner and land developer John P. Gist founded the eponymous town in the early 20th century. PO 30 Aug 1912, PM Caddo A. Tomme.

GIVENS (Lamar) Asbury Bunyan Whitten, who kept the area's first general store, chose the name for the family of his wife, Evaline Givens. PO 2 May 1891, PM Marcus L. Russell.

GLADEWATER (Gregg, Upshur) Gladewater grew around a water tank and station established by the Texas & Pacific Railway in 1873 and named from Glade Creek, a stream that ran through a low swampy area known as The Glades. By one local legend a family had found a lovely camping spot and one young lady remarked, "This is a beautiful glade, now if we could only find some water!" By another, a saloon keeper who sold whiskey by the pint began diluting his product with water from Glade Creek, causing at least one customer to complain that he was "sick and tired of paying for that damn glade water." PO 22 Aug 1873, PM John B. Crookston.

GLADYS (Jefferson) Pattillo Higgins, a community promoter and the force behind the Spindletop Oil Field, named the town for Gladys Bingham, reportedly one of his favorite Sunday School students.

GLASSCOCK (County) Created 1887, organized 1893. Named for George Washington Glasscock (1810–1868), born in Kentucky. Glasscock fought in the Black Hawk War in Illinois in 1832, moved to Texas in 1834, and was a soldier in the Texas Revolution. He was instrumental in the formation of Williamson County, donating land for the county seat that was named GEORGETOWN in his honor.

GLEN ROSE (Somervell) Known from about 1850 as Barnard's Mill for the gristmill operated by Charles Barnard, formerly an Indian trader along the Brazos with his brother George, the namesake of GEORGES CREEK. By local tradition the name was changed in 1874 to Rose Glen at the suggestion of Annie Jordan, wife of the new site owner, who claimed that the landscape reminded her of Rose Glen mentioned in stories she had heard of her ancestral Scotland. PO 23 Oct 1871 as Barnard's Mill; changed to Glen Rose 4 May 1874, PM James M. Brown.

GLIDDEN (Colorado) The Galveston, Harrisburg & San Antonio Railway established switching yards, a depot, and a roundhouse at the site in the mid-1880s. The source of the name is uncertain; several accounts credit the name to an F. G. Glidden, identified in local documents as "a railroad engineer." PO 24 Mar 1888, PM John Patterson.

GLOBE (Lamar) Thomas Henry Wheeler opened a general store in what became known as the Wheeler Settlement about 1876. His son, William Alvis Wheeler, opened the Globe PO 9 Mar 1899. He was reportedly inspired by the globe (chimney) on a kerosene lamp.

GOBER [GO ber] (Fannin) George Wisdom Gober and his son James established the first "gritter," a gristmill, in the area in the 1870s. PO 24 Nov 1879, PM James D. Christian.

GODLEY (Johnson) Robby B. Godley, a Cleburne lumber dealer, donated land in 1886 for the right of way and a station on the Gulf, Colorado & Santa Fe Railway in 1886. PO 6 Jan 1888, PM James N. King.

GOFORTH (Hays) James Taylor Goforth established a cotton gin shortly after the end of the Civil War. Goforth was the first PM 16 May 1890.

GOLD (Gillespie) Founded by German settlers from Fredericksburg before 1878 when Willian Grobe established the Rheingold post office. That office was discontinued in 1907 and the Gold office was opened by John Ottens 25 Mar 1908. Gold is a shortening of Rheingold, a choice strongly influenced by the presence of several Gold families.

GOLDEN (Wood) Although settlement began in the 1870s, the community was not organized until 1882 when the Missouri–Kansas–Texas Railroad established a station named for John Golden, a construction engineer. PO 10 Feb 1885, PM Julius C. Lambertson.

GOLDSMITH (Ector) When the Permian Basin oilfields began producing in the 1920s, Ector City, named for the county, grew on the Charles Goldsmith Ranch northwest of Odessa. When the name Ector City was rejected by the Post Office Department, Imogene Dunn resubmitted the application and opened the Goldsmith PO 13 May 1937.

GOLDTHWAITE [GOL thwayt] (Mills) In 1885 the Gulf, Colorado & Santa Fe Railway employed Joseph G. Goldthwaite, a Galveston businessman, to organize the sale of town lots. PO 11 Jan 1887, PM Willis Marshall.

GOLIAD (County) Created 1836, organized 1837. Named from the city of Goliad.

GOLIAD [GOL ee ad] (Goliad) Established as Santa Dorotea about 1750, a Spanish fort and community that became known as *La Bahía del Espíritu Santo* "the Harbor of the Holy Spirit." In the late 1820s Rafael Antonio Manchola, a member of the legislature of the Mexican state of Coahuila and Texas, petitioned his government to change the name to Goliad, an anagram of (H)idalgo, to honor Don Miguel Hidalgo y Costilla, a Catholic priest and a hero of the Mexican War for Independence. By this time *La Bahía del Espíritu Santo* had been shortened to La Bahia and in 1829 La Bahia was changed to Villa de Goliad. PO 14 Feb 1779 as Richmond; changed to Goliad 18 Jan 1847, PM John T. Price.

GOLINDA [guh LIN duh] (Falls, McLennan) Father Ignacio Galindo [*sic*] was granted the site in the early 1830s. PO 16 May 1860 as Golindo, PM Ebenezer Hatch.

GOLLY (DeWitt) Antoine Louis Golly, born in Haut-Rhin, Alsace, France, emigrated to Texas in the 1850s and soon took the name Antonio Golly.

GOMEZ (Terry) Gomez is generally considered the first settlement in Terry County, surveyed in 1902 by Joseph Blankenship who was also the first Terry postmaster in February 1903. Apparently the name of the office was proposed by the Post Office Department in honor of Máximo Gómez y Báez, a military commander and hero of Cuba's War for Independence that evolved into the Spanish-American War of 1898.

GONZALES (County) Created 1836, organized 1837. Named from the city of Gonzales.

GONZALES (Gonzales) In 1825 Gonzales was the capital of Empresario Green DeWitt's Colony and named for Rafael Gonzales (1789–1857), governor of the Mexican state of Coahuila and Texas from its creation in 1824 until 1826. PO 22 May 1846, PM Benjamin B. Peck.

GOOBER HILL (Shelby) Little is known of the origin of this tiny community except that it was named for goobers or ground peas, the peanuts that were once associated with the area.

GOOD HOPE (Lavaca) The origin of this optimistic name is uncertain; it may have been taken from the Good Hope Missionary Baptist Church established in the 1870s.

GOODLETT [GUD lit] (Hardeman) Named for James Booth Goodlett, a QUANAH rancher and banker, and Quanah PM in 1918. PO 20 May 1889 as Gypsum, named for the local mineral; changed to Goodlett 6 Apr 1909, PM Charles S. Shires.

GOODLOW (Navarro) Named for Harry Goodlow who began farming in the area about 1880.

GOODNIGHT (Armstrong) Charles Goodnight, often called the Father of the Texas Panhandle, was born in Illinois and brought to Texas as a child in 1845. He and Oliver Loving drove cattle along the route that became known as the Goodnight-Loving Trail from Texas through what is now New Mexico and Colorado to rangeland in Wyoming. In 1877 Goodnight and his business partner, Englishman John Adair, founded the JA Ranch that grew to more than a million acres by the mid-1880s. PO 19 Nov 1888, PM Sam Dyer. Goodnight himself was postmaster in the 1890s. See Loving.

GOODNIGHT (Navarro) Probably named for landowners John J. and Millie Goodnight who came to the area from Kentucky in the 1890s.

GOODRICH (Polk) About 1880 the Houston East & West Texas Railway established a station named for site owner William M. Goodrich. PO 12 Apr 1882, PM Warren J. Foyles.

GORDONVILLE (Grayson) Silas Gordon was a "bushwacker," a Confederate guerrilla fighter, in Missouri during the Civil War and was probably associated with Quantrill's Raiders in Texas. After the war Gordon lived near present Gordonville. PO 7 Aug 1876, PM George W. Crump.

GOREE [GOR ee] (Knox) Robert D. Goree was a promoter of Knox County and instrumental in establishing several settlements in the area. PO 2 June 1888, PM George Benedict.

GORMAN (Eastland) The community of Shinoak was renamed for Patrick A. Gorman, general manager of the Waco & Northwestern Railroad, and roadmaster of the Texas Central. PO 24 Oct 1888 as Shinoak; changed to Gorman 18 Jan 1890, PM Hughes O. Thomas.

GOSHEN (Parker) Named from the Goshen Meetinghouse, itself named from the Biblical Goshen, the land of rich soil and bountiful crops. The church was one of several founded in the 1850s by pioneer Methodist minister Pleasant Tackitt, known as the "Fighting Parson" for his battles with Texas Indians.

GOUGH (Delta) Named for one or more Gough families, perhaps that of Rio Lycurgus Gough, a minister of the Christian Church who emigrated from Kentucky to Lamar County in the mid-1850s. PO 29 May 1888, PM John Bailey.

GOULD (Cherokee) Founded in the late 1870s as a station on the International–Great Northern Railroad. Probably named for financier Jay Gould, one of the richest men in America at the time. Gould invested heavily in a number of Texas railroads including the I–GN. PO 9 Feb 1905, PM Richard Yancey.

GOULDBUSK [GOOLD buhsk] (Coleman) Founded in the early 1900s by Horace Starkweather, president of the Farmers State Bank of Coleman, acting as agent for William Gould Busk, a British entrepreneur who had purchased the property in the 1880s. PO 19 Dec 1905, PM Thomas Smith.

GRACETON (Upshur) When the Marshall & East Texas Railway built through the area about 1909 the station was named from the Graceton Church, itself named for Grace Simpson, 10-year-old daughter of district judge Robert P. Simpson of Gilmer. PO 24 Mar 1882 as Diana; changed to Graceton 20 Feb 1909, PM Edgar M. Mattox.

GRAFORD [GRAY ferd] (Palo Pinto) Graford was named for its location midway between *Gra*ham and Weather*ford* (leaning toward Graham). PO 17 Aug 1894, PM Willis S. Green.

GRAHAM (Young) Brothers Edwin Smith and Gustavus Adolphus Graham emigrated from Louisville, KY, shortly after the Civil War. The Grahams held title to more than 100,000 acres of Young County, part of which was surveyed by Gustavus Graham and in 1872 became the town of Graham and the Young County seat two years later. PO 30 Sept 1873, PM Julius H. Wilson.

GRANBURY [GRAN behr ee] (Hood) In 1858 brothers Jacob and Jesse Nutt came to Texas from Bradford County, TN. In 1866 they donated forty acres along the Brazos River for the townsite named for Hiram Bronson Granbury, a Civil War hero from Waco who was killed in action at the Battle of Franklin, TN, in 1864. (His military records spelled his name Granberry, the usual spelling of the town name until the mid-1870s when the PO spelling Granbury was adopted.) The original home of the Nutt brothers is the site of the present Nutt House Hotel, established about 1880 by a third brother, David Nutt. PO 15 June 1869, PM Calaway Landers.

GRAND PRAIRIE (Dallas, Tarrant) Known as Deckman (or Dechman) from the early 1860s when the site was bought by Alexander McRae Deckman from Halifax, Nova Scotia. The name Grand Prairie invites inventive speculation. By one romantic account, a gentlelady on her way to Dallas paused at the Texas & Pacific station, marveled at the scene around her and exclaimed "My, what a grand prairie." PO 27 Oct 1874 as Deckman; changed to Grand Prairie 13 Aug 1877, PM William M. Haskett.

GRAND SALINE (Van Zandt) About 1840 John Jordan began to harvest the salt deposits on Saline Prairie and the area became known as Jordan's Saline. That name lasted until 1873 when the Grand Saline station was established by the Texas & Pacific Railway. PO 17 May 1849 as Jordans Saline; discontinued 23 Jan 1872; reestablished 19 Feb 1874 as Grand Saline, PM Samuel Q. Richardson.

GRANDFALLS (Ward) Named for the upper falls, the "grand falls" of the Pecos River. PO 10 May 1897, PM James G. Baker.

GRANGERLAND (Montgomery) Founded in the early 1900s by Edwin Granger, an "electropathic physician" from Chicago. Shortly after the Conroe Oilfield began producing in the early 1930s, Edwin Granger's son, Don, created the community to provide housing for oilfield workers.

GRANJENO [gran JEE no] (Hidalgo) Settled from about 1870; named for *granjeño* (*Celtis pallida*), the spiny shrub (desert hackberry), that grows in the area.

GRAPELAND (Houston) Founded as Grapevine in 1872 with construction of the Houston & Great Northern Railroad, named from the wild grapevines along the railroad right of way. The name was changed 26 May 1873 when Thomas Beasly opened the Grapeland PO.

GRAPETOWN (Gillespie) Settled in the 1850s and named from South Grape Creek. PO 11 Nov 1885, PM Wilhelm Hohenberger.

GRAPEVINE (Tarrant) Organized about 1855 when merchant Archibald Leonard proposed the name Leonardville and his brother-in-law Henry Suggs proposed Suggsville. Each agreed to abide the decision of notary James Moorehead, who satisfied (or frustrated) both parties by choosing the name Grapevine Springs. PO 4 Aug 1858 as Grape Vine; changed to Grapevine 12 Jan 1914, PM Minerva Austin Hendrickson.

GRAY (County) Created 1876, organized 1902. Named for Peter W Gray (1819–1874), born in Virginia. Gray came to Texas in 1838 and studied law under his father. He was appointed district attorney by Sam Houston, was a member of the first Republic of Texas Legislature, a founder of the Houston Public Library, and a justice of the Texas Supreme Court in 1874. (The "W" in Peter W Gray stands alone and abbreviates no name.)

GRAYBACK (Wilbarger) Probably named for "graybacks," the body lice that were the bane of cowboy camps. The name was likely brought to the area by Civil War veterans for whom lice were a part of army life. The lice were called "graybacks" by Union soldiers and "bluebellies" by Confederates.

GRAYBURG (Hardin) The Thompson-Ford Lumber Company founded Grayburg about 1907, so named "because all of the buildings in the town will be painted gray." PO 2 Mar 1909, PM Frederick L. Thompson.

GRAYSON (County) Created and organized 1846. Named for Peter Wagener Grayson (1788–1838), born in Virginia. About 1830 Grayson brought a number of his family's slaves from Kentucky to Matagorda where he became a planter, attorney, and poet. Grayson was an advisor to Stephen F. Austin and Austin's aide-de-camp in the 1830s, Attorney General of the Republic of Texas under President Sam Houston, and special envoy to the US in 1837 to argue for Texas statehood.

GRAYTOWN (Wilson) Founded by James W. Gray from Edinburgh, Scotland, who fought at San Jacinto in 1836. Gray married Simona Fernández Seguín and Graytown was built upon her inheritance. PO 6 Aug 1861, PM James W. Gray.

GREEN (Karnes) Founded about 1900 as Pullin, probably named for landowner Hiram Pullin. In 1907 William Green, a partner in the construction firm of Green and Welhausen of Yoakum, laid out the town that he named for himself. PO 19 Oct 1907, PM Amry Starr Barbee.

GREEN HILL (Titus) Probably named for Edward Hollister Green who reportedly founded the first Presbyterian church in the area about 1860. PO 22 Jan 1857, PM William S. Coffey.

GREENOCK (Bosque) Perhaps a transfer from Greenock on the western coast of Scotland, but more likely from Greenock,

Crittenden County, AR, itself named for Greenock, Scotland. PO 17 Jan 1882, PM Susan Green.

GREENVILLE (Hunt) When Hunt County was created in 1846 there was some sentiment for naming the seat Pinckneyville in honor of the sitting Texas Governor, James Pinckney Henderson, but Henderson apparently suggested the name of his friend, Thomas Jefferson Green. PO 8 Mar 1847, PM Samuel C. Hooker. See Tom Green County.

GREGG (County) Created and organized 1873. Named for John Gregg (1828–1864), born in Alabama. Gregg was a Freestone County newspaper publisher, lawyer, and district judge in the 1850s. In the summer of 1861 he recruited, organized, and led the Seventh Texas Infantry in several Civil War engagements. He was killed in action at New Market Road in Virginia in October 1864.

GREGGTON (Gregg) Founded as Willow Springs with construction of the Texas & Pacific Railway in the early 1870s. The town was renamed for Gregg County when Richard Hall established the PO 10 Feb 1933. Greggton is now part of Longview.

GREGORY (San Patricio) Founded about 1887 when the Coleman-Fulton Pasture Company donated a thousand acres for a townsite and for cattle pens along the San Antonio & Aransas Pass Railway. Named for Thomas Watt Gregory, an Austin lawyer, promoter of the University of Texas, and US Attorney General in the 1910s. PO 17 July 1893, PM Cecil F. Williams.

GRESHAM [GRESH uhm] (Smith) Named with construction of the St. Louis Southwestern Railway (Cotton Belt) in the 1870s and probably named for Walter Gresham, chief attorney for the railroad.

GRICE (Upshur) John Jefferson Grice, born in Georgia, moved to Upshur County at the end of the Civil War and established the first general store, in which he opened the Grice post office in 22 Apr 1890. Formerly known as Hamil's Chapel.

GRIFFIN (Cherokee) Founded in 1853 by Isaac Kendrick, son of the first site owner, also Isaac Kendrick. Reddick Jennings, the first schoolteacher, was offered the job of postmaster reportedly because he was one of the few people in the area who could read and write. Jennings established the office 15 Apr 1853 as Troutman, perhaps named for Troutman, GA, in Jennings's home state. The name was changed 27 Dec 1855 for Griffin, GA, the Kendricks's former home.

GRIFFITH (Cochran) In 1934 Cochran County land agent Henry D. Chipley founded Oasis, a hopeful name suggesting a garden in the desert. The name was changed in 1950 for Karl Griffith, a founder of the First Bank of Morton.

GRIMES (County) Created and organized 1846. Named for soldier and politician Jesse Grimes (1788–1866), born in North Carolina. Grimes came to Texas from Alabama in 1826 as part of Stephen F. Austin's Second Colony. Grimes signed the Texas Declaration of Independence and served in five of the nine congresses of the Republic of Texas and the first four legislatures of the State of Texas.

GRIT (Mason) John Warren Hunter, editor of the *Moran Herald*, is credited with choosing the name, reportedly for the gritty nature of the soil. PO 29 June 1901, PM Loyd Sanders.

GROESBECK [GROZ bek] (Limestone) Founded in 1870 when the Houston & Texas Central Railway extended a line from Kosse. Named for Abraham (Abram) Groesbeek [*sic*] of Houston, a director of the H&TC. PO 12 Apr 1871, PM James N. Bartholow.

GROOM (Carson) In the 1880s Benjamin B. Groom, a noted Kentucky cattle breeder, relocated to the Texas Panhandle and began purchasing land for the Francklyn Land and Cattle Company, an English syndicate headed by Charles G. Francklyn. In 1902 the town of Groom was founded on the line of the Chicago, Rock Island & Gulf Railway. PO 4 June 1902, PM Thornton Dysart.

GROSVENOR [GROS vuhn er] (Brown) Probably named for Charles Henry Grosvenor, a multi-term US Representative from Ohio. The name may have been chosen by Efram E. McClain, a fellow Ohioan when Grosvenor was at the height of his political career. Though Grosvenor was a Union Army officer in the Civil War and few Union soldiers are remembered in Southern place names, the passing of years and the fact that Grosvenor would have been unknown to many settlers in Brown County would have made the name acceptable. PO 11 May 1900, PM Efram E. McClain.

GROVES (Jefferson) Founded as Pecan Grove about 1915. The name was modified to Groves when the community was organized by the Port Arthur Land and Development Company in the late 1910s. PO 4 Nov 1929, PM William R. Burt.

GROVETON (Trinity) William Peters, a director of the Trinity County and Sabine Pass Land and Railway Company, laid out the townsite in 1881. Peters asked for naming suggestions and "Grandfather" Cox reportedly looked out at a grove of impressive Black Jack oaks and said no better name could be found than Grovetown, subsequently recorded as Groveton. PO 18 Dec 1882, PM John P. Backshear.

GRUENAU (DeWitt) Probably named by settlers from Grünau, Germany, southeast of Berlin. German for "green field."

GRUENE [GREEN] (Comal) When the International–Great Northern Railroad built through the area in the 1880s the station was named for Heinrich (Henry) Gruene who kept a general store, established a school, and managed a dance hall. PO 6 June 1890 as Goodwin, PM Henry D. Gruene; discontinued 31 Mar 1904.

GRUVER (Hansford) About 1907 Joseph Hezkiah and Adeline Gruver established a ranch several miles west of the present town that was named in their honor when Blanche Jones opened the Gruver PO 19 Oct 1927.

GUADALUPE (County) In 1842 the Congress of the Republic of Texas created Guadalupe County but never authorized its organization. In 1846 the legislature recreated and organized Guadalupe County, named from the Guadalupe River, itself named in the 1680s by the Alonso de León Expedition, *Nuestra Señora de Guadalupe* "Our Lady of Guadalupe," in honor of the Virgin Mary who had appeared in a vision to a Mexican peasant in the 1530s.

GUDA (Falls) Named for one or more of the Guderian families who emigrated from Germany to Texas about 1870. PO 28 Apr 1891 as Gurley; changed to Guda, a shortening of Guderian, 28 Feb 1912, PM Gus J. Guderian.

GUERRA [GWEHR uh] (Jim Hogg) Reportedly named for landowner Antonio Guerra. PO 30 Apr 1906, PM Joseph J. Lodovic.

GUFFEY (Jefferson) Founded in 1901 shortly after drilling began in the nearby Spindletop Oil Field. Named for James M. Guffey of Pittsburgh who organized oilfields in Pennsylvania and financed oil exploration in Texas. Guffey was a primary organizer of the Gulf Oil Corporation in the 1900s. PO 28 June 1901, PM Bertie J. VanVleck.

GUN BARREL CITY (Henderson) When the Cedar Creek reservoir was constructed in the 1960s the community took the name of Texas Highway 198, known as Gun Barrel Lane, straight as a gun barrel (almost) between MABANK and PAYNE SPRING. The city's slogan: "We Shoot Straight With You."

GUNSIGHT (Stephens) The source of the name is unknown but, as we might expect, it has generated a number of popular etymologies. By one, a slot in a nearby hill resembles a rifle's peep sight; by another a ridge in a range of nearby hills is as straight as a gun barrel; and by still another a peak at the end of the ridge resembles a gunsight. PO 31 Mar 1880, PM John W. Shephard.

GUNTER (Grayson) Named for cattleman, lawyer, and businessman John "Jot" Gunter who donated land for the townsite when the St. Louis, San Francisco & Texas Railway established a station. PO 24 May 1898, PM Charles Holman.

GUSTINE [GUHS teen] (Comanche) Named from the PO established 6 Jan 1888 by merchant Samuel Gustine.

GUTHRIE (King) The namesake is generally taken to be a W. H. Guthrie, investor and part owner of the Louisville Land and Cattle Company that purchased the townsite and several hundred surrounding acres in the early 1880s. More likely, however, Andrew Tackett, who platted the townsite in 1891, chose the name for David P. Guthrie, a Cincinnati lawyer, officer of the Chesapeake & Ohio Railway in Covington, KY, and an investor in the Louisville Land and Cattle Company. PO 25 Sept 1891, PM John Frazier.

GUY (Fort Bend) Named from the Guy PO opened by Orr Rowland 31 May 1898. Rowland named the office for his daughter, Una Guy Rowland.

H

HACKBERRY (Cottle) About 1918 William Q. Richards, owner of the 3D and Moon Ranches, sold the townsite to William Moss and Walter Liedkte who laid out the community named for a cluster of hackberry trees on the Little Wichita River. PO 4 Mar 1925 as Stewart, named PM George B. Stewart.

HACKBERRY (Edwards) Named from the Hackberry Store opened in the early 20th century, and itself named from Hackberry Creek. PO 7 Jan 1914, PM Joseph Mathews; discontinued 30 Sept 1931.

HACKBERRY (Lavaca) Named for several large hackberry trees in the front yard of Ludwig Eduard Neuhaus, a German immigrant who opened the area's first steam sawmill-gristmill in the early 1850s and was the first PM 4 July 1862.

HAGERVILLE [HAY ger vil] (Houston) Farmer and blacksmith James W. Hager and his wife Naoma settled in the area in the 1840s. Their son, James Polk Hager, was the first PM 21 Sept 1891.

HAIL (Fannin) Hail was founded about 1850 as Clarksville, named for early settlers Elijah and Nancy Clark. According to local sources, when Clarksville was rejected as a name for the PO, several names were written on slips of paper, tossed into a hat, and Elijah Clark picked Hail, reportedly suggested for a recent, especially damaging hail storm. PO 28 Apr 1894, PM James T. Clark.

HAINESVILLE (Wood) First known as DuPree for William J. DuPree who established a medical practice in the 1850s. Christian Haines built a gristmill and opened a general store on Mill Race Creek in the 1860s. PO 25 June 1892 as DuPree; changed to Hainesville 31 July 1893, PM William J. Bankston.

HALE (County) Created 1876, organized 1888. Named for Virginian John C. Hale (1806–1836), about whom little is known. Hale, a lieutenant in the Second Regiment Texas Volunteers, died in action at the Battle of San Jacinto in April 1836.

HALE CENTER (Hale) Founded north of Epworth in 1891 as Hale City. After the great grasshopper plague of 1892 many people left Hale City and Epworth. Those who remained moved to a site between the two towns that they called Hale Center. PO 3 June 1884 as Epworth; changed to Hale City 16 Apr 1891; changed to Hale Center 19 Sept 1893.

HALFWAY (Hale) Halfway was so named because it was taken to be equidistant between Olton at the western edge of Hale County and the county seat at Plainview. PO 4 May 1910, PM Edgar Howard.

HALL (County) Created 1876, organized 1890. Named for Warren DeWitt Clinton Hall (1794–1867), born in South Carolina. A soldier, lawyer, and Texas pioneer, Hall served as an officer in the Mexican Army, fought with the Americans in the War of 1812, was Adjutant General during the Texas Revolution, and acting Secretary of War for the Republic of Texas.

HALL (San Saba) The Hall Ranch was established in the mid-1850s by John Mabin Hall and operated by his sons Nathan, James, and William. The community was formally named for the Hall family when the Gulf, Colorado & Santa Fe Railway established Hall Station. PO 14 Sept 1911, PM William Hudson.

HALLETTSVILLE (Lavaca) John Hallett, an English merchant seaman who received a land grant from Stephen F. Austin in 1831 and donated land for the townsite about 1838. PO 26 Feb 1849, PM Colatinus Ballard.

HALLSBURG (McLennan) Waco physician William E. Hall donated part of his ranch for a townsite when the International–Great Northern Railroad established a station in 1902.

HALLSVILLE (Harrison) Probably named for Elijah Hall, a surveyor for the Southern Pacific Railroad. PO 17 Dec 1849 as Ash Spring; changed to Hallsville 29 Nov 1869, PM Wilford Ferrell.

HALTOM CITY [HAWL tuhm] (Tarrant) Founded in 1932. Named for George W. Haltom, a public benefactor who moved his jewelry store from Bowie to Fort Worth in the early 20th century.

HAMBY (Taylor) The counties of Callahan, Jones, Shackelford, and Taylor meet at Hamby, giving the community its first name, Corners. PO 3 Mar 1902, PM general store owner Hamby W. Richardson.

HAMILTON (County) Created and organized 1858. Named for James Hamilton (1786–1857). Hamilton represented South Carolina in the US Congress in the 1820s and was Governor of South Carolina in the 1830s. His greatest service to Texas was securing a substantial loan from the US for the Republic of Texas.

HAMILTON (Hamilton) Founded in 1858, named from the county and made the county seat. PO 22 Sept 1859 as Hampton; changed to Hamilton 9 Dec 1874, PM Thomas D. Neel.

HAMLIN (Jones, Fisher) Hamlin was founded about 1906 with construction of the Kansas City, Mexico & Orient Railway and named for Hamlin Stilwell, a builder of the Erie Canal, a founder of Western Union Telegraph, and the grandfather of Arthur Stillwel, founder of the KCM&O and the namesake of PORT ARTHUR. PO 19 Dec 1904, PM Barton Burnham.

HAMMOND (Robertson) Benjamin F. Hammond, a planter from Alabama, brought some 100 slaves to his new plantation on the Brazos River in the early 1850s. PO 5 July 1870, PM Robert Furniss Martin.

HAMON [HAY muhn] (Gonzales) In the 1850s, Abraham Obediah Hamon relocated from Tennessee and opened a general store at South Riverside. The South Riverside PO was discontinued in 1881; reopened 20 May 1884, PM Abraham Hamon.

HAMSHIRE (Jefferson) Named for farmer, stock raiser, and land developer Lovan Hamshire (whose name is often misreported as Hampshire). Born and raised in Calcasieu Parish, LA, Hamshire emigrated to what was then known as the Taylor Bayou Settlement in the 1860s. PO 16 Sept 1897, PM John E. Caruthers.

HANCOCK (Comal) Reportedly named for John Hancock, an early settler who received a land grant about 1850. PO 15 Oct 1914, PM Theodore Heise.

HANDLEY [HAN lee] (Tarrant) Handley was founded about 1880 with construction of the Texas & Pacific Railway on the plantation established by Confederate Army officer James Madison Handley. Fort Worth annexed Handley in 1946. PO 10 July 1876, PM Cheatle C. Wood.

HANKAMER (Chambers) Named for Johann Wilhelm (John William) Hankamer who emigrated from Prussia in 1845. Hankamer was a farmer, local official, and justice of the peace. Ira Hankamer, son of John and Lurenda Hankamer, opened the PO in his general store 24 May 1904.

HANOVER (Milam) Edward Coleman Orthofer emigrated from Hanover, Germany, in 1873. He proposed the name for the Hanover PO, opened by Junius Gregory 17 Jan 1890. Orthofer followed Gregory as PM in 1891.

HANSFORD (County) Created 1876, organized 1889. Named for jurist and politician John M. Hansford who relocated from Glasgow, KY, to Texas in 1837. Hansford represented Shelby County in the Third and Fourth Congresses of the Republic of Texas in the late 1830s. He was shot and killed by a mob during disturbances in East Texas in 1844.

HANSFORD (Hansford) The town of Hansford, named from the county and now a ghost town, was founded by James Wright and Fred Bonfill in 1887. PO 26 Aug 1887 as Hansford; discontinued 31 Mar 1920.

HAPPY (Randall, Swisher) Happy, "the town without a frown," takes its name from Happy Draw, said to be named by thirsty cowboys who were happy to find fresh water after a long cattle drive. PO 14 Mar 1891, PM David Currie.

HAPPY UNION (Hale) Named from the Happy Union Baptist Church, founded about 1900. The church was reportedly named from the harmony that existed between church and community.

HARBIN (Erath) Probably named for Young and Sarah Harbin who began farming in the area in the 1870s. PO 1 Oct 1890 as Bishop; changed to Harbin 3 June 1892, PM John M. Harbin.

HARDEMAN (County) Created 1858, recreated 1876, organized 1884. Named for brothers Thomas Jones and Blackstone Hardeman (Hardiman) who emigrated from Hardeman County, TN, in 1835. (Hardeman County, TN, was named for Thomas Jones Hardeman in 1823 in recognition of his service in the War of 1812.)

HARDIN (County) Created and organized 1858. Named for the Hardin family of Liberty, William Hardin being the most well-known. After a murder indictment in Tennessee Hardin relocated to Texas in the mid-1820s. He developed an extensive plantation and became alcalde of Anahuac and later of Liberty.

HARDIN (Hardin) Founded as the seat of Hardin County in 1858. The town began its decline when it was bypassed by the Sabine & East Texas Railway in the 1880s and the county seat was moved to Kountze. PO 31 May 1860, PM John J. Dollard.

HARDY (Montague) Ruben Hardy established a sawmill, gristmill, and cotton gin about 1877. Several years later Hardy founded Ardmore, OK. PO 20 Dec 1880, PM Reuben Hardy.

HARE (Williamson) Local lore claims that the town was named Hare because of the abundance of cottontail rabbits. This explanation was the basis for the community nickname, "Fuzzy." More likely the name is for one or more Hare families. PO 14 Apr 1900, PM Charles W. McKinney.

HARGILL (Hidalgo) Hargill was founded in the 1910s by William Apsey *Har*ding and lawyer Samuel Lamar *Gill*. Harding and Gill also founded the town of LASARA in Willacy County, named for their wives, Laura Harding and Sarah Gill. PO 20 Apr 1915 as Filigonio, named for landowner Filigonio Cuellar; changed to Hargill 1 Sept 1926, PM Claude L. Pollock.

HARKER HEIGHTS (Bell) In the late 1950s property owners Harley Kern and Pinckney Cox combined their land holdings and laid out a community that was formally named in 1960 for *Har*ley *Ker*n. Harker Heights is now a Killeen suburb.

HARKEYVILLE (San Saba) Named for Mathias and Catherine Harkey who began farming in the area in the mid-1850s.

HARLETON (Harrison) In the early 1890s the Paris, Marshall & Sabine Pass Railway established Harleton Station, named for brothers Robert H. and James W. Harle, organizers and operators of the Hope Lumber Company. PO 28 Apr 1891 as Fontana; changed to Harleton 17 Nov 1892, PM John M. Miller.

HARLINGEN [HAR lin juhn] (Cameron) Harlingen, known in its early years as "Six Shooter Junction," was laid out in 1904 by Leonidas C. (Lon) Hill, Sr. and Uriah Lott and named for Lott's ancestral homes, Harlingen in the northern Netherlands and Harlingen in Somerset County, NJ. PO 24 June 1904, PM James Lockhart. See Lott.

HARMON (Lamar) Warner and Mirah Harrell moved to the area from North Carolina in the 1840s. Warner Harrell probably chose the name for his father, Harmon Harrell. PO 15 Jan 1900, PM Benjamin Drummond.

HARMONY (Anderson) Named from the Harmony Missionary Baptist Church established in 1891.

HARMONY (Hopkins) Local lore claims the name was appropriate because the townspeople lived in harmony with their neighbors.

HARMONY (Karnes) Probably named from the Harmony Baptist Church whose congregation formed in the mid-1860s and built its first church in the mid-1870s.

HARMONY (Kent) The local story is that the town was so named after disagreements between families were peaceably resolved.

HARPER (Gillespie) Founded about 1850 by George Franklin Harper from Sangamon

County, IL. Harper established the PO 21 Nov 1883 and was a Gillespie County commissioner in the 1890s.

HARPERSVILLE (Stephens) Named for James and Mary Harper, from Hart County, KY, who established a farm and ranch in the late 1870s. PO 16 Apr 1894, PM Thomas McLachlan.

HARRIET (Tom Green) Charles P. Lovelace opened the PO 27 Aug 1909, named for Harriett [*sic*] Malone, teenage daughter of James Malone, a San Angelo banker.

HARRIS (County) Created 1836, organized 1837. Named for John Richardson Harris (1790–1829), born in upstate New York. Harris was living in Missouri in the early 1820s when he met Moses Austin, who convinced him to move to Texas.

HARRISBURG (Harris) In 1826 John Richardson Harris laid out the town of Harrisburg(h), named for the Harris family with a nod to Harrisburg, PA, which was founded by his grandfather, John Harris, Jr., in 1785. PO c. 1836 as Harrisburgh; changed to Harrisburg 15 Nov 1892. Harrisburg is now part of Houston.

HARRISON (County) Created 1839; organized 1842. Named for Jonas Harrison (1777–1836), born in New Jersey. Harrison was a customs official in New York when he was bankrupted by the panic of 1819. He moved to Texas and became a lawyer and local official in the Nacogdoches area in the 1820s.

HARRISON (McLennan) Harrison, also known as Harrison's Switch, was founded on James Harrison's plantation in 1872 with construction of the Houston & Texas Central Railway. PO 28 Apr 1879, PM James W. Moore.

HARROLD (Wilbarger) Known informally as Cottonwood, the name was formalized as Harrold for Ephraim Harrold, an owner of the Bar-X Ranch when the Fort Worth & Denver City Railway built through the area in the mid-1880s. PO 10 July 1885, PM Raymond Starr.

HART (Castro) Tivis Winfield Hart, farmer and stock raiser, moved to Texas from Kentucky in the 1890s. He was the first PM 31 May 1900.

HARTBURG (Newton) John T. Hart, an Orange attorney, was instrumental in securing the Hartburg PO, opened 4 Dec 1896 by William B. Ellis.

HARTLEY (County) Created 1876, organized 1891. Named for brothers Oliver C. (1823–1859) and Rufus K. Hartley (1825–1871), distinguished Texas jurists and legislators. Oliver Hartley served in the Texas House in the early 1850s and Rufus Hartley served in both the House and Senate in the 1860s.

HARTLEY (Hartley) Founded in the late 1880s with construction of the Fort Worth & Denver City Railway and named for the county. PO 9 Apr 1888, PM W. W. Latham.

HARVARD (Camp) The name may have been proposed by Henry Goldmark, an 1878 Harvard graduate who was instrumental in attracting the Texas & St. Louis Railway in the early 1880s.

HARVEY (Brazos) Named about 1880 for Harvey Mitchell, a hotelier, shopkeeper, and town promoter. PO 31 July 1886, PM James W. Barron. Also known as Bethel, named from the Bethel Church.

HARWELL POINT (Burnet) Harwell's [*sic*] Point on the Colorado River was named for James Seaborn Harwell, who began farming in the area in the 1850s. Now a Kingsland neighborhood.

HARWOOD (Gonzales) The Galveston, Harrisburg & San Antonio Railway station was named for Thomas Moore Harwood, a Gonzales lawyer and close friend of Thomas Wentworth Peirce, part owner of the GH&SA. PO 13 Nov 1872 as Mule Creek; changed to Harwood 26 Aug 1874, PM William A. Hodges.

HASKELL (County) Created 1858, re-created 1876, organized 1885. Named for Charles Ready Haskell (1817–1836), born in Nashville, TN. Haskell came to Texas with a company of Tennessee volunteers in 1835 and lost his life at age 19 in the 1836 Goliad Massacre.

HASKELL (Haskell) Settlement at Willow Pond Springs began about 1880. The community was named for Haskell County shortly after the county was first created in 1858. PO 31 Mar 1884, PM Rebecca A. Standefer.

HASLAM [HAZ luhm] (Shelby) Named for Lee F. Haslet, general superintendent of the William R. Pickering Lumber Company of Springfield, MO, that founded Haslam in 1912. PO 30 Dec 1914, PM John Thorn.

HASLET [HAS lit] (Tarrant) Reportedly named for Haslett [*sic*], MI, the former home of a contractor for the Gulf, Colorado & Santa Fe Railway. PO 26 Apr 1887, PM Frank Moore.

HASSE [HAH see] (Comanche) About 1890 the Fort Worth & Rio Grande Railway established the Cordwood Junction siding; renamed for Otto H. Hasse, station agent for the FW&RG. John Hardin, the first PM 12 Apr 1900, suggested Hasse's name.

HATCHEL (Runnels) Known from the 1880s as Vogelsang for farmers Otto and Helena Vogelsang. Renamed when Elijah W. Hatchel opened the PO 21 Apr 1904.

HATCHETTVILLE (Hopkins) Named for landowner and merchant Edward L. Hatchett who opened a general store about 1908.

HAVANA (Hidalgo) The name dates from the 1760s when José Matías Tijerina named his land grant for Havana, Cuba. PO 18 Feb 1886, PM Andres Salinas.

HAWKINS (Wood) Founded in 1873 when the Texas & Pacific Railway established Hawkins Station. The local account is that a member of the surveying crew named Hawkins carved his name on a tree, which travelers took to be the station's name. The T&P employed several surveyors named Hawkins; one in particular, A. D. Hawkins, is reported to have surveyed several of the T&P lines in Arkansas and Texas. PO 22 Aug 1873, PM James H. Sullivan.

HAWKINSVILLE (Matagorda) In the 1840s James Boyd Hawkins brought his family and slaves to Caney Creek and established a cotton and sugarcane plantation. The station on the New York, Texas & Mexican Railway was named for the Hawkins plantation in 1903. PO 23 Feb 1876, PM Edgar Hawkins.

HAWLEY (Jones) Fletcher Scott surveyed the site for the Wichita Valley Railway in 1906 and suggested the name for Edward Hawley of New York, a member of the first board of directors of the WV in 1905. PO 2 May 1903 as Zelo; changed to Hawley 23 Jan 1907, PM Dollie R. Cooper.

HAWTHORNE (Walker) Presumably named for the local hawthorn bushes. PO 16 June 1902, PM Payton Daniel.

HAYMOND (Brewster) Creed Haymond was general solicitor for the Central Pacific Railroad in the 1880s. PO 30 Oct 1883 as McLeary; changed to Haymond 23 Oct 1884, PM Charles W. Brown.

HAYNESVILLE (Wichita) Henry H. Haynes moved to Texas from Kentucky in the early 1900s. Haynes kept a general store and served several terms as Wichita County commissioner. Haynesville was also known as Mount Carmel and Punkin Center.

HAYS (County) Created and organized 1843. Named for legendary Texas Ranger John (Jack) Coffee Hays (1817–1883). A native of Tennessee and a surveyor by training, Hays came to Texas in 1836, developed the image of the Texas Rangers as an independent, irregular force, and distinguished himself in the Mexican War. He spent his later years in California where he was a founder and promoter of the city of Oakland and the first elected sheriff of San Francisco in 1850.

HAYS (Hays) Founded in 1908 as the future seat of Hays County. When San Marcos remained the county seat, Hays began its decline. Also known as Hays City.

HEARNE [HERN] (Robertson) In the early 1850s, Christopher Columbus Hearne brought several generations of Hearneses and several generations of slaves from Alabama and Louisiana and established a plantation on some ten thousand acres along the Brazos River. The Houston & Texas Central Railway established Hearne Station in 1868 on land donated by C. C. Hearne.

HEATH [HEETH] (Rockwall) Named for John Oswell Heath, Kaufman County deputy sheriff in the early 1850s and PM of the Rockwall PO in the late 1880s. PO 27 Apr 1886, PM Thomas B. Owens.

HEBBRONVILLE [HEB ruhn vil] (Jim Hogg) Founded by the Texas Mexican Railway in the early 1880s. When Francisco Peña refused to sell land for the townsite, the railroad bought acreage from James R. Hebbron, an Englishman who had spent much of his life as a California miner before becoming a Texas rancher about 1878. PO 24 May 1882 as Peña Station, named for Francisco Peña; changed to Hebbronville 12 Feb 1895, PM Andrew J. McGovern.

HECKVILLE (Lubbock) Named for Henry and Grace Heck who built a cotton gin and grain elevators about 1948. Henry was the grandson of German immigrant John Hecht.

HEDLEY (Donley) Merchant Alfred Rowe established the RO Ranch in the late 1870s and founded the town of Rowe on the line of the Fort Worth & Denver City Railway a decade later. In the early 20th century James E. M. Hedley, a hotelier from Indiana, persuaded the railroad to relocate its tracks a mile southeast of Rowe to his new town of Hedley. Buildings were moved to trackside and Rowe disappeared. PO 20 Feb 1907, PM John H. Ramsey.

HEDWIG VILLAGE (Harris) Named from Hedwig Road, east of the village, itself named for Hedwig Jankowski Shroeder, who, with her husband Henry, began farming the area in the early 20th century.

HEDWIGS HILL (Mason) Founded in the early 1850s by German settlers from Fredericksburg, one of whom was Ludwig (Louis) Martin, one of the organizers of Gillespie County who opened the Hedwig's Hill PO 29 June 1858, named for his mother and daughter, both named Hedwig.

HEGAR (Waller) Sophia and Otto Hegar from Darmstadt, Germany, began farming in the area by 1880. Their son, also Otto Hegar, was the first postmaster 18 Jan 1899.

HEIDELBERG (Hidalgo) Named for Heidelberg, Germany by Mercedes real estate developer Frank Grosshaisser, who laid out the community in 1920.

HEIDENHEIMER [HEYED uhn heye mer] (Bell) In the early 1880s the Gulf, Colorado & Santa Fe Railway established Heidenheimer Station, named for Sampson Heidenheimer, a director of the railroad and who, with his brothers Abraham and Isaac, was owner of Heidenheimer and Company, one of the largest grocery-store chains in Texas. PO 5 Sept 1881, PM David Beckham.

HELBIG (Jefferson) Founded in 1900 on the line of the Gulf, Beaumont & Kansas City Railway. Named for Fred A. Helbig, a GB&KC secretary. PO 11 Oct 1890 as Rosedale; changed to Helbig 6 Mar 1901, PM James McLain.

HELENA [HEL uh nuh] (Karnes) About 1850 Thomas Ruckman, who would be instrumental in organizing Karnes County, established a trading post in Alamita on the San Antonio–Goliad Road. He became business partners with physician Lewis Owings and together they laid out Helena, named for Owings's wife, Helen. PO 7 Nov 1853, PM Lewis Owings. Ruckman was the second PM in 1854.

HELMIC (Trinity) Founded about 1908 as Alabama Station, a stop on the Groveton, Lufkin & Northern Railway. In 1810, the name was changed for William J. Helmick [*sic*], a director of the GL&N. PO 11 July 1910, PM George W. Richardson.

HELOTES [he LO teez] (Bexar) Nahuatl (Aztec) *elotl* "roasting ears, corn on the cob" was taken into American Spanish as *elotes* or *olotes* with the extended meaning "cornfields." Helotes referred to the general area from at least the early 1700s and gained official status in 1873 when Charles (Carl) Mueller established the Helotes PO 12 Sept 1873. As a place name, Helotes is unique to Texas.

HEMMING (Cooke) Founded about 1889 and named for Charles C. Hemming, president of the Gainesville National Bank. PO 7 May 1894, PM William Pipkin.

HEMPHILL (County) Created 1876, organized 1887. Named for John Hemphill (1803–1862), born in South Carolina. Hemphill emigrated to Texas in 1838, established a law practice at Washington on the Brazos, became a justice on the Supreme Court of the Republic of Texas, and was Chief Justice of the Supreme Court of the State of Texas in the late 1840s and 1850s. He succeeded Sam Houston as US Senator in 1859 and was expelled in 1861 at the outset of the Civil War.

HEMPHILL (Hemphill) Founded in 1859 when John Hemphill (see Hemphill County) was a newly elected US Senator, several decades before the county was created. PO 26 July 1859, PM Michael Watson.

HEMPSTEAD (Waller) Late in 1856 James McDade and Richard Peebles organized the Hempstead Town Company and purchased land on the projected line of the Houston & Texas Central Railway. Peebles chose the name to honor his brother-in-law, Giles Samuel Booth Hempstead, a Portsmouth, OH, physician. PO 7 June 1877, PM Robert P. Faddis.

HENDERSON (County) Established April 27, 1846, created from parts of Houston and Nacogdoches counties. Named for James Pinckney Henderson (1808–1858), born in North Carolina. Henderson joined the Texas Revolution in 1836, was Attorney General and Secretary of State for the Republic of Texas, the first Governor of the State of Texas (1846–1847), and US Senator (1857–1858).

HENDERSON (Rusk) Platted in 1843 by John C. Miller and named for James Pinckney Henderson, the first Governor of Texas (1846–1847). PO 14 June 1843, PM John C. Miller. See Henderson County.

HENKHAUS [HENGK haws] (Lavaca) Named for one or more Henkhaus families, several of whom had settled in southeast Texas by the early 1830s. PO 16 Apr 1898, PM Aloysius Henkhaus.

HENRIETTA (Clay) The Texas Legislature created Clay County in 1857 and specified that the county seat be named Henrietta, but no reason was given and the source of the name is uncertain. Because the county was probably named for Henry Clay (see Clay County), a Texas legislator, perhaps on a whim, may have suggested that the seat should also be named for Henry Clay, although disguised by the feminine form of his name, Henrietta. Also, Henry Clay and his wife, Lucretia Hart, had eleven children, the first of which was Henrietta, born in 1800. Perhaps her name was proposed to a Texas legislator by a Clay admirer. PO 12 Aug 1862, PM William T. Waybourn.

HEREFORD (Deaf Smith) Named for the registered Hereford cattle introduced to the Texas Panhandle by Lewis Bradley and George Jowell in 1897. When the Pecos & Northern Texas Railway established a station at Hereford in 1899, most of the town of La Plata, then the seat of Deaf Smith County, was physically moved to trackside and Hereford became the new county seat. PO 22 Nov 1898, PM Lyman Montgomery. Also known as Blue Water.

HERMLEIGH (Scurry) The town was originally called Hermlin, a blend of the names of banker Robert *Herm* and grain merchant Harry Har*lin* who donated land for the townsite when the Roscoe, Snyder & Pacific Railway built through the area in 1907. Columbus Rea established the PO as Wheat 9 Sept 1890; the name was changed to Hermleigh 29 Mar 1907; to Foch 31 Dec 1918 in honor of French General Ferdinand Foch, the Supreme Allied Commander in World War I; and back to Hermleigh 16 Dec 1920.

HERTY (Angelina) Founded as a company town about 1940 by the Southland Paper Mill and named for Charles H. Herty, the Georgia chemist who developed the first efficient process for producing newsprint from Southern pine in the early 1930s.

HESTER (Navarro) Hester was organized in the 1880s. PO 14 Apr 1890, PM Ira Pickering who chose the name for Thomas J. Hester, a partner in the Barth and Hester stock raising and poultry company of Corsicana.

HEWITT (McLennan) John A. Warren, an early businessman, suggested the name for George A. Hewitt, a director of the Missouri–Kansas–Texas Railroad when the Hewitt station was opened in 1882. PO 13 Nov 1884, PM Thomas McMurry.

HEXT (Menard) Known as Marengo from the 1870s. The Marengo PO operated 28 Apr 1894–27 Dec 1894; reopened as Hext 8 Nov 1897, PM Enis Stark. Named for farmer and land speculator Joseph Robert Hext.

HICKSBAUGH (Tyler) Founded in 1917 by the Lodwick Lumber Company of Shreveport, LA. Hicksbaugh is a blend of the names of Samuel Bailey *Hicks* and John T. Wurts*baugh*, lumbermen and directors of the East Texas & Gulf Railway. PO 21 Feb 1918, PM Chester V. McGee.

HICO [HEYE ko] (Hamilton) Physician John Rankin Alford chose the name for Hico, Calloway County, KY, his childhood home. Hico may be from a Cherokee word with the general meaning "clear water." PO 4 Oct 1860, PM John R. Alford.

HIDALGO [hi DAL go] (County) Created and organized 1852. Named for Miguel Hidalgo y Costillo (1753–1811), a Jesuit priest in what is now Dolores Hidalgo, Mexico. He was politically and socially active in the early 1800s and is known as the "Father of Mexican Independence."

HIDALGO (Hidalgo) The Hidalgo townsite, occupied from the mid-18th century, went by several names before 1852 when John Young laid out Edinburgh, which was renamed Hidalgo in the mid-1880s. PO 19 Jan 1876, PM Nathaniel H. Evans. See Edinburg.

HIDEAWAY (Smith) Hideaway is a developer's promotional name given to the residential and resort community founded by James Fair, the mayor of Tyler, in 1967.

HIGGINBOTHAM (Gaines) John James and Lucy Ann Higginbotham brought their family from Mississippi in 1880. Their sons Rufus and Joseph established the Higginbotham Ranch and were prominent Seagraves businessmen from the 1900s.

HIGGINS (Lipscomb) Founded in the late 1880s when the Panhandle branch of the Santa Fe Railroad extended a line from Wichita, KS. Named by Edward B. Purcell, vice president of the railroad, for financier G. H. Higgins, a stockholder in the SF. PO 13 Aug 1887, PM James J. Patton.

HIGH (Lamar) McDaniel High relocated from Mississippi in the 1870s, established a general store in 1889, and opened the PO 26 Feb 1891.

HIGHTOWER (Liberty) The Lamb PO, opened 6 Apr 1899 by Charles Lamb, was changed to Hightower 26 Feb 1912, named for Lewis Buckner Hightower, a Huntsville lawyer, Texas state legislator, and district court justice from 1888 until his death in 1918.

HILDA (Mason) Established in the 1850s by German settlers from Fredericksburg and New Braunfels. PO 26 Sept 1901, PM Emma Schulze. Named for Hulda Dina Eckert, daughter of farmers Louis and Caroline Eckert. The Post Office Department likely changed the name on the application from Hulda to the more familiar Hilda.

HILL (County) Created and organized 1853. Named for George Washington Hill (1814–1860), born in Tennessee. Hill came to Texas in 1836 and served as a surgeon at Fort Houston. He was a four-term Texas Congressman and concurrently Texas Secretary of War and Secretary of the Navy under President Sam Houston 1843–1844.

HILLISTER (Tyler) Founded as Hollister, named for William H. Hollister, trustee of the Texas & New Orleans Railroad during its reorganization in the 1870s. The PO application was apparently misread and the office was approved as Hillister 8 Jun 1882, PM William R. McCarty.

HILLJE [HIL jee] (Wharton) In the late 1880s Frederick Hillje from Oldenburg, Germany, with several business partners, laid out the community and founded the Weimar Land Company to attract settlers, in particular those of German and Czech origin. PO 1 Sept 1899, PM Louis C. Wychopen.

HILLSBORO (Hill) When Hill County was created, the seat was established as Hillsborough. PO 2 Aug 1854 as Hillsborough, PM Cincinnatus N. Brooks; changed to Hillsboro 25 July 1888. See Hill County.

HILSHIRE VILLAGE (Harris) The area was first known as Hilshire Manor, named about 1950 by developer and Houston businessman Frank Bruess who reportedly took the name from Hillshire [*sic*] Village, a name he came across in a book on English country estates. The community became known as Long Point Town and was incorporated in 1955 as the somewhat confusing "City of Hilshire Village."

HINCKLEY (Lamar) Hinckley was named for John F. Hinckley, chief engineer for the Paris & Great Northern Railroad that was chartered in 1881 with the intention of building a line from Paris to the Red River and connecting with the Frisco Line. PO 27 Oct 1902, PM James T. Darby.

HINDES [HEYENZ] (Atascosa) By 1870 George and Caroline Hindes had emigrated from Alabama to Atascosa County. About 1912 they donated land for a station on the San Antonio, Uvalde & Gulf Railroad and for the townsite. PO 13 Jan 1913, PM James O. Branch.

HIRAM (Kaufman) James Hiram Hughes moved from Louisiana to Texas in the 1860s and opened the Hiram PO 29 Sept 1893.

HITCHCOCK (Galveston) Organized in the early 1870s when the Gulf, Colorado & Santa Fe Railway built Hitchcock's Station, named by Emily Hitchcock in honor of her late husband, Lent Hitchcock, landowner, businessman, Galveston alderman, and community benefactor from the 1840s. PO 19 Mar 1884, PM Arthur Walker. Previously known as Highland.

HITCHLAND (Hansford) In the 1890s James and Charles Hitch established the Hitch Ranch on the Texas-Oklahoma border. The brothers founded Hitchland when the Chicago, Rock Island & Gulf Railway built through the area in the 1920s. PO 28 July 1930, PM Myrtle McComas.

HOBAN (Reeves) Father Joseph Hoban was appointed pastor of the St. Joseph Catholic Church at Fort Davis in 1876. PO 31 Oct 1911, PM William C. Sisco.

HOBBS (Fisher) Known informally as Red Town, reportedly for the color of John Cavender's store, until 26 May 1888 when Robert Martin opened the Hobbs post office, named for Vachel Hobbs Anderson, the postmaster at Roby.

HOBSON (Karnes) Founded in 1898 as Castine, likely named by settlers from the Castine Bayou area of St. Tammany Parish, LA. Renamed the following year when Rear Admiral Richard Pearson Hobson, who received the Medal of Honor for his service in the Spanish-American War, spoke at the site during one of several whistle-stop tours after the war. Hobson City in Alabama, Hobson's home state, is also named in his honor. PO 1 Nov 1898 as Castine; changed to Hobson 15 Mar 1899, PM Rudolph J. Polasek.

HOCHHEIM [HO heyem] (DeWitt) German "hoch's home." Possibly named for Hochheim, Germany; most likely named for Volentine (Valentine) Hoch who built one of the first homes in the area in 1848 soon after he arrived in Texas from Hesse, Germany. PO 17 Aug 1870, PM Theodore Schwab.

HOCKLEY (County) Created 1876, organized 1921. Named for George Washington Hockley (1802–1854), born in Pennsylvania. Hockley met Sam Houston in Washington, D.C. and followed him to Tennessee and to Texas in 1835. He was Houston's Chief of Staff, Commander of Artillery at San Jacinto, and Secretary of War under President Houston in the late 1830s and early 1840s.

HOCKLEY (Hockley) George Washington Hockley established the town of Hockley, now a northwest Houston suburb, about 1836. PO 9 Sept 1853 as Houseville; changed to Hockley 24 Aug 1858, PM Alexander M. Walker. See Hockley County.

HODGSON (Bowie) Informally known as Harkey's Mill for the cotton gin and sawmill operated by Lee Harkey from the 1860s. Formally named from the PO opened 6 June 1893, PM John J. Hodgson.

HOEN [HO uhn] (McLennan) Founded in the 1890s as Hoehn by J. H. George Hoehn, a Waco banker. When the International–Great Northern Railroad tracks were laid through the area in 1903, railroad officials re-spelled the name—likely influenced by local Hoen families. PO 20 Apr 1912, PM William Pate.

HOGEYE (Hunt) Named in the 1850s from the nearby Masonic lodge. The local account is that the "Eye of Providence" associated with Freemasonry looked to "some of the unlettered" like the eye of a pig.

HOGG (Burleson) Named from the PO opened 26 June 1893 by Andrew Pillow who named the office for James Hogg, sitting Governor of the State of Texas. See Jim Hogg County.

HOLDER (Brown) Founded by David Dawson Holder who relocated from Franklin County, TN, about 1865. PO 3 Oct 1896, PM Willis C. Strickland.

HOLLAND (Bell) James R. Holland settled in the early 1870s and introduced steam-powered cotton gins to the area. PO 10 Apr 1879, PM Alfred Evans.

HOLLIDAY (Archer) In 1841, while a member of the ill-fated Texan Santa Fe Expedition, John J. Holliday carved his name on a tree trunk. Early settlers took the name on the tree, applied it to a nearby stream, and from there to the community. The town was laid out about 26 Nov 1890 when Willard P. Smith established the PO.

HOLLY (Houston) Probably named for Washington and Porter Holley [*sic*], brothers from Alabama who established a large farm near Pennington in the 1860s. Washington Holley represented the district in the Texas Legislature in the late 1870s. PO 6 May 1886, PM Charles R. Brannen.

HOLMAN (Fayette) Named for George and John Holman (Hollman), brothers from Virginia who established a cotton plantation in the mid-1840s in an area they called Holman Valley. PO 11 Dec 1891, PM George Lewis. Earlier known as Pecan, named from Pecan Creek.

HOLT (Hutchinson) Benjamin and Birdie May Holt settled about 1900 and donated land for the first school and first cemetery.

HONDO (Medina) Spanish "deep." Hondo was founded in the early 1880s with construction of the Galveston, Harrisburg & San Antonio Railway; reportedly named for a deep valley crossed by and likely named by the Alonzo de León Expedition of 1689. PO 12 Apr 1882 as Hondo City, PM George Everts.

HONEA (Montgomery) Named from the PO established 30 Mar 1894 by town constable William H. Honea.

HONEY GROVE (Fannin) According to local lore Davy Crockett made camp in the area in 1835 and found so many bee trees that he called the site Honey Grove. PO 22 May 1846, PM Samuel Erwin.

HOOD [HUD] (County) Created and organized 1866. Named in honor of John Bell Hood (1831–1879), born in Kentucky. Bell served as a US and Confederate Army officer who commanded Hood's Texas Brigade that served with great distinction throughout the Civil War as part of the Army of Northern Virginia. Camp Hood, now Fort Hood in Killeen, TX, also named for John Bell Hood, was established in 1942.

HOOD (Cooke) Named from the PO opened 4 Dec 1889 by Adolphus Porter Hood.

HOOKS [HUKS] (Bowie) Named for Warren and Elizabeth Hooks who brought their eight children and 100 slaves from Alabama in the late 1840s. Warren Hooks became one of the most successful plantation owners in northeast Texas and represented the district in the Texas Legislature in the late 1860s. PO 9 Apr 1884, PM James Smith.

HOOT (Bowie) Reportedly named for one "Hoot" White. Details are unknown.

HOOVER (Gray) Laid out in 1908 near a switch on the Panhandle & Santa Fe Railway. Named for Harvey Hoover, a lawyer and president of the First National Bank of Canadian. PO 31 Jan 1910, PM Joseph Heare.

HOOVER (Lamar) Samuel Preston Hoover emigrated from Missouri in the mid-1870s. PO 9 Dec 1897, PM Olive Beasley. Samuel Hoover was the second PM 7 Apr 1899.

HOPKINS (County) Created 1846, organized 1848. Presumably named for David Hopkins, born in Indiana in the mid-1820s. He and his wife, Ann, first appear in the Texas census of 1850 and for the next several decades his occupation is given simply as "farmer." The reasons for naming a county in his honor are unknown.

HORTENSE (Polk) John and Susannah Handley relocated from Alabama in the late 1850s and kept a general store in Moscow. John Handley opened the PO 2 Jan 1891, named for the Handley's nine-year-old daughter, Hortense.

HORTON (Delta) Named from the Horton School, founded in 1867. The community was organized in the late 1890s with construction of the Texas Midland Railroad. PO 12 Apr 1900, PM Richard Horton.

HORTON (Panola) Organized in the mid 1880s and named for Thomas Horton, PM at Ingleside who donated land for the first school in what was then the Tacoma area in December 1885.

HOSTYN (Fayette) First known as Bluff for the precipices along the Colorado River. A Czech settlement began in the mid-1850s and about 1925 the community was named for Hostýn Hill, a holy site in Moravia, Czech Republic. PO 26 Apr 1869 as Bluff, PM Paul Naudhauser.

HOUSTON (County) Created and organized 1837. Named in honor of Sam Houston (1793–1863), born in Virginia. Houston was Governor of Tennessee (1827–1829), the first and third President of the Republic of Texas (1836–1838, 1841–1844), US Senator from Texas (1846–1859), and the seventh

Governor of the State of Texas (1859–1861). Elijah and Andrew Gossett, prosperous landowners who had served with Houston in the Texas War for Independence, proposed the name for the man who came to be known as the hero of San Jacinto. See Crockett.

HOUSTON [YOOS tuhn, HYOOS tuhn] (Harris) In 1832 brothers Augustus Chapman and John Kirby Allen left upstate New York for Texas. The Allens bought the Houston site and began advertising its advantages and virtues in 1836. They engaged Thomas Borden and his brother Gail, the founder of BORDEN, to survey the townsite they named for Sam Houston, an iconic figure in Texas history. PO 1837, Jacob W. Cruger. See Houston County.

HOVEY (Brewster) Founded in 1913 with construction of the Kansas City, Mexico & Orient Railway. Named for Smith B. Hovey, receiver when the railroad bankrupted in 1912.

HOWARD (County) Created 1876, organized 1882. Named for Volney Erskine Howard (1809–1889), born in Maine. Howard served in the Mississippi Legislature in the 1830s and the Texas Legislature in the 1840s. He ended his career as a justice on the Superior Court of Los Angeles, CA. Howard County was named in his honor more than 20 years after he left Texas, never to return.

HOWARD (Ellis) Named in 1896 for Howard Williams, eight-year-old son of Blanche Williams and Thomas Bestor Williams, a Texas State Representative in the late 1890s. PO 29 July 1896, PM John W. Miles.

HOWARDS (Newton) About 1906 the Orange & Northwestern Railroad established Howard's Switch, named for Thad Howard, foreman and part owner of the Fleming sawmill.

HOWE (Grayson) In the early 1870s the Houston & Texas Central Railway established the Summit Switch, taken to be the highest point between the Red River and the Gulf of Mexico. About 1875 Jabes Haning (various spellings) donated land for the town named for Milton G. Howe, chief engineer and general superintendent of the H&TC. PO 29 Feb 1876, PM Samuel W. Young.

HOWLAND (Lamar) Henrietta Howland "Hetty" Green, considered the richest woman in America at the time, bought the Texas Midland Railroad and installed her son, Edward Howland Robinson Green, as president and general manager. The town was named for Edward Howland Robinson Green when the TM built through the area in the 1890s. PO 18 Mar 1880 as Grove; changed to Howland 21 July 1897, PM Aaron V. Bost. Also known as Pleasant Grove. See Atlas, see Cash, see Jiba.

HOWTH [HOWTH] (Waller) Named for Edwin Howth (Houth), a grocer, or his brother William, a saloon keeper, or both. One or both of the Howths donated land for the Houston & Texas Central Railway about 1870. PO 1 Aug 1872 as Howth Station, PM Terah M. Freeman; changed to Howth 24 Dec 1895.

HOXIE (Williamson) John Randolph Hoxie, a businessman with headquarters in

Chicago, was a major landowner in Central and West Texas in the last half of the 19th century. PO 2 Jan 1900, PM John Hoxie's nephew, Mortimer, who supervised the Hoxie Ranch.

HRANICE [huh RAN uhs] (Lee) Settled largely by Czechs from Fayette County in the 1880s and named from Hranice in the Czech Republic.

HUB (Parmer) The town sees itself as the center or "hub" of the county, from which everything radiates outward.

HUBBARD (Bowie) Named for one or more of the prominent Hubbard families of northeast Texas, perhaps for the Smith County family that included Richard Hubbard, Governor of Texas in the 1870s, or for the Bowie County family that included Robert Moss Hubbard, a New Boston attorney and Texas legislator in the early 1930s.

HUBBARD (Hill) The local account is that Richard B. Hubbard, Governor of Texas (1876–1879), was present at a meeting to organize the town in 1881 and in honor of his visit the town was named in his honor. Informally known as Slap Out. By one account, the local store was so poorly stocked that when the storekeeper was asked for a certain product he would answer, "I'm slap out of that." PO 17 Feb 1873 as McLainsboro; changed to Hubbard 28 Nov 1881, PM George W. Bishop.

HUCKABAY (Erath) John and Martha Huckabay began farming in the area about 1870. John Huckabay established the PO 17 May 1888.

HUDD (Scurry) Named for James Bailey "Hud" Hudnall who kept a general store from the 1890s. Hudnall opened the PO 8 July 1901.

HUDSON (Angelina) John Thornberry Bolton Hudson and his wife, Cinthia (several spellings), brought their family to the area from Butler County, AL, and began farming in 1866. The community was named for the Hudsons after they donated land for the first school in 1880.

HUDSPETH (County) Created and organized 1917. Named for Claude Benton Hudspeth (1877–1941), born in Medina, Bandera County. Hudspeth was a rancher, newspaper editor, politician, and oilman who served in the Texas House (1902–1906), Texas Senate (1906–1918), and the US House of Representatives (1919–1931).

HUFFINS (Cass) Named for Robert M. Huffines [*sic*], a Cass County surveyor in the late 19th century. PO 17 Mar 1881, PM James McConnell. Also spelled Huffines.

HUFFMAN (Harris) Probably named for David Huffman, the first known settler, who arrived about 1840. PO 24 Dec 1888, PM James F. T. Pruett.

HUFSMITH (Harris) Frank Hufsmith was superintendent of motive power and rolling stock for the International–Great Northern Railroad that established a station about 1872. PO 26 June 1902, PM Henry L. Mueller.

HUGHES SPRINGS (Cass) Named from the chalybeate springs near the cabins built about 1840 by Reese and Robert Hughes, brothers from Tennessee. PO 30 Oct 1878, PM John Jones.

HULL (Liberty) Robert C. Duff, president of the Beaumont, Sour Lake & Western line of the International–Great Northern Railroad chose the name for William F. Hull, personal secretary to Benjamin Franklin Yoakum, vice president of the San Antonio & Aransas Pass Railway. PO 6 July 1908, PM Samie Edgar Bevers. See Yoakum.

HUMBLE [UHM buhl] (Harris) Beginning about 1870 Pleasant Smith Humble purchased a San Jacinto River ferry and opened a general store and took over the failing town of Lord. The Humble townsite was formally laid out in 1904 with the discovery of oil. The Humble Oil and Refining Company (Esso, Exxon) was organized in 1911, shortly before the headquarters moved to Houston. PO 14 Sept 1886, PM Pleasant S. Humble.

HUMBLE (Hopkins) Probably named from the Humble Oil and Refining Company which drilled a discovery well in the Pickton Oil Field in 1944.

HUNGERFORD (Wharton) Quinan was founded in the early 1870s, named for George E. Quinan, a Wharton lawyer who served in the Texas State Senate in the late 1850s. When the New York, Texas & Mexican Railway built through the area in 1882, the town was moved slightly to the east and renamed Hungerford for Daniel Elihu Hungerford, vice president of the NYT&M. PO 25 June 1874 as Quinan; changed to Hungerford 10 Sept 1883, PM William McKinney.

HUNT (County) Created and organized 1846. Named for Memucan Hunt (1807–1856), born in North Carolina and named for a Persian prince in the Biblical book of Esther. Hunt moved to Texas in 1836 and was instrumental in securing US recognition of the Republic of Texas in 1837. He was Secretary of the Texas Navy in 1839.

HUNT (Kerr) Robert Finley Hunt moved from Tennessee to Texas in 1890 and to Karnes County where he established the Choate PO in 1904. Hunt bought the Kerr County townsite in 1911 and sold a plot to Alva Joy who named the PO for Hunt 13 Dec 1913.

HUNTER (Comal) Andrew Jackson Hunter moved from Louisiana and established a cotton plantation in 1867. About 1880 the International–Great Northern Railroad established the Hunter shipping platform. PO 25 June 1883, PM general store owner Gustavus A. Schleyer.

HUNTINGTON (Angelina) Collis Potter Huntington was a director of the Central Pacific and Southern Pacific railroads and one of the "Big Four" of 19th century railroading with Leland Stanford, Mark Hopkins, and Charles Crocker, all of whom have communities or counties named in their honor. Several dozen towns in the US are named for Collis Huntington, the best known is probably Huntington, WV. PO 23 July 1900, PM Robert D. Chapman.

HUNTOON [huhn TOON] (Ochiltree) Huntoon was founded about 1920 on the line of the Panhandle & Santa Fe Railway; named for Joel Huntoon, an organizer of the Atchison, Topeka & Santa Fe

Railway in the late 1850s. PO 28 Sept 1921, PM Robert Morris.

HUNTSVILLE (Walker) Huntsville was founded by brothers Pleasant and Ephraim Gray who opened a small store in 1836. The Grays traded first with Bedai Native Americans and later with settlers from the Southeastern states. The name was chosen by Pleasant Gray for Huntsville, AL, the Gray's family home. PO 9 June 1837, PM Ephraim M. Gray.

HURLWOOD (Lubbock) In 1925 Claude B. *Hurlbut*, a Lubbock real estate agent, and business partner W. M. *Wood* founded the town and blended their names into Hurlwood. PO 23 Jan 1926, PM Guy K. Horton.

HURNVILLE (Clay) Site owner William Hurn, a Welsh coal miner, emigrated to the US in 1869 and began farming in the area in the late 1870s. PO 11 June 1891, PM Isaac Lowry.

HURON (Hill) In the early 1880s Jehu McPherson Gist opened a general store where he established a PO 2 June 1897, named for his son, Huron Franklin Gist.

HURST (Tarrant) William Letchworth and Mary Lynch Hurst from Claiborne, TN, were early settlers in the 1860s. The Rock Island Railroad station was named in their honor in 1903. PO 16 Sept 1904 as Ormel; changed to Hurst 14 Jan 1909, PM Jackson B. D. Loughridge.

HUTCHINS (Dallas) William J. Hutchins was owner, president, and general manager of the Houston & Texas Central Railway that built through the area in the early 1870s. PO 29 June 1872, PM Rene Henry.

HUTCHINSON (County) Created 1876, organized 1901. Named for Anderson Hutchinson (1797–1853). Hutchinson, a native Virginian, opened a law office in Austin in 1840 and became a Texas district judge. It is doubtful that he ever came near the county that bears his name.

HUTTO [HUHT o] (Williamson) In 1847 James Emory Hutto came to Travis County from Greenville, SC, by way of Madison County, AL. By 1855 he had become an established farmer and stock raiser in Williamson County. He conveyed land for Hutto Station to the International–Great Northern Railroad in 1876 and opened the Hutto PO 27 June 1877.

HYE [HEYE] (Blanco) About 1875 Hiram G. Brown (known as Hi or Hye Brown) moved from Mississippi to the settlement known as Rocky, named from Rocky Creek. The name became Hye 7 May 1886 when Brown became PM and moved the Martinsburgh PO (Gillespie County) to his general store.

HYLTON (Nolan) Elisha Hylton established a general store and a blacksmith shop about 1874. He is probably responsible for carving the name Hylton on Hylton Mountain, the prominence southwest of the town. Hylton opened the PO 5 June 1886.

HYMAN (Mitchell) Apparently named for Harry and Sarah Hyman who donated land for the schoolhouse in the early 1920s. PO 3 Sept 1924, PM Sarah M. Hyman.

J

IAGO [eye AY go] (Wharton) Iago was named from the Iago post office established by storekeeper Clarence D. Kemp in July 1891. Kemp apparently chose the name for Iago, the antagonist of Shakespeare's *Othello*, making this one of the few places in the US named for a literary villain rather than a hero. This is the only Iago in the US.

IATAN [EYE tan] (Mitchell) According to local accounts crews building the Texas & Pacific Railway in the early 1880s called the area "Satan's Flat" because it was "hot as hell." The name of the station was to have been "Satan," but the sign painter misread the "S" for an "I." Alternatively, the station may have been chosen by officials of the Texas & Pacific Railway for Iatan, Platte County, MO, the only other Iatan in the US. The Missouri community is supposedly named for Iatan, an Oto and Missouri leader of the 1830s. PO 20 Mar 1890, PM Daniel Crowe.

IDA (Grayson) PO 27 May 1884, PM Susan R. Matthews who chose the name for her 12-year-old daughter, Ida.

IDALOU [EYE duh LOO] (Lubbock) Julian Bassett, rancher, land developer, railroad builder and principle founder of CROSBYTON laid out the town of Idalou about 1916. According to Bassett's own report, he named Idalou for his sisters, *Ida* Eugena and Marie *Lou*ise. See Kitalou.

IKE (Ellis) Ike and Emma Hendley relocated from Tennessee and began farming in the area in the late 1880s. PO 30 Mar 1898, PM Archibald J. Rice.

ILLINOIS BEND (Cooke, Montague) From the early 1860s the community was known as Wardville for Carter Ward who kept the first general store. Settlers from Illinois suggested the name Illinois Bend for the turn in the Red River that forms a half circle around the town. PO 17 Sept 1877, PM William Wickliffe.

IMPACT (Taylor) Founded in 1960 north of the Abilene city line as a "wet" community where liquor sales were legal, in direct competition with the "dry" city of Abilene. The community was named for Impact, Incorporated, the advertising business of the town's mayor, Dallas Perkins. Impact is now an Abilene suburb.

IMPERIAL (Pecos) Englishman Alexander Edmondson Williamson White, known as A. E. W. White or Alphabet White, established the Imperial PO 11 May 1910, said to be named for the Imperial Valley of California. The following year the town of Imperial was platted for site owner Benjamin Bush. See Clauene.

INADALE [EYE nuh dayl] (Scurry) Founded in 1922 with construction of the Roscoe, Snyder & Pacific Railway. Named for Ina Wooten, daughter of Horace O. Wooten, an Abilene businessman and vice president of the RS&P. Some reports claim that Dale was the daughter of Edward Smallwood Hughes who financed much of the RS&P, but this cannot be verified and Dale was probably added for romantic effect. PO 31 May 1924, PM Egan N. Cummings.

INARI [eye NAHR ee] (Refugio) Inari was suggested by Arthur Edward Spohn, a

Corpus Christi physician who had visited Lake Inari, India, as a youth.

INDEPENDENCE (Washington) In 1833 Dr. Asa Hoxey brought his family and several dozen slaves from Montgomery, AL, to a site then known as Coles Settlement. The local story is that Hoxey, a strong proponent of Texas independence, chose the name in recognition of the signing of the Texas Declaration of Independence in 1836. However, according to the Texas Historical Marker at Independence, the name was in use at least a year earlier. PO 22 May 1846, PM John Root.

INDIAN CREEK (Brown) The local story is that the name arose from an incident in the 1840s when William S. Wallace (not to be confused with Bigfoot Wallace) and his Bexar County surveying crew were forced to take refuge from a Comanche raid near the stream later named for the incident. By an alternate account the surveying crew named the creek when they came upon Delaware Indian victims of a Comanche attack. PO 11 Sept 1876, PM Francis Harris, general store owner.

INDIAN GAP (Hamilton) Reportedly named for a pass through the hills used by Indian trading and later raiding parties. PO 23 Jan 1879, PM James G. Robinson.

INDIANOLA (Calhoun) Founded in the mid-1840s as the port city of Karlshaven "Carl's haven," named for Prince Carl of Solms-Braunfels. The name became Indian Point shortly thereafter and Indianola in 1849. Mary Mitchel Brown is credited with creating the name that retained the "Indian" of Indian Point and added Spanish *ola* "wave" to suggest that Indianola was "the wave of the future." Indianola would not have a future, however. After hurricanes of the 1870s and 1880s, the town was abandoned. PO 7 Sept 1847 as Indian Point; changed to Indianola 10 May 1849, PM Archibald C. Hyde.

INDUSTRY (Austin) Industry is considered by many to be the first permanent German settlement in Texas. In 1831 Johann Friedrich Ernst arrived in the area and planted fruit orchards and vegetable gardens and established Industry's first industry, turning locally grown tobacco into marketable cigars. The town was laid out by Ernst in 1838 and according to local reports was named by acclamation for "the enterprising and industrious spirit of Friedrich Ernst." PO 1 Jan 1842, PM John G. Seiper.

INEZ [eye NEZ] (Victoria) The area was first known as Arenosa, named from Arenosa (Spanish "sandy") Creek. In 1882 the New York, Texas & Mexican Railway established Inez Station, named for Inez Telfener, daughter of Count Joseph Telfener, an owner of the railroad. PO 10 July 1884, PM Henry Clay Koontz. See Telferner [*sic*].

INGLESIDE (San Patricio) John W. Vineyard, a rancher, businessman, and investor, is credited with choosing the name Ingleside (Scots for "fireside"), reportedly for his ancestral home in Ayrshire, Scotland. PO 17 Mar 1858, PM Henry Nold.

INGRAM (Kerr) Founded by John Charles Wesley Ingram, a storeowner and Baptist preacher who arrived from California in the early 1880s. PO 31 Oct 1882, PM John C. W. Ingram.

IOLA [eye OL uh] (Grimes) An early account claims Iola was an Indian maiden (beautiful, of course); another that Iola was the wife (or daughter) of an early settler; still another that Iola is a shortening of Ariola. Indeed, several Ariola families were settled in the area by 7 Aug 1871 when William F. Irvine opened the Iola PO. More likely, however, the name is a transfer from Iola, Allen County, KS, founded by Josiah Colborn and named for his wife, Iola, in 1859.

IOWA COLONY (Brazoria) Founded in 1908 by George I. Huffman (Hoffman) and Robert Beard, agents for the Immigration Land Company of Des Moines, IA. PO 25 Sept 1919, PM Anna Ford.

IOWA PARK (Wichita) David and Andrew Kolp founded Iowa Park in the late 1880s. The Kolps reportedly promoted the site by running excursion trains from Iowa and by laying out the community to suggest a small Iowa town. Although the town is named for the state of Iowa, it is unclear if the Kolps had Iowa connections or if the name was chosen to appeal specifically to Iowans. PO 12 Nov 1888, PM Andrew J. Kolp.

IRA (Scurry) In the early 1890s Ira Newton Green opened a general store on the site of what was first known as "Green's Place." The name was changed when Ira Green opened the PO 28 Feb 1899.

IRAAN [eye ruh AN] (Pecos) About 1927 Ira Yates, on whose ranch oil had recently been discovered, sponsored a naming contest, offering a free building lot to the winner. Clement Hallmark submitted the winning entry by blending the names of *Ira* Yates and his wife, *An*nie Yates. PO 6 Jan 1928, PM Mattie Randolph.

IREDELL [EYE ruh del] (Bosque) Ward Keeler, a miller and surveyor from New York state, founded Iredell in the late 1860s. The accepted story is that Ward and Barbara Ann Keeler named the town for their son, Ira, with "dell" added for romantic effect, but Iradell was misread by the Post Office Department and the application was returned as Iredell. Iredell, TX, may also be a transfer, from Iradell [*sic*], NY, or from Iredell County, NC, founded in 1788 and named for James Iredell, a US Supreme Court Justice appointed by President George Washington. PO 21 Dec 1870, PM William G. Keeler.

IRELAND (Coryell) Informally known as Hamco for its location on the *Ham*ilton–*Co*ryell county line. The community was officially named in 1911 with construction of the Stephenville North & South Texas Railway for John Ireland, mayor of Seguin in 1858, and the 18th Governor of Texas (1883–1887). PO 8 May 1911, PM Robert M. Studer.

IRION [EYE ruhn] (County) Created and organized 1889. Named for Robert Anderson Irion (1804–1861), born in Tennessee. Irion moved from Mississippi to Texas in 1832 and established a medical practice in

San Augustine and later in Nacogdoches. He was a member of the first Republic of Texas Legislature and Texas Secretary of State under President Sam Houston in the late 1830s. (Irion, a rare American family name, is a form of German *Gereon* from St. Gereon of Cologne, a 4th century Christian martyr.)

IRONTON [EYERN uhn] (Cherokee) Charles H. Martin, a Jacksonville lawyer and immigration agent for the International–Great Northern Railroad, named the town in the early 1900s, apparently for the Chapel Hill Manufacturing Company that used local iron ore to produce kitchen tools and farm implements to support the Confederacy during the Civil War. PO 17 Sept 1904, PM Samuel Roach.

IRVING (Dallas) In the beginning the town of Gorbet, founded in the 1840s by John Gorbet (Gorbit), was joined by Kit, founded by Jonathan Story who arrived in the mid-1850s. In 1902, Otis Brown and Julius Schulze, surveyors for the Chicago, Rock Island & Gulf Railway, bought a third site and laid out the town of Irving, named by Schultz for writer Washington Irving. For many years Schultz had been an active member of the Washington Irving Literary Society. PO 2 Aug 1889 as Gorbet, PM Mary Story; changed to Kit, 2 Apr 1894; changed to Irving 2 May 1904, PM Robert M. Hudson.

ISRAEL (Polk) Named from the New House of Israel, a church established by the Utopian Society of Israelites who emigrated from Michigan in 1895 to await the coming of Jesus.

ITALY (Ellis) Waxahachie postmaster Gabriel Penn suggested the name, reportedly because he found the climate of the area similar to that of Italy which he had recently visited. PO 24 Mar 1880, PM Robert Aycock.

ITASCA [eye TAS kuh] (Hill) Founded about 1880. The local account is that Itasca was named by a Missouri–Kansas–Texas Railroad engineer who reportedly saw a mirage that reminded him of Lake Itasca, MN. Itasca is a manufactured name, coined by 19th century ethnologist Henry Rowe Schoolcraft from pseudo-Latin *veritas caput*, a description of the lake in northern Minnesota that he and William Boutwell took to be the "true head" of the Mississippi River. Schoolcraft blended the final two syllables of *veritas* with the first syllable of *caput* and created Itasca. PO 9 Feb 1882, PM Thomas C. Carlisle.

IUKA (Atascosa) Charles Franklin Simmons, a promoter of Atascosa County, probably chose the name for his birthplace, Iuka, Tishomingo County, MS. Iuka is likely from a Choctaw or Chickasaw personal name derived from a Choctaw war name meaning "great one" or "prisoner killer." PO 6 May 1886, PM James R. Goodwin.

IVAN [EYE vuhn] (Stephens) Named for Ivan Oliver Brockman, son of Stephens County physician James Brockman and Katie Brockman. PO 27 Feb 1900, PM William O. Brockman (relationship to Ivan or James not determined).

IVANHOE (Fannin) Known as Hawkins Prairie for pioneer settler Strother Moses

Hawkins until the mid-1880s when Joseph Dupree suggested the name be changed for a book he admired, Walter Scott's *Ivanhoe*. The Hawkins Prairie PO, opened 20 Sept 1877, was changed to Ivanhoe 8 June 1885, PM James F. Reed.

IZORO [eye ZOR uh] (Lampasas) Probably named for Izoro (Isora, Izore) Gilliam, daughter of David Gilliam, a private in the Alabama cavalry who moved to Texas after the Civil War and became a farmer and community benefactor. PO 18 Aug 1888, PM Thomas J. Upton.

J

JACINTO CITY [juh SIN to] (Harris) Houston developer Frank W. Sharp established several subdivisions in the Houston area following World War II; one was Jacinto City, named for the Battle of San Jacinto that led to Texas's independence in 1836; another was Lucille Place for his wife, Lucille. See San Jacinto.

JACK (County) Created 1856, and organized 1857. Named for William Houston Jack (1806–1844) and Patrick Churchill Jack (1808–1844) whose family moved from Alabama to Texas about 1830. The brothers, both lawyers, distinguished themselves militarily and politically during and after the Texas Revolution. William Jack was Secretary of State and served in the Republic of Texas Legislature in the 1830s; Patrick Jack was district attorney and justice of the Supreme Court of the Republic of Texas in the 1840s. The brothers died of yellow fever within weeks of one another in the summer of 1844.

JACKSBORO (Jack) Mesquiteville, the first county seat, was renamed Jacksborough from Jack County in 1858. PO 30 June 1858 as Jacksborough, PM William A. Nix; changed to Jacksboro 21 Oct 1889.

JACKSON (County) An original Texas county created in 1836. Named for Andrew Jackson, US President 1829–1837.

JACKSON (Shelby) Named about 1900 for Thomas and Rebecca Jackson who began farming in the area in the 1860s.

JACKSON (Van Zandt) Reuben Andrew Jackson Kennedy established a medical practice in the 1870s and opened the PO 12 Jan 1889.

JACKSONVILLE (Cherokee) The name resulted from the happy union of two Jacksons. In 1847 Jackson Smith from Kentucky established a smithy on Gum Creek. He laid out the townsite early in 1850 and the first house was built by Dr. William Jackson. PO 15 June 1848 as Gum Creek; changed to Jacksonville 20 June 1850, PM Jackson Smith.

JACOBIA [juh KO bee uh] (Hunt) Formerly known as Jacobs' Prairie, likely named for Stokley Jacobs from Tennessee. The name was changed to Jacobia, a Latinized form of Jacob, when Benjamin Wall opened the post office 21 Feb 1887.

JAMAICA BEACH (Galveston) In the mid-1950s the Jamaica Corporation founded and named the resort community of Jamaica Beach on Galveston Island.

JAMES (Shelby) James J. Rushing opened the James PO in his general store 9 May 1901.

JAMESTOWN (Newton) James W. Westbrook opened the Jamestown PO in his general store 10 May 1911.

JARDIN [JARD uhn] (Hunt) Spanish "garden, flower garden." Founded about 1880; naming circumstances unknown. PO 25 July 1881, PM Foster A. Lane.

JARRELL [JEHR uhl] (Williamson) In 1909 Orlando Jarrell, a real estate developer from Temple, and Ernest Haeber, a businessman from Bartlett, founded Jarrell on the proposed line of the Bartlett Western Railway. PO 9 July 1855 as Corn Hill; changed to Jarrell 8 Mar 1912, PM Thomas B. Thomas.

JASPER (County) Created 1836, organized 1837. Named in honor of William Jasper (c. 1750–1779). During the Revolutionary War siege of Charleston Harbor in 1776, a British warship shot an American flag from its staff. At great personal risk, Sergeant William Jasper retrieved the flag, remounted it on a ramrod and saw to its care until a more permanent flagpole could be found. Jasper was mortally wounded at Savannah in 1779. His name has long been linked with that of a Sergeant Newton and the pairing of the names Jasper and Newton is one of the marvels of American naming, largely because of the folklore that has grown around them. The myth was provided by Mason Weems, a Protestant Episcopal minister of the early 19th century better known for his biography of George Washington in which he made up the "I cannot tell a lie" story of Washington and the cherry tree, which became an indispensable part of Americana. In *The Life of Francis Marion*, Weems tells the fictitious and highly romanticized story of how Sergeants Jasper and Newton—by themselves of course—followed and subdued a squad of British soldiers who were marching American troops to Savannah to be hanged. The book went through many editions, each one embellishing and enlarging the exploits of Marion, Jasper, and Newton. Thus, it was natural if not inevitable that when Jasper County was divided in 1846, the new county would be named Newton.

JASPER (Jasper) The municipality of Bevil, named for farmer, land developer, and judge John Randolph Bevil, was organized in the late 1820s. The community was first known as Bevil's Settlement and renamed for Jasper County when the county was created in 1836. The Bevilport PO, with the ominously named Randolph Doom as PM, opened 16 Dec 1854 and closed 15 Dec 1899. The Jasper office was opened by PM John Bevil in Dec 1836.

JAVA (Cherokee) Several entertaining but likely imaginative stories have been created to explain the origin of this intriguing name. By one, often credited to local historian Lem Brown, at a community dance a young lady happened to lose her petticoat (the reasons for this tragedy are never mentioned) and other dancers noticed that the garment bore the name "Java" and thus had been repurposed from a Java coffee sack. "Java" then became a community byword and was well known when the post office was established in 1895. A related story claims that the garment monogrammed "Java" was found in a local stream, which generated a number of stories of its own. Since the early 1700s coffee beans were the primary export of the Indonesian island of Java and bags embossed with the name "Java" were common in the US and retailored into clothing. PO 28 Dec 1895, PM John L. Watson.

JAYTON (Kent) In the 1870s Daniel Marfet Jay brought his family from Benton, AR, to what became known as Jay Flat. He opened the Jayton PO 20 Feb 1886.

JEAN (Young) In 1875 Benjamin (or Benoni) and Martha Ann Lamar, with several of their ten children, moved from Kentucky to Young County where they founded the town of Jean. According to local accounts, their son James, the first postmaster

30 Nov 1906, chose the name for his first sweetheart; which must have pleased his wife, Mary.

JEDDO [JED o] (Bastrop) Jeddo (Yeddo) is a romanization of Edo, for Edo, Japan (renamed Tokyo in 1868). Largely because of its associations with the exotic East, Jeddo became a popular place name in the US in the decades following Commodore Matthew Perry's "opening" of Japan to the West in the early 1850s and his published account of the expedition in which he refers to Edo as "Yedo." A dozen or so places in the US are named Jeddo, one of which may have been transferred to Texas but more likely the name was chosen directly from Jeddo, Japan, by a prominent citizen or by the first PM, Asa Bellamy, who established the Jeddo PO 13 Feb 1874.

JEFF DAVIS (County) Created and organized 1887. Named for Jefferson Davis (1808–1889), US Secretary of War and Mississippi Senator in the 1850s, and President of the Confederate States of America (1861–1865). Fort Davis and the Davis Mountains are also named for Jeff Davis.

JEFFERSON (County) Created 1836, organized 1837. Named for Thomas Jefferson (1743–1826). Jefferson, a true American polymath, was principle author of the Declaration of Independence and third US President (1801–1809).

JEFFERSON (Marion) Founded on adjacent sites laid out by Allen Urquhart and Daniel Alley in 1842. Named by the Jefferson Township Company, but the source of the name is uncertain. The city is generally claimed to be named for President Thomas Jefferson or for the Jefferson family of Monticello, VA, but formal evidence is lacking. For a discussion of the naming of Jefferson, see Jacques Bagur, *Antebellum Jefferson, Texas*, 36–41. PO 22 May 1846, PM William Bishop.

JENKINS (Madison) This tiny community northeast of Madisonville was named about 1885 for Anguish [*sic*] Jasper Jenkins from Alabama, who donated land for a school and a non-denominational church.

JENNINGS (Lamar) Named for landowners Wiley Jennings and his sons, James and William, from Tennessee, who began farming there in the 1850s. PO 16 Nov 1885, PM Thomas Morgan.

JERICHO (Donley) Jericho was founded in 1902 as a station on the Chicago, Rock Island & Gulf Railway. Jericho is likely a transfer from one of the fifty or so Jerichos in the US, perhaps from Alabama or Missouri. PO 9 Aug 1902, PM James P. Altizer.

JERMYN [JER muhn] (Jack) Joseph J. Jermyn was president and principle financier of the Gulf, Texas & Western Railroad, which built through the area in 1909. PO 7 Feb 1910, PM Frank McClure.

JERSEY VILLAGE (Harris) The northwest Houston suburb of Jersey Village was founded in 1953 by LeRoy Kennedy and site owner Clark W. Henry, who probably named the community after his dairy herd of Jersey cattle.

JEWETT [JYOO it] (Leon) The International-Great Northern Railroad founded Jewett in 1871, named for lawyer and politician Henry J. Jewett. As a Robertson County state senator Jewett was instrumental in creating Leon County from Robertson in 1846. PO 29 Dec 1871, PM George M. Skipper.

JIBA [HEE buh] (Kaufman) Founded in the early 1900s as Green, probably named for Edward Howland Robinson Green, an owner of the Texas Midland Railroad. The name was changed in 1905, probably by a railroad employee, to Jiba, from Spanish *giba* "hump," named for a small hill on the railroad line or more likely from railroad jargon where a hump was an artificial hill that used gravity to switch cars onto different tracks. The Green PO, opened 1 Feb 1901, was changed to Jiba 30 Aug 1905, PM James M. Gibson. See Atlas, see Cash, see Howland.

JIM HOGG (County) Created and organized 1913. Named for James Stephen Hogg (1851–1906), the first native Texan to become governor (1891–1895). Hogg is known by many Americans less for his politics than for naming his only daughter Ima. The Hogg family insisted that she was named for a character in the Civil War epic poem, *The Fate of Marvin*, written by her uncle, Thomas Hogg. Ima Hogg became a respected Texas philanthropist and patron of the arts. Contrary to pulp media reports she did not have a sister named Ura.

JIM WELLS (County) Created 1911, organized 1912. Named for James Babbage Wells, Jr. (1850–1923), born in Aransas County. Wells, a Brownsville lawyer, specialized in land claims along the Rio Grande. From the 1880s until the 1920s Wells was arguably the most powerful political figure in South Texas. See Norias.

JOAQUIN [waw KEEN] (Shelby) Founded about 1885 with construction of the Houston East & West Texas Railway. Land for the HE&WT right of way was donated by Benjamin Franklin Morris and the station was named for his grandson, Joaquin Morris. PO 5 May 1884 as Sarat; changed to Joaquin 16 June 1886, PM Erastus F. Sayers.

JOHNSON (County) Created and organized 1854. Named for Middleton Tate Johnson (1810–1866), born in South Carolina. Johnson was a member of the Alabama Legislature in the 1830s and the Republic of Texas Legislature in the 1840s. He was a Texas Ranger who served with the Texas Mounted Volunteers during the Mexican War. He helped establish and name Fort Worth and was an organizer of Tarrant County.

JOHNSON CITY (Blanco) Founded in the late 1870s by site owner James Polk Johnson, a nephew of Samuel Ealy Johnson, Sr., grandfather of President Lyndon Baines Johnson. PO 12 Feb 1878, PM John B. Liggett.

JOHNSONS STATION (Tarrant) Named from the homesite of Middleton Tate Johnson. See Johnson County.

JOHNSVILLE (Erath) John Zacharius Martin relocated from Georgia to Texas in the 1850s and to Erath County where he opened the PO in his general store 7 Jan 1901.

JOHNTOWN (Red River) Named about 1900, reportedly for the unusually large number of residents named John, including John Rodgers, the first postmaster 13 Nov 1901.

JOINERVILLE (Rusk) Known informally as Cyril and as Miller until 1930 when Columbus Marion "Dad" Joiner brought in the discovery well of the East Texas Oil Company. Esther Berry named the PO for Joiner 21 Jan 1932.

JOLLY (Clay) About 1890 the Fort Worth & Denver City Railway established a shipping station named for rancher and site owner William H. Jolly. PO 3 Nov 1891, PM David Rogers.

JOLLYVILLE (Williamson) Founded in the mid-1860s by John Gray Jolly, who relocated from TN about 1853.

JONAH (Williamson) Known as Water Valley until the late 1850s when James Warnock and Joseph Mileham established a town and gristmill on the San Gabriel River that became known as Eureka Mills. In the 1880s when the post office application was submitted, the names Water Valley and Eureka Mills were rejected. A local account claims that Jonah was then suggested since the people were having as much bad luck in acquiring a post office as Jonah had with the whale. PO 31 Mar 1884, PM John Walker.

JONES (County) Created 1858, recreated 1876, organized 1881. Named for Anson Jones (1797–1858), born in Great Barrington, MA. Jones made his way to Texas in 1833 and established a medical practice at Brazoria. He was a surgeon in the Texas Army, Secretary of State under President Sam Houston, and the last President of the Republic of Texas (1844–1846).

JONES PRAIRIE (Milam) Joseph Patterson Jones came to Texas from Illinois to join Sterling Clack Robertson's Colony in 1833. Jones was killed in a fight with Kickapoo Indians while surveying Navarro County in 1838. PO 27 Nov 1876, PM Benjamin F. Whitfield.

JONESBORO (Coryell, Hamilton) William Levi Jones, born in Mississippi, established a steam sawmill and gristmill in the 1860s. PO 12 Apr 1871 as Jones Mill; changed to Jonesboro 9 July 1877, PM Pleasant Williams.

JONESVILLE (Harrison) Probably named for Martin William Jones, the site owner and the area's first storekeeper. PO 18 Jan 1847 as Border; changed to Jonesville 13 Nov 1849, PO Beman H. Martin.

JOPLIN [JAHP luhn] (Jack) Site owner Johnnie Joplin laid out the town in 1882. PO 28 May 1891, PM James B. Key.

JOPPA [JAHP uh] (Burnet) The area was known as Pool Branch until William Childers opened the Joppa PO 24 Nov 1891. Joppa is probably a transfer, likely from Joppa, Cullman County, AL, itself named for the Biblical Joppa (Jaffa), now part of Tel Aviv, Israel.

JOSEPHINE (Collin) Named for Josephine (Josie) Hubbard, daughter of Jesse and Ellen Hubbard who donated land for a station on the Cotton Belt Railroad in 1887. PO 25 July 1888, PM Joseph M. Stubblefield.

JOSHUA (Johnson) Laid out in 1880 on the anticipated line of the Gulf, Colorado & Santa Fe Railway. A rejected application for a PO named Caddo Peak was resubmitted and approved as Joshua. Daniel McMillan, a local physician and the first postmaster 28 Mar 1882, is credited with suggesting the name for the Biblical Joshua.

JOSSELET (Haskell) Founded about 1910 as a station on the Wichita Valley Railway. Named for site owner Victor Joseph Josselet who, along with two brothers, emigrated from Belgium in the early 1870s.

JOSSERAND (Trinity) Peter and Frank Josserand, sons of French immigrant Pierre Josserand, established their first sawmill in the early 1880s. Peter Josserand was the first PM 3 Aug 1887, followed by his wife, Fidelia Louisa, in 1905.

JOT 'EM DOWN (Delta) In 1936 Dion McDonald opened a general store that was familiarly known as the Jot'Em Down Store, named after the fictional establishment co-owned by Lum Edwards and Abner Peabody on the immensely popular hillbilly comedy show *Lum and Abner* in the 1930s and 1940s. The name took root and Jot'Em Down became the name of a local ginning corporation and then of the community.

JOURDANTON [JERD uhn tun] (Atascosa) In 1909 Jourdanton was established as Cam-Zan on the line of the Artesian Belt Railroad, named for founders Jourdan *Cam*pbell, son of John Campbell, founder of Campbellton, TX, and Theodore H. *Zan*derson, a San Antonio businessman. The PO was opened 30 Apr 1909 by PM Thomas D. Harrison as Jourdanton for Jourdan Campbell. See Campbellton.

JOY (Clay) Settlers from Fannin County named the community Fannintown about 1880. The name was changed in January 1895 when John Smith established the Joy post office. The motivation for the name is unknown although local accounts say the people were joyful because of the bountiful crops.

JUD (Haskell) Hiram Franklin "Jud" Roberson was a stock breeder and ginner in the late 19th and early 20th centuries. PO 2 Mar 1895, PM William C. Allen.

JUDKINS (Ector) Andrew Lafayette Judkins was an Odessa farmer and stock raiser from the 1870s. PO 26 Dec 1906, PM Hiram Graham.

JUDSON (Gregg) Founded in the early 1880s. Named from the Judson Missionary Baptist Church, itself named for Adoniram Judson, a Baptist missionary who spent most of his life serving the church as a foreign missionary in the country then known as Burma. PO 4 Mar 1890, PM Francis M. Whitehurst.

JULIFF [JOO lif] (Fort Bend) Organized in the 1850s on the line of the Houston Tap & Brazoria Railway. Named for John J. Juliff, born in Middlesex, England, a farmer and the first PM 26 Sept 1891.

JUMBO (Panola) Named for Jumbo, the massive elephant that was a star of P. T.

Barnum's circus. Jumbo met an untimely death from a railroad catastrophe in 1885 and this highly publicized event, along with memories of Jumbo's successful tour of East Texas in the early 1880s, led to businessman James Brady's choosing the name when he opened the PO 8 Sept 1888.

JUNCTION (Kimble) Laid out in the mid-1870s as Denman by Marcellus Denman. The name was later changed to Junction City for the site where the South and North Llano rivers join. PO 5 June 1876 as Denman; changed to Junction City 18 June 1877, PM Harriett S. Kountz; changed to Junction 6 May 1894, PM Frank Vickery.

JUNO (Val Verde) According to a local story saloon owner Henry Stein's menu consisted solely of frijole beans and beer. When his Mexican barkeepers were asked what was on the menu, the reply was "ju know." Stein chose the name when he opened the PO 21 Jan 1886.

JUSTICEBURG (Garza) Arthur E. Tuffing from Portage County, OH, opened the Leforest PO in March 1902, named for his sons Lee and Forest Tuffing. The office was changed to Justiceburg 25 June 1910, PM William A. Chaney, named for site owner and Garza County treasurer Jefferson Davis Justice.

JUSTIN (Denton) Justin was founded in 1848 as a French utopian community organized by followers of Étienne Cabet. The town was known by several names, most notably New Icaria, until 25 Jan 1887 when Thomas J. Wheeler opened the Justine [*sic*] PO named for Walter Justin Sherman, chief engineer for the Santa Fe Railroad; changed to Justin 4 Oct 1887, PM John W. Berry.

K

KADANE CORNER [kuh DAYN] (Wichita) Named for and probably by George Kadane who emigrated from Syria in 1896. With his son Jack, Kadane brought in oil fields on the Ikard Ranch in 1937. The Kadanes were later partners in the Kadane-Griffith Oil Company.

KAFFIR [KAF er] (Swisher) Named about 1905 for the Kaffir grain elevator and the Kaffir school, themselves named for kaffir (usually spelled kafir) corn, a locally grown sorghum.

KALGARY (Crosby) According to a local account, when Sallie Greer Reed assumed postal duties 1 May 1927 she named the office from a news story of the Canadian Mounted Police who were searching for a lost trapper near Calgary, Canada. The reason for the change in spelling is unknown.

KAMAY [KAY em ay] (Wichita) About 1912 local businessmen Joseph Kemp, Hamilton Munger, and Reese Allen formed the Kemp-Munger-Allen Oil Company. The name of the company and the oilfield was shortened to K-M-A and the community was known as Kemp or Kemp City. Thoughts of a post office (which never materialized) led to the name Kamay, a pronunciation of the letters K-M-A, in the late 1930s.

KAMEY (Calhoun) Founded by John William McKamey, a Port Lavaca rancher who relocated from Arkansas about 1908. PO 13 Apr 1910, PM Elijah T. Johnson.

KANAWHA [KAHN uh wah] (Red River) Charles P. Brown, community founder and the first postmaster, chose the name in 1886 for his birthplace, Kanawha County, WV.

KAREN (Montgomery) John Bauer opened the PO 30 Mar 1909, named for his two-year-old daughter, Karen.

KARNACK (Harrison) By a local account a classically educated family (that of Thomas Jefferson Taylor, father of Claudia Taylor, better known as Lady Bird Johnson, has been suggested), chose the name because the townsite was approximately the same distance from Port Caddo as Karnack was from Thebes in ancient Egypt. PO 29 Sept 1898, PM Charles C. Baker.

KARNES (County) Created and organized 1854. Named for Henry Wax Karnes (1812–1840), born in Tennessee. Karnes settled in Texas in 1835 where he distinguished himself in the Texas Revolution, enlisting as a private and rising to the rank of colonel by the end of the war.

KARNES CITY (Karnes) Founded as the county seat about 1890. When the post office application was submitted in 1891 as Karnes, named from the county, the Post Office Department added "City."

KARON [kuh RON] (Live Oak) Karon is a respelling of Caron for Ralph Harry Caron, the first postmaster 3 Aug 1923.

KATEMCY [kuh TEM see] (Mason) Named from Katemcy Creek, itself named for Katemcy (Ketemoczy, Ca-tumsie), a Penateka (Southern) Comanche leader of the mid-19th century. Katemcy is best known for the treaty he signed with John Meuseback on behalf of the German settlers of Texas in 1848. The town was founded on land purchased about 1870 by physician William Flemon Cowan and his wife Mary, a midwife. Their son, Alfred Cowan, opened the Katemcy PO 17 Nov 1884.

KATY (Fort Bend, Harris, Waller) Although some say the namesake is the wife (or friend) of a local bartender, the town is named for the Missouri–Kansas–Texas Railroad, known from its early days in the 1870s as the KT—the KATY—that built through the area in the early 1890s. PO 23 Jan 1896, PM James O. Thomas.

KAUFMAN (County) Created and organized 1848. Named for David Spangler Kaufman (1813–1851), born in Pennsylvania. Kaufman came to Texas in the late 1830s, established a law practice in Nacogdoches, served in the Republic of Texas Congress, was chargé d'affaires to the US, and a US Representative from Texas (1846–1851).

KAUFMAN (Kaufman) Founded in the early 1840s as Kingsboro, named for Dr. William King; renamed Kaufman in 1852. PO 18 Dec 1849 as Kaufman, PM John W. Fields.

KEECHI [KEE cheye] (Leon) Founded about 1870 with construction of the Missouri Pacific Railroad. Named for the Keechi (Kichai), Native American Caddoan speakers who lived in Texas, Oklahoma, and Louisiana. Other than designating a group of people, the name has no apparent meaning, surely not "land of peaceful waters" as a local legend claims. Keechi Creek in Anderson County, Quihi in Medina County, Kechi in KS, and Keatchie in LA are variants. PO 25 Jan 1872, PM Francis Eldridge.

KEELERSVILLE (Williamson) Keeler is a phonetic spelling of Keliehor, for William Keliehor who established a sheep ranch in the early 1870s. PO 4 May 1895, PM Frederick Zahn.

KEETER (Wise) Albert Lafayette Keeter, a Missionary Baptist minister relocated from Georgia in the 1870s. PO 11 May 1880 as Kuter (a misspelling); changed to Keeter 7 Sept 1883, PM Phoebe L. Keeter.

KEITH (Grimes) Named for one or more Keith families, likely that of Reuben and Mary Keith who brought their family from Georgia about 1865. PO 26 May 1881, PM John D. Keith.

KELLER (Tarrant) Founded about 1880 as Athol, likely named by settlers from an Athol in Kentucky or Missouri both named from Athol, Scotland. About 1882 the Texas & Pacific Railway changed the name for John C. Keller, a T&P construction foreman. PO 11 Jan 1871 as Double Springs; changed to Keller 16 June 1888, PM John H. Wallace.

KELLERVILLE (Wheeler) Pittman and Ida Keller began farming in the area in the early 1900s. PO 4 Apr 1935, PM Frankie Bradford.

KELLYVILLE (Marion) Named about 1870 for George Addison Kelly, owner of the Kelly Plow Company, makers of farm equipment, cast iron stoves, and cooking utensils from the early 1850s. PO 27 May 1878 as Kellysville, PM George A. Kelly; changed to Kellyville 17 Oct 1883.

KELSEY (Upshur) About 1900 John and Jim Edgar, brothers from Alabama, founded Kelsey, a Mormon colony named from Kelsey Creek, itself named in the 1850s for early physician and public official William Kelsey. PO 25 July 1902, PM Alonzo Cantrell.

KELTYS (Angelina) In the mid-1880s Charles L. Kelty, a New York City merchant, built a sawmill on the line of the Kansas & Gulf Short Line Railroad. Keltys is now part of Lufkin. PO 26 May 1890, PM Joseph H. Kurth.

KEMAH [KEE muh] (Galveston) Kemah was founded as Evergreen on the line of the Texas & New Orleans Railroad in the late 1890s and renamed in the mid-1900s. Kemah, from a Peoria (Miami) word meaning "leader," is probably a transfer from Kema, Ottawa County, OK. PO 12 Nov 1907, PM John H. Kipp.

KEMP (Kaufman) Levi Noble founded Kemp about 1850, named for his mother, Sarah Kemp Noble. PO 27 May 1851, PM Levi Noble.

KEMPER CITY (Victoria) After serving in the Texas Army, John Frederick Kemper established a trading post at Kemper's Bluff on the Guadalupe River in 1836. He was killed in a skirmish with Indians in 1845. PO 2 June 1860, PM William P. Graves.

KEMPNER (Lampasas) The area was known from the early 1870s as Taylor's Creek for rancher Dan Taylor, and later as Slaughtersville for site owner Philip Slaughter. The Gulf, Colorado & Santa Fe Railway established Kempner Station in 1882, named for Harris Kempner, a Galveston financier and one of the first directors of the GC&SF. PO 25 Mar 1878 as Slaughtersville; changed to Kempner 14 Aug 1882, PM John F. Rutledge.

KENDALIA (Kendall) An adaptation of Kendall. Kendalia was founded in the early 1880s by Boerne journalist Charles Gustav Vogel who established the PO 13 Nov 1882.

KENDALL (County) Created and organized 1862. Named for George Wilkins Kendall (1809–1867), born in New Hampshire. Kendall became part owner of the New Orleans *Picayune* newspaper in the 1830s and promoted the annexation of Texas. He joined and reported the ill-fated Texan Santa Fe Expedition of 1841, was a noted war correspondent during the War with Mexico, and in later years he developed and promoted the Texas sheep industry.

KENDLETON (Fort Bend) In the late 1860s William Kendall, a Richmond lawyer, divided his plantation into 100-acre farms that were sold exclusively and cheaply to slaves freed after the Civil War. PO 15 Apr 1884, PM Benjamin Williams.

KENEDY (County) Created and organized 1921. Named for Mifflin Kenedy (1818–1895). Kenedy, a Pennsylvania Quaker, was a riverboat pilot, rancher, and business partner of Richard King, founder and namesake of the King Ranch.

KENEDY (Karnes) Established in 1886 with construction of the San Antonio & Aransas Pass Railway. Named for Mifflin Kenedy, a financier and promotor of Texas railroads who invested heavily in the SA&AP. PO 12 Mar 1887 as Kenedy Junction, PM Christopher Dailey; changed to Kenedy 21 June 1887. See Kenedy County.

KENEFICK [KEN uh fik] (Liberty) In the early 1900s the Kenefick Construction Company of Kansas City, MO, founded by and named for William Kenefick, contracted to build a section of the Beaumont, Sour Lake & Western Railway in Liberty County.

KENNARD [kuh NAHRD] (Houston) About 1900 the Central Coal and Coke Company, with headquarters in Kansas City, MO, founded Kennard, probably named for John R. Kennard of Navasota, a distinguished Civil War veteran and judge of the 4th District that included Grimes and Houston counties in the 1880s. PO 16 Jan 1902, PM Alexander MacTavish.

KENNEDALE (Tarrant) Founded in 1886 in anticipation of the Southern Pacific Railroad; named for Fort Worth lawyer Oliver S. Kennedy, with "dale" added for romantic effect. PO 8 Feb 1884, PM John D. Hudson.

KENNEY (Austin) Named for John Wesley Kenney, a Methodist minister who founded and promoted Methodist congregations in the 1830s. Kenney's evangelical efforts have been credited for Methodism's becoming a major denomination in Texas in the 19th century. PO 9 Nov 1880 as Thompson; changed to Kenneyville 25 June 1884; changed to Kenney 14 June 1892. James E. Thompson was PM under each of the three office names. Also spelled Kinny.

KENSING (Delta) In 1896 merchant David Flenni*ken* married Mene [*sic*] San*sing* of Lamar County.

KENT (County) Created 1876, organized 1892. Named for Andrew Kent (1791?–1836), born in Kentucky. Kent moved to Missouri, then to Texas about 1830. Little is known of his life in Texas until 1836 when he joined the Gonzales Ranging Company of Mounted Volunteers which arrived at the Alamo on March 1, 1836. He died five days later.

KERENS [KERNZ] (Navarro) In 1881 the Cotton Belt Railroad established Kerens Station, named for Richard C. Kerens of St. Louis, an investor in the CB, and US Ambassador to Austria-Hungary in the early 20th century. PO 30 Aug 1871 as Wadeville; changed to Kerens 26 May 1882, PM Saunders P. Day.

KERMIT (Winkler) Early in 1910 Kermit Roosevelt, second son of former President Theodore Roosevelt and like his father a devoted big game hunter and conservationist, spent time at the T Bar Ranch hunting antelope. The community was named in honor of Kermit Roosevelt and the Roosevelt family when Marvin Scott opened the Kermit PO 18 July 1910.

KERR (County) Created and organized 1856. Named for James Kerr (1790–1850), who probably pronounced his name [kar]. Born in Kentucky, Kerr moved to Missouri at an early age, became a county sheriff, and served several terms in the Missouri Legislature in the 1810s and early 1820s. About 1825 he joined Erastus (Deaf) Smith in Texas in selecting a site for the DeWitt Colony's center of government. Kerr was Surveyor General for the DeWitt Colony in the late 1820s and an active participant in the Texas governmental conventions of the 1830s.

KERRICK (Dallam) Kerrick was laid out in 1930 and named for Harrison Summers Kerrick who owned land in the area. Kerrick was an army colonel and the author of the code of conduct for the US flag.

KERRVILLE (Kerr) Founded about 1850 as Brownsborough, named for shingle maker and first settler Joshua Brown. The name was changed to Kerrsville at Brown's request. When Hance Burney opened the PO 9 June 1858, he dropped the "s" from Kerrsville.

KIAM [KEYE am] (Polk) Apparently named for Edward Kiam, a Houston businessman and namesake of the Kiam Building in Houston constructed in 1893. PO 14 May 1901, PM James McKee.

KILDARE (Cass) Likely named for County Kildare in eastern Ireland, perhaps by Irish workers building the Texas & Pacific Railway in the 1870s. PO 24 June 1874, PM Clement Galloway.

KILGORE (Gregg, Rusk) In 1872 the International–Great Northern Railroad established a line between Palestine and Longview that passed through land owned by Constantine Buckley Kilgore for whom the station was named. Kilgore, a Rusk County lawyer, was a Texas Representative in the US Congress in the late 1880s and early 1890s. PO 4 Feb 1873, PM Virgil H. Kilgore.

KILLEEN [kuh LEEN] (Bell) In 1881 the Gulf, Colorado & Santa Fe Railway bypassed the town of Palo Alto and named the station for Frank Patrick Killeen, an Irish immigrant who had worked his way from railroad clerk to assistant general manager of the GC&SF. PO 8 Nov 1872 as Palo Alto; changed to Killeen 4 Aug 1882, PM Edmund M. Spencer.

KIMBLE (County) Created in 1858, organized in 1876. Named for George C. Kimble (1803–1836). Kimble, born in Pennsylvania, moved to TX in 1825 as a member of Green DeWitt's Colony. He later established a hat factory in Gonzales with his business partner, Almaron Dickenson. Kimble and the Gonzales Ranging Company entered the Alamo on March 1, 1836 where he and Dickenson died five days later.

KING (County) Created 1876, organized 1891. Named for William Philip King (1820–1836), born in Mississippi. The King family became part of Green Dewitt's Colony in 1830 and established a farm near Gonzales. In 1836 William King joined the relief force from Gonzales and at age fifteen was the youngest defender to die at the Alamo.

KING (Coryell) Earlier known as Stringtown, presumably so called because the buildings were "strung out" along Cowhouse Creek. Named for shopkeeper Henry King when John Seay opened the PO 24 Mar 1882.

KINGS MILL (Gray) In the mid-1880s the White Deer Lands Trust, a consortium of

British investors represented by London banker Andrew Kingsmill, took over the failed Francklyn Land and Cattle Company. The community grew around the Kings Mill Station established by the Southern Kansas Railroad of Texas in the early 1900s. The station was most likely named for Andrew Kingsmill's nephew, Montague Kingsmill Brown, a businessman with interests in ranching and railroad construction. Brown was mayor of Pampa in the 1920s. PO 4 Apr 1916 as Ecla; changed to Kings Mill 3 June 1922, PM Marguerite E. Massey.

KINGSBURY (Guadalupe) Founded about 1875 with construction of the Galveston, Harrisburg & San Antonio Railway. The station was named for William Gilliam Kingsbury, Texas Commissioner of Immigration, and an advocate of townsites along the line of the GH&SA. PO 13 Aug 1875, PM Mark W. Izard.

KINGSLAND (Llano) James Madison Trussell, a diarist and poet, brought his family from Mississippi in 1877. About 1890 Trussell and his son-in-law, Martin King, laid out the town of Kingsville, named for the King family. The name was changed when the Austin & Northwestern Railroad established Kingsland Station in the early 1890s. PO 25 June 1892 as Kingsville; changed to Kingsland 29 June 1893, PM Andrew L. Jones.

KINGSTON (Hunt) Benjamin "Nick" Hodges donated land for a station on the Missouri–Kansas–Texas Railroad in 1880. Hodges said he chose the name for Kingston in northwest Georgia where he and other Confederate soldiers surrendered to the Union Army in May 1865. PO 4 Oct 1880, PM J. W. Maynard.

KINGSVILLE (Kleberg) In 1903 Robert Justus Kleberg organized the Kleberg Town and Improvement Company to establish a community on the King Ranch and to attract a station on the St. Louis, Brownsville & Mexico Railway. The station and town were named for the ranch and for its founder, Richard King, who built the 800,000-acre ranch over several decades before his death in 1885. PO 15 July 1904, PM Leonard Thomas. See Kleberg County.

KINNEY (County) Created 1850, organized 1874. Named for Henry Lawrence Kinney (1814–1862), born in Pennsylvania. Kinney came to Texas about 1838 after some questionable real estate dealings in Illinois. He was a founder of Corpus Christi and a four-term representative in the Texas Legislature in the 1850s and 1860s. Against secession, Kinney resigned his seat in the Texas House and moved to Mexico in 1861. See Corpus Christi.

KIOMATIA [keye uh MAY shuh] (Red River) Named from the Kiomatia Plantation of Miller County, AR, bought by George Washington Wright about 1830. The plantation was named from the Kiamichi River of southeast Oklahoma. Kiamichi was apparently the name of one or more Caddo villages. PO 5 July 1850, PM Travis G. Wright.

KIRBY (Bexar) By 1900 Kirby Station was a stop on the Southern Pacific Railroad, named from the Kirby yard where railroad ties cut by the Kirby Lumber Company of

East Texas were stored. PO 12 Sept 1907, PM Louise Stolte.

KIRBYVILLE (Jasper) John Henry Kirby of Houston was a major figure in the East Texas lumber industry in the late 19th and early 20th centuries. Kirby partnered in the creation of the Gulf, Beaumont & Kansas City Railway, organized the Texas Pine Land Association, and founded the Southern Pine Association. He also served in the Texas House in the 1910s and 1920s. Several towns in East Texas owe their names and their existence to the Kirby Lumber Company, including Bessmay, Blox, and Browndell. PO 10 June 1895, PM Robert L. Frazer.

KIRKLAND (Childress) John Quincy Adams brought his family from Kentucky to an area known as Kirkland in 1880. Adams laid out the town of Kirkland in 1887 with construction of the Fort Worth & Denver City Railway. PO 6 Nov 1883, PM M. C. Williams.

KIRVIN (Freestone) The Trinity & Brazos Valley Railway established Kirvin Station in 1906, named for district judge Oliver C. Kirvin who donated land for the T&BV right of way. PO 30 Nov 1907, PM George Everett.

KITALOU [KIT uh loo] (Lubbock) In 1928 Frank Clarity, vice president and general manager of the Fort Worth & Denver City Railway, coined Kitalou by blending the name of his wife, Katherine (*Kit*ty) with Id*alou*, the town two miles northeast. See Idalou.

KITTRELL [KI truhl] (Walker) Founded in the early 1850s by pioneering physician Pleasant Williams Kittrell. Kittrell was Sam Houston's personal physician, a Texas legislator in the 1850s, and instrumental in founding the University of Texas. PO 2 May 1904, PM Eugene C. Woods. See Madison County; see Normangee.

KLEBERG (County) Created and organized 1913. Named for Robert Justus Kleberg, father (1803–1888) and son (1853–1932). The elder Kleberg emigrated from Prussia in 1834, fought at San Jacinto, and was Chief Justice of Austin County in the 1840s. The younger Kleberg was Richard King's lawyer and business associate and, after King's death in 1885, manager of the King ranch. He married King's daughter, Alice Gertrudis, the namesake of Alice, and became ranch manager in 1932. Rudolph Kleberg, also a son of Robert Justus Kleberg the elder, is the namesake of Rudolph in Kenedy County.

KLEBERG [KLEE berg] (Dallas) Named for Robert Justus Kleberg, the namesake of Kleberg County, who was granted several thousand acres in the area for his service in the Texas Revolution. PO 9 Feb 1882 as Kleburgh, PM James Capehart; changed to Kleburg 28 Nov 1887; changed to Kleberg 1 Apr 1926, PM Ira Floyd.

KLONDIKE (Delta) The Klondike, Yukon Territory, was in the news because of the Alaska Gold Rush in the late 1890s. PO 20 Sept 1897, PM Joel J. Hunt.

KLUMP (Washington) Named for Wilhelm August Klump who emigrated from Germany and settled in the area about 1850. PO 11 Sept 1899, PM George Schulze. Louis

Klump, son of Wilhelm and Anna Klump, was the second PM in 1900.

KNICKERBOCKER (Tom Green) In the 1870s Joseph Tweedy, Edwin Grinnell, and several others brought sheep herding to the area and established a settlement they named for Diedrich Knickerbocker, a pseudonym of 19th century writer Washington Irving who shared summer residences with Tweedys and Grinnells in Tarrytown, NY. PO 17 Aug 1881, PM Edwin Grinnell.

KNIPPA [kuh NIP uh] (Uvalde) Formerly known as Chatfield, a siding on the Galveston, Harrisburg & San Antonio Railway. (Chatfield Hill preserves the name.) About 1887 George Knippa, who had emigrated from Prussia in the 1850s, brought his family to the area from Fayette County and became a local benefactor and community namesake when the PO was established by Olive Woodard, 16 Feb 1898.

KNOTT [NAHT] (Howard) Named for Calvin Stevenson Knott, a livestock dealer and later a Fort Worth businessman and tour guide. PO 15 Mar 1907, PM Jerome B. Kerr.

KNOX (County) Created 1858, re-created 1876, organized 1886. Named for Henry Knox (1750–1806), born in Boston, MA. Knox was Commander-in-Chief of the Continental Army and President George Washington's first Secretary of War. Knox was a Revolutionary War hero and a popular political figure. At least a dozen counties and towns in the US are named in his honor and one of these may have influenced the naming of Knox County, Texas.

KNOX CITY (Knox) Lewis Riter opened the Orient PO 19 Sept 1903, named for the Kansas City, Mexico & Orient Railway. The name was changed to Knox City when William Pope became PM 16 Sept 1904.

KOERTH [KERTH] (Lavaca) Named for Carl Gottlieb (Charles) Koerth who kept a general store and was master of the Antioch PO in 1879. PO 27 May 1884 as Koerth's, PM Columbus Franks; changed to Koerth 10 Apr 1893.

KOHRVILLE [KOR vil] (Harris) Former slaves from Alabama and Mississippi founded Kohrville in the late 1860s. Named for Paul and Agnes Kohrmann from Baden, Germany, who established a general store about 1869. PO 20 June 1881, PM Paul Kohrmann.

KOKERNOT (Gonzales) David Levi Kokernot was a junior officer in the Texas Army in the 1830s. After the Texas Revolution he settled in Gonzales County and became the owner of several thousand acres of land along the Guadalupe River. Eventually, much of his land holdings were sold to Henry Dreyer, for whom the town of DREYER is named.

KOKOMO [KO kuh mo] (Eastland) Kokomo, founded in the 1890s on the line of the Texas & Pacific Railway, is a transfer by settlers from a Kokomo in Arkansas or Mississippi, themselves named for the original Kokomo in Howard County, IN. Kokomo was a 19th century Miami leader whose name may translate as "bear chief." PO 23 June 1899, PM Mary E. Comer.

KOMENSKY (Lavaca) Czech settlers named the community about 1895 in honor of Jan Amos Komensky (John Amos Comenius), a 17th century Czech teacher, writer, and educational philosopher.

KOOCKVILLE (Mason) Wilhelm (William) and Wilhelmina (Minnie) Koock (Kooch) from Hanover, Germany, established a trading post about 1867. Koockville is now a suburb of Mason.

KOPPERL [kuh PERL] (Bosque) Moritz Kopperl emigrated from Moravia in 1848, settled in Galveston, and became a wealthy merchant, president of the Texas National Bank, and president of the Gulf, Colorado & Santa Fe Railway. PO 5 Sept 1881, PM David A. Geisler.

KOSCIUSKO [kuh SHOOS ko] (Wilson) Kosciusko was organized by Polish settlers in the early 1890s with construction of the San Antonio & Gulf Railroad and named in June 1896 when Frank Nieschwietz established the Kosciusko PO, named in honor of Andrzej Tadeusz Bonawentura Kościuszko, usually Americanized as Thaddeus Kościuszko (1746–1817), one of George Washington's trusted aides during the Revolutionary War and a fighter for Polish independence in the 1790s.

KOSSE [KAH see] (Limestone) Founded in the late 1860s with construction of the Houston & Texas Central Railway; named by the H&TC for surveyor and chief engineer Theodore W. Kosse, who emigrated from Prussia in the late 1840s. PO 4 Oct 1856 as Eutaw; changed to Kosse 18 Oct 1870, PM Smith P. Young.

KOSSUTH [KAHS uhth] (Anderson) Lajos Kossuth was a leader of the 1848 Hungarian Revolution and president of Hungary in 1850. At least a dozen places in the US have been named in his honor, primarily during or shortly after his tour of the US in the early 1850s when he addressed a joint session of Congress. The Texas name was probably suggested by László Újházy, a compatriot of Kossuth who became a US citizen and settled near San Antonio in the mid-1850s.

KOUNTZE [KOONTSZ] (Hardin) In 1881 the Sabine & East Texas Railway laid track between Beaumont and Kountze, named by the S&ET for Herman, Charles, and Augustus Kountze, bankers and financiers with offices in New York, Omaha, and Denver, and major investors in Texas railroads, especially the S&ET. PO 28 Mar 1882, PM James E. Snelling.

KOVAR [KO ver] (Bastrop) Named for the Martin Kovar family who emigrated from Bohemia in the late 1870s. PO 4 Feb 1903, PM Frank Rundus.

KRESS (Swisher) Known as Wright for rancher Ryan Wright until 1906 when the Pecos & Northern Texas Railway built through the area. The namesake is reportedly one George H. Kress, about whom little is known. PO 30 Jan 1891 as Wright, PM Henrietta Wright; changed to Kress 23 July 1908, PM John F. Moore.

KREUTZBERG (Kendall) In the late 1840s Joseph Vincent Phillip, a carpenter from Pilsen, Bohemia, raised a large wooden cross on a hill overlooking the Guadalupe

River. The site became known as Kreutzberg (German "hill of the cross").

KRUGERVILLE (Denton) Founded in the mid-1960s by Denton homebuilder L. H. (Larry Holland) Kruger.

KRUM (Denton) Founded in 1884 by the Gulf, Colorado & Santa Fe Railway. Likely named for a railroad employee or official. A. R. Krum, reportedly a vice president of the Santa Fe, has been suggested, but some Santa Fe publications say the station was named for Charles K. Krum, a railroad official. PO 28 June 1888, PM Stephen D. Chadwell.

KURTEN (Brazos) Kurten was a German community founded by Henry Kurten (Curtin, Kertin). Kurten, born in Prussia, was in Galveston on leave from the German Army in the early 1850s and decided to stay. PO 29 Jan 1890, PM Horace H. Raymond.

KYLE (Hays) In 1880 the New York and Texas Land Company, a subsidiary of the International–Great Northern Railroad, laid out the town of Kyle, named for Ferguson Kyle who donated land for the townsite and the I-GN station. Kyle represented the district in the Texas House in 1870 and again in 1901. His father, Claiborne Kyle, served in the Texas House and Senate in the 1850s and 1860s. PO 5 Jan 1880, PM Nicholas Schlemmer.

KYOTE [KEYE ot] (Atascosa) Kyote was a phonetic respelling of "coyote" by PM William O. Rogers who established the office 23 Mar 1927. Rogers varied the spelling because there was a town in Bosque County also named for the abundant coyote population, though it too was misspelled, but as Cayote.

L

LA BAHIA [lah bah HEE uh] (Washington) Named from the La Bahía Road, also known as the Opelousas Road, established by the Spanish in the mid-18th century. The road, in several sections, ran from southwestern Louisiana to southeastern Texas. PO 16 June 1879, PM Edward Matejowsky.

LA BLANCA [lah BLAHNK uh] (Hidalgo) Named from the La Blanca Ranch, the "white" ranch established in the late 18th century, itself likely named for the white ranch house. PO 15 Nov 1927, PM Verna Pridmore.

LA CERDA (Nacogdoches) Named for the original land grantee, Juan Nepomuceno de la Cerda, born 1752 in Spanish Louisiana.

LA COSTE [luh KAHST] (Medina) The Galveston, Harrisburg & San Antonio Railway established the town of Fernando in the early 1890s. The name was later changed in honor of Jean Baptiste La Coste, a San Antonio businessman most remembered for establishing the first ice plant in San Antonio in 1868. PO 29 Nov 1893 as Fernando; changed to LaCoste 23 May 1898, PM James M. Cook.

LA FERIA [LAH fe REE uh] (Cameron) The name dates from at least 1777 when Rosa Hinojosa de Ballí received the La Feria ("the fair, the market") land grant from Spain. PO 19 May 1909, PM William Pittman.

LA GRANGE [luh GRAYNJ] (Fayette) From the 1820s the site was known as Moore's Fort for early settler John Henry Moore, one of Stephen F. Austin's original settlers. The town was platted in 1837 with the creation of Fayette County and named for La Grange (French "the barn"), the chateau and estate of the Marquis de Lafayette in central France. PO 27 Feb 1839, PM Hiram Ferrill. See Fayette County.

LA GRULLA [lah GROO yuh] (Starr) Founded in the 1780s on a site that extended to both sides of the Rio Grande. From Spanish *grulla* "crane," named for the sandhill cranes once common in the area. PO 17 Sept 1897, PM Lucas Hinojosa.

LA JOYA [luh HOY yuh] (Hidalgo) Spanish "the jewel." The name is said to have been inspired by a small lake west of the community whose waters "shone like a jewel in the sun." PO 3 Nov 1905 as Samfordyce; changed to La Joya 16 Sept 1931, PM Mary M. Solis.

LA JUNTA [luh HOON tuh] (Presidio) Spanish "meeting, joining." First known as *La Junta de los Ríos*, the site was at the confluence of the Río Conchos and Rio Grande rivers. See Presidio County.

LA MARQUE [luh MAHRK] (Galveston) Formerly known as Highland the name was changed 25 Jan 1887 when Patrick McPhillips opened the La Marque PO (French for "the mark"). Origin of the name is unknown.

LA PALOMA (Cameron) Spanish "the dove." Site owner Manuel Saldana chose the name in the early 20th century, reportedly for the flocks of doves that nested in the nearby oak and willow groves. PO 12 July 1912, PM Fred Aiken.

LA PRYOR (Zavala) Isaac (Ike) Pryor, a drover on the cattle trails of the 1870s, organized the Zavala Land and Water Development Company in the early 20th century to promote the area and market personal and professional building lots. Pryor laid out the community and established a station on the Crystal City & Uvalde Railroad on his ranch in 1909. Why Pryor combined his name with the Spanish feminine article "la" is unknown. PO 22 Jan 1910, PM Morell D. Reeso.

LA SALLE (County) Created 1858, organized 1880. Named for René-Robert Cavelier, the Sieur de La Salle (1643–1687). Hoping to establish a French commercial empire on the Gulf Coast, La Salle's armada sailed from France in the summer of 1684. He failed to locate the mouth of the Mississippi River and landed at Matagorda Bay where he attempted to plant a French colony. Most of the colonists were killed by Indians and La Salle himself was murdered by one of his own men near the Trinity River in March 1687.

LA SALLE (Jackson) La Salle was founded in the early 20th century when the Missouri Pacific Railroad established Benwest Station, a blend of the names of the site owners, ranchers John M. *Ben*nett and his business partners, brothers George, Solomon, and Isaac *West*. When the Wests withdrew from the partnership, the name became Bennview. The community was formally laid out in the mid-1920s and the name was changed to La Salle in 1937, presumably for the Sieur de La Salle, for whom La Salle County is named. PO 24 May 1928 as Bennview, PM John J. Stepan; changed to La Salle 1 Aug 1937.

LA VERNIA [lah ver NEE uh] (Wilson) In the early 1850s William Robert Wiseman and William Claiborne Rector laid out the community and organized the Cibolo Presbyterian Church. The source of the name is unknown. There is no evidence to connect La Vernia with the Franciscan monastery of Lavernia near Camaldoli, Tuscany, Italy and attempts to relate the name to Spanish *verde* "green" quickly become popular etymologies. PO 2 Feb 1853 as Post Oak; changed to Lavernia 7 May 1859, PM Connally F. Henderson.

LA WARD (Jackson) *La*fayette *Ward*, a businessman and rancher who introduced Brahma and other exotic cattle breeds to Texas in the early 20th century, founded the town about 1905 on the line of the St. Louis, Brownsville & Mexico Railway. PO 4 Oct 1897 as Buhler; changed to La Ward 31 July 1906, PM George R. Joines.

LABELLE (Jefferson) French "beautiful one." Named by Joseph Eloi Broussard, instrumental in developing the Texas rice industry. Broussard opened the LaBelle PO 16 June 1888, named for his fiancée, Mary Belle Bordages.

LACEYVILLE (Nacogdoches) Lacey (Lacy) Hunt was co-owner with Tilden Tilford of the Tilford-Hunt Lumber Company of Nacogdoches established in 1904.

LACY-LAKEVIEW (McLennan) Lacy was organized in the 1880s, named for Waco businessmen William D. Lacy and his son, Walter G. Lacy. Lacy became a stop on the Texas Electric Railway; the next station was

Lakeview. The Lacy and Lakeview governments merged in 1953.

LADONIA [luh DON yuh] (Fannin) In 1855 James Cole laid out the townsite as McCowansville, named for early settler Francis McCowan. The source of the name Ladonia is unknown but has generated a number of local stories. By one, Ladonia is an English phonetic spelling of Spanish *La Doña*, but who "the lady" might have been is uknown. By another, in the late 1850s Donald Millsap (or Millsay) and his family stopped at Francis McCowan's store where LaDonna, his young daughter, entertained the customers with songs and recitations. On 27 July 1858, PM Daniel S. Redner changed the name of the post office (established by Francis McCowan 1 Oct 1853 as North Sulphur) to Ladonia to memorialize LaDonna's performance.

LAFAYETTE (Upshur) Matthew Fielding Locke, born in Tennessee, moved to Upshur County in the early 1850s, served in the Texas House, and founded LaFayette in 1858, named for his eight-year-old son, LaFayette Calhoun Locke. PO 12 Feb 1858, PM Samuel M. Talkington.

LAGARTO (Live Oak) In 1856 John Ramey from Fort Merrill, a maker of saddle trees, laid out the community on Lagarto Creek. *Lagarto* (Spanish "lizard") referred to alligators, and the stream was noted for its alligator population. PO 17 Aug 1874, PM Frank H. Church.

LAGUNA SECA (Hidalgo) Spanish "dry lake." Named from the Laguna Seca Ranch established in 1867 by Macedonio Vela. The Delfina PO, named for Vela's daughter, opened 11 Jan 1893, PM Richard Marsh.

LAGUNA VISTA (Cameron) Spanish "lake view." Apparently so named because the site overlooked Laguna Madre.

LAHEY (Terry) Named about 1915 by the Panhandle & Santa Fe Railway in honor of Thomas H. Lahey, a Hartley County rancher. PO 27 May 1926, PM Edward J. Purcell.

LAIRD HILL (Rusk) Named for site owner Shirley Spurgeon "Shack" Laird, a farmer and oilman during the East Texas oil boom of the 1930s. PO 1936, PM Ignatius S. Cutcher. Known informally as Pistol Hill.

LAJITAS [lah HEE tis] (Brewster) Spanish "little flat stones." Presumably named for the local paving stones. PO 26 May 1904, PM Josephine Navarro McGuirk.

LAKE VICTOR (Burnet) A former railroad camp on the line of the Houston & Texas Central Railway was platted as Lake Victor in 1903. The name was apparently chosen by Ophelia Gilmore, daughter of early settlers George and Carolina Gilmore, for Victor Kellogg, foreman of the railroad construction crew. PO 12 Feb 1903, PM Francis A. Ramsey.

LAMAR (County) Created 1840, organized 1841. Named for Mirabeau Buonaparte Lamar (1798–1859), younger brother of Lucius Quintus Cincinnatus Lamar and cousin of Gazaway Bugg Lamar. A native Georgian, Lamar came to Texas in 1835, fought in the Texas Revolution, and was the second President of the Republic of Texas (1838–1841). Lamar was a painter, a poet, and a founder of the Philosophical Society of Texas. Lamar, the seat of Barton County, MO, and the birthplace of President Harry S. Truman, is also named for Mirabeau Lamar.

LAMAR (Aransas) James W. Byrne, the clerk of Refugio County, founded Lamar in 1839 named for Mirabeau B. Lamar, then President of the Republic of Texas. Byrne reportedly asked Lamar to personally lay out the town. PO 30 May 1839, PM George Armstrong.

LAMASCO [luh MAS ko] (Fannin) Lamasco, in Vanderburgh County, IN, was named in the 1830s by blending the names of early settlers, John and William *La*w, James *Mac*-Call, and Lucius *Sco*tt. Settlers from Indiana brought the name to Lamasco, Lyon County, KY, the former home of the founders of Lamasco, TX. PO 15 Feb 1886, PM Fred Owen.

LAMB (County) Created 1876, organized 1908. Named for George A. Lamb (1814–1836). At age 20 Lamb moved to Texas from South Carolina and began farming west of Huntsville in Walker County. In March 1836 he joined the Second Regiment of Texas Volunteers and was killed the following month at San Jacinto.

LAMESA [luh MEE suh] (Dawson) Rancher Arthur L. Wasson, apparently impressed by the surrounding flat land, proposed the name *La Mesa* (Spanish "the table"), which was soon compressed to Lamesa. The Chicago PO, opened 15 May 1889, was changed to Lamesa 9 Apr 1904, PM Harrison B. Oliver.

LAMKIN (Comanche) George Washington Lamkin relocated from Georgia to Texas in the 1860s. Lamkin donated land for the townsite and opened the PO named for his family 9 May 1884.

LAMPASAS [lam PAS is] (County) Created and organized 1856. Named from the Lampasas River, itself named by Spanish explorers of the early 1720s, probably for Lampazos, Mexico, now the city of Lampazos de Naranjo, Nuevo León, itself founded in the late 17th century and apparently named from the local growth of *Xanthosoma robustum*, called *lampazos* and commonly known as elephant ears. George Scott laid out the town of Burleson in 1855, named for Scott's father-in-law, early settler John Burleson (Berleson).

LAMPASAS (Lampasas) When Lampasas County was created, Burleson was made the county seat and the name was changed to Lampasas. PO 4 May 1857 as Lampasas, PM Francis Fletcher.

LANARK (Cass) Founded in the early 1870s with construction of the Texas & Pacific Railway. Lanark is a transfer name, perhaps from a Lanark in Arkansas or Illinois, or more likely directly from Lanark, Scotland, location of the offices of several financiers who underwrote construction of a number of Texas railroads. PO 15 Dec 1873, PM Calisto Woodward. See Queen City.

LANCASTER [LANGK is ter] (Dallas) Abraham Bledsoe laid out the townsite in 1852, named for his birthplace, Lancaster, Garrard County, KY, which was platted by

Bledsoe's father in 1798 and named by settlers from Lancaster, PA, which was named for Lancaster, England in the early 1730s. PO 20 July 1848 as Pleasant Run; changed to Lancaster 19 Apr 1860, PM Samuel T. Bledsoe.

LANDRUM (Cameron) About 1913 the San Benito & Rio Grande Valley Railroad established Landrum Station, named for James L. Landrum, known as the Father of SAN BENITO.

LANE (Hunt) Robert Ward Lane, a farmer and stockman from Tennessee, opened a general store in 1866 and established the PO 17 Jan 1879.

LANE CITY (Wharton) Named for Jonathan Lane, a Texas State Senator in the late 1880s and president of the Cane Belt Railroad when the CB terminal was constructed in 1900. PO 26 Sept 1901 as Arnim, named for Edward Alexander Arnim of Flatonia, Jonathan Lane's business partner; changed to Lane City 13 Feb 1911, PM Frank M. Ryon.

LANELY (Freestone) Lanely is an adaptation of Lane. The community was named for Methodist minister James King Lane who opened the Lanely PO 1 Mar 1899.

LANEVILLE (Rusk) Laneville was named in the early 1880s, apparently for the intersection where roads provided four lanes of travel, one in each direction. PO 26 Sept 1888, PM Philetus R. Williamson.

LANGTRY (Val Verde) Named for George Langtry, a construction engineer for the Southern Pacific Railroad that built through the area in 1882. Several years later Roy Bean, a justice of the peace who referred to himself as "the law west of the Pecos," arrived and claimed that he had chosen the name for Lillie Langtry, a socialite and actress he greatly admired. He named the saloon-courtroom where he administered frontier justice the Jersey Lilly in her honor. Other than Bean's word there is nothing to support his claim, but the myth abides. PO 8 Dec 1884, PM William F. Robinson.

LANIER [luh NIHR] (Cass) Named from the Lanier PO established 3 Nov 1873 by native Georgian Alexander Collins, who named the office for Lanier County, GA, itself named for Georgia poet Sidney Lanier.

LANNIUS [LAN ee is] (Fannin) In the 1870s Benjamin Franklin Stephens relocated from Georgia and founded the town of Stephensville. The name was changed for businessman William Lannius when Blackmore H. Gay opened the Lannius PO 17 Apr 1891.

LANTANA (Denton) A planned community developed by the Dallas-based Republic Property Group beginning in 1999, named for Texas Lantana or Calico Bush, a perennial flower of the verbena family noted for its attraction to butterflies.

LAREDO [luh RAY do] (Webb) Tomás Sánchez de la Barrera y Garza, born in Nuevo León, Mexico, founded Laredo in 1755. A delightful popular etymology claims that Spanish priests built a church with three bells, tuned to the musical notes "la," "re," and "do," which became the name of the town. Rather, Laredo is named from

Nuevo Laredo, Tamaulipas, Mexico, itself named for Laredo on the Bay of Biscay in northern Spain, perhaps the birthplace of José de Escandón, the first governor of Nuevo Santander, who authorized the founding of Laredo. PO 3 Feb 1849, PM Augustin Soto.

LARIAT (Parmer) Lariat was established on the former XIT Ranch by the Pecos & Northern Texas Railway in 1913 and named by a railroad official, probably William Simpson, who was impressed by the roping skills of the cowboys who worked the XIT. PO 9 Dec 1925, PM Maggie L Robertson.

LARISSA (Cherokee) In 1847 the Rev. Thomas McKee with a group of Cumberland Presbyterian settlers from Lebanon, TN, founded Larissa. Named by McKee's son, Thomas N. McKee, also a Presbyterian minister, for Larissa, the ancient Greek city of learning and the home of Hippocrates. Present Larissa includes the remains of Talladega, founded about 1837 and named by settlers from Talladega, AL. PO 23 Dec 1847, PM Jesse Davidson. See Mount Selman.

LARUE (Henderson) In the late 1850s a community formed around Morrison Chapel, named for John D. Morrison. The name was changed in 1901 when the Texas & New Orleans Railroad established LaRue Station, named for Joseph T. LaRue, an Athens banker and businessman. PO 27 May 1901, PM Charles F. Regester.

LAS TIENDAS (Webb) Spanish "the stores." Apart from the obvious, the source of the name is unknown.

LASARA [luh SEHR uh] (Willacy) Founded in 1924 by William A. Harding and Samuel Lamar Gill, the founders of Willamar. Lasara is a blend of *La*ura and *Sara*h, for their wives, Laura Harding and Sarah Gill. PO 28 Oct 1926, PM Andrew Watson. See Willamar.

LASSATER [LAS uht er] (Marion) In the late 1870s the East Line & Red River Railroad established Lasater [*sic*] Station, named for Joseph and Josephine Lasater who settled in the area in the late 1860s. PO 9 June 1875 as Sidney; changed to Lasater Station 9 Nov 1877, PM Joseph D. Lasater.

LATCH (Upshur) Lewis A. Latch, who operated a sawmill and cotton gin from the late 1870s, was sheriff of Upshur County from about 1907. PO 26 Feb 1904, PM James Long.

LATEX (Harrison) Located on the Louisiana-Texas border.

LATEXO [luh TEKS o] (Houston) Known as Bethel from the Bethel Church and School and later as Starks Switch for the siding built by the International–Great Northern Railroad to handle lumber from the Starks Sawmill. In the early 1900s the Louisiana–Texas Orchard Company, known as Latexo, organized the town to market the local fruit crops. PO 10 Dec 1907, PM James Patton.

LATIUM [LACH uhm] (Washington) Latium is the region of west central Italy surrounding Rome and was the capital of the Roman Empire. Latium is one of a half dozen "Latin" colonies founded in Texas by German political, artistic, and social refugees following the German revolutions of the late 1840s. PO 8 Apr 1884, PM Hermann Otto Cornitius.

LAUREL (Newton) In 1890 the Sabine Tram Company established a lumber camp named for Laura Gilmer, daughter of Alexander Gilmer, major stockholder of the STC and later owner and operator of the Alexander Gilmer Lumber Company. The name may have been influenced by the local growth of laurel trees. PO 21 June 1889, PM George W. Smyth.

LAURELES [luh RAY lis] (Cameron) Named from the *Rincón de los Laureles* "corner, valley of the laurels" land grant from which the Laureles Ranch was also named.

LAVACA [luh VAK a, luh VAH kuh] (County) Named from the Lavaca River that begins in Gonzales County and flows southeast for more than one hundred miles before emptying into Lavaca Bay in Calhoun County. About 1685 the expedition of René-Robert Cavelier, the Sieur de La Salle, named the river *Rivière de Les Veches* "river of cows" for the local buffalo herds. Later Spanish explorers translated the name as *la vaca* "the cow." In January 1842 the Republic of Texas Legislature modified the name and established La Baca County. After much legislative and judicial wrangling, in 1846 the name La Vaca County replaced La Baca County. The Bovine PO, a translation of *vaca*, opened 16 May 1860, PM Patrick May.

LAVON [luh VAHN] (Collin) Named for Olen Lavon Thomson, son of the first postmaster, Elbert C. Thomson who opened the office 1 May 1888.

LAWSON (Dallas) Known as Haught's Store for the general store kept by Samuel and Isabelle Haught in the 1850s, or as Slapfoot, reportedly for the community's uninhibited weekend dance parties. Renamed for Henry Lawson who bought Haught's store in the early 1890s. PO 22 Oct 1866 as Haught's Store; changed to Lawson 17 July 1897, PM Archibald B. Lanier.

LAWSONVILLE (Rusk) Named for Henry and Amanda Lawson, planters from Georgia, about 1845. Henry Lawson represented the district in the Texas Legislature in the early 1850s. Amanda Lawson established the PO 4 June 1877.

LAZARE [luh ZAHR] (Hardeman) Lazare was established in the early 20th century by the Quanah, Acme & Pacific Railway and named for Lazare Baker, grandson of Samuel Lazarus, organizer and president of the QA&P. Lazare is the French form of Lazarus. PO 12 July 1909, PM William A. Dorsey.

LAZBUDDIE [LAZ buhd ee] (Parmer) Luther Green, known as "Laz," and Andrew Sherley, known as "Buddie," established a general store called the Lazbuddie Commissary on land they purchased from the Star Ranch in the mid-1920s. PO 4 May 1926, PM John H. Hennington.

LEADAY [luh DAY] (Coleman) Mabel Day, widow of William Day, married Joseph Lea and combined her two husbands' names when the town was platted on the Day Ranch in 1904. PO 8 Apr 1905, PM John R. French.

LEAGUE CITY (Galveston) Galveston businessman and community benefactor John C. League founded League City about 1890. PO 19 Feb 1874 as Clear Creek; changed to League City 8 Apr 1896, PM George W. Butler.

LEAGUEVILLE (Henderson) Likely named from the league of land (about 4,400 acres) surveyed by Aaron York about 1850. PO 30 Mar 1899, PM Wellborn B. Cooper.

LEAKEY [LAY kee] (Real) John Leakey from Tennessee is regarded as the first permanent settler in what is now Real County in the 1850s. PO 14 May 1884, PM Arthur G. Vogel.

LEANDER [lee AN der] (Williamson) After the Austin & Northwestern Railroad built through the area in 1882 many of the homes and businesses of the bypassed community of Bagdad were moved a mile east to the railroad town of Leander. Although a Karl Leander, reported to be the station manager of the A&N, is often claimed to be the namesake, the station and community were named for Leander Brown, mayor of Austin in the late 1860s and one of the first directors of the A&N in 1881. Leander includes the former town of Bagdad, founded in 1854 by innkeeper Charles Babcock and named by settlers from Bagdad, TN. Bagdad Road in Leander preserves the name. The Bagdad PO, opened 8 May 1855, was changed to Leander 6 Oct 1882, PM John F. Heinatz.

LEARY (Bowie) Named for Daniel T. Leary, a Texarkana lawyer and the site owner. PO 6 Mar 1894, PM James Wiggins.

LEBANON (Collin) Lanson Clark (often misspelled Danson Clark) named the community for his former home, Lebanon, TN, itself named for the Biblical prophecy that "Lebanon shall be turned into a fruitful field." PO 1 Mar 1860, PM Philip A. Huffman.

LEBANON (Hill) Named from the Lebanon Methodist Church organized in 1872.

LEDBETTER (Fayette) Named for the Ledbetter family from Tennessee. Plantation owners Hamilton and Jane Ledbetter brought 30 slaves to Texas, first to Victoria County and to Fayette County in 1845. The Ledbetter's son, William Hamilton Ledbetter, was a Texas State Senator in the 1870s and mayor of La Grange in the 1880s. PO 27 June 1871, PM Robert Leiswitz.

LEE (County) Created and organized 1874. Named for Confederate General Robert E. Lee. As a US Army officer Lee served in Texas on several occasions from 1856 until 1861.

LEES (Glasscock) Lees grew around a tuberculosis sanatorium founded in 1907 by Georgia physician Edward A. Lee. PO 1 Apr 1907, PM Samuel Polk.

LEESBURG (Camp) Probably named for Englishman John Lee who emigrated to Texas in 1857, fought in the Civil War, and farmed in Camp County from the mid-1870s. PO 25 June 1874 as Leesburgh, PM James G. Credille.

LEESVILLE (Gonzales) Known as Capote from the Capote Hills west of the town, themselves named from Spanish for "cape, cloak." In the early 1870s Newburn William Guinn laid out the community of Leesburg, named for either his wife or daughter. PO 3 Mar 1873 as Capiote [*sic*]; changed to Leesville 25 Aug 1874, PM James A. Nance.

LEFORS [luh FORZ] (Gray) Site owner James Isham "Perry" LeFors, born in Dade County, MO, came to Texas in 1870. LeFors was foreman of the Diamond F Ranch and the first town sheriff. PO 12 Oct 1892, PM Henry Thut.

LEGGETT (Polk) Ralph McGee Leggett moved from Moscow, TX, in the 1880s and opened a general store. The Leggett House, built by his brother, John Calvin Leggett in 1886, is a Texas Historic Landmark. PO 27 Oct 1882, PM James R. Freeman.

LEGION (Kerr) The community was known as Legion from 1922 when the property was owned by the Texas Department of the American Legion. Now part of Kerrville. PO 2 Dec 1922, PM Charles A. Duff.

LEHMAN [LEE muhn] (Cochran) In 1923 Christopher Columbus Slaughter laid out the town of Ligon south of present Morton, named for his daughter-in-law, Carrie Ligon Slaughter. When the South Plains & Santa Fe Railway built through the area, Ligon moved south to trackside and changed its name to Lehman for Frank A. Lehman, general manager of the SP&SF. PO 21 Jan 1924 as Ligon; changed to Lehman 16 May 1925, PM Alvin O'Pry. See Morton, see Whiteface.

LEIGH [LEE] (Harrison) John W. Furrh, the townsite owner and a Marshall shopkeeper, founded Leigh about 1900, named for his wife, Leigh Loftus Furrh. PO 10 Mar 1884 as Blocker, PM Albert B. Blocker; changed to Leigh 2 Feb 1901, PM John T. Winston.

LELA [LEE luh] (Wheeler) The Chicago, Rock Island & Gulf Railway station was established as Story in the early 1900s. The name was changed to Lela at the request of Bedford Forrest Bowers, who would become the second postmaster, for Lela H. Smith, sister-in-law of his brother Isaac Newton Bowers. PO Sept 1902, PM Hezekiah J. McGehee.

LELIA LAKE [LEEL yuh] (Donley) About 1888 Gibson A. "Gyp" Brown, the first judge of Donley County, established a flag station on the Fort Worth & Denver City Railway named for his sister-in-law, Lelia Payne. PO 18 Dec 1906, PM Philip Jackson.

LEMING (Atascosa) The site was known as Las Gallinas (Spanish "the hens"), presumably for the local prairie chickens, until 1912 when the San Antonio, Uvalde & Gulf Railroad established Leming Station, named for Merit E. Leming, vice president of the SAU&G. Merit Leming's son, Paul, is often miscredited as the town's namesake. PO 13 Sept 1880 as Gallinas; changed to Leming 1 July 1912, PM James S. Neill.

LENORAH (Martin) Named for Lenorah Epley, wife of John Epley, eleven-term Martin County clerk. After John Epley's death in office in 1941 Lenorah Epley became Martin County clerk. PO 2 July 1924, PM Joseph F. Willingham.

LEO (Cooke) The local account is that Martin Stamper, an Era physician, suggested

Leo, Latin "lion" because the town was "a very tough place." PO 7 May 1894, PM Thomas McBride.

LEON (County) Created and organized 1846. Named for empresario Martín de León (1765–1833). After being rebuffed several times by the Spanish governor at San Antonio in the early 19th century, De León's Colony was approved by the Mexican government in 1824, along with authority to found the city of Victoria.

LEONA [lee ON uh] (Leon) In the early 1880s the Texas Legislature directed the founding of Leona and adapted the name from Leon County. PO 30 Jan 1845 as Leona Mills, PM James Mitchell.

LEONARD (Fannin) In 1880 the Denison & Southeastern Railway laid tracks on land owned by the heirs of Solomon Langdon Leonard, a lawyer and local judge who bought the tract in 1859. PO 9 Nov 1880, PM William B. Patterson.

LEROY [LEE roy] (McLennan) Leroy was founded about 1897 with construction of the International–Great Northern Railroad and named for Leroy Trice, vice president and general manager of the I–GN. PO 5 Mar 1900, PM Joseph Lumbley.

LESLEY (Hall) Stock raiser James Patterson Montgomery opened the PO 17 Oct 1902 named for his two-year-old son, Samuel Leslie Montgomery. The spelling has alternated between Lesley and Leslie.

LEVELLAND (Hockley) The community was organized as Hockley City about 1912 by Charles W. Post, founder of the C. W. Post cereal empire and the namesake of POST in Garza County. Renamed for the local landscape by Post's wife and daughter when James A. Stroud, the first Hockley County sheriff, opened the Levelland PO 30 Sept 1924. See Post.

LEVERETT'S CHAPEL (Rusk) Marshall and Eliza Ann Leverett settled at the site in the early 1850s.

LEVI (McLennan) Named for Levi Robinson, brother of John Robinson, the namesake of ROBINSON. PO 7 July 1897, PM John Young.

LEVITA [luh VEYET uh] (Coryell) From about 1870 the town was known as Simpsonville for Montaville Simpson who operated a general store and a gristmill. The name became Levita when Charles Henry Martin Jaye opened the Levita PO 3 June 1886. The source of the name is unknown.

LEWISVILLE (Denton) John Holford, a shopkeeper from Missouri and early settler in the 1840s, gave the town its first name, Holford's Prairie. Basdeal (or Basdell) W. Lewis bought the site in the early 1850s and the name was changed to Lewisville. PO 14 June 1855 as Lewisville, PM Theodore J. Dorsett.

LEXINGTON (Lee) James Shaw is generally regarded as the first permanent settler on String Prairie in the 1840s. According to local accounts the town was named for Lexington, MA, site of one of the first confrontations of the Revolutionary War. PO 16 Aug 1849 as String Prairie; changed to Lexington 20 May 1853, PM Shadrack B. Owen.

LIBERTY (County) Created 1836, organized 1837. In 1831 the Mexican government created the *Villa de la Santísima Trinidad de la Libertad* "Community of the Most Holy Trinity of Liberty." By 1836 the name had been compressed to Liberty, partly a translation of *Libertad*; partly inspired by the connotations of "liberty"; and partly from towns in eastern states named Liberty.

LIBERTY (Liberty) Originally part of a Mexican municipality, the community was known as Liberty by 1836 when Liberty County was created and William Hardin opened the Liberty PO.

LIBERTY HILL (Titus) By a local story the town was named for the Liberty Church when it got its "liberty" from another congregation with which there were disagreements. The new church was built on a hill, thus the name.

LILBERT (Nacogdoches) Named from the Lilbert post office, opened by Rev. John Lilbert Wortham 19 July 1899.

LILLIAN (Johnson) According to local accounts the town was named for Lillian Renfro and Lillian Cunningham, wives of George J. Renfro and William J. Cunningham who laid out Lillian about 1903. Rather, the namesake is Lillian Hunter Noble, sister-in-law of George Lawrence Noble, general manager of the International–Great Northern Railroad that established a station in 1902. PO 20 Oct 1875 as Pleasant Point; changed to Lillian 12 July 1904, PM Alice P. Braswell.

LIMESTONE (County) Created and organized 1846. Named for the abundance of local limestone.

LINCOLN (Lee) John A. Lincoln, a Campbellite minister, moved to Evergreen about 1880. The name was changed when Adolph Boscamp opened the Lincoln PO 14 Sept 1886.

LINDALE (Smith) Elijah Lindsey, brother-in-law of Richard Hubbard, Governor of Texas in the late 1880s, opened the first general store in the late 1860s. Lindsey's name was shortened and modified to Lyn and "dale" was added for romantic effect when John Davis opened the Lyndale PO in 1873. The spelling was changed to Lindale in 1874.

LINDEN (Cass) Jeremiah Preston Wood laid out the townsite in 1848, named for his former home, Linden, TN, itself named from Thomas Campbell's popular 1803 poem, "The Battle of Hohenlinden," which begins "On Linden, when the sun was low/ All bloodless lay the untrodden snow." PO 25 May 1852, PM Ward Taylor.

LINDENAU [LIN duh now] (DeWitt) Named in 1893, perhaps by early settlers from Lindenau in east central Germany; more likely from "Lindenau," a popular German polka at the time. PO 29 July 1895, PM Gustav Markowsky.

LINDSAY (Cooke) In 1887 the Gainesville, Henrietta & Western Railway established a switching station named for James Menees Lindsay, a district judge and a founder of the Gainesville National Bank. PO 27 May 1891, PM Anton Flusche. See Muenster.

LINGLEVILLE (Erath) Named for Illinoisans Jacob and Annie Lingle who established a farm in the 1860s. PO 6 Nov 1885, PM Redick Campbell. Informally known as Needmore.

LINN (Hidalgo) Linn was founded in the late 1920s by developer William Dougherty; reportedly named for Linn Dougherty, son of William and Orpha Dougherty. PM 11 Aug 1928, PM Andrew C. Doughty.

LIPAN [li PAN] (Hood) The Lipan were one of the two main Apache groups in Texas. Thomas Burns, from Ireland, laid out the community in the early 1870s and opened the PO in his general store 24 May 1875.

LIPSCOMB (County) Created 1876, organized 1887. Named for jurist Abner Smith Lipscomb (1789–1856), born in South Carolina. Lipscomb, former chief justice of the Alabama Supreme Court and a member of the Alabama Legislature, moved to Texas and established a law practice in Brenham in 1839. He was Texas Secretary of State under President Mirabeau Lamar and justice of the Texas Supreme Court in the 1840s and 1850s.

LIPSCOMB (Lipscomb) James W. Arthur established the town of Lipscomb, named from the county, and opened the PO in his general store 20 Dec 1886.

LISSIE (Wharton) New Philadelphia was founded on the line of the Buffalo Bayou, Brazos & Colorado Railway in 1878. PO 17 Jan 1878 as Philadelphia; discontinued 3 Nov 1891; reestablished 31 Oct 1894 as Lissie, probably named by PM Alma Coats Adams in honor of Melissa Cassandra Leveridge Stockton, a revered teacher known as Lissie.

LITTIG [LIT ig] (Travis) In 1883 Jackson Morrow, a former slave, donated land for an African American community that was named for Augustus Ward Littig, trainmaster of the Houston & Texas Central Railway. PO 20 May 1889; PM Thomas B. Fowler.

LITTLE HOPE (Wood) The local story is as pessimistic as the name suggests. When the Little Hope Missionary Baptist Church was founded in 1881, several parishioners thought there was little hope for the success of the church or for the town. More hopefully, the Little Hope Baptist church was probably named for an established Hope Baptist Church, perhaps in another state. There are also Little Hope churches in Angelina, Panola and Van Zandt counties.

LITTLE RIVER (Bell) The Leon River and Lampasas River join at the site to form Little River, a tributary of the Brazos River. In 1989 Little River and Academy merged as Little River-Academy. PO 26 Feb 1886, PM Cornelius Burks.

LITTLEFIELD (Lamb) Founded in 1912 by George Washington Littlefield, rancher, banker, and University of Texas benefactor. Littlefield, a UT regent in 1911, built the Alice P. Littlefield Dormitory in 1927, named for his wife, Alice Payne Littlefield, who donated the family home, the Littlefield House on Whitis Ave., to the university in 1935. PO 5 Feb 1913, PM Campbell Duggan.

LIVE OAK (County) Created and organized 1856. Named for *Quercus Virginiana*, the Southern live oak, prominent in the county and in much of South and Central Texas.

LIVELY (Kaufman) According to local lore there were so many dances that the town became known as a "lively little place." Rather Lively was named for Joel T. Lively, part owner of the Lively and Doss grocery and dry goods store from the early 1900s and the Lively and Kellum store from the 1910s.

LIVERPOOL (Brazoria) Laid out in 1837 for Englishman Thomas C. Nelson of Galveston, known as the Commodore. According to tradition, Nelson named the town for Liverpool, England. PO 1 Mar 1845, PM Warren D. C. Hall who platted the town of Liverpool and for whom HALL COUNTY was named.

LIVINGSTON (Polk) Moses Livingston Choate, a landowner and cabinet maker from Tennessee, founded the town as Springfield about 1840. When Polk County was created in 1846, Choate donated land for the county seat, named Livingston in his honor. PO May 1838 as Fulton; changed to Livingston 19 May 1847, PM John Davis.

LLANO [LA no] (County) Created and organized 1856. Named from the Llano River whose two parent forks join in northeast Edwards County and flow for 100 miles, emptying into the Colorado River at Kingsland in Llano County. As early as the 1710s the river was known to Spanish explorers as *Río de los Chanes* or *Río de los Sanas* for the Chane (or Sana), a Tonkawan people. Through spelling changes, Chanes became Llanes, which through popular etymology became Llano (Spanish "plain, flat land").

LLANO (Llano) The Texas Legislature established the community of Llano along with Llano County in 1856. PO 1 Sept 1857, PM John Oatman.

LOCKER (San Saba) In the mid-1870s James Monroe Locker established a cotton gin on the Colorado River at BOWSER BEND. His son, Thomas H. Locker, opened the post office 15 June 1899.

LOCKETT (Wilbarger) Brothers Tilman (Tillmon) and Jeremiah Lockett emigrated from Tennessee in the late 1880s.

LOCKETTVILLE (Hockley, Terry) Founded in the mid-1930s by Aubrey Locket(t), agriculturist and philanthropist. In 1997 the Texas A&M Agricultural Experiment Station in Vernon announced the development of Lockett Wheat, a hardy winter variety named for Aubrey Lockett who donated land for the research station in the early 1970s.

LOCKHART (Caldwell) About 1826 Byrd Lockhart, with his brothers Andrew and Charles, arrived in Texas as part of Green DeWitt's Colony. Byrd Lockhart became one of the principle surveyors in the area around Gonzales and he is known to history as one of the two defenders of the Alamo who were ordered to Gonzales to arrange for supplies and reinforcements shortly before the battle. PO 14 June 1847 as Plum Creek; changed to Lockhart 27 July 1848, PM James Dougherty.

LOCKNEY (Floyd) By local tradition, in 1899 Crosby County surveyor Henry C. Knight named the community for James Henry Lockney and his son, Johnson Frederick Lockney, about whom little is known. PO 16 July 1890, PM William Davis.

LOCO (Childress) Spanish *loco* "mad." Named from the loco weed. Chronic ingestion of this toxic plant that grows in much of the western US causes animals, especially cattle and horses, to grow weak and lose muscular control, acting, as described in early accounts, as though they were crazy. PO 11 Nov 1892, PM John S. Hill.

LODI [LO deye] (Marion) By most reports the name was suggested by Jessie Lopresto for his former home, Lodi, Italy. From one account to another Mr. Lopresto is claimed to be a railroad worker, an early settler, or a sawmill operator. Alternatively, Lodi may be a transfer, perhaps from Lodi, MS, or Lodi, TN. Lodi, a popular place name occurring in more than a dozen states, is ultimately from the province and city in northern Italy where Napoleon defeated an Austrian army in 1796. PO 23 Nov 1876, PM Dudley Warner.

LOEB [LOB] (Hardin) Founded in the 1850s as Concord and renamed about 1900 when Henry Loeb established the Diana Brick and Tile Company. PO 4 Aug 1858 as Concord; discontinued 4 Dec 1877; reestablished as Loeb 16 Sept 1903, PM Simon Hyman.

LOEBAU (Lee) Organized by German settlers in the late 1880s and named for Löbau in East Saxony. PO 13 Dec 1898, PM John Matthijetz who was succeeded by his son August in 1901.

LOHN [LAHN] (McCulloch) William and Harriet Lohn, German immigrants, began farming in the area in 1879. PO 4 Mar 1890, PM Morgan J. Stacy.

LOIRE (Wilson) James Merrill Swindler from Pointe Coupee Parish, LA, was the first PM in July 1895. He is credited with bringing settlers to the site from the Loire Valley of France, hence the name.

LOIS (Cooke) Lois was named from the PO established 24 Dec 1897 by Daniel Wilson. The office was probably named for Lois Stamper, four-year-old daughter of Martin and Elizabeth Stamper of Era. Elizabeth Stamper was Era PM at the time.

LOLAVILLE (Collin) Lolaville was a predominantly African American community established in the 1940s and named for teacher and benefactor Lola Kelsey Dunafan.

LOLITA (Jackson) Named for Lolita Reese, granddaughter of Charles Keller Reese who joined Stephen F. Austin's Colony in 1830 and fought at San Jacinto. Many of the houses and businesses of nearby Red Bluff were moved to Lolita when the St. Louis, Brownsville & Mexico Railway built through the area in 1909. PO 3 Mar 1910, PM Mary Cole.

LOMA ALTA (McMullen) Spanish "high hill." PO 3 Jan 1910 as Lomo Alto [*sic*], PM John W. Womack.

LOMAX (Howard) Named about 1930 from the Lomax School, established on the Lewis Lomax farm in the 1920s.

LOMETA [lo MEET uh] (Lampasas) Spanish *lomita* "little hill." The Senterfitt PO was established in the summer of 1877 on land donated by rancher Reuben Senterfitt. In 1885 when the Gulf, Colorado & Santa Fe Railway built through the area Senterfitt moved to trackside two miles away. The Senterfitt PO was changed to Lometa 23 July 1886, PM Frank McKean.

LONE GROVE (Llano) Lone Grove was organized in the 1870s and probably named for an isolated cluster of pecan trees on the Little Llano River. PO 8 May 1876, PM John R. Coggin.

LONE STAR (Morris) The Lone Star Steel Company of Dallas established a mill and adopted the Texas nickname in the 1930s. PO 1 May 1948, PM Charles H. Abernathy.

LONG LAKE (Anderson) Named from Long Lake Plantation, itself named for Long Lake, the body of water on the plantation's western edge. The site was alternately known as Monington for Hugh Moning (Monnig) who bought the plantation in 1911, and his son Joseph, the plantation manager. PO 30 Aug 1918 as Monington, PM Louise A. Gaught.

LONG MOTT (Calhoun) Mott is a Texas term for an isolated grove, especially one with live oaks or elms, on an otherwise open prairie. Settlers in the 1850s named two such groves Upper Mott and Lower Mott. The PO opened by George De Cloudt 24 May 1887 took the name of the more elongated Upper Mott.

LONGVIEW (Gregg) Named in the early 1870s with the arrival of the Texas & Pacific Railway. Local naming stories have in common the unobstructed view for many miles in all directions. One account attributes the name to Ossamus Hitch Methvin who claimed that anyone standing on Rock Hill would have "a long view indeed." PO 27 Jan 1871, PM Oliver H. Pegues.

LONGWORTH (Fisher) Founded about 1902 and named from the Long Ranch, operated from the early 1880s by brothers Andrew and Frank Long. PO 26 Jan 1907, PM Jefferson Salter.

LOONEYVILLE (Nacogdoches) John Robert Looney relocated from South Carolina in the 1850s and opened a dry goods store. By coincidence Looneyville is just northwest of Little Bayou Loco. PO 10 July 1874, PM Robert J. Lester.

LOOP (Gaines) The local story is that Edgar Belcher, the first postmaster in March 1905, was toying with his lariat and mulling over possible names when he recalled the old cowboy trick of making a loop with the lasso and jumping through the twirling circle. Thus inspired, he submitted the post office application requesting the name "Loop."

LOPENO [lo PEN yo] (Zapata) Named for Antonio López, husband of Doña Ysabel María Sánchez who received a land grant from the king of Spain in the mid-1700s.

The site of Old Lopeno is now under Falcon Lake. The new Lopeno includes the former communities of San Jose, Santa Fe, San Pedro, and El Tigre. PO 9 July 1901 as Lopena; changed to Lopeno 26 Oct 1909, PM Manuel G. Salinas.

LORAINE (Mitchell) In 1872, Cornelius F. Crandall founded the town of Crandall in Harrison County, IN. By 1880 he was in Kaufman County, TX, where he founded a second Crandall. In 1890 he established the Loraine PO in Mitchell County and 15 years later platted the town of Loraine. The source of the name is unknown.
See Crandall.

LORENA (McLennan) Founded in 1881 when the Missouri–Kansas–Texas Railroad laid tracks between Taylor and Hillsboro. Named for Lorena Westbrook, daughter of Charles and Mary Virginia Westbrook, plantation owners and community benefactors. PO 19 June 1882, PM Charles Schaefer.

LORENZO (Crosby) The Crosbyton-South Plains Townsite Company founded Lorenzo in 1911 on land owned by the CB (Coonley Brothers) Livestock Company of Chicago. Named for Lorenzo Dow, an attorney for the cattle company. PO 28 Sept 1911, PM Alice McGuire.

LOS ANGELES (La Salle) Founded in 1923 by the Frank Z. Bishop Land Company of San Antonio. The name was chosen for its promotional value and to suggest that the climate and living conditions were similar to those of Los Angeles, CA. PO 22 Oct 1923, PM Louise Sladek.

LOS EBANOS (Hidalgo) Spanish "the ebonies." Named for the thorny shrub known as Texas Ebony, native to South Texas. PO 21 May 1910, PM Maximo Diaz.

LOS FRESNOS (Cameron) Founded in 1913 by Leonidas C. (Lon) Hill, Jr., son of Eustacia and Leonidas Hill, Sr., a founder of HARLINGEN. Earlier known as "Mose," Hill's nickname, the community was formally named Los Fresnos (Spanish "the ash trees"). The name may have originated with Hill or it may be from an earlier school or a Spanish land grant. PO 2 Jan 1919, PM Harry H. Whipple.

LOS HUISACHES (Webb) Named for the huisache shrub, also known as the Sweet Acacia widespread in South Texas. See Weesatche.

LOS INDIOS (Cameron) Literally "the Indians." By one local story the name originally referred to a rock formation that looked like a (south Asian) Indian with a turban. More likely Los Indios was the name of an 18th century land grant and ranch. PO 3 Sept 1913, PM William F. Shaler.

LOS NOPALITOS (Webb) Named from nopales, the pads of the prickly pear cactus often used in soups and salads.

LOS OJUELOS (Webb) Spanish "little eyes, little springs." The site was first settled in the early 19th century by Eugenio Gutiérrez, the original land grantee and probably the person who chose the name for the seep springs. PO 26 Oct 1894 as Ojuelos, PM Cayetano Ochoa.

LOS YBANEZ (Dawson) Los Ybanez was founded in 1980 on the site of a 1930s Civilian Conservation Corps camp by Israel Ybanez and named for his extended family.

LOSOYA [luh SAW yuh] (Bexar) Leon Lecomte established the Losoya post office 24 Feb 1879, named for José Toribio Losoya, a Tejano defender of the Alamo and whose family is the namesake of Losoya Street, which borders San Antonio's famous Riverwalk.

LOTT (Falls) The San Antonio & Aransas Pass Railway station was established about 1890 and named for Uriah Lott, SA&AP president. PO 28 May 1890, PM Sylvester J. Crump.

LOTTA (Harrison) James Edgar McLemore opened the Lotta PO 5 Apr 1915, named for his wife, Lottie Dixon McLemore, or their daughter, Lottie Dorothy McLemore, or both.

LOUISE (Wharton) In 1882 the New York, Texas & Mexican Railway established Louise Station, named for Marie Louise Antoinette Hungerford Mackay, daughter of Daniel Elihu Hungerford, vice president of the NYT&M and the namesake of HUNGERFORD. Marie Louise Mackay was the spouse of John W. Mackay, part owner of the NYT&M and the namesake of MACKAY. PO 26 Apr 1888, PM Alexander McDow.

LOVELACE (Hill) About 1885 the Missouri–Kansas–Texas Railroad built a switch on property owned by James, Quinton, and William Loveless, whose name was misspelled as Lovelace. At one time Lovelace was informally known as Frog Liver, for unknown reasons. PO 2 Oct 1893, PM Jerry S. Redman.

LOVELADY (Houston) Founded on the line of the Houston & Great Northern Railroad in 1872 on land originally granted to Cyrus Lovelady. His son, Henry Cyrus Lovelady, donated land for the railroad right of way. PO 4 Aug 1858 as Pennington; changed to Lovelady 8 Nov 1872, PM August Hofmann.

LOVING (County) Created 1887, organized 1931. Named for Oliver Loving (1812–1867), rancher and cattle driver. Born in Kentucky, Loving arrived in Texas in 1845 and worked his way to Jack County. He and Charles Goodnight developed the Goodnight-Loving Trail in the late 1860s, over which cattle were driven from Young County through New Mexico and Colorado to grazing land in Wyoming. See Goodnight.

LOVING (Young) The townsite was once part of the Lost Valley Loving Ranch on the Goodnight-Loving Trail. The community was named for the family of Oliver Loving for whom Loving County is named. PO 7 Mar 1905, PM John S. Stratton.

LOWAKE [lo WAY kee] (Concho) In 1909 local farmers John *Lowe* and Charles Schl*ake* donated both land and their names for a station on the Concho, San Saba & Llano Valley Railroad. Schlake was the first PM, 28 Oct 1909.

LOYAL VALLEY (Mason) Founded in 1869 by Baron Otfried Hans Freiherr von Meusebach, the founder of Fredericksburg, known as John O. Meusebach after his arrival in Texas in 1845. According to local sources, Meusebach chose the name to reflect the loyalty early settlers showed to one another. PO 28 May 1868, PM Solomon Wright. See Fredericksburg.

LOYOLA BEACH (Kleberg) In the 1930s Orlando Underbrink opened a grocery store and rental cabins on an arm of Baffin Bay that he named for his father, Ignatius Loyola Underbrink, an architect who designed Our Lady of Consolation Church in Riviera.

LUBBOCK (County) Created 1876, organized 1891. Named for Thomas Saltus Lubbock (1817–1862), born in South Carolina. Lubbock was a cotton trader in New Orleans before he joined the Texas Revolution. He participated in the Siege of Bexar, was a member of the Texan Santa Fe Expedition, and, with Benjamin Franklin Terry, organized Terry's Texas Rangers during the Civil War. Lubbock was in command of Terry's regiment when he died of typhoid in Kentucky in 1862. His younger brother, Francis Richard Lubbock, was the ninth Governor of Texas (1861–1863).

LUBBOCK (Lubbock) Lubbock grew from the competing towns of Monterey, founded early in 1890 by Whitfield Rayner, for whom the now ghost town of Rayner in Stonewall County is named, and Lubbock, founded about the same time by Frank Wheelock, manager of the IOA Ranch. The communities joined as Lubbock in December 1890. The Lubbock PO had been established several years earlier, in June 1884 by PM George W. Singer. See Lubbock County.

LUCAS (Collin) Peter Lucas brought his family to the area from Kentucky in the mid-1840s. His son Gabriel established the PO in his general store 11 May 1888.

LUCKENBACH [LOO KIN bahk] (Gillespie) Jacob Luckenbach and five siblings arrived in Texas from Germany in December 1845. Jacob Luckenbach was granted land in Fredericksburg that he sold in 1852 and moved to the site of present Luckenbach. About 1860 the family of August Engel, Sr., a circuit-riding Methodist minister, opened a general store nearby. When August Engel, Jr. applied for a post office in April 1886 he asked his sister Wilhelmina "Minnie" Engel to fill out the appropriate form, on which she wrote the name Luckenbach for her fiancé Carl Albert Luckenbach, son of Jacob and Justina Luckenbach. In 1892 Wilhelmina Engel (now Wilhelmina Luckenbach) named the Albert post office for her husband, Carl Albert Luckenbach. See Albert.

LUEDERS [LOOD erz] (Jones, Shackelford) The Webb and Hill Land and Cattle Company laid out the townsite in 1899, named for Frederick Lueders who had been granted the property for his military service during the Texas Revolution. Leuders was killed at San Jacinto. PO 4 May 1900, PM Richard Newman.

LUELLA (Grayson) John L. Hughes opened the PO 12 Jan 1888, named for his daughter Luella.

LUFKIN (Angelina) Lufkin was founded in 1881 with construction of the Houston East & West Texas Railway. The station was named for Abraham P. Lufkin, a Galveston cotton merchant, local politician, and friend of Paul Bremond, president of the HE&WT. There is little to support the claim that the namesake is Edwin P. Lufkin, a civil engineer employed by the HE&WT. PO 12 Apr 1882, PM William A. Abney.

LULING (Caldwell) James Converse, chief construction engineer of the Galveston, Harrisburg & San Antonio Railway, laid out the townsite in 1874. It has been suggested that the name Luling was a transfer from Luling, LA; that Luling was the family name of the wife of a railroad official; or that Luling was a Chinese launderer named Lu Ling who followed the railroad construction crew. More likely, however, the namesake is Charles Luling, a New York banker and railroad financier and probably a friend of Thomas Wentworth Peirce, part owner of the GH&SA. PO 30 Nov 1848 as Plum Creek; changed to Luling 26 Aug 1874, PM Carnot Bellinger.

LUMKINS (Ellis) The James W. Lumpkins [*sic*] family moved from Arkansas and began farming in the area in 1874.

LUNA (Freestone) Named for Gertrudis Luna who was granted a league of land (about 4400 acres) by the Galveston Bay and Texas Land Company in 1835. PO 17 Aug 1880, PM Richmond Driver.

LUND (Travis) Lund is a Swedish community, settled in the 1880s as Pleasant Hill and renamed for Lund, Sweden, when Joseph Rivers established the post office 13 Dec 1895.

LUSK (Throckmorton) Robert Lusk began farming in the area about 1880. PO 12 May 1900, PM Lucie Lusk.

LUTHER (Howard) Luther F. and Mary M. Lawrence relocated from Kentucky about 1903. The town was named for the post office opened by PM Luther F. Lawrence 1 July 1909. See Fairview.

LUTIE [LOOT ee] (Collingsworth) Lutie was organized about 1900 as Anderson, named for John Anderson, the first clerk of Collingsworth County. In September 1909 Chester Aldridge opened the PO, named for Lutie Belle Templeton, wife of district attorney and county judge Robert H. Templeton, and known for her work on the *Wellington Times* newspaper.

LUXELLO (Bexar) In the early 20th century entrepreneur Charles Lux opened Luxello Hall, a combination train station, saloon, and dance hall. Luxello has now been absorbed by San Antonio. PO 6 July 1915, PM Charles Lux.

LYFORD [LEYE ferd] (Willacy) Founded in the early 1900s by the Chicago & Eastern Illinois Railroad and named for William H. Lyford, a Chicago lawyer and an attorney for the C&EI. PO 10 Apr 1907, PM William G. Schlect, a partner in the Hood and Schlect grocery store.

LYNCHBURG (Harris) About 1822 Nathaniel Lynch established a ferry across the San Jacinto River. A decade later he laid out the town of Lynchburg. PO 23 Dec 1847 as San Jacinto; changed to Lynchburg 1836, PM Nathaniel Lynch.

LYNN (County) Created 1876, organized 1903. There is a great deal of uncertainty regarding the namesake of Lynn County. Most sources agree that the county is named for an Alamo defender named Lynn (Linn) but otherwise his identity is conjectural. The Texas Almanac says only that the county was named "for Alamo victim W. Lynn." Panhandle historian Donald R. Abbe, in his article in the *Handbook of Texas Online*, claims the namesake is George Washington Lynn, about whom little is known. Alamo records show only William Linn, a private from Massachusetts.

LYNN GROVE (Grimes) Lynn is apparently a popular etymology of Lin. The town was named in the late 1860s for the local clusters of Linden (Lin) trees (basswoods).

LYONS (Burleson) William A. Lyon (or Lyons), a landowner and shopkeeper, donated 50 acres to the Gulf, Colorado & Santa Fe Railway about 1880. PO 23 Aug 1872 as Krohne, PM George Krohne; changed to Lyons 21 May 1886, PM Alonzo J. Radford.

LYTLE (Atascosa, Bexar, Medina) About 1860 John Thomas Lytle from Adams County, PA, and his cousin, Thomas McDaniel, established the Lytle-McDaniel Ranch. Lytle was instrumental in attracting the International–Great Northern Railroad in 1882. PO 10 Sept 1883, PM William Garnand.

LYTTON SPRINGS [LIT uhn] (Caldwell) Named for John Lytton (Litton) who came to Texas from North Carolina by way of Missouri about 1827. Litton joined Stephen F. Austin's Colony and established a homestead around the springs that came to bear his name in the 1830s. PO 4 Mar 1859 as Albade; changed to Lytton Springs 24 Mar 1888, PM Henry Clay Harris.

ML

MABANK [MAY bangk] (Kaufman) About 1900 the Southern Pacific Railroad established a station on ranchland owned by George *Ma*son and Thomas Eu*bank*. PO 10 Nov 1887 as Lawndale; changed to Mabank 2 Jan 1900, PM James F. Tolbert.

MABELLE (Baylor) Founded as a station on the Wichita Valley Railroad in the early 20th century. Named for Ma(y)belle Thompson, daughter of James T. Thompson who established the PO 13 Dec 1906.

MABRY (Red River) In 1848 William Mabry settled in Red River County after stops in North Carolina, Indiana, and Missouri. He was a Deputy US Marshal, a justice of the peace, a teacher, the PM at Mill Creek in 1868, and a Texas State Representative in 1872.

MACBAIN (Motley) Probably named for John MacBain, manager of the Matador Ranch. MacBain was instrumental in attracting the Quanah, Acme & Pacific Railway to Motley County in the early 1910s.

MACDONA (Bexar) Founded about 1886 as a station on the Galveston, Harrisburg & San Antonio Railway and named for the site owner, George Macdona. PO 13 Sept 1886, PM Mary K. Meredith.

MACEY (Brazos) Site owner William Macey (Macy) laid out and named the town about 1870. PO 13 July 1874, PM Samuel J. Lipscomb. Also known as Murphysboro.

MACKAY (Wharton) The New York, Texas & Mexican Railway built through the area in 1881 and named the station for John William Mackay, part owner of the NYT&M. The town of LOUISE is named for his wife, Marie Louise, daughter of Daniel Hungerford. PO 28 Jan 1885, PM Charles Nelson. See Hungerford.

MACUNE [muh KOON] (San Augustine) Probably named for Charles William Macune, Methodist pastor, lawyer, and editor, best known for his political populism and for founding the National Farmers Alliance and Cooperative Union in the late 1880s. PO 15 Dec 1888, PM William C. Wade.

MADISON (County) created 1853, organized 1854. Credit for the creation of Madison County is usually given to Dr. Pleasant Williams Kittrell who chose the name in honor of James Madison, fourth President of the United States (1809–1817). See Kittrell.

MADISONVILLE (Madison) The city, named from the county, was founded in 1853 as county seat. PO 29 Aug 1854, PM Ledford L. Swindler.

MADRAS (Red River) In the 1870s Thomas J. Dozier established a general store in which he opened the Madras post office in July 1887. Probably named for Madras (now Chennai), the coastal city in southeast India that was often in the news because it was experiencing severe food shortages and social upheavals at the time.

MAGNOLIA (Montgomery) Founded in the 1840s as Mink's Prairie, presumably named for Joseph Mink, a cattle forager for the Texas Army in the 1830s and trading post proprietor by 1850. The name was changed to Magnolia, apparently for the local magnolia trees, when the International–Great Northern Railroad built through the area in the early 20th century. PO 15 Apr 1893, PM Wilbur F. Fisher.

MAHA (Travis) Maha is a shortening of Mayhard, named from Mayhard Creek, itself named for an early Mayhard settler or family.

MAHL (Nacogdoches) Mahl was founded about 1900 with construction of the Texas & New Orleans Railroad. According to a local story, Mahl is a reverse spelling of Lham, an agent employed by the T&NO. Although Lham is indeed a (rare) American family name, Mahl was named for either William Mahl, assistant to the president of the T&NO, or John T. Mahl, a director and general baggage agent. PO 10 Feb 1902, PM William Henry Stuskey.

MAHOMET [muh HAHM it] (Burnet) PO 14 Dec 1857, PM George Ater who chose the name for Mahomet, Champaign County, IL, his former home. Coincidentally, August G. Mahomet was postmaster for several weeks in the summer of 1879.

MAHONEY (Hopkins) George W. Mahoney was an agent for a Seattle land consortium that bought and subdivided the Kimberly Ranch in 1900. See Brashear.

MAJORS (Franklin) Farmer and merchant Benjamin Franklin Majors relocated from Alabama and opened the Majors PO 11 July 1899.

MALAKOFF [MAL uh kawf] (Henderson) Named for the battle of Malakoff, a major engagement of French-British and Russian forces during the Crimean War in 1855. The name was most likely suggested by John Collins, an Athens physician and businessman. PO 20 July 1855, PM James A. Mitcham.

MALONE (Hill) In the early 20th century the tracks of the International–Great Northern and the Trinity & Brazos railroads intersected at Malone, named for William Malone, president of the I-GN. Malone includes the former community of Walling, founded in the mid-1880s by site owner Alonzo Dru Walling. PO 24 Oct 1903, PM Jesse L. Zachary.

MALTA (Bowie) Probably named by early settler Lynn Tucker for Malta, DeKalb County, IL, itself likely named for the island of Malta in the Mediterranean Sea. PO 2 Dec 1896, PM Jeff D. Norman.

MALVADO (Terrell) Spanish "bad, malicious." Reportedly named from an incident in which supplies of a US Army patrol were washed away in a flash flood at a Lozier canyon crossing.

MAMBRINO [mam BREYE no] (Hood) The source of the name is uncertain. The town may have been named for the line of Standardbred racing horses that dates to the mid-18th century and the original sire, Mambrino. Mambrino is also a legendary Moorish king whose golden helmet made him invulnerable. PO 26 May 1904, PM James A. McCarty.

MANCHACA [MAN chak, MAN shak] (Travis) Named from the Manchaca Springs, themselves named for José Antonio

Manchaca (Menchaca), a Tejano officer in the Texas Revolution, serving under Juan Seguin. After the war Manchaca was a San Antonio alderman and mayor pro tem in 1838. PO 19 Apr 1851 as Manchac House; discontinued and reopened 24 June 1874 as Manchac; discontinued and reopened 28 Feb 1881 as Manchaca, PM George E. Miller.

MANCHESTER (Red River) The name of the Taylor post office, established in 1871, was changed to Manchester in 1880 by postmaster Joseph Elvadus Srygley for Manchester, IL, the home of several of his family members, itself a transfer from Manchester, England.

MANDA (Travis) The largely Swedish community was settled in the late 1880s and named for Amanda (Manda) Bengtson, sister of Otto Bengtson, the first PM 15 Apr 1893.

MANGUM [MANG guhm] (Eastland) James and Mary Ann Mangum from Mississippi began farming in the area in the 1880s. Their son, Robert Mangum, opened a general store in the 1890s and was the first PM 9 Mar 1899.

MANHEIM (Lee) Probably named for Mannheim, Germany, by Adolf Wachsmann who opened the PO 23 Oct 1900 in his combination store and saloon.

MANKINS [MAN kinz] (Archer) In 1890 the Wichita Valley Railway built a spur to the Sam Lazarus Ranch. In 1908 Charles Mangold of Dallas bought the ranch and platted the townsite named for ranch foreman Tom Mankins. PO 28 Apr 1909, PM Horace A. Nicholson.

MANOR [MAY nuhr] (Travis) James B. Manor came to Texas from Tennessee with Sam Houston in 1832 and settled near the present town of Manor in 1836. Manor was the only postmaster of the Grassdale office, serving from 15 Sept 1859 until 21 Mar 1860. The settlement was known as Manor's Stage Stand until Manor donated land to the Houston & Texas Central Railway that established Manor Station in the early 1870s. The Gregg PO, opened 15 June 1871, was changed to Manor 5 July 1872, PM Woody Browning.

MANSFIELD (Tarrant) Named for Ralph *Man* and Julian *Feild* [*sic*] who built a gristmill in the late 1850s. Feild was the first Fort Worth PM (as Field) 28 Feb 1856 and also the first Mansfield PM 1 Mar 1860.

MANSON (Jackson) A cattle loading site northeast of Edna was known as the Edna Stock Pens until 1900 when the Texas & New Orleans Railroad established Manson Station, named for Alphonse Manson, a T&NO dispatcher.

MANVEL [MAN vuhl] (Brazoria) Known as Pomona from 1887 when the Gulf, Colorado & Santa Fe Railway built through the area until 22 Sept 1892 when William Pugh opened the Manvel PO, named for Allen Manvel, president of the GC&SF.

MAPLE (Bailey) Lafayette Greenhill Wilson, an early settler, rancher, attorney, and district judge, provided legal services to small towns in the Panhandle at the turn of the 20th century. His son, Maple Wilson, began ranching about 1915 and donated land as well as his name for the school and the community. PO 29 Aug 1934, PM William L. Blaylock.

MAPLETON (Houston) Named about 1920 for the Thomas Maples family, area landowners. The area was also known as Stumpville for the tree stumps that remained after the pine forest was clear cut.

MARAK (Milam) Founded in the early 1880s as Maraksville, named for Frantisek and Rosalia Kozova Marak who emigrated to Texas from Horni Sklenov, Moravia, in the late 1850s. PO 26 Oct 1897 as Marak, PM Joseph Matula.

MARATHON [MEHR uh thun] (Brewster) Marathon was established with construction of the Galveston, Harrisburg & San Antonio Railway in 1882. The name was chosen by Albion Shepard, one of the surveyors hired by the GH&SA to locate the route and lay out the town. Shepard, the first PM 13 Feb 1883, was a retired sea captain who said the local terrain, especially the valley and surrounding hills, reminded him of Marathon, Greece.

MARBLE FALLS (Burnet) William S. Gaston opened the Marble Falls PO 25 July 1884. The area had been known for some time as Marble Falls for the falls on the Colorado River created by the hard limestone shelf that was taken—perhaps metaphorically—for marble. Confederate General Adam Rankin Johnson founded the town of Marble Falls in July 1887.

MARFA (Presidio) Marfa was founded in 1882 or 1883 as a water replenishing station on the Galveston, Harrisburg & San Antonio Railway and named by Hanna Maria Strobridge, wife and traveling companion of James Harvey Strobridge, construction superintendent for the Southern Pacific Railroad. Etymologist Barry Popik has shown that Strobridge took the name Marfa, the Russian form of Martha, from the 1876 Jules Verne novel *Michael Strogoff: The Courier of the Czar*, in which Marfa Strogoff is the widowed mother of the protagonist. PO 3 Apr 1883, PM Russell C. Norton.

MARGARET (Foard) The original settlement in Hardeman County was known as Pease for its location on the Pease River (named for Elisha Pease, Governor of Texas when the river was first systematically charted in 1856). The name was changed about 1884 for Margaret Wesley, then four years old and considered the first non-Indian child born in the area. When Margaret was bypassed by the Kansas City, Mexico & Orient Railway in the late 1900s the community packed up and moved several miles southwest to trackside. PO 11 May 1880 as Pease; changed to Margaret 15 June 1885, PM Mary F. Wesley.

MARIETTA (Cass) Known as Oak Ridge until 5 Apr 1880 when Robert Newton Wommack established the Marietta post office, named for his wife, Mary Ellen, affectionally known as Marietta.

MARION (County) Created and organized 1860. According to most sources the county was named in honor of Francis Marion, the South Carolina "Swamp Fox" whose unconventional methods of warfare made him a hero of the American Revolution. However, historian Lucille Bullard has convincingly argued that the namesake is Marion DeKalb Taylor who represented the district in the Texas House (1849–1851); the Texas Senate (1851–1859); and again in the Texas House (1859–1861). During his last term Taylor was elected Speaker of the House and in this capacity was instrumental in the creation and organization of the county that would likely have been called Taylor if Texas did not already have a Taylor County.

MARION (Angelina) The site on the Angelina River was known as McNeill's Landing from the 1820s until 1846 when the growing community was made the seat of Angelina County and renamed for Revolutionary War General Francis Marion. PO 8 Mar 1847, PM John D. Gann.

MARION (Guadalupe) Marion was founded about 1877 with construction of the Galveston, Harrisburg & San Antonio Railway. The standard story is that Joshua W. Young, a Seguin builder, donated land for the railroad and proposed the name in honor of his granddaughter, Marion Dove. However, the town was platted by Thomas Wentworth Peirce, part owner of the GH&SA and father of a daughter, Marion, born in the summer of 1874. Both Marions may be commemorated by the name. PO 31 May 1877, PM George Weber.

MARKHAM (Matagorda) Markham was founded about 1901 as Cortes, named for Henry William Cortes, a Houston businessman and co-owner of the Cortes–Moore Canal Company. In 1903 Cortes was renamed for Charles Henry Markham, a director of the Southern Pacific Railroad, parent of the Texas & New Orleans, which established a station at Markham. PO 14 Mar 1901 as Cortes; changed to Markham 16 Apr 1903, PM Thomas Smith.

MARKLEY (Young) Probably named for Brigadier General Alfred C. Markley. After serving at a number of frontier posts, Markley retired in Young County in the early 20th century. PO 30 Aug 1888 as Manle (Manlee); changed to Markley 30 Nov 1888, PM Stephen Munderback.

MARLIN (Falls) About 1835 Sterling Clack Robertson, the empresario of Robertson's Colony, named the community Sarahville de Viesca in honor of his mother, Sarah Robertson, and Agustín Viesca, the governor of Coahuila and Texas. The town was renamed for early settler John Marlin when Falls County was created in 1850. PO 29 Nov 1851, PM John Jarvis. Informally known as Bucksnort.

MARQUEZ [mahr KAY] (Leon) Founded about 1870 on the line of the International–Great Northern Railroad and named for María de la C. Marquez, the first site owner. PO 25 Mar 1872, PM Joseph R. Brown.

MARSHALL (Harrison) In 1841 Isaac Van Zandt, a Harrison County lawyer and future namesake of Van Zandt County, chose the name apparently for John Marshall, Chief Justice of the US Supreme Court in the early 19th century. PO 13 Sept 1841, PM W. W. O. (William Wall Oliver) Stanfield.

MARSTON (Polk) Founded in the 1880s with construction of the Houston East & West Texas Railway and named for New York financier Edgar L. Marston, a director of the HE&WT and later president of the Texas-Pacific Coal Company. PO 27 July 1901, PM Robert L. Collier.

MART (McLennan, Mart) Mart was probably named by Hiram Breland or his son, Albert, generally regarded as the first settlers, who expected the town to become a marketing and trading center. PO 6 Apr 1880, PM William B. Stodghill.

MARTHA (Liberty) Robert C. Duff, president of the Beaumont, Sour Lake & Western line of the International–Great Northern Railroad, named the town for Martha Mills, wife of site owner William Mills.

MARTIN (County) Created 1876, organized 1884. Named for Wylie (Wyly) Martin (1776–1842), born in Georgia. Martin became a career military officer, and joined Stephen F. Austin's Colony in 1825. After participating in the Texas Revolution, he was justice of Fort Bend County and a Republic of Texas Senator.

MARTINDALE (Caldwell) George and Nancy Martindale donated land for the townsite in 1855. PO 1 July 1875, PM Robert Martindale.

MARTINS MILL (Van Zandt) The town formed about 1873 from the mill and cotton gin operated by Daniel G. Martin from the late 1850s. PO 14 Jan 1879, PM John C. Burrage.

MARTINSVILLE (Nacogdoches) Founded by John Daniel Martin, a pioneering physician who practiced medicine in the area for fifty years beginning in the mid-1860s. PO 25 Oct 1867, PM Robert B. Crawford.

MARVIN (Lamar) Enoch Mather Marvin, a Methodist Episcopal bishop, was a Confederate Army chaplain and a founder of Marvin College in Waxahachie that opened in 1870 and closed in 1874.

MARYNEAL (Nolan) Founded on the line of the Kansas City, Mexico & Orient Railway in 1907. Named for Mary Doran and her husband, Neal, who was secretary and auditor of the KCM&O. PO 9 Oct 1907, PM James S. Arledge.

MARYSTOWN (Johnson) Established about 1870 as Marysville, named by Thomas W. Hollingsworth for his wife, Mary. The application for a Marysville PO was rejected and resubmitted as Marystown. PO 13 Mar 1874, PM John M. McKinney.

MARYSVILLE (Cooke) Marysville may have been named for Marysville, CA, or for Mary Corn, wife of Richard Corn who established a gristmill in the 1860s. The name was probably chosen by John Kelly who opened the PO 13 Jan 1873.

MASON (County) Created and organized 1858. Named from Fort Mason, established by the US Army in 1851. The post was named for either Lt. George T. Mason who was killed in the first skirmish of the War with Mexico on the Rio Grande near Brownsville in April 1846, or Brevet Brigadier General Richard Barnes Mason. When Fort Mason became operational General Mason had been dead less than a year and would have been the better known, having been military governor of California in the late 1840s. (Several decades later, Fort Mason in San Francisco was named in his honor.) However, in 1851 the conflict of memory was the War with Mexico, which would favor Lt. Mason.

MASON (Mason) The town of Mason developed near Fort Mason from the early 1850s. PO 8 Mar 1858 as Fort Mason; changed to Mason 26 June 1858, PM George W. Todd. See Mason County.

MASTERSON (Moore) Robert Benjamin Masterson had ranching and business interests in a number of Texas counties, especially in Amarillo and Fort Worth, where he was a director of the First National Bank. Masterson was named in his honor in the late 1920s. PO 1 Jan 1950, PM Robert L. Knox.

MATADOR (Motley) In the late 1870s Spottswood Lomax and Henry Campbell organized the Matador Cattle Company and established the Matador Ranch. The name was apparently chosen by Lomax whose interests outside of ranching lay in Spanish literature and culture. Campbell laid out the townsite shortly after John Biddle opened the Matador PO 21 Jan 1886.

MATAGORDA (County) Matagorda is an original Texas county, created in 1836 and named for the Mexican municipality of Matagorda established in 1834, itself named from Matagorda Bay or from the town of Matagorda.

MATAGORDA (Matagorda) The town of Matagorda was founded in 1827 by appointees of Stephen F. Austin and likely named by Austin's primary surveyor, Elias Wightman. The source of the name is uncertain. Several writers have suggested that Matagorda is a compound of Spanish *mata* "thicket" and *gorda* "dense"; thus, *matagorda* would translate as "dense thicket," referring in particular to the formidable canebrakes reported by early explorers. Others have claimed the name is from obsolete Spanish *mata* "slaughter" and *gorda* "large," without explanation. A more direct source may be Matagorda, Spain. PO 1836, PM J. S. Clements.

MATHIS (San Patricio) Thomas Henry Mathis, a businessman and rancher, donated land for the townsite when the San Antonio & Aransas Pass Railway built through the county in 1887. Mathis founded ROCKPORT, the seat of Aransas County, in 1867. PO 14 Apr 1890, PM Samuel B. Carnes.

MATINBURG (Camp, Upshur) Settled in the 1880s as Martinsburg, named for Abram Dallas Martin who represented the district in the Texas House 1889–1891. Martin was intentionally misspelled Matin to avoid post office conflicts when the PO was opened by Simeon Harris 7 Sept 1893.

MATTHEWS (Colorado) John Matthews migrated to the area from Virginia in the mid-1830s. He managed a large plantation and at the outbreak of the Civil War owned some 150 slaves, many of whom stayed on the plantation after emancipation. PO 28 June 1895, PM Mary McRee.

MAUD (Bowie) When the Cotton Belt Railroad built through the area in the early 1870s, Samuel Knapp donated land for the station and the townsite; reportedly named for Maud Knapp, daughter of Samuel and Arrepsy Glennora Knapp. PO 18 Jan 1881, PM Samuel D. Knapp.

MAUDLOWE (Refugio) Dennis Martin O'Connor founded Maudlowe, named for his wife, Maud Lowe O'Connor, in 1912 when a branch of the St. Louis, Brownsville & Mexico Railway established a station on the O'Connor Ranch. PO 12 Feb 1915, PM Francis P. Marberry.

MAURICEVILLE [muh REES vil] (Orange) Mauriceville was founded by the Beaumont Land Corporation shortly after construction of the Orange & Northwestern Railroad in 1902. Named by Leopold Miller, president of the O&N, in honor of his son, Maurice. PO 2 Nov 1906, PM John P. Hilliard.

MAVERICK (County) Created 1856, organized 1871. Named for Samuel Augustus (Sam) Maverick (1803–1870), born in South Carolina. His family moved to Texas in 1810 and he became a cattleman, lawyer, mayor of San Antonio, and Texas state legislator. Maverick's calves often went unbranded and were called "mavericks," a name that now refers to anyone with an independent mind.

MAVERICK (Runnels) Named for Samuel Augustus Maverick, the namesake of Maverick County. PO 10 Oct 1883, PM Marion Thomas Cobb.

MAXEY (Lamar) Named for Samuel Bell Maxey, United States Army lieutenant, Confederate Army General, and US Senator. Thomas E. Nixon, an early settler who served under General Maxey in the Civil War, suggested the name. The PO was established 9 Mar 1880 by Benjamin Wilhite when Maxey was serving in the US Senate.

MAXWELL (Caldwell) Earlier known as New Martindale, Maxwell was formally laid out when the Missouri–Kansas–Texas Railroad was extended from San Marcos to Lockhart in the late 1880s. Named for Thomas Maxwell, the first site owner in 1845. PO 10 July 1888, PM Elbert Laney.

MAY (Brown) In the 1860s David May brought his family to Texas and began farming in Freestone County. His son, Nathan Lumpkin May, moved to Brown County and opened the May PO 30 Nov 1881.

MAYDELLE (Cherokee) Named for Maydelle Campbell, daughter of Thomas M. Campbell, Texas Governor 1907–1911. PO 27 May 1910, PM James Holsomback.

MAYFIELD (Hill) In the early 20th century the Trinity & Brazos Valley Railway established a shipping station named for John Mayfield, farmer and ginner.

MAYFLOWER (Newton) Formerly known as Survey or Surveyville, regarded as the site of the first survey in Newton County. Presumably named for the local wildflowers. PO 19 Sept 1890 as Surveyville; discontinued 2 Nov 1898; reestablished as Mayflower 26 Oct 1912, PM John Wells.

MAYPEARL (Ellis) Known as Eyrie "the eagle's nest" until 1903 when the International–Great Northern Railroad established Maypearl Station. The name was probably proposed by Thomas Jefferson Trammell, a civil engineer employed by the I–GN, for his wife, Mary (May) combined with the name of the daughter or wife of an I-GN official. PO 24 Aug 1894 as Eyrie; changed to Maypearl 25 June 1903, PM Gertrude Dumas.

MAYSFIELD (Milam) Named for Thomas Newton Mayes (Mays) who began farming in the area in the 1850s. PO 20 Aug 1868, PM Simon Whitley.

McADOO (Dickens) Named about 1915 for William Gibbs McAdoo, a leader of the Progressive Movement of the early 20th century. When the community was organized, McAdoo was US Secretary of the Treasury under President Woodrow Wilson. PO 6 Mar 1915, PM Benjamin Hines.

McALLEN (Hidalgo) In 1904 John McAllen and his son, James Ballí McAllen, organized the McAllen Townsite Company to plat and promote the community established on the McAllen (formerly Santa Anita) Ranch. PO 26 Apr 1907, PM Edward Mullen.

McCAMEY [muh KAY MEE] (Upton) George Port, land agent for the Kansas City, Mexico & Orient Railway, proposed the name for George B. McCamey who brought in the McCamey Discovery oil well on September 27, 1925. PO 5 Mar 1926, PM Amzi Carothers.

McCAULLEY (Fisher) Founded with construction of the Kansas City, Mexico & Orient Railway in 1906. Named for Robert Lee McCaulley, a Sweetwater banker and investor in the KCM&O. PO 16 July 1890 as Taopi (named for Taopi, MN, or for Chief Taopi, a Sioux leader of the 1850s for whom the Minnesota town is named); changed to McCauley [*sic*] 6 July 1903, PM William L. Glascock; changed to McCaulley, 2 June 1906.

McCLANAHAN (Falls) Named for John and Katherine McClanahan who began farming in the area in the 1870s. PO 22 Mar 1887, PM Azro D. Smith.

McCOY (Atascosa) Probably named for William Abner McCoy, born in Louisiana, a prominent rancher who donated land for a station on the San Antonio, Uvalde & Gulf Railroad line in 1913. PO 28 July 1914, PM Walter Tausch.

McCOY (Floyd) Named from the McCoy School District established in 1908 and named for Andrew J. McCoy who donated land for the schoolhouse.

McCOY (Red River) Named for early settler Jasper McCoy, who relocated from Georgia about 1852.

McCULLOCH [muh KUHL uhk] (County) Created 1856, organized 1876. Named for Benjamin McCulloch (1811–1862), a family friend of Sam Houston in Tennessee. McCulloch, a veteran of the Battle of San Jacinto, was a Texas Ranger, a member of the Republic of Texas Legislature, and a chief of scouts in both the Mexican and Civil wars. He was killed in the Battle of Pea Ridge in Arkansas in 1862.

McDADE (Bastrop) Founded in 1860 by James W. McDade, Texas State Representative and Senator in the 1850s and a lawyer for the Houston & Texas Central Railway. PO 29 Nov 1871, PM Augustus W. May.

McFADDIN (Victoria) Named from the McFaddin Ranch, established by Refugio cattleman James McFaddin in the mid-1870s. PO 13 Aug 1907 as Marianna;

changed to McFaddin 12 July 1923, PM William R. McFaddin.

McGREGOR (McLennan) McGregor was founded in 1882 where the lines of the Gulf, Colorado & Santa Fe and the Texas & St. Louis railways crossed. Gregor Carmichael McGregor, vice president of the Waco State Bank, sold land to the railroads for a station called McGregor's Springs. PO 12 Apr 1882 as Banks; changed to McGregor 6 Oct 1882, PM Thomas H. Baker.

McKINNEY (Collin) In the summer of 1846 the town of Buckner, founded and named by shopkeeper John McGarrah for Buckner, AR, was selected as the seat of Collin County. Two years later McKinney, named for Collin McKinney, was founded to replace Buckner as the county seat. By 1850 Buckner had become a ghost town. PO 25 Nov 1846 as Buckner; changed to McKinney 31 May 1848, PM Joel F. Stewart. See Collin County.

McKINNEY SPRINGS (Brewster) Previously known as Boquillas (Spanish "little mouths"), named for the springs that were formally named for Thomas Devine McKinney. McKinney was foreman of the Gage Ranch and was instrumental in developing the local mercury industry. PO 30 Dec 1896 as Boquillas; changed to McKinney Springs 22 Dec 1913, PM Walter K. Ellis.

McLEAN [muh KLAYN] (Gray) McLean grew around a water well and switch established by the Choctaw, Oklahoma & Texas Railroad in 1901. The site was named for William P. McLean, a US Congressman from Texas in the early 1870s and appointed to the first Texas Railroad Commission by Governor Jim Hogg in 1891. PO 4 Aug 1902, PM William McLaughlin.

McLENDON-CHISHOLM (Rockwall) About 1870 Preston McLendon opened a general store and blacksmith shop and was the first McLendon PM in March 1880. Several years later Enoch and Frank Chisholm laid out a community near the site of McLendon's store that included the Chisholm PO, opened in April 1891. The towns of McLendon and Chisholm lived side by side, apparently in harmony, until October 1969 when they incorporated as McLendon-Chisholm.

McLENNAN (County) Created and organized 1850. Named for early settler Neil McLennan (1777–1867), whose family left the Isle of Skye, Scotland in 1801. McLennan made his way from North Carolina to Texas in 1835, surveyed with George Erath, and began farming in what is now McLennan County in the mid-1840s.

McMAHAN [mik MAN] (Caldwell) The area was first known as Whizzerville and also as Wildcat, named for a saloon on Tinney Creek kept by German immigrant Ambrose Tinney. Edward McMahan opened the first general store and his son, Robert McMahan, established the PO 12 July 1898.

McMULLEN (County) Created 1858, organized 1862. Named for Irish emigrant John McMullen (1785–1853), a merchant in Matamoros, Mexico, in the 1820s when he met James McGloin. In 1828 the two empresarios were authorized to settle 200 families along the Nueces River. The McMullen-McGloin Colony was promoted largely to Irish immigrants and was known as the Irish Colony.

McNARY (Hudspeth) In 1923 the Galveston, Harrisburg & San Antonio Railway established McNary Station, named for James G. McNary, an El Paso banker, a director of the Rio Grande & El Paso Railroad, and a director of the McNary Lumber Company. McNary, Rapides Parish, LA, and McNary, Apache County, AZ, are also named for James McNary. PO 16 Aug 1926, PM Charles Stillwell.

McNEIL (Travis) Named in the mid-1880s for George McNeil, section foreman for the Austin & Northwestern Railroad. PO 17 Dec 1888, PM Addison Sheppard.

McQUEENEY (Guadalupe) With construction of the Southern Pacific Railroad station, merchant Charles Blumberg named the site McQueeney in honor of John Thomas McQueeney, division superintendent of the SP. PO 16 July 1900, PM Charles F. Blumberg.

MEDICINE MOUND (Hardeman) Named from the four rounded hills west of the town reported to be Comanche ceremonial sites. The town was laid out in 1908 by the Orient Land Company for the Kansas City, Mexico & Orient Railway. PO 3 Nov 1908, PM William H. Bellamy.

MEDINA [muh DEE nuh] (County) Created and organized 1848. Named from the Medina River, itself probably named for Spanish engineer Pedro Medina by Alonso de León during his 1689 expedition.

MEDINA (Bandera) Medina was settled from the mid-1860s and named for its location at the junction of the north and west prongs of the Medina River. PO 2 Mar 1880, PM Floyd Benton. See Medina County.

MEEKER (Jefferson) George W. Meeker was president of the Beaumont, Sour Lake & Western Railway in the 1900s.

MEGARGEL (Archer) Roy C. Megargel was president of the Gulf, Texas & Western Railroad when the town was founded in 1910. PO 14 Apr 1910, PM Hugh Brown.

MELDRUM (Shelby) Norman S. Meldrum was general manager of the Houston East & West Texas Railway that built through the area in 1885.

MELON (Frio) The town was first known as Mellon, a spelling that suggests a personal name, but no Mellon associated with the area has been identified. The local account is that the spelling was changed in recognition of the many watermelons grown in the area. PO 5 Oct 1906 as Mellon; changed to Melon 20 Feb 1909, PM John D. Eldridge.

MELROSE (Nacogdoches) Melrose was named about 1840 by Thomas Jefferson (T. Jeff) Johnson, a local businessman and physician (or dentist). The local account is that Johnson chose the name for Melrose, Scotland. PO 15 June 1846, PM Augustus Stephens.

MELVIN (McCulloch) The Melvin Land Company founded the community in 1904 on the sheep ranch that William Melvin had operated from the 1870s. PO 16 Apr 1906, PM Joseph A. Johnson.

MEMPHIS (Hall) Early in 1890 James Montgomery and William Robertson, along with several others, bought and platted the townsite. Later that year, when Robertson applied for a post office, the suggested names were rejected. According to the local story, James Wilson Brice, a Methodist minister and one of the site owners, remembered visiting Austin where he happened upon a letter addressed to Memphis, TX, with the notation "no such town in Texas." Brice thought there should be such a town in Texas and proposed the name Memphis, which was met with general approval.

MENARD [muh NAHRD] (County) Created 1858, organized 1871. Named for Michel Branamour Menard (1805–1856), born in Quebec, Canada. Menard established himself in Texas about 1830 and built a sawmill and gristmill on what became known as Menard Creek. Menard later organized the Galveston City Company and founded Galveston in the late 1830s.

MENARD (Menard) Founded in 1858 as Menardville, named from the county. The name was changed to Menard about 1910 when the Fort Worth & Rio Grande Railway established a station. PO 6 Apr 1910, PM Hugo E. Schuchard.

MENLOW (Hill) Likely a transfer from Menlo [*sic*], GA, itself named from Menlo Park, NJ. PO 26 June 1895, PM Henry H. McCall.

MENTONE (Loving) The original Mentone was established in 1893 by the Loving Canal and Irrigation Company, formed to irrigate farmlands using Pecos River water. The local account is that a surveyor for the company suggested the name for his former home, Menton, France. A more immediate source is likely Mentone in DeKalb County, AL, itself named for Menton, France. Present Mentone was founded in 1905 ten miles south of the first Mentone by the Stratton Land Company of Chicago. PO 29 Sept 1893, PM John J. Combs.

MENTZ (Colorado) Mentz is an adaptation of Mainz from Neu Mainz, the name first given to the town by settlers from Mainz, Germany, in the mid-1840s. PO 21 June 1853 as San Barnard; changed to New Mainz 1 Aug 1860, discontinued and reestablished as Mentz 17 June 1889, PM Joseph Burttschell. The name was probably influenced by the presence of several local Mentz families.

MERCEDES (Hidalgo) About 1904, real estate agent Lon C. Hill, Jr. laid out Lonsboro. Hill sold his interests to the American Rio Grande Land and Irrigation Company that renamed the town Mercedes. The source of the name is unknown. Although an abundance of local stories claim the namesake is Mercedes Díaz, wife of Porfirio Díaz, president of Mexico (1884–1911), local historian Beatrice de León Edwards has shown there is no evidence that Díaz was ever married to a woman named Mercedes. PO 26 Dec 1906, PM William Price. See Beatrice de León Edwards, *Mercedes*.

MERETA [muh RET uh] (Tom Green) Wade Fisher, who opened the PO 12 Apr 1902, named the office for Metta and Retta Burns, seven-year-old twin daughters of Sid and Sarah Burns of Van Zandt County.

MERIDIAN (Bosque) In 1854 the Texas Legislature created Bosque County and appointed six commissioners to locate the county seat.

Commissioner Jasper Mabry suggested the name Meridian for Meridian Creek, itself named several decades earlier by surveyor George Erath, for whom Erath County is named, for the proximity of its source to the 98th meridian. PO 12 June 1856, PM Joseph W. Smith.

MERRICK (Martin) Named for landowners and merchants Griffith and Rhoda Merrick who moved to the area in the early 20th century.

MERRILLTOWN (Travis) Named for Nelson Merrill who relocated from Ohio to Texas in 1837. Merrill opened the Merrillton PO in his general store 19 Mar 1851. Merrilltown is now part of north Austin.

MERTENS (Hill) Named for financier William Mertens, a major bondholder of the St. Louis Southwestern Railway (Cotton Belt) that established a station in 1887. PO 4 Apr 1888, PM John Taylor.

MERTZON [MERTS uhn] (Irion) Mortimer Lovejoy Mertz was president of the San Angelo National Bank and a director of the Kansas City, Mexico & Orient Railway, which established a station about 1910. PO 7 Dec 1908, PM Ira M. Wood.

MESQUITE (Dallas) Mesquite, founded in 1873 by the Texas & Pacific Railway, was named from Mesquite Creek, itself named for the spiny desert shrub with edible pods that provided food and fiber for Native Americans and now provides fuel and flavor for backyard barbeques. From Nahuatl (Aztec) *mizquitl* through Spanish. PO 16 Mar 1874, PM William Bradfield.

METCALF GAP (Palo Pinto) Metcalf Gap, a pass through the Palo Pinto Mountains, was named for John Jones Metcalf(e) and his son William who established ranch headquarters near the site in 1856.

MEXIA [muh HEE uh] (Limestone) Named for the estates of Enrique Guillermo Antonio Mexía and his sister, Adelaida Matilda Mexía. The land in what is now Limestone and bordering counties was granted by the state of Coahuila and Texas in 1833. The town was named by the Houston and Texas Central Townsite Company in 1871. PO 1 Mar 1872, PM James N. Bartholow.

MEYERSVILLE (DeWitt) Founded by Pierre "Peter" Bluntzer who brought a group of Alsatian families to Coleto Creek in the 1840s and 1850s. The town was named for Adolph Meyer who settled in the area about 1846 and was the first PM 22 Dec 1851.

MIAMI [meye AM uh] (Roberts) The townsite was surveyed in 1877 on the proposed route of the Southern Kansas Railroad. Samuel Edge, the "Father of Miami," and Mark Huselby formed the Miami Township Company to promote the community and to sell building lots. Some local accounts claim that Miami is from a Native American language meaning "sweetheart" or "beautiful." Rather, Miami, with the general meaning "downstream people," is a transfer, probably from Miami, KS, that was named about 1860 for the Miami people who had been removed from Indiana in the 1830s. Both Edge and Huselby are reported to have had Kansas connections. PO 20 Jan 1890, PM Andrew J. Montgomery.

MICO [MEE ko] (Medina) Although *mico* can mean a long-tailed monkey in Spanish, here the name is derived from the *M*edina *I*rrigation *Co*mpany, created by Alex Walton to divert water from Lake Medina after the Medina River was dammed in 1911. PO 21 Aug 1911, PM Claude Gilliam.

MIDDLE WATER (Hartley) Middle Water was organized as a division of the XIT Ranch in the late 1880s and named for its location near Middle Water Creek. PO 10 July 1902, PM Edith Dyer.

MIDDLETON (Leon) In the early 1840s William B. Middleton came to Texas from Illinois and opened a general store. He survived the Mier Expedition, was the first sheriff of Leon County, and served two terms in the Texas Legislature in the late 1850s. PO 25 Oct 1867, PM Sampson Holleman.

MIDKIFF (Midland, Upton) In 1902 John Rufus Midkiff opened a general store in Midland County north of the Upton County line and established the Midkiff PO 12 May 1904. The town of Midkiff disappeared when the PO was discontinued in 1911. Oil was discovered south of the ghost town of Midkiff in 1950 and, according to local lore, the drilling camp was known as Hadacol Corners for a welder named Hadacol Dardis, so called because "they had to call" him something. Hadacol Corners was an unacceptable name for the post office in 1952 so the community appropriated the name of the vanished town of Midkiff. PO 16 Sept 1952, PM W. L. Williams.

MIDLAND (County) The Texas Legislature carved Midland County out of Tom Green County on February 28, 1885. Named for its location halfway between Fort Worth and El Paso on the Texas & Pacific Railway.

MIDLAND (Midland) Originally Midway, the name Midland was chosen because Midway was already established in another county. Early in 1884 the Midland Town Company, made up largely of Northern businessmen, was created to promote the town of Midland and to sell buildings lots. PO 4 June 1884, PM Charles H. Welch.

MIDWAY (Dawson) The origin of the name is uncertain. Mark Odintz, writing for the *Handbook of Texas Online*, suggests the name was chosen because the community lay nearly equidistant between the Mount Olive and Mullins schools.

MIDWAY (Lavaca) Reportedly named for its location halfway between Shiner and Yoakum on the Southern Pacific Railroad line.

MIDWAY (Titus) Reportedly named from the school located midway between the Gladewater and Mt. Sylvia districts that were consolidated in the 1920s.

MIDYETT (Panola) Named for Spencer Midyett (several spellings) who opened the post office in his dry goods store 1 June 1887.

MIKESKA [muh KES kuh] (Live Oak) Named for Peter and Anna Mikeska who emigrated from central Europe in the early 1870s. PO 14 Nov 1903, PM Peter Mikeska.

MILA DOCE (Hidalgo) Spanish for "mile 12." Named from East Mile 12 N Road, which runs through East Oliveras.

MILAM [MEYEL uhm] (County) Created 1836, organized 1837. Named for Benjamin Rush Milam (1788–1835), born in Kentucky. Milam came to Texas about 1818 as an Indian trader and became a major figure in the Texas Revolution. He was killed at the Battle for San Antonio in December 1835.

MILAM (SABINE) Red Mount (Red Mound) established about 1830 by merchant John Roberts, was renamed in 1835 in honor of Benjamin Rush Milam. Milam PO May 1838, PM William H. Harris. See Milam County.

MILANO [muh LAN o] (Milam) Founded east of the present site by the International–Great Northern Railroad in 1874. The name was probably chosen by a railroad official for Milano (Milan), Italy. PO 25 June 1874, PM James F. Buck. This is the only Milano in the US.

MILBURN (McCulloch) Named for Andrew J. Milburn who established the PO 2 May 1878.

MILES (Runnels) Earlier known as Miles City, named for Jonathan Miles, a San Angelo rancher who was instrumental in attracting a station on the Gulf, Colorado & Santa Fe Railway in 1888. PO 21 Mar 1890 as Miles Station, PM John McLeod; changed to Miles 11 Aug 1908.

MILFORD (Ellis) Founded about 1853 by William Hudson, Arvin Wright, and James Higgins. The local story is that Hudson chose the name for Milford, MA. PO 3 Aug 1854, PM William Hudson.

MILLERSVIEW (Concho) Named for rancher Edward D. Miller who co-founded the town with real estate agent Henry Barr. Barr was the first PM 3 Sept 1903.

MILLETT (La Salle) Founded with construction of Cibola Station on the line of the International–Great Northern Railroad in 1881 and named from the Millett Ranch, established in the mid-1870s by brothers Alonzo, Eugene, and Hiram Millett. PO 29 Mar 1888, PM Alonzo Millett.

MILLHEIM (Austin) Founded in the late 1840s by settlers from Mülheim ("mill home") in west central Germany. PO 22 May 1845 as Swearingen's, PM Samuel Swearingen; changed to Millheim 12 June 1856, PM Ferdinand F. Engelking.

MILLICAN (Brazos) In 1821 Robert and Nancy Millican brought their children and slaves from South Carolina and were among Stephen F. Austin's early settlers. The Millican's son Elliott was a pioneer physician and a Texas state legislator in the 1840s and 1850s. PO 12 May 1849, PM Arthur Edwards.

MILLS (County) Created and organized 1887. Named for John T. Mills (1817–1871). Born in Ireland, Mills emigrated to the US as a child, studied law in South Carolina and moved to Texas in 1837. He was a Clarkesville lawyer, circuit judge, district judge and a justice of the Supreme Court of the Republic of Texas in the early 1840s.

MILLSAP (Parker) In 1880 when the Texas & Pacific Railway established a station, the small towns of Mineral City, Peck City, and Millsap merged at trackside as Millsap, named for Cicero Fuller Millsap(s), a native Georgian who moved to Palo Pinto County about 1850 and to Parker County in the 1860s. PO 16 Jan 1877, PM Benjamin Porter.

MILO CENTER (Deaf Smith) Probably named for milo (sorghum), a local grain crop. The name was reportedly suggested by Hardy Benson at a community picnic in the early 1960s.

MILTON (Lamar) Milton was founded in the 1860s as Minton, named for one of several Minton families who were farming in the area before 1870. Through misreading or illegibility the name became Milton when Moses Mowrey opened the PO 28 Dec 1874.

MILVID (Liberty) Milvid was founded in the early 1900s and named for Anson W. *Mil*ler and Charles Shelton *Vid*or, owners of the Miller-Vidor Lumber Company of Galveston. PO 26 Apr 1907, PM Paul Zimmerman. See Vidor.

MIMS (Brazoria) Named from the Fannin-Mims Plantation established in the early 1830s by James Walker Fannin and Joseph Mims, one of Stephen F. Austin's Old Three Hundred settlers. See Fannin County.

MINDEN (Rusk) Probably a transfer brought to Texas by settlers from Minden, LA, itself named from Minden, Germany. PO 14 Mar 1850, PM William H. Pate.

MINEOLA [min ee OL uh] (Wood) When the Houston & Great Northern Railroad and the Texas & Pacific Railway established stations in 1873, the community was laid out by Ira Hobart Evans, secretary of the H&GN and later president of the New York and Texas Land Company. Mineola may be a blend of Min, for Minnie Wesley Patten, daughter of Dr. Adolphus Leander Patten and Emeline Patten, and Ola, reportedly a relative of Ira Evens, or it may be a transfer from Mineola, Alabama or Missouri. PO 13 May 1875, PM Thomas L. Scruggs. Formerly known as Sodom.

MINERA [muh NEHR uh] (Webb) Minera (Spanish "mining") was probably a continuation of an earlier settlement known as Carbon, a center of coal mining along the Rio Grande from the early 1880s. PO 11 May 1891, PM David D. Davis.

MINERAL (Bee) In the late 1870s water from the local springs, once claimed to be unfit for humans or animals, was said to have phenomenal healing powers and medicinal benefits of all kinds. A prosperous spa was envisioned and the community became known as Mineral City. The spa soon closed but the community endured. PO 2 Sept 1878 as Mineral City, PM Porter M. Neel; changed to Mineral 7 Aug 1895, PM Benjamin O'Neal.

MINERAL WELLS (Palo Pinto) James Alvis Lynch laid out and named the community in 1881. Water from the early wells was said to be unfit to drink but was later promoted for its medicinal properties claimed to cure ailments from rheumatism to hysteria. The PO was established by Horatio Barnett 4 Apr 1881 as Ednaville, named for his daughter, Edna; changed to Mineral Wells 20 Sept 1882, PM James C. Haynes.

MINERVA [muh NERV uh] (Milam) Minerva was founded in 1891 on land donated by the Sharrod Sanders family for a station on the San Antonio & Aransas Pass Railway.

The station was named for Sharrod Sanders's widow, Minerva Amanda, his daughter, Minerva Mae, or more likely both. PO 29 Apr 1892, PM Mittie Jones.

MINGS CHAPEL (Upshur) Jessie Daniel Mings, known as "Grandpa," brought his family and slaves from Alabama and established a plantation in the late 1850s. A chapel that gave the community its name was built in the early 1860s.

MINGUS [MING guhs] (Palo Pinto) Mingus was founded in 1881 with construction of the Texas & Pacific Railway. By local accounts the town was named for a William Mingus who reportedly settled in the area in the mid- 1850s. This may be the William Mingus who served as a Texas Ranger for a decade in the late 1850s and early 1860s. PO 16 Sept 1897, PM Joel Brock.

MINTER (Lamar) Named for Minter H. Parker from Missouri who established a farm in the late 1840s and opened the Minter PO 10 Apr 1882.

MIRANDO CITY (Webb) About 1920 Oliver W. Killam, an oilman and community benefactor, founded Mirando City, named for Nicolás Mirando, owner of the original land grant. PO 18 May 1922 as McCaslin; changed to Mirando City 24 May 1922, PM Lee McCaslin.

MISSION (Hidalgo) In 1907 John Conway bought the site from the French Oblates of Mary Immaculate, caretakers of *La Lomita* "the little hill" *Mission*, founded in the early 1860s. PO 13 Sept 1907, PM James L. Dougherty.

MISSION VALLEY (Victoria) Named for the *Nuestra Señora del Espíritu Santo de Zúñiga Mission* (Mission La Bahía), established by Spain in 1722; relocated from Garcitas Creek by Franciscan missionaries about 1726. PO 26 Aug 1854, PM Stephen S. Harris.

MISSOURI CITY [muh ZOR uh] (Fort Bend, Harris) Founded in the early 1890s by Houston-area real estate investors Reuben Cash, Louis Luckle, and William McElroy. Named for the state of Missouri where the community was widely advertised and promoted, especially in the St. Louis area. PO 21 Aug 1897, PM William Watts.

MITCHELL (County) Created 1876, organized 1881. Named for Asa and Eli Mitchell, born in Somerset County, PA. The Mitchell brothers came to Texas as part of Stephen F. Austin's Old Three Hundred in 1824 and were politically and militarily involved during the Texas Revolution. Eli participated in the Battle of Gonzales; Asa fought at San Jacinto.

MIXON (Cherokee) Named for Alza and Susan Mixon from Alabama by way of Missouri who began farming in the area in the mid-1850s. PO 11 Sept 1889, PM Thomas Stovall.

MOBEETIE [mo BEET ee] (Wheeler) From about 1874 the Mobeetie settlement grew around a buffalo hunters camp and supply store known as Hidetown. With the establishment of Fort Elliott in 1875, the town became known as Sweetwater for its location on Sweetwater Creek. As William Coy Perkins tells the story, when the post office application with the name Sweetwater was rejected, Indian scouts from Fort Elliott offered the name Mobeetie, which they said was their word for "sweet water." The application was resubmitted and accepted. After Fort Elliott closed, a cyclone destroyed much of the town and the county seat was moved to Wheeler. What was left of Old Mobeetie was moved to New Mobeetie on the Panhandle & Santa Fe Railway line in 1929. PO 16 Jan 1878 as Fort Elliott, PM William M. D. Lee; discontinued 19 Apr 1880. The Mobeetie office opened 4 Sept 1879, PM George A. Montgomery.

MOBILE CITY (Rockwall) Mobile City began as a mobile home park sometime prior to January 1990 when it was incorporated in order to allow liquor sales.

MOFFAT [MAHF it] (Bell) Moffat was founded about 1857 by Chauncey and Amelia Moffet [*sic*]. Chauncey Moffet was the first doctor in the area and in the years preceding the Civil War he bought slaves, taught them to read and write, and relocated them in Northern and western free states. PO 22 Aug 1872, PM James Valiant.

MOLINE [mo LEEN] (Lampasas, Mills) Moline grew from the mid-1880s around a cluster of gristmills and later a cotton gin. The town was probably named from the Texas Moline Plow Company, itself named for the Moline Plow Company of Moline, IL. PO 29 July 1910, PM Annie D. Spivey.

MONAHANS (Ward) Originally known as Monahan's Well for the well and water tank established by Thomas J. (Pat) Monahan about 1881. Monahan, a surveyor for the Texas & Pacific Railway, dug the first water well in the area. PO 4 Dec 1883, PM Silas Hogg.

MONAVILLE (Waller) Daniel Culpepper Singletary, born in Georgia, established a general store and opened the Mona PO 26 May 1886, named for his newborn daughter, Mona.

MONKSTOWN (Fannin) Named for James and Amanda Monk who began farming in the area in the 1860s. PO 3 June 1878, PM James Monk.

MONROE (Rusk) Likely a transfer from Monroe County, GA, perhaps brought to Texas by native Georgian John Robertson who opened the PO 4 Dec 1860.

MONROE CITY (Chambers) Known from the 1840s as White City for James Taylor White, the "Cattle King of Southeast Texas," until the mid-1930s when oil was discovered and the community was formally named for White's grandson, Robert Monroe White. PO 25 June 1936, PM Thelma L. Thames.

MONT (Lavaca) Mont is likely a shortening of Monserate, the name of the PO opened by Thomas Dew in March 1894, itself probably a phonetic spelling of Montserrat, the island in the Caribbean. The present name was in use by the time the Mont school was opened in 1908.

MONT BELVIEU (Chambers) The PO application requesting the name Barber's Hill for first settler Amos Barber was rejected in May 1890. The application resubmitted as Mont Bellview, an older name for the site and apparently an attempt at French for "hill of the pleasant view," was approved by the Post Office Department and by Zachary Winfree, the first postmaster 28 May 1890. The reason for the change from Bellview to Belvieu is unknown.

MONTAGUE [MAHN tag] (County) Created 1857, organized 1858. Named for Daniel Montague (1798–1876), a surveyor, plantation owner, and slave holder in Louisiana before moving to Texas in 1836. He was an officer of the Texas Mounted Volunteers during the Mexican War and was elected to the Texas Senate in 1863. The town of Montague, the county seat, was created by the Texas Legislature in 1858. PO 31 May 1860, PM John H. Cox.

MONTALBA [mahn TAL buh] (Anderson) The local account is that Montalba, which can be interpreted as "white mountain," was named for the summit east of the town when it was dusted with snow. The Beaver PO operated from 27 July 1848 until 25 July 1881; reestablished as Montalba 20 Mar 1882, PM William J. Hamlett.

MONTELL [mahn TEL] (Uvalde) Charles DeMontel was a colonizer, engineer, and local official from the 1840s through the 1870s in Medina, Bandera, and Uvalde counties. He established Camp Montel, which provided the nucleus for the town of Montell, on the Nueces River as a base for his surveying party in 1870. The second "l" was apparently added to Montel by George Clarke, the first PM 13 Nov 1879.

MONTEOLA [mahn tee OL uh] (Bee) Founded as Butlers on the Butler Ranch about 1880. The origin of the name Monteola is unknown. By a local account James Lynch, keeper of the general store and the second postmaster, created Monteola by blending Monte, the name of a traveling salesman, with Ola, the name of Monte's wife. An abandoned community in Lewis County, NY, is the only other Monteola in the US. PO 9 Mar 1907, PM John C. Armistead.

MONTGOMERY (County) Created by the Republic of Texas in December 1837 and named for the town of Montgomery.

MONTGOMERY (Montgomery) William Watters Shepperd, who relocated from North Carolina in 1831, and his business partner, John Wyatt Moody, laid out the town of Montgomery in June 1837. The origin of the name has long been debated; the traditional story is that Shepperd or Moody took the name from the Montgomery trading post, established in the early 1820s by soldier and adventurer Andrew Jackson Montgomery, a third generation relative of Brigadier General Richard Montgomery, a hero of the American Revolution. However, the name was probably suggested by Moody for Montgomery County, AL, where he had lived for a decade before moving to Texas in 1835 and where he had served as county clerk in the late 1820s. PO 17 May 1837, PM W. W. Shepperd.

MONTHALIA [mahn THAL yuh] (Gonzales) The origin of the name is uncertain. There is the usual claim that Monthalia is from an "Indian" word, here said to mean "little mountain," and also a local account that Phelps White, an early settler, left his fiancée, Thalia, in Georgia while he homesteaded in Texas. When she died before he could make the return trip he named the site in her honor. Perhaps the name is from Greek *thalia* "to bloom, to flourish," the source of THALIA in Foard County. PM 6 Dec 1893, PM Mark Potts.

MONTICELLO [mahn tuh SEL o] (Titus) Monticello, for Thomas Jefferson's plantation home in Virginia, is a popular place name occurring in some 30 states. By a local account an early settler suggested the name after a visit to Jefferson, TX, where he was impressed by an exhibit on Jefferson's estate. Alternatively, Monticello may have been brought to Texas by settlers from Monticello, Alabama, Georgia, or Mississippi. PO 5 May 1857, PM Cicero J. Corder.

MOODY (McLennan) The Gulf, Colorado & Santa Fe Railway established Moody Station in 1881; named for William Lewis Moody, a Galveston businessman and a director of the GC&SF. PO 13 Apr 1855 as Perry; changed to Moody 21 Nov 1881, PM J. H. Morrison.

MOORE (County) Created 1876, organized 1892. Named for Edwin Ward Moore (1810–1865), a native Virginian. Moore resigned his lieutenancy in the US Navy and became commander of the Texas Navy in 1839. He served until 1843 when he was dismissed by Texas President Sam Houston. Litigation by both Moore and Texas resulted in a court's finding Moore guilty of minor offenses but not the disobedience and piracy with which he was initially charged. Despite the acrimony between Moore and Texas there were apparently few objections to naming a county in his honor.

MOORE (Frio) The New York and Texas Land Company founded Moore Hollow about 1880, presumably named for Robert Moore, known as "Mustang" Moore, an early settler from NC about whom little is known except that he was killed in a Comanche raid. A local folk tale claims the name arose when a jaded traveler from the East showed up at the train station, shouted "no more; I can take no more of Texas," hurried to the nearest saloon, downed a shot of whiskey, and promptly hanged himself. PO 14 Jan 1879 as Moore Hollow, PM John B. McMahon; discontinued and reopened as Moore's Station 8 June 1882; changed to Moore 13 Oct 1897.

MOOREVILLE (Falls) The town grew around a general store opened by Irish immigrant Robert Moore in the 1850s. PO 4 Mar 1878 as Mooresville, PM William Murphy; changed to Mooreville 10 June 1892.

MORALES [muh RAHL uhs] (Jackson) Earlier known as Morales de Lavaca, for blacksmith Frank Morales and the nearby Lavaca River. PO 12 Dec 1849 as Morales de Lavaca, PM James Kerr; changed to Morales in the early 1860s.

MORAN [muh RAN] (Shackelford) First known as Hulltown for Mary and George Washington "Swope" Hull who established a general store in the early 1880s. The name was changed to Hicks about 1890, then to Moran in 1892 for John J. Moran, a stockholder and officer of the Texas Central Railway. PO 29 Aug 1883 as Hulltown, PM Swope Hull; changed to Hicks 2 Jan 1890; changed to Moran 2 Mar 1892, PM Allen D. Spain (D'Spain).

MORAVIA (Lavaca) Ignac (Ignatz) Jalufka's general store provided the nucleus for Moravian settlers beginning about 1880. PO 20 Sept 1882, PM Isaac E. Clark.

MORGAN (Bosque) The Gulf, Colorado & Santa Fe, and Houston & Texas Central Railways built through the area in the late 1870s; the station was named for Santa Fe Railroad stockholder Thomas Morgan. PO 26 Aug 1879 as Steele's Creek, PM John W. Simms; changed to Morgan 22 Dec 1879, PM Elizabeth J. Nichols.

MORGAN MILL (Erath) George Morgan established a gristmill early in 1877. PO 1 Aug 1877 as Morgan's Mill, PM Royston Andrews.

MORITA (Howard) Spanish "little mulberry." Named in the 1850s for Milton Faver's La Morita Ranch, itself named from La Morita, the name of one of several springs on the property. PO 23 July 1907, PM Hersey Blaisdell.

MORRILL [MAHR uhl] (Cherokee) Roland Morrill came to East Texas from Michigan in 1901, founded the Morrill Orchard Company, and developed the local peach industry. Morrill's company closed in the 1930s. PO 24 Feb 1903, PM F. J. Franklin.

MORRIS (County) Created 1875, organized 1877. Named for William Wright Morris (1805–1883), born in North Carolina. Morris was a plantation owner who brought his extended family and slaves from Alabama to Texas in 1847. He was a tireless promoter of East Texas railroads and represented Rusk County in the Texas House in 1861 and again in 1873.

MORRIS RANCH (Gillespie) The townsite was the headquarters of the Morris Ranch, noted for its thoroughbred horses, owned from 1856 by New York businessman Francis Morris and managed by his nephew, Charles Morris. PO 30 June 1893, PM Guy D. Anderson.

MORSE (Hansford) Morse was organized in the late 1920s with construction of the North Texas & Santa Fe Railway and named for Charles A. Morse, chief engineer for the Chicago & Rock Island Railroad. PO 1 Mar 1929, PM Ruth Etta Powers.

MORTON (Cochran) Morton J. Smith, a Cochran County land agent, founded the community in the 1920s. The townsite is part of the ranch of Christopher Columbus Slaughter, a prominent rancher and banker. PO 22 Mar 1924, PM Mary Winder. See Whiteface, see Lehman, see Vealmoor.

MOSCOW [MAHS ko] (Polk) Born in Bell Buckle, TN, David Griggs Green moved to Texas in 1835. After participating in the Texas Revolution he settled in what is now Polk County, opened a general store and established the PO as Green's 19 May 1847. The office was changed to Moscow in January 1853, probably named by Green for Moscow, Fayette County, TN, where he apparently had lived before moving to Texas.

MOSHEIM [mo SHEEM] (Bosque) Mosheim is probably a transfer from Mosheim, Greene County, TN, itself named by German Lutherans in the early 1870s in honor of Johann Lorenz von Mosheim, an 18th century German theologian and church historian. PO 21 July 1887, PM Jefferson David Howard.

MOSS BLUFF (Liberty) Named for Nathaniel Moss and from the location overlooking the Trinity River. Moss, a native of Louisiana, settled near the site in the early 1830s. PO 22 Dec 1869, PM Samuel S. Firth.

MOSTYN [MOST uhn] (Montgomery) Named for one or more Mostyn (Moston) families. Henry and Alice Mostyn from County Sligo, Ireland, were established farmers by 1850. PO 20 Aug 1908, PM Peter Josserand.

MOTLEY (County) Created 1876, organized 1891. Named for Junius William Mottley (c. 1812–1836), a native Virginian who arrived in Texas by way of Kentucky in 1835. Mottley [*sic*] signed the Texas Declaration of Independence, was surgeon for the Texas Army post at Goliad, and died from a wound received during the Battle of San Jacinto in 1836.

MOUND (Coryell) Named from a nearby white chalky hill when the Texas & St. Louis Railway built through the area in the early 1880s. PO 9 June 1884, PM Isaac Franks.

MOUNT BLANCO (Crosby) Named from Blanco (Spanish for "white") Canyon and an elevation on the Caprock escarpment. The town was founded about 1878 by Henry Clay Smith, a Fort Griffin hotelier at the time and later a rancher at Blanco Canyon. Smith's wife, Elizabeth, opened the PO 1 Sept 1879.

MOUNT CALM (Hill) By one local account Mount Calm is a popular etymology of Montcalm, the name of a local French blacksmith and wheelwright; by another Mary Johns chose the name for the Marquis de Montcalm after reading a book about the French and Indian War. PM 30 June 1858, Hardy Jones.

MOUNT ENTERPRISE (Rusk) The local account is that the name was coined by combining "mount," from a nearby hill, with the vision of the town's growth expressed by businessman Charles Vinzent who established several furniture factories and retail outlets in the 1840s. PO 12 Sept 1846 as Mulberry Grove; changed to Mount Enterprise 9 Apr 1849, PM Charles Vinzent.

MOUNT JOY (Delta) According to the local story, the site was named by Francis (Fanny) Buford. After a long journey from Virginia with her husband, Simeon, she surmounted a small hill and expressed her joy at reaching their journey's end. PO 21 Nov 1876, PM Matthew Keen.

MOUNT PLEASANT (Titus) Mount Pleasant was founded in 1846 with the creation of Titus County. Local stories explaining the name abound. By one, early travelers found the mound near a spring a "pleasant" place to camp for the night; by another, a large hill was a favorite and "pleasant" hunting ground for local Indians; by another, the name was suggested by the fact that the local hills were pleasant to look upon; and by still another, Caddo Indians revered a burial site known as the "pleasant mound" that was modified by settlers to Mount Pleasant. PO 18 Jan 1847, PM Daniel McCall.

MOUNT SELMAN (Cherokee) In the mid-1880s the Kansas & Gulf Short Line Railroad bypassed Larissa. William McKee, son of Thomas McKee, the founder of Larissa, laid out a town on the line of the K&G named for Dr. James Selman who donated land for the townsite. Mount was added when McKee established the PO 2 July 1884. See Larissa.

MOUNT VERNON (Franklin) The area was known as Mount Vernon from at least the 1850s, although the name did not become official until 1875. The townsite was probably donated by the family of George and Rebecca Keith who were settled in the area by the early 1840s. The name may be a transfer, brought to Texas from a Mount Vernon in Alabama, Arkansas, or Mississippi or the town may have been named directly for George Washington's estate, Mount Vernon, Virginia, itself named by Washington's half-brother, Lawrence, for British Vice Admiral Edward Vernon. PO 20 July 1848 as Keith's, PM William S. Keith; changed to Lone Star 19 Nov 1850; changed to Mount Vernon 21 Sept 1875, PM John L. Rutherford.

MUELLERSVILLE [MIL erz vil] (Washington) Named from the post office established by William F. Mueller 1 Mar 1899.

MUENSTER [MYOON ster] (Cooke) In the 1880s Franz Emmerick "Emil" Flusche and his brother, Friederick August Flusche, founded the German Catholic colonies of Muenster, Lindsay, and Pilot Point in Texas and colonies in Kansas and Iowa. Named for Müenster, Westphalia, Germany, birthplace of the Flusches. PO 19 Dec 1889, PM August Flusche.

MULDOON (Fayette) Established in 1886 with construction of the San Antonio & Aransas Pass Railway on land granted to Miguel (Michael) Muldoon, an Irish Catholic priest who came to Texas from Mexico in the early 1820s and who counseled Stephen F. Austin during his imprisonment in Mexico City in the 1830s. PO 18 Jan 1888, PM James Kerr.

MULESHOE (Bailey) The Bailey County seat was founded in 1913 with construction of the Pecos & Northern Texas Railway and named from the Muleshoe Ranch, established in 1903 by Edward K. and Charles Warren, father and son, corset manufacturers from Michigan. Their spread, originally part of the XIT Ranch, grew to several hundred thousand acres. According to the local account, on one of his rides Charles Warren happened upon an old mule shoe and thought this would be a good name for the ranch and would also make a distinct, easily recognizable brand. However, there had been several Muleshoe ranches and several Muleshoe brands registered in Texas since at least the mid-1840s, one of which may have influenced Warren's selection of the name. PO 7 Jan 1913 as Janes, named from the John N. Janes Ranch; changed to Muleshoe 25 May 1914, PM Melville P. Smith.

MULLIN [MUHL uhn] (Mills) In 1858 Charles Mullin built a ranch house on Jim Ned Creek that became the nucleus for the town of Mullin that was organized with construction of the Santa Fe Railroad station in 1885. PO 26 July 1886, Thomas S. Baird.

MUMFORD (Robertson) Jeffrey Mumford, with sons Jeptha and David, emigrated from Georgia through Florida to Texas where Jeptha "Jesse" Mumford (who claimed the family name was Mountford but was mistakenly written Mumford), established a ferry across the Brazos River near the site in the 1830s. PO 28 Jan 1878, PM Bryant B. Bailey.

MUNCY (Floyd) About 1892, the Robert E. Lee Muncy family moved from Lee County, VA, to Texas. Muncy, a Baptist minister, was instrumental in organizing the Missionary Baptist Church and Sunday School. The community was named for the Muncy family in 1897.

MUNDAY (Knox) First known as Maud, reportedly named for a Miss Maud Isbell. Reuben Munday, who established the PO 8 Aug 1894, chose the name for his former home, Mundys [*sic*] Landing, Woodford County, KY, named for the Munday family in the 1880s.

MUNGER (Limestone) Munger had its start in 1902 when Henry Martin Munger donated land for a station on the Trinity & Brazos Valley Railway. PO 19 Sept 1899 as Condor; changed to Munger 13 Apr 1905, PM William H. Ellington.

MUNSON (Rockwall) Named for William B. Munson, a lawyer, rancher, and a founder of DENISON. PO 22 May 1900, PM Daniel Columbus Canup.

MURCHISON [MERK i suhn] (Henderson) Named about 1880 with construction of the St. Louis Southwestern Railway (Cotton Belt) for Thomas Frank Murchison who established the first bank in Athens in 1890. PO 28 Feb 1881 as Lindsey; changed to Murchison 23 Aug 1883, PM John B. Murphree.

MURPHY (Collin) Earlier known as Decatur and Maxwell, the town was named for landowners William Murphy and his sons, William and James, who donated land for the right of way and for a station on the line of the St. Louis Southwestern Railway (Cotton Belt) that was extending a line connecting Plano and Greenville in 1888. PO 30 Jan 1891, PM James T. Murphy.

MURRAY (Young) James J. Murray and Thomas Price, farmers from New York and Ohio, respectively, were the first settlers in 1874. Mary C. Cusenbary established the post office named for James Murray 12 Jan 1880.

MYKAWA [mi KAH wuh] (Harris) Named for Shunpei Mykawa, a former Japanese naval officer who brought rice cultivation to the area in 1906. Now part of Houston. PO 22 June 1907, PM Mamie Murchison.

MYRTLE SPRINGS (Van Zandt) William Austin Thomas Murrey (Murry), a nurseryman and publisher of *The Fruit Grower* magazine named the town for the crepe myrtle trees that grew in his family's yard. Murry established the PO 8 Apr 1887 and five years later he named his first-born daughter Myrtle.

N

NACLINA [nuh KLEE nuh] (Nacogdoches) A blend of *Nac*ogdoches and Ange*lina* for the location of the town near the line between the two counties.

NACOGDOCHES [nak uh DO chuhs] (County) An original Texas county created by the Republic of Texas 1836, organized in 1837. The mission of *Nuestra Señora de Guadalupe de los Nacogdoches* was established by Spanish missionaries in 1716, named from the Nacogdoche, the "Paw Paw people," a division of the Caddo confederacy who lived in the Nacogdoches area in the 17th and 18th centuries.

NACOGDOCHES (Nacogdoches) The city of Nacogdoches grew around the Old Stone Fort, a Spanish administration building built in 1779. PO 9 Feb 1837, PM Henry Raguett. Natchitoches [NAK i tish], LA, is a variant.

NADA [NAY duh] (Colorado) Organized about 1890 by Czechs and Germans from the area around Frelsburg. Named from Czech *naděje*, "hope." PO 17 Apr 1894, PM William Engbrock.

NANCY (Angelina) Named for Nancy Thompson, daughter of Dave Thompson who was secretary and treasurer of the Angelina County Lumber Company in the 1920s. PO 14 Feb 1901 as Dunkin, PM Harrison Dunkin; changed to Nancy 1 June 1926, PM Ralph C. Arnett.

NAPLES (Morris) The area was known as Wheatville until the early 1880s when the Texas & St. Louis Railway established Belden Station. The local story is that several names were submitted with the PO application in 1895 and the Post Office Department in Washington chose Naples. PO 7 Dec 1868 as Wheatville; changed to Station Belden 9 Jan 1882; changed to Naples 16 Feb 1895, PM Franklin E. Baker.

NARUNA [nuh ROO nuh] (Burnet) William Marion Spitler, a farmer and later a furniture salesman, bought the site in 1876. Spitler opened the PO 19 June 1878, choosing the name for the steamship Naruna, most likely the vessel that brought him to Texas from New Orleans in the early 1850s.

NASH (Bowie) Martin Manny Nash was division superintendent of the Texas & Pacific Railway that established a station in the early 1870s. PO 12 Mar 1884 as Park, named for PM John N. Parker; changed to Nash 8 June 1906, PM James Kenney.

NASH (Ellis) Probably named for Newton John Nash, an Ellis County attorney and mayor of Waxahachie in the mid- and late 1870s. PO 12 July 1883, PM Benjamin Reed.

NAT (Nacogdoches) Nathaniel (Nat) Jarrell was a dry goods salesman and the first postmaster 12 Apr 1895.

NATALIA (Medina) The Medina Irrigation Company founded Natalia in 1912, named for Natalie Pearson, daughter of engineer Frederick Stark Pearson who built the dam that created Medina Lake in 1913. PO 19 Mar 1913, PM Thomas Ragsdale. See Pearson.

NAVARRO [nuh VAHR o] (County) Created and organized 1846. Named for José Antonio

Navarro (1795–1871), a hero of the Texas Revolution. Navarro, a San Antonio lawyer and friend of Stephen F. Austin, supported Texas independence from Mexico and admission to US statehood. Before Texas independence he served in the Coahuila and Texas Legislature and the Mexican Federal Congress; after independence he served in the senate of the Republic of Texas. See Corsicana.

NAVARRO (Navarro) The town of Navarro was organized in the late 1870s as Hopewell, named from the Hopewell Baptist Church. In 1907 when the Houston & Texas Central Railway built north of Hopewell many of the structures were moved to trackside and the community was renamed Navarro. PO 18 Nov 1908, PM John B. Cole.

NAVASOTA [nav uh SOT uh] (Grimes) Francis Holland, one of Stephen F. Austin's Old Three Hundred, settled near what is now Holland Creek in the early 1820s. Known briefly as Hollandale, the community developed as Nolansville, named for James Nolan who donated land for the Houston & Texas Central Railway in 1859. Nolansville was renamed for the Navasota River when Jeremiah Lee opened the post office June 24, 1854. Navasota is a Spanish rendering of a Native American name for the river, usually written Nabasoto. Pedro de Rivera y Villalón was apparently the first person to record the name while on an inspection tour of the frontier defenses of New Spain in the 1720s.

NAVIDAD (Jackson) Navidad, settled from the 1840s, was named from the Navidad River, from Spanish "nativity, birth of Christ." PO 26 Apr 1869, PM William W. Williford.

NAZARETH (Castro) Joseph Reisdorff, a Catholic priest instrumental in attracting German settlers to the area, established the colony in 1902, named for the Biblical Nazareth. PO 6 Mar 1903, PM Frances McCormick. See Rhineland.

NECESSITY (Stephens) By one local account townspeople could not agree on a name for the post office so they chose this one out of necessity. PO 19 July 1893, PM Thomas Edwards.

NECHANITZ [NEK uh nits] (Fayette) Named for Nechanitz, the German form of Nechanice, a town now in the north central region of the Czech Republic. The name was likely chosen by Wenzel Matejowsky who emigrated from Bohemia in the early 1850s. Matejowsky represented the district in the Texas Legislature in the late 1870s and opened the PO in his general store 29 Jan 1874.

NECHES [NAY chis] (Anderson) Neches was founded in 1872 by Murdock McDonald and Jack Davis who donated parts of their properties for a station on the International–Great Northern Railroad. The town was named from the Neches River, itself named *Río de los Neches* "River of the Neches" by one of the expeditions led by Alonso de León in the 1680s. (The Neche were a Caddoan people who lived in the area until the middle of the 19th century. The name may translate as "Osage orange.") PO 23 Dec 1872 as Nechesville, PM John Quincy Adams Capps.

NEDERLAND [NEE der luhnd] (Jefferson) Nederland, literally "lowland," the Dutch name for The Netherlands, was founded about 1895 by the Port Arthur Land Company on the line of the Kansas City, Pittsburg & Gulf Railroad. Arthur Stilwell, the namesake of Port Arthur, named the community for the Dutch investors who had financed many of his business enterprises, including the KP&G. PO 19 Apr 1898, PM Gerardus Willebrodus Joannes Kilsdonk.

NEEDVILLE (Fort Bend) August Schendel, from Brandenburg, Germany, founded Schendelville about 1892. The PO application requested the name Needmore that the Post Office Department in Washington changed to Needville since there was an established Needmore PO in Texas. PO 14 Apr 1894, PM August Schendel.

NEGLEY (Red River) The community was first known as Gough for the sawmill operated by William Churchill Gough in the early 1880s and renamed when George W. Mitchell established the PO 13 June 1892. Reportedly named for early settler Oliver P. Negley.

NELSON CITY (Kendall) In the late 1920s rancher and site owner Edwin Nelson opened a convenience store and gas station. In 1929 he added a dance hall and named the site Nelson City.

NELSONVILLE (Austin) In the mid-1860s namesake David Nelson opened a general store. He was shortly joined by Isaac Lewis who built a sawmill and gristmill. Lewis opened the PO 8 July 1872 that he named for Nelson.

NEMO (Somervell) The local story is that the PO application asked for the name Cleburne, Johnson Stop because the town was midway between Cleburne and Johnson Stop on the Santa Fe line. That name was rejected for being too long, which infuriated Jimmy Johnson (the Johnson of Johnson Stop) who declared that if the town wasn't worthy of the name Cleburne, Johnson Stop then it might as well be named for no one. That remark inspired the local schoolteacher to suggest Nemo, Latin for "no one." PO 20 Dec 1893, PM Arthur Francis Rinker.

NERI [NEHR ee] (Hood) Perhaps named for the Biblical Neri, an ancestor of Jesus; probably named for Felipe Enrique Neri, the Baron de Bastrop. PO 19 Apr 1892, PM Jesse J. Mann. See Bastrop County.

NESBITT (Harrison) Founded by twin brothers Robert Jameison and Nathan Littleton Nesbitt who left Tennessee for Arkansas in the mid-1840s, moving on to Harrison County and founding the town of Nesbitt soon after the War with Mexico.

NEUVILLE [NYOO vil] (Shelby) Founded in the late 1880s and named for the Stephen de Neuville family who emigrated from France in the 1840s. Through popular etymology the name is often recorded as Newville. PO 11 May 1901, PM William J. Neuville.

NEVADA [nuh VAY duh] (Collin) First known as McMinn Chapel, named for the family of John McMinn, early settlers in the 1840s. In the early 1860s Granville Stinebaugh purchased a farm and laid out a community that he named Nevada. Although Nevada, MO, has been suggested as the source of the name, more likely Stincbaugh named his town for the Territory of Nevada that he likely would have passed through on his way to or from the California gold fields.

PO 3 Aug 1880, PM Samuel Stinebaugh (brother of Granville).

NEW BADEN [nyoo BAYD uhn] (Robertson) In 1881 John George Meyer, director of the Texas Land and Immigration Company, organized the community named for Baden, Germany. PO 12 Apr 1882, PM Phillip Reichert.

NEW BERLIN [nyoo BER luhn] (Guadalupe) Carl August "Edward" Tewes emigrated from Waldeck-Frankenberg, Germany in the 1860s, opened a general store in which he established the PO 1 Apr 1878.

NEW BIELAU (Colorado) New Bielau was settled largely by Texas Germans in the 1850s and 1860s who named the town for Bielau in Silesia.

NEW BLOX (Jasper) See Blox.

NEW BRAUNFELS [nyoo BRAHN fuhlz] (Comal) The *Verein zum Schutze deutscher Einwanderer in Texas* "Society for the Protection of German Immigrants in Texas," better known as Adelsverein "nobility society," was organized in 1842 to establish German colonies in Texas. In 1844 Carl, Prince of Solms and Lord of Braunfels, better known as Prince Carl of Solms-Braunfels, was appointed commissioner general to lead the Adelsverein-sponsored settlements to Texas. In 1845 Nicolaus Zink led an immigrant group to the site that was named Neu Braunfels by Prince Carl for Braunfels in west central Germany, site of the Solms-Braunfels family castle since the 13th century. *Braunfels* is literally "brown rocks." PO Nov 1845, PM Charles Thomas.

NEW CANEY (Montgomery) In the late 1870s the Houston, East & West Texas Railway established Caney Station, named from Caney Creek, itself named for the local cane forests. The PO application requested the name Caney; when this was rejected the application was resubmitted as New Caney. PO 7 July 1882, PM James Robinson.

NEW COLONY (Bell) Founded in 1905 by Czech settlers from the Elgin area. New Colony is a translation of Czech "Nova Osada," apparently the town's original name.

NEW DEAL (Lubbock) The Santa Fe Railroad founded Monroe, named for Monroe G. Abernathy, chief engineer of the SF and the namesake of ABERNATHY in 1909. The name was changed in 1935 when four local school systems formed the New Deal district, named for President Franklin Roosevelt's New Deal programs. PO 28 Apr 1910 as Monroe; discontinued 15 Nov 1910; reopened 1 June 1949 as New Deal, PM Grady Henly.

NEW HARMONY (Smith) In 1867 the community organized the Harmony Baptist Church. To avoid confusion with an existing Harmony Church the name was changed to New Harmony Baptist Church which provided the name for the town of New Harmony.

NEW HOME (Lynn) A one-room school, built about 1907, was known as the Deuce of Hearts School for its location on the Deuce of Hearts Ranch. When a proposal for building a church was considered, several citizens questioned the appropriateness of the name Deuce of Hearts Church. Lorenzo DePriest, a teacher at the school, suggested "New Home" since most of the people were recent arrivals. PO 6 Mar 1913, PM Fred P. Thomas.

NEW MOORE (Lynn) New Moore is a blend of the names of the founders, George A. *New*man, owner of the Newman Land and Development Company of O'DONNELL and McCarty *Moore* who laid out the community in 1924 on a site formally part of the Slash-L ranch.

NEW SALEM (Rusk) Oscar Wilson named the town Salem in honor of his former home in Victoria County. To avoid duplication of POs the name was changed to New Salem by Poindexter Payne, the first PM, 19 Sept 1849.

NEW SUMMERFIELD (Cherokee) Caley Amos Summers donated land for a schoolhouse in 1895. The school, built on Summer's Field, was appropriately named the Summerfield school. The community took the name of the school when Isaac Tipton opened the PO in his general store 11 Dec 1897. The office was discontinued in 1905 and reopened as New Summerfield 25 Oct 1838.

NEW SWEDEN (Travis) Named from the New Sweden Lutheran congregation formed in 1877. PO 23 Aug 1887 as New Sweeden [*sic*], PM Axel O. Sjoholm (Seaholm). The spelling was changed to Sweden in January 1893. Earlier known as Knights Ranch.

NEW TAITON [nyoo TAYT uhn] (Wharton) Named for Dr. Charles William Tait who brought his family and at least 65 slaves to Texas from Georgia in the 1840s. Tait was a surgeon during the Mexican War, a Texas State Representative in the 1850s, and an organizer of the Buffalo Bayou, Brazos & Colorado Railway, the first railroad to operate in Texas. PO 24 Feb 1892 as Tait; changed to Taiton 25 Feb 1896, PM William S. Delany, Jr.

NEW ULM (Austin) Named for the city of Ulm in Baden-Würtemberg, southwest Germany. By one local account, Lorenz Mueller proposed the name, bolstering his suggestion by treating his fellow citizens to generous samples of Rhine wine. PO 1 Oct 1853, PM Lawrence Miller. Formerly known as Duff's Settlement for pioneer James Duff.

NEW WAVERLY (Walker) New Waverly was founded in 1870 some ten miles west of the original Waverly (now Old Waverly) with construction of the Houston & Great Northern Railroad. Francis Maxey Lewis is generally credited for suggesting the name from Walter Scott's "Waverly" novels. PO 12 Mar 1872 as Phelps; changed to New Waverly 21 Jan 1873, PM William Whitley.

NEWBURG (Comanche) The community was known as South Leon, named from the South Leon River, until the mid-1880s when the name was changed to Newburg. The source of the name is uncertain. Newburg may be a transfer from Newburg in Alabama or Missouri. PO 21 Nov 1881 as South Leon, PM Columbus Addison Lee; changed to Lee 6 Nov 1883; changed to Newburg 28 Mar 1884, PM John W. Womack.

NEWCASTLE (Young) Late in 1851 the US Army established Fort Belknap, named for William G. Belknap, breveted Brigadier General during the Mexican War. In the early 20th century the Belknap Coal

Company was incorporated, taking the name of the fort. In 1908 the name was changed to Newcastle at the request of Samuel Hardy, the superintendent of mining operations, for Newcastle-upon-Tyne in northeast England, not only his birthplace but the center of a major coal mining area. PO 14 Aug 1856 as Fort Belknap; discontinued 5 Nov 1866; reestablished 20 Jan 1874 as Belknap; changed to Newcastle 13 Nov 1908, PM Thomas J. McCrary.

NEWGULF (Wharton) The Texas Gulf Sulphur Company, owned by financiers Bernard Baruch and J. P. Morgan, founded Gulf, a company town, south of Bay City in Matagorda County in 1919. In 1928 Texas Gulf Sulphur laid out a second town, creatively named Newgulf. PO 25 Oct 1928, PM William J. O'Rourke.

NEWPORT (Clay) According to the local account Newport is an acronym created by the initials of seven prominent early citizens: Newton, Ezell, Welch, Portwood, Owsley, Reiger, and Turner (or others; the names vary from source to source). Just as likely Newport is a blend of the names *New*ton and *Port*wood; the others being added fortuitously (or conveniently) at a later date. PO 11 July 1878, PM William Looney.

NEWSOME (Camp) Named from the Newsome PO, opened by John M. Newsome in his general store 2 Jan 1902.

NEWTON (County) Created and organized in 1846. Named for a Revolutionary War soldier, traditionally assumed to be Sergeant John Newton. For his story and the frequent pairing of his name with that of William Jasper, see Jasper County.

NEYLAND and **NEYLANDVILLE** (Hunt) These communities, within a mile of one another, were founded in the 1870s on Robert Neyland's plantation, established in the 1840s. Neylandville was primarily an African American community organized by freed slave Jim Brigham in 1865. Neyland PO 13 June 1892, PM John D. Moore. Neylandville PO 8 Mar 1888, PM Benjamin F. Brown.

NICKLEBERRY (Cass) Nickleberry, southeast of Marietta, was settled in the late 19th century as a predominantly African American community. The likely namesake is Tip Nickleberry who farmed in the area in the early 1900s.

NIEDERWALD [NEE der wawld] (Caldwell, Hays) German "brush, undergrowth." Named in the late 1860s by German settlers who were surrounded by what they described as "low forests of mesquite." PO 5 Apr 1902, PM Hugo Albert Buaas.

NIGTON (Trinity) Founded in 1873 by former slaves including Jefferson Carter, a landowner, a teacher, and a leader of the Negro Business League in the early 1930s. PO 14 June 1894, PM Robert H. Massie.

NIMROD (Eastland) The community was known as Monroe until March 1888 when William Munn opened the PO in his general store. The office was apparently named for the Biblical Nimrod, a Mesopotamian king often associated with the Tower of Babel, whose name has come to mean clueless if not dimwitted.

NIX [NIKS] (Lampasas) According to local lore the community could not agree on a name when "an old German settler" said, "why not call it *nichts* 'nothing' because there is nothing here." After some laughter the name was agreed upon in its Americanized form, Nix. PO 21 Nov 1883, PM Elizabeth Wallace.

NIXON (Gonzales, Wilson) Founded in 1906 when the Galveston, Harrisburg & San Antonio Railway established Nixon Station on John Nixon's ranch. PO 20 Oct 1906 as Nixonville, PM Charles Curry; changed to Nixon 3 Apr 1908.

NOACK [NO ak] (Williamson) In 1870 Peter Zieschang founded Hochkirk, the German name of Bukecy, Sorbian for the Wendish region of Germany. Renamed when John E. Noack established the PO 12 July 1902.

NOBILITY (Fannin) When the Post Office Department denied William Gentry's request for a Gentry post office, Gentry resubmitted the application with the roughly synonymous name, Nobility, which was approved in Nov 1881.

NOCKENUT (Wilson) Nockenut is likely an adaptation of mockernut, the smooth-barked hickory tree also known as the white-heart hickory. Naming details are unknown. PO 10 Nov 1858, PM William W. Cockrum.

NOCONA [no KO nuh] (Montague) In the late 1870s the Missouri–Kansas–Texas Railroad established Nocona Station. Benjamin Wathen, a KATY engineer, is credited for proposing the name for Peta Nocona, the Comanche leader married to Cynthia Ann Parker and father of Quanah Parker. From Comanche *nookoni* "wandering, moving about." PO 2 May 1887, PM Wade Horton. See Quanah.

NOELKE [NOL kee] (Irion) The Kansas City, Mexico & Orient Railway established Monument Switch in 1910, renamed in 1933 for rancher and site owner Walter Montgomery Noelke.

NOGALUS PRAIRIE [no GAL uhs] (Trinity) According to a local folk tale, Nogalus Prairie came to be associated with the community when horse thieves had to be hanged from a tree limb because there were "no gallows." Through popular etymology "no gallows" became Nogalus. Rather, the name is from Spanish *nogal* "walnut." PO 27 Nov 1894, PM Sam Franklin Kenley.

NOLAN (County) Created in 1876, organized in 1881. Named for Philip Nolan (1771–1801), an irregular military adventurer who led at least four unauthorized expeditions into Texas from Louisiana in the last decade of the 18th century, ostensibly to capture wild mustangs for the Louisiana militia and for private sale. The Spanish military commander at Nacogdoches considered him a troublemaker and probably a spy. Nolan was killed in a fight with Spanish troops in 1801. PO 13 June 1890 as Sowell, PM Archibald Sowell; changed to Nolan 10 Mar 1892, PM William C. Lee.

NOLANVILLE (Bell) First known as Nolan Valley, named from Nolan Creek, itself named for Philip Nolan, for whom Nolan

County is named. Nolan likely set up headquarters in the area about 1800. PO 19 Dec 1883, PM Frank S. Box.

NOME (Jefferson) The Texas & New Orleans Railroad established Congreve Station in 1860, named for Charles Congreve, treasurer of the T&NO. By one hoary folk tale, the name became Nome when a lady passenger stepped onto the T&NO platform and asked a young man "is this Liberty Station?" He replied "No'm," a gracious Southern "no m'am," and this struck bystanders as a good name for their town. More likely, since the Sour Lake oil reserves were booming at the time of the Alaska gold strikes, the source of the name is Nome, AK. PO 19 Apr 1894 as Buttfield for Joseph B. Buttfield of Sour Lake; changed to Nome 18 May 1903, PM Tennie Patrick.

NOODLE (Jones) Named from Noodle Creek. The local account is that "noodle" meant "nothing," in particular, a dry creek. The site was named when a lone, thirsty Indian looked at the streambed and plaintively sighed "no water," translated as noodle. PO 4 June 1900, PM Anthus Claud Gist.

NOONAN (Medina) George Henry Noonan was a local ranch owner and Medina County lawyer. Noonan represented Texas in the US Congress 1895–1897. PO 8 Apr 1910, PM Valentine Mangold.

NOONDAY (Harrison) Noonday was formerly known as Shortview, perhaps to contrast with Longview. According to the local story, in 1876 a meeting to choose a name was held at twelve o'clock, so Noonday was the obvious choice.

NOONDAY (Smith) The town was named from the Noonday post office opened 3 May 1880 by Edward W. Smith, itself named for the Noonday Baptist church of Noonday, Cobb County, GA.

NOPAL [NO puhl] (DeWitt, Presidio) Spanish "prickly pear." Nopal in DeWitt County was named in 1896 when Merrill W. Smith opened the Nopal PO. Nopal in Presidio County was named in the early 1880s with construction of the Galveston, Harrisburg & San Antonio Railway.

NORDHEIM (DeWitt) In 1895 William Frobese, president of H. Runge and Company, a Cuero shipping and banking firm that owned the townsite, suggested the name for his birthplace, Nordheim, Germany. PO 23 Jan 1896, PM Henry Schlosser. See Runge.

NORIAS [NOR ee uhs] (Kenedy) The townsite was owned and administered by the King Ranch and provided a shipping point for King Ranch cattle on the St. Louis, Brownsville & Mexico Railway from the early 1900s. Probably named through clever wordplay for Jim Wells, the namesake of Jim Wells County. Norias is Spanish for "wells."

NORMAN (Williamson) In the late 1870s Martin B. Norman arrived from Alabama. He bought property in the area and established a farm, a cotton gin, and a general store.

NORMANGEE [NOR muhn jee] (Leon) Norman G. (Goree) Kittrell was a lawyer, district and appellate court judge, and author of books on Texas law and government. He was the son of pioneer physician Pleasant Kittrell for whom the town of Kittrell, north of Huntsville in Walker County, was named. Normangee was founded in 1905 with construction of the Houston & Texas Central Railway. PO 10 July 1874 as Rogers Prairie; changed to Normangee 20 Oct 1906, PM John A. Heath.

NORMANNA [nor MAN uh] (Bee) About 1886 the San Antonio & Aransas Pass Railway established Walton Station, named for David Alfred Theophalis Walton, the sheriff of Bee County. When Walton was rejected as a name for the post office, first PM Andrew Peterson submitted Normanna, named for the local Norwegian colony and taken to mean "far north, home of the Norsemen." PO 26 Apr 1894.

NORSE (Bosque) Cleng Peerson, more than anyone else responsible for Norwegian settlements in the US, founded communities in Wisconsin, Minnesota, and Illinois and moved to Bosque County in the mid-1850s where he established the town of Norse. PO 27 Dec 1880, PM Ole K. Langren.

NORTH COWDEN [KOWD uhn] (Ector) In the mid-1880s William Henry Cowden and his brothers, John Motherwell and George Edgar, established the Cowden Ranch (the JAL). The community was named from the ranch after oil was discovered in 1930. (The origin of the JAL brand is a mystery, but it provided the name of the Jal PO that opened on the ranch in 1910 and the town of Jal in Lea County, NM.) PO 16 May 1848, PM Anna H. Dyer.

NORTH ZULCH (Madison) Julius Zulch emigrated from Kassel, Germany, in the late 1840s and established a general store in the area that became known as Zulch. About 1907 the Trinity & Brazos Valley Railway established a station north of Zulch, named, appropriately, North Zulch. PO 24 Feb 1908, PM James C. Parker.

NORTHRUP (Lee) Northrup grew around the San Antonio & Aransas Pass Railway established about 1890. Probably named for fruit grower Robert H. Northrup, PO 16 June 1894, PM Matthaus Tschatschula.

NORTON (Runnels) Named for site owner George Washington Norton, a Louisville, KY, banker and financier. PO 27 Nov 1894, PM Marion A. Wilkerson.

NOTLA [NAHT luh] (Ochiltree) Notla, Alton spelled backward, was created by site owner Frank Hamilton about 1920. Hamilton was part owner of the Alton Mercantile Company of Enid, OK. PO 21 Dec 1920, PM Mary Hamilton.

NOTREES (Ector) According to a local story shopkeeper and first postmaster Charles Brown chose the name in 1946. Brown reportedly noticed that the town once had a single tree which was removed to make way for the Shell gas plant; thus, leaving the town with "no trees."

NOTTAWA [NAHT uh way] (Wharton) Nottawa is probably a transfer from Nottawa, Monroe County, AL, itself named from the Nottaway River of Virginia and North Carolina. PO 16 June 1904, PM Frank C. Boyden.

NOVICE [NAH vuhs] (Coleman) Novice developed from the earlier communities of Tyro and Atoka, both founded in the early

1880s. Novice is a clever translation of Tyro, Latin for "beginner." PO 31 Mar 1880 as Pock; changed to Tyro 24 May 1880; changed to Novice 29 Sept 1884, PM Don W. Ward.

NOVICE (Lamar) According to a local story, the establishment of a church and school around 1900 provided a basis for the town that was a novice among existing communities.

NOVOHRAD [NO vuh rahd] (Lavaca) Novohrad was apparently named by settlers from Bohemia in central Europe for what is now Novohgrad-Volynsky in northern Ukraine. PO 31 Oct 1894, PM John Vrazel.

NOXVILLE (Kimble) Named for Noah and Persis Nox who arrived in the area from Missouri in the 1870s. Noah Nox was a Kimble County commissioner in the late 1870s and early 1880s. PO 16 Dec 1879, PM Persis Nox who kept the office in the family's general store.

NUECES [nyoo AY sis] (County) Created 1846, organized 1847. Named from the Nueces River, the name of which appeared on Spanish maps as the *Río Escondido* "hidden river" as early as the 1520s. The name *Río Nueces*, "river of nuts" from the flourishing pecan trees along its banks, was recorded by a member of Alonso de León's expedition of 1689.

NUNNELEE (Fannin) Named for Robert and Ella Nunnelee from Arkansas who kept a general store from the early 1900s.

NURSERY (Victoria) In 1883 Gilbert Onderdonk founded and named the town for his fruit nursery. Onderdonk was an influential South Texas fruit scientist who created several new varieties including the Texas Peach and the Victoria Mulberry. PO 18 Nov 1884, PM Gilbert Onderdonk.

NYE [NEYE] (Webb) Named for Thomas Carter Nye who established the Bermuda onion industry in the Laredo area around the turn of the 20th century. PO 4 May 1905, PM Thomas Delbridge.

O

OAKALLA [o KAL uh] (Burnet) The application for an Oak Valley PO was mistranscribed or misread by postal officials and approved as Oakalla. The name of Ocala, FL, is unrelated. PO 19 May 1879, PM James Kincaid.

OAKLAND (Colorado) Amasa Turner opened the Oakland PO in 1848, named for Oakland, the estate of his friend David Burnet, the first President of the Republic of Texas.

OAKWOOD (Leon) In 1872 the International–Great Northern Railroad established Oakwoods Station, named for the nearby stands of post oaks. The name was shortened to Oakwood when John Perrin opened the PO 1 July 1872.

OATMEAL (Burnet) The community was named from Oatmeal Creek but the origin of the name is uncertain. By one account Oatmeal is a popular etymology of Oathneil or Otneal, reportedly the name of the owner of the first local gristmill; by another Oatmeal is a translation based upon German *Hafer* "oats." Perhaps the name is a popular etymology of Habermehl (Habermill, Havermill), the family name of several German settlers, or even a direct translation since Habermehl (literally "oats" + "flour") is a German family name originally associated with producers or sellers of oatmeal. PO 13 Dec 1853, PM John Scott.

OBREGON (Coleman) Obregon was organized in the 1920s and was probably named for Álvaro Obregón Salido, a general in the Mexican Revolution of 1910 and president of Mexico 1920–1924.

O'BRIEN (Haskell) When the Kansas City, Mexico & Orient Railway built through Haskell County in 1906, the station was named for vice president and general manager Nick J. O'Brien. PO 19 Mar 1902 as Mid; changed to Carney 20 June 1905; changed to O'Brien 19 Oct 1908, PM James McWhirter.

OCAW [O kaw] (McLennan) "Waco" spelled backward. Ocaw is part of Bellmead in the greater Waco metropolitan area.

OCEE [o SEE] (McLennan) Fleming S. Ewing, the first PM 4 Dec 1895, named the office for Ocee W. Ewing, his two-year-old son.

OCHILTREE [AHK uhl tree] (County) Created 1876, organized 1889. Named for William Beck Ochiltree, a Nacogdoches lawyer, district judge, Secretary of the Treasury, and the last Attorney General of the Republic of Texas. PO 13 Sept 1886, PM Adalaska L. Rusk.

OCHOA [o CHO uh] (Presidio) Named for Esteban Ochoa who ran the Ochoa Ranch and who introduced irrigated farming to the area in the mid-1910s.

OCKER (Bell) Ocker was a largely Czech community, settled in the early 1880s and named for Bennet Ocker who opened the PO 8 Sept 1888.

ODDS (Limestone) Perhaps the name was brought to Texas by settlers from Odds in Johnson County, KY. (Kentucky also has a town called Oddville.) The name is not as unusual as we might think. There are places named Odd in Virginia and West Virginia and there have been a dozen or so Odd or

Odds POs. While the Odds are well represented, there are no Evens, oddly enough. PO 14 Oct 1899, PM Frank R. Adair.

ODELL (Wilbarger) In 1908 the Kansas City, Mexico & Orient Railway established Odell Station, named for Jabez T. Odell of New York, vice president of the KCM&O. PO 27 Apr 1909, PM Charles W. Stults.

ODEM (San Patricio) Odem was founded in 1909 shortly after the St. Louis, Brownsville & Mexico Railway built through San Patricio County. Site owners John Welder and David Odem named the town for Odem, a rancher and former county sheriff. Odem was also part owner of the SINTON townsite. PO 10 Dec 1909, PM Jarrad Birdsong Clark.

ODESSA (Ector) The seat of Ector County was founded on the line of the Texas & Pacific Railway in the summer of 1881 and promoted by the Odessa Land and Townsite Company of Zanesville, OH. The source of the name is uncertain. According to local stories, Odessa was the name of a beautiful Indian princess (or in later versions a "dazzling Texas maiden"), or the city was named for the Ukrainian Black Sea port of Odessa by Russian railroad crews who were reminded of their homeland by the West Texas landscape. To further speculate, Odessa may have been the name of a wife or daughter of a railroad official, early settler, or rancher. When the site was named, Odessa was becoming a popular female given name. According to census data, in 1880 six women in Texas were named Odessa but in 1900 there were 190. PO 19 Aug 1885, PM Elza White.

ODLAW (Kinney) Waldo spelled backward. Named for Jedediah Waldo, vice president of the Missouri–Kansas–Texas Railroad in 1893 and president of the Galveston, La Porte & Houston Railway.

O'DONNELL (Dawson, Lynn) Thomas J. O'Donnell was a railroad contractor largely responsible for attracting a station on the Pecos & Northern Texas Railway in 1910. PO 30 Oct 1905 as Central; changed to O'Donnell 23 Jan 1911, PM Charles H. Doak.

OENAVILLE [o EE nuh vil] (Bell) Oenaville was apparently named by Cullen D. Johnson who established the Oenaville PO 2 May 1872. Oenaville is one of Texas's mystery names; the origin is unknown but the exotic spelling has occasioned a number of speculations. By one, the namesake is Oena Griffin, reportedly the first European child born in the area but whose existence has not been verified; by another, Oena was a local Indian maiden (beautiful, of course); by another, Oenaville was the hometown of Cullen Johnson in Alabama (or Florida, or Georgia, take your pick); and by still another—and certainly the most romantic—Oena was a Seminole beauty that Johnson left behind when he came to Texas.

OGBURN (Wood) Known as Jim Hogg for the 20th Governor of Texas until 19 June 1909 when Simon Richardson opened the Ogburn post office, named for Josiah W. Ogburn who established a sawmill in the late 1890s.

OGDEN (Baylor) Nancy and William Ogden from southern Illinois established a farm in the 1870s.

OGDEN (Cottle) In the late 19th century, Alfred Ogden, born in Pinchbeck, England, developed a herd of pure-bred Hereford cattle and promoted the breed nationally. Ogden's prize bull, Jim Hogg, named for the 20th Governor of Texas, was calved in 1897 shortly after Governor Hogg left office. It is unclear if ex-governor Hogg was informed of his namesake, PO 28 Jan 1911, PM Laurence L. Driggs.

OGLESBY [O guhlz bee] (Coryell) Founded in 1882 with construction of the St. Louis Southwestern Railway (Cotton Belt) as Hilltop, presumed to be the highest point on the railroad line. The name was changed for William Oglesby who donated part of his ranch for the townsite. PO 22 May 1883, PM Joseph J. Hackney.

OHIO (Hamilton) William Thatcher Baker moved to Texas from Liking County, Ohio, about 1850. PO 12 Apr 1882, PM William Baker who chose the name for his home state.

OILLA (Orange) With the discovery of oil in 1913, site owners Ernest Williams and Robert Walles named the town Oilla. The accepted story is that Oilla is a blend of "oil" and "la" from Louisiana, probably added by Louisiana native Jesse Eugene Juban who opened the PO 31 Dec 1913.

OILTON (Webb) Founded as Torrecillas "little towers" for the local limestone formations when the Texas Mexican Railway established a station about 1900. With the oil boom of the 1920s, the Torrecillas PO, opened 30 Aug 1901, was changed to Oilton 19 June 1922, PM Francisco Guerra.

OKLAUNION (Wilbarger) In the late 1880s Joseph Spaulding "Buckskin Joe" Works bought a settlement known as Mayflower. Works apparently saw the site as a connection point or "union" for railroads of North Texas and Oklahoma and changed the name to Oklaunion. Works was fond of such names. Buckskin Joe founded Navajoe [*sic*], now an Oklahoma ghost town, and created the name by blending the name of the Navajo mountains with his own. PO 20 May 1889, PM Epaminondas Brooks (known as Nondae Brooks).

OKRA (Eastland) Named for okra, a veg-etable associated with the South in general and gumbo in particular. Naming details are unknown. PO 28 Feb 1899, PM Henry R. House.

OLD GLORY (Stonewall) German settlers founded Brandenburg in 1903. Given the anti-German sentiment generated by the First World War, the name was changed to the patriotic Old Glory at the request of seamstress and prominent citizen Emma Carr. PO 13 July 1908 as Brandenberg [*sic*]; changed to Old Glory 9 Aug 1918, PM Verina M. Holloman.

OLDEN (Eastland) Probably named for Robert F. Olden, the Eastland PM, in 1889. PO 2 Sept 1891, PM Luther Miller.

OLDENBURG (Fayette) Gustav Steenken and Johann Schmitt founded Oldenburg in 1886, named for their former home in Germany. PO 16 Mar 1887, PM Reinhard Aschen.

OLDHAM (County) Created 1876, organized 1880. Named for Williamson Simpson Oldham (1813–1868), born in Tennessee. Oldham was speaker of the Arkansas General Assembly and an Arkansas Supreme Court justice. He moved to Texas in 1849, was a member of the Congress of the Confederate States of America, and author of an early history of the Confederacy.

OLFEN (Runnels) In the early 1900s the German Catholic community was named Maas for Father Frank Maas, the area's first priest. The name was changed to Olfen, the ancestral home of Elizabeth Matthiesen in North Rhine-Westphalia, Germany. She and her husband, Bernard Matthiesen, were early settlers in the 1890s.

OLIVIA (Calhoun) Founded in the early 1890s when Rev. Carl Johan Emil Haterius brought a colony of Swedish Lutheran settlers from Galesburg, IL. Haterius named the community for his wife, Olivia Olson Haterius. PO 4 Nov 1892, PM Jonas Williams.

OLLIE (Polk) Nelson and Margaret Rice were the first known settlers, arriving from Alabama in the mid-1850s. The community was named for Mittie Ollie Rice, PM in 1913; granddaughter of Nelson and Margaret Rice and sister of David Rice, the first PM 14 May 1901.

OLMITO [ol MEET uh] (Cameron) Spanish "little elm." Named from the Olmito Ranch. PO 9 Mar 1905, PM Charles Lindsey.

OLMOS [OL muhs, AHL muhs] (Bee) The original name, Los Olmos (Spanish "the elms"), was shortened to Olmos in 1917.

OLMOS PARK (Bexar) Founded about 1927 by site developer Herman Charles Thorman who named the community from Spanish *olmos* "elms." Now part of San Antonio.

OLNEY [AHL nee] (Young) Possibly named for Olney, IL; more likely named for Massachusetts statesman Richard Olney, President Grover Cleveland's Attorney General in 1893 and Secretary of State in 1895. PO 17 Jan 1891, PM James M. Briscoe.

OLTON [OLT uhn] (Lamb) William Pulver Soash and the Soash Land Company founded Olton in the early 1900s. Named in 1 Sept 1903 by PM Joseph Z. (Jozy) Powell for his son, Walter Olton Powell.

OMAHA [OM uh haw] (Morris) Omaha has been known by at least four names: Elliott's Mills for the gristmill and sawmill established by David Elliot in the early 1850s; Morristown for Thompson Morris of Mt. Pleasant who donated land for the station on the St. Louis Southwestern Railway (Cotton Belt) in the 1870s; Gavett for the PO established in 1881; and Omaha. According to local accounts, to choose a name for the PO seven citizens each wrote a name on a piece of paper and dropped it into a hat. The slip with "Omaha" was drawn, reportedly submitted by William Noah Ellis or his son,

Daniel Hugh Ellis, for their former home, Omaha, Randolph County, AL. The Gavett PO was changed to Omaha 20 Apr 1886, PM John M. Witt.

OMEN (Smith) Formerly known as Round Hill and also as Canton. Albertus Wellington Orr, master of the Summer Hill Select School, chose the name "omen" for its positive associations with 1876. PO 8 June 1880, PM Michael Cayler.

ONALASKA [o nuh LAS kuh] (Polk) Thomas Rowe founded Onalaska, WI, in 1850, taking the name from Thomas Campbell's 1799 poem *The Pleasures of Hope*, which includes the line "The wolf's long howl from Onalaska's shore." (Onalaska is one of the eastern Aleutian Islands, now spelled Unalaska.) William Carlisle founded a lumber company in Onalaska, WI, in the 1880s and established lumber camps successively in Arkansas, Texas, and Washington state, naming each one Onalaska. PO 2 Aug 1805, PM Lawrence O. Jackson.

OPDYKE (Hockley) The Atchison, Topeka & Santa Fe Railway built through the area in the mid-1920s and the town was named for one of several officials of the AT&SF in the 19th century: George Opdyke, Charles Opdyke, or Stacy Opdyke.

OPELIKA [o puh LEYE kuh] (Henderson) A transfer from Opelika, Lee County, AL. From Muskogee "big swamp." PO 18 Dec 1912, PO John Vickery.

ORA (Angelina) George Medford established the Breaker PO 23 Sept 1884. Two months later, he changed the name to Ora in honor of his one-year-old daughter, Ora Lee Medford.

ORAN [o RAN] (Palo Pinto) Named for Oran Milo Roberts, 17th Governor of Texas (1879–1883). PO 6 Jan 1886, PM Daniel B. Matheny. See Roberts County.

ORANGE (County) Created and organized 1852. By one account the county was named for an orange grove established by farmer and first Orange County judge, George Pattillo. However, the name may be a transfer from Orange, NJ, the birthplace of A. H. Reading, the Jefferson County surveyor who laid out the town of Orange about 1858.

ORANGE (Orange) The community was founded by Resin (Reason) Green, plantation owner and early settler of Kenefik and known as Green's Bluff until 1852 when the Green's Bluff PO was changed to Madison. The Madison office was changed to Orange, apparently named for Orange County 18 Aug 1858, PM David C. Hewson.

ORANGE GROVE (Jim Wells) In 1908 James Fennell Dibrell and Max Starcke of GUADALUPE subdivided a portion of the Ventana Ranch and laid out the town of Orange Grove. The name was chosen to reflect and promote the growing citrus industry of the Lower Rio Grande Valley. PO 13 Mar 1909, PM Nehemiah Templeton. Dibrell and Starcke also laid out the town of SANDIA.

ORANGEDALE (Bee) Founded in the early 1900s with the expectation that the area would become a leading producer of citrus fruit, especially oranges, thus the name.

ORANGEFIELD (Orange) Named for the Orange oilfield with establishment of the post office by Fred Bland 27 Dec 1922.

ORANGEVILLE (Fannin) According to one account visitors to the area were fascinated by the fruit of the bois d'arc trees that they called oranges. This so amused the locals that they named the town Orangeville. PO 22 Sept 1858, PM George Elrod. See Bois D'Arc.

ORCHARD (Fort Bend) Dr. William Steenberger Chenoweth and Theophilus Walter Oyler founded Fruitland in 1891 on a site owned by Samuel K. Cross of Topeka, KS. A post office application for Fruitland was rejected; resubmitted and approved as Orchard 12 Apr 1893, PM William Chenoweth.

ORE CITY (Upshur) Named from the iron ore deposits that had been informally mined from the 1860s. Plans for organized industrial mining began about 1910 with construction of the Port Bolivar & Iron Ore Railroad. PO 18 Apr 1912, PM John Carroll.

ORELIA (Frio) Collin deVilbiss established the Orelia PO 9 Apr 1900, named for his one-year-old daughter, Ora.

ORIENT (Tom Green) Named for the Orient of Texas Railroad, part of the Kansas City, Mexico & Orient Railway system, created to build a line from Kansas City to Topolobampo on the Mexican Pacific coast. The railroad built through Tom Green County in the early 20th century. PO 7 May 1909, PM Thomas F. Harris.

ORLA (Reeves) In 1890 the Pecos Valley Railway, chartered by James Hagerman and his business associates as the Pecos River Railroad Company, established a section house just south of the Texas–New Mexico border named for the location from Spanish *orla* "border, fringe." PO 12 Oct 1910 as Angeles; changed to Orla 26 Dec 1906, PM Josh D. McAdams.

OROZIMBO [or uh ZIM bo] (Brazoria) Orozimbo Plantation, established in the 1820s, was the home of Dr. James Aeneas Enos Phelps, one of Stephen F. Austin's Old Three Hundred and a surgeon in the Texas Army. Santa Anna was held prisoner at Orozimbo in 1836. The origin of the name is uncertain. The plantation may have been named for an individual; Orozimbo is a personal name found frequently in Latin America, especially in Brazil. This is the only Orozimbo in the US. PO 1836, PM J. A. E. Phelps.

ORRS (Marion) Charles E. Orr opened the Orrville post office in his general store 27 June 1881.

OSAGE (Colorado) Pioneer physician Dr. Samuel D. McLeary founded the town of Osage about 1855, named for the local bois d'arc or Osage orange trees. The name comes from the Osage Nation who found the wood of these particular trees especially valuable for making bows. PO 30 Oct 1862, PM Samuel Davies McLear.

OSCAR (Bell) Founded about 1890 by Oscar Jones, the first postmaster 20 June 1892.

OSCEOLA [o see OL uh] (Hill) Founded in the mid-1870s. Probably named for Osceola, a Seminole leader who fought US forces in the Seminole Wars of the 1830s in Florida. PO 13 June 1878, PM James L. Burgess.

OTIS CHALK (Howard) Founded as Chalkton in 1926 when oil was discovered on the ranch of Otis Chalk. PO 18 Jan 1939 as Chalkton; changed to Otis Chalk 1 June 1939, PO Helen N. Splain.

OTTINE [ah TEEN] (Gonzales) Adolph and Theresia Otto established a farm on the San Marcos River in the 1870s. Their son, John August Otto, opened the post office 12 Oct 1892 and coined the name Ottine by blending his family name with that of his wife, Christine.

OTTO (Falls) When the International–Great Northern Railroad built through the area in 1901 the communities of Needmore and Lonestar merged as Otto, probably named for Henry Otto Stansbury, a local teacher and the PM at Rosebud in 1907. PO 13 July 1900, PM Cornelius J. Thomas.

OVALO [o VAL uh] (Taylor) Founded in 1909 by Percy Jones, construction engineer and later president of the Abilene & Southern Railway Company that built through the area in 1909. Spanish for "oval," Ovalo was named from the shape of the valley in which it lies. PO 26 Oct 1894 as Lawn; changed to Ovalo 11 Mar 1 909, PM Dana Harkrider.

OVERTON (Rusk) John Franklin Overton donated land for the townsite in 1873. PO 17 Mar 1873, PM James Harper.

OVILLA [o VIL uh] (Ellis) Martha Molloy, wife of Cumberland Presbyterian minister Daniel Gideon Molloy of Waxahachie, chose the name about 1870. Local accounts claim that she created Ovilla by prefixing "O" to Spanish *villa*. However, Ovilla is a Spanish family name, a 19th century female given name, and the name of several communities in Tennessee, one of which may have been transferred to Texas. PO 7 Feb 1871, PM Robert M. Chapman.

OWENS (Crosby) Tom B. Owens, the site owner, was vice president of the Fort Worth Cotton Exchange, director of the Western National Bank, and a community benefactor who donated land for the first school in the 1920s.

OWENSVILLE (Robertson) In 1856, county records were moved from Wheelock to the new county seat at Owensville, named for Harrison Owen, the first county clerk. PO 19 Sept 1856, PM John T. Young.

OWENTOWN (Smith) Owentown began as a switch on the St. Louis Southwestern Railway (Cotton Belt) about 1877. The community developed in the 1940s when the site became a supply center for Camp Fannin during World War II. The town was named in the late 1940s for Cliff Owen, a Tyler hardware dealer.

OXFORD (Llano) Andrew Jackson Johnson founded Oxford in 1877, named for Oxford,

MS, his childhood home. PO 3 Aug 1880, PM George W. Wilson.

OZONA [o ZO nuh] (Crockett) Ozona was founded in 1891 as Powell Well, named for Dallas surveyor Ernest M. Powell who drilled a well, built a windmill, and provided free water. Ozona was a promotional name, based on the belief that the more ozone in the air, the more invigorating and more healthful it was. PO 3 Sept 1891, PM Frank M. Boykin.

P

PACIO (Delta) The PO application asked for the name Patio, but because of illegibility or misspelling the office was approved as Pacio and the PM accepted this name rather than return the application. PO 12 Jan 1892, PM James P. Mote.

PADUCAH [puh DYOO kuh] (Cottle) Named by early settler and landowner Richard Potts for his former home, Paducah, KY. Paducah is a French transcription of a Native American name and referred to several different peoples of the southern plains, notably Apaches and Comanches. PO 19 Sept 1891, PM Charles Scott.

PAIGE (Bastrop) Named for Norman Paige who surveyed the route of the Houston & Texas Central Railway that built through the area in the early 1870s. PO 13 Mar 1874, PM Thomas D. Gorman.

PAINT ROCK (Concho) Named about 1878 from Paint Rock, a limestone cliff two miles southeast of the town that bears more than a thousand Native American pictographs. PO 1 July 1879, PM William Proctor.

PAKAN [PAYK uhn] (Wheeler) Named for Sam Pakan who brought a dozen Bohemian families to the area from Chicago in 1904.

PALACIOS [puh LASH uhs] (Matagorda) Palacios is a shortening of *tres palacios* (Spanish "three palaces"), named from Tres Palacios Bay, an arm of Matagorda Bay. According to an early story the name arose when a sudden storm in Matagorda Bay blew Spanish sailors off course and they were guided to safety by steering toward what they took to be three palaces in the distance. The palaces were mirages but the name endured. More likely, however, the namesake is José Félix Trespalacios who led an eventful life in Texas and Mexico in the early decades of the 19th century. He fought for Mexican independence and in 1822 he became the first governor of Coahuila and Texas, then part of the United Mexican States. PO 20 May 1903, PM Joseph E. Pybus.

PALESTINE [PAL uhs teen] (Anderson) Founded in 1846 as the seat of Anderson County. The community was apparently named by associates of Daniel Parker for Palestine, Crawford County, IL, Parker's home before moving to Texas. Parker was a minister of the Primitive Baptist church and a primary organizer of the Union Primitive Baptist Association of Texas in 1840. PO 8 Mar 1847, PM Charles Shelton.

PALITO BLANCO [puh LEE to BLANG ko] (Jim Wells) Spanish "little white stick, little white sapling." Named for the light gray bark of the young Palo Blanco trees, also known as Sugar Hackberrys or Texas Sugarberrys, found primarily in Central and East Texas. PO 25 Oct 1904 as Eva; changed to Palito Blanco 15 May 1928, PM Angelita de Gonzalez.

PALMER [PAH mer] (Ellis) Possibly named for Edward Albert Palmer of Houston, a Harris County state representative and senator in the 1850s, and a judge of the district court in Harris County. Palmer was a stockholder in the Houston & Texas Central Railway. PO 5 Jan 1874, PM Martin Hill.

PALO ALTO (Nueces) From American Spanish, literally "tree tall." The town was named from an 1834 land grant to Matias Garcia.

PALO PINTO [PAL o PIN to] (County) Created 1856, organized 1857. Named from Palo Pinto Creek, from Spanish "painted tree." PO 15 Mar 1858 as Golconda; changed to Palo Pinto 12 July 1860, PM Samuel A. Oxford.

PALODURO [PAL uh DOR o] (Armstrong) The community grew around the post office opened in November 1882 by PM Charles M. Hinsdale. The office was named from Palo Duro Canyon. In American Spanish *palo* "stick, pole" became generic for "tree," and *palo duro* "hard tree" referred to the stands of hardwoods in the canyon.

PALUXY [puh LUHK see] (Hood) The Paluxy River, from which the town takes its name, begins in Erath County where the north and south branches of the river meet, and runs southeast for some thirty miles to where it joins the Brazos in Somervell County. Paluxy is a transfer from the Biloxi River, Harrison County, MS, as earlier spellings such as Poluxey and Baloxey suggest. PO 7 July 1873, PM William Ethridge.

PAMPA (Gray) In the summer of 1887 the Southern Kansas Railroad of Texas established Glasgow Station, later known as Sutton. George Tyng, manager of the White Deer Lands Trust that owned the site, suggested the name Pampa because the local landscape reminded him of the Pampas, the treeless plains of Argentina that he had recently visited. PO 29 Oct 1892, PM Thomas Lane.

PANCAKE (Coryell) Rancher John Russell Pancake came to Texas from Virginia in 1858 and established the Pancake PO 19 June 1884. The office was closed in 1886; reestablished as Bush 29 Mar 1894; and renamed Pancake 7 June 1901. Following family tradition, John Pancake's son, William Pancake, was PM from 18 July 1905 until the office was discontinued 31 Jan 1908.

PANDALE (Val Verde) The local story is that settlers combined ordinary "pan," from the town's location in a pan-shaped valley, with romantic "dale." PO 25 Sept 1909, PM Ida J. Bates.

PANDORA [pan DOR uh] (Wilson) The San Antonio & Gulf Railroad built through the area and Wesley Irvin opened the area's first general store about 1890. Local lore claims that townspeople could not agree on a name and shortly after the SA&G established a station an employee delivered a package addressed to "Pandora's Box." That name was readily accepted even though opening the mythical Pandora's Box released a swarm of troubles upon the world. PO 27 Apr 1893 as Lorenz; changed to Pandora 8 Nov 1906, PM Jonathan Montgomery.

PANHANDLE (Carson) Formerly known as Carson City, named from Carson County, the community was platted in 1887 with construction of the Panhandle & Santa Fe Railway and named for the twenty-six northwestern counties that form the Texas Panhandle and gave the P&SF its name. PO 13 Aug 1887, PM Albert L. Mayfield.

PANNA MARIA [PAN uh muh REE uh] (Karnes) Polish "Virgin Mary." Panna Maria is claimed to be the oldest permanent Polish settlement in the US, founded in 1854 by Leopold Moczygemba, a Franciscan priest from Upper Silesia. The name honors the Church of the Virgin Mary in Krakow, Poland. PO 30 Aug 1856, PM Samuel Hedges.

PANOLA [puh NO luh] (County) Created and organized 1846. The name was probably suggested by John Allison, a cotton planter who brought his family and some 30 slaves from Panola County, MS, in the early 1840s. From Choctaw *ponola* "cotton." See Fair Play.

PANTEGO [pan TAY go] (Tarrant) Frederick Foscue, site owner and Texas politician, donated land for a church and school. According to a local legend, Pantego was a "loyal and trusted" Indian friend of Foscue. However, Pantego may be a transfer from Pantego, Suffolk County, NY, originally a Native American place name on Long Island. Pantego is now part of Arlington.

PANTEX (Carson) Pantex, named from the *Pan*handle of *Tex*as, was founded in 1942 as a company town for employees of the Panhandle Ordnance Plant that produced bombs and gunshells for the armed forces during World War II. Pantex was deactivated in 1945 and reactivated by the Atomic Energy Commission in 1951. PO 15 Jan 1945, PM Mary Newman Lemmons.

PAPALOTE [pah puh LO tee] (Bee) Present Papalote is the result of an 1850s merger of Steenville, Cravenville, and Murdock Place, each named for a family of early settlers. The town was named from Papalote Creek, itself named from Mexican Spanish, ultimately from Nahuatl (Aztec). *Papalote* has the general meaning of flying or blowing. By one local account the name comes from a wind-powered gristmill; by another from stones shaped like kites found in the stream bed. PO 29 Feb 1860 as Papalota, PM William B. Burditt; discontinued 10 July 1862. PO 8 Apr 1870 as Popolote; changed to Papalote 20 June 1883.

PARADISE (Wise) Founded in 1873 as El Dorado on land owned by Oliver Henry Perry Read. The Post Office Department required a different name and early settler William Burress suggested Paradise Prairie, reportedly because the location to him was a "paradise on earth." PO 10 Mar 1876 as Paradise, PM Lundy B. Hiatt.

PARIS (Lamar) In 1844 Pin Hook was considered an inappropriate name for the Lamar county seat and Thomas Poteet, an employee of merchant George Wright who donated land for the townsite, suggested the name Paris, for Paris, France. PO 1 Apr 1843, PM George W. Wright.

PARKER (County) Created and organized 1855. Named for Isaac Parker (1793–1883), born in Georgia. Parker located in Texas by way of Tennessee and Illinois in 1835. He was the uncle of Cynthia Ann and John Parker who were captured by a Comanche war party in 1836; he led several unsuccessful attempts to recapture them in the 1840s. Parker served in both houses of the Texas Legislature and introduced the bill that created Parker County in the legislative session of 1855–56.

PARKER (Collin) William Claiborne Parker established a gristmill and cotton gin in the late 1860s. PO 12 Apr 1888, PM George W. Kennedy.

PARKER (Johnson) The community developed in the 1880s and was organized about 1905 when the Trinity & Brazos Valley Railway built through the area. The name Kennard for the Kennard family who donated land for the railroad was suggested but the town was named for Alexis Dupont Parker, president of the Colorado & Southern Railway which had controlling interest in the T&BV. PO 14 Sept 1887 as Nathan; changed to Parker 12 May 1906.

PARMER (County) Created 1876, organized 1907. Named for Martin Parmer (1778–1850), born in Virginia. Parmer moved first to Kentucky, then to Tennessee, then to Missouri where he served in the state legislature. Parmer emigrated to Texas in the mid-1820s, was a delegate to the Constitutional Convention of 1836, a signatory to the Texas Declaration of Independence, and Chief Justice of Jasper County.

PARNELL [pahr NEL] (Hall) Founded about 1905. Named for Henry Silee and Arkadelphia Parnell who began farming in the area in the early 1900s. PO 9 Sept 1912, PM James A. Adams. Also known as Greasy Neck.

PARVIN [PAHR vuhn] (Denton) By 1860 the community was known as the Rue Settlement for brothers Jacob and Lewis Rue and by the mid-1870s as Good Hope, named from the Good Hope Baptist Church. The church was destroyed by a tornado and rebuilt on land donated by Henry Parvin. PO 8 May 1884, PM Isom King.

PASADENA (Harris) Founded in 1893 by John H. Burnett, president of the Galveston National Bank and a major investor in Texas railroads. Either Burnett or Charles Munger, who was instrumental in organizing the community, chose the name for Pasadena, CA, itself named in 1874 from pieces of Ojibwa words reported to mean "valley." PO 6 Dec 1893, PM Jasper F. Hays.

PASTURA (Jones) Spanish "pasture." Naming details are unknown. PO 6 Oct 1911, PM Martin Olson.

PATONIA (Polk) Brantley M. Pate, a turpentine distiller, opened the PO 31 Aug 1912.

PATRICK (McLennan) Named from the PO opened by Patrick Gallagher in his general store 28 July 1882. Earlier known as Stark Grove.

PATROON [puh TROON] (Shelby) Founded in the early 1860s. Named from Patroon Bayou. In colonial French and Dutch America, a patroon was a landowner with a large estate roughly equivalent to an English manor. The particular patroon for whom the bayou was named is unknown. PO 14 Nov 1840, PM Joseph Mason.

PATTISON (Waller) James Tarrant Pattison came to Texas from South Carolina via Florida in the late 1820s and became a major cotton planter and slaveholder with a large plantation on the Brazos River. The townsite was laid out about 1877 with construction of the Texas Western Narrow-Gauge Railroad and named, according to legend, for Pattison because his horse bested a rival's in a race where the winner won the right to name the town. PO 27 May 1879 as Patterson's [*sic*] Station, PM Thomas N. Bemus; changed to Patterson 2 Apr 1883; changed to Pattison 8 Mar 1916.

PATTON VILLAGE (Montgomery) Hugh L. Patton operated a sawmill near Splendora from the late 1820s. He became a noted oil well firefighter with Red Adair in the 1930s. In the early 1950s Patton purchased the site and the city of Patton Village developed in the 1960s.

PATTONVILLE (Lamar) Robert J. Patton, born in Alabama, opened a general store in the 1850s and was the first PM 25 Oct 1860.

PAWELEKVILLE [puh WAH luhk vil] (Karnes) Named for the Lawrence Pawelek family that settled in the area in the 1860s.

PAWNEE (Bee) The local account is that early explorers, for unknown reasons, painted the word "pawnee" on a board and nailed it to a tree. Travelers and later settlers saw the sign and took it to be the name of the town. PO 1 June 1948, PM Mary O. Ryan.

PAXTON (Shelby) Founded in the mid-1880s with construction of the Houston East & West Texas Railway. Named for one or more Paxton families. William and Nancy Paxton from Tennessee by way of Kentucky were established in the area by the late 1850s. PO 1 Sept 1892, PM Peter Herrington.

PAYNE SPRING (Henderson) William K. Payne from Alabama settled in the area about 1850. He was a delegate to the Texas Secession Convention and signed the Texas Ordinance of Secession in 1861. PO 27 Aug 1890, PM John Q. Hamond.

PAYTON (Blanco) Peyton Roberts, a former slave, founded the community as Freeman or Freemen's Colony at the close of the Civil War. PO 20 Dec 1898, PM Alfred W. Walker. Alternate spelling: Peyton.

PEACOCK (Stonewall) About 1902 Braxton Bragg Peacock and his brothers John and James opened a general store that housed the PO established by James Morgan Peacock 4 May 1908. For a time the town was known as Alluvia for the station on the Stamford & Northwestern Railroad line.

PEARL (Coryell) The area was formerly known as Swayback, named from Swayback Mountain, reportedly so named because it resembled the sagging back of an overburdened burro. The application for a Swayback PO was misread and the office was opened as Wayback 17 Nov 1884 in the general store kept by Ephraim Davenport and his cousin Overton. When Ephraim Davenport became PM in March 1890 the Wayback PO was renamed Pearl in honor of Overton's son, William Pearl Davenport.

PEARL CITY (DeWitt) Reportedly named for the Pearl Brewery of San Antonio, brewers of Pearl Beer, or for the quantity of Pearl Beer sold in the local saloons.

PEARLAND (Brazoria) The community developed in the 1880s along a siding on the Gulf, Colorado & Santa Fe Railway and was first known as Mark Belt, named for Marcus Lindsey Belt, an official of the Brazoria Land and Cattle Company of Missouri. (Belton, MO, is named for Mark Belt.) The name was formalized as Pear Land [*sic*] about 1893, reportedly chosen by "Count" Witold von Zychlinski, for whom Zychlinski Park in Pearland is named. Zychlinski is said to have been struck by the beauty of the local pear trees in flower. PO 4 Oct 1893 as Markbelt; changed to Pearland 20 Nov 1893, PM John T. Lacy.

PEARSALL (Frio) Pearsall was founded in 1881 by the New York and Texas Land Company, a subsidiary of the International–Great Northern Railroad and named for Thomas W. Pearsall of New York, a director and later vice president of the I-GN. PO 29 Aug 1881, PM Charles Cox.

PEARSON (Medina) Pearson was founded in 1912 by the Medina Irrigation Company and named for Frederick Stark Pearson, a leading civil engineer at the turn of the 20th century. In Texas he is best remembered for his work on the Medina Dam and the system of irrigation wells and canals he developed in Hale and Medina counties. See Natalia.

PEASTER [PEES ter] (Parker) Elizabeth Peaster and her brother Henry, South Carolina natives, began farming in the area in the 1870s. PO 6 Aug 1886 as Fremont; changed to Peaster 2 July 1890, PM Newton M. Howard.

PEAVY (Angelina) Anderson Jasper Peavy was a noted logger in Angelina County and a partner in the Bonner, Peavy and Bonner Logging Company.

PECOS (County) Created 1871, organized 1872. Named for the Pecos River that begins in northern New Mexico and flows for some 900 miles before entering the Rio Grande north of Del Rio. *Pecos*, with the general meaning "place of water," first recorded in reports of the Juan de Oñate Expedition of 1598, is a Spanish adaptation of the Keres Native American name for Pecos Pueblo east of Santa Fe, NM.

PECOS [PAY kuhs] (Reeves) George A. Knight, president of the Pecos Valley Land and Irrigation Company, laid out the town in the early 1880s when the Texas & Pacific Railway established Pecos Station, named from the Pecos River or Pecos County. PO 17 Nov 1882, PM William J. Leader; changed to Pecos 20 June 1884, PM Alvin M. Callahan.

PEELTOWN (Kaufman) In the 1850s James and Martha Peel brought their family from Tishomingo County, MS. The town was named for Peel's son, farmer James Monroe Peel, probably in the late 1870s.

PEERLESS (Hopkins) The community has had its share of names: In the 1850s, Gay's Mills for miller John Gay; in the 1870s, Hilldale; in the 1880s, Fairyland, named from dances where young girls pretended to be fairies; in the 1890s, Peerless. The local account is that the town was named Peerless ironically when a family planted a large crop of Peerless potatoes but because of heavy rains, the crop could not be harvested and the potatoes rotted in the field, releasing an unpleasant odor that could be smelled for miles in all directions. PO 29 Jan 1880 as Fairyland; changed to Peerless 20 Mar 1891, PM Joseph P. Arnold.

PEGGY (Atascosa) Soon after John Mowinkle settled in the area in the early 1930s, Clara Mae Nichols opened the Hollywood store. The community was known as Hollywood until 3 Oct 1935 when Nichols became PM of the Peggy PO. Probably named for Peggy Pander (Ponder), John Mowinkle's niece.

PELHAM [PEL uhm] (Navarro) About 1866 Louis and Laura Richie, former slaves, founded the community named for their former home, Pelham, Shelby County, AL. PO 22 Sept 1900, PM Louis R. Richie.

PENDLETON (Bell) Named in the early 1880s with construction of the Santa Fe Railroad for George Cassety Pendleton who represented the district in the Texas Legislature 1883–1889; was Texas Lieutenant Governor in Governor Jim Hogg's administration 1890–1892; and two-term US Congressman 1893–1896. PO 12 June 1883 as Pendletonville, PM George C. Pendleton; changed to Pendleton 14 Jan 1908.

PENIEL [puh NEYEL] (Hunt) Founded about 1900 as Holiness, named for Texas Holiness University, sponsored and operated by the Pentecostal Church of the Nazarene. The name was changed for the Biblical Peniel, where Jacob wrestled with an angel and "saw the face of God." The university moved to Oklahoma in 1920 and the town of Peniel became part of Greenville in the late 1950s. PO 27 Sept 1901 as Holiness; changed to Peniel 17 Mar 1902, PM Henry M. Hills.

PENITAS [puh NEET uhs] (Hidalgo) From *peñitas* (Spanish "small stones"). Naming circumstances are unknown. PO 4 Sept 1909, PM Narcisa Zamora.

PENNINGTON (Houston, Trinity) Pennington was named from the PO established by Daniel Dailey and named for early merchant Isaac Hill Pennington. Dailey, a Houston land speculator and developer, laid out the community in 1866. PO 4 Aug 1858 as Pennington, PM Daniel Dailey; changed to Lovelady 8 Nov 1872.

PENWELL (Ector) Robert R. Penn, a reporter covering the Texas oil industry for the *Dallas Morning News*, became an oilman in his own right, bringing in a gusher in 1929. The town was laid out in September of that year as Penn's Well and known by that name until Walter Bates opened the Penwell PO 30 June 1930.

PEORIA [pee OR ee uh] (Hill) According to the local account a transient named Stewart, who regularly camped at the site, suggested the name for his permanent home, Peoria, IL. PO 3 Oct 1856, PM Henry Young.

PERCILLA (Houston) In 1891 Henry Robertson submitted a PO application requesting the name Procella for early landowner Jose Procella. The name was either unclear or misread and the office was approved as Percilla. PO 26 Dec 1891, PM Henry T. Robertson. Known from the 1870s as Evergreen, named from the Evergreen Church and School.

PERICO [peh REE ko] (Dallam) Farwell Park was founded in 1888 on the line of the Fort Worth & Denver City Railway, named for Charles B. Farwell, owner of the XIT Ranch and his son, Walter, the ranch manager. For unknown reasons the name was changed to Perico (Spanish "parakeet") in 1905. PO 16 Nov 1907, PM A. H. Mohler. Perhaps appropriately, the Perico PM in 1913 was Harry Bird.

PERRIN (Jack) Perrin was organized about 1913 with construction of the Gulf, Texas & Western Railroad line between Seymour and Weatherford on land owned by Louis Perrin whose father, Levi, was an early settler. PO 3 Sept 1913, PM John Harman.

PERRY (Falls) Founded with construction of the Houston & Texas Central Railway in the early 1870s. Named for Falls County judge Albert G. Perry. PO 12 June 1876 as Peyton, probably named for Presbyterian minister Charles W. Peyton; changed to Perry 21 May 1883, PM Frank B. Chilton.

PERRYTON (Ochiltree) In 1919 the Panhandle & Santa Fe Railway station was named for George Morgan Perry from Grinnell, IA, a county judge who was instrumental in organizing Ochiltree County. PO 23 Aug 1919, PM Madora Vernon McGee.

PERRYVILLE (Wood) Founded in the 1860s as Parryville [*sic*] for the sawmill operated by W. J. Perry (Parry). PO 27 July 1860, PM John Shrum.

PERSONVILLE (Limestone) Benjamin Davis Persons, a native North Carolinian, moved to the area from Tennessee and founded Personville in the early 1850s. PO 24 Sept 1855, PM William Persons.

PESCADITO [pes kuh DEE to] (Webb) Spanish "little fish." The town was probably established with construction of the Texas Mexican Railway about 1880 and was reportedly named for the small fish found in a stock tank.

PETERS (Austin) In the early 1880s the Gulf, Colorado & Santa Fe Railway established a spur named for early settler Albert Peters who opened the post office 10 Oct 1883. Alas, poor Peters. Three years later he was accused of misusing postage stamps, found guilty, and fined fifty dollars.

PETERSBURG (Hale) Margaret Peters opened the Petersburg PO 39 Sept 1891. Edwin White opened a general store in 1902 and founded Petersburg about 1909.

PETROLIA [puh TROL yuh] (Clay) Oil City was the first community in the area, established about 1903. In 1904 the Wichita Falls & Oklahoma Railway laid tracks northwest of Oil City and founded Petrolia, named for Petrolia, Butler County, PA, itself named from the Pennsylvania oil fields. PO 14 Nov 1904, PM Henry Dunn.

PETRONILA [pe truh NIL uh] (Nueces) Named from the Santa Petronila Ranch, established in the early 1760s by Blas María de la Garza Falcón, a decade after he founded Camargo, Mexico. The ranch was named from Petronila Creek and the Petronila land grant, named for Saint Petronila, an early Christian martyr.

PETTEWAY [PET uh way] (Robertson) Michael Petteway, born in Alabama, opened a general store in the 1880s and established the post office that he named for himself in December 1887.

PETTIBONE (Milam) Pettibone was a flag stop on the Gulf, Colorado & Santa Fe Railway from 1881, named for Frank G. Pettibone, assistant to the general manager of the GC&SF.

PETTIT [PET it] (Hockley) A feature of the area was a limestone bluff with a number of caves known as *Las Casas Amarillas*, the "yellow houses." The caves gave their name to the Yellow House Ranch, part of which was bought by John Henry Pettit who established the town in 1922. PO 10 Apr 1935, PM Truett Mauldin.

PETTUS (Bee) Pettus was named in the 1880s with construction of the San Antonio & Aransas Pass Railway for John Freeman Pettus, cattle rancher, horse breeder, and son of Freeman Pettus, one of Stephen F. Austin's Old Three Hundred settlers. PO 29 Sept 1886 as Pettus City, PM David Hodges; changed to Pettus 6 July 1896.

PETTY (Lamar) Known as Lookout from the late 1860s to the early 1880s when the Texas & Pacific Railway established a stop called Dowlin. According to the local story the name was changed because passengers did not know how to react when the conductor called "Lookout." PO 23 Jan 1882 as Dowlin; changed to Petty for landowner James Madison Petty 13 Dec 1886, PM David W. Yarbrough.

PETTY (Lynn) Petty was founded about 1900 to support the farming and ranching operations of the T Bar Ranch, managed by William T. Petty.

PFLUGERVILLE [FLOO ger vil] (Travis) Henry Pfluger brought his family from Kassel, Germany, and settled in the area in the early 1850s. Farmer and shopkeeper Wilhelm Bohls from Oldenburg, Germany, named the community for Pfluger. The name became official when Bohls's son, Louis, opened the Pflugerville PO 19 July 1893. (Henry Pfluger's ancestors, like himself, were probably farmers; *pfluger* is German for "plowman.")

PHALBA [FAL buh] (Van Zandt) Joseph W. Jordan, the first postmaster 21 Sept 1897, named the office for his two-year-old daughter, Phalba.

PHARR [FAHR] (Hidalgo) About 1910 John Connally Kelley laid out the town of Pharr, named for his business partner, Henry Newton Pharr, a Louisiana sugarcane grower and founder of the Louisiana and Rio Grande Canal Company that constructed a diversion system using water from the Rio Grande to irrigate the area's vegetable and cotton crops. PO 18 Mar 1911, PM William Cage.

PHELAN (Bastrop) In 1903 John C. Phelan, son-in-law of Robert D. Hunter, president of the Texas and Pacific Coal Company, organized the Independence Mining Company to develop the lignite coal industry in Bastrop County. Phelan founded the community the following year. PM 7 July 1905, PM Eli H. Perkins.

PHELPS (Walker) When the Houston & Great Northern Railroad laid tracks between Conroe and Trinity in the early 1870s the station was named for Anson G. Phelps, co-founder of the Phelps Dodge Corporation that built much of the H&GN. PO 12 Mar 1872 as Phelps, PM William Whitley; changed to New Waverly 21 Jan 1873. PO 24 Nov 1874 as Phelps, PM Andrew Winter. See Dodge, see New Waverly.

PHILLIPS (Hutchinson) Founded as Whittenburg by rancher James Whittenburg in 1926.

The town of Pantex (*Pan*handle of *Tex*as) was established about the same time. In 1938 Pantex and Whittenburg merged as Phillips, named for the Phillips Petroleum Company whose Alamo Refinery was opened at Pantex in 1927. PO 6 June 1925 as Pantex, PM Robert F. Smith; discontinued 31 Dec 1929; reopened 1 Jan 1938 as Phillips, PM Arvel O. Pickens.

PICKENS (Henderson) John Mires Pickens began farming in the area in the mid-1850s. About 1900 the Texas & New Orleans Railroad established the Pickens Spur flag station.

PICKTON (Hopkins) There are two local naming stories, both having to do with the arrival of the East Line & Red River Railroad in 1879. By one, a railroad official asked townspeople to "pick a name," which they did. By the other, the picks of the workers laying the railroad bed could be heard for a great distance and the site became known as "pick town," compressed to "pickton." PO 29 Aug 1881, PM William Richardson.

PIDCOKE [PID KOK] (Coryell) Named for Methodist minister Richard Burton Pidcocke from Staffordshire, England, who brought English colonists to Cowhouse Creek in 1850. The first community name, Pidcocke, was respelled Pidcock when Thomas Williamson opened the Pidcock Ranch PO in Jan 1875; the name was further altered to Pidcoe in June 1892 and to Pidcoke in Sept 1893.

PIEDMONT [PEED mahnt] (Grimes) First known as Sulphur Springs for the local mineral springs and spa established in the 1840s by William Willis Arrington. The source of the name is uncertain. Piedmont is likely a transfer, perhaps from Piedmont, AL, perhaps from Piedmont, VA, the home state of Cooper S. Taliaferro, who opened the Piedmont Springs PO 30 June 1858; changed to Piedmont 16 Apr 1908.

PIERCE (Wharton) Abel Head Pierce, a South Texas cattleman known as "Shanghai" Pierce (so named, according to some, because he resembled a scrawny Shanghai rooster) built Pierce Station for the New York, Texas & Mexican Railway on his ranch in 1881. PO 15 Nov 1886 as Pierce Station, PM George S. Hamilton; changed to Pierce 18 June 1895.

PIKE (Collin) Charles L. McGowan, the first PM 11 Nov 1885, chose the name for his former home, Pike County, KY, itself named in 1821 for western explorer Zebulon Pike.

PILGRIM (Gonzales) Named from Pilgrim Lake, itself named for the first land grantee, Thomas Jefferson Pilgrim, a Baptist minister and Spanish translator for Stephen F. Austin. Pilgrim is often credited with founding the first Sunday school in Texas. PO 27 Oct 1879 as Pilgrims Lake; changed to Karney 18 July 1894, PM Rudolph Karney; changed to Pilgrim 5 July 1900, PM James T. Dawson.

PILOT KNOB (Travis) Pilot Knob is a small hill several miles south of Austin, named from the residue of an extinct volcano and used as a navigation marker by early settlers.

PILOT POINT (Denton) Pilot Point was founded by James Pierson in 1854 and named for its location on a prominence that had been used for decades as a geographic location and navigational aide. PO 12 June 1855, PM general store owner James D. Walcott.

PIN HOOK (Lamar) The first settlers came to the area in the 1830s. The name Pin Hook was in general use by the 1860s, named from the Pin Hook general store. Pin Hook is a remarkably common place name, occurring more than one hundred times in the US, almost exclusively in the Midwest and South. The origin of the name is unknown; it may be from "pinhooker," a slang term for a produce broker (originally a tobacco merchant) who refuses to buy until prices are low and then resells to distributers at a higher price; it may refer to a sharp bend in a local road; or from using a bent pin as a fishing hook. There was also the practice of selling a customer an alcoholic drink with a bent pin hooked over the edge of the glass to circumvent prohibition laws by allowing the merchant to claim that the pin was the item of sale and the liquor was free. As recently as 1988, some residents wanted to change the name of the town to Faulkner, but Pin Hook remained the official designation. See Faulkner.

PINE (Camp) Known from the late 1840s as Pine Tree for the local pine forests. The community was renamed Cannon Switch by the Texas & St. Louis Railway, probably in honor of Burrell Cannon, inventor of the Ezekiel Airship, a heavier-than-air craft that is claimed to have flown in PITTSBURG in 1902, a year before the Wright brothers' first flight. PO 26 Oct 1902, PM Matthew Harris Nicholson.

PIRTLE (Rusk) Charles Wood, who opened the PO 25 Apr 1884, chose the name to honor George W. Pirtle, the first Belleview postmaster in 1849.

PITTSBURG (Camp) William Harrison Pitts brought his family and several dozen slaves from Georgia in the early 1850s. He was soon joined by several other Pitts families. The Pitts became so numerous that the Rev. Harvey Hamill, when establishing a Methodist mission at the site later in the 1850s, is said to have remarked "this must be Pittsburgh." W. H. Pitts donated land for the townsite and the community was named for him when William C. Loving established the Pittsburgh PO 23 May 1855. The spelling was changed to Pittsburg in 1893.

PLACEDO [PLAS uh do] (Victoria) Plácido Benavides, a settler in Martín de León's Colony who played an important role in the Texas Revolution, established a ranch on what became known as Placedo Creek in the early 1830s. The first formal use of the name was about 1860 when the San Antonio & Mexican Gulf Railroad established by a station that was later known as Placedo Junction. The Placedo PO was established, PM Philip McLaughlin 8 Aug 1906.

PLACID [PLAS id] (McCulloch) Joseph F. Gault founded the community about 1902 when the Fort Worth & Rio Grande Railway built through the area. Two names were submitted with the PO application: Gaultville and Placid. The Post Office Department chose Placid. PO 18 Apr 1908, PM Owen H. Robbins.

PLAINS (Yoakum) Stockman William J. Luna, who founded Plains in 1905, reportedly chose the name for the rolling plains of West Texas. Luna was the first PM 4 Sept 1906.

PLAINVIEW (Hale) Site owners Edwin L. Lowe and Zachariah T. Maxwell laid out Plainview about 1885. Lowe, the first PM 28 Mar 1887, chose the name Plainview for the treeless flatlands that "could be seen for miles in all directions."

PLANO [PLAY no] (Collin) The name was suggested in the early 1850s by Henry Dye who had recently established the first medical practice in the area. Dye explained that *plano* was Spanish for "flat" or "level," which described the local terrain. PO 9 Oct 1852, PM William Forman.

PLANTERSVILLE (Grimes) Plantation owners, many from Alabama, settled in the area in the 1830s. The community was organized a decade later and named by Sarah Green for the local planters, one of whom was her husband, James. PO 12 Aug 1856, PM Peter W. Walton.

PLASKA (Hall) Apparently Plaska was intended to be Pulaski, suggested by members of one of the several Orr families in the area for their former home, Pulaski, TN, but the name was misread or changed by the Post Office Department. The Lodge PO, opened 7 Mar 1905, was discontinued 1909 and reestablished as Plaska 1 June 1920, PM Bernice Vallance.

PLEAK (Fort Bend) Named for Arthur E. Pleak of Rosenberg, a real estate investor and community benefactor of the 1900s and 1910s.

PLEASANTON [PLEZ uhn tuhn] (Atascosa) John Bowen, San Antonio PM in the mid-1840s, donated land for the community he named for his friend John Balthasar Plaisance whose name had been Anglicized to Pleasants. PO 4 Aug 1858, PM Elijah Thomas. North Pleasanton was laid out in 1913 by the Nueces Valley Townsite Company, of which Merit Leming, the namesake of LEMING, was president.

PLEDGER (Matagorda) Dr. John Walton Brown, the first PM in 1880, named the office for the family of his deceased wife, Narcissa Pledger, who came to Texas from South Carolina with her parents, William and Mary Ann, in 1838.

PLEMONS (Hutchinson) Plemons was founded about 1900 and named for site owner Barney Plemons, son of William Buford Plemons, Texas State Representative from Amarillo 1895–1897. PO 29 May 1901, PM Mattie Sams.

PLUCK (Polk) Founded about 1850 as Stryker for George Stryker, a partner in the Angle Lumber Company. For unknown reasons the name was changed to Pluck about 1918. According to one local account the name is appropriate because it took pluck to settle in this part of East Texas. One wag suggested that Pluck described the "general orneriness" of the people. PO 17 Feb 1885 as Stryker; discontinued in 1913; reopened as Pluck 25 Oct 1918, PM Howard L. Mallott.

POETRY (Kaufman) From at least the middle of the 1840s the town was known as Turner for Elisha Turner who received a labor of land for his service in the Texas Revolution. By 1880 the name had been changed to

Poetry. The source of the name is uncertain. By one popular etymology a peddler passing through the area came upon a ragged boy and an even more ragged dog. The peddler remarked "Now that's a poor Tray if I ever saw one"; over time "poor Tray" became Poetry. PO 29 Jan 1880, PM William Allen.

POINT (Rains) Known as Rice's Point for early settler William Rice until 1879 when the Missouri–Kansas–Texas Railroad built through the area and Hattie Ann Ballew opened the Point PO 16 Dec 1879.

POINT BLANK (San Jacinto) Founded by Robert Tod Robinson who moved to Texas from Alabama by way of Mississippi in the 1840s. Florence Dissoway, a governess for the Robinson children, named the site "Pointe Blanche," French for White Point, the landing dock along the white hills of the Trinity River. Robinson requested the post office be named Point Blanc, which popular etymology quickly turned into Point Blank. PO 13 May 1884, PM Tod Robinson.

POLK (County) Created and organized 1846. Named for James Knox Polk, US President (1845–1849). Polk's Vice President was George Mifflin Dallas, considered by many to be the namesake of DALLAS.

POLLOK [PAHL uhk] (Angelina) Reportedly named for Harold D. Pollok, a doctor working for either an Angelina County lumber company or for the Tyler Southeastern Railway to care for the prisoners who built the TS line. PO 9 Nov 1886, PM James G. McKnight.

PONDER (Denton) The Santa Fe Railroad established Gerald Station in 1889. To avoid duplication of post offices the name was changed to Ponder for landowner and Denton banker William A. Ponder. PO 17 June 1893, PM Jesse H. McWhorter.

PONE (Rusk) Also known as Corn Pone. In the final months of the Civil War when food was scarce the town was called Short Pone. PO 31 Oct 1898, PM Luther O. Neeley.

PONTA (Cherokee) The site was known as Hub for surveyor Hubbard Guinn until shopkeeper Robert Montgomery opened the Ponta PO 1 Apr 1903. Montgomery may have chosen the name (Latin for "bridge") in recognition of the bridges over Mud Creek.

PONTOTOC [PAHN tuh tahk] (Mason) Robert Kidd, the first shopkeeper, chose the name for his former home, Pontotoc County, MS. Pontotoc is probably from Choctaw for "hanging grapes." PO 5 Jan 1880, PM Benjamin Willis.

POOLVILLE (Parker) Poolville was apparently named for a spring-fed pond known as the "Big Pool" that provided washing water for the people and served as a waterhole for cattle and wild animals. PO 6 Nov 1883, PM James T. Scott.

PORFIRIO (Willacy) Named in the mid-1920s for Porfirio García, a merchant and rancher who operated the Reforma Ranch.

PORT ARANSAS [PORT uh RAN zuhs] (Nueces) Called Port A by locals. The community had its beginning in 1853 when Robert Ainsworth Mercer, an English merchandiser, established El Mar Rancho on Mustang Island. PO 12 July 1888 as Ropesville; changed to Tarpon 17 July 1896; changed to

Port Aransas 23 Dec 1910, PM Emma A. Roberts. See Aransas County and Aransas Pass.

PORT ARTHUR (Jefferson) Founded about 1895 by railroad magnate Arthur Edward Stilwell whose Kansas City, Pittsburg & Gulf Railroad was organized in 1889 to link the middle US with the Gulf of Mexico. PO 19 June 1896, PM Mate Strong.

PORT BOLIVAR [BAH luh ver] (Galveston) First known as Parrville for Samuel Parr, who surveyed the site in 1838. A land development consortium platted the site in 1893 as Port Bolivar, named from Bolivar peninsula, itself named for Simón Bolívar, for whom the country of Bolivia is named. PO 15 Feb 1876 as Gabion; changed to Port Bolivar 2 June 1893, PM Eldridge H. Clinton.

PORT ISABEL (Cameron) Named from the 1828 *Potrero de Santa Isabel* "Pasture (Paddock) of Saint Isabel" land grant to Rafael García. The small community of *El Frontón de Santa Isabel* "The Pediment of Saint Isabel," shortened to *El Frontón* and also known as *Punta de Santa Isabel* "Point of Saint Isabel," shortened to Point Isabel, developed in the early 1830s. Point Isabel became officially Port Isabel with incorporation in 1928. PO 3 Feb 1849 as Brazos Santiago, PM Richard Schuyler; changed to Port Isabel 1 Aug 1930, PM John Mahurin.

PORT LAVACA (Calhoun) Founded by Thomas McConnell, a Victoria merchant who lost his home and business in the 1840 Comanche raid on Linnville. Shortly thereafter McConnell bought the site and laid out the town of La Vaca "the cow." PO Dec 1841, PM L. M. McKinzie. See Lavaca County.

PORT MANSFIELD (Willacy) Both Port Mansfield and the Port Mansfield Channel that cuts through Padre Island were named in the 1950s for Joseph J. Mansfield, US Representative from Texas, who introduced a bill in Congress to extend the Gulf Intracoastal Waterway from Corpus Christi to the Rio Grande.

PORT SULLIVAN (Milam, Robertson) In the mid-1830s Augustus Sullivan opened a general store at a site that became a landing for steamboats on the Brazos River. PO 24 Mar 1852, PM Hawthorne Chamberlin.

PORTER (Montgomery) Named for James Porter, who operated a sawmill in the late 1870s and early 1880s. PO 30 Mar 1891 as Entre; changed to Porters 20 Aug 1892, PM William H. Epperson; changed to Porter 1 Jan 1951.

PORTLAND (San Patricio) Named for Portland, ME, by the New England Land Company about 1890. The community was organized largely through the efforts of John G. Willacy, the namesake of Willacy County. PO 9 Mar 1891, PM Walter Willett.

POSEY (Hopkins) Leeaiden (several spellings) and Sarah Posey brought eleven children from Missouri to Texas and began farming in 1846. PO 15 May 1902 as Reuben; changed to Posey 27 Sept 1902, PM Henry C. Glossup.

POSEY [PO zee] (Lubbock) Named for Walter S. Posey, banker and civic leader. Posey organized the Lubbock Chamber of Commerce in the 1920s and was president of the First National Bank of Lubbock in the 1940s.

POST (Garza) Charles William Post of Michigan, founder of Post cereals, established

Post City in 1907 as a model town where alcohol and all forms of licentious behavior were prohibited. Post died in 1914, the year Post City became simply Post. PO 18 July 1907, PM Frank L. Curtis. See Close City.

POSTOAK (Jack) Apparently named for a remarkable post oak tree, where, legend has it, citizens hid during Indian raids. PO 25 Sept 1876, PM William Hutchison.

POTEET [po TEET] (Atascosa) Francis Marion Poteet came to Texas from Tennessee by way of Los Angeles, CA, in 1866. Poteet was a merchant, blacksmith, farmer, and the first PM 9 Apr 1886.

POTH [POTH] (Wilson) In the late 1850s James Rumsey Skiles emigrated from Kentucky and laid out the town of Marcelina named from Marcelina Creek. The Marcelina Switch on the San Antonio & Aransas Pass Railway and the community were renamed Poth when Arnold H. Poth (Path) established the post office 22 Aug 1901. According to the local story, rancher Robert Dilworth offered seven acres to the first person who would build a home at the site; Arnold Poth accepted Dilworth's offer.

POTOSI [puh TO see] (Taylor) Robert A. Pollard, brother of Fouchee T. Pollard who opened the PO 19 July 1883, chose the name about 1890, reportedly from a book he was browsing to help his brother find a name for the PO. Pollard may have come across Potosi, MS, or San Luis Potosí, Mexico, itself named from the Potosí silver mine in Bolivia.

POTTER (County) Created 1876, organized 1887. Named for Robert Potter (1799–1842), born in North Carolina. Potter represented North Carolina in the US Congress (1829–1831). After resigning from Congress, he was again elected to the North Carolina House but was expelled for fighting, cheating at cards, and threatening other players with guns and knives. Finished with North Carolina, he came to Texas in 1835, signed the Texas Declaration of Independence, and was Secretary of the Texas Navy and a Republic of Texas Senator.

POTTSBORO (Grayson) In the early 1870s James A. Potts from Alabama donated a site for a station on the Denison & Pacific Railway and laid out the town of Pottsborough in 1878. PO 19 May 1879, PM William P. Richelieu. The spelling was changed to Pottsboro in 1893.

POTTSVILLE (Hamilton) Founded in 1878 on land donated by farmer Edmond Goggin with the stipulation that alcoholic beverages would not be sold or consumed on the site. Named for John S. Potts, a farmer and sheep rancher from 1872. PO 2 Jan 1879, PM Thomas Burks.

POWDERLY (Lamar) First known as Lenoir, likely named for the Thomas Lenoir family who settled in the area in the 1860s. When the St. Louis–San Francisco Railway established a station in the late 1880s the name was formalized as Powderly for Terence Powderly, a leading figure in the American labor movement of the late 19th century. Powderly was head of the Knights of Labor in the 1880s. PO 14 Feb 1888, PM John W. Pearce.

POWELL (Navarro) When the Cotton Belt Railroad built through the area in 1881 the station was built on land donated by farmer Charles Fredrick "Bud" Powell. PO 24 Feb 1892, PM Thomas J. Brookshire.

POYNOR (Henderson) Civil engineer David Poynor laid out the route for the Texas & New Orleans Railroad in 1901. PO 10 May 1902 as Poyner, PM Dan Dickerson; changed to Poynor 8 Apr 1919.

PRAESEL [PRAZ uhl] (Milam) Rockdale developer Floyd Praesel laid out the community in 1951.

PRAHA [PRAH hah] (Fayette) Praha, a variant of Prague, replaced the earlier name, Mulberry, about 1860 as the number of Bohemian settlers increased. PO 20 Mar 1884, PM Edward Knesek.

PRAIRIE LEA (Caldwell) The oldest community in Caldwell County, Prairie Lea was named by Sam Houston, probably in 1839, in honor of Margaret Moffette Lea who would become his third wife in 1840. PO 23 Aug 1851, PM James Callahan.

PRATTVILLE (Delta) In 1878 William B. Pratt moved to the area and opened a wagon and buggy shop. He established the Prattville PO 27 June 1881.

PREMONT (Jim Wells) Charles Premont, a livestock breeder, and Andrés Canales, a rancher and storekeeper, laid out the town in 1908. PO 13 Jan 1909, PM Frank Ayers.

PRESIDIO [pruh SID ee o] (County) Created 1850, organized 1875. Presidio is a shortening of *Presidio del Norte* "Fortress of the North," itself a shortening of *Presidio del Norte de la Junta de los Ríos* "Fortress of the North at the Junction of the Rivers," for the Spanish outpost built in 1860 where the Río Conchos flows into the Rio Grande at Ojinaga, Chihuahua, across the river from Presidio, TX.

PRESIDIO (Presidio) The modern city of Presidio has been known by several names in its recorded history, from La Junta de los Rios "the joining of the rivers" where the Rio Conchos flowing north from Mexico joined the Rio Grande in 1680 to Presidio del Norte "fortress of the north" by 1830, named from the military garrison and penal colony established in the 1760s. The name was shortened to Presidio by the time shopkeeper Hiram Kelly opened the PO 30 Apr 1868.

PRICE (Rusk) In March 1884 William Pirtle opened the Carlysle [*sic*] PO. The office, changed to Carlisle in 1889, was discontinued in 1904 and reestablished by 1940 as Price, named for merchant Joseph M. Price.

PRIDDY (Mills) Named for Thomas Jefferson Priddy, a Baptist minister, Texas Ranger, and first PM 31 Mar 1891.

PRIMERA [pree MEHR uh] (Cameron) Primera was settled in the early 20th century and organized in the late 1920s when the San Antonio & Aransas Pass Railway established Primera Station named, according to local sources, from Spanish "first" since this was the first stop west of Harlingen.

PRINCETON (Collin) Princeton was organized in 1881 when the Missouri–Kansas–Texas Railroad extended its line from

Greenville to McKinney. Named for Prince Alexander Dowlen, founder and head of the Farmersville Academy. PO 24 Nov 1888, PM Walter Harrelson.

PRINGLE (Hutchinson) In 1929 the Chicago, Rock Island & Gulf Railway extended a line north from Stinnett and William H. Pringle donated land for the Pringle school. PO 13 Sept 1929, PM Benjamin Cook.

PRITCHETT (Upshur) According to local accounts, the post office was to have been named Pritchard after early settler John M. Pritchard, but through misspelling or misreading the office was established as Pritchett. This may be true but there were several Pritchett families in the vicinity at the time, including that of Alonzo Griffen Pritchett, the area's pioneer doctor. PO 26 June 1893, PM Charlie Warren.

PROCTOR (Comanche) Proctor grew around a general store opened by Alexander Proctor and Thomas Moore in the early 1870s. The Fort Worth & Rio Grande Railway built through the area in the early 1890s, bypassed Proctor, and established a station called Camden. So many Proctor dwellings and businesses were disassembled and moved to trackside that Camden Station was renamed Proctor. PO 25 June 1874, PM Thomas Moore.

PROFFITT (Young) Rancher and site owner John W. Proffitt laid out the community in the 1870s. PO 20 Jan 1880, PM James G. Armstrong. John W. Proffitt was postmaster in 1881; his son, Spain Proffitt, kept the office for a short time in 1911.

PROGRESO (Hidalgo) Founded on the Toluca Ranch established by Florencio Saenz in the early 1880s. When the request for a Toluca post office was rejected the application was resubmitted with the name Progreso, Spanish "progress," presumably to show that this was a progressive community. PO 2 Apr 1900, PM Edward Jefferds.

PROGRESS (Bailey) Joshua Blocher founded Progress about 1915 and presumably chose the name to suggest a dynamic, progressive commercial center on the Texas plains. When the town failed to develop, Blocher became an eccentric and a recluse. He was beaten to death by thieves who thought he must be rich from the sale of building lots. PO 21 Apr 1927, PM William A. Kennedy.

PROSPER (Collin) A hopeful name chosen about 1880 apparently by officials of the St. Louis, San Francisco & Texas Railway to reflect and promote the potential of the area. PO 22 May 1893, PM Larkin Adamson.

PROVIDENCE (Floyd) William J. Lovvorn chose the name about 1890, probably for Providence, Marengo County, AL, his former home.

PROVIDENT CITY (Colorado) Founded and named in 1909 by the Provident Land Company of Kansas City, MO. PO 17 Jan 1895 as Goldenrod; changed to Provident City 1 Apr 1910, PM Anderson R. Knight.

PRUITT (Van Zandt) Adelia Corasandra Pruitt (Pruett) established the PO 18 Aug 1888.

PULLMAN (Potter) Pullman, now part of Amarillo, was reportedly named for a Pullman sleeping car that housed a construction crew building the Fort Worth & Denver City Railway in 1887. Alternatively, the name may have been chosen by William Henry Bush, the namesake of BUSHLAND for George Pullman, inventor of the Pullman sleeping car. The headquarters of Bush's hat company was in Chicago where Pullman sleeping cars were built, and Bush was likely associated with Pullman professionally or personally.

PUMPHREY (Runnels) Founded in the 1890s as New Hope; renamed in 1901 for site owner William M. Pumphrey who emigrated from Alabama shortly after the Civil War. PO 4 Oct 1901, PM Marquis Hill.

PUMPVILLE (Val Verde) Named from the pumping station established by the Galveston, Harrisburg & San Antonio Railway in the 1880s. PO 27 Nov 1899, PM James M. Morgan.

PURDON (Navarro) In 1881 the St. Louis Southwestern Railway (Cotton Belt) came through the town of Belle Point. According to local lore Belle Point was renamed by a railroad employee who was attracted to a local grocery store cashier named Ada Purdon. Rather the namesake is Charles de la Cherois Purdon, chief engineer for the St. Louis Southwestern Railway (Cotton Belt). PO 7 Nov 1881, PM Owen E. Highsmith.

PURSLEY (Navarro) William H. Pursley, a farmer and stockman, brought his family from Arkansas in 1858 and opened a general store. Pursley later donated land for the school and cemetery. PO 4 Apr 1872, PM Samuel L. Swindal.

PURVES [PER vuhs] (Erath) Reportedly named for William Washington Purves (Purvis) and his son John, who moved to the area in the 1870s and donated land for the first church in 1890. Most likely named for James Morgan Purves, generally considered the town founder. PO 13 Sept 1897, PM Jesse G. Conner.

PUTNAM (Callahan) Charles M. Putnam was president of the Texas, Louisiana & Eastern Railroad when the TL&E built through the area in the early 1880s. PO 5 Sept 1881 as Cat Claw; changed to Putnam 25 July 1882, PM Theron M. Taber.

PYOTE [PEYE ot] (Ward) Pyote was the name of the area by 1881 when the Texas & Pacific Railway extended its line from Odessa and established a water tower and the Pyote Tank telegraph office. A local legend claims that Pyote was a mispronunciation of "coyote" by Chinese railroad builders. More likely Pyote is a phonetic transcription of *peyote*, the cactus from which the hallucinogen is derived. PO 20 Mar 1907, PM Albert D. Pigman.

Q

QUAIL (Collingsworth) The first settlers arrived around 1890 and reportedly named the community for the abundance of quail. The bird motif was continued in 1910 when Wade Arnold published the first newspaper, the *Quail Feather*. PO 7 July 1902, PM Sam Wilson.

QUANAH [KWAH nuh] (Hardeman) Comanche "scent, fragrance." Quanah Parker, son of Nocona and Cynthia Ann Parker, was the leader of the Quahada "antelope" Comanches in the late 19th and early 20th centuries. When the community was named in the early 1880s Parker had settled his people on the Kiowa-Comanche Reservation in Indian Territory. PO 11 Jan 1886, PM John A. Johnson. See Nocona; see Parker.

QUEEN CITY (Cass) In January 1877 postmaster John C. Hutchinson moved the Lanark PO to the site and changed the name to Queen City, presumably to attract settlers. Beyond the positive associations of "queen," Hutchison's reasons for choosing the name may have been influenced by the fact that Queen Victoria of Britain was in the news, having added to her titles "Empress of India" on 1 May 1876. See Lanark.

QUEMADO [kuh MAH do] (Maverick) Spanish "burned, scorched." Named from the Quemado Valley, itself reportedly named for grass fires that burned the prairie but more likely from an ancient volcanic eruption that left the area parched and barren. PO 22 Dec 1903, PM Louise Lehman.

QUICKSAND (Newton) Named from Quicksand Creek and Little Quicksand Creek, themselves named for the actual or perceived presence of the wet loose sand that entraps heavy objects.

QUIHI [KWEE HEE] (Medina) Founded in 1845 by Empresario Henri Castro, the namesake of Castro County. Named from Quihi Lake, itself named for the white necked Mexican eagle buzzard. Also written Keechie or Quichie. PO 24 June 1854, PM Louis Bohle.

QUINLAN (Hunt) The Texas Central Railway founded the community in the mid-1880s as Roberts, named for Texas Governor Oran Milo Roberts. With reorganization of the railroad in the late 1880s, Edward Howland Robinson Green, president of the Texas Midland Railroad, moved the station and changed the name to Quinlan for George Austin Quinlan, vice president and general manager of the Houston & Texas Central Railway. PO 3 Aug 1874 as Payne's Store, PM John Payne; changed to Quinlan 15 Oct 1894, PM John H. Cooke. See Howland.

QUINTANA (Brazoria) Founded about 1830 opposite Velasco on the Brazos River. Probably named for Andrés Eligio Quintana Roo who was instrumental in drafting the Mexican Declaration of Independence in 1813. PO 1836 as Velasco, PM Isaac C. Hoskins; changed to Quintanna [*sic*] 1 June 1853, PM Reuben R. Brown.

QUITAQUE [KIT uh kway, KIT ee kway] (Briscoe) Named from Quitaque Creek, itself named from the Quitaca, Native Americans who inhabited West Texas and eastern New Mexico, some of whom accompanied soldier-colonist Juan Domínguez de Mendoza into the interior of Texas in the 1680s. In the early 1880s Charles Goodnight claimed that Quitaque was an Indian word meaning "end of the trail." More likely Quitaque is from Nahuatl through American Spanish *cuita* "excrement," reportedly the source of the name of the Quitaque Peaks in Motley County whose shape resembled piles of horse manure. PO 6 Sept 1882 in Floyd County, PM John E. Farrington; moved to Briscoe County 3 July 1891. See Goodnight.

QUITMAN (Wood) John Anthony Quitman served in the Texas Revolution and the Mexican War. When Quitman was organized in 1850, John Quitman was Governor of Mississippi. Quitmans in Mississippi, Georgia, and Missouri are also named for John Quitman. PO 20 Oct 1851, PM Howard Keys. See Fort Quitman.

R

RABB [RAB] (Nueces) Named for Green A. Rabb, a late 19th century stockman and a descendant of the William Rabb family who settled on what became known as RABBS PRAIRIE.

RABBS PRAIRIE (Fayette) William and Mary Rabb, after stops in Pennsylvania, Illinois, and Arkansas, joined Stephen F. Austin's Colony in the early 1820s. Rabb is generally considered the first planter and miller in what is now Fayette County. PO 17 Aug 1900 as Rabb, PM Ernst A. Franke.

RACHAL [ruh SHEL] (Brooks) Founded about 1913 and named for Edward R. Rachal, cattleman and Brooks County assessor. Edward was the brother of rancher and businessman Darius Cyriaque Rachal, the founder of Rosita in San Patricio County, now a ghost town.

RADIUM (Jones) Radium grew around a general store kept by James M. Williford from the early 1900s. The name was likely chosen for radium, the element often in the news since its discovery by Marie and Pierre Curie in 1898.

RAGTOWN (Lamar) According to local lore, the citizens of Ragtown, because of their high standards of cleanliness, washed their clothes so often that they quickly became rags.

RAINBOW (Somervell) According to the local story, during a divisive discussion to choose a name for the post office, a rainbow followed a torrent; a citizen called out "let's name our town Rainbow." The motion was apparently approved enthusiastically. PO 6 Dec 1899, PM William Stewart.

RAINS (County) Created and organized 1870. Named for Emory Rains (1800–1878), born in Warren County, TN. Rains came to Texas in 1826. He served in several early congresses of the Republic of Texas and represented the district in the state legislature from the mid-1840s into the 1860s. After leaving the legislature Rains was instrumental in the creation of Rains County. The county seat, EMORY, is also named in his honor.

RAISIN (Victoria) Raisin was founded as Lucy on the Gulf, Western Texas & Pacific Railway in 1889. By one account the town was named by railroad employees who noticed the vineyards (or wild grapes, depending on the story) that grew around the station. By another, townspeople were discussing possible names in the general store when viticulturist James Reeves walked in with a handful of grapes; one of the group remarked "these grapes would make good raisins." It is unclear if this comment was praise or ridicule, but Reeves obviously agreed. PO 22 Sept 1892, PM Charles G. T. Friedrichs.

RALLS (Crosby) About 1910, with construction of a short line railroad through his ranch, John Robinson Ralls laid out the town, built homes and offices, and donated land for a school and churches. The success of Ralls led to the decline of the nearby communities of Emma and Cedric. PO 29 Dec 1890 as Emma; changed to Ralls 1 Aug 1911, PM Alice Brown.

RAMBO (Cass) By local tradition, in the 1850s Gale Rambo, a white US military officer, and his African American wife, Lydia, established the community for free African Americans.

RAMIRENO (Zapata) Ramireno was named for site owner José Luis Ramírez who was granted the land by the king of Spain in the 1780s. The town was originally located several miles south on the Rio Grande and relocated in 1953 when the Falcon Dam was built. *Ramireño de Arriba* (upper) and *Ramireño de Abajo* (lower) communities flourished until the early 1910s. See Falcon.

RAMIREZ (Duval) Named from the Rafael Ramírez land grant of the 1850s. PO 12 Dec 1910, PM Pedro Chapa.

RAND (Kaufman) Edmund and Katherine Rand emigrated from Wisconsin and began farming in the area in the 1860s.

RANDADO [ran DAH do] (Jim Hogg) Founded on the Randado Ranch established by Hipólito Garcia in the 1830s. The town was named for *randas*, the intricately braided, ornate lassos for which the Randado Ranch was famous. PO 5 June 1882, PM Juan Ruiloba.

RANDALL (County) Created 1876, organized 1889. Named for Horace Randal (respelled Randall in official documents). Randal (1833–1864), whose family moved from Tennessee to Texas in 1839, was a West Point graduate and a Confederate officer who died of wounds suffered at the battle of Jenkins Ferry, AR, in April 1864.

RANDOLPH (Fannin) Known as Lindsey School House from the school built on land donated by Thomas Lindsey in the 1840s. In 1887 the Louisiana, Arkansas & Texas Railway established Randolph Station, named for Tom Randolph, a Sherman banker and community benefactor. PO 2 Dec 1887, PM James F. Reed.

RANGER (Eastland) Ranger had its beginning as a tent city in the 1870s in Ranger Camp Valley where Texas Rangers established temporary quarters. The Texas & Pacific Railway built through the area about 1880 and James Davis opened the Ranger PO 27 Dec 1880.

RANKIN (Ellis) In 1879 Thomas Alston applied for a PO named Alstonia. Through misreading or misinterpretation the request was approved as Astonia. PM Alexander Marshall Rankin changed the name 7 Mar 1900 in honor of his grandfather, Frederick Harrison Rankin, one of Stephen F. Austin's Old Three Hundred.

RANKIN (Upton) About 1908 Midland rancher Henry Halff founded Upland ten miles north of present Rankin. When the Kansas City, Mexico & Orient Railway built through the area south of Upland in 1911, businesses and homes were disassembled and moved to Rankin Station, named for Finis Ewing Rankin, a rancher and livestock dealer who brought his family from Bell Buckle, TN, to Midland, TX, in 1897. PO 9 Mar 1912, PM Opal Nix.

RATCLIFF (Houston) Jesse Ratcliff emigrated from Georgia about 1875 and established a sawmill. He opened the Ratcliff PO 6 Feb 1885 that provided the nucleus for the town of Ratcliff.

RATIBOR [RAT uh bor] (Bell) Founded by Czech settlers about 1900. Named for

Ratibořr, the town now in southern Poland near the border with the Czech Republic.

RATTAN (Delta) Clarence Volney Rattan, the PM at Cooper, was instrumental in establishing the Rattan PO, opened 10 Apr 1893 by PM McLee Parrish. Rattan in Pushmataha County, OK, was named about 1910 by settlers from Rattan, TX.

RAVENNA [ri VEN uh] (Fannin) The traditional story is that Ravenna was named for the many ravines in the area, especially a notable gully that ran through the center of town. However, considering the spelling, Ravenna may be a borrowing, perhaps from the better-known Ravenna in northeast Ohio. Alternatively, Lewis B. Grogan, a preacher and headmaster who established the Ravenna PO 6 June 1879, may have chosen the name for Ravenna, Italy.

RAWLINS (Dallas) The Rev. Roderick Rawlins, a major figure in the religious restoration movement of the mid-19th century, founded the town as Hardscrabble in the 1840s. Rawlins sold part of his land to his son-in-law, Abraham Bledsoe, who established Lancaster in the 1850s. PO 8 Feb 1890, PM Thomas E.Conn.

RAYBURN (Liberty) Rayburn was founded about 1900 with construction of the Gulf, Colorado & Santa Fe Railway and named for site owners Minter and Edna Rayburn. Minter Rayburn was a Liberty County judge in the early 1900s. PO 6 May 1902, PM Lucius White.

RAYLAND (Foard) Founded about 1885 by Presley Smith Ray and his son James who emigrated from Kentucky about 1880. PO 14 Mar 1891, PM Presley Ray.

RAYMONDVILLE (Willacy) In 1904 Edward Burleson Raymond (named for Edward Burleson, the namesake of Burleson County), working with representatives of the King Ranch, established the Raymond Town and Improvement Company to lay out a town, sell building lots, and promote the community. PO 2 Dec 1904, PM James Kimball.

RAYWOOD (Liberty) Raywood is a compression of the name of *Ray*mond Har*wood*, a rice grower and miller. PO 6 Mar 1894, PM Hiram D. Fellows.

RAZOR (Lamar) Razor was apparently named from the Razor Store where Razor Tobacco was a popular item. PO 26 Sept 1904, PM Alexander K. Haynes who owned the Razor Store from the early 1900s.

REAGAN [RAY guhn] (County) Created and organized 1903. John Henninger Reagan (1818–1905), born in Tennessee, arrived in Nacogdoches, TX, in 1838. He is best known for having served as Postmaster General of the Confederacy and for a brief time as Confederate Treasurer. Less known, he was a prominent Texas politician on both sides of the Civil War. From 1858 until 1861 he was a Texas Representative to the US Congress and after the war he returned to Congress, serving in the 1870s and 1880s.

REAGAN (Falls) When the Houston & Texas Central Railway built through the area in the early 1870s, lawyer and landowner

William Reason Reagan, brother of John H. Reagan, the namesake of Reagan County, donated land for the townsite. PO 23 June 1873, PM Robert Harper.

REAGAN WELLS (Uvalde) Named for John Reagan (not the John Henninger Reagan for whom Reagan County was named), who developed and promoted the area's mineral waters in the early 20th century. PO 3 Jan 1912, PM Lewis B. Herington.

REAGOR SPRINGS [RAY ger] (Ellis) Named for the John Bascom Reagor family who settled in the area in the late 1840s. PO 18 Mar 1878 as Reager's, PM Fountain P. Ray.

REAL (County) Created and organized 1913. Named for Julius Real (1860–1944), born at his parents' ranch on Turtle Creek seven miles south of Kerrville. He became a county judge, county commissioner, and county superintendent of schools. When the county was created, Julius Real was in his second term as a Texas State Senator.

REALITOS [ree uh LEET is] (Duval) Named from the *realitos*, the small army camps housing Mexican troops. PO 15 Feb 1886, PM Charles Shaw.

RED LICK (Bowie) Named in the late 1870s for the red clay salt lick frequented by deer and other fauna. Now part of Texarkana.

RED RIVER (County) An original Texas county created by the Republic of Texas in 1836 and organized in 1837. Named for the Red River that marks the northern extent of the county and forms much of the boundary between Texas and Oklahoma. Red River is a direct translation of Spanish *Río Rojo*; the river was named from the reddish hue given off by the ferric oxide washed from the sedimentary rocks that line its banks.

REDWATER (Bowie) Formerly known as Ingersoll, named for orator and agnostic Robert Ingersoll. With the religious revival of the late 19th century, the name was changed through the efforts of Ernest T. Page for the red-tinted water of the local springs. PO 27 June 1881 as Ingersoll; changed to Redwater 13 Dec 1894, PM Ernest T. Page.

REEDVILLE (Caldwell) Laid out in 1887 with construction of the Missouri–Kansas–Texas Railroad and named for site owners Absalom and Margaret Reed, farmers who relocated from Mississippi in the late 1870s. PO 21 Jan 1890, PM John C. Reed.

REESE (Cherokee) The Texas & New Orleans Railroad established Reese Switch, named for conductor Reese Lloyd, about 1900. PO 12 Apr 1895 as Andy; changed to Reese 19 Sept 1904, PM John H. Henderson.

REEVES (County) Created 1883, organized 1884. Named for George Robertson Reeves (1826–1882), born in Tennessee. Reeves moved to Grayson County, TX, in 1846 and represented the district in the state legislature in the mid-1850s and again in the 1870s and 1880s.

REFUGIO [ruh FYOO ree o] (County) An original Texas county created by the Republic of Texas in 1836, named from the villa and Mexican municipality of Refugio.

REFUGIO (Refugio) In 1793 Spanish Franciscans established the *Nuestra Señora del Refugio* "Our Lady of Refuge" mission near Tivoli. The mission was moved several years later to the present site of Refugio on Mission River. PO 1836, PM Patricio Fitzsimmons.

REHBURG (Washington) Settled primarily by Germans from Rehburg (now Rehburg-Loccum) in northwest Germany in the late 1840s. PO 4 Apr 1898, PM Paul Ranft.

REILLY SPRINGS (Hopkins) James Reily, aide to Thomas J. Rusk during the Texas Revolution and Sam Houston's special envoy to the United States, was a major landowner in the area and the namesake of the community in the 1860s. PO 29 Sept 1871 as Reily Springs, PM William F. Kilgore; renamed Reilly Springs 31 Oct 1906.

REINHARDT (Dallas) In 1886 the Gulf, Colorado & Santa Fe Railway established Reinhardt Station, named for Joseph W. Reinhardt, general auditor and later president of the GC&SF. PO 9 May 1884 as Ola; changed to Reinhardt 30 Dec 1886, PM Emil H. Ueckert. Now part of Dallas.

REK HILL (Fayette) Named for one or more Rek families from Moravia, perhaps that of Ignatz Rek, established farmers by 1880.

REKLAW (Cherokee, Rusk) Reklaw, Walker spelled in reverse, was named for site owner Margaret L. Walker when the Texas & New Orleans Railroad established a station in 1902. PO 5 Oct 1903, PM John O. McCarter.

RELAMPAGO [ray LAHM puh go] (Hidalgo) In the 1850s Thaddeus Rhodes and José Mora combined their properties into the Relampago Ranch, named from Spanish "flash of lightening." The townsite, named from the ranch, was platted about 1908 by Lon Hill's Capisallo Town and Improvement Company. PO 30 Apr 1910, PM Jésus García.

RENDON (Tarrant) Apparently named for Joaquin Rendon, a sheep rancher considered the first landowner. PO 9 Jan 1891, PM general store owner Washington Norwood. The settled area is often considered as one community, Rendon-Retta.

RENNER (Collin) The St. Louis Southwestern Railway (Cotton Belt) established Renner Station in the late 1880s, named for John A. Renner, hired to develop townsites along the route of the St.LS. PO 13 July 1888, PM George F. Hudson. Renner officially became part of Dallas in 1977.

RENO (Lamar) Reno Station, established in 1876 on the line of the Texas & Pacific Railway, was named for Reno, NV, itself named in 1868 for Jesse Reno, a Union Army officer who was killed during the Civil War battle of South Mountain, MD, in 1862.

RETREAT (Navarro) First known as Beeman's School House, named for benefactor William H. Beeman. The local story is that the school's location changed many times, whenever a population shift required yet another move, to which some wag said, "let's just call it the Retreat School."

RHEA [RAY] (Parmer) Brothers John and Joseph Rhea bought a portion of the XIT Ranch in 1901, which they sold in 1906. The

Rheas were nephews of William and James Rhea, namesakes of RHEA MILLS. PO 5 Mar 1909, PM John W. Barnett.

RHEA MILLS (Collin) In the late 1850s William and James Rhea, brothers from Tennessee, built a flour and corn mill at what became known as Rhea's Mills. William Rhea represented the district in the Texas Legislature in the 1860s. PO 27 Jan 1876, PM James Rhea. See Rhea.

RHINELAND (Knox) Rhineland, named for the German Rhineland, was founded in 1895 by Hugo Herchenbach and Father Joseph Reisdorff as a refuge for German Catholics. Reisdorff, born in Rheinprovinz, Germany, was also instrumental in the founding of NAZARETH in Castro County and UMBARGER in Randall County. PO 15 June 1895, PM Hugo Herchenbach.

RHOME (Wise) Prairie Point, founded in the late 1850s, was deserted by the late 1860s and replaced by Rhome in the early 1880s when the Fort Worth & Denver City Railway established Rhome Station, named for Byron Crandall Rhome who introduced Hereford cattle to Texas in the 1870s and was instrumental in developing the area as a major ranching center. PO 9 Feb 1883, PM Samuel Snead

RHONESBORO (Upshur) William M. Rhone established the first sawmill in the area about 1900. PO 27 Sept 1902, PM James Barton.

RICARDO (Kleberg) Probably named for Richard Kleberg, son of Robert Justus Kleberg, Sr. The name was changed to the Spanish form, Ricardo, about 1911. PO 8 Feb 1909 in Nueces County as Richard, PM Walter H. Thompson. See Kleberg.

RICE (Navarro) Founded in 1872 with construction of the Houston & Texas Central Railway; named for Massachusetts businessman William Marsh Rice, part owner of the H&TC. Rice endowed the William Marsh Rice Institute for the Advancement of Literature, Science and Art that opened in Houston in 1912 and was renamed Rice University in 1960. PO 2 Oct 1872, PM Joseph Calloway Bartlett.

RICHARDS (Grimes) Founded on the line of the Trinity & Brazos Valley Railway in 1906 and named for William E. Richards, a Houston banker and financier. PO 18 Sept 1906, PM James J. Lieb.

RICHARDSON (Dallas) In the early 1870s the Houston & Texas Central Railway established Richardson Station north of the town of Breckinridge. Named for Alfred S. Richardson, a Houston lawyer who was secretary and treasurer of the H&TC. PO 27 Sept 1858 as Breckenridge [*sic*]; changed to Richardson 8 June 1874, PM Charles C. Blandford.

RICHMOND (Fort Bend) Robert Eden Handy and William Lusk, Brazoria real estate investors and promoters, founded Richmond in 1837. According to the Historic Richmond Association the community was named for Richmond, England, now Richmond upon Thames, London. PO 4 Jan 1838, PM John Levering.

RIDINGS (Fannin) Charles Calvin Ridings, born in South Carolina, established a blacksmith shop in the late 1850s. His grandson, also Charles Calvin Ridings, was the first PM 11 June 1900.

RIESEL [REES uhl] (McLennan) The area was first known as Roddy for Stephen G. Roddy who established a gristmill and cotton gin in the 1870s. William H. Riesel, for whom the town is named, bought and remodeled Roddy's gin in 1890. PO 29 Mar 1890 as Prospect; changed to Riesel 8 June 1891, PM Eugene Kauffman. See Roddy.

RINGGOLD (Montague) Founded in 1892 where the tracks of the Chicago, Rock Island & Texas Railway crossed those of the Missouri–Kansas–Texas Railroad. The application for a PO requested the name Harrisonia in honor of Joseph Harris who donated land for the townsite. When that name was rejected the application was resubmitted as Ringgold, the family name of Harris's wife, Olivia. PO 21 Dec 1892, PM Robert J. Liston.

RIO FRIO (Real) Newman McCollum Patterson relocated from Fayette, AL, in 1847. About 1869 he established a sawmill and gristmill on the Frio River and platted the town of Rio Frio. Joseph James Henry Patterson, third son of Newman and Lucy Ann Patterson, opened the Rio Frio PO 9 Dec 1875. See Frio.

RIO GRANDE CITY (Starr) Henry Clay Davis founded Rio Grande City on the Rio Grande opposite Ciudad Camargo about 1847. Davis, a survivor of the 1842 Mier Expedition, was the first Starr County clerk in 1848, established the PO 3 Feb 1849, and was a Texas State Senator in the 1850s.

RIO HONDO (Cameron) Spanish "deep river." Named from the Arroyo Colorado or Rio Hondo River. The town was probably founded by James Robinson George, a hardware merchant who settled in 1909. PO 15 Apr 1911, PM Charles Boomer.

RIO VISTA (Johnson) The community was known by several names, including Kimball and Grange Hall, until 1881 when the Gulf, Colorado & Santa Fe Railway built through the area. Rio Vista was named for its location overlooking the Nolan River, itself named for filibuster Phillip Nolan. PO 4 Nov 1885, PM Hezekiah Hughes. See Nolan County.

RIOMEDINA (Medina) Named from the Medina River. Early settlers were Armin Boehm and his son Frederick, the first PM, who kept a saloon and general store and operated a cotton gin from the early 1900s. PO 16 Apr 1908 as San Geronimo; changed to Rio Medina 6 Oct 1908, PM Frederick Alex Boehme. Also spelled Rio Medina.

RIOS (Duval) Known as La Gloria, named from the Rancho La Gloria until Felipe Rios opened the PO in December 1938; named for Francisco Rios whose family had settled in the area by 1900.

RISING STAR (Eastland) The community informally known as Copperas Creek was formally named in 1880 when George W. Hardin opened the Rising Star PO. The name was chosen by Downs D. McConnell, the PM at Eastland, who saw the area as a "rising star" of agricultural production and general prosperity.

RIVERSIDE (Walker) Founded with construction of the Houston & Great Northern Railroad in 1872 on the west bank of the Trinity River. PO 15 Jan 1855 as Newport; changed to Riverside 23 Feb 1872, PM William D. Shaw.

RIVIERA (Kleberg) Theodore F. Koch, a land developer from St. Paul, MN, laid out Riviera on the line of the St. Louis, Brownsville & Mexico Railway in 1907. Koch claimed the area reminded him of the French Riviera. PO 27 May 1907, PM Henry C. Horstman. See Vattman.

ROANE [RON] (Navarro) Roane is probably a transfer from Roane, Lafayette County, AR, or Roane County, TN, both named for members of the same Roane family. PO 1 Feb 1892, PM John Cohagen. Formerly known as Post Oak for the Post Oak School.

ROANOKE (Denton) Roanoke, named for Roanoke, VA, was founded on the line of the Texas & Pacific Railway in 1881. PO 19 Dec 1870 as Elizabeth; changed to Roanoke 3 Aug 1881, PM August F. Wiggs.

ROANS PRAIRIE (Grimes) Willis and Margaret Roan, planters from Georgia and Alabama, brought their family and slaves to the Rocky Creek area about 1835. The community was formally named in May 1846 when Willis Ivey Roan opened the PO. For a short time in the early 20th century, when the International–Great Northern Railroad extended a branch line, the town was known as Steadmanville, probably named for Nathan Steadman, an original director of the Calvert, Waco & Brazos Valley Railway which was acquired by the I-GN in 1901.

ROARING SPRINGS (Motley) Founded about 1912 with construction of the Quanah, Acme & Pacific Railway. Named from the cluster of springs several miles south of the town, themselves apparently named from the reports of buffalo hunters that the roar of the falls was audible a mile away. PO 26 Oct 1912, PM Joseph Shelton.

ROBERT LEE (Coke) Site owner Leasel Bobo Harris platted the community in 1891. Although several sources claim the town was named in honor of Confederate General Robert E. Lee, the namesake is Harris's grandson, Robert Lee Cartledge, born in 1890. PO 9 Feb 1891, PM Hubert Henry Pearce.

ROBERTS (County) Created 1876, organized 1889. Named jointly for John S. Roberts (1796–1871), born in Virginia, a signer of the Texas Declaration of Independence in 1836; and Oran Milo Roberts (1815–1898), born in South Carolina, Chief Justice of the Texas Supreme Court (1874–1879) and the 17th Governor of Texas (1879–1883).

ROBERTSON (County) Created 1837, organized 1838. Named for Sterling Clack Robertson (1785–1842), born in Tennessee. Robertson was an empresario of Robertson's Colony in 1834. He signed the Texas Declaration of Independence and the Constitution of the Republic of Texas and served in the first and second congresses of the Republic of Texas.

ROBERTSON (Crosby) In the early 20th century community benefactors that included William Robertson donated land and built what became known as the Robertson School.

ROBINSON (McLennan) In 1852 John Robinson brought his family from Alabama to what became known as Robinsonville. He was joined in 1854 by his brother, Levi, for whom LEVI, six miles south of Robinson, was named. PO 17 Apr 1878 as Hague; changed to Robinson 14 Jan 1879, PM Leonidus B. Foster.

ROBSTOWN (Nueces) George Paul, an Iowa land developer, platted Robstown in the early 1900s, named for Robert Driscoll, president of the Corpus Christi National Bank and an incorporator of the St. Louis, Brownsville & Mexico Railway. PO 3 Aug 1905, PM August Kuehn. See Driscoll.

ROBY [RU bee] (Fisher) Brothers Dewitt and Marcus Roby, land developers and site owners, laid out the town in 1885. After the Robys donated land for parks and civic buildings, their namesake town became the county seat in 1886. Fisher, Roby's contender for the seat, then changed its name to North Roby. PO 3 Mar 1886, PM Vachel Hobbs Anderson, for whom Hobbs in Fisher County is named.

ROCHELLE [ro SHEL] (McCulloch) The local story is that the name was chosen for La Rochelle, France, by a "lonely, homesick" French traveler who, in the words of a local historian "begged that the small settlement . . . be named for the historical French city of which he dreamed and to which he longed to return." PO 19 May 1879, PM Fred Fetter.

ROCHESTER [RAH ches ter] (Haskell) About 1905 Amsey B. Carothers, a local businessman and the site owner, donated land for a station on the Kansas City, Mexico & Orient Railway. Carothers chose the name for Rochester, NY, birthplace of Arthur Edward Stilwell, organizer of the KCM&O and the namesake of PORT ARTHUR. PO 29 Aug 1900 as Marcy; changed to Rochester 3 May 1906, PM Richard H. Greenwade.

ROCK ISLAND (Colorado) In the mid-1890s the Texas & New Orleans Railroad promoted the new town of Crasco, named from Crasco Creek. Real estate agent and landowner Charles Peterson changed the name for the Rock Island Railroad when he became PM 9 Aug 1897.

ROCKDALE (Milam) Landowners George Green, Benjamin Ackerman, and Frank Smith sold 400 acres to the International–Great Northern Railroad in 1873. When the track was completed Ackerman's wife, Nancy, proposed the name for a nearby rock, reported to be 12 feet high and 20 feet around, with dale added for romantic effect. PO 20 Oct 1873, PM James Muir.

ROCKETT (Ellis) Known in the 1840s as Liberty. The name was changed in the early 1850s for shopkeepers John and Anna Rockett from North Carolina. PO 29 Mar 1894, PM James A. Rawlins.

ROCKNE [RAHK nee] (Bastrop) First known as Walnut Creek and later as Lehman or Lehmanville for John and Rosina Lehman who settled in the area in the 1870s. In 1931, after a vote by area schoolchildren, Lehmanville was renamed for Knute Rockne, the legendary Notre Dame football coach who was killed in an airplane crash in March 1931. PO 1 Feb 1900 as Lehman, PM Martin Lehman.

ROCKPORT (Aransas) Founded in the mid-1860s as an abattoir, beef processing center, and shipping station. The town was laid out in 1867 by John Doughty and cousins Thomas and John Mathis and named from the rock ledge that makes up much of the shoreline. PO 6 May 1868, PM Don M. M. Turner.

ROCKSPRINGS (Edwards) Founded by Joseph Sweeten and named from the area's natural springs. PO 3 July 1891, PM Joseph R. Sweeten.

ROCKWALL (County) Created and organized 1873; named from the community of Rockwall.

ROCKWALL (Rockwall) Founded in the spring of 1854 on land donated by Elijah Elgin and named for the wall-like underground sandstone formations that appeared to 1840s settlers as artificial walls. PO 3 Aug 1854, PM Daniel J. Thomas.

ROCKWOOD (Coleman) Rockwood grew around a store opened by Leonidus Shield in the mid-1880s. Disagreement over the name led to Discord when Henry Faulk established the Discord PO in May 1889. Discord was changed to Rockwood in 1890, reportedly at the request of music teacher Flossie Thompson, for the Adolph Wood family that lived on a rocky hill. PO 24 May 1889 as Discord; changed to Rockwood 31 Jan 1890, PM Mary A. Wainwright.

RODDY (Van Zandt) Named for Stephen Goven Roddy who opened a general store in the mid-1880s. PO 6 Nov 1885, PM Willy L. Morrison. Stephen G. Roddy was PM in 1887. See Riesel.

ROGANVILLE (Jasper) When the Gulf, Beaumont & Kansas City Railway laid tracks in 1899 the nascent town was named for Charles Rogan, an Austin attorney and commissioner of the Texas General Land Office. PO 19 Oct 1899, PM Robert Mann.

ROGERS (Bell) Founded about 1880 with construction of the Gulf, Colorado & Santa Fe Railway and named for John D. Rogers, a Galveston businessman and a director of the GC&SF. PO 26 Apr 1881 as Rodgers, PM Francis M. Edwards; changed to Rogers 2 Apr 1908.

ROLAND (Collin) Founded by Lite Townsend Morris who brought his extended family to Texas from Missouri in 1855. Local accounts claim that Morris was a great reader and named the community for one of his favorite epic poems, *The Song of Roland*. Just as likely, Morris chose the name for one of several relatives named Roland (Rowland) Morris. PO 14 Dec 1887, PM Thomas Webb.

ROLLA [RAHL uh] (Collingsworth) James A. Smith opened the Rolla PO 29 June 1894, named in honor of his 12-year-old son, Rolla.

ROMA-LOS SAENZ (Starr) Roma (Spanish "Rome") was named about 1820, probably by Catholic missionaries in honor of the Roma Mission first established near the site in the early or mid-1750s. At some point the community of Los Saenz "the Saenz people" joined with Roma. PO 15 Apr 1850 as Roma, PM Henry Hollister.

ROMAYOR [ro MAY er] (Liberty) Romayor, a misspelling of Rumayor, was named for Joaquín Fernández de Rumayor, the original land grantee. PO 2 June 1903, PM Samuel K. Stanfield.

ROMERO (Hartley) Eugenio Romero, a New Mexico pastore, moved his sheep to the area and founded Romero Springs about 1876. The Rock Island Railroad established a shipping station in the early 1900s named for Romero. PO 6 Mar 1903, PM Robert P. Church; order rescinded; established 7 Aug 1908, PM Isaac Newton Vincent.

ROOSEVELT [ROOZ velt] (Kimble) William Wagoner founded Roosevelt in 1898; named for Theodore Roosevelt who was in the news at the time for leading his "Rough Riders" up San Juan Hill in Cuba in July 1898. PO 22 Aug 1898, PM Alice Clara Ella Wag(g)oner, spouse of William Wagoner.

ROPESVILLE (Hockley) In 1917 the South Plains & Santa Fe Railway extended a line from Lubbock to Seagraves and named the station Ropes, apparently for the rope pens on the Spade Ranch used to contain cattle awaiting shipping. PO 15 June 1920, PM James R. Evans.

ROSANKY [ro ZANG kee] (Bastrop) In the early 1890s the Missouri–Kansas–Texas Railroad established a station on land donated by Edward Rosanky, a farmer and merchant who emigrated from Prussia in the 1860s. PO 13 Mar 1884 as Eagle Branch, PM James F. Ward; changed to Rosanky 2 Oct 1893, PM William E. Nash.

ROSCOE (Nolan) Reportedly named for Roscoe Costello, a conductor on the Texas & Pacific Railway. PO 24 Nov 1890, PM John A. Thompson.

ROSE HILL (Harris) Dr. Pleasant W. Rose established the first medical practice in the area in the early 1830s. PO 27 Feb 1839 as Spring Creek; changed to Crofts Mills 17 Oct 1840; changed back to Spring Creek 19 July 1848; changed to Rose Hill 2 Aug 1852, PM Christian F. Duer.

ROSEBUD (Falls) Greer's Horsepen, the first settlement in the area, became known as Mormon when several Mormon families arrived. John Tarver opened the Mormon PO in the summer of 1884. Allin Taylor became PM in 1877 and changed the name to Rosebud, according to local accounts for the extraordinary roses grown by Jennie Mullins.

ROSENBERG (Fort Bend) Founded in the early 1880s shortly after the Gulf, Colorado & Santa Fe Railway built through the area. Named for Henry Rosenberg, a Swiss-born Galveston businessman, banker, and philanthropist. Rosenberg was president of the GC&SF in the mid-1870s. PO 1 Nov 1881, PM Holman Ham.

ROSEWOOD (Upshur) Probably named for Alice Rose Carson who opened the Essex PO 22 Dec 1891 and changed the name to Rosewood 29 Oct 1902.

ROSHARON [ro SHEHR uhn] (Brazoria) In the early 1910s George Wetmore Colles, Jr., a mechanical and electrical engineer born in New York City, established the Rose of Sharon Ranch, apparently named for the local abundance of Cherokee Roses. The name was compressed to Rosharon when Antonio Arcaro established the PO 9 Feb 1912.

ROSITA [ro SEE tuh] (Duval) Four area features share the name: Rosita Creek, Rosita Ranch, Rosita School, and the community of Rosita. The name was in use by at least 1906 when it appears in Rosita School records. Naming details are unknown.

ROSS (McLennan) In 1874 the Houston & Texas Central Railway established Ross Station; named for Lawrence Sullivan "Sul" Ross, then sheriff of McLennan County and later the 19th Governor of Texas (1887–1891). PO 8 Jan 1880, PM Charles Kingsbury.

ROSSER [RAWS er] (Kaufman) John Damron founded Trinidad, named from the Trinity River, in 1851. The Texas & Pacific Railway built through the area in the early 1870s, bringing with it the demise of Trinidad and the rise of Rosser. In 1886 businessman Robert S. Rosser submitted a PO application requesting the name Burton. The application was rejected, resubmitted, and approved as Rosser. The Trinidad PO operated 24 June 1854–5 Nov 1866. The Rosser office opened 26 June 1886, PM John Cochran.

ROSSTON (Cooke) Brothers Orpheus and Theodore Ross, from Missouri by way of Grayson County, kept the Ross department store in Pilot Point from about 1870. Orpheus and Margaret Ross's son, Orus Orpheus Ross (known as "O. O.") became a noted Wichita Falls lawyer and jurist. PO 16 Jan 1877, PM Theodore A. Ross.

ROSSVILLE (Atascosa) In 1867 John Clark Ross, who had worked in both England and Scotland, and his brother William, arrived in Galveston and settled on land owned by his wife, María Antonia Navarro, originally granted to her grandfather, José Antonio Navarro, the namesake of Navarro County. John and William Ross platted Rossville in 1873. PO 11 Jan 1877, PM William Frazer Mather Ross.

ROTAN [ro TAN] (Fisher) Earlier known as White Flat for the local gypsum deposits. The Texas Central Railway established Rotan Station in 1906, named for Edward Rotan, president of the First National Bank of Waco and a director of the TC. PO 29 Dec 1906 as Rotando; changed to Rotan 22 Jan 1907, PM Thomas N. Penick.

ROUND ROCK (Williamson) Named from a large, oval rock in Brushy Creek near the site where Jacob Harrell, mayor of Austin in 1847, opened a blacksmith shop in 1848. PO 27 May 1851 as Brushy Creek; changed to Round Rock 24 Aug 1854, PM Thomas C. Oatts.

ROUNDUP (Hockley) Roundup grew around a shipping station established by the Atchison, Topeka & Santa Fe Railway in 1912. The name was proposed by William H. Simpson, chief of the Santa Fe's advertising department, who claimed the name would promote tourism.

ROWDEN [ROD uhn] (Callahan) The local account is that storekeeper Walter Roberts asked representatives of all the nearby families to put their names in a hat, out of which he drew "Rowden," for farm owners Smith and Elizabeth Rowden. PO 22 June 1906, PM Walter V. Roberts.

ROWENA [ro EE nuh] (Runnels) In 1888 the Gulf, Colorado & Santa Fe Railway established a section house known as Rowena Station, named for the wife and daughter of James Spillane of Galveston, private secretary to Webster Snyder, general manager of the railroad. The community was laid out in 1898 as Baronsville by local land developer Paul J. Baron. PO 19 Jan 1900 as Bolf, named for land agent John Bolf (Bolfik); changed to Rowena 1 July 1901, PM Gustav Schuhmann.

ROWLAND (Montague) Named for John T. Rowland, mayor of GAINESVILLE in the late 1880s and district representative in the Texas Legislature 1901–1905.

ROWLETT (Dallas) Named for Daniel Rowlett, legislator, lawyer, surveyor, cartographer, and physician of the 1840s and 1850s. PO 5 Apr 1880 as Morris, PM Austin Morris; changed to Rowlett 19 Feb 1889, PM Benjamin H. Harris.

ROXTON (Lamar) Fred Tarpley suggests that the local white limestone outcroppings gave the community its name which was earlier spelled Rockston and Rockstown. Alternatively, Roxton may be a transfer from Roxton, Madison County, AR. PO 9 Sept 1853 as Prairie Mount; changed to Roxton 2 Feb 1869, PM Richard B. Hamlet.

ROYALTY (Ward) Apparently the name is from royalties earned from the oil pumped at GRANDFALLS from the mid-1920s. PO 26 Aug 1929, PM Naomi M. Lewis.

ROYSE CITY (Collin, Rockwall) Garrett Burgess "Byrd" Royse emigrated from KY in 1850s, platted the townsite, sold the first building lots, and attracted the Missouri–Kansas–Texas Railroad in the mid-1880s. PO 25 Oct 1886, PM Knud M. Peterson. Also known as Fay.

ROYSTON (Fisher) Cady Royston, daughter of Clara and Richard Royston of Bastrop, founded Royston in 1907 on the section of land she had been given by her uncles, Kenner Keener Rector and district judge John Benjamin Rector. PO 1 Apr 1907, PM William J. Jackson.

ROZNOV (Fayette) John M. Halamicek who established the PO 18 Nov 1892, chose the name for Rožnov, his former home, now in the eastern Czech Republic.

RUCKER (Comanche) Apparently named for Calvin Rucker who was operating a cotton gin near the site by 1890. PO 2 Apr 1900, PM David Gregory.

RUDOLPH (Kenedy) Named in the early 1900s for Rudolph Kleberg, son of Robert Justice Kleberg and grandson of Richard King, founder of the King Ranch. After serving in the Texas Legislature, Kleberg was a US Representative 1896–1903. PO 5 Nov 1904, PM James R. Burt. See Kleberg County.

RUGELEY (Matagorda) Named about 1902 for planter and physician Henry Lowndes

Rugeley who established a medical practice in Bay City at the end of the Civil War.

RUIDOSA [ree uh DO suh] (Presidio) Spanish "noisy." Naming details unknown. PO 17 Oct 1914, PM Jesus Nunez.

RULE (Haskell) Jesse L. Jones, a cashier at the Haskell National Bank, named the community for his friend and business advisor, William A. Rule, vice president of the Commercial National Bank of Kansas City and a director of the Kansas City, Mexico & Orient Railway that established a station in the early 1900s. PO 2 May 1903, PM Angie A. Baker.

RUMLEY (Lampasas) Rumley was named from a farm equipment line manufactured by the Rumely [*sic*] company of La Porte, IN. The Advance-Rumely thrashing machine of the late 19th and early 20th centuries, brought to the area by Ross Smart and Buck Simon about 1915, was highly regarded.

RUNGE [RUHNG ee] (Karnes) Henry Runge, an Indianola businessman, banker, and community benefactor, platted the town in 1886. One of Runge's sons, also named Henry, founded ARCADIA in Galveston County. PO 20 Sept 1887, PM Walter Lokey. See Nordheim.

RUNNELS (County) Created 1858, organized 1880. Named for Hiram George Runnels (1796–1857), born in Georgia. Runnels was a prominent Mississippi politician in the 1820s and 1830s, elected governor in 1833. He moved his family and some 50 slaves to Texas in 1842, established a plantation on the Brazos River, and was a delegate to the Convention of 1845. He was elected to the Texas Senate in 1857 but died before he could take the oath of office. His nephew, Hardin Richard Runnels, was the 6th Governor of Texas (1857–1859).

RUSK (County) Created and organized 1843. Named for Thomas Jefferson Rusk (1803–1857), born in South Carolina. Rusk emigrated to Nacogdoches early in 1835, signed the Texas Declaration of Independence, was the first Secretary of War of the Republic of Texas, and was instrumental in forcing the remaining Cherokees from East Texas into Oklahoma after the battle of the Neches in the summer of 1839. Rusk, the seat of Cherokee County, is also named for Thomas Jefferson Rusk.

RUSK (Cherokee) Cherokee County and Rusk, its seat, were authorized simultaneously by the Texas Legislature in April 1846. The town was named for Thomas Jefferson Rusk, for whom neighboring Rusk County had been named three years earlier. PO 8 Mar 1847, PM Edward L. Givens. See Rusk County.

RUSSELL (Leon) Thompson Daniel Russell and Harriett Malinda Russell began farming in the area about 1885. PO 16 Feb 1885, PM Thompson Russell.

RUSSELTOWN (Cameron) Known as Barreda for one or more Barreda families until the late 1930s when Frank and Martha Russell relocated from Alabama and established Russell Plantation.

RUTERSVILLE [ROOT erz vil] (Fayette) Martin Ruter, a pioneer Methodist minister from New England, was a leading figure in establishing Methodism in Texas in the late 1830s. PO 27 Feb 1839, PM William Paris Smith.

RUTLAND (Angelina) Merchant William P. Rutland was the first postmaster at Diboll in 1897 and one of the first directors of the Texas South-Eastern Railroad, chartered in 1900.

RYE (Liberty) Organized about 1900 with construction of the Gulf, Colorado & Santa Fe Railway; named for farmer Morgan Calvin Rye who relocated from Georgia to Texas about 1858. PO 11 Aug 1902, PM William H. Kelly; rescinded 22 Nov 1902; reestablished 19 June 1906, PM William Emanuel.

RYLIE (Dallas) In the mid-1840s James and Mary Rylie moved to Texas from Illinois and settled on what became known as Rylie Prairie, where James Rylie established a smithy. PO 8 Feb 1883, PM Hartwell Cox.

L

SABANNO [suh BAN uh] (Eastland) Named from the Sabana [*sic*] River, from Spanish *sabana* "savanna, treeless plain." PO 14 Feb 1901, PM James E. Broyles.

SABINAL [SAB uh nahl] (Uvalde) Spanish "juniper grove." Sabinal, named from the Sabinal River and Sabinal Canyon, grew around a rest stop on the San Antonio–El Paso stagecoach line established in October 1854 by Thomas Burton Hammer. Hammer, who relocated from Bedford County, PA, in the mid-1840s, established the PO 19 Oct 1854. See Sabine County.

SABINE [suh BEEN] (County) An original Texas county created 1836, organized 1837. Named from the Sabine River that marks the eastern edge of the county and forms much of the boundary between Texas and Louisiana. The name first appears as *Río de Sabinas* "river of junipers (or cypress)" on a 1721 map associated with the Aguayo Expedition.

SACHSE [SAKS ee] (Collin, Dallas) William and Elizabeth Sachse donated land for the townsite and the right of way for the Gulf, Colorado & Santa Fe Railway in 1866. PO 3 Nov 1886 as Saxie, PM William Sachse; changed to Sachse 29 May 1892, PM Elias W. Shepherd.

SACUL [SA kuhl] (Nacogdoches) Soon after the Texas & New Orleans Railroad built through the area about 1900, a PO application was submitted requesting the name Lucas for the first site owners, brothers John and Newton Lucas. When that name was rejected the application was resubmitted as Sacul, Lucas spelled backward. PO 29 June 1903, PM William Greer.

SADLER (Grayson) John and Geraldine Sadler donated land for a station on the Missouri–Kansas–Texas Railroad in the 1870s. PO 9 May 1891 as Talley, PM Hugh Sadler; changed to Sadler 27 June 1892, PM Joseph S. Cariker.

SAGERTON [SAY ger tuhn] (Haskell) William M. Sager, a trail driver and cattleman from Missouri, settled in the area in the early 1870s. PO 31 Oct 1903, PM Herbert Posey.

SAGINAW [SAG uh naw] (Tarrant) Formerly known as Dido, named either for the mythical queen Dido, the founder of Carthage, or, according to some accounts, for a local mare famous for her antics, her "didos." Formally named in 1882 by Jarvis J. Green for Pontiac, MI, his former home. When this name was rejected by the Post Office Department, Jarvis suggested Saginaw, another Michigan city. PO 5 Jan 1888, PM William W. Gilley.

SALADO [suh LAY do] (Bell) Named from Salado (Spanish "salty") Creek. The site was a rest stop on the Austin-Waco stagecoach line from the early 1850s. About 1860 the town of Salado and Salado College were founded on land donated for an educational institution by Elijah Sterling Clack Robertson, son of Sterling Clack Robertson, the empresario of Robertson's Colony. PO 29 Apr 1852, PM Lewis A. Ogle.

SALEM (Newton) Seth Swift established the Salem PO 8 Mar 1847, named for his birthplace, Salem, MA.

SALEM (Rusk) See New Salem.

SALESVILLE (Palo Pinto) Edmond and Anita Sale brought their family from Kentucky in the mid-1870s. Edmond T. Sale established a general store and opened the PO 17 May 1879 as Anita. Sale changed the name to Salesville 15 Apr 1880.

SALINE (Menard) Spanish "salty place." Settled in the 1870s; named from Saline Creek.

SALINENO (Starr) In 2008, after the US government began allowing diacritics in place names, the Salineno PO was changed to Salineño. PO 11 Oct 1899, PM Adolph Oosterveen; never opened; established 20 Nov 1911, PM Patricio G. Canales.

SALMON [SAL muhn] (Anderson) Named for PM Meredith D. Salmon, who opened the PO 1 July 1902.

SALTILLO [sal TIL o] (Hopkins) Spanish "jump, little leap." John Arthur from Franklin County, VA, opened a grocery store, gristmill, and cotton gin in 1849. Arthur suggested the name for Saltillo, Mexico, which was occupied by US troops in November 1846 during the Mexican War. PO 13 Feb 1860, PM Moses F. Russell.

SALTY (Milam) Named from Salty Creek. PO 6 July 1894, PM Francis M. Amason.

SAM FORDYCE [sam FORD is] (Hidalgo) The St. Louis, Brownsville & Mexico Railway built through the area in 1904 and named the station for Samuel Wesley Fordyce, a banker and financier who underwrote construction of much of the SLB&M. Fordyce in Dallas County, AR, was also named for Sam Fordyce. PO 18 Feb 1886 as Havana; renamed Samfordyce 3 Nov 1905, PM Charles S. Schunior. See Fodice.

SAMNORWOOD [sam NOR wud] (Collingsworth) Samuel Willis Norwood and Temperence Viola Norwood brought their family from Jackson County, AL, in 1899. Sam Norwood was a rancher and president of the local Farmers & Merchants bank. The community was organized and formally named in 1931 when the Fort Worth & Denver Northern Railway extended its line to Pampa. PO 5 Dec 1932, PM Robert Jason Young.

SAMPLE (Gonzales) Named for one or more Sample (Semple) families who were established in the area before 1870. PO 1 Aug 1905, PM Grover Sample.

SAN ANGELO (Tom Green) San Angelo was founded by merchant Bartholomew J. DeWitt, who established a trading post in the late 1860s that became associated with his wife, Carolina Angela, sister of José Rafael de la Garza, for whose family Garza County is named. Carolina Angela was known as Santa Angela, shortened to San Angela. After the San Angela PO was opened by Nathan Osmer 20 Jan 1881 and the grammatical incorrectness of combining the Spanish masculine San with the feminine Angela was pointed out, the office was renamed San Angelo 25 Oct 1883. See Garza County.

SAN ANTONIO (Bexar) Named from the San Antonio River, itself named by Domingo

Terán de los Ríos, the first governor of Spanish Texas, on an exploratory expedition in the summer of 1691. The river was approached on or about 13 June 1691, the feast day of the Franciscan friar San Antonio de Padua (Saint Anthony of Padua). Early in May 1718 the *San Antonio de Valero* Mission, named from San Antonio and the Marqués de Valero, the Viceroy of New Spain, was founded by provincial Governor Martín de Alarcón and the Franciscan priest Antonio de San Buenaventura y Olivares. About the same time Alarcón established the San Antonio de Béxar Presidio. The community of San Fernando de Béxar, likely named for Fernando III, king of several Spanish provinces in the 13th century and canonized in 1671, was founded near the mission about 1730. The community was generally known as Béxar until 1837 when John William Smith opened the San Antonio PO. Smith would later be a multi-term mayor of San Antonio in the late 1830s and early 1840s.

SAN ANTONIO VIEJO (Jim Hogg) The San Antonio Viejo "Old San Antonio" Ranch, from which the town takes its name, was granted to Francisco Xavier Vela in 1805.

SAN AUGUSTINE (County) An original Texas county created 1836, organized 1837; named for the town and Mexican municipality of San Augustine.

SAN AUGUSTINE (San Augustine) In 1830 William McFarland and his son Thomas, both surveyors, settled on Ayish Bayou (named from the Ayish or Ais, a Caddoan people who lived in the area in the 18th century). Thomas McFarland platted the townsite in 1833; the following year Mexico established the municipality of San Augustine, probably named for St. Augustine of Hippo. PO 22 May 1846, PM Travis G. Brooks.

SAN BENITO (Cameron) In 1907 James Landrum, the namesake of LANDRUM, Samuel Robertson, and Benjamin Hicks laid out the town of Bessie, named for Bessie Yoakum, daughter of Benjamin Franklin Yoakum, a visionary Southwest railroad executive and the namesake of YOAKUM. The name San Benito was apparently coined by Rafael Moreno, an associate of Hicks, by combining the given names of Robertson (Sam, altered to San) and Hicks, known informally as "Don Benito." PO 2 Apr 1907 as Diaz, PM Samuel Robertson; changed to San Benito 11 May 1907.

SAN DIEGO (Duval, Jim Wells) Named from the *San Diego de Arriba* and *San Diego de Abajo* (upper and lower San Diego) land grants conveyed to Julián and Ventura Flores, father and son, by the Spanish government about 1800. The town of San Diego, first known as Perezville, was authorized by the Flores family in the early 1820s. PO 8 July 1867, PM George Warden.

SAN ELIZARIO [san el uh ZAHR ee o] (El Paso) In 1789 the Spanish presidio of *San Elceario* near present Fort Hancock was moved to the *Hacienda de los Tiburcios*, renamed San Elzearo and later San Elizareo for Saint Elzéar of Sabran, the patron saint of soldiers. PO 17 Apr 1851 as San Elizario, PM Henry L. Dexter.

SAN FELIPE [san fuh LEEP] (Austin) Founded by Stephen F. Austin in 1824 as the governmental and commercial center of the Austin colony. The name was likely chosen by Felipe de la Garza, Mexican governor of the Eastern Interior Provinces, which included Austin's Colony. In retrospect San Felipe de Austin was an especially well-chosen name. Being a triple honorific the name at once honored the local authority, Stephen F. Austin; the regal authority, Felipe de la Garza; and the religious authority, St. Philip the disciple. PO 1826 as San Felipe de Austin (in Mexico), changed to San Felipe 1835.

SAN GABRIEL (Milam) Jesse and Peter Mercer, soldiers in the Texas Revolution; founded San Gabriel in the mid-1840s, named from the San Gabriel River, known to Spanish explorers from at least 1716 as the *Río de San Francisco Xavier* for Saint Francis Xavier. Javier, the Spanish spelling of Xavier, was misread or misrecorded by, among others, Stephen F. Austin, who wrote "San Javriel" on his 1829 map. Through popular etymology Javriel became Gabriel. PO 13 Aug 1850, PM Thomas J. Allen.

SAN ISIDRO (Starr) Santiago Peña, the first permanent settler in the 1870s, named the site for San Isidro (St. Isidore) of Seville, the patron saint of farmers. PO 21 Apr 1904, PM Amado Peña.

SAN JACINTO [san juh SIN to] (County) Created 1869, organized 1870. Named for the April 21, 1836 Battle of San Jacinto fought between the Texas Revolutionary Army of Sam Houston and the Mexican forces of Santa Anna. The Texas victory led to independence and the Republic of Texas. The conflict was named from the San Jacinto River, Spanish for "hyacinth," itself probably named for the 13th century Dominican Saint Hyacinth, patron saint of those in danger of drowning.

SAN JACINTO (Walker) Named for the Battle of San Jacinto, the decisive engagement of the Texas Revolution. PO 19 Jan 1858, Harrison G. Carlile. See San Jacinto County.

SAN JUAN [san WAN] (Hidalgo) In the early 20th century, John T. Closner, often called the "Father of Hidalgo County," established the San Juan Plantation, reportedly named by Closner's wife by translating his given name into Spanish and adding *San* "saint" for effect. PO 6 Feb 1909, PM Robert Savage.

SAN MARCOS [san MAHR kuhs] (Hays) The Alonso de León Expedition gave the name San Marcos (St. Mark) to a Central Texas river in 1689. Why the river is so named is uncertain but by the early 18th century the name referred to the current San Marcos River. The first settlement at the site, *Villa de San Marcos de Neve*, was founded in 1808 and abandoned four years later. The present city, named from the San Marcos springs and the river, was surveyed by Edward Burleson shortly before his death in 1851. PO 28 Dec 1846, PM Eli Merriman.

SAN PATRICIO (County) Created 1836, organized 1837, reorganized 1847; named from the town of San Patricio.

SAN PATRICIO [san puh TRISH ee o] (San Patricio) James McGloin and John McMullen, empresarios authorized by Mexico to settle some 200 families along the Nueces River, founded the *Villa de San Patricio de Hibernia* "town of Saint Patrick of Ireland" about 1830. PO 17 May 1848, PM John Ross.

SAN PERLITA [san per LEET uh] (Willacy) In 1926 Charles Rene Johnson founded San Perlita, the "little pearl," named for his wife, Olga Pyrle. PO 13 July 1929, PM Lillian Beeraft.

SAN SABA (County) Created and organized in 1856; named from the San Saba River.

SAN SABA [san SAB uh] (San Saba) The community of San Saba was organized in the mid-1850s and named from the San Saba River. In December 1732, on the feast day of Saint Sabbas, members of the Juan Antonio Bustillo y Ceballos Expedition came to a river they named *Río de San Sabas de las Nueces* "River of Saint Sabbas of the Nuts," later shortened to San Saba. PO 5 May 1857, PM Wiley T. Murray.

SAN YGNACIO [san ig NAH see o] (Zapata) About 1830 Jesús Treviño brought settlers from what is now Ciudad Guerrero, Tamaulipas, Mexico, and established a community named for St. Ignatius Loyola, the patron saint of Guerrero. PO 3 Jan 1876, PM Fernando Uribe.

SANCO [SAN ko] (Coke) Sanaco, probably meaning "sap" or "gum," was a leader of the Penateka (southern) Comanches in the mid-19th century. Sanaco had shrunk to Sanco by 10 July 1888 when John Durham established the Sanco PO.

SAND (Dawson) Apparently a shortening of "Sands of Texas," an early name for the area. PO 23 Oct 1935, PM Ebbie Lee.

SANDERSON (Terrell) Originally named Strawbridge Station, a popular etymology of Strobridge, named for James Harvey Strobridge, superintendent of construction of the Central Pacific Railroad. Renamed in 1882 for Thomas P. Sanderson who built the roundhouse at Strawbridge.

SANDIA [san DEE uh] (Jim Wells) James Fennell Dibrell and Max Starcke of Guadalupe, TX, laid out Sandia in 1907 on what was originally the Casa Blanca land grant of José de la Garza. Dibrell and Starcke likely chose the name Sandia, Spanish for "watermelon," in recognition of an important local cash crop. PO 22 Apr 1907, PM James Kring. See Orange Grove.

SANDJACK (Newton) Probably named for the stands of Sandjack Oak (*Quercus incana*), also known as Bluejack Oak or Cinnamon Oak, common along the Gulf Coast and inland rivers such as the Sabine.

SANDOW (Milam) In 1922 the McAlester Fuel Company of Oklahoma, an investor in the local lignite industry, named the community Sandow, apparently for Eugene Sandow, a German strongman and body builder who was a major attraction in Florenz Ziegfeld's productions at the turn of the 20th century. Known as Freezeout and also as Millerton for benefactor Emil Miller.

SANDUSKY (Grayson) Sandusky may have been named for William Sandusky, a Texas artist and draftsman who drew one of the first maps of Austin in 1839, but more likely Sandusky is a transfer from Sandusky, OH, itself named from Wyandot *sandesti* "water." There being no clear source for the name, several stories have been invented to explain its origin. By one particularly clever popular etymology, at a meeting to choose a name for the town there suddenly arose a great wind that blew so much sand that the room became dusky; thus Sandusky. PO 19 Nov 1875, PM William Miller.

SANFORD (Hutchinson) Sanford was founded in 1927 with construction of the Rock Island Railroad on ranchland owned by James McEuin Sanford, an early settler and one of the organizers of Hutchinson County. PO 26 Sept 1927, PM James B. Michener.

SANGER [SANG er] (Denton) Sanger was founded as a refueling stop on the Gulf, Colorado & Santa Fe Railway in 1886 and named for Alexander Sanger, a partner in the Sanger Brothers chain of dry goods stores in North Texas. PO 18 Feb 1887 as New Bolivar, PM Francis M. Ready; changed to Sanger 25 Mar 1887. See Adell.

SANTA ANNA (Coleman) Named from the Santa Anna Mountains, twin peaks north of the community, themselves named for Santa Anna (Santana), a Penateka Comanche leader of the mid-19th century. PO 7 Apr 1879, PM Jacob Walton.

SANTA CRUZ (Duval) Santa Cruz was named from the *Santa Cruz de la Concepción* land grant, conveyed to Francisco Cordente by the Spanish government in the early 19th century. The town of CONCEPCION was named from the same land grant. PO 21 Mar 1906, PM Crescencio Leal.

SANTA FE (Galveston) After 1877 when the Gulf, Colorado & Santa Fe Railway built through the area, the towns of ALGOA, ALTA LOMA, and ARCADIA were established along the railroad line. In the 1900s the three communities merged many of their services and were known collectively as Santa Fe, named for the GC&SF. PO 31 Dec 1982, PM Clyde W. Singleton.

SANTA MARIA [san tuh muh REE uh] (Cameron) Named from *El Rancho de Santa María*, owned by Lawrence J. Hynes who donated land for Our Lady of Visitation Catholic Church in the early 1880s. Hynes was the first PM 25 Feb 1878.

SANTA MONICA (Willacy) Clarence Ayres of Hidalgo, president of the American Life Insurance Company that underwrote much of the development in the area in the 1920s, chose the name for the company's headquarters, Santa Monica, CA, itself named for Ste. Monica, mother of St. Augustine.

SARAGOSA [sehr uh GO suh] (Reeves) Perhaps named for an early settler; Saragosa is more likely a transfer from one of the several Zaragozas in Mexico or in Spain, or from Saragossa [*sic*], Walker County, AL. PO 23 Jan 1844, PM James K. Dempsey.

SARATOGA (Hardin) Pinkney Watts, an early settler in the 1850s and later the town sheriff, developed and promoted the medicinal value of the local spring water and changed the name from New Sour Lake to Saratoga to capitalize on the notoriety of Saratoga Springs, the well-known New York spa. PO 3 June 1884, PM William A. Richardson.

SARGENT (Matagorda) George Sargent, who emigrated from Cornwall, England, in the mid-1830s, and his son, John Sargent, were prominent area ranchers in the 1860s and 1870s. PO 31 Dec 1912, PM Mary C. Montgomery.

SARITA [suh REET uh] (Kenedy) Named about 1904 for Sarita Kenedy, daughter of John and Marie Turcotte Kenedy and granddaughter of Mifflin Kenedy, founder of the La Parra Ranch and namesake of KENEDY COUNTY. The town of TURCOTTE is named for Marie Turcotte Kenedy. PO 19 Dec 1904, PM Claude G. Arnold.

SARON [SAY ruhn] (Trinity) Saron was established about 1882 on the Trinity & Sabine Railway as a shipping station for William Cameron's sawmill. The name is a variant of the Biblical Sharon and likely a shortening of *Rosa de Sarón* "the rose of Sharon." PO 25 Aug 1894, PM Charles H. Pillney.

SASPAMCO [suh SPAM ko] (Wilson) Saspamco is an acronym derived from the name of the San Antonio Sewer Pipe Manufacturing Company. The town was formally named when the PO was established by George J. Ball 22 Aug 1901.

SATIN (Falls) As Falls County historian Lillian St. Romain tells the story, twenty names for the post office had been suggested. "While a group of citizens were in a local dry goods store discussing [a] twenty-first [name], a clerk, handling a bolt of satin cloth, remarked that satin was pretty. The group took notice and placed 'satin' on the list" (113). PO 20 Dec 1917, PM John Hamilton. Formerly known as Laguna.

SATSUMA [sat SOOM uh] (Harris) James T. Thompson, president of the Satsuma Land Company, laid out the town of Satsuma in 1910, named for Satsuma oranges, expected to be a major export of the area, which, unfortunately, did not materialize. (The oranges were named for Satsuma, Kyushu, Japan, where they were developed.) PO 19 June 1909, PM James T. Thompson.

SATTLER (Comal) Heinrich (Henry) Sattler, son of Wilhelm Sattler, one of the first settlers of New Braunfels, opened the Sattler's PO 16 Sept 1856. The office was established and discontinued several times before William Sattler opened the Sattler PO 3 May 1880.

SAVAGE (Crosby) Enoch Ellis Savage of Littlefield owned the site on which the first local cotton gin was built in 1924.

SAVOY (Fannin) Site owner William Louis Marshall Savoy, known as Colonel Savoy, donated land for the Texas & Pacific Railway station in 1872. PO 25 Feb 1839 as Big Creek; changed 12 Apr 1871 to Blackberry Plain, PM William Savoy; changed to Savoy 6 June 1873, PM John Slaughter.

SAYERS (Bexar) Joseph Draper Sayers was US Representative in the 1880s and 1890s and the 22nd Governor of Texas (1899–1903). PO 6 Nov 1885, PM William D. H. Saunders. See Sayersville.

SAYERSVILLE (Bastrop) David Sayers, a physician born in Virginia, settled in the area in the 1850s. His son, Joseph Draper Sayers, was the 22nd Governor of Texas and the namesake of SAYERS in Bexar County. PO 20 Feb 1889, Henry M. Green. See Sayers.

SCHATTEL [SHAT uhl] (Frio) William and Caroline Schattel brought their twelve children to the area from East Bernard in Wharton County early in 1924. Site owner William Schattel laid out the town and established the PO 2 Dec 1924.

SCHERTZ (Guadalupe) The Galveston, Harrisburg & San Antonio Railway established Schertz Station in 1876, named for Sebastian Schertz who had emigrated from Alsace-Loraine in the 1840s and kept a general store from the mid-1870s. PO 23 May 1884 as Cutoff; changed to Schertz 6 Apr 1899, PM William Schertz, Sebastian's son.

SCHLEICHER [SHLEYE ker] (County) Created 1887, organized 1901. Named for Gustaves Schleicher (1823–1879), born in Hesse, Germany. Schleicher was an engineer, politician, social idealist, and freethinker, and a founder of the utopian community of Bettina, named for German writer, artist, and composer, Bettina von Arnim in Llano County in 1847. Schleicher served in the Texas Legislature in the 1850s and the US Congress in the 1870s. At the same time Schleicher was a San Antonio lawyer, surveyor for the Bexar Land District, and a railroad executive. See Cuero.

SCHOOLERVILLE (Hamilton) Joseph and Laura Ann Schooler from Kentucky began farming in the area about 1890.

SCHROEDER [SHRAY der] (Goliad) The PO was established 30 June 1890 as Germantown for the many German settlers in the 1840s. The office was changed to Schroeder 21 Oct 1918 in honor of Paul Schroeder, the first local son to be killed in World War I; PM Rudolph Toerck.

SCHULENBURG [SHOOL in berg] (Fayette) Thomas Peirce, an owner of the Galveston, Houston & San Antonio Railway, named Schulenburg for the site owner and town founder, August Louis Herman von Schulenburg, who emigrated from Hannover, Germany in the 1840s. PO 22 May 1846 as Lyons, PM Dewitt Lyons; changed to Schulenburg 18 Jan 1886, PM Charles Kessler.

SCHUMANSVILLE [SHOO muhnz vil] (Guadalupe) August Wilhelm Schumann emigrated from Prussia in 1846, bought several hundred acres of land from which he established the townsite, then subdivided the remaining acreage which he sold to the next wave of Prussian immigrants. PO 4 Jan 1904, PM Diedrich A. Klenke.

SCHWAB CITY (Polk) Named for Dick Schwab, an oil wildcatter from Livingston, TX, who drilled a discovery well in 1937 that turned out to be a gusher.

SCHWERTNER [SWERT ner] (Williamson) Named for the Bernhard Schwertner family that emigrated from Austria in 1877. The town was founded by Bernhard and Franziska

Schwertner's son Adolph who donated land for the Bartlett Western Railway in 1909. PO 30 Aug 1912, PM Gustav A. Matejowsky.

SCOTLAND (Archer) Henry J. Scott, an English diplomat with headquarters in Toronto, Ontario, owned several thousand acres in Archer County. About 1907 Scott's agent, John Henry Meurer (whose home is now a historical site in Scotland, TX), laid out the town named for Henry Scott. PO 3 June 1908, PM Fritz Frerich.

SCOTTSVILLE (Harrison) Founded by William Thomas Scott, a wealthy East Texas planter who emigrated from Mississippi in 1840. By 1850 Scott owned a lavish mansion, at least five cotton plantations, and more than one hundred slaves. He represented the district in the Texas State Legislature both before and after the Civil War. PO 4 Aug 1869, PM Washington Mathis.

SCROGGINS (Franklin) Scroggins' Switch was a spur on the East Line & Red River Railroad established in the 1870s to serve the Scroggins Brothers Sawmill operated by Milton Mills Scroggins and several family members from the 1850s. PO 30 Oct 1891, PM Samuel Thomas.

SCURRY (County) Created 1876, organized 1884. Named for William Read Scurry (1821–1864), born in Tennessee. Scurry came to Texas in 1839, served as district attorney, and was a member of the Republic of Texas Congress in the 1840s. He was a Confederate General in the Civil War and was mortally wounded in the battle of Jenkins Ferry in Arkansas in April 1864.

SCURRY (Kaufman) Richard Scurry Dean was granted a section of land near present Scurry for his service in the Texas Revolution. Known as Scurry Dean, he was mortally wounded in 1862 during the Battle of Pea Ridge, Arkansas. PO 16 Apr 1883, PM William L. Upton.

SCYENE [seye EEN] (Dallas) In 1854 James J. Beeman, the Prairie Creek PM, petitioned to change the name of the office to White Rock. When that name was rejected Beeman proposed the name Scyene, for the city in ancient Egypt now known as Aswan and mentioned several times in the Bible. PO 17 Sept 1852 as Prairie Creek; changed to Scyene 1 June 1854, James J. Beeman.

SEABROOK (Chambers, Galveston, Harris) Seabrook was named for founder and promoter John Seabrook Sydnor. Sydnor was mayor of Galveston in the 1840s and a Galveston slave trader until the Civil War. His home, Powhatan House in Galveston, is on the National Register of Historic Places. PO 14 May 1892 as Lakeside; changed to Seabrook 28 Aug 1895, PM Edward F. Palms.

SEADRIFT (Calhoun) Roberta Dierlam, the winner of a naming contest, likely chose the name for the debris that washed through the area after the hurricane that destroyed Indianola in 1886. PO 4 Sept 1891, PM Jessie Dierlam.

SEAGOVILLE [SEE go vil] (Dallas) Tillman Kimsey Seago moved from Georgia to Texas in 1851, opened a general store in 1876, and established the Seagoville PO 7 Nov 1881.

Seago was elected to the Texas Legislature on the Populist ticket in 1894.

SEAGRAVES (Gaines) Named about 1917 with an extension of the Santa Fe Railroad for Charles Seagraves, general colonizing agent for the SF. PO 11 Sept 1909 as Blythe, PM Samuel Blythe; changed to Seagraves 21 Nov 1921, PM Lora M. Wicker.

SEALE (Limestone, Robertson) Joshua and Mariah Seale, planters from Mississippi, moved to the area following the Civil War. PO 26 Jan 1885, PM Henry Shaw. Mike Seale, son of Joshua and Mariah, was PM in 1912.

SEALY (Austin) The Gulf, Colorado & Santa Fe Railway founded Sealy about 1875, named for George and John Sealy. About 1880 George Sealy bought the GC&SF and saved the line from bankruptcy; his brother, John Sealy, was president. PO 2 Mar 1880, PM Robert P. Josey.

SEAWILLOW (Caldwell) Named for Seawillow Margaret Ann Pipkin Wells. A disastrous flood on the Neches River forced the Pipkins to abandon their home and Seawillow's mother gave birth sheltered only by a large willow tree, thus the name. Seawillow's husband, Littleberry Wells, established the Seawillow PO 4 Aug 1899. Their daughter was Seawillow Lemon Wells.

SEBASTIAN (Willacy) Formerly known as Stillman, named from the Stillman Ranch operated by Charles Stillman, the founder of BROWNSVILLE. The name was formally changed about 1912 for John Sebastian, vice president of the Chicago, Rock Island & Pacific Railway. PO 11 Jan 1908, PM William Henry Rowell.

SEBASTOPOL [suh BAS tuh pool] (Trinity) Sebastopol is the name of about a dozen communities in the US, all named in the 1850s when Sebastopol on the Black Sea was under siege by British, French, Turkish, and other troops during the Crimean War, widely reported in American newspapers. PO 13 Apr 1860, PM Isaac A. Felker. Earlier known as Bartholomew.

SECLUSION (Lavaca) The local account is that the community was named for its isolation. PO 28 Apr 1879, PM Mary Ann Speake.

SECURITY (Montgomery) Founded about 1890 as Pocahontas. In the early 20th century the name was changed to Bennette for site owner James O. H. Bennette, a Conroe sawmiller and businessman. Several years later the property was bought by the Security Land Company of Arizona that laid out and renamed the community. PO 9 Mar 1910, PM James C. Walker.

SEDALIA [suh DAYL yuh] (Collin) The name was brought to Texas from Sedalia, MO, itself named in the mid-1850s by George Smith who created Sedalia from Sed, the nickname of his daughter, adding the suffix "alia." PO 15 Jan 1889, PM David Martin.

SEDWICK (Shackelford) The town was first known as Vesta Switch, established by the Texas Central Railway in the early 1880s. About 1900 the name became Sedwick for farmer and stock raiser John Francis Sedwick. PO 4 May 1905, PM Maude Sophronia Randolph.

SEELIGSON [SEE lig suhn] (Jim Wells) Probably named for Michael Seeligson, mayor of Galveston in the early 1850s.

SEGNO [SEG no] (Polk) Segno was named by Henry S. Knight who moved to the area from Mississippi in the 1870s. Although Segno is a town in Liguria, northwest Italy, Knight, with his musical background, probably chose the name for the *dal segno* (D.S.), Italian "from the sign," the musical sign marking the beginning and end of a repeat. PO 28 July 1911, PM Willis Knight.

SEGOVIA [suh GO vee uh] (Kimble) Apparently named for Segovia, Spain. According to a local story George Van Buren, a relative of President Martin Van Buren, was visiting the area and suggested the name because the Texas landscape reminded him of Spain. PO 29 June 1900, PM John Charles Wesley Ingram. See Ingram.

SEGUIN [si GEEN] (Guadalupe) In August 1838 some 30 investors calling themselves the Gonzales Rangers laid out the town of Walnut Springs, named from Walnut Branch. In February 1839, probably at the suggestion of John King, the name was changed to honor Juan Nepomuceno Seguín, a military leader during the Texas War for Independence and a political leader in the early years of the Texas Republic. PO 1838 as Comanche; changed to Seguin 29 Sept 1839, PM James Campbell.

SEJITA [suh HEET uh] (Duval) Sejita is probably an Anglicized spelling of Spanish *cejita* "little eyebrow," reportedly referring to a semi-circular dam that created a watering hole for livestock. PO 25 Sept 1914, PM William Smith.

SELDEN (Erath) Named for John Selden who established a gristmill in 1855. PO 18 Feb 1886, PM Henry Mosley.

SELFS (Fannin) Adam and Mahala Self settled in the area in the late 1840s. Their son George and grandson, also named George, built a gristmill and cotton gin in the 1880s. PO 3 Aug 1887, PM William E. Whittenberg.

SELMA (Bexar) Early settlers included Martha Jane and John Sobiesky Koontz Harrison, part owners of the Harrison and McCulloch Stage Line that linked Galveston and points west from the mid-1840s. John Harrison opened the Cibolo PO 21 June 1852; changed to Selma 5 Feb 1856, likely for Selma, AL, by PM Arthur Foster. See Cibolo.

SELMAN CITY (Rusk) Oil was discovered on Silas Selman's farm in the 1930s. PO 22 Sept 1939, PM Raymond A. Crawford.

SEMINOLE (Gaines) Formerly known as Caput, Latin for "head," named from the Caput post office established by William B. Austin 19 Dec 1904. Austin renamed the office 22 Jan 1906 Seminole Wells, the fresh water sources named for the African Americans and Seminoles who scouted for the US Army in the Texas Indian Wars following the Civil War.

SERBIN [SER bin] (Lee) Founded about 1855 by Wendish (Sorbian) settlers, many from Saxony and Prussia. Pastor Johann Kilian, under whose leadership the colony was organized, was apparently the first to use the name Serbin, generally taken to mean "Sorbian lands." PO 17 Aug 1860, Fredrick A. Engelke.

SETH WARD (Hale) In 1910 the Methodist Church bought Central Plains College and Conservatory of Music. The school was renamed Seth Ward College for the first Texas Bishop of the Southern division of the Methodist Episcopal Church South. After two fires in the 1910s the college was abandoned but the community endures as a suburb of Plainview.

SETTEGAST (Harris) Brothers Julius and Joseph Settegast emigrated from Prussia in the 1850s, opened a slaughterhouse in the 1870s, and founded the community in the 1890s. Settegast was annexed by Houston in 1949.

SEVEN SISTERS (Duval) A translation of *Siete Hermanas*, the area was named for seven small nearby hills or, as some have claimed, for the seven daughters (or granddaughters) of influential landowner Rufugio Serna. The town was named for the Seven Sisters oilfield, brought in about 1935. PO 9 Sept 1936, PM Olivia Solis.

SEXTON (Sabine) Probably named for Franklin Barlow Sexton, a Sabine County landowner who served in both houses of the Texas Legislature and the Confederate House of Representatives. Sexton ended his legal career as a justice on the Texas Supreme Court in the 1890s. PO 4 Oct 1860, PM William P. Polley.

SEYMORE (Hopkins) Named for Mary and Isaac Hart Seymore from Tennessee who began farming in the area in 1847.

SEYMOUR (Baylor) Reportedly named for a ranch hand named Seymour Munday (for whom Seymour Creek may have been named). PO 14 Jan 1879 as Oregon City; changed to Seymour 1 Apr 1879, PM Ida R. Morris.

SHACKELFORD (County) Created 1858, organized 1874. Named for Jack Shackelford (1790–1857), born in Virginia. He was a physician and planter who served in the Alabama Legislature before joining the Texas Revolution in 1835 as commander of the Alabama Red Rovers. He survived the Battle of Coleto Creek and escaped the Goliad Massacre.

SHAFTER (Presidio) Sporadic silver mining had characterized the area since the 1600s, but in 1880 prospector John Spencer discovered a major site. He and William R. Shafter, a US Army officer stationed at Fort Davis, leased mining rights that resulted in the formation of the Presidio Mining company in the early 1880s. The mining town was named for Shafter when the PO was established 3 Mar 1885.

SHALLOWATER (Lubbock) Founded about 1910 with the proposed name Ripley for Edward Ripley, president of the Santa Fe Railroad. In order to avoid duplication of post offices, the name was changed to Afton and a short time later to Shallowater, presumably because the town was located in an area with a high water table that contributed to the ease of drilling wells. PO 11 Aug 1913, PM Emmett B. Porter.

SHAMROCK (Wheeler) George Washington Nickel opened the PO 6 Oct 1890, named for the luck and good fortune associated with the Shamrock. Nickel was not, as some say, from Ireland; he was born in Missouri and his parents were born in Pennsylvania. The PO was discontinued 30 May 1903 and the nearby Exum PO was changed to Shamrock 19 June 1903, PM Frank Exum.

SHANKLERVILLE (Newton) Founded by former slaves Jim and Winnie Shankle. The town was settled largely by emancipated African Americans after the Civil War. Also spelled Shankleville.

SHANNON (Clay) Earlier known as Stampede Springs, the community grew around a general store kept by Rachel and Morgan Ivie from about 1878. Reportedly named for several families who had recently emigrated from Shannon, Ireland. PO 22 Nov 1893, PM James T. Gates.

SHARP (Milam) William Franklin Sharp practiced medicine in Davilla for forty years, beginning in the late 1860s. PO 19 May 1900, PM Charles R. Campbell.

SHARYLAND (Hidalgo) John Shary, a Corpus Christi land developer who turned the area into a major citrus-producing center, founded Sharyland in the mid-1910s.

SHAVANO [SHA vuh no] (Bexar) First known as Locke Hill for the William Jackson Locke family who moved to the area from Illinois in the 1850s. By several local accounts Shavano is a phonetic spelling of Charbonneau, for a local French rancher. More likely, Shavano is a misspelling or mishearing of Shawano, a form of *Shawnee*, the name of an Algonquian people that translates as "southern." The Shawnee were resident in parts of Texas from the 1820s until about 1840 when they were forcibly removed to Indian Territory. PO 17 Mar 1869 as Locke Hill, PM Lewis M. Lacey; changed to Shavano 21 Nov 1881, PM Augustine de Zavalla. Also Shavano Park.

SHAWS BEND (Colorado) About 1840 Josiah Shaw emigrated from Kentucky and established a large plantation called Sunnyside. Shaw represented the district in the Texas Legislature in the late 1860s and early 1870s.

SHEFFIELD (Pecos) Founded by site owner William F. Sheffield, a rancher, shopkeeper, and the first PM 9 May 1898.

SHELBY (County) An original Texas county, created 1836, organized 1837. Named for Isaac Shelby (1750–1826), born in Hagerstown, MD. Shelby was a hero of the American Revolution and the War of 1812. Twice Governor of Kentucky, Shelby was a popular politician and soldier. Some two dozen US counties and towns are named in his honor.

SHELBY (Austin) In 1822 David Shelby moved from Pennsylvania to Texas and was one of the Old Three Hundred settlers of Stephen F. Austin's First Colony. About 1840 Otto von Roeder built a mill on Mill Creek and by the mid-1840s the community was known as Roedersmühle "Roeder's mill." The Post Office Department rejected this name but approved the office as Shelby for David W. Shelby, who was the first PM 1 May 1839.

SHELBYVILLE (Shelby) Settlers from Tennessee began arriving in the 1820s, giving the community its first name, Nashville. That name was changed to Shelbyville by the Texas Legislature when Shelby County was organized in 1837. PO 20 Dec 1836 as Criswell's; changed to Shelbyville Aug 1837, PM Joseph Peeve.

SHELDON (Harris) Named for Henry K. Sheldon of Brooklyn, NY, a director of the Texas & New Orleans Railroad elected in 1879. PO 20 Dec 1887, PM James M. Harrington.

SHEP (Taylor) Named for Andrew Martin Sheppard, know as Shep, a shopkeeper and the first PM 21 Nov 1903.

SHEPHERD (San Jacinto) Benjamin Armistead Shepherd laid out the community in 1875 as a station on the proposed line of the Houston East & West Texas Railway. Shepherd, founder of the First National Bank in Houston, is the namesake of the Shepherd School of Music at Rice University. PO 22 Dec 1879, PM Jack B. Noble.

SHEPTON (Collin) Shepton is a modification of Shepard, for Joseph W. Shepard who established a general store at the site in 1890. PO 27 Dec 1894, PM John L. Huffman. Shepton is now part of Plano.

SHERIDAN (Colorado) Hugh Sheridan, the site owner and namesake, sold a substantial part of his land holdings to the San Antonio Loan and Securities Company in 1908. The loan company, along with the San Antonio & Aransas Pass Railway, divided the site into building lots and small farms.

SHERMAN (County) Created 1876, organized 1889. Named for Sidney Sherman (1805–1873), born in Massachusetts. In 1835 Sherman raised a company of volunteers in Kentucky to aid in the Texas Revolution. Sherman distinguished himself at San Jacinto where he is credited with creating the battle cry "Remember the Alamo." He later served in the Republic of Texas Legislature and was instrumental in organizing several early Texas railroads.

SHERMAN (Grayson) Named in 1846 for Sidney Sherman. PO 8 Mar 1847, PM James Thompson. See Sherman County.

SHERWOOD (Irion) Reportedly named for landowner Granville Hudson Sherwood, the town of Sherwood flourished until 1910 when it was bypassed by the Kansas City, Mexico and Orient Railway in favor of Mertzon. PO 10 Aug 1881, PM William S. Kelly.

SHIELD (Coleman) Leonidas Lafayette Shield, born in Mississippi, relocated to Texas in the 1870s, was elected to the Texas House for the 1887–1889 session, and opened the Shield store in the early 1900s, from which the town took its name. PO 19 Mar 1907, PM Miles W. Vance.

SHILOH (Limestone) Shiloh is a popular place name in the US. There are about one thousand Shiloh churches—predominantly in the Southern states—and more than one hundred towns named Shiloh. Shiloh, TX, may be a transfer or may be named for the 1862 Civil War battle in Tennessee. PO 23 June 1894 as Lo, perhaps a shortening of Shiloh, PM Gideon Luther Jordan; changed to Luther 14 Oct 1897; changed to Shiloh 1 Oct 1906.

SHINER (Lavaca) Known as Halfmoon from the Halfmoon Trading Post, reportedly named for the shape of a local stand of timber, until 1887 when farmer and stockman Henry B. Shiner donated land for a station on the San Antonio & Aransas Pass Railway. PO 6 Nov 1885 as Halfmoon; changed to Shiner 31 Mar 1888, PM John M. Krueger.

SHIRO [SHEYE ro] (Grimes) Shiro was founded in January 1902 when the Trinity & Brazos Valley Railway established Shiro Station and Francis Mayfield opened the Shiro PO. Mayfield, a distributor of exotic fruit trees and shrubs, chose the name for the Shiro plum, which was novel to the US at the time, having been introduced in the late 1880s.

SHIVE [SHEYEV] (Hamilton) James Wilson Shive and his son Robert Leroy Shive relocated from North Carolina about 1855 and opened a general store. Both were PMs; Robert established the office 18 Jan 1884, followed by James 14 Apr 1886.

SHORT (Shelby) Daniel McDowell Short was a Shelbyville lawyer who participated in the War with Mexico and the Civil War and represented the district for three discontinuous terms in the Texas Legislature in the 1850s, 1860s, and 1870s. PO 4 Jan 1885, PM Frank Powell.

SHOVEL MOUNTAIN (Burnet) According to local lore the name arose when an early settler found a shovel on a nearby hilltop. PO 11 Nov 1869, PM Ottilie Giesecke.

SIDNEY (Comanche) PO 6 Jan 1886, PM John Stapp who named the office for his four-year-old son, Sidney.

SIENNA PLANTATION (Harris) In the early 1900s Lillian and Stella Scanlan, daughters of former Houston mayor Thomas Howe Scanlan, bought the Waters Plantation which they renamed for Siena, in Tuscany, Italy.

SIERRA BLANCA (Hudspeth) Sierra Blanca "white mountain," is the highest peak in the Sierra Blanca range north of the community, 6900 feet above sea level. The Southern Pacific and Texas Pacific railroads met in Sierra Blanca in December 1881, providing the second transcontinental railroad route. A silver spike marked the occasion. PO 8 June 1882, PM William J. McFee.

SILAS (Shelby) Charles Silas Baines, born in Tuscaloosa, AL, opened the PO in his general store 11 Apr 1892.

SILOAM [SEYE lom] (Bowie) Named directly or indirectly for the Biblical Siloam, the pool where Jesus made the blind man to see. Because of its Biblical associations Siloam is a popular place name; some eighty US towns are named Siloam, and about one hundred churches, mostly in Southern states. One of these is the likely source of Siloam in Bowie County. PO 20 Feb 1895, PM George Wright.

SILSBEE (Hardin) Named about 1900 for Nathaniel D. Silsbee of Boston, M.A. Silsbee and John H. Kirby, owner of the Kirby Lumber Company, were on the first board of directors of the Gulf, Beaumont & Great Northern Railroad that established a station in the 1890s. PO 6 July 1894, PM Basil M. Kimbrel. See Kirby.

SILVER CITY (Navarro) Local lore claims the name came from an incident during the Civil War when a merchant refused to recognize Confederate money as legal tender and demanded silver coins instead.

SILVERTON (Briscoe) Businessman Thomas Jefferson Braidfoot, who was instrumental in the creation of Briscoe County, founded Silverton in 1890. The name was reportedly chosen by his wife, Olivia Braidfoot, for the shimmering reflections of moonlight on the local lakes. PO 21 July 1891, PM Leonard C. Fisher.

SIMMONS (Live Oak) In the early 1900s Charles Franklin Simmons (born Calvin Franklin Simmons), using money from the sale of his father's Vegetable Liver Medicine, bought a ranch in which he laid out Simmons City in 1907. PO 13 Dec 1907, PM Dave E. Goodwin (declined); established 5 Mar 1908, PM Charles M Wedding. See Christine, see Iuka.

SIMMS (Bowie) Brothers James Harvey and Abram Lemuel Simms from Alabama established a general store in the late 1880s. PO 4 Aug 1890, PM James Simms.

SIMMS (Deaf Smith) Named from the Simms School, established in 1915 on a site donated by a local Simms family.

SIMONTON (Fort Bend) About 1840 Henry Smith Simonton and his sons Theophilus, Robert, and Henry brought their families and a hundred slaves to the area from Iredell County, NC, and established a plantation on the Brazos River. The town was named after the Civil War when the plantation was subdivided and the units sold as farms or building lots. PO 30 Mar 1894, PM Alonzo Williams.

SIMSBORO (Freestone) In the mid-1850s Sterling Sims and his three brothers brought their families from South Carolina.

SINCLAIR CITY (Smith) The first productive oil well was drilled in the area in the early 1930s and Sinclair City grew around and was named for the pumping station established by the Sinclair Oil and Refining Company.

SINTON (San Patricio) In the late 1880s a consortium of businessmen that included George W. Fulton, a partner in the Coleman-Fulton Pasture Company; John J. Welder, a founder of EWELDER; and David Odem, for whom ODEM is named, laid out the town of Sinton, named for David Sinton, a Cincinnati pig-iron industrialist who was a major stockholder in the Coleman-Fulton Pasture Company. PO 8 Dec 1888, PM Margaret E. Camp.

SIPE SPRINGS [SEEP] (Comanche) Organized in the early 1870s and named from the local sluggish springs, or sipes. Sipe was a 19th century variant pronunciation of seep. PO 4 Feb 1873 as Siep [*sic*] Springs, PM John Buckmaster; changed to Sipe Springs 9 July 1883.

SISTERDALE (Kendall) Nicolaus Zink, the surveyor of New Braunfels, founded Sisterdale in 1847 at the confluence of East and West Sister Creeks. PO 23 Oct 1851, PM Ottmar von Behr.

SIVELLS BEND [SIV ulz BEND] (Cooke) About 1860 Simon B. and William T. Sivells, born in Kentucky, moved from Kentucky Town in Grayson County and opened a general store at a bend in the Red River. PO 8 May 1872, PM William Midkiff.

SKEETERVILLE (San Saba) Roy Douglas "Dougie" Wilson coined and popularized the name in the early 1900s to let everyone know that whenever he rode through the area his horse would be "covered with skeeters."

SKELLYTOWN (Carson) Henry Schafer, the site owner, founded Skellytown about 1926; named for William Grove Skelly, founder of the Skelly Oil Company of Tulsa, OK. When the Panhandle & Santa Fe Railway established a station in 1927 the nearby towns of Roxana and Noelette merged with Skellytown. PO 18 Feb 1927, PM Inez P. Paulsen.

SKIDMORE (Bee) In the late 1850s Samuel Skidmore moved his family from Hardy County, VA (now in West Virginia), to a site on Aransas Creek. About 1886 his son, Francis (Frank) Skidmore, a rancher and real estate dealer, donated land for the town and for a station on the San Antonio & Aransas Pass Railway. The Aransas PO, established 30 Aug 1870, was changed to Skidmore 2 June 1887, PM William R. Hay.

SLATE SHOALS (Lamar) Apparently named for the slate deposits that created shallows in the local waters.

SLATON (Lubbock) William B. Story, then chief engineer for the Santa Fe Railroad system, later president of the Atchison, Topeka & Santa Fe Railway, chose the site in 1910. The station was named for landowner Oscar L. Slaton. PO 1 Nov 1910, PM George F. Higbee.

SLAYDEN (Gonzales) Slayden was founded in the late 1880s as a station on the San Antonio & Aransas Pass Railway, named for James Luther Slayden, a San Antonio merchant and politician. Slayden served in the state legislature in the mid-1890s and was a Texas Representative to the US Congress for ten terms in the late 19th and early 20th centuries. PO 12 Nov 1889, PM Nathan Brelsford.

SLIDE (Lubbock) The local story is that a survey of the site in the early 1900s showed that most dwellings were one to two miles east of their recorded locations so residents had to "slide" their homes and businesses to their proper places. PO 12 July 1904, PM James S. Slover.

SLIDELL [sleye DEL] (Wise) The area was known as Hackberry Grove until 1884 when the first businesses were established and John M. Campbell opened the Slidell post office, named for John Slidell, a New York City merchant who became a New Orleans businessman and politician. Slidell, a US Congressman and Senator from Louisiana in the 1840s and 1850s, was a strong supporter of Southern and states' rights. He was later the Confederate ambassador to France. The city of Slidell in St. Tammany Parish, LA, was named for John Slidell in 1882.

SLIGO (Yoakum) Pat McHugh founded Sligo, named for his former home, Sligo, Connacht, Ireland, in the early 1900s. PO 31 August 1903, PM Kate McHugh, Pat's sister.

SLOCUM (Anderson) According to local lore the name was created about 1898 by Edgar Threadgill McDaniel, who predicted "Fortunes will be made here, but they will be slow in coming." By popular etymology "slow in coming" became "slowcome" became Slocum. There were, however, several Slocum families in the area at the time. PO 4 Jan 1898, PM Edmond T. McDaniel.

SMELTERTOWN (El Paso) Created in 1887 as a company town for employees of the Kansas City Consolidated Smelting and Refining Company that established a smelter to process the local copper and lead ore. PO 25 Mar 1939, PM Royal G. Martin.

SMETANA [SMET nuh] (Brazos) The area west of Bryan was settled by Bohemian families in the early 1880s. Smetana (Czech "sweet cream") may have been named for a Smetana family or in honor of Czech composer Bedrich Smetana who died in 1884. PO 25 Apr 1896, PM Jacob Sramek.

SMILEY (Gonzales) James W. Smiley, reportedly a sheepherder, settled on what became known as Smiley's Lake in the 1850s. PO 29 Oct 1884, PM Duncan Livingston.

SMITH (County) Created and organized 1846. Named for James Smith (1792–1855), a native of Spartanburg, SC. Smith fought at the battle of New Orleans and served with Sam Houston in the Tennessee militia. Smith is often credited with suggesting and promoting the use of the five-point star now identified with Texas.

SMITHFIELD (Tarrant) When the St. Louis Southwestern Railway (Cotton Belt) laid tracks south of Zion in 1887 the station was named for Eli Smith who donated land for a church in Zion. PO 21 Feb 1878, PM John G. Walker. North Richland Hills annexed Smithfield in 1958.

SMITHLAND (Marion) A number of Smiths (several of whom were named Francis or Frank) were in the area by the early 1840s. Credit for founding and naming the community has been given to Francis (Frank) P. Smith who settled in the late 1830s, and John Frank Smith (apparently a son of Francis P.). PO 13 Nov 1850, PM Hezekiah Horner.

SMITHSON VALLEY (Comal) Named for Benjamin and Augusta Smithson who began farming in the area in the mid-1850s. PO 17 Feb 1857, PM Benjamin Smithson.

SMITHVILLE (Bastrop) A nameless community had existed from about 1830. In the mid-1870s Franklin Smith and his business partner, Murray Burleson, decided to formally lay out the town and apply for a post office. Smith, having won a coin toss to choose the town's name, became the namesake. PO 23 Aug 1876, PM John P. Jones.

SMITHWICK (Burnet) Noah Smithwick established Smithwick Mills in the 1850s. Smithwick, a pioneer blacksmith, gunsmith, soldier, and miller, was the author of *The Evolution of a State*, an early history of Texas published in 1900. PO 21 Aug 1871 as Smithwick Mills, PM Thomas Stinnett; changed to Smithwick 9 Feb 1882.

SMYER [SMEYE er] (Hockley) In 1925 the Santa Fe Railroad established a station named for Clinton E. Smyer, a Santa Fe division superintendent. PO 28 May 1926, PM Eunice McCullough.

SMYRNA (Cass) Smyrna was named about 1880, probably by Elder Nelson Porterfield, minister of the Baptist Church of Christ, for a Smyrna church in Alabama or Georgia. Smyrna is a Biblical name, mentioned by John in the Book of Revelation. There are about 150 churches in the US named Smyrna, as well as several dozen places concentrated in the Southern states.

SNAP (Panola) Named for Fred William Cariker, known as "Snap," a physician from Georgia who established a medical practice in the 1890s. PO 11 Oct 1899, PM Charles W. Thomas.

SNEEDVILLE (Cottle) Likely named for Joseph Sneed, a pioneer Methodist circuit rider from the 1840s who was instrumental in establishing Methodism in Texas. PO 19 Dec 1912, PM Jesse Swagerty.

SNIPE (Brazoria) The name was chosen in 1921 when Robert Weems established the Snipe PO. According to local lore Weems chose the name because his father's hunting partners were fond of a practical joke played on young hunters where a neophyte would be taken into the woods on a "snipe hunt." The innocent was told to make bird calls until a snipe jumped into his sack. The jokers would then leave the woods and bet on how long it would be until the victim realized he had been tricked.

SNOOK (Burleson) Robert E. Hoskins opened the PO 20 Feb 1895, named for John S. Snook, PM of the Caldwell PO.

SNYDER (Hale) Founded by Peter Snyder who settled several Mennonite families from the Upper Midwest in 1907.

SNYDER (Scurry) Adventurer and soldier William H. Snyder left Pennsylvania in the 1850s, wandered through the West, fought for the North in the Civil War, and opened a trading post on Deep Creek in 1878. In its early years Snyder went by several informal names, including "Hide Town" for the buffalo hide shanties that housed prospectors and early settlers, and "Robber's Roost" for its citizens of less than acceptable behavior. PO 21 Nov 1883, PM Houston B. Patterson.

SOCORRO [suh KOR uh] (El Paso) Founded by Spaniards and Piro Indians fleeing the pueblo at present-day Socorro, NM, during the 1680 Pueblo Revolt. The pueblo was named *Socorro* "help, aid" in 1598 by Don Juan de Oñate in recognition of the food and water the Piro had given the exhausted Spanish expedition. PO 20 Sept 1869, PM Juan Armendaris.

SODVILLE (San Patricio) The Paul Land Company founded Sodville about 1905 by dividing ranchland into small farms. The source of the name is uncertain but may be related to "sodbusters," a derogatory term for farmers who plowed the grazing lands.

SOLINO (Hidalgo) The local story is that a monolingual sign painter working for the Texas & New Orleans Railroad misheard Salina (Spanish "salt mine"), the intended name for the salt works, and wrote Solino. PO 14 Dec 1932, Estella P. Lane.

SOLMS (Comal) Named about 1880 for Prince Carl of Solms-Braunfels who was instrumental in establishing German settlements in Texas. PO 27 Aug 1894, PM Friedrich E. Hoffmann. See New Braunfels.

SOMERSET (Bexar) Old Somerset was founded in 1848 several miles south of the present town and named by settlers from Somerset, Pulaski County, KY. Most of the homes and businesses of Old Somerset and many of those in neighboring Bexar were moved to trackside when the San Antonio Southern (Artesian Belt) Railroad established a station at the present site about 1910. PO 12 Aug 1920, PM Walter Kurz.

SOMERVELL (County) Created and organized as Somerville 1875 (the spelling was changed the following year). Named for Alexander Somervell (1796–1854), born in Prince George's County, MD. Somervell came to Texas in 1833, enlisted in the Texas Army, took part in the Battle of San Jacinto, was David G. Burnet's Secretary of War, and served in the first two congresses of the Republic of Texas. At the request of Sam Houston, Somervell organized and led the Somervell Expedition, a punitive strike against Mexico in 1842.

SOMERVILLE (Burleson) Named in 1873 for Albert Somerville, first president of the Gulf, Colorado & Santa Fe Railway. PO 28 Apr 1894, PM Laura Seal.

SOMMERS MILL (Bell) Founded by DeWitt Clinton Summers who established Summer's Mills, a gristmill complex, about 1880. PO 21 Dec 1881, PM DeWitt C. Summers. The reason for the change in spelling is unknown.

SONOMA [suh NOM uh] (Ellis) By a local account an early settler saw ice glistening on tree branches in the moonlight and was reminded of *sonoma*, an "Indian" word meaning "valley of the moon." Rather, Sonoma is most likely a transfer, probably from Sonoma, CA, possibly from Sonoma, AL. Sonoma, TX, is now part of Ennis.

SONORA [suh NOR uh] (Sutton) Spanish "sonorous." Merchant and cattleman Charles G. Adams chose the name about 1887 in recognition of Sonora, Mexico, reportedly the home of one of his domestic employees. PO 19 Sept 1889, PM Robert Wiley Callahan.

SORRELLE [suh REL] (Wharton) Richard Henry Douglass Sorrel established the Sorrel Plantation in the 1850s. PO 7 Apr 1894 as Sorella, PM Zenos Smith.

SOUR LAKE (Hardin) Water from the local springs was at first thought to be undrinkable because of its mineral content but was later promoted for its medicinal value and became a major export in the 1860s. PO 7 Nov 1866, PM Charles S. Beach. See Saratoga.

SOUTH BEND (Young) Apparently named for a bend of the Clear Fork of the Brazos River between Graham and Eliasville. Formerly known as Arkansas, the name was formalized as South Bend when John Kirby established the PO 7 May 1878.

SOUTH PADRE ISLAND (Cameron) Known from the early 16th century as *Isla Blanca* "white island" and later as *Isla del Padre Ballí*, for Padre José Nicolás

Ballí, a Catholic priest of the late 18th and early 19th centuries who established a mission on the southern part of the island about 1805.

SOUTHLAND (Garza) Founded in the early 20th century by rancher, businessman, and banker Andrew Briggs Robertson on the southern part of the V ranch; thus, the name. PO 14 June 1905 as Bresford, named for Bresford, England, by PM Job Davies; changed to Southland 15 July 1910.

SOUTHMAYD [SAUTH MAYD] (Grayson) Founded in the late 1870s when the Texas & Pacific Railway laid tracks on property originally granted to Daniel Starr Southmayd, a Presbyterian minister and South Texas missionary of the 1830s. PO 6 Dec 1881, PM John A. Bohrer.

SOWERS (Dallas) Edmund and Freelove Sowers moved to the area from Pulaski County, IL, and began farming in 1856. PO 14 June 1881, PM Edmund Sowers.

SPADE (Mitchell) In 1880 Judson Warner and John Evans began operations on what became known as the Spade Ranch, named for the brand that resembled a shovel, registered in 1889. The community of Spade developed in the 1890s and took the name of the ranch 6 July 1909 when the Herbert PO was renamed Spade by PM Robert H. Crump. Spade in Lamb County was founded in the late 1920s, also on the Spade Ranch.

SPANISH FORT (Montague) The site was originally a fortified Taovaya Indian town known as San Teodoro by Spanish militia and traders from the 1770s. The Taovaya left the area and their town fell into ruins that were misidentified by American visitors as those of a Spanish presidio, thus the name. PO 16 Jan 1877, PM Lewis Cass McNatt.

SPARENBERG (Dawson) William H. Gartin opened the PO 20 May 1903, named for George Sparenberg, the PM at Big Spring in Howard County, in appreciation for his help in establishing the PO.

SPARKS (Bell) Sam Sparks was Bell County sheriff in the late 19th century; he was succeeded by his son, also Sam Sparks. PO 15 Sept 1897, PM George Hagler.

SPEAKS (Lavaca) The community of Bearden, settled in the early 1850s, became known as Speaksville when Thomas Speake, Sr. opened a general store in the early 1860s. The Bearden PO, opened 4 Aug 1851, was changed to Speakeville 9 July 1866 when Thomas Speake became PM. In the late 1870s and early 1880s, the office operated as Boxville, named for Speake's wife, Priscilla Box Speakes.

SPEARMAN (Hansford) Thomas C. Spearman was vice president of the North Texas & Santa Fe Railway that built through the area in 1917. PO 17 May 1917, PM Hattie Maize.

SPEEGLEVILLE (McLennan) Israel Washington Speegle moved to the area from Missouri and opened a blacksmith shop in 1848. He opened the PO 27 May 1879.

SPLENDORA [splen DOR uh] (Montgomery) Splendora was founded in the mid-1890s as Cox's Switch, named for Charles Cox who was instrumental in attracting the Houston, East & West Texas Railway in the 1890s. Cox's Switch was renamed when Milton Z. King established the Splendora post office in May 1896. King is credited with recognizing the community "for the splendor of its floral environment."

SPRABERRY (Midland) Named from the Spraberry Oil Fields developed in the 1940s by the Seaboard Oil Company on Abner Spraberry's ranch in Dawson County.

SPRING HILL (Navarro) Named for the local springs and Hill's Trading Post, established shortly before 1840 by Dr. George Washington Hill. Hill was a Texas Army surgeon with an illustrious career in the Texas Revolution and the Republic of Texas and PM for the first Spring Hill PO 5 Nov 1849. Hill County was named in Hill's honor in 1853. See Hill County.

SPUR (Dickens) In the early 20th century the Espuela Land and Cattle Company, named from Spanish *Espuela* "spur," one of its several brands, sold the Spur Ranch to a syndicate that named Charles Adam Jones ranch manager. Jones laid out the community of Spur in 1909 on the line of the Stamford & Northwestern Railroad. PO 15 Sept 1909, PM Norton A. Baker.

SQUAW MOUNTAIN (Jack) According to a local legend the mountain northeast of the community was the site of a battle between Native Americans and Texas Rangers about 1875. An Indian woman was killed in the fighting and was buried where she fell. PO 30 Dec 1892 as Squaw, PM David Connor.

ST. HEDWIG (Bexar) Named in the 1850s for Saint Hedwig, the 13th century patron saint of Silesia. The Cottage Hill PO was changed to Saint Hedwig 18 June 1877, PM Frank Felix.

ST. JO (Montague) In 1872 local shopkeepers Irby Boggess and Joseph Howell laid out the community that Boggess named for Howell, adding "Saint" for reasons known only to him. The PO 30 Oct 1860 as Head of Elm; renamed Saint Jo 7 Aug 1873, PM Irby Boggess.

ST. JOHN (Fayette) Named from the St. John Catholic Church dedicated on 24 June 1894, the nativity of St. John the Baptist.

ST. PAUL (San Patricio) Master real estate promoter, George H. Paul, bought and sold several hundred thousand acres of former ranchland in the early 20th century. He laid out the community early in 1910. Apparently George Paul was known as "Saint Paul." PO 3 Dec 1910, PM Elard R. Howard.

STACY (McCulloch) Brothers Morgan J. and William T. Stacy kept a general store from about 1890. The town was known informally as Brown Town for Julia and Susan Brown, widows of settlers who had moved into the area in the 1870s. PO 13 Sept 1897, PM William T. Stacy.

STAFFORD (Fort Bend) William Stafford, one of Stephen F. Austin's Old Three Hundred settlers, operated a flour mill and cotton gin as early as 1830. The town was formally named in 1853 when the Buffalo Bayou, Brazos & Colorado Railway established Stafford Station. PO 16 Mar 1854 as

Stafford's Point, changed to Stafford 26 Feb 1869, PM Lorohama Gossett.

STAIRTOWN (Caldwell) Oscar Stair, the site owner and proprietor of the general store, founded the community in the 1920s to accommodate oilfield employees.

STALEY (San Jacinto) Named for John C. Staley who opened the PO in his general store 13 Aug 1913.

STAMFORD (Haskell, Jones) About 1899 Henry King McHarg, president of the Texas Central Railway, named Stamford in honor of his adopted hometown, Stamford, CT. PO 2 Dec 1899, PM Nathan Leavitt.

STAMPEDE (Bell) Named about 1880 from Stampede Creek. There are a number of local stories that attempt to explain the name. By one, a herd of steers was spooked by a thunderstorm on a cattle drive; by another, in the 1830s a party of Texas Rangers surprised a group of Indians butchering buffalo and killed them all, causing the Indian ponies to stampede. PO 29 Sept 1893, PM Silas J. Clark.

STAMPS (Upshur) Founded and named by William O. Stamps who established a sawmill and syrup mill in the early 1900s.

STANDART (Kinney) Named for businessman Charles Walbor Standart in recognition of his contributions to the schools of Kinney County in the late 19th century. PO as Amanda 13 Mar 1888; changed to Standart 23 Oct 1890, PM Julius L. Stambaugh. See Amanda.

STANFIELD (Clay) Named from the Stanfield Brothers Ranch operated by William and Leander Stanfield from about 1870. PO 26 June 1903, PM Mariana Mayes.

STANTON (Martin) In the early 1880s the community was named *Marienfeld* (German "Mary's field") at the suggestion of Father Anastasius Peters, a Carmelite priest. The Marienfield PO, opened 28 Dec 1882 by PM John Konz, was changed to Stanton 1 Jan 1890. The reasons for the change and identity of the namesake are uncertain. The generally accepted account is that the town was named for Edwin McMasters Stanton. However, it would be highly unusual for a Southern community to be named for President Abraham Lincoln's Secretary of War, especially one who was a harsh critic of what he saw as the North's "lenient" treatment of the South during Reconstruction. More likely the name was proposed by settlers from an existing Stanton and one not named for Edwin Stanton. Likely candidates are Stanton, AL, named for railroad official Myron Stanton and Stanton, KY, named for Congressman Richard Stanton.

STAPLES (Guadalupe) John Douglas Staples, born in Tennessee, began farming in the area in the 1850s and later kept a general store. PO 19 May 1879 as Staples Store, PM Edward P. Waller; changed to Staples 20 Mar 1891.

STAR (Mills) Named about 1885 from Star Mountain, itself named by shopkeeper Alec Street who claimed the mountain was shaped like a star. PO 5 Aug 1884, PM William E. Reid.

STARR (County) Created and organized 1848. Named for James Harper Starr (1809–1890), born in Connecticut. Starr settled in Nacogdoches in 1837. He was a physician, banker, treasurer of the Republic of Texas, and president of the board of land commissioners, appointed by President Sam Houston.

STARRVILLE (Smith) Methodist minister Joshua Starr bought the site in 1852 and established Starrville, with deed restrictions prohibiting liquor and gambling. Starrville flourished until the late 1870s when the Tyler Tap Railroad established a station at Winona. PO 15 Feb 1849 as Gum Spring, PM Rice Wells; changed to Starrville 16 June 1857, PM Edward P. Wells.

STARTZVILLE (Comal) Named for one or more descendants of Johann Starz (Startz) who emigrated from Germany in 1844 and was instrumental in the founding of New Braunfels.

STEPHENS (County) Created June 1858 as Buchanan, named for sitting US President James Buchanan; renamed in December 1861 for Alexander H. Stephens, the only Vice President of the Confederate States of America.

STEPHENS CREEK (San Jacinto) Named from the stream that flowed on the land granted to Miles G. Stephen(s) in the mid-1830s.

STEPHENVILLE [STEV uhn vil] (Erath) John M. Stephen donated land for the seat of Erath County in 1856. Stephen opened the post office 28 July 1857 in the store he kept jointly with his brother William. The townsite was surveyed by George B. Erath for whom the county was named.

STERLEY (Floyd) William F. Sterley was passenger agent when the Fort Worth & Denver City Railway was built through the area in the late 1920s. PO 23 Jan 1929, PM Luther W. Gregg.

STERLING (County) Created and organized 1891. Named for W. S. Sterling (a somewhat mythical character of vague background and known by initials only). Sterling was a noted buffalo hunter and Indian fighter who was in Texas by the 1850s. Later, according to local reports, he was a US Marshal in Arizona and was killed in a fight with Apaches.

STERLING CITY (Sterling) Robert C. Stewart donated land for Sterling City, named for Sterling County. Many of the businesses and residents of nearby Cummings were moved to the new site when Sterling City was designated the county seat in 1891. PO 4 Nov 1885 as Montvale; changed to Sterling City 12 Oct 1891, PM George D. Hines.

STERRETT [STEHR it] (Ellis) When the Missouri–Kansas–Texas Railroad built through the area in 1889 the town was platted and named for pioneer settler James Sterrett. PO 8 Apr 1890, PM Isaac C. Culbertson.

STEVENS (Sherman) About 1900 the Chicago, Rock Island & Gulf Railway established Stevens Switch, reportedly named for Steve Stevens, said to be a conductor on the CRI&G. PO 11 Apr 1929, PM Josie F. Compton.

STEWARDS MILL (Freestone) George Washington Steward built a gristmill on Grindstone Creek about 1852. Steward later donated land for a church and cemetery. His son,

Jeremiah Terry Steward, established the PO 26 Nov 1872.

STILES (Reagan) William Gordon Stiles opened the PO 17 Apr 1894. He would later be president of the First National Bank of Wheeler and a director of the First State Bank of Mobeetie.

STINNETT (Hutchinson) Merchant Albert Sidney Stinnett of Amarillo, a leading booster and promoter of Amarillo and the Texas Panhandle in the 1920s, platted the town of Stinnett in 1925, the seat of Hutchinson County from 1926. PO 13 Oct 1926, PM Preston Walker.

STOCKDALE (Wilson) Founded in 1863; named for Fletcher Summerfield Stockdale, Lieutenant Governor of Texas (1864–1865) and interim governor in 1865. PO 12 Oct 1871, PM Jethro Bunker.

STOCKMAN (Shelby) Peter Stockman, born in Alabama, began farming in the area in the 1840s. He was followed by his son, also Peter Stockman, and grandson, Hiram Stockman, who founded the community in the 1890s. PO 9 Sept 1899, PM William Wallace.

STONEBURG (Montague) Stoneburg was organized in 1893 with the arrival of the Chicago, Rock Island & Texas Railway. Named for rancher James M. Stone who donated land for the townsite. PO 19 Jan 1893 as Riley, PM William Williams; changed to Stoneburg 11 May 1893.

STONEHAM [STON uhm] (Grimes) John H. Stoneham, born in Alabama, settled in the area in the 1840s and donated land for the right of way of the Central & Montgomery Railway in 1879. PO 4 Nov 1885, PM John Oscar Stoneham.

STONEWALL (County) Created 1876, organized 1888. Named for Confederate General Thomas Jonathan "Stonewall" Jackson.

STONEWALL (Gillespie) Founded in 1870 by Israel Moses Nunez who donated land for the first school. Nunez, a Civil War veteran known as Major, chose the name for Confederate General and Civil War hero Stonewall Jackson. PO 5 Mar 1875, PM James White.

STOUT (Wood) Henry Stout, from Tennessee by way of Illinois and Arkansas, fought in the Texas Revolution, was instrumental in the organization of Wood County, was an early county sheriff, and served in the Texas State Legislature in the 1850s. PO 2 Apr 1884, PM William L. Richards.

STOWELL [STOWL] (Chambers) Founded in the 1890s with construction of the Gulf & Interstate Railway. Named for H. C. Stowell, a railroad engineer and associate of Fox Winnie, the namesake of WINNIE. PO 22 Jan 1900, PM Wesley Hunefelt.

STRAIN (Hardin) Strain was founded about 1908 with construction of the Beaumont, Sour Lake & Western Railway. Named for Cyrus W. Strain, agent for several railroads in the Missouri Pacific system, including the BSL&W.

STRANGER (Falls) The local story is that a representative of the Post Office Department, while passing through, asked the village blacksmith the name of the town and the blacksmith, in poor English, replied that he was a stranger. The representative, sure of only one word, wrote "Stranger" on the application. PO 24 Nov 1879, PM Harris Kay.

STRATFORD (Sherman) Stratford was laid out in the mid-1880s by Walter Colton, a Civil War veteran, who likely chose the name for Stratford Hall, Westmoreland County, VA, the plantation home of the Lee family and the birthplace of Robert E. Lee, whom Colton greatly admired. PO 27 May 1901, PM Edwin Parks.

STRATTON (DeWitt) Named for John Stratton of Cuero. A newspaper ad from 1880 described Stratton as "a saddler and harness maker and dealer in buggies, hacks and spring and platform wagons." PO 16 Nov 1887, PM Charles Middlebrook.

STRAWN (Palo Pinto) In 1880 Stephen Bethel Strawn, a partner with James Nesbit Stuart in the Strawn and Stuart Ranch, donated land for the Texas & Pacific Railway station. PO 11 Aug 1880 as Everton; changed to Strawn 13 Sept 1880, PM Harvey E. Johnson.

STREETER (Mason) Settled in the 1850s. Known as Honey Creek and Bluff Creek until 5 Dec 1890 when Joseph A. Black established the Streeter post office, reportedly named for Samuel T. Streeter, an early settler.

STREETMAN (Navarro, Freestone) Streetman, founded in 1905 with construction of the Trinity & Brazos Valley Railway, was named for Samuel Streetman, at the time a prominent Houston lawyer who was later instrumental in establishing what is now the South Texas College of Law. PO 21 Nov 1883 as Cade (Navarro County), named for Cade Hayes; changed to Streetman (Freestone County) 9 Apr 1907, PM Joseph J. Hood.

STRINGTOWN (Newton) According to local lore, the town was named from the remarks of itinerant salespeople and travelers who noticed that houses were "strung out" along the road. PO 15 Mar 1880 as Rainbow, PM William Martin Clark.

STUBBLEFIELD (Houston) Named about 1890 for farmer Wyatt Stubblefield who donated land for the first school.

STYX [STEYEKS] (Kaufman) According to Fred Tarpley, Styx was named by a Dr. Gordon for the river Styx that in Greek mythology forms the boundary between Earth and Hades. However, the pronunciation suggests that Styx is an intentional or inadvertent misrecording of the family name Stykes. There were several Stykes families in Kaufman County when the town was named and at one time there was a Stykes street in the city of Kaufman. PO 18 Jan 1899, PM William C. Flint.

SUBLIME (Lavaca) As the name of a populated place, Sublime is unique to Texas and the origin of this intriguing name is unknown. The town grew around a store opened by Dietrich Strunk about 1855. Either Strunk or Robert Miller, who donated land for the townsite, likely chose the name to attract settlers. After all, who wouldn't want to live in Sublime, Texas? PO 14 June 1875, PM Dietrich Strunk.

SUDAN [SOO dan] (Lamb) Founded in the early 1910s by the Furneaux brothers, Joseph, John, and William, Dallas-based ranchers. Peter Boesen, who opened the PO 14 June 1917, named the office for Sudan grass, a drought resistant forage crop of the sorghum family that was brought to the US from Khartoum, Sudan, Africa in 1909.

SUGAR LAND (Fort Bend) In 1828 Stephen F. Austin granted Oakland Plantation to his personal secretary, Samuel Williams, who sold the site to his brothers Nathaniel and Matthew who planted sugarcane and established a raw sugar mill, giving rise to the name Sugar Land, which became official 16 Dec 1858 when the Hodge's Bend PO was changed to Sugar Land by PO John Crump.

SULLIVAN CITY (Hidalgo) Founded in the late 1820s on the Ed W. Sullivan Ranch as a loading station on the Missouri Pacific Railroad. PO 8 Mar 1935, PM Olivia Diaz Villegas.

SULPHUR SPRINGS (Hopkins) From the 1870s the local mineral springs were advertised as health enhancements and the area was promoted as a resort and spa. PO 17 May 1854 as Bright Star; changed to Sulphur Springs 1 Mar 1871, PM Daniel Gunn.

SUMMERFIELD (Castro) When the Pecos & Northern Texas Railway built through the area in the late 1890s Summerfield was founded as Boom, so named, according to one writer, because it was a boomtown. The name was changed in 1907 for John S. Summerfield, a Sherman surveyor who had participated in determining the boundaries of the XIT Ranch in the 1880s. PO 12 Feb 1903 as Boom; changed to Summerfield 27 Nov 1907, PM Gilbert J. Ness.

SUMNER (Lamar) Moses and Lucinda Sumner began farming in the area in the 1850s. PO 6 Nov 1885, PM James Cox.

SUNDOWN (Hockley) According to an oft-repeated popular etymology a group of ranchers discussed and debated the choice of a name for hours until one said, "It's sundown; let's go home." Rather, Robert Slaughter chose the name from the movie *Sundown*, part of which was filmed on his ranch in Sonora, Mexico, in the late 1920s. PO 29 Mar 1938, PM Walter E. Miller.

SUNNYSIDE (Castro) Named from the Sunnyside School, itself named with the 1912 merger of the Axtell and Roush schools. Jeff Gilbreath reportedly proposed the name for a Sunnyside in Tennessee. According to local promotions, Sunnyside aptly describes the character of the community.

SUNRAY (Moore) Rancher and financier Jack Clarence Collins founded the town as Altman in 1929, named for a relative, Annie Margaret Altman. The name was changed when the Sunray Oil Company (later Sunoco) established a gas and oil refinery in the early 1930s. The Altman PO, opened 11 July 1930, was changed to Sunray 15 Mar 1931, PM Oscar T. Griffith.

SUTHERLAND SPRINGS (Wilson) In 1850 John Sutherland, a physician specializing in herbal medicine, established a laying-in facility where he treated a variety of maladies, especially cholera. He later added a school and a church to his medical complex. PO 27 Jan 1851, PM John Sutherland.

SUTTON (County) Created 1887, organized 1890. Named for John Schuyler Sutton (c. 1822–1862), born in New York. Sutton moved to Texas in 1836 and was associated with the Texas military most of his adult life. He was part of the Texan Santa Fe Expedition, participated in the Mexican War, commanded a company of Texan Rangers, was an officer in the Seventh Texas Cavalry during the Civil War, and was mortally wounded at the battle of Valverde, NM, in February 1862.

SWAN (Smith) The area was known as Hopewell from at least 1887. The name was changed about 1890 for William D. Swann [*sic*], who would represent the district in the Texas Legislature in the early 1900s and again in the 1920s. PO 7 Feb 1884 as Swann, PM William N. Shamburger; discontinued 4 Nov 1885; reopened as Hopewell 8 Apr 1887; changed to Swan 20 Mar 1891, PM Frank Nelson.

SWEARINGEN (Cottle) Ohio-born rancher Doss D. Swearingen bought the site on the OX Ranch in 1894. PO 2 Nov 1898, PM Eliza Dulaney.

SWEENY (Brazoria) Named from the sugar plantation established on the San Barnard River by John Sweeny (father), who brought his family and more than two hundred slaves from Tennessee in the early 1830s. PO 25 Nov 1895, PM John Sweeny (son).

SWEET HOME (Lavaca) Sweet Home developed around a store and hotel operated by George West, for whom George West, the seat of Live Oak County, is named. The local story is that the name was appropriate because "early residents felt they had found ideal conditions for home life." PO 14 July 1852, PM Alfred Patton. See George West.

SWEETWATER (Nolan) Sweetwater, founded shortly after Nolan County was created in 1876, took its name from Sweetwater Creek, earlier known as Blue Goose Creek. Sweetwater is reportedly a translation of MOBEETIE. PO 27 Mar 1879 as Sweet Water, PM L. B. Perry.

SWENSON (Stonewall) In 1908, on news that the Stamford & Northwestern Railroad would be extending a line through the area, Thomas C. Hoy laid out the community named for Swante Magnus Swenson, founder of the SMS Ranch and considered the first Swedish immigrant to Texas, arriving in 1838, and his cousin's sons, Eric Pierson and Swen Albin Swenson, New York financiers and officers of the S&N. PO 20 July 1910, PM Warren A. Huntsman.

SWIFT (Nacogdoches) Named for one or more Swift families who had established farms in the area by 1850. PO 7 Sept 1883, PM William H. Swift.

SWISHER (County) Created 1876, organized 1890. Named for James Gibson Swisher (1794–1862), born in Tennessee. Swisher was a prominent figure in the Texas Revolution and the early years of the Texas

Republic. He settled in Texas in 1833, was a member of the Convention of 1836 and signatory to the Texas Declaration of Independence and the Constitution of the Republic of Texas. After Texas independence, Swisher became an Austin hotelier and tavern keeper. Swisher Street north of the LBJ Presidential Library in Austin is named in his honor.

SYCAMORE (Wise) Reportedly named for the sycamore trees that were once abundant in the area. PO 17 Aug 1894, PM Davis S. Cox.

SYLVESTER (Fisher) The Compere Brothers real estate firm of Abilene founded Sylvester in 1903 on news that the Kansas City, Mexico & Orient Railway would be building through the area. The community was laid out on the AJ Ranch and named for William W. Sylvester, vice president of the KCM&O. PO 2 May 1903, PM James W. Tune.

T

TABOR [TAY ber] (Brazos) Named from one or more Tabor families who had settled in the area by the 1880s, including John and Martha Jane Tabor from Alabama. PO 24 May 1888, PM Millard F. Jackson.

TACUBAYA [ta koo BAH yuh] (Brooks) Named from the Tacubaya section of Mexico City, probably by Eligio Garcia who established the Tacubaya Ranch in the 1870s. From Nahuatl (Aztec), reportedly meaning "where water is collected."

TADMOR (Houston) Probably named from the nearby Tadmor church, itself ultimately named for the Biblical Tadmor (modern Palmyra), the city built by Solomon. PO 6 Feb 1885, PM Richard Harvin.

TAFT (San Patricio) Founded in 1900 by Joseph French Green who was appointed manager of the Coleman-Fulton Pasture Company by David Sinton for whom Sinton, the San Patricio county seat, is named. Green chose the name for Charles P. Taft of Cincinnati, OH, Sinton's son-in-law and the half-brother of future US President William Howard Taft. PO 5 May 1904, PM Imogene Warburton. See Sinton.

TAHOKA [tuh HO kuh] (Lynn) Founded in 1903 as the seat of Lynn County by the Tahoka Townsite Company, organized by Benjamin Sweet, Jack Alley, and William Petty (the namesake of PETTY). The town was named from Tahoka Lake, several miles northeast of the community. Several writers suggest the name is from Spanish *ojo tejas* "eye of Texas," an interpretative name for Tahoka Springs; others say the source is Choctaw *taha oka* "the water is all gone"; and still others claim that Tahoka is from a Comanche word having to do with "one's enemies." If the source is Comanche it may refer to "clear water." PO 30 Apr 1903, PM Fannie N. Henderson.

TALCO (Titus) The oft-repeated story is that a shopkeeper named Brown took the name from a box of sweets produced by the *T*exas, *A*rkansas and *L*ouisiana Candy *Co*mpany. However, efforts to verify the company's existence have been unproductive. PO 12 Jan 1856 as Gouldsboro, PM Nehemiah C. Gould; changed to Talco 4 Aug 1910, PM Quinton S. Loveless.

TALPA [TAL puh] (Coleman) Talpa has been claimed to be a shortening of catalpa, a local tree also known as Indian Cigar, and a shortening of talpatate, the crusty Texas soil, but more likely Talpa is a transfer from Talpa, Jalisco, Mexico, named from Nahuatl (Aztec) "on the land." Any relationship between the name Talpa and that of Talpacata Creek in Bee County is unknown. The town of Talpa grew around the Gulf, Colorado & Santa Fe Railway station, established in 1892. PO 13 June 1883 as Vale; changed to Talpa 28 Jan 1887, PM R. Henry Henderson.

TALTY (Kaufman) Michael Francis Talty emigrated from County Clare, Ireland, and settled in the area known as Irish Ridge in 1895. Peter Elder opened the PO in Talty's general store 11 Oct 1899.

TAMINA [TAM uh nee] (Montgomery) Tamina grew around a Houston & Great Northern Railroad station established in the early

1870s. James H. Berry, a Houston civil engineer and town promoter, apparently chose the name for Tammany Hall, headquarters of the Tammany Society, a New York City benevolent and political organization whose name had become associated with corruption and cronyism. The name on the post office application was either misspelled or misread and the office was approved as Tamina. PO 17 July 1897, PM John D. Moore.

TANGLEWOOD (Lee) Sisters Bettie and Frances Williams were apparently reading Nathaniel Hawthorne's *Tanglewood Tales*, a book retelling Greek myths for children, and decided that Tanglewood would be a good name had for their growing community. The west Houston neighborhood of Tanglewood is reportedly named for Hawthorne's book as well. PO 12 Apr 1880, PM Robert Griffith.

TANKERSLEY (Tom Green) Richard Franklin and Annie Ellen Allen Tankersley moved to Texas from Mississippi in 1853. Richard Tankersley donated land for the townsite and Annie Tankersley established the Concho House, the first hotel in San Angelo, in the late 1870s. PO 6 Apr 1910 as McGrath; changed to Tankersley 23 July 1910, PM Theodore D. Boyd.

TARKINGTON PRAIRIE (Liberty) Burton Benton and Sarah Berry Tarkington came to the area from Indiana about 1840. Tarkington Prairie and Tarkington Bayou are named for the family. PO 11 Aug 1853, PM Andrew Isaacks.

TARPLEY (Bandera) Postmaster Wiley J. Prickett changed the Hondo Canyon (*Cañon*) PO to Tarpley, 31 Jan 1899, named for his stepson, William Tarpley Prickett, and other Tarpley relatives.

TARRANT (County) Created 1849, organized 1850. Named for Edward H. Tarrant (1796–1858), born in South Carolina. Tarrant moved to Texas from Tennessee in the mid-1830s but apparently did not take part in the Texas Revolution. He resigned his seat in the Republic of Texas Congress in 1837 to become an Indian fighter and is best known for the attacks he led on Caddo and Cherokee camp sites on Village Creek in present Tarrant County in the summer of 1841.

TARZAN (Martin) Named in 1927 for the series of Tarzan books written by Edgar Rice Burroughs. At that time the series was approaching a dozen volumes and was at the height of its popularity. Tarzana, the estate (now city) in southern California that Burroughs bought and named in 1917, may have influenced the choice of the Texas name. PO 31 Mar 1927, PM Tant Lindsay.

TASCOSA [tas KO suh] (Oldham) When an Atascosa post office was denied early in 1878 the application was resubmitted without the initial A. PO 24 June 1878, PM George Julius Howard. See Atascosa.

TATE SPRINGS (Tarrant) Evan Calaway Tate and his cousin David Tate, both born in Georgia, established farms in the area about 1870. Now part of Arlington.

TATUM (Rusk, Panola) About 1850 Albert Tatum brought his family and some 50 slaves from Alabama to the area where he established a cotton plantation and later a sawmill and gristmill. His son Paul was the first PM 6 Jan 1886.

TAWAKONI (Hunt, Rains) West Tawakoni in Hunt County and East Tawakoni in Rains County were founded in the 1960s shortly after construction of the Iron Bridge Dam on the Sabine River that created Lake Tawakoni, named for the Tawakoni, a Caddoan people related to the Wichita who were resident in the area from the 18th century until the late 1850s when they were moved onto the Wichita Reservation in Indian Territory.

TAYLOR (County) Created 1858, organized 1878. Named for George, Edward, and James Taylor, brothers from Tennessee who arrived in Texas in the early 1830s. It is generally accepted that the brothers perished at the Alamo but there is some evidence that they died a short time later in the Goliad Massacre.

TAYLOR (Williamson) In 1876 on news that the International–Great Northern Railroad would be building through Williamson County the Texas Land Company founded Taylorsville, named for Edward Moses Taylor, an official of the Houston Belt & Terminal Railway. PO 9 Aug 1876 as Taylorville; changed to Taylor 31 Aug 1880, PM John O. Frink.

TAYLORSVILLE (Caldwell) Hugh and Mary Taylor brought their family from Kentucky and began farming in the early 1850s. PO 24 Sept 1874 as Elm Grove, PM John Peacock; changed to Taylorsville 27 Dec 1890, PM Madison Taylor, son of Hugh and Mary Taylor.

TAZEWELL (Hopkins) According to local lore, in 1887 Granville Kemper, the town physician, was applying for a post office and asked his wife, Estelle, for an appropriate name. For unknown reasons she replied "Tase," he said "Well," and Tazewell it was. More likely the name is a transfer from Tazewell, Virginia, Tennessee, or Georgia, themselves named for Henry Tazewell, or his son, Littleton, both US Senators from VA.

TEAGUE (Freestone) Teague was founded in the early 20th century as a distribution center for the Trinity & Brazos Valley Railway. Named for Narcissa Elizabeth Teague Yoakum, mother (possibly stepmother) of Benjamin Franklin Yoakum, the namesake of Yoakum and director of the Colorado & Southern Railway that bought the T&BV in 1905. PO 30 June 1880 as Brewer; changed to Teague 20 Apr 1906, PM Gordon King.

TEASELVILLE [TEEZ uhl vil] (Smith) The area was known as Loftin, named for the William Pitt Loftin family, until about 1912. Reportedly named for John Teasdale (Tasdale), a Bullard-area grocer.

TECULA [tuh KOO luh] (Cherokee) Tecula was founded as Reynolds about 1872 with construction of the International–Great Northern Railroad. By 1917 the name Reynolds had been replaced by Tecula, a name of uncertain origin. Tecula may be a transfer from the municipality of Tecuala in the state of Nayarit in west central Mexico; said to mean "place of wild animals." PO 8 July 1873 as Reynolds; discontinued and reestablished 15 May 1917, PM Omera D. Burns. This is the only Tecula in the US.

TEHUACANA [tuh WAW kuh nuh] (Limestone) Tehuacana is an adaptation of Tawakoni, the Caddoan people resident in Texas and Oklahoma from the 18th century. PO 8 Mar 1847 as Tewockony Springs; discontinued 5 Nov 1866; reopened as Tehuacana 9 Oct 1869, PO Matt Honeycutt. See Tawakoni.

TELEGRAPH (Kimble) Named from Telegraph Canyon where telegraph poles were cut to support the lines used for communication among army forts. PO 17 Feb 1900, PM Ruth Holmes.

TELEPHONE (Fannin) The local story is that several names for the post office (including "Telegraph") were rejected when James Knox Polk Hindman offered "Telephone," since he had the only working telephone in town. PO 26 Feb 1886, PM J. K. P. Hindman.

TELFERNER [TELF ner] (Victoria) Founded in 1882 with construction of the New York, Texas & Mexican Railway. Named for Italian Count Joseph Telfener, financier, and builder of the NYT&M. How the name gained the medial "r" is unknown. PO 19 Dec 1895 as Jasmine; changed to Telferner 17 Dec 1908, PM William L. Bailey.

TELICO [TEL uh ko] (Ellis) The community was known as Trinity City, named from the Trinity River, until 1856 when Thomas Hamilton McCray established the Telico Manufacturing Company to produce finished cotton and woolen products. McCray chose the name for his former home, Tellico, Monroe County, TN, itself named for the Tellico River. PO 10 Mar 1856 as Tellico, PM Thomas McCray; discontinued 23 Jan 1867, reopened as Telico 29 Oct 1894, PM George Hogge.

TELL (Childress) Tell is a shortening of Tell Tale Flats, so named, according to Fred Tarpley, "because some residents were exceedingly eager...to report unsolicited information about their neighbors." (*1001 Texas Place Names*) PO 4 May 1905, PM James Ira Sandifer.

TEMPLE (Bell) Known informally as Tanglefoot and as Mud Town. The name Temple became official when the Gulf, Colorado & Santa Fe Railway established Temple Junction Station in 1880, named for Bernard Moore Temple, surveyor and chief engineer for the GC&SF and one of the most influential railroad engineers in Kansas, Nebraska, and especially Texas in the 1870s and 1880s. PO 18 Jan 1881, PM Edmond G. Pendleton.

TENAHA [TEN uh hah] (Shelby) Tenehaw [*sic*] was a Mexican municipality that included much of present Shelby County. Tenaha has been taken to be from an unidentified Indian language meaning "muddy water." However, an early spelling, Tenaja, suggests a derivation from Spanish *tinaja* "large jar," a reference to the rock basins created by intermittent streams or dripping water that functioned as stone waterholes. PO 7 Apr 1886, PM James N. Woodfin.

TENERYVILLE [TEN er ee vil] (Gregg) Founded in 1931 with the discovery of oil on the site owned by George B. Tenery. Now part of Longview.

TENNESSEE COLONY (Anderson) Founded in 1847 by settlers from Tennessee with a few

Alabamans included for variety. PO 24 Mar 1852, PM John Woolverton.

TENNYSON (Coke) Samuel Sayner emigrated from Bubwith, Yorkshire, England in 1870. He was instrumental in organizing Coke County in 1889 and suggested the name Tennyson for Alfred, Lord Tennyson, Poet Laureate of the United Kingdom. PO 26 June 1894, PM Sarah E. Kiser.

TERLINGUA [ter LING gwuh] (Brewster) Named from Terlingua Creek. The source of the name is unknown but has generated its share of speculations, guesses, and popular etymologies. By one, Terlingua is the name of a narcotic plant used in Indian rituals; by another it is the name of a vanished Indian village. Several writers have argued that early spellings—Terlingo, Las Lingas and especially Tres Linguas—suggest that Terlingua is derived from Spanish *tres lenguas* for the "three languages" spoken in the area: Spanish, English, and "Indian." However, spellings such as these may themselves be popular etymologies. PO 15 Aug 1899, PM William Bell.

TERRELL (County) Created and organized in 1905. Named for Alexander Watkins Terrell (1827–1912), born in Virginia. Terrell moved to Missouri in 1831 and to Austin, TX, in 1852 where he became a noted courtroom lawyer. After distinguished service in the Civil War, Terrell served four terms in the Texas Senate and two terms in the Texas House. He was President Grover Cleveland's minister plenipotentiary to the Ottoman Empire in the 1890s, a University of Texas regent in the early 1910s, and president of the Texas Historical Association in 1912.

TERRELL [TEHRL] (Kaufman) Terrell was founded in 1873 with construction of the Texas & Pacific Railway and named for surveyor Robert A. Terrell. One of Terrell's legacies is Terrell House, an octagonal structure Terrell built in 1864. PO 13 June 1871 as Johnson's Point; changed to Terrell 23 Sept 1873, PM Jasper W. Johnson.

TERRELL WELLS (Bexar) Named in the 1920s for developer and promoter Frederick Terrell, a prominent political figure who was mayor of San Antonio in 1903. PO 1 Oct 1932, PM Helen A. Milhan.

TERRY (County) Created 1876, organized 1904. Named for Benjamin Franklin Terry (1821–1861), a partner in the consortium that built the first railroad in Texas, the Buffalo Bayou, Brazos & Colorado Railway, chartered in February 1850. In August 1861 Terry organized and led the Eighth Texas Cavalry, known as Terry's Texas Rangers, into the Civil War. He was killed at the Battle of Woodsonville in Kentucky on December 17, 1861.

TERRYVILLE (DeWitt) James and John Terry, brothers from Tennessee, opened a general store in the 1850s. James Terry was a DeWitt County judge in the early 1880s. PO 15 Feb 1869, PM Eli F. McDonald.

TESNUS [TES nuhs] (Brewster) After the names Tabor and Sunset were rejected by post office officials, Sunset was spelled backward and the application was resubmitted requesting the name Tesnus. PO 2 Feb 1912, PM Clara Gould.

TEXARKANA (Bowie) Texarkana was established in 1873 in anticipation of the Cairo & Fulton and Texas & Pacific railways. While Texarkana is a blend of three state names, *Tex*as, *Ark*ansas and Louisi*ana*, the direct source of the name is uncertain. There are several local stories. By one, the name was taken from the Texarkana, a Red River steamboat; by another, the name was coined by a northwest Louisiana saloon keeper who offered a drink he called "the Texarkana" (no record of what it included); and by another, Gus Knobel, a surveyor for the St. Louis, Iron Mountain & Southern Railway, created the name and made it "official" by writing Texarkana on a gateway sign. PO 2 Feb 1886, PM Willis Whitaker.

TEXAS (State) According to tradition the name Texas is from a Caddo word with the general meaning "friend, ally," claimed to be used as a greeting among members of the confederated Caddo tribes of East Texas. The reputed source is based largely on a 1690 letter of Damián Massanet, a Franciscan priest who accompanied the Alonso De León Expedition. Massanet wrote that a group of Indians, fearful of the Spanish, found the courage to leave their hiding places shouting "*techas, techas*, which means 'friends, friends.'" Over time *techas* became Texas and "friendship" became part of Texas lore and the Texas state motto in 1930. Notably, several lines later Massanet wrote of being with "the Tejas Indians" and later he founded the *San Francisco de los Tejas* mission, suggesting that Tejas was in common use as a name for the local people. (By 1600 the name could be written either Tejas or Texas; De León wrote Texas; Massanet wrote Tejas.) These findings, among others, led historian Jorge Luis García Ruiz to question the traditional origin of the name Texas. In 2018 García Ruiz argued that Texas derived ultimately from the Río Tejas, the name early Spanish explorers had given to the Nueces River. Tejas, from the river, became a name for the Tejas people and for their territory. He further argued that the river was named from *taxus* (*teja* in Spanish), Latin for the bald cypress tree found throughout the Southeastern US. A full account can be found in García Ruiz, *Texas: The False Origin of the Name*.

TEXAS CITY (Galveston) Named by Jacob, Benjamin, and Henry Myers of Duluth, MN, who organized the Texas City Improvement Company and founded the community in 1893. Texas City includes the early settlement of Shoal Point. PO 11 May 1893, PM Frank B. Davison.

TEXHOMA [teks OM uh] (Sherman) Located on the *Tex*as-Okla*homa* state line, Texhoma was established with construction of the Chicago, Rock Island & Mexico Railway in 1901. Most of the community's businesses are on the Oklahoma side due to a 1932 survey that moved the state line several hundred feet south of its former location. The PO operated in Texas 11 Dec 1909–30 Apr 1910, PM Andy Young Ingham.

TEXLA (Orange) Texla, a blend of the state abbreviations of Texas and Louisiana, grew around a sawmill the Robert W. Wier Lumber Company bought from the Harrell–Votaw Lumber Company in 1905. PO 21 Sept 1905 as Bruce, PM Charles G. Bruce; changed to Texla 10 July 1906.

TEXLINE (Dallam) Texline, located on the Texas–New Mexico border and a shortening of "Texas state line," was founded by the Fort Worth & Denver City Railway in 1888 and organized as the Dallam County seat in 1891. PO 24 Oct 1888, PM Abbie Matlock.

TEXON [TEKS ahn] (Reagan) Texon was founded in 1924 by Levi Smith, vice president and general manager of the Big Lake Oil Company, and named for the Texon Oil and Land Company organized by Frank Pickrell and Haymon Krupp of El Paso in 1921. PO 28 Apr 1926, PM Willie H. McGonagle.

TEXROY (Hutchinson) Founded in the late 1920s; named for Sherman D. McIlroy, known as *Tex* McIl*roy* from his days prospecting for gold in Alaska. He and his brother, White McIlroy, formed the Duck Creek Oil Company and brought in a gusher in 1926. Texroy is now part of Borger.

THALIA [THAL yuh] (Foard) About 1910 grocer William Washington Pigg donated land for the townsite. The Pigg name, coupled with the town's location on Paradise Creek, led to a great deal of amusement; a local preacher is said to have remarked "I can now say something that few if any others can. I have baptized pigs in Paradise." When the Post Office Department rejected the name Paradise, someone suggested Thalia for the Greek goddess of poetry and festivity. PO 3 Mar 1890, PM Josie Wells.

THEDFORD (Smith) Named for Lemuel (Lem) Thedford, a landowner who was instrumental in organizing the local school district. Now part of Lindale.

THELMA (Bexar) Englishman James Watson opened the PO 3 May 1906 in his general store and named the office for his two-year-old daughter, Thelma.

THEON [THEE ahn] (Williamson) The Holy Trinity Catholic Church was established in 1889 northeast of Theon and it is generally assumed that the name, from Greek *theo* "god," was chosen to signify the relationship between the church and the town. PO 12 Sept 1890, PM Fritz Krauss.

THERMO (Hopkins) Named from the Thermo Fire Brick Company about 1910. Also known as Crush for the local rock crusher.

THICKET (Hardin) Founded about 1900 as a flag station on the Gulf, Colorado & Santa Fe Railway; named from the Big Thicket, the ill-defined, heavily wooded area of Polk, Tyler, and adjacent counties. The Williams PO, opened 22 Jan 1906, was changed to Thicket 25 June 1906 by PM Henry Geisendorff.

THOMASTON (DeWitt) Nathan Thomas, a planter who moved to Texas from Tennessee in the 1830s, represented the district in the Texas Republic Legislature in the early 1840s and served in the Texas State

Legislature in the late 1860s. Thomas sold land for a townsite to the Gulf, Western Texas & Pacific Railway in 1872. PO 25 Apr 1854 as Price's Creek; changed to Thomaston 23 Nov 1877, PM Humphrey Heard.

THOMPSONS (Fort Bend) In the 1830s Jesse Thompson and his sons—Hiram, James, and Jack—emigrated from North Carolina and established a ferry across the Brazos River. Hiram Thompson, who would later be a Fort Bend commissioner and tax assessor, inherited the site of Thompsons from his wife, Mary Ann Bohannon. PO 31 Aug 1881 Helinora; changed to Thompsons 17 Oct 1888, PM James M. Cassil.

THOMPSONVILLE (Gonzales) Preston and Lucy Thompson purchased land in the area in the late 1850s and kept a general store from the early 1860s. PO 15 June 1869, PM Hilliard Polley; changed to Waelder 29 Oct 1874. See Waelder.

THOMPSONVILLE (Jim Hogg) Probably named for Oscar Thompson, the first sheriff of Jim Hogg County in the 1910s. PO 8 May 1925, PM Marie Reeves.

THORNBERRY (Clay) Known as the Illinois Colony until April 1891 when Emma Butler established the PO named for farmer and stockman Amos Thornberry who introduced fruit farming to the area in the 1880s.

THORNDALE (Milam) Thorndale was founded in the late 1870s with construction of the International–Great Northern Railroad. The local account is that the name recalls the thorns of the ubiquitous prickly pear, sagebrush, and mesquite. PO 18 Apr 1878, PM Miscipsia A. O. Moore.

THORNTON (Limestone) The community grew around the station established by the Houston & Texas Central Railway in 1871. Named for Nathaniel Macon Thornton who donated land for the H&TC right of way. PO 6 Feb 1873, PM William L. Wright.

THORP SPRING (Hood) Pleasant Thorp laid out the site in the mid-1850s. In the 1860s the town became a resort and spa, capitalizing on the reported medicinal properties of the spring water. Thorp Spring was the original site of AddRan Male and Female College, forerunner of Texas Christian University. PO 13 Aug 1874, PM William Haynes. See Addran.

THRALL (Williamson) In 1876 the International–Great Northern Railroad established Stiles Switch, named for landowners James and Frank Stiles. About 1900 the town that grew around Stiles Switch was named for writer, historian, and Methodist minister Homer Spellman Thrall, a prominent figure in Texas Methodism from the 1840s through the 1880s. Among his books are *History of Methodism in Texas* and *History of Texas*, both widely read in the late 19th century. PO 19 Dec 1901, PM Rolley Riley.

THREE RIVERS (Live Oak) "Where the Atascosa, Frio & Nueces Rivers meet, midway between San Antonio and Corpus Christi" is the slogan of the Three Rivers Chamber of Commerce. In 1913 the San Antonio, Uvalde & Gulf Railroad established Hamiltonburg Station, named for site owner

Annie Hamilton and her son Thornton. In 1914 the name was changed to Three Rivers at the suggestion of Charles Tips, a real estate agent and village promoter. PO 30 Oct 1913 as Hamiltonburg; changed to Three Rivers 1 May 1914, PM Harry H. Whitworth.

THREE STATES (Cass) Named for the junction of Texas, Arkansas, and Louisiana.

THRIFT (Wichita) Named from the Thrift–Waggoner Bank, one of several banks in which Dan Waggoner and his son, William Thomas Waggoner, were officers and investors. PO 21 May 1925, PM Myrtle Anthony. See Electra.

THRIFTY (Brown) Thrifty was settled shortly after the Civil War as Jim Ned, named from Jim Ned Creek, itself probably named for Jim Ned, a Native American leader and US Army scout in the 1840s. The origin of the name Thrifty is unknown. White suggests the name arose because "there must have been some tightwads in the neighborhood at the time" (White, 84). PO 10 June 1875 as Jim Ned; discontinued 13 Oct 1879; reopened as Thrifty 9 Nov 1880, PM George W. Allen.

THROCKMORTON (County) Created 1858, organized 1879. Named for William Edward Throckmorton (1795–1843), a native Virginian who moved to Collin County in 1841 where he practiced medicine until his death in 1843. When Throckmorton County was created, his son, James Webb Throckmorton (1825–1894), was a rising Texas politician who had just finished his third term in the Texas Legislature. He was the 12th Governor of Texas (1866–1867) and served in the US Congress (1874–1888).

THURBER (Erath) Thurber was founded in 1888 by Robert Dickey Hunter, owner of the Texas and Pacific Coal Company. Hunter named the community for his business partner, New York financier Horace K. Thurber. PO 1 May 1888 as Johnson Mines; changed to Thurber 2 Jan 1889, PM Fred R. Young.

TIFFIN (Eastland) Tiffin, British slang for a small shot of whiskey, came to mean lunch, especially when accompanied by mild liquor. The local story is that a British railroad worker announced one noon that he would be taking "tiffin" which at least some people thought would be a good name for their town. The Bull Creek PO, opened 20 May 1919, was changed to Tiffin 8 July 1920 by PM Bryant L. Dulin.

TIGERTOWN (Lamar) By one local story, a large picture of a circus tiger hung over the bar in one of the town's saloons, leading to the invitation "let's get a shot at the tiger"; by another, broadsides advertising a coming circus were posted throughout the town and a group of inebriated riders saw the signs and galloped through the streets shouting "Tigertown! Tigertown!"; and by still another, local boys attending a dance were involved in fisticuffs with boys from Bonham and pictures of tigers were painted on buildings to show the fierceness of the fight. The Cathron's Store PO operated from 5 Sept 1878 until 15 Nov 1905.

TIGUA [TIG wuh] (El Paso) Tigua, Soccoro, and Ysleta were named for Albuquerque, (present-day NM) area pueblos when Spaniards and Indians fled south during the Pueblo Revolt of 1680. Tigua was the Spanish name for the Tiwa. See Soccoro; see Ysleta.

TILDEN (McMullen) The community was first known as Dog Town, so named by one account for the feral dogs that roamed the streets and by another for the marauding canines that were shot and left lying in the town's only street. Dog Town, however, was not considered an appropriate name for a respectable community so Rio Frio was formally named in 1858. Politics then intervened and Rio Frio was renamed Tilden in 1877 for Samuel J. Tilden, Governor of New York, the defeated candidate in the 1876 presidential election. PO 12 June 1871 as Dog Town; changed to Tilden 14 Sept 1877, PM Robert W. Johnson.

TILMON (Caldwell) General store owner and first postmaster Joseph Putnam (Putman) opened the PO 5 Apr 1890, named for his business partner, druggist Tilmon Monk.

TIMPSON (Shelby) Founded with construction of the Houston East & West Texas Railway in the mid-1880s. Probably named for Paul B. Timpson, son of Samuel C. Timpson of Houston, a director of the HE&WT. PO 4 Nov 1885, PM James H. Blankenship.

TIN TOP (Matagorda) Founded in the late 1920s and apparently named for the first businesses in the area, a cotton gin and a general store, both notable for their tin roofs.

TIN TOP (Parker) Tin Top dates from about 1949 when residents of Balch, Horse Shoe Bend, and Hightower merged with the existing Tin Top, named about 1910 for a cotton gin with a galvanized metal roof.

TIOGA [teye O guh] (Grayson) According to local sources a crew working on the Texas & Pacific Railway in the early 1880s was struck by the purity of the local well water and named the site for Tioga in New York state, known for its mineral springs. However, Tioga, TX, was founded by Dr. Jacob Stevenson Nichols who may have chosen the name for Tioga, Hancock County, IL, near his birthplace. PO 29 Aug 1881, PM Jacob Nichols.

TIRA [TEYE ruh] (Hopkins) Tira was first known as Chapman Arm(s) for William Chapman, a Methodist Episcopal minister who brought his family from Indiana in the early 1850s. The name was changed when Allen Payton opened the Tira PO 24 Dec 1898. Tira is taken to be a form of Tyre, mentioned in the Bible. One wag is reported to have remarked, "It should be named for Tyre because it is just as wicked as the biblical city."

TITLEY (Brewster) James W. Titley was superintendent of bridges and buildings for the Fort Worth & Denver City Railway in the 1890s and 1900s.

TITUS (County) Created and organized 1846. Named for Andrew Jackson Titus (1814–1855), born in Alabama. Titus settled in Texas in 1839. He established the Savanna, TX, post office in 1846, served in the War with Mexico, and was a representative in the Texas Legislature in the early 1850s.

TIVOLI [TEYE vuh lee, teye VOL ee] (Refugio) Business partners Preston Austin and Jesse McDowell, founders of AUSTWELL, laid out the Tivoli townsite in 1907, named for the Tivoli Ranch that Austin and several others had bought from the heirs of Newton Gullett in the early 20th century. In 1876 Gullett's wife, Charlotte, an aristocratic New Orleanian, named the ranch for one of the several Tivolis in New Orleans, most likely the Place Du Tivoli on St. Charles Avenue (now Lee Circle). PO 31 July 1893, PM Herman J. Landgraf.

TIVYDALE (Gillespie) Canadian Joseph Tivy, a surveyor and prospector, came to Texas about 1840. Tivy was elected to the Texas House in 1873 and was the first mayor of Kerrville in 1890. Tivydale is also knownas Pumpkinville.

TOCO (Lamar) Toco is a transfer with shortening, perhaps from Tacoa, Shelby County, AL; more likely from Tocowa, Panola County, MS, from Choctaw "broken trees." Formerly known as Shady Grove.

TODVILLE (Chambers, Harris) John Grant Tod, Jr. founded Todville in 1900. Grant was a Harris County judge in the 1890s and Texas Secretary of State under Governor Joseph Sayers in the early 20th century.

TOKIO [TO kee o] (Terry) Belle Ware, who established the PO 21 Sept 1912, apparently chose the name for her attraction to Japanese culture.

TOLAR (Hood) Tolar was founded about 1890 with construction of the Fort Worth & Rio Grande Railway. State Representative William McGaughey proposed the name to honor his friend Alfred H. H. Tolar, publisher of the *Colorado City Courant* newspaper who had served with him in the Texas Legislature in the late 1880s. PO 21 June 1890, PM John R. Powell.

TOLBERT (Wilbarger) In the 1880s the Fort Worth & Denver Railway established a shipping station called Wheatland. The application for a Wheatland PO was rejected and resubmitted with the name Tolbert, for Wilbarger county judge James R. Tolbert. PO 30 June 1890, PM George S. Tomlinson.

TOLEDO (Newton) By one local account, Toledo was named for a local Indian leader; by another, for José Álvarez Toledo y Dubois, an early 19th century freelance fighter for the independence of Spain's New World possessions; and by yet another, for Toledo, Spain. More likely Toledo was brought to Texas by settlers from Toledo, OH, itself named for Toledo, Spain. PO 21 Dec 1885, PM William C. Lenahan.

TOLOSA [tuh LO suh] (Kaufman) A transfer from Tolosa, Zacatecas, Mexico, itself named from Tolosa in northern Spain. PO 11 Oct 1880, PM Charles A. Jenkins.

TOM BEAN (Grayson) Thomas C. Bean, a Bonham landowner and surveyor, donated land for the townsite as a station on the St. Louis Southwestern Railway (Cotton Belt) in 1887. PO 24 Jan 1888, PM William Grindstaff.

TOM GREEN (County) Created 1874, organized 1875. Named for Thomas Green

(1814–1864), born in Virginia. Green moved to Texas to join the revolution in late 1835. He fought at San Jacinto, recruited a company of riflemen during the War with Mexico, and commanded the Fifth Texas Volunteer Cavalry in the early years of the Civil War. He was mortally wounded on April 12, 1864 during the Red River Campaign.

TOMBALL (Harris) Founded in the early 1900s as Peck, reportedly named for a Trinity & Brazos Valley Railway civil engineer. In 1907 the town was renamed for Thomas Henry Ball, multi-term mayor of Huntsville in the 1880s and US Representative from Texas at the turn of the 20th century. PO 5 Mar 1908, PM Claude T. Smith.

TOMLINSON HILL (Falls) Named for the rise to which James K. Tomlinson brought his family and slaves from Alabama in 1859.

TOOL (Henderson) Farmer and cattleman George Tool, born in GA, relocated to Texas in the late 1860s. PO 2 Aug 1901, PM Joe Stewart.

TOPSEY (Coryell) Local lore claims that the town was named for Topsey, a well-known mule. PO 13 Apr 1901, PM Henry Moore.

TORNILLO [tor NEE o] (El Paso) Tornillo was founded by the Tornillo Townsite Company, organized by El Paso businessmen in 1909. From Spanish *tornillo* "screw, clamp," the town was named for the local Tornillo tree, a subspecies of mesquite of the genus *prosopis*; also known as screwbean mesquite. PO 27 Mar 1909, PM Monico Jimenez.

TOURS (McLennan) Settlers from Illinois arrived on November 11, 1874, the feast day of St. Martin, Bishop of Tours, and named the community St. Martinsville. The name was changed when Joseph Loftin opened the Tours PO 10 Nov 1891.

TOW [TAW] (Llano) Brothers William and Wilson Tow brought their families to the area from Missouri via Fannin County, TX, about 1850. PO 26 Feb 1886 as Tow Valley, PM Matt B. Clendenen, discontinued 11 May 1887, reestablished as Tow 15 Jan 1896.

TOYAH, TOYAHVALE [TOY yuh] (Reeves) The Toyah settlement developed in the early 1880s. Toyavale was established 25 miles south of Toyah with construction of the Pecos Valley Southern Railway that linked Toyavale with the town of Pecos. Railroad officials created Toyahvale by adding the poetic "vale" to Toyah. Toyah is often claimed to be from a Native American word meaning "flowing water" or "abundant water." PO 30 Dec 1881 as Toyah, PM Hiram Lightner. The Lyles PO was changed to Toyahvale 31 July 1894, PO Charles A. Hutchins.

TRACY (Milam) Known as Shields Gin for the cotton gin established by William Shields in the early 1890s until 11 Dec 1986 when Wiley Sanders opened the Tracy PO, named for grocer Nathaniel Tracy.

TRAVIS (County) Created 1840, organized 1843. Named for William Barret Travis (1809–1836), born in South Carolina. Travis practiced law in Alabama and Georgia before coming to Texas in 1831 and opening a law office near

Galveston. Travis was one of the first volunteers to join the Texas Army. His martyr's death at the Alamo made him a Texas hero.

TRAVIS (Falls) Travis Fleming Jones surveyed the site for the San Antonio & Aransas Pass Railway about 1890. PO 21 July 1880 as Lang, probably named for rancher and financier John J. Lang; changed to Travis 21 Nov 1891, PM James F. Miller.

TRAWICK [TRAY wik] (Nacogdoches) John Trawick relocated from Alabama in the 1860s and donated land for the townsite and a Texas & New Orleans Railroad station in the early 1900s. PO 24 Nov 1902, PM Marion Bates.

TRENT (Taylor) Named for Eskota rancher Isaac Riley Trent about 1881 with construction of the Texas & Pacific Railway. In an oft-told story an employee for the T&P is supposed to have mistakenly left the sign for Trent at the Eskota site and the sign for Eskota at the Trent site. Apparently Isaac Trent did not mind the mix-up. PO 7 May 1883, PM William G. Canon.

TRENTON (Fannin) Dr. William Cox Holmes is generally regarded as the "Father of Trenton" for his organization of the town about 1880. The name Trenton is probably a transfer. By one local story, early settler Andrew Russell suggested the name for a Louisiana hospital where he had received treatment during the Civil War; by another, the town was named for Trenton, NJ. Equally likely the name was brought to Texas by settlers from Trenton, Grundy County, MO. PO 29 Aug 1881, PM George Sanders.

TREVAT [truh VAT] (Trinity) Thomas Leander Trevathan moved from Pike County, AL, to San Augustine County, TX, in the 1840s and to Trinity County about 1860. Trevathan's name was shortened when Walter Jones established the Trevat PO 15 June 1892.

TRICKHAM [TRIK uhm] (Coleman) The town grew from the mid-1850s around the area's first general store. By local tradition, the name Trickham arose because of the jokes, practical and otherwise, played on customers, such as hiding mouse traps in the cracker barrel or diluting whiskey with creek water and watching cowboys become tipsy by suggestion. The storekeeper claimed he played these pranks on his customers to "trick'em." PO 10 Apr 1879, PM Theron Taber.

TRINIDAD (Henderson) John Schultz Damron from Tennessee platted the town of Trinity named from the Trinity River in 1851. When Trinity was rejected as a name for the PO, the application was resubmitted and approved as Trinidad. PO 27 Oct 1891, PM David C. Legg. See Trinity County.

TRINITY (County) Created and organized 1850. Named from the Trinity River. Alonso de León, a Spanish officer with orders to locate and expel a French colony from the Texas coast, is generally credited with naming the river *Río de la Santísima Trinidad* "River of the Most Holy Trinity" about 1690.

TRINITY (Trinity) Trinity was founded as Trinity Station, named from Trinity County, with construction of the Houston & Great

Northern Railroad. The name was changed in February 1872 when Samuel Robb opened the Trinity PO.

TROUP (Cherokee, Smith) Troup was organized in the early 1870s on the line of the International–Great Northern Railroad and named by settlers from Troup County, GA, or for George McIntosh Troup, US Representative from Georgia in the 1810s, Governor of Georgia in the 1820s, and the namesake of Troup County, GA. PO 7 June 1854, PM Daniel P. Fowler.

TROY (Bell) Troy (Old Troy) was settled in the 1860s several miles north of present Troy and known as Elm Creek until the late 1870s. When the Missouri–Kansas–Texas Railroad built through the area in the early 1880s many of the homes and businesses of Old Troy were disassembled and moved to trackside. Troy is probably a transfer name, likely from Troy, Pike County, AL, itself named from Troy, NY. PO 16 Jan 1854 as Elm Creek; changed to Troy 10 May 1876, PM Edmund G. Pendleton.

TRUMBULL (Ellis) Known as Switch for the railroad switch installed by the Houston & Texas Central Railway in the early 1870s and subsequently known as Ghost Hill, apparently because several ranch hands had been killed by a passing train. Trumbull was formally named in the early 20th century for Nathan Franklin Trumbull, president of the Fort Worth & Denver City Railway and a director of the Missouri–Kansas–Texas Railroad. PO 12 May 1894 as Clemma; changed to Trumbull 20 Apr 1904, PM Louis N. Lee.

TRUSCOTT (Knox) At the end of the Civil War James Joseph Truscott moved his family from Illinois to Arkansas and, in the late 1870s, to Texas. Truscott was the first judge of Knox County and later mayor of Maud, OK. PO 2 Dec 1889, PM Arizona Truscott.

TUCKER (Anderson) Shortly after the end of the Civil War a group of emancipated African Americans established a community known as Green Bay which became part of Prairie Point when the International–Great Northern Railroad built through the area in 1872. Prairie Point was renamed in the early 1880s for William H. Tucker, a local landowner and newly-elected state representative from Anderson County. PO 26 Feb 1873 as Prairie Point; changed to Tucker 31 Jan 1882, PM John Young, Jr.

TULETA [too LEET uh] (Bee) In 1906 Rev. Peter Unzicker led a group of Mennonites to the area from Livingston County, IL, and founded a community named for Tuleta Maude Chittum, daughter of James Chittum, part owner of the Chittum-Miller Ranch from which Unzicker purchased the townsite. PO 14 Sept 1907, PM James J. Miller.

TULIA [TOOL yuh] (Swisher) The post office application requested the name Tule (Spanish "cattail reeds") for Middle Tule Creek. The name was miswritten or misread and the office was approved as Tulia. PO 22 Aug 1887, PM James Parrish.

TULIP (Fannin) In the middle 1830s Daniel Rowlett, who was instrumental in the creation of Fannin County, established the town of Lexington. The name was changed about 1840 for the Tulip Bend of the Red River, itself reportedly named from the local wild tulips. PO 5 June 1878 as Tulip, PM Thomas Lawrence.

TULSITA [tuhl SEET uh] (Bee) About 1930 site owner James L. Courtney laid out the town of Tulsa, named for his former home in Oklahoma. When that name was rejected by the Post Office Department, Courtney modified Tulsa to Tulsita "little Tulsa." PO 15 Apr 1931, PM Victor E. Nelson.

TURCOTTE (Kenedy) Named in the early 1900s for Marie Stella Turcotte Kenedy, wife of John Kenedy and daughter-in-law of Mifflin Kenedy, the namesake of Kenedy County. See Sarita.

TURKEY (Hall) Settled in the 1890s as Turkey Roost, named for the birds that gave Turkey Creek its name. PO 3 Mar 1893, PM Alfred P. Hall.

TURLINGTON (Freestone) Joseph M. Parker opened the Turlington PO 3 August 1901, named for Marcellus (Marcus) Turlington from Alabama who established a medical practice in the 1890s.

TURNERSVILLE (Coryell) The Turnersville Spring and Campground, well known to travelers and cattle drovers, was formally named in the 1870s for local blacksmith Calvin Turner. PO 24 May 1875, PM Joseph Black.

TURNERTOWN-SELMAN CITY (Rusk) Turnertown was founded in the East Texas oilfield in the 1930s by brothers Roger and Horace Turner, Henderson businessmen. Selman City was named for Silas Selman, an owner of property where oil was discovered in the 1930s. Turnertown and Selman City merged by 1970. PO 22 Sept 1939 as Selman City, PM Raymond A. Crawford.

TURNEY (Cherokee) Joseph and Nancy Turney brought their family from Alabama in the early 1850s. The PO was established by Lenon Bownds (various spellings) 20 Nov 1903 and the postmastership became a family tradition. Lenon Bownds was followed by Homer Bownds in 1904, Nellie Bownds in 1905, and Ira Bounds [*sic*] in 1909.

TUSCOLA [tuhs KOL uh] (Taylor) Dr. Clarence McClellan Cash, a horseback doctor who practiced rural medicine for half a century, founded Tuscola about 1889 and chose the name for Tuscola, IL, where he had spent much of his childhood. The Illinois name is a transfer from Tuscola, MI, where it was coined by the 19th century ethnologist Henry Rowe Schoolcraft who created a number of pseudo-Indian names based loosely on native language roots. At one time, Schoolcraft claimed Tuscola meant "warrior prairie" and at another that it meant "level lands." PO 6 Apr 1899, PM David H. Cole.

TWICHELL (Ochiltree) Twichell, founded in 1919 as a station on the Panhandle & Santa Fe Railway, was named for Ginery Bachelor Twichell, US Representative from Massachusetts in the 1860s and president of the Atchison, Topeka & Santa Fe Railway, parent of the P&SF, from the 1870s.

TWIN SISTERS (Blanco) The Twin Sisters are two prominent hills south of Blanco that served as landmarks for travelers and early settlers. PO 24 Dec 1856, PM Otto Wupperman.

TWITTY (Wheeler) Named from the Twitty PO, opened by Asa Linton Twitty 26 Oct 1912. Country singer Harold Lloyd Jenkins, his musical career stagnating, changed his name in 1957 and became famous as Conway Twitty, for Conway, AR, and Twitty, TX.

TYE (Taylor) The Texas & Pacific Railway established Tebo Station in 1881, likely named for Tebo, MO. The community was named Tye when PM George W. Bennett changed the name of the Hines PO to Tye 9 Nov 1901, for John P. Tye, who had opened the Hines PO 6 Apr 1899.

TYLER (County) Created and organized 1846. Named for John Tyler (1790–1862), 10th President of the US (1841–1845). On March 1, 1845, during his last days in office, Tyler signed the bill annexing Texas to the United States.

TYLER (Smith) Named for John Tyler, 10th President of the US. PO 8 Mar 1847, PM Elisha E. Lott.

TYNAN [TEYE nuhn] (Bee) Probably named for John Tynan, an employee of the San Antonio & Aransas Pass Railway that built through the area in the late 1880s. PO 14 Nov 1911, PM Arnold J. Shary.

U

UHLAND [YOO luhnd] (Caldwell, Hays) Louis Scheh chose the name in honor of Ludwig Uhland, 19th century poet, literary critic, lawyer, politician, and, like Scheh, from Wertemburg, Germany. PO 1 Feb 1900, PM Herman Seelinger.

UMBARGER [UHM bahr ger] (Randall) About 1898 the Panhandle & Santa Fe Railway established a switch on Stephen G. Umbarger's ranch. PO 11 Sept 1902, PM Joe H. Hall.

UNCERTAIN (Harrison) A number of stories have been created to explain the origin of Uncertain, unique among American place names. By one, the site was known as Uncertain Landing because of the difficulty of docking steamboats plying Caddo Lake; by another, when the first settlers arrived the boundary between the US and the Republic of Texas at Caddo Lake had not been firmly established and residents were uncertain of where they lived; and by still another the town was incorporated to allow liquor sales, but it was uncertain if the ordinance would be approved.

UNITY (Lamar) The local account is that the name was chosen to reflect the spirit of togetherness shown by everyone in the community.

UNIVERSAL CITY (Bexar) Developer Aubrey Milner founded Universal City in 1931 next to Randolph Air Force Base. Milner expected the airfield and the community to become internationally recognized. PO 31 Jan 1970, PM Elmo W. Ullrich.

UPSHUR [UHP sher] (County) Created and organized 1846. Named for Abel Parker Upshur (1790–1844), born in Virginia. Upshur was US Secretary of State in the early 1840s and worked with Texas Ambassador Isaac Van Zandt on the agreement that led to Texas statehood. In 1844, Upshur and US Secretary of the Navy Thomas Gilmer were killed aboard the USS Princeton when one of its guns exploded. See Gilmer.

UPTON [UHP tuhn] (County) Created 1887, organized 1910. Named for brothers John and William Upton who emigrated from Franklin County, TN, to Texas in the 1850s. Both brothers rose to the rank of Colonel in the Confederate Army. John was mortally wounded at the second Battle of Bull Run in 1862; William survived the war and served in the Texas Legislature in 1866 and again from 1879 through 1885.

URBANA [er BAN uh] (San Jacinto) When the Houston, East & West Texas Railway built through the area in the early 1900s, Simon P. Coughlin, assistant superintendent of the HE&WT, chose the name for his birthplace, Urbana, OH, itself named from Latin "of the city." PO 7 Aug 1914, PM George W. Jordan.

UTLEY [YOOT lee] (Bastrop) Storekeeper James Harvey Wilbarger, who founded Utley in the 1850s, chose the name in honor of his mother-in-law, Nancy Utley Olive. James Wilbarger is remembered as the son of Josiah Wilbarger, who lived for twelve years after being scalped by Comanches in the early 1830s. PO 8 Feb 1892, PM Goodloe Drisdale.

UTOPIA [yoo TOP ee uh] (Uvalde) Utopia was first known as Waresville, named for William Ware, a Republic of Texas soldier.

In 1884 the town of Montana was platted north of Waresville. When Montana was rejected as a name for the post office, George A. Barker changed the name of the Waresville PO to Utopia in 1885. By some accounts Barker found the area both healthful and satisfying, his personal "Utopia." Others claim the name was suggested by Dr. J. W. Whittaker for Thomas More's fictitious and satirical book, *Utopia*. Perhaps the name resulted from the vision of Victor Prosper Considerant, an attempt to found a Fourierist phalanx—a Utopia—in Sabinal Canyon, a vision that was cut short by the failure of Considerant's Réunion Colony in Dallas.

UVALDE [yoo VAL dee] (County) Created 1850, re-created and organized 1856. Named for Juan de Ugalde (1729–1816). In 1776 Ugalde was appointed governor of the Spanish province of San Francisco de Coahuila, which included Texas. Ugalde led a number of campaigns against Lipan and Mescalero Apaches including a decisive battle in 1790 at what became known as Cañon de Ugalde near present Utopia.

UVALDE (Uvalde) Uvalde, the seat of Uvalde County, was founded as Encina (Spanish "live oak"), about 1854 by Reading Wood Black, and renamed Uvalde for the county in 1856. PO 22 Aug 1853 as Fort Inge; changed to Uvalde 23 Mar 1857.

L

VAHLSING [VAHL sing] (San Patricio) In the 1950s Fred H. Vahlsing (Valsing) was one of the world's leading producers of vegetables; his main farm north of Mathis included irrigated fields with vegetable storage and preparatory facilities. Production slumped in the 1960s when cotton and corn became major crops.

VAL VERDE (County) Created and organized 1885. Named for the Civil War battle fought in late February 1862 at Valverde Creek, now in Socorro County, NM, where Confederate General Henry Hopkins Sibley's Texas cavalry defeated Colonel Edward Canby's Union forces. The stream was named either from Spanish *Val Verde* "green valley" or for an early Spanish governor of New Mexico. Val Verde in Milam County was founded about 1868, and also named for the Civil War battle at Valverde Creek.

VALDASTA [val DAS tuh] (Collin) The petition for a PO in 1886 asked for the name Valdosta, for Valdosta, GA. The name was either unclearly written or misread and the office was approved with the name Valdasta and was never corrected. Valdosta, from the Aosta Valley, the Valle d'Aosta in northern Italy, was the name of Georgia Governor John Troup's estate. PO 2 June 1886, PM Tandy W. Smith. See Troup.

VALENTINE (Jeff Davis) The local account, repeated many times because of its sentimental appeal, is that the town was named when a crew laying tracks for the Southern Pacific Railroad reached the site on Valentine's Day in 1882. However, there are several more likely sources of the name. Charles Crocker, one of the "Big Four" of 19th century western railroad builders and a director of Wells Fargo, was one of the investors with controlling interest in the Southern Pacific. Crocker's only daughter was Harriet Valentine Crocker. Even more likely, the namesake is John J. Valentine, who succeeded Charles Crocker at Wells Fargo in 1882 and was also a major investor in the Southern Pacific. PO 22 Jan 1886, PM Daniel Carr.

VALLEY WELLS (Dimmit) Named for the local artesian wells and promoted nationwide from about 1910 as the Good Luck Colony by the Texas Land and Loan Company. PO 24 Jan 1914, PM William Shumate.

VAN (Van Zandt) The early settlement went by such names as Swindle, for settler George Swindall, and "Who'd a Thought It," the response of many when the disreputable "Ratty Towns" attempted to open a general store. These informal names were replaced 28 June 1894 when James Vance established the Van post office, named for Van Zandt County, for Vance himself, or for both.

VAN ALSTYNE [van AWL steen] (Grayson) Named about 1873 by the Houston & Texas Central Railway for Maria and William Ashley Van Alstyne of Houston. William Van Alstyne was treasurer and director of the H&TC and the Van Alstynes were major stockholders. PO 17 Apr 1873, PM Charles P. Pattie.

VAN HORN (Culberson) The town of Van Horn was founded about 1880 and named from the Van Horn Wells, mineral springs ten miles south of the present townsite.

The springs were apparently first described by Maj. Jefferson Van Horne in the 1840s but are more likely named for Lt. James J. Van Horn (no relation) who was in command of an infantry company that occupied Van Horn Wells at the outbreak of the Civil War. PO 14 Jan 1886.

VAN RAUB (Bexar) Byron H. Robb, a confidence man wanted for fraud and deception in Ohio, made a midnight move to Texas in 1882, changed his name to Van Raub (apparently unaware that in German, *Raub* means "robbery") and founded the community in the mid-1880s. PO 20 May 1889, PM Frank A. Newton.

VAN VLECK (Matagorda) Hardeman, named for Bailey Hardeman, the namesake of Hardeman County, was renamed in 1901 for Will G. Van Vleck, manager and vice president of the Galveston, Harrisburg & San Antonio Railway. PO 14 Feb 1860 as Hardeman; changed to Van Vleck 3 Jan 1901, PM Leander W. Brown.

VAN ZANDT (County) Created and organized 1848. Named for Isaac Van Zandt (1813–1847), born in Tennessee. A lawyer and politician, Van Zandt relocated to Texas in 1838, served in the Texas House and was appointed by Sam Houston as a delegate to Washington to arrange for the annexation of Texas. Van Zandt county was named in his honor shortly after his death from yellow fever.

VANCE (Real) Vance was first known as Bullhead, named from Bullhead Creek, itself named for the Mudcat or Bullhead fish. The townsite was surveyed in 1883 and formally named in 1886 for François Xavier Wantz who emigrated from Offendorf, Bas Rhin, France, in 1845. The German pronunciation of Wantz, [VAHNTS], was Anglicized to [VANS] and the name was respelled when the Bull Head [*sic*] post office was changed to Vance in 18 May 1886 by PM Lavania C. Jackson.

VANCOURT (Tom Green) Lumberman William S. Kelly named the town in the early 20th century for the family of his wife, Mary Ann Van Court. PO 19 Mar 1906, PM Florence E. Webb.

VANDERPOOL (Bandera) Informally known as Bugscuffle, a name that reportedly came about when a revival meeting (or church picnic or community social, depending on the story) became so infested by flying insects that the occasion degenerated into a "scuffle with the bugs." The town was formally named for Littleberry Vanderpool who opened the PO 10 Feb 1886.

VANDYKE (Comanche) Nixon VanDyke Frost and Florida Lucinda Frost, farmers from the 1870s, donated land for a schoolhouse about 1880. PO 5 Jan 1903, PM Deroll Nabers.

VARISCO [vuh RIS ko] (Brazos) Biagio Varisco, who went by the name Brazos Varisco, was born in Sicily and emigrated to Bryan, TX, in 1907. An agriculturalist and businessman, Varisco was a director of the Bryan Chamber of Commerce and namesake of the Varisco building erected in 1947.

VASCO (Delta) When the request for a PO named Velasco was denied the application was resubmitted with the name shortened to Vasco. PO 9 May 1903, PM Zou Kelley Anderson. See Velasco.

VASHTI [VASH tee] (Clay) Jane Turner established the PO 10 June 1892, named for her niece Jo Vashti(e) Strahan, daughter of Cicero and Catherine Strahan, the first local merchants.

VATTMAN (Kleberg) Theodore Koch, a Minnesota real estate investor, founded Vattman in 1909. Koch and Father Edward Vattman, then secretary of the Catholic Colonization Society of America, promoted the site to attract German Catholic families from Texas and from the Upper Midwest. Riviera was founded by Koch about the same time. Also spelled Vattmanville.

VAUGHAN (Hill) Bascom Hamilton Vaughan established a medical practice about 1880. PO 3 Sept 1885, PM Robert Middleton.

VEACH (San Augustine) Named for John A. Veach, a member of the 3rd Consultation in 1835. PO 27 Oct 1916, PM Willie C. McKnight.

VEALMOOR (Howard) Founded on Christopher Columbus Slaughter's ranch by the Lone Star Land Company, established by Slaughter's sons, Richard and Robert, and his daughter and town namesake, Minnie Slaughter Veal, who married Slaughter's business partner, George T. Veal. PO 9 June 1926, PM Mae Zant.

VEGA [VAY guh] (Oldham) Vega, Spanish "lowland, plain," was laid out in 1903 with construction of the Choctaw, Oklahoma & Texas Railroad. Andrew Miller, who surveyed the townsite with Howard Trigg, opened the first store and was the first postmaster 30 Jan 1904.

VELASCO [vuh LAS ko] (Brazoria) The original Velasco was founded in 1831 as a Mexican customs port on the site of what is now Surfside Beach, probably named for José María Gómez de Cervantes y Altamirano de Velasco Padilla y Obando, an army officer in the Mexican War of Independence. After a hurricane destroyed much of the original town, Velasco was reestablished several miles northwest in 1891.Velasco became part of Freeport in 1957. The PO was first established in 1836, PM Isaac C. Hoskins.

VENUS (Johnson) Known as Gossip until the 1880s. Jabe C. Smyth, a real estate agent from Alabama, platted Venus in the late 1880s and according to some accounts chose the name for one of his relatives or for Venus Hosby, claimed to be the daughter of a local doctor, but Venus Hosby's existence is difficult to verify. Perhaps Smyth chose the name for Venus, the Roman goddess of love and fertility. The Gossip PO, opened 4 Oct 1888, was changed to Venus 12 Dec 1888, PM James A. Burgess.

VERA (Knox) Reportedly named for Vera Kellog, daughter of an early settler. PO 1 Jan 1891, PM George Ballard.

VERBENA (Garza) Probably named by settlers from Verbena, Chilton County, AL, itself named for the local verbena, the plant used in an herbal tea commonly prescribed in folk medicine. PO 16 Dec 1901, PM Jacob Benjamin Cotton.

VERDI (Atascosa) By a local account the name was proposed by Joseph Peyragrosse, a French settler in the 1880s, for a river in his native country, perhaps the Verdon, which became Verdi by popular etymology. PO 10 Jan 1891, PM Sidney S. Smith.

VERHALEN (Reeves) Probably named for Raymond Patrick Verhalen, born in Wisconsin. Verhalen emigrated to Texas in the 1900s and by 1930 was an established Reeves County nurseryman and grape arborist.

VERHELLE (DeWitt) In 1872 the Gulf, Western Texas & Pacific Railway established Burns Station, named for Arthur and Sarah Burns and their son Joseph Columbus Burns, among the first settlers on Irish Creek in the 1820s. The name was changed in the early 1900s for Eugene Verhelle, a machinist for the GWT&P.

VERIBEST [VEHR ee best] (Tom Green) Veribest was earlier known as Mullins for Isaac Mullins, one of the organizers of Tom Green County and a Texas state legislator in 1880. When the Post Office Department rejected the name Mullins in the 1920s, the town was renamed for the Veribest "Very Best" line of meat products, preserves, and cooking accessories produced by the Armour packing company of Chicago. The local story is that homemaker Sue Rister was grocery shopping when the mayor of Mullins asked her to suggest a new name and she replied Veribest, not only for the products but because Veribest would provide a positive image for their town. PO 12 June 1926, PM Annie M. Roberson.

VERNON (Wilbarger) The town developed in the 1870s. When the request for an Eagle Flat PO was rejected, the name Vernon was submitted and approved. The origin of the name is unknown. Several writers have suggested the PO was named for George Washington's estate, Mount Vernon; others claim the namesake was a more personal figure, one Vernon Brown, a whiskey drummer whose visits were eagerly anticipated. PO Sept 1880, PM George W. Darby.

VESSEY (Red River) Settlement began in the 1850s and the town was named in the late 1890s for John Vesey who moved to Clarksville, TX, from Mississippi by way of Tennessee in 1869. Vesey was a teacher, lawyer, and Red River County judge from 1888. PO 6 May 1899 as Vesey, PM Walter H. Colvert. Also spelled Vesey.

VIBORAS [vee BOR uhs] (Starr) Spanish "vipers, rattlesnakes." The town developed about 1890 on the ranch of Don Manuel Guerra. PO 9 June 1909, PM Rafael Trevino.

VICTORIA (County) An original Texas county created 1836 and named from the city of Victoria.

VICTORIA (Victoria) Founded in 1824 by empresario Martín de León as the *Villa Nuestra Señora de Guadalupe de Jesús Victoria*, shortened to *Guadalupe Victoria* for José Miguel Ramón Aducto Fernández y Félix, or Guadalupe Victoria, a Mexican political leader and the first president of the United Mexican States, 1824–1829. PO c. 1836, PM John Linn. Victoria in Limestone County was probably named about 1900 in honor of Queen Victoria of Britain.

VICTORY CITY (Bowie) This optimistically named community developed near the Lone

Star Army Ammunition Plant established by the Lone Star Defense Corporation at the beginning of the Second World War.

VIDAURRI [veye DEHR uh] (Refugio) Earlier known as Redlew, "Welder" spelled backward, for German settler Francis Welder who settled in the area in the mid-1840s. The town was formally named for José Jesús Vidaurri, an official of the Mexican government authorized to issue land grants to eligible settlers of the Power and Hewetson Colony in the early 1830s. PO 14 Dec 1911, PM Albert L. Hail.

VIDOR [VEYE der] (Orange) Charles Shelton Vidor of Galveston bought the Beaumont Sawmill Company and with Anson W. Miller established the Miller-Vidor Lumber Company around 1900. The community was officially named for Vidor when Joseph A. Payment opened the post office 1 Feb 1909. See Milvid.

VIENNA [vee EN uh] (Lavaca) First known as the Cheney Settlement, named for John Cheney who emigrated from Georgia in 1830 and became a local official and town constable. Formally named for Vienna, Austria, when Benjamin Milby opened the PO 21 July 1873.

VIEW (Taylor) View was laid out in 1910 for the Santa Fe Railroad by the Western Development Company. The name was apparently chosen from the vista provided from the nearby hills. PO 10 Oct 1910, PM William M. Safford.

VIGO PARK [VEYE go] (Swisher) The Indiana–Texas Land Company laid out Vigo Park in 1906, named for Vigo and Parke counties, Indiana. PO 15 Nov 1907 as Vigo, PM Charles R. Gardner; changed to Vigo Park 7 Dec 1908. A town named Vigo—named for Vigo, Spain—existed for 20 years in the late 19th century in Concho County. PO 23 Dec 1887, PM John T. Pruitt.

VILAS [VEYE lis] (Bell) Vilas may have been named for William Freeman Vilas of Wisconsin. George Tillman who established the Vilas, TX, PO 14 Mar 1888 would have known that Vilas was the US Postmaster General.

VINCENT (Howard) Reportedly named for Vincent Vinson, who arrived in the area in the early 1890s. More likely named for grocer Vincent Clement Easley. Turner L. Clayton opened the PO in Easley's store 1 Apr 1907.

VINEGARONE [vin i guh RON] (Val Verde) About 1882 the Southern Pacific Railroad established a construction camp named for the vinegaroons [*sic*], whip scorpions common to the area, so named for the vinegar-like smell of their secretions. PO 27 Jan 1926, PM Beatrice N. Lowry.

VINEYARD (Jack) Vineyard was founded in the early 1880s by George Washington Vineyard. When he discovered that the spring water on his property had medicinal value, Vineyard changed the name to Wizard Wells and promoted the water as a cure for everything from arthritis to bleeding ulcers. The Chicago, Rock Island & Texas Railway established Vineyard Station several miles south of Wizard Wells about 1900. PO 26 July 1882 as Vineyard, PM James Knox White;

changed to Wizard Wells 2 Oct 1914, PM James T. Hopper.

VINTON (El Paso) John C. Vinton, a Southern Pacific Railroad surveyor, laid out the railroad route through the area in the early 1880s. PO 1 Nov 1892, PM John Morce. Also known as Morceville.

VIOLET (Nueces) The site was purchased about 1905 by Erwin Cushman and Louis Petrus. John Fister opened the PO in his general store 10 Sept 1913, named for his wife, Violet.

VIRGINIA POINT (Galveston) Named from the Virginia Point plantation and cotton gin operated by lawyer William Jefferson Jones, a newspaper editor and Texas Supreme Court justice born in Virginia. PO 30 Jan 1845, PM unknown; discontinued; reopened 23 Nov 1875, PM Wilhelmine Johnson.

VISTULA (Houston) Probably named for the Vistula, the longest and largest river in Poland. Naming details are unknown. PO 20 Mar 1900, PM John Smith.

VOCA (McCulloch) Voca is a shortened form of Avoca, brought to TX by brothers William and John Deans from Avoca, Benton County, AR, itself named for Avoca, Ireland. PO 19 Dec 1878, PM Walter P. Anderson. See Avoca.

VOLENTE (Travis) Volente grew around a grist mill established about 1860 by Thomas Anderson who opened the Anderson's Mills PO 21 Aug 1876. That office was discontinued in 1884 and reestablished 8 Feb 1886 as Volente by Andrew J. Stanford. The source of the name is uncertain. By a local story generally regarded as a folk tale, Volente was suggested by Lucy Anderson, the miller's wife, who claimed she found the name in a book and that it originated in an Indian language and meant "God willing." There may be more than a grain of truth in this; *volunté* is Latin for "willing, permitting."

VON ORMY (Bexar) In 1886 Norbert von Ormay [*sic*], presenting himself as Count Norbert von Ormay Auffenberg, an Austrian nobleman, arrived with a show of splendor and elegance that was widely reported. PO 14 Jan 1879 as Mann's Crossing, PM Anton F. Krause; changed to Von Ormy 4 Dec 1886, PM Branson Bywaters.

VOSS (Coleman) Founded on the William Day Ranch in 1904 and named for William Voss, business manager for ranch owner Mabel Lea Day. PO 27 Apr 1904, PM Henry Morgan. See Leaday.

VOTAW [VO taw] (Hardin) Clark Mordecai Votaw was assistant land commissioner for the Kirby Lumber Company and vice president of the Santa Fe Townsite Company that laid out the community on the line of the Gulf, Colorado & Santa Fe Railway about 1900. PO 19 Nov 1901, PM John W. Waldrop.

VOTH [VOTH] (Jefferson) Known as Elwood until 1902 when the Keith Lumber Company of Beaumont established the Voth Mill, named for lumberman Henry L. Voth. PO 2 Jan 1903, PM John H. Broome.

VSETIN (Lavaca) Settled in the 1880s largely by Moravians from Vsetín in the eastern Czech Republic.

W

WACO [WAY ko] (McLennan) The Waco townsite was surveyed in 1849 by George B. Erath, namesake of Erath County. The community was to have been called Lamartine, for the French poet and politician, Alphonse de Lamartine; instead Erath wrote Waco on the town plat, the name of the Wichita Native Americans whose main village was near the site of the present city. PO 27 July 1850 as Waco Village, PM Shapley Prince Ross, father of Sul Ross. See Ross; see Erath County.

WADSWORTH (Matagorda) William Bryant Wadsworth, born in Matagorda County in 1843, was a long-time community benefactor and promoter. The town was formally named in his honor when Christian Zipprian opened the PO 29 Aug 1907.

WAELDER [WEL der] (Gonzales) Founded about 1874 with construction of the Galveston, Harrisburg & San Antonio Railway; named for Frederick Jacob Waelder, a San Antonio lawyer and promoter of Texas railroads, especially the GH&SA. PO 15 June 1869 as Thompsonville; changed to Waelder 29 Oct 1874, PM Weldon J. Williamson.

WAKA [WAH kuh] (Ochiltree) Waka is a shortening of Wawaka, a town in Noble County, IN, probably named by rancher John N. Stump who came to Ochiltree County from Indiana by way of Missouri and Miami, TX. About 1920 the original Waka moved several miles north and replaced Burnside, a stop on the Panhandle & Santa Fe Railway. PO 23 Sept 1901 as Wawaka, PM Seraph Elizabeth Stump, whose husband, David (and John's brother), donated land for the office; changed to Waka 1 May 1927, PM Edward R. Stump, a third brother of John's.

WAKE (Crosby) Wake was founded in 1902 by site owner William Andrew Jackson Jones. John W. Smith chose the name for the Pacific Island of Wake that he had occupied with American forces in 1898 during the Spanish-American War. Smith opened the PO 2 May 1903.

WAKE VILLAGE (Bowie) Founded at the height of the Second World War to house employees of the Lone Star Army Ammunition Plant and the Red River Army Depot. The town was named in late 1944 for Wake Island in the Pacific, the site of bitter fighting between American and Japanese forces in December 1941. See Victory City.

WALBURG (Williamson) In 1880 Henry Doering (Daering) emigrated from Walburg, Germany. He opened a general store in 1882 and established the Walburg PO 10 July 1886.

WALDECK (Fayette) In the early 1840s the Adelsverein, a German Emigration Society, founded Waldeck, named for Count Ludwig Joseph von Boos-Waldeck, a German nobleman instrumental in the formation of the Adelsverein (see Fredericksburg). PO 29 Aug 1860 as Long Prairie; discontinued in 1876 and reestablished as Waldeck 24 Oct 1881, PM Reiner Aschen.

WALDRIP (McCulloch) Anderson Marion Waldrip emigrated from Tennessee by way of Mississippi in the 1840s. PO 24 Nov 1879, PM Hardy F. England.

WALHALLA [wahl HAH luh] (Fayette) Named by German settlers who began arriving in the 1830s. Walhalla is a variant of Valhalla, Germanic "home of the gods." PO 29 Sept 1886, PM Gustav Schuhmann.

WALKER (County) Created and organized 1846. Walker County was originally named for Robert J. Walker, US Senator from Mississippi in the late 1830s and early 1840s. Although Walker was a vigorous supporter of Texas annexation, his pro-Union views before and during the Civil War led to an 1863 Texas Legislature resolution that the namesake of the county would henceforth be Samuel Hamilton Walker, a captain of the Texas Rangers who died in 1847 in the War with Mexico.

WALL (Tom Green) Named for James Wall, father and son, who together kept a general store from the mid-1890s. PO 19 Mar 1906, PM James M. Wall, Jr.

WALLER (County) Created and organized 1873. Named for Edwin Waller, Sr. (1800–1881), born in Virginia. Waller moved to Texas in the early 1830s. He was signatory to the Texas Declaration of Independence and one of the framers of the Constitution of the Republic of Texas. He was later supervisor of the crew that surveyed the city of Austin and Austin's first mayor in 1840.

WALLER (Harris, Waller) Waller was laid out in 1884 and named for Waller County by King Hiram Faulkner. PO 21 Jan 1884, PM John T. Sanders.

WALLIS (Austin) Joseph E. Wallis, a Galveston merchant, was instrumental in building the Gulf, Colorado & Santa Fe Railway and was a director in the 1880s. PO 13 Oct 1873 as Bovine Bend; changed to Wallis Station 7 June 1886, PM William Guyler; changed to Wallis 1 July 1911.

WALLISVILLE (Chambers) In 1825 Elisha Henry Roberts Wallis brought his family from Nachitoches Parish, LA, to what became known as Wallis Hill. Wallis's descendants laid out the townsite in 1854. PO 25 Nov 1857, PM Albert G. Van Pradelles.

WAMBA [WAHM buh] (Bowie) PO 20 Oct 1897, PM Laurell B. Fort who reportedly chose the name for Wamba coffee, a popular brand in East Texas at the time.

WARD (County) Created 1887, organized 1892. Named for Thomas William Ward (1807–1872), born in Ireland. Ward fought in the Texas Revolution, built the 1837 Texas capital in Houston, was a three-term mayor of Austin in the 1840s and 1850s, and US consul to Panama in 1853. Wardville, the first seat of Johnson County and now a ghost town, was also named in honor of Thomas Ward.

WARDA (Fayette) Andreas Falke emigrated from Germany in the 1860s, opened a general store, and named the town Warda, a form of Wartha, his former home in Germany. PO 27 June 1877, PM William W. Lunn.

WARESVILLE (Uvalde) Founded in 1852 by William Ware, a soldier in the Texas Revolution, cited for his heroism at the Battle of San Jacinto. PO 13 Jan 1876, PM Charles F. Durbon.

WARFIELD (Midland) In the early 1880s the Texas & Pacific Railway established a flag stop named for J. F. Warfield, associated with the land surveys of the T&P. PO 11 Jan 1884, PM Harry A. Rathvon.

WARING (Kendall) In 1887 Robert Percival Maxwell Waring donated right-of-way land to the San Antonio & Aransas Pass Railway. Waring named the site for himself and for his ancestral home, Waringford, County Down, Ireland. PO 26 Apr 1880 as Windsor; changed to Waringford 20 Apr 1888, PM Richard Hunnan; changed to Waring 14 Mar 1891.

WARREN (Tyler) Founded on the line of the Sabine & East Texas Railway in 1882 by Alexander Young, who organized the Warren Land and Lumber Company the same year. Named for his former home, Warren, PA. PO 7 Sept 1883, PM John C. Tyrrell.

WARREN CITY (Gregg, Upshur) Founded and named in 1952 for the Warren Petroleum Corporation of Tulsa, OK, the town's largest employer.

WARRENTON (Fayette) Warrenton was named by shopkeeper Wilhelm (William) Neese for Warren Baker Burton Ligon (Legan), an early settler in the 1850s. PO 22 Nov 1866 as Neese's Store; changed to Warrenton 7 May 1873, PM Albert C. Lenert.

WASHBURN (Armstrong) In 1876 when the Fort Worth & Denver City Railway was building through the area, Robert Montgomery laid out the town of Washburn, named for Daniel Weston Washburn, an FW&DC construction engineer. PO 20 Mar 1888, PM James Logue.

WASHINGTON (County) An original Texas county, created 1836, organized 1837 and named for the town of WASHINGTON.

WASHINGTON (Washington) John Hall laid out the town of Washington in 1833 on a site that was then the Mexican Department of Nacogdoches, to become the Department of Brazos in 1834. The name was chosen about 1835 when Hall, with Asa Hoxey and several others, organized the Washington Townsite Company to develop and promote the community. Hoxey, a physician and planter, proposed the name for Washington, Wilkes County, GA, his former home, itself named for President George Washington. Over time, and likely to distinguish this Washington from Washington, DC, the town became known as Washington-on-the-Brazos. PO 22 May 1846, PM Alfred Moore.

WASKOM [WAHS kuhm] (Harrison) Founded in the late 1840s as Powell Town. The name was changed in 1872 when the Southern Pacific Railroad established Waskom Station, named for John Waskom, president of the SP. PO 18 May 1850 as Powellton, PM Thomas D. Powell; changed to Waskom Station 18 Mar 1872, PM William Sill.

WASTELLA [wahs TEL uh] (Nolan) PO 1 Apr 1907, PM store owner William H. Neely who chose the name for his teenage daughter, Kansas Wastella Neely. The next year he donated land for the Wastella station on the Roscoe, Snyder & Pacific Railway.

WATAUGA [wuh TAW guh] (Tarrant) Founded about 1880 with construction of the Texas & Pacific Railway. Watauga is a transfer from Watauga, Tennessee, Kentucky, or North Carolina, themselves named from the Watauga River of NC and TN. Watauga was apparently the name of a Cherokee village. PO 12 Dec 1883, PM Samuel A. Drysdale.

WATERLOO (Williamson) Josiah Rainwater came to Texas from Kentucky in the late 1880s, opened a general store and founded Waterloo, named for his birthplace, Waterloo, Pulaski County, KY. PO 12 May 1893, PM Patrick G. Tartar.

WATERMAN (Shelby) Founded about 1905 by the Waterman Lumber Company. PO 19 Mar 1906, PM William M. Waterman.

WATTERSON (Bastrop) Charles and Martha Watterson began farming in the area about 1852. PO 17 Jan 1878 as Live Oaks; changed to Watterson 7 Nov 1891, PM Charles Coffin Watterson.

WAXAHACHIE [wahks uh HACH ee] (Ellis) Founded in 1850 on land donated by early settler and hotelier Emory W. Rogers. The name is of Native American origin and is either a transfer from Waxahatchee Creek in Shelby County, AL, or from Wichita, a Caddoan language of the people who lived in the area until they were removed to Indian Territory in the mid-19th century. The name of Waxahatchee, AL, is probably a compound of *waksee*, a Muskogee clan name, and *hahchee* "creek, river." The Wichita source is claimed to be a compound based upon *waks* and *hahch*, meaning either "fat monster" or "fat wildcat." Circumstantial evidence supports the Alabama origin since a number of Texas names of the middle 19th century were transfers from the Southeastern US, and Emory Rogers, who played a leading role in organizing Waxahachie, was an Alabama native who brought his family to what is now Waxahachie in the 1840s. PO 13 Aug 1850, PM Joseph N. Whittenburg.

WAYLAND (Stephens) The local story is that Wayland was so named because it was "on the way" to more important places. PO 29 May 1877, PM William C. Hightower.

WAYSIDE (Armstrong) The area was first known as Beulah for the Beulah school, named for Beulah McSpadden, daughter of David McSpadden who donated land for the schoolhouse in 1893. By local lore the town was named for its location on the wayside (roadside) of Palo Duro Canyon when Harvey J. Bradford opened the Wayside PO 15 Sept 1897, PM Harvey J. Bradford.

WEALTHY (Leon) Jesse Quinn established the Poor PO 3 Sept 1888. Apparently the townspeople were reluctant to live in a town called Poor, so they changed the name to the more appealing Wealthy. PO 18 Apr 1894, PM John Barker.

WEATHERFORD (Parker) In 1855 Jefferson Weatherford, a Texas State Senator, and Isaac Parker, a Texas State Representative, co-sponsored a bill creating a new county to be called Parker with the seat at Weatherford. PO 18 Sept 1856, PM David Norton. See Parker County.

WEAVER (Hopkins) Founded about 1887 with construction of the St. Louis Southwestern

Railway (Cotton Belt). Named for James A. Weaver, banker, Hopkins County sheriff, and community benefactor of the 1870s and 1880s. PO 2 Nov 1847 as White Oak; changed to Weaver 27 Dec 1888, PM Charles W. Bryant.

WEBB (County) Created and organized 1848. Named for James Webb (1792–1856). Webb resigned his position as US district judge in Florida and moved to Houston in 1838. He was Texas Secretary of State and Attorney General under President Mirabeau Lamar, a state senator in the 1840s, and the first judge of the Texas Fourteenth Judicial District (Corpus Christi area) in the 1850s. (Webbville, now a ghost town in Jackson County, FL, was named for James Webb in 1827 when he was a practicing attorney and community benefactor and shortly before he was appointed district judge.)

WEBBERVILLE (Travis) John Ferdinand Webber left Vermont and joined Stephen F. Austin's Colony about 1825. He was the first settler on Webber's Prairie and later established a ranch on the Rio Grande in what is now Hidalgo County. PO 30 Jan 1845 as Webber's Prairie, PM Noah Smithwick.

WEBSTER (Harris) Founded about 1875 as Websterville for one James Webster who apparently either led or welcomed a colony of English settlers to the community about 1880. PO 9 June 1875 as Websterville; changed to Gardentown 15 Aug 1890; changed to Webster 15 July 1893, PM James W. Thompson.

WEBSTER (Wood) In 1856 Gilbert Smith Matthews bought the site and changed the name from Prospect Hill to Webster, for New England politician and statesman Daniel Webster. PO 19 May 1855 as Prospect Hill; changed to Webster 10 Jan 1856, PM Thomas C. Sadler.

WECHES [WEE chiz] (Houston) Joshua J. Hennes founded the town of Neches in the mid-1840s, named from the Neches River. Hennes opened the Neches PO 29 Jan 1847 that was discontinued in the early 1860s. When the request to reopen the Neches office was denied, the spelling was changed and the Weches PO opened 9 Aug 1887, PM Gedie S. Harrison. See Neches.

WEEDHAVEN (Jackson) Rather than a suburban homeowner's worst fear, Weedhaven was named for civil engineer James F. Weed, who bought the property in the 1930s.

WEEPING MARY (Cherokee) Weeping Mary was founded at the close of the Civil War as a community for newly emancipated African Americans. A local story relates the name to a freedwoman named Mary who lost her land to a cheating plantation owner, but a more likely source is the weeping Virgin Mary, *Stabat Mater Dolorosa*.

WEESATCHE [WEE sach] (Goliad) First known as Middleton since the town was thought to be midway between Goliad and Clinton. The name was changed in 1860 to Weesatche, a phonetic spelling of Spanish *huisache*, the "sweet acacia," itself a borrowing from Nahuatl (Aztec) meaning "many thorns." PO 22 Nov 1855 as Middleton; discontinued and reopened as Weesatche 16 May 1860, PM William Cartwright.

WEHDEM (Austin) Wehdem, originally known as New Wehdem, was named by

German settlers in the 1890s for Wehdem, now part of Stemwede in northwest Germany. PO 8 Apr 1904, PM Henry Poeppelmeyer.

WEIMAR [WEYE mer] (Colorado) Daniel W. Jackson donated land for the townsite and for a station on the Galveston, Harrisburg & San Antonio Railway in the early 1870s. In 1873 the town was named by Thomas Wentworth Peirce, part owner of the GH&SA who claimed fond memories of a visit to Weimar, Germany. PO 23 Dec 1873, PM Henry Windrow.

WEINERT [WEYE nert] (Haskell) Founded in 1906 with construction of the Wichita Valley Railway. Named for jurist and politician Ferdinand C. Weinert of Seguin. Weinert was Texas Secretary of State in 1913 and served in four state legislatures from the early 1890s through the mid-1930s. PO 28 Dec 1906, PM William M. Webb. Weinert in Guadalupe County is also named for Ferdinand Weinert.

WEIR [WIHR] (Williamson) Weir grew around a Missouri–Kansas–Texas Railroad station established in 1903. Named for the Thomas Calvin Weir family, settlers from Tennessee in the mid-1850s. PO 6 May 1895 as Townsville, named for PM James Towns; changed to Weir 27 May 1903, PM Lucy A. Weir, daughter-in-law of T. C. Weir.

WELCOME (Austin) Johann Schmidt from Oldenburg, Germany, chose the name about 1852. Schmidt was reportedly struck by the hospitality shown to the new settlers. PO 20 Nov 1871, PM Henry Meyer.

WELDON (Houston) Some say Weldon is a reflex of the lumberman's cry "well done" for a good job or for an accident avoided; others say the namesake is Weldon Morrow who reportedly operated a sawmill in the Magnolia area and donated land for the townsite. Rather the town is named for Weldon Jones Murchison who relocated from Mississippi in the 1860s. Newton L. Stepp transferred the Calhoun's Ferry PO to Murchison's store and renamed the office Weldon 13 Aug 1869; Murchison was the 2nd PM beginning April 1874.

WELFARE (Kendall) Welfare is a direct translation or a popular etymology of either German *Wohlfahrt* "welfare, well-being" or Wohlfahrt, a German family name of the same meaning. Several Wohlfahrt families had settled in the area when the community was formally named in 1880. PO 15 Nov 1875 as Bonton; changed to Joseway 3 Feb 1880; changed to Welfare 25 Mar 1880, PM Charles Beseler.

WELLINGTON (Collingsworth) Founded in 1890, largely through the efforts of owners and operators of the Rocking Chair Ranch. The name was chosen to honor the Duke of Wellington, the hero of Waterloo, by one or more of the Rocking Chair's English investors. PO 9 Jan 1891, PM Carrie Barton. See Aberdeen.

WELLMAN (Terry) Founded in 1918 as a shipping point on the South Plains & Santa Fe Railway, a subsidiary of the Atchison, Topeka & Santa Fe Railway. Named for Augustus Ogden Wellman, assistant treasurer of the AT&SF. PO 11 Mar 1925, PM Alvan L. Burnett.

WELLS (Cherokee) The Kansas & Gulf Short Line Railroad founded Wells in 1885, named for Elija H. Wells, the railroad's chief engineer and surveyor. PO 8 Aug 1857 as Cheeseland in the now vanished town of Cheeseland (reportedly named for Caroline Hillenkamp's unforgettable cheeses); changed to Wells 29 Mar 1886, PM Eureka Spinks.

WELLS CREEK (Anderson) Named from Wells Creek, itself named for Samuel G. Wells, the first site owner in the 1830s.

WESCO (Gray) Named for the *Wes*tern Carbon *Co*mpany, manufacturer of carbon black, used in the production of tires and printer inks, from the mid-1820s.

WESER [WEEZ er] (Goliad) Apparently named for the Weser, a ship that brought many German and Polish settlers from Bremen to the US in the 1860s. The ship was named from the Weser River in northwest Germany. PO 4 Apr 1881, PM Henry Cook.

WESLACO [WES luh ko] (Hidalgo) Weslaco is a compression of *W. E. S*tewart *La*nd *Co*mpany that sold the townsite to Edmund Cooper Couch and Robert Lee Reeves who founded Weslaco in 1917. The company was founded by Walter Edgar Stewart, a banker, financier, and benefactor of several East Texas communities. The Stewart Airport in Tyler is named in his honor. PO 17 Mar 1920, PM Allie Reeves.

WESLEY (Washington) Wesley is a popular etymology of Veseli, a Czech settlement of the 1850s named for a Veselí in the Czech Republic. The Rev. Joseph Opocensky organized one of the first Moravian congregations in the US at Veseli in 1864 and was the first Wesley PM 12 Aug 1867.

WEST (McLennan) Thomas Marion West, a businessman and landowner from Kentucky, opened a general store in the early 1880s and organized the West Bank a decade later. PO 23 June 1852 as Bold Springs; changed to West 28 Aug 1882, PM Thomas West.

WESTBROOK (Wood) Founded about 1880 by landowner and community benefactor Sampson Westbrook who had relocated from Georgia in the early 1850s.

WESTFIELD (Harris) Named for site owner Gadi F. West in 1870 with construction of the International–Great Northern Railroad. PO 25 Aug 1873, PM Herman Tautenhahn.

WESTHOFF (DeWitt) Founded as Bello in 1906 when the Galveston, Harrisburg & San Antonio Railway extended a line from Cuero. Formally named for lumber merchant William Westhoff, Sr. of Indianola, an early settler from Hanover, Germany. PO 10 Dec 1906, PM William L. Moore.

WESTMINSTER (Collin) The Methodist church bought a private school in the town of Severn Points in the early 1890s and changed the name of the school to Westminster College, named from Westminster, Carroll County, MD, itself named from the London borough of Westminster. PO 15 June 1899, PM George Hullinger.

WESTON (Collin) Larkin Adamson, who established the PO 16 Jan 1854, chose the name for his former home, Weston, Platte County, MO.

WESTOVER (Baylor) The name was changed from Seaborn in 1910 when the Gulf, Texas & Western Railroad established a station on land owned by cattleman John Wesley Stevens. Stevens and his wife, Martha, chose the name for her mother's family. PO 18 Jan 1907 as Seaborn, PM James Seaborn Gore; changed to Westover 1 Jan 1911, PM James H. B. Kyle.

WESTPHALIA (Falls) Named in the late 1870s by settlers with family roots in Westphalia, Germany. PO 20 May 1887, PM Pius Heckman, pastor of St. Mary Catholic Church in Temple.

WESTVILLE (Trinity) James M. West came to Texas from Mississippi in 1880. He became a successful lumberman, banker, newspaper publisher, and Houston businessman, and he served as the first PM of the Westville office 11 June 1900.

WESTWAY (Deaf Smith) John Slaton, a Hereford lawyer, chose the name in the early 1920s, reportedly because the town was a few miles west on the way to Hereford, the Deaf Smith county seat.

WESTWORTH VILLAGE (Tarrant) Westworth, named for its location west of Fort Worth, was founded in 1942 as a military aircraft construction site that became Carswell Air Force Base in 1948, named for World War II Medal of Honor recipient Horace S. Carswell, Jr.

WETMORE (Bexar) Founded in 1880 with construction of the International–Great Northern Railroad. Named for Jacob S. Wetmore, a director of the I-GN. PO 13 Feb 1890, PM Rosa Claridge.

WETSEL (Collin) In the late 1840s Henrich Wetzel (Henry Wetsel), a cabinet maker from Pennsylvania, moved to Collin County where he became a millwright and landowner. Now part of Allen.

WHARTON (County) Created and organized 1846. Named for brothers John Austin Wharton and William Harris Wharton, lawyers from Nashville, TN. William Wharton was appointed first minister to the United States by Republic of Texas President Sam Houston in 1836. John Wharton was captain and later commander of Terry's Texas Rangers during the Civil War.

WHARTON (Wharton) The town of Wharton was founded with the creation of Wharton County in 1846. The Peach Creek PO, opened 27 Feb 1837, was changed to Wharton 1 July 1847, PM Gabriel Eagan.

WHEELER (County) Created 1876, organized 1879. Named for Royal Tyler Wheeler (1810–1864), born in Vermont. Wheeler moved to San Augustine in 1839 and had an influential legal career as district attorney, professor of law at Austin College, and Chief Justice of the Texas Supreme Court from 1857, when he succeeded John Hemphill for whom Hemphill County is named, until his death in 1864.

WHEELER (Wheeler) Founded and named for Wheeler County in 1904 by ranchers Robert Rogers and James Stanley. Rogers was the first PM 9 Nov 1905.

WHEELOCK (Robertson) Eleazar Louis Ripley Wheelock founded and named the town for himself in the mid-1830s. Wheelock was an Indian agent, surveyor, and Texas land commissioner. PO 12 Sept 1846, PM Simon W. Kellogg.

WHITE CITY (Wilbarger) Named for James Franklin White, who emigrated from Georgia and began farming in the area in the early 1870s.

WHITE DEER (Carson) Named from the White Deer Lands, the name of the reorganized Francklyn Land and Cattle Company. The name was taken from White Deer Creek where, according to legend, a hunting party happened across an albino deer drinking from the stream. PO 17 Dec 1888 as Whig; changed to White Deer 7 Jan 1889 by PM Charles D. Hawes.

WHITE ROCK (Hunt) White Rock was named from the local Austin chalk geological formations, themselves named for the outcroppings near Austin. The community was known as Tidwell Creek from the 1840s until the Tidwell Creek PO was changed 13 Apr 1868 to White Rock, PM Jones Kennedy.

WHITE SETTLEMENT (Tarrant) By some accounts the settlement was so named to distinguish a community for Anglos from a nearby town of largely Native Americans; by others, the town was named for the many settlers with the family name White (more than 100) who moved to the county in the 1870s. A 2005 referendum to change the name to West Settlement failed by a ten to one margin. PO 13 Sept 1886, PM David R.Tinsley.

WHITEFACE (Cochran) Founded in 1924, northeast of its present location; named from Whitecamp and Whiteface Pasture on Christopher Columbus Slaughter's Lazy S Ranch, themselves named from his white-faced (Hereford) cattle. When the South Plains & Santa Fe Railway built through the area in the mid-1920s the town was physically moved several miles southwest to trackside. PO 1 Feb 1926, PM Mary L. Word.

WHITEHOUSE (Smith) Whitehouse was apparently named in the mid-1840s when a lone building was whitewashed and became the most visible structure in the town. Some say it was the Methodist church. PO 9 June 1873, PM Thomas B. Fowler. Whitehouse is now a Tyler suburb.

WHITESBORO (Grayson) Ambrose and Sarah White brought their family from Illinois in the summer of 1848. Ambrose White, a surveyor of the site that became known as White's Colony, opened the PO as Whitesborough 12 May 1860.

WHITEWRIGHT (Grayson) In 1878 William Whitewright of New York purchased the site and donated land for a station on the Missouri–Kansas–Texas Railroad, in which he was a major investor. PO 8 Apr 1878 as White Wright, PM James A. Batsell.

WHITHARRAL [WIT hehrl] (Hockley) John Whitfield Harral, whose name was compressed to Whitharral, was a trustee of the Yellow House Land Company that was organized in the 1920s to oversee the subdivision and sale of the Littlefield Ranch. PO 12 Apr 1926, PM Carradine B. Edgar.

WHITNEY (Hill) Whitney was founded in 1879 with construction of the Houston & Texas Central Railway and named for Charles A. Whitney of New York, son-in-law of railroad magnate and financier Charles Morgan and a major shareholder in the H&TC. PO 5 Jan 1880, PM John S. Napier.

WHITSETT [WIT sit] (Live Oak) In 1913 land for the townsite and for a station on the San Antonio, Uvalde & Gulf Railroad was donated by Taylor Whitsett and Walter Reiffert; each hoping to have the town named in his honor. Reiffert tossed a coin, called correctly by Whitsett. PO 3 Sept 1913, PM Robert H. Weatherly.

WHITSON (Coryell) Named for Numa Whitson, a former steamboat engineer who moved to the area in the 1870s and established a cotton gin and gristmill. PO 8 Oct 1891, PM James Holt.

WHITT (Parker) Likely named for local landowner and surveyor John Roger Witt [*sic*]. PO 5 Feb 1877, PM Washington W. Hopkins.

WHON [WAHN] (Coleman) Whon is an English phonetic spelling of "Juan." The particular Juan who provided the name is unknown, perhaps a cowboy on the McCain ranch. PO 16 June 1903, PM Bertha McCain.

WICHITA [WICH uh taw, WICH un tah] (County) Created 1858, organized 1881. Named from the Wichita River and for the Wichita, a Caddoan people who lived in Texas from the Red River south to the Waco area from the early 18th century until the 1850s when the few remaining Texas Wichitas were moved to a reservation in Oklahoma.

WICHITA FALLS (Wichita) Founded in 1876 by the heirs of John Scott who, according to legend, won the site of Wichita Falls in a poker game. The town was named for a small Wichita River waterfall that was washed away by a flood in the 1880s, leaving the name without a referent. A century later, in 1987, city engineers recreated the falls as a series of steps with recirculating water. PO 5 Mar 1879, PM Charles G. Convers.

WICKETT (Ward) In 1881 the Texas & Pacific Railway established Arroya Switch. With the discovery of oil in 1927 the community flourished as Wickett, named for oilfield developer and town promoter Fred H. Wickett. PO 14 June 1927, PM Onnie Mae O'Brien.

WIED [WEED] (Lavaca) Wied was settled largely by Germans beginning in the 1870s. The community was named for Wied in the German Rhineland, or more likely for a family named Wied. Henry and Antonia Wied were established farmers by 1880. PO 28 Dec 1889, PM William Kruse.

WIEDEVILLE (Washington) Wiedeville grew around Wiedes Store established by Johann George Christian Wiede, Heinrich Wilhelm Christian Wiede, and Christian Heinrich Wiede, sons of Carl and Louise Wiede who brought their family from Brandenburg, Germany, in the 1860s.

WIERGATE (Newton) Wiergate was founded in 1917 for employees of the Wier Longleaf

Lumber Company owned by Houston lumberman Robert W. Wier. PO 5 Sept 1918, PM Harold Hopkins.

WIGGINS (McLennan) A stop on the Texas Central Railway from the early 1880s, first known as Tokio. Because of resentment toward Japan during the Second World War the name was changed to Wiggins for one of the several local Wiggins families.

WILBARGER (County) Created 1858, organized 1881. Named for pioneer settlers Josiah and Mathias Willbarger. In the 1820s Josiah Wilbarger moved from Missouri to Texas and settled in Stephen F. Austin's Colony. He was joined by his brother, Mathias, a surveyor for Austin's colony, and by the early 1830s the brothers had established a settlement north of present Bastrop. Josiah Wilbarger is a Texas legend if for no other reason than he lived for twelve years after being scalped by Comanches in 1833.

WILCO (Hartley) Wilco, a blend of *Wil*son and *Co*rporation, was named from the ranch operated by brothers James, Frank, and John Wilson from the 1860s.

WILDERVILLE (Falls) Ervin M. Wilder, Captain of the 2nd Regiment of Texas Mounted Volunteers in the Mexican War, bought the site in 1860. PO 25 June 1874, PM Thomas Sims.

WILKINS (Upshur) Founded as Wilkins Mills in the late 1870s on the Texas & Pacific Railway line, named for the sawmills operated by William Scrivner Fitzowens Wilkins, who was also the first postmaster 7 July 1879. The Wilkins Mills PO was discontinued 1880; reestablished as Wilkins 9 Nov 1903, PM James Lee Dunagan.

WILLACY (County) Created 1911, organized 1921. Named for John G. Willacy (1859–1943), born in Louisville, KY. Willacy came to the Corpus Christi area in 1892 and served in the Texas Legislature as representative or senator from 1899 to 1914. He introduced the bill to create the county that bears his name.

WILLAMAR (Willacy) Willamar is a blend of *Wil*liam and *Lamar* for William Harding and Samuel Lamar Gill who laid out the town in 1921. They blended their wives' names, Laura and Sarah, to name the next town they founded, LASARA.

WILLIAM PENN (Washington) John Eldridge chose the name about 1848 for the William Penn, a steamboat that operated on the Brazos River in the 1840s and 1850s. PO 13 May 1873, PM Abner Lay.

WILLIAMSBURG (Lavaca) In the 1840s John Williams laid out the town adjacent to his general store and gristmill. In April 1876 Williams moved the Petersburg PO to his store and renamed the office Williamsburgh.

WILLIAMSON (County) Created and organized 1848. Named for Robert McAlpin Williamson (c. 1805–1859), born in Georgia. Williamson was known as "Three Legged Willie" because of an illness in his teen years that left him with a right leg useless from the knee down and permanently frozen at a right angle. He wore a wooden prosthesis attached to the knee that gave him the appearance of having three legs. Williamson came to Texas in the late 1820s and became a major figure in Texas law and politics. He was a Texas Ranger, a newspaper editor, a Republic of Texas Supreme Court justice, and a multi-term state representative and senator. When Williamson County was created in 1848 Williamson had just completed his second term in the Texas State Senate.

WILLIS (Montgomery) Peter J. and Richard S. Willis kept the P. J. Willis general store from about 1850. The brothers donated land for the townsite and for the Houston & Great Northern Railroad station in the early 1870s. The Danville PO, named for PM Daniel Robinson, was changed to Willis 29 Apr 1872, PM Fannie E. George.

WILLS POINT (Van Zandt) William Wills, an early settler in the 1840s, operated a rest stop for travelers and stagecoaches on the Dallas-Shreveport road from the mid-1850s. The community was apparently known as Iola until Thomas White opened the Wills Point PO 23 Sept 1870, named for William Wills, who by this time had become a Van Zandt tax assessor.

WILMER (Dallas) In 1872 the Houston & Texas Central Railway established the Prairie Valley station. The name was changed to Wilmer when James W. Johnson established the PO 5 May 1884, reportedly for A. J. Wilmer, a conductor on the H&CT.

WILMETH (Runnels) Named for Joe B. Wilmeth, a Ballinger banker and businessman. PO 1 Apr 1907, PM Mary L. Smith.

WILSEY (Parmer) In 1905 the consortium overseeing the XIT Ranch appointed Frederick W. Wilsey to the office of land commissioner in charge of sales.

WILSON (County) Created and organized 1860. Named for James C. Wilson (1816–1861) who emigrated from Yorkshire, England, in 1837. A lawyer and Methodist minister, he was a local official and served in the Texas Legislature in the 1840s and 1850s.

WILSON (Lynn) Founded by William Green and business associates from Shiner in 1912. Named from the Wilson County School Lands, surveyed in the last years of the 19th century. PO 19 Jan 1912, PM Lonnie Lumsden.

WIMBERLEY (Hays) In the late 1840s Pleasant Wimberley arrived in Texas from North Carolina by way of Mississippi and Arkansas. He established the complex known as Wimberly Mills—a gristmill, sawmill, molasses mill, and cotton gin. PO 10 Feb 1880, PM Robert Moore.

WINCHELL (Brown) The Fort Worth & Rio Grande Railway established Winchell Station in the early 1900s, named for Benjamin L. Winchell, vice president and general manager of the FW&RG. PO 9 Apr 1903, PM Charles Wilson.

WINCHESTER (Fayette) Laid out about 1857 by John Grom (Groome) and reportedly named for his former home, Winchester, Franklin County, TN. PO 4 June 1866, PM Thomas Moore.

WINDOM (Fannin) Founded in the 1870s on the line of the Texas & Pacific Railway. The traditional stories are that the name was chosen because the site was the highest and windiest point between Texarkana and Fort Worth, or for one Thomas Windom, reported to be the engineer who drove the first T&P train through the area. Perhaps a more likely namesake is William Windom, US Representative and Senator from Minnesota from the late 1860s into the 1880s and later US Secretary of the Treasury. Windom was a well-known politician and several communities and natural features are named for him, including Windom Peak in Colorado. PO 18 Jan 1885, PM Howard Bowman.

WINDSOR (McLennan) The town of Windsor was named from the Windsor Ranch, itself named about 1900 by owner Harry Chauncey Chamberlin for his former home, Windsor, VT.

WINDTHORST [WIN thorst] (Archer) In 1891 Fred Ledergerber and the first settlers founded Windthorst as a refuge for persecuted German Catholics. The community was named for Ludwig Windthorst, a leader of the German Catholic political party in the 1870s and 1880s. PO 12 Mar 1892, PM John Andres.

WINFIELD (Titus) When the Texas & St. Louis Railway built through the area in the early 1880s, the station was called Barrett for site owner William C. Barrett. The community was known as Winfield from 1892for William H. Winfield of Texarkana, general passenger agent for the T&SL. PO 10 Oct 1887 as Carr, PM Patrick H. Carr; changed to Winfield 13 Dec 1892, PM Emma S. Faver.

WINGATE (Runnels) Named for Walter J. Wingate, a Ballinger attorney. PO 14 Mar 1892, PM Mary F. McKandles.

WINK (Winkler) Wink, at first a collection of shacks, tents and dugouts, grew around the Hendrick oilfield, part of the 1920s oil boom in Winkler County. Originally called Winkler for the county, the name was shortened to Wink when Marvin Beasley opened the post office 18 June 1927.

WINKLER (County) Created 1887, organized 1910. Named for Clinton McKamy Winkler (1821–1882), born in North Carolina. Winkler moved to Texas in 1840, served in the state legislature, rose to the rank of lieutenant colonel during the Civil War, and was an associate justice on the Texas appellate court in the 1870s. Winkler in Navarro County was also named in his honor.

WINKLER (Navarro) Clinton McKamy Winkler was a Corsicana lawyer who was instrumental in the creation of Navarro County. PO 28 Apr 1879, PM America M. Chastain. See Winkler County.

WINNIE (Chambers) Founded in 1895 by the Gulf & Interstate Railway and named for Fox Winnie, a contractor, part owner, and officer of the G&I. PO 6 Sept 1895, PM Zachariah Guess.

WINNSBORO (Wood) By one popular etymology, a Mr. Wynn often rode to town on a burro. Wynn's burro gave its name to the town of Wynnsboro and when the local newspaper ran out of "y"s it was forced to print the name as Winnsboro. Rather, the town was founded in 1854 by Dr. William R. McMillan and his stepfather John E. Winn (Wynn), who gave rise to a second popular etymology. The story went around that John Winn, being English, insisted on calling his land a borough and not a farm. William McMillan opened the Winnsborough PO 6 Mar 1855; changed to Winnsboro 1893.

WINONA [weye NO nuh] (Smith) Named for Winona Douglas, daughter of James P. Douglas, Civil War hero, railroad promoter, and state senator from Smith County for most of the 1870s. PO 2 Jan 1878, PM John R. Nolan.

WINTER HAVEN (Dimmit) Apparently named by settlers from Winter Haven, FL. PO 2 Apr 1927, PM Samuel Young.

WINTERS (Runnels) Founded in the early 1890s; named for Fort Worth real estate agent John Nichols Winters. PO 7 Mar 1891, PM Frederick Plate.

WISE (County) Created and organized 1856. Named for Henry A. Wise (1806–1876), a native Virginian. Wise was US Representative in the 1830s and 1840s, Governor of Virginia in the 1850s, and a Brigadier General in the Confederate Army. As a US Representative Wise was a strong supporter of statehood for Texas.

WISE (Van Zandt) Henry A. Wise (not the Henry A. Wise for whom Wise County was named), established the Wise PO 20 May 1889.

WITTING (Lavaca) Named for George Witting, a Columbus, TX, merchant and landowner. PO 12 Apr 1880, PM Fritz Gehrels.

WIZARD WELLS (Jack) See Vineyard.

WODEN (Nacogdoches) Named for Woden, the chief Teutonic god, with establishment of the PO 25 Jan 1886 by William Parrish. The name was reportedly suggested by the second PM, Anna Dodds.

WOKATY [WO kuht ee] (Milam) Named for one or more Wokaty families who emigrated from Bohemia in the 1870s. PO 7 Mar 1900, PM Anthony Wokaty.

WOLFE CITY (Hunt) Lemuel Pinckney Wolfe and Abbey Wilson established a gristmill in the early 1870s. PO 8 Apr 1878 as Wolf's Mill, PM Lemuel P. Wolfe.

WOLFFORTH [WUL forth] (Lubbock) Founded about 1916 as Wolffarth [*sic*], named for brothers George Wolforth [*sic*], a rancher and president of the Citizens National Bank of Lubbock, and Eastin Wolfforth [*sic*], a rancher and a Lubbock County sheriff. PO 14 Feb 1924, PM Jesse D. Perkins.

WOMACK (Bosque) Hugh Anderson established the PO 25 Feb 1880 as Mornack, probably a mistranscription of Womack; changed to Womack 25 Feb 1880. Thomas J. Womack followed Anderson as postmaster in 7 Feb 1881.

WOOD (County) Created and organized 1850. Named for George Thomas Wood (1795–1858), a native Georgian who moved to Texas in 1839. Wood was an officer in the Mexican War, and the second Governor of Texas (1847–1849).

WOOD HI (Victoria) William A. Wood, a prominent rancher and the brother of Tobias Wood for whom Woodsboro in Refugio County is named, died in 1900. In his honor his wife, Nellie Borland Wood, donated land for a school that opened in 1918. The town took the name of the William A. Wood Memorial High School.

WOODROW (Lubbock) Founded in the 1910s when Thomas Woodrow Wilson was President of the United States. There was considerable discussion over whether the community should be named Woodrow or Wilson but since the name Wilson was common and Woodrow less so, Woodrow was chosen.

WOODS (Panola) Edwin Hull from North Carolina established a general store in the early 1850s. The town, first known as Hull's Store, was formally named when Theodrick Wood opened the Woods PO 16 Jan 1854.

WOODSBORO (Refugio) The land development firm of Johnson and Pugh of Danville, IL, laid out Woodsboro in 1906, named for Tobias DeCantillon Wood who sold part of the Bonnie View Ranch to Johnson and Pugh. PO 8 Apr 1907, PM William D. Holloman. See Bonnie View.

WOODSON (Throckmorton) Oliver Josephus Wood and Roxana Penelope Wood began farming in the area in the 1870s; their son, Currier L. Wood, opened the Woodson PO 31 Aug 1905.

WOODVILLE (Tyler) In 1847 Dr. Josiah Wheat donated land for the townsite that he named in honor of George Thomas Wood, the second Governor of Texas (1847–1849). PO 6 Jan 1843 as Collard's; changed to Woodville 7 Sept 1847, PM James H. Fulgham. See Wood County.

WOODWARD (La Salle) Named in the early 20th century for land developer and real estate promoter David J. Woodward, founder of the Woodward Carriage Company of San Antonio and the Woodward Body Works in Austin. His home in San Antonio is on the National Register of Historic Places. PO 27 Aug 1907, PM Edwin E. Oliver.

WOOSLEY (Rains) James Woosley, born in Virginia, lived in Tennessee, Illinois, Missouri, and Arkansas before settling in Texas. Woosley and several of his sons were farmers and storekeepers from the 1870s.

WORTHAM (Freestone) Founded about 1870 as Tehuacana. The name was changed to Long Bottom, a popular etymology of Longbotham. Robert Longbotham from Durham, England, was the original land grantee in the 1830s. In 1874 the community was formally named for farmer and merchant Luther Rice Wortham, who was instrumental in securing a station on the Houston & Texas Central Railway. PO 20 Nov 1871 as Long Bottom; changed to Wortham 14 July 1874, PM Samuel C. Denton.

WORTHING (Lavaca) Namesake Fabian Worthing opened the Worthing PO 12 Apr 1882. The name was changed to Orsack 7 July 1882 by PM Joseph Orsack and changed back to Worthing 29 Apr 1892 when Fabian Worthing again became PM.

WRIGHT CITY (Rusk, Smith) Named from Wright's Candy Factory established by grocer Theophilus O. Wright in the 1920s.

WRIGHTSBORO (Gonzales) According to a local popular etymology, now told tongue in cheek, in the 1850s farmer Leroy Wright owned several burros that had free range. When one was spotted it was customary to say, "that's Wright's burro." And thus,

Wrightsboro received its name. Leroy and Margaret Wright were indeed local farmers, but the extent of their burro population is unknown. PO 27 Apr 1869, PM Joseph Swearingen.

WUTHRICH HILL (Williamson) Christian Gottfried Wuthrich emigrated from Bern, Switzerland, in the early 1870s and settled in the area in the late 1880s.

WYLIE (Collin, Dallas, Rockwall) In 1888, when the Gulf, Colorado and Santa Fe Railway bypassed the town of Nickelville and established a station named for William D. Wylie, right-of-way agent for the GC&SF, Nickelville and its nickel store, forerunner of the five and dime, moved a half mile north to trackside where it was joined by the small towns of Eureka, St. Paul and Lone Elm. PO 29 Aug 1883 as Nickelville; changed to Wylie 10 June 1886, PM John F. Butler.

WYLIE (Taylor) About 1902 Mary Varina Wylie donated land for a school and a church. A decade later she donated additional land and requested that the school be named in honor of her deceased husband, early settler James Jackson Wylie. The town was named from the Wylie school in the mid-1910s. PO 19 Dec 1904 as Sambo, named by PM John Vance for his friend Sam Little, known as "Sambo."

Y

YANCEY (Medina) About 1890 ranchers John J. Strait and John J. Kilgore founded Yancey; named for their sons, Yancey Clarence Strait and William Yancey Kilgore. PO 1 Dec 1897, PM Benjamin F. Moss.

YANTIS (Wood) Settled in the 1860s and formally named by miller and ginner George R. Yantis from Kentucky. Yantis established the post office 28 Jan 1885.

YARBORO [YAHR ber uh] (Grimes) James Quincy Yarboro (Yarborough), a merchant from Alabama, established a cotton gin and gristmill on Yarboro Creek shortly after the end of the Civil War. PO 27 Dec 1871 as Wallace Prairie; changed to Yarboro(ugh) 24 Sept 1879, PM James Q. Calhoun.

YARD (Anderson) The local story is that when merchant Bruce Gray applied for a post office his list of possible names inadvertently included a customer's request for a yard of cloth. The Post Office Department dutifully approved the office as Yard, 21 July 1903.

YARRELTON (Milam) Thomas Yarrell, a merchant from North Carolina, opened the Yarrellton PO in his dry goods store 10 Feb 1880. For unknown reasons the name was changed to Yaralton 20 Aug 1886 and back to Yarrellton 4 Dec 1886.

YOAKUM (County) Created 1876, organized 1907. Named for Henderson King Yoakum (1810–1856), born in Claiborne County, TN. Yoakum, mayor of Murfreesboro, TN, in 1837, relocated to Huntsville in 1845 and was instrumental in establishing Huntsville as the seat of Walker County. He was professor and librarian at Austin College and wrote one of the first comprehensive histories of Texas, *History of Texas from its First Settlement in 1685 to its Annexation to the United States in 1846*, first published in 1856.

YOAKUM [YO kuhm] (DeWitt, Lavaca) Yoakum was founded in 1887 with construction of the San Antonio & Aransas Pass Railway and named for Benjamin Franklin Yoakum, general manager and traffic manager of the SA&AP at the time and later president of the St. Louis–San Francisco Railway. Yoakum was a visionary railroad executive and an important figure in Texas railroading in the late 19th century. The Conroy PO, opened 25 July 1884, was changed to Yoakum 6 Sept 1887, PM John P. Jamieson.

YORKTOWN (DeWitt) The town was named for site owner John York, a Kentuckian who joined Stephen F. Austin's colony in the mid-1820s, was granted land for his service in the Texas Revolution, and moved to the area in the 1840s. York was killed in a fight with Indians at Escondido Creek in 1848. PO 10 Mar 1851, PM John King.

YOUGEEN [yoo JEEN] (Bee) About 1910 Eugenia O'Callahan McGloin, daughter of a pioneer Bee County family and in-law of one of the founders of the McMullen-McGloin Colony, donated several acres for the railroad station, which she named for herself through a phonetic spelling of Eugene.

YOUNG (County) Created 1856, organized 1874. Named for William Cocke Young (1812–1862), born in Tennessee. Young, a soldier and jurist, moved to Texas in 1837. He was the first sheriff of Red River County, a district attorney for the Republic of Texas, and a US Marshal.

YOUNG (Freestone) Dr. Tolbert Fannin Young from Memphis, TN, practiced medicine in the area from 1875 and was a prominent community leader and benefactor. Young was the first PM, 6 Nov 1883.

YOUNGSPORT (Bell) Named for one or more Young families, likely the first permanent settlers in the area. Michael Young brought his family from Alabama as part of Robertson's Colony in the 1820s. PO 7 Aug 1871, PM John Bruce.

YOWELL [YOL] (Delta, Hunt) Brothers John W. and James F. Yowell, farmers and shopkeepers from the 1880s. PO 22 Jan 1898, PM Ida V. Spears.

YSLETA [is LET uh] (El Paso) Ysleta was founded by Isleta Pueblo Indians and Spaniards from Isleta Pueblo south of present-day Albuquerque, NM, fleeing the Pueblo Revolt of 1680. *Isleta* "little island" was named by 16th century Spanish explorers for its location on the Rio Grande. The Texas settlement first called *Ysleta del Sur* "Little Island of the South," is generally regarded as the oldest extant settlement in Texas. Ysleta is now part of El Paso. PO 29 June 1857 as Isleta, PM Henry Dexter, discontinued in 1868. The Socorro PO was changed to Ysleta 10 Mar 1874.

YTURRIA [ee TER yuh] (Willacy) Named from the Yturria Ranch, developed over several decades following the Civil War by Francisco Yturria (1830–1912), a Brownsville businessman and banker. PO 1907, PM James Bryden.

YZNAGA [iz NAH guh] (Cameron) Antonio José Yznaga y Castillo emigrated from Cuba in the late 1830s and to Texas in the mid-1840s. He was a cattle rancher, businessman, and civic leader. His daughter, Yrene, was the daughter-in-law of Mifflin Kenedy, the business partner of Richard King, founder of the King Ranch. See Kenedy.

Z

ZABCIKVILLE [ZAHB chik vil] (Bell) Zabcikville was settled largely by Texas Czechs, many from RATIBOR. The community was first known as Lugoville for John Lugo who kept a general store in the 1900s. Lugo sold the store to Frank Marek who changed the name to Marekville. About 1932 the name became officially Zabcikville for Frank Zabcik who bought the store and added a saloon.

ZAPATA [zuh PAHT uh] (County) Created and organized 1858. Named for Antonio Zapata (c. 1800–1840), a pioneer rancher and military leader who fought against Santa Anna and the Mexican Centralist government in the 1830s.

ZAPATA (Zapata) Founded in the late 18th century when settlers from south of the Rio Grande established the town of Habitación, later known as CARRIZO after a Native American group known as the "reed people" by early Spanish explorers. The name was changed to Bellville in 1858 for Texas Governor Peter Hansborough Bell and changed again in 1898 for its location in Zapata County. Englishman Henry Redmond, a local trader and rancher who donated land for the Zapata County courthouse, established the Carrizo post office 16 Jan1854. The name was changed to Zapata 2 May 1901.

ZAVALA (County) Created 1858, organized 1884. Named for Manuel Lorenzo Justiniano de Zavala y Sáenz (1788–1836), an important figure in Mexican politics in the 1820s and in Texas politics in the 1830s. Zavala signed the Texas Declaration of Independence and was the first Vice President of the Republic of Texas in 1836.

ZAVALLA [zuh VAL uh] (Angelina) Zavalla was organized in 1900 on the line of the Texas & New Orleans Railroad, named for its location on land granted by Mexico to empresario Lorenzo de Zavala [*sic*] in 1829 and authorizing Zavala to settle some 500 families in southern Texas. PO 19 Jan 1901, PM Jesse C. Fondren. See Zavala County.

ZELLA (McMullen) Howard Bland, from Muskingum County, OH, was a pioneer sheep rancher and part owner of the Zella Townsite Company that laid out the community on the line of the San Antonio, Uvalde & Gulf Railroad in 1913. Named for Bland's daughter, Zella. PO 13 Mar 1914, PM Emmons C. Williams.

ZEPHYR (Brown) A zephyr is a gentle breeze, a soft west wind. A blue norther (a classic Texasism) is just the opposite, a sudden dramatic drop in temperature under a blue-black sky. The local story is that the town was named ironically about 1850 when a group of surveyors was caught in a blue norther and one remarked "this is some zephyr we have run into." PO 29 Dec 1879, PM John M. Wilson.

ZIMMERSCHEIDT (Colorado) Frederick Adolph Zimmerscheidt emigrated from Rhineland-Palatinate, Germany in 1838. Zimmerscheidt was particularly involved with educational institutions in the area, donating land for the first schoolhouse and promoting Hermann University in Frelsburg (which never materialized).

ZIONVILLE (Washington) The community grew around the Zion Lutheran Church founded by Rev. William Pfennig in 1870.

PO 4 Apr 1872, PM Adolph Streckert. Also spelled Zionsville.

ZIPPERLANDVILLE (Falls) This small community was named from the Zipperlen store, opened by Otto Wilhelm Zipperlen in the 1920s.

ZORN (Guadalupe) Probably named for Joseph Zorn, Jr., Seguin postmaster in the 1870s and mayor of Seguin in the 1890s and 1900s. PO 3 Sept 1891, PM John F. Timm.

ZUEHL [ZEEL] (Guadalupe) Ferdinand Zuehl (Fred Zuhl) from Prussia established a general store in the 1860s. PO 16 June 1888 as School; changed to Zuehl 19 Oct 1906, PM Willie H. Zuehl.

ZUNKERVILLE (Karnes) Named for the Zunker family from Prussia headed by August and Amilia Zunker. August Zunker was a local farmer and his son, Harry, was a farmer and merchant from the early 1920s.

REFERENCES AND COUNTY INDEX

This bibliography is organized into statewide and county-specific resources. It's worth noting that all should be used with caution: Our experience was that new or updated print and digital sources appeared almost daily, especially for statewide references, and some county-specific resources dating from the 1920s can be found only in special collections of university libraries. However, each will provide a starting point for anyone wishing to pursue the history of Texas towns or counties.

County references are followed by the names of the communities whose naming history is included in the book. Much thanks is owed to master's degree-seeking scholars who chose to document the history of a county, and county historical societies that prepared keepsake centennial books.

A singularly valuable resource is *The Handbook of Texas*, a true Texas treasure. This six-volume collection, updated regularly online, includes more than 25,000 entries on Texas geography, history, and culture from the 16th century. First published in 1952 and made available online in 1999, the *Handbook* was the brainchild of Walter Prescott Webb, a Professor of History at the University of Texas and President of the Texas State Historical Association who claimed the *Handbook* was "a reference to practically anything on Texas history." It is indeed that—and much more.

General References

Bright, William. *Native American Placenames of the United States*. Norman: University of Oklahoma Press, 2004.

Coulet du Gard, René. *Dictionary of Spanish Place Names of the Northwest Coast of America, Vol. IV*. Newark, DE: Editions des deux mondes, 1983.

Hines, Robert R., ed. *Doing History in Small-Town Texas*. Palo Alto College, 2018. pacweb.

alamo.edu/interactivehistory/projects/town/projects_town.htm.

Madison, Virginia, and Hallie Crawford Stillwell. *How Come It's Called That?: Place Names in the Big Bend Country*. Marathon, TX: Iron Mountain Press, 1997.

Pizzola, Gail Carle. "A Sociolinguistic Study of the Folk Etymology of Selected Texas Place Names." PhD dissertation, Indiana University of Pennsylvania, 2000.

Ruiz, Jorge Luis García. *Texas: The False Origin of the Name*. Ruiz, 2019.

St. Clair, Kathleen E., and Clifton R. St. Clair. *Little Towns of Texas*. Jacksonville, TX: Jayroe Graphic Arts, 1982.

Stewart, George R. *American Place-Names: A Concise and Selective Dictionary for the Continental United States of America*. New York: Oxford University Press, 1985.

Tarpley, Fred. *1001 Texas Place Names*. Austin: University of Texas Press, 1980.

Tarpley, Fred. *Place Names of Northeast Texas*. Commerce: East Texas State University, Educational Research and Field Services, 1969.

Texas State Historical Association, and University of Texas at Austin. *The Handbook of Texas*. Austin: Texas State Historical Association, 1999. tshaonline.org.

Counties

ANDERSON

Avera, Carl L. *Wind Swept Land*. San Antonio: Naylor, 1964.

Hohes, Pauline Buck. *A Centennial History of Anderson County, Texas*. Tucson, AZ: Americana Unlimited, 1976.

ANDREWS

Andrews County Heritage Committee. *Andrews County History, 1876–1978*. Andrews, TX: n.p., 1978.

ANGELINA

Angelina County Historical Survey Committee. *Land of the Little Angel: A History of Angelina County, TX*. Lufkin, TX: n.p., 1977.

Boon, Effie Mattox. "The History of Angelina County." Master's thesis, University of Texas, 1937.

ARANSAS

Aransas County-Rockport Centennial, Inc. *A Glimpse at Our Past*. Corpus Christi, TX: Coastal Printing, 1971.

ARCHER

Loftin, Jack. *Trails Through Archer: A Centennial History—1880–1980*. Burnet, TX: Nortex, 1979.

ARMSTRONG

Armstrong County Historical Association. *A Collection of Memories: A History of Armstrong County, 1876–1965*. Hereford, TX: Pioneer, 1965.

ATASCOSA

Clover, Margaret (Gidley). "The Place-Names of Atascosa County, Texas." Master's thesis, University of Texas, 1952.
Robert H. Thonhoff Collection, and Atascosa History Committee. *Atascosa County History*. Pleasanton, TX: The Committee, 1984.

AUSTIN

Biesele, Rudolph Leopold. *The History of the German Settlements in Texas 1831–1861*. Austin: Eakin, 1998.

BAILEY

McKillip, LaVonne. *Early Bailey County History: Paleo-man to Plow-man, 12,000 B.C. to 1930 A.D.* Muleshoe, TX: B. Stovall, 1978.

BANDERA

Bandera County History Book Committee. *History of Bandera County, Texas*. Dallas: Curtis Media, 1986.
Hunter, J. Marvin. *A Brief History of Bandera County, Covering One Hundred Years of Intrepid History*. Baird, TX: Baird Star, 1949.
Tobin, Peggy. *Bandera Pass*. N.d. tshaonline.org/handbook/online/articles/rkb01.

BASTROP

Korges, William Henry. "Bastrop County: Historical and Educational Development." Master's thesis, University of Texas, 1933.
Moore, Bill. *Bastrop 1691–1900*. Wichita Falls, TX: Nortex, 1977.

BAYLOR

Baylor County Historical Society. *Salt Pork To Sirloin: Vol. II/The History of Baylor County, Texas from 1878 to 1976*. Wichita Falls, TX: Nortex, 1977.

BEE

Bauer, Grace. *Bee County Centennial 1858–1958*. Beeville, TX: Beeville Publishing, 1958.
Ezell, Camp. *Historical Story of Bee County, Texas*. Beeville, TX: Beeville Publishing, 1973.

BELL

Atkinson, Bertha. "The History of Bell County, Texas." Master's thesis, University of Texas, 1929.
Bell County Historical Commission, and E. A. Limmer. *Story of Bell County, Texas*. Austin: Eakin, 1998.

BEXAR

Green, David P. *Place Names of San Antonio: Plus Bexar and Surrounding Counties*. N.p.: Maverick Publishing, 2015.
Hines, Robert R., ed. *Doing History in Small-Town Texas*. Palo Alto College, 2018. pacweb.alamo.edu/interactivehistory/projects/town/projects_town.htm.
St. Clair, Kathleen E., and Clifton R. St. Clair. *Little Towns of Texas*. Jacksonville, TX: Jayroe Graphic Arts, 1982.

BLANCO

Moursund, John Stribling. *Blanco County History*. Burnet, TX: Nortex, 1979.

Speer, John W., and Henry C. Armbruster. *History of Blanco County.* Austin: Pemberton Press, 1965.

BORDEN

Frantz, Joe B. *Gail Borden: Dairyman to a Nation.* Norman: University of Oklahoma, 1951.

BOSQUE

Bosque County History Book Committee, and Bosque County Historical Commission. *Bosque County: Land and People: A History of Bosque County, Texas.* Dallas: Curtis Media, 1986.
Pool, William C. *Bosque Territory: A History of an Agrarian Community.* Kyle, TX: Chaparral, 1964.
Radde, Rebecca D. *Bosque Primer: An Introduction to the History of Bosque County.* N.p.: Radde, 1976.

BOWIE

Chandler, Barbara Susan Overton. "A History of Bowie County." Master's thesis, University of Texas, 1937.
Tarpley, Fred. *Place Names of Northeast Texas.* Commerce: East Texas State University, Educational Research and Field Services, 1969.

BRAZORIA

Brazoria County Federation of Women's Clubs. *History of Brazoria County.* N.p.: n.p., 1940.
Creighton, James A. *A Narrative History of Brazoria County.* Waco: Texian Press, 1975.

BRAZOS

Brundidge, Glenna Fourman, Langston James Goree, Paul David McKay, and Paul Robert Scott. *Brazos County History: Rich Past, Bright Future.* Bryan, TX: Family History Foundation, 1986.

BREWSTER

Casey, Clifford B. *Mirages, Mysteries and Reality: Brewster County, Texas, the Big Bend of the Rio Grande.* Seagraves, TX: Pioneer, 1974.

Madison, Virginia, and Hallie Stillwell. *How Come It's Called That?* Marathon, TX: Iron Mountain Press, 1997.

BRISCOE

Briscoe County Historical Survey Committee. *Footprints of Time in Briscoe County.* Vol. 2. Silverton, TX: Briscoe County Historical Survey Committee, 1992.

BROOKS

Lasater, Dale. *Falfurrias: Ed C. Lasater and the Development of South Texas.* College Station: Texas A&M University Press, 1985.

BROWN

Havins, Thomas Robert. *Something About Brown: A History of Brown County, Texas.* Brownwood, TX: Banner Printing, 1958.

White, James C. *The Promised Land: A History of Brown County, Texas.* Brownwood, TX: Brownwood Banner, 1941.

BURLESON

Burleson County Historical Society. *Astride the Old San Antonio Road: A History of Burleson County, Texas.* Caldwell, TX: Burleson County Historical Society, 1980.

BURNET

Bowden, M. G. "History of Burnet County." Master's thesis, University of Texas, 1940.

Debo, Darrell. *Burnet County History.* Burnet, TX: Eakin, 1979.

CALDWELL

Historical Society of Caldwell County. *Historical Caldwell County: Where Roots Inter-*

twine. Wolfe City, TX: Hennington, 2003.
O'Banion, Maurine O. "The History of Caldwell County [Texas]." Master's thesis, University of Texas, 1931.

CALHOUN

Calhoun County Historical Commission. *The Shifting Sands of Calhoun County, Texas*. Port Lavaca, TX: Port Lavaca Wave, 1981.
Hayes, John Benjamin. *An Administrative Survey and Proposed Plan of Reorganization of the Schools of Calhoun County, Texas*. Austin: University of Texas, 1939.

CALLAHAN

Chrisman, Brutus Clay. *Early Days in Callahan County*. [Baird, TX]: n.p., 1996.

CAMERON

Hildebrand, Walter W. "The History of Cameron County, Texas." Master's thesis, North Texas State College, 1950.
Thompson, James Heaven. "A Nineteenth Century History of Cameron County, Texas." Master's thesis, University of Texas, 1965.

CAMP

Camp County History Book Committee. *Camp County, Texas: Customs and Characters*. Pittsburg, TX: Pittsburg Camp County Library, 1986.

CARSON

Randel, Mrs. Ralph E., and Carson County Historical Survey Committee. *A Time to Purpose: A Chronicle of Carson County*. Hereford, TX: Pioneer, 1966.
Robertson, Pauline D., and R. L. Robertson. *Cowman's Country: Fifty Frontier Ranches in the Texas Panhandle, 1876–1887*. Amarillo, TX: Paramount, 1981.

CASS

Cass County Genealogical Society, and Kathryn McAlexander. *History of Cass County People.* Atlanta, TX: The Society, 1982.

Tarpley, Fred. *Place Names of Northeast Texas.* Commerce: East Texas State University, Educational Research and Field Services, 1969.

CASTRO

Castro County Historical Commission. *Castro County, 1891–1981.* Dallas: Taylor, 1981.

CHAMBERS

Harry, Jewel Horace. "A History of Chambers County." Master's thesis, University of Texas, 1940.

CHEROKEE

Cherokee County Historical Commission (Tex.). *Cherokee County History,* Jacksonville, TX: 2001. texashistory.unt.edu/ark:/67531/metapth354360.

CHILDRESS

Ord, Paul, Susie Ord, Verdel Davis, and D. O. Nash. *They Followed the Rails: A History of Childress County.* Childress, TX: Childress Reporter, 1970.

CLAY

Taylor, William Charles. *A History of Clay County.* Austin: Jenkins, 1974.

COCHRAN

Fleming, Elvis E., and David J. Murrah. *Texas' Last Frontier: A New History of Cochran County.* Morton, TX: Cochran County Historical Society, 2001.

COKE

Yarbrough, Jessie Newton. *A History of Coke County, Home of the Rabbit Twisters: The Early Years to 1953.* Robert Lee, TX: J. N. Yarbrough, 1979.

COLEMAN

Coleman County Historical Commission (Tex.). *A History of Coleman County and Its People.* San Angelo, TX: Anchor, 1985.

COLLIN

Stambaugh, J. Lee, and Lillian J. Stambaugh. *A History of Collin County, Texas.* Austin: Texas State Historical Association, 1958.

COLLINGSWORTH

Collingsworth County History Book Committee. *Collingsworth County 1890–1984.* Dallas: Taylor, 1985.

COLORADO

Colorado County Historical Commission. *Colorado County Chronicles: From the Beginning to 1923.* Austin: Eakin, 1986.
Hinton, Mary. *Weimar, Texas: First 100 Years, 1873–1973.* N.p.: n.p., 1973.

COMAL

Haas, Oscar. *History of New Braunfels and Comal County, Texas 1844–1946*. Austin: Steck Company, 1968.
Penshorn, Lillian E. "A History of Comal County." Master's thesis, Southwest Texas State Teachers College, 1950.

COMANCHE

Lightfoot, Billy B. "The History of Comanche County, Texas, to 1920." Master's thesis, University of Texas, 1949.

CONCHO

LeFevre, Hazie Davis. *Concho County History 1858–1958*, Vol. 2. Eden, TX: Hazie Davis LeFevre, 1959.

COOKE

Jones, C. N. *Early Days in Cooke County 1848–1873*. Gainesville, TX: Cooke County Heritage Society, 1977.

CORYELL

Coryell County Genealogical Society. *Coryell County, Texas, Families, 1854–1985*. Dallas: Taylor, 1986.
Scott, Zelma. *A History of Coryell County, Texas*. Austin: Texas State Historical Association, 1965.

COTTLE

Bennett, Carmen Taylor. *Our Roots Grow Deep: A History of Cottle County*. Floydada, TX: Blanco Offset Printing, 1970.

CRANE

Hooper, Gordon L. *Pioneer History of Crane County Before 1925*. Bloomington, IN: iUniverse, 2012.

CROCKETT

The Crockett County Historical Society. *A History of Crockett County*. San Angelo, TX: Anchor, 1976.

CROSBY

Crosby County Pioneer Memorial Museum, and Crosby County Historical Commission. *Crosby County History: 1876–1977*. Dallas: Taylor, 1978.

CULBERSON

Wylie, Rosa Lee. *History of Van Horn and Culberson County, Texas*. Hereford, TX: Pioneer, 1973.

DALLAM

Dallam and Hartley Counties Historical Association. A *Tale of Two Counties: Dallam-Hartley Counties*. N.p.: n.p., 1985.

Hunter, Lillie Mae. *The Book of Years: A History of Dallam and Hartley Counties*. Hereford, TX: Pioneer, 1969.

Mauldin, William David. "History of Dallam County, Texas." Master's thesis, University of Texas, 1938.

DALLAS

Lewis Publishing Company. *Memorial and Biographical History of Dallas County, Texas . . . Containing a History of This Important Section of the Great State of Texas, from the Earliest Period of its Occupancy to the Present Time . . . and Biographical Mention of Many of its Pioneers, and Also of Prominent Citizens of Today*. Chicago: Lewis, 1892.

Mesquite Historical Committee. *A Stake in the Prairie*. Mesquite, TX: Mesquite Historical Committee, 1984.

Popik, Barry. *Dallas*, 2009. barrypopik.com/index.php/new_york_city/entry/dallas_summary.

Stark, Anne. "A History of Dallas County." Master's thesis, University of Texas, 1935.

Tarpley, Fred. *Place Names of Northeast Texas*. Commerce: East Texas State University, Educational Research and Field Services, 1969.

DAWSON

Lindsey, M. C. *The Trail of Years in Dawson County, Texas.* Baltimore, MD: Gateway Press, 1987.

DEAF SMITH

Deaf Smith County Historical Society. *Deaf Smith County, Texas, 1876–1981: The Land and Its People.* N.p.: The Society, 1982.

DELTA

Tarpley, Fred. *Place Names of Northeast Texas.* Commerce: East Texas State University, Educational Research and Field Services, 1969.

DENTON

Bates, Edmond Franklin. *History and Reminiscences of Denton County.* Denton, TX: McNitzky Printing, 1975.
Hervey, Hollace. *Historic Denton County: An Illustrated History.* San Antonio: Historical Publishing Network, 2002.

DEWITT

Murphree, Nellie, and Robert W. Shook. *A History of DeWitt County.* [Victoria, TX]: n.p., 1962.

DICKENS

Arrington, Fred. *A History of Dickens County: Ranches and Rolling Plains.* Burnet, TX: Nortex, 1971.

DIMMIT

Tidwell, Laura Knowlton. *Dimmit County Mesquite Roots.* Austin: Wind River Press, 1984.

DONLEY

Browder, Virginia. *Donley County: Land O'Promise.* Wichita Falls, TX: Nortex, 1975.

Ashtola
Clarendon
Giles
Hedley
Jericho
Lelia Lake

DUVAL

McCoy, Dorothy Abbott. *Oil, Mud and Guts.* Brownsville, TX: Springman-King Lithograph, 1977.

Benavides
Concepcion
Freer
Ramirez
Realitos
Rios
Rosita
San Diego
Santa Cruz
Sejita
Seven Sisters

EASTLAND

Cox, Edwin T. *History of Eastland County, Texas.* San Antonio: Naylor, 1950.
Lindsey, Robert Yancy. "A History of Eastland County, Texas." Master's thesis, University of Texas, 1940.

Carbon
Chaney
Cisco
Desdemona
Dothan
Eastland
Gorman
Kokomo
Mangum
Nimrod
Okra
Olden
Ranger
Rising Star
Sabanno
Tiffin

ECTOR

Horton, Finas Wade. "A History of Ector County, Texas." Master's thesis, University of Texas, 1950.

Douro
Goldsmith
Judkins
North Cowden
Notrees
Odessa
Penwell

EDWARDS

Rocksprings Woman's Club. *Edwards County History.* San Angelo, TX: Anchor, 1984.

Barksdale
Carta Valley
Hackberry
Rocksprings

EL PASO

Porter, Eugene O. *San Elizario: A History.* Austin: Jenkins, 1973.
Sonnichsen, C. L. *Pass of the North.* El Paso: Texas Western Press, 1968.

Anthony
Canutillo
Clint
El Paso
Fabens
San Elizario
Smeltertown
Socorro
Tigua
Tornillo
Vinton
Ysleta

ELLIS

Ellis County History Workshop, and Edna Davis Hawkins. *History of Ellis County, Texas.* N.p.: Ellis County History Workshop, 1972.
Tarpley, Fred. *Place Names of Northeast Texas.* Commerce: East Texas State University, Educational Research and Field Services, 1969.

Alma
Alsdorf
Avalon
Bardwell
Boyce
Boz
Bristol
Britton
Byrd
Creechville
Crisp
Ennis
Ferris
Forreston
Garrett
Howard
Ike
Italy
Lumkins
Maypearl
Milford
Nash

ERATH

Eoff, Vallie. "A History of Erath County, Texas." Master's thesis, University of Texas, 1937.

FALLS

Old Settlers and Veterans Association of Falls County, Texas, and Roy Eddins. *History of Falls County, Texas.* N.p.: n.p., 1947.
St. Romain, Lillian Schiller. *Western Falls County, Texas.* Austin: Texas State Historical Association, 1951.

FANNIN

Bonham Public Library. *Fannin County Folks and Facts: Fannin County, Texas: A Collection of Historical Sketches and Family Histories.* Bonham, TX: Taylor, 1977.
Tarpley, Fred. *Place Names of Northeast Texas.* Commerce: East Texas State University, Educational Research and Field Services, 1969.

FAYETTE

Lotto, Frank. *Fayette County: Her History and Her People.* Schulenburg, TX: Sticker Steam Press, 1902.
Williams, Marjorie L. *Fayette County: Past & Present.* La Grange, TX: Marjorie L. Williams, 1976.

Rek Hill
Roznov
Rutersville
Saint John
Schulenburg
Waldeck
Walhalla
Warda
Warrenton
Winchester

FISHER

Yeats, E. L., and Hooper Shelton. *History of Fisher County, Texas*. Sweetwater, TX: Shelton Press, 1975.

Celotex
Claytonville
Eskota
Hamlin
Hobbs
Longworth
McCaulley
Roby
Rotan
Royston
Sylvester

FLOYD

Hall, Claude V. "The Early History of Floyd County." Master's thesis, University of Texas, 1922.

Aiken
Allmon
Barwise
Dougherty
Floydada
Lockney
McCoy
Muncy
Providence
Sterley

FOARD

Phelps, Bailey P. *They Loved the Land: Foard County History*. Quanah, TX: Quanah Tribune-Chief, 1969.

Crowell
Foard City
Margaret
Rayland
Thalia

FORT BEND

Bridges, Jim L. "The History of Fort Bend County, 1822–1861." Master's thesis, University of Texas, 1939.

Wharton, Clarence R. *History of Fort Bend County*. Houston, TX: Anson Jones Press, 1939.

Arcola
Beasley
Booth
Cinco Ranch
Crabb
Dewalt
Fairchilds
Fifth Street
Foster
Fresno
Fulshear
Guy
Juliff
Katy
Kendleton
Missouri City
Needville
Orchard
Pleak
Richmond
Rosenberg
Simonton
Stafford
Sugar Land
Thompsons

FRANKLIN

Hicks, Billy, and Doris Meek. *Historical Records of Franklin County, Texas*. Mount Vernon, TX: Franklin County Historical Survey Committee, 1972.

Majors
Mount Vernon
Scroggins

FREESTONE

Browne, Philip Dale. "The Early History of Freestone County to 1865." Master's thesis, University of Texas, 1925.

Freestone County Historical Commission. *History of Freestone County Texas*. N.p.: n.p., 1978.

Avant Prairie
Bonnerville
Butler
Cotton Gin
Dew
Fairfield
Freestone
Kirvin
Lanely
Luna
Simsboro
Stewards Mill
Streetman
Teague
Turlington
Wortham
Young

FRIO

Frio Pioneer Jail Museum Association. *Frio County, Texas: A History*. Dallas: Taylor, 1979.

GAINES

Coward, Margaret, ed. *The Gaines County Story: A History of Gaines County, Texas*. Seagraves, TX: Pioneer, 1974.

GALVESTON

Graham, Samuel B, and Ellen Newman. *Galveston Community Book*. Galveston: Arthur H. Cawston, 1945.
McComb, David G. *Galveston: A History*. Austin: University of Texas Press, 1986.
Webb, Jesse Owen. "The History of Galveston to 1865." Master's thesis, University of Texas, 1924.

GARZA

Didway, Charles. *Wagon Wheels: A History of Garza County*. Burnet, TX: Eakin, 1980.

GILLESPIE

Curtis, Sara Kay. "A History of Gillespie County, Texas, 1846–1900." Master's thesis, University of Texas, 1943.
Gillespie County Historical Society. *Pioneers in God's Hills*. Austin: Von Boeckmann-Jones, 1960.

GLASSCOCK

Greenwood, Max H. "A Brief History of Glasscock County." Master's thesis, Texas Technological College, 1937.

GOLIAD

Pruett, Jackie L. *History and Heritage of Goliad County*. Austin: Eakin, 1985.

GONZALES

Gonzales County Historical Commission. *The History of Gonzales County, Texas*. Dallas: Curtis Media, 1995.

Tarpley, Fred. *1001 Texas Place Names.* Austin: University of Texas Press, 1980.

GRAY

Gray County History Book Committee. *Gray County Heritage.* [Pampa, TX?]: Gray County History Book Committee, 1985.

Prouse, Frances Darlene. "A History of Gray County, Texas." Master's thesis, University of Texas, 1957.

GRAYSON

Grayon County Frontier Village. *The History of Grayson County, Texas.* Dallas: Curtis Media, 1981.

Tarpley, Fred. *Place Names of Northeast Texas.* Commerce: East Texas State University, Educational Research and Field Services, 1969.

GREGG

Dickson, John Britain. "History of Gregg County, Texas." Master's thesis, University of Texas, 1957.

Tarpley, Fred. *Place Names of Northeast Texas.* Commerce: East Texas State University, Educational Research and Field Services, 1969.

GRIMES

Blair, E. L. *Early History of Grimes County.* N.p.: n.p., 1930.

Grimes County Historical Commission. *History of Grimes County, Land of Heritage and Progress.* Dallas: Taylor, 1982.

Tarpley, Fred. *1001 Texas Place Names.* Austin: University of Texas Press, 1980.

GUADALUPE

Moellering, Arwerd Max. "A History of Guadalupe County, Texas." Master's thesis, University of Texas, 1938.

Weinert, Willie Mae. *An Authentic History of Guadalupe County*. Seguin, TX: The Seguin Enterprise, 1951.

HALE

Cox, Mary L. *History of Hale County, Texas.* Plainview, TX: n.p., 1937.

Wofford, Vera Dean. *Hale County Facts and Folklore, Volume II.* Dallas: Taylor, 1986.

HALL

Baker, Inez. *Yesterday in Hall County, Texas.* Dallas, TX: The Book Craft, 1940.

HAMILTON

Pool, Oran Jo. "A History of Hamilton County." Master's thesis, University of Texas, 1954.

HANSFORD

Hansford County Historical Commission. *Hansford County, Texas.* Spearman, TX: Hansford County Historical Commission, 1983.

HARDEMAN

Jones, J. Paul. "History of Hardeman County, Texas." Master's thesis, North Texas State College, 1949.

Neal, Bill. *The Last Frontier: The Story of Hardeman County*: Quanah Tribune-Chief, 1966.

HARDIN

Schaadt, Robert L. *The History of Hardin County, Texas.* Dallas: Curtis Media, 1991.

HARRIS

American Association of University Women (North Harris County Branch). *The Heritage of North Harris County*. 1986. texashistory.unt.edu/ark:/67531/metapth611550.

McComb, David G. *The City in Texas: A History*. Austin: University of Texas Press, 2015.

HARRISON

Armstrong, James Curtis. "The History of Harrison County, Texas, 1839 to 1880." Master's thesis, University of Colorado, 1930.

HARTLEY

Dallam and Hartley Counties Historical Association. *A Tale of Two Counties: Dallam-Hartley Counties*. N.p.: n.p., 1985.

Hunter, Lillie Mae. *The Book of Years: A History of Dallam and Hartley Counties*. Hereford, TX: Pioneer, 1969.

HASKELL

Felker, Rex A. *Haskell County and Its Pioneers*. Quanah, TX: Nortex, 1975.

HAYS

Dobie, Dudley Richard. "The History of Hays County." Master's thesis, University of Texas, 1932.

Popik, Barry. *Buda*. 2008. barrypopik.com/index.php/new_york_city/entry/buda_summary.

Stovall, Frances. *Clear Springs and Limestone Ledges: A History of San Marcos and Hays County for the Texas Sesquicentennial*. [San Marcos, TX?]: Hays County Historical Commission, 1986.

Buda
Dripping Springs
Goforth
Hays
Kyle
Niederwald
San Marcos
Uhland
Wimberley

HEMPHILL

Riley, Glyndon M. "The History of Hemphill County." Master's thesis, West Texas State Teachers College, 1939.

Canadian
Gageby
Gem
Hemphill

HENDERSON

Faulk, J. J. *History of Henderson County Texas: Recording Names of Early Pioneers, Their Struggles and Handicaps, Condition and Appearance of the County, Advancement and Progress to the Present.* Athens, TX: Athens Review, 1929.

Athens
Brownsboro
Chandler
Eustace
Fincastle
Gun Barrel City
Larue
Leagueville
Malakoff
Murchison
Opelika
Payne Spring
Pickens
Poynor
Tool
Trinidad

HIDALGO

Edwards, Beatrice L. *Mercedes*, 2014. Internet resource.

Hidalgo County Centennial Corp. *The Centennial Celebration of the Organization of Hidalgo County in Texas, December 7–13, 1952.* Mission, TX: Times Publishing, 1952.

Abram
Alamo
Cipres
Citrus City
Donna
Edcouch
Edinburg
Elsa
Faysville
Granjeno
Hargill
Havana
Heidelberg
Hidalgo
La Blanca
La Joya
Laguna Seca
Linn
Los Ebanos
McAllen
Mercedes
Mila Doce
Mission
Penitas
Pharr
Progreso
Relampago
Sam Fordyce
San Juan
Sharyland
Solino
Sullivan City
Weslaco

HILL

Bailey, Ellis. *A History of Hill County, Texas 1838–1965.* Waco: Texian Press, 1966.

Reed, Ruth B., Walton Smith, Celeste Varnell Dodd, and Hill County Historical Commission. *A History of Hill County, Texas, 1853–1980.* N.p.: The Commission, 1980.

Reese, James Verdo. "A History of Hill County, Texas to 1873." Master's thesis, University of Texas, 1961.

Abbott
Aquilla
Birome
Blum
Chatt
Covington
Derden
Files Valley
Hillsboro
Hubbard
Huron
Itasca
Lebanon
Lovelace
Malone
Mayfield
Menlow
Mertens
Mount Calm
Osceola
Peoria
Vaughan
Whitney

HOCKLEY

Brasher, Lillian. *Hockley County: 1921–1971 The First Fifty Years.* Canyon, TX: Staked Plains Press, 1978.

Watkins, Orville R. "History of Hockley County." Master's thesis, Texas Technological College, 1941.

HOOD

Ewell, Thomas T. *History of Hood County*. Granbury, TX: Junior Woman's Club, 1956.
Smith, Shirley Robert. *Cresson Community Crossroads*. N.p.: S. R. Smith, 1988.

HOPKINS

Adams, Florene Chapman. *Hopkins County and Our Heritage*. Sulphur Springs, TX: Florene Chapman Adams, 1970.
Orren, G. G. "History of Hopkins County." Master's thesis, East Texas State Teachers College, 1938.
Tarpley, Fred. *Place Names of Northeast Texas*. Commerce: East Texas State University, Educational Research and Field Services, 1969.

HOUSTON

Aldrich, Armistead Albert. *The History of Houston County Texas*. San Antonio: Naylor, 1943.
Bishop, Eliza, and History Book Committee. *History of Houston County, Texas 1687–1979*. Tulsa, OK: Heritage Publishing Company, 1979.

HOWARD

Pickle, Joe. *Gettin' Started: Howard County's First 25 Years*. Big Spring, TX: Howard County Heritage Museum, 1980.

HUDSPETH

Acala
Allamoore
Arispe
Cornudas
Dell City
Esperanza
Etholen
Fort Hancock
Fort Quitman
McNary
Sierra Blanca

HUNT

Harrison, W. Walworth. *History of Greenville and Hunt County, Texas.* Waco: Texian Press, 1976.
Tarpley, Fred. *Place Names of Northeast Texas.* Commerce: East Texas State University, Educational Research and Field Services, 1969.

Aberfoyle
Boles Home
Caddo Mills
Campbell
Cash
Celeste
Clinton
Commerce
Dixon
Fairlie
Greenville
Hogeye
Jacobia
Jardin
Kingston
Lane
Neyland and Neylandville
Peniel
Quinlan
Tawakoni
White Rock
Wolfe City

HUTCHINSON

Hutchinson County Historical Commission. *A Hutchinson County History Book Featuring Local History, Photographs, Illustrations, and Biographies.* N.p.: n.p., 1980.

Borger
Bunavista
Dial (Gulf Dial)
Electric City
Fritch
Holt
Phillips
Plemons
Pringle
Sanford
Stinnett
Texroy

IRION

Irion County Historical Society. *A History of Irion County, Texas.* San Angelo, TX: Anchor, 1978.

Arden
Barnhart
Mertzon
Noelke
Sherwood

JACK

Huckabay, Ida Lasater. *Ninety-Four Years in Jack County: 1854–1948.* Waco: Texian Press, 1949.
Jack County Genealogical Society. *The History of Jack County Texas.* Dallas TX: Curtis Media, 1986.

Bryson
Cundiff
Gibtown
Jacksboro
Jermyn
Joplin
Perrin
Postoak
Squaw Mountain
Vineyard
Wizard Wells

JACKSON

Taylor, Ira Thomas. *The Cavalcade of Jackson County.* San Antonio: Naylor, 1938.

Carancahua
Cordele
Edna
El Toro
Francitas
Ganado
LaSalle
La Ward
Lolita
Manson
Morales
Navidad
Weedhaven

JASPER

McReynolds, James M. "A History of Jasper County, Texas, Prior to 1874." Master's thesis, Lamar State College of Technology, 1968.

Bessmay
Blox
Bonami (Bon Ami)
Browndell
Buna
Call
Curtis
Evadale

Gist
Jasper
Kirbyville
New Blox
Roganville

JEFF DAVIS

Madison, Virginia, and Hallie Crawford Stillwell. *How Come It's Called That?: Place Names in the Big Bend Country.* Marathon, TX: Iron Mountain Press, 1997.

Chispa
Fort Davis
Valentine

JEFFERSON

East, Lorecia. *History and Progress of Jefferson County.* Dallas: Royal Publishing Company, 1961.

Beaumont
Cheek
China
Fannett
Gladys
Groves
Guffey
Hamshire
Helbig
La Belle
Meeker
Nederland
Nome
Port Arthur
Voth

JIM HOGG

Hebbronville Chamber of Commerce. *50th Anniversary Jim Hogg County.* Hebbronville, TX: The Chamber, 1963.

Agua Nueva
Cuevitas
Guerra
Hebbronville
Randado
San Antonio Viejo
Thompsonville

JIM WELLS

Pollard, Neva Virginia. *The History of Jim Wells County.* N.p.: n.p., 1945.

Alfred
Alice
Amargosa
Ben Bolt
Casa Blanca
Orange Grove
Palito Blanco
Premont
Sandia
Seeligson
San Diego

JOHNSON

Abernathy, Frances Dickson T. "The Building of Johnson County: And the Settlement of the Communities of the Eastern Portion of the County." Master's thesis, University of Texas, 1936.

Block, Viola. *History of Johnson County and Surrounding Areas.* Waco: Texian Press, 1970.

Smith, Shirley Robert. *Cresson Community Crossroads.* N.p.: S. R. Smith, 1988.

Alvarado
Bono
Burleson
Cleburne
Cresson
Crowley
Godley
Joshua
Lillian
Marystown
Parker
Rio Vista
Venus

JONES

Shelton, Hooper, and Homer Hutto. *First 100 Years of Jones County, Texas.* Stamford, TX: Shelton Press, 1978.

Abilene
Anson
Avoca
Hamlin
Hawley
Lueders
Noodle
Pastura
Radium
Stamford

KARNES

Didear, Hedwig Krell. *A History of Karnes County and Old Helena.* Austin: San Felipe Press, 1969.

Thonhoff, Robert H. "A History of Karnes County." Master's thesis, Southwest Texas State University, 1963.

Bainville
Burnell
Cestohowa
Choate
Coy City
Ecleto
El Oso
Falls City
Gillett
Green
Harmony
Helena
Hobson
Karnes City
Kenedy
Panna Maria
Pawelekville
Runge
Zunkerville

KAUFMAN

Kaufman County Historical Commission. *A History of Kaufman County.* Terrell, TX: Kaufman County Historical Commission, 1978.
Tarpley, Fred. *Place Names of Northeast Texas.* Commerce: East Texas State University, Educational Research and Field Services, 1969.

Ables Springs
Abner
Becker
Cobb
College Mound
Colquitt
Crandall
Elmo
Forney
Gastonia
Hiram
Jiba
Kaufman
Kemp
Lively
Mabank
Peeltown
Poetry
Rand
Rosser
Scurry
Styx
Talty
Terrell
Tolosa

KENDALL

Kendall County Historical Commission. *A History of Kendall County, Texas: Rivers, Ranches, Railroads, Recreation.* Dallas: Taylor, 1984.

Bankersmith
Bergheim
Boerne
Comfort
Kendalia
Kreutzberg
Nelson City
Sisterdale
Waring
Welfare

KENEDY

Allhands, J. L. *Gringo Builders.* N.p.: n.p., 1931.

Armstrong
Norias
Rudolph
Sarita
Turcotte

KENT

Pritchett, Jewell G., and Erma Barfoot Black. *Kent County and Its People.* Rotan, TX: Rotan Advance, 1983.

Clairemont
Girard
Harmony
Jayton

KERR

Bennett, Bob. *Kerr County, Texas, 1856–1956.* San Antonio: Naylor, 1956.
Real, Matilda Marie. "A History of Kerr County, Texas." Master's thesis, University of Texas, 1942.

Camp Verde
Center Point
Hunt
Ingram
Kerrville
Legion

KIMBLE

Fisher, O. C. *It Occurred in Kimble: The Story of a Texas County.* Houston: Anson Jones Press, 1937.

Cleo
Junction
Noxville
Roosevelt
Segovia
Telegraph

KING

King County Historical Society. *King County: Windmills & Barbed Wire.* Quanah, TX: Nortex, 1976.

Dumont
Guthrie

KINNEY

Kinney County: 125 Years of Growth, 1852–1977. N.p.: Kinney County Historical Commission, 1978.

KLEBERG

Bass, Stirling Wesley. "The History of Kleberg County." Master's thesis, University of Texas, 1931.

Kleberg County Historical Commission. *Kleberg County Texas.* Austin: Hart Graphics, 1979.

KNOX

Knox County Historical Society. *Knox County History.* Haskell, TX: Haskell Free Press, 1966.

LA SALLE

Ludeman, Annette Martin. *La Salle: South Texas Brush Country, 1856–1975.* Quanah, TX: Nortex, 1976.

LAMAR

Tarpley, Fred. *Place Names of Northeast Texas.* Commerce: East Texas State University, Educational Research and Field Services, 1969.

LAMB

Scott, Evalyn Parrott. *A History of Lamb County.* N.p.: n.p., 1968.

LAMPASAS

Lampasas History Book Committee. *Lampasas County, Texas: Its History and Its People.* Marceline, MO: Walsworth, 1991.

LAVACA

Boethel, Paul C. *The History of Lavaca County.* Rev. ed. San Antonio: Naylor, 1959.

LEE

Killen, James C. *History of Lee County, Texas.* N.p.: Lee County Historical Survey Committee, 1974.

LEON

Leon County Historical Book Survey Committee. *History of Leon County Texas.* Dallas: Curtis Media, 1986.

LIBERTY

Fincher, Rosalie. "The History of Liberty County." Master's thesis, University of Texas, 1937.

Partlow, Miriam. *Liberty, Liberty County, and the Atascosito District.* Austin: Pemberton Press, 1974.

LIMESTONE

Walter, Ray A. *A History of Limestone County.* Austin: Von Boeckmann-Jones, 1959.

LIPSCOMB

Lipscomb County Historical Survey Committee. *A History of Lipscomb County, Texas 1876–1976.* Lipscomb County Historical Survey Committee, 1976.

LIVE OAK

Sparkman, Ervin L., and Mary Sparkman Roberts. *The People's History of Live Oak County, Texas*. Mesquite, TX: Ide House, 1981.

LLANO

Fry, Tillie Badu Moss. "A History of Llano County, Texas." Master's thesis, University of Texas, 1943.

Oatman, Wilburn. *Llano, Gem of the Hill Country: A History of Llano County, Texas*. Hereford, TX: Pioneer, 1970.

LOVING

Dunn, Robert W. "The History of Loving County, Texas." Master's thesis, University of Texas, 1948.

LUBBOCK

McDonald, Mary Louise. "The History of Lubbock County, Texas." Master's thesis, University of Texas, 1942.

LYNN

Abbe, Donald R. "The History of Lynn County." Master's thesis, Texas Tech University, 1974.

Hill, Frank P., and Pat Hill Jacobs. *Grassroots Upside Down: A History of Lynn County, Texas*. Austin: Eakin, 1986.

MADISON

Madison County Historical Commission. *A History of Madison County, Texas*. Madisonville, TX: The Commission, 1984.

MARION

Bagur, Jacques D. *Antebellum Jefferson, Texas: Everyday Life in an East Texas Town*. Denton, TX: University of North Texas Press, 2012.

Bullard, Lucille Blackburn. *Marion County, Texas, 1860–1870*. Jefferson, TX: n.p., 1965.

Tarpley, Fred. *Jefferson: Riverport to the Southwest*. Wolfe City, TX: Henington Publishing, 1983.

MARTIN

Haggard, Ruby J. H. *Martin County, Texas: Its Land and Its People, 1881–1978*. Dallas: Taylor, 1979.

Liles, Vernen. "Pioneering on the Plains: The History of Martin County, Texas." Master's thesis, University of Texas, 1953.

MASON

Eilers, Kathryn Burford. "A History of Mason County, Texas." Master's thesis, University of Texas, 1939.

Polk, Stella G. *Mason, and Mason County: A History*. Austin: Pemberton Press, 1966.

MATAGORDA

Brown, Shirley Ledwig, Carol Sue Gibbs, and Mary B. Ingram. *Historic Matagorda County*. Houston: D. Armstrong Co., 1986.

Jeter, Lorraine Bruce. *Matagorda: Early History*. Baltimore, MD: Gateway Press, 1974.

MAVERICK

Pingenot, Ben E. *Historical Highlights of Eagle Pass and Maverick County*. Eagle Pass: Eagle Pass Chamber of Commerce, 1971.

McCULLOCH

Barfoot, Jessie Laurie. "A History of McCulloch County, Texas." Master's thesis, University of Texas, 1937.

Spiller, Wayne. *Handbook of McCulloch County History*. Seagraves, TX: Pioneer, 1976.

McLENNAN

Kelley, Dayton. *Handbook of Waco and McLennan County, Texas*. Waco: Texian Press, 1972.

Poage, William Robert. *McLennan County Before 1980*. Waco: Texian Press, 1980.

McMULLEN

McMullen County History Book Committee. *McMullen County History.* Tilden, TX: McMullen County History Book Committee, 1981.
Smyer, Joe Pate. "A History of McMullen County, Texas." Master's thesis, University of Texas, 1952.

MEDINA

Castro Colonies Heritage Association. *The History of Medina County, Texas.* Dallas: National ShareGraphics, 1980.
History of Medina County, Texas. Dallas, TX: National ShareGraphics, 1980.

MENARD

Menard County Historical Society. *Menard County History: An Anthology.* San Angelo, TX: Anchor, 1982.

MIDLAND

Midland County Historical Commission & Midland County Historical Society. *The Pioneer History of Midland County, Tex. 1880–1926.* Dallas: Taylor, 1984.

MILAM

Batte, L. M. A. *History of Milam County, Texas.* San Antonio: Naylor, 1956.
Milam County Heritage Preservation Society. *Matchless Milam: History of Milam County, Texas.* N.p.: Milam County Heritage Preservation Society, 1984.

MILLS

Bowles, Flora Gatlin. *A No Man's Land Becomes a County.* Goldthwaite, TX: Eagle Press, 1978.

MITCHELL

Bradford, Giles. "A History of Mitchell County, Texas." Master's thesis, University of Texas, 1937.

MONTAGUE

Donnell, Guy Renfro. "The History of Montague County, Texas." Master's thesis, University of Texas, 1940.

MONTGOMERY

Montgomery County Genealogical Society. *Montgomery County History*. Conroe, TX: The Society, 1981.

Montgomery, Robin Navarro. *Historic Montgomery County: An Illustrated History of Montgomery County, Texas*. Conroe, TX: Montgomery County Genealogical & Historical Society, 2003.

MOORE

Thomas, Myrna Tryon. *The Windswept Land: A History of Moore County, Tx*. Dumas, TX: Myrna Tryon Thomas, 1967.

MORRIS

Connor, Jean. *A Short History of Morris County*. Daingerfield, TX: Daingerfield Bicentennial Commission, 1976.

Tarpley, Fred. *Place Names of Northeast Texas*. Commerce: East Texas State University, Educational Research and Field Services, 1969.

MOTLEY

Campbell, Harry H. *The Early History of Motley County*. Wichita Falls, TX: Nortex, 1958.

NACOGDOCHES

Haltom, Richard W. *The History of Nacogdoches County Texas*. Austin: Jenkins, 1972.

Partin, James Galloway. "A History of Nacogdoches and Nacogdoches County, Texas to 1877." Master's thesis, University of Texas, 1968.

La Cerda
Laceyville
Lilbert
Looneyville
Mahl
Martinsville
Melrose
Naclina
Nat
Sacul
Swift
Trawick
Woden

NAVARRO

Love, Annie Carpenter. *History of Navarro County*. Dallas: Southwest Press, 1970.

Putnam, Wyvonne. *Navarro County History*. Quanah, TX: Nortex, 1975.

Angus
Barry
Chatfield
Cheneyboro
Corbet
Corsicana
Cryer Creek
Dawson
Dresden
Emhouse
Frost
Goodlow
Goodnight
Hester
Kerens
Navarro
Pelham
Powell
Purdon
Pursley
Retreat
Rice
Roane
Silver City
Spring Hill
Streetman
Winkler

NEWTON

Peavy, Josephine Cochrum. "A History of Newton County, Texas." Master's thesis, University of Texas, 1942.

Adsul
Belgrade
Bleakwood
Bon Wier
Burkeville
Call
Deweyville
Farrsville
Fawil
Hartburg
Howards
Jamestown
Laurel
Mayflower
Quicksand
Salem
Sandjack
Shanklerville (Shankleville)
Stringtown
Toledo
Wiergate

NOLAN

Bradford, Louise. *A History of Nolan County, Texas*. Master's thesis, University of Texas, 1934.

Yeats, E. L., and Hooper Shelton. *History of Nolan County, Texas*. Sweetwater, TX: Shelton Press, 1975.

Blackwell
Eskota
Hylton
Maryneal
Nolan
Roscoe
Sweetwater
Wastella

NUECES

Deviney, Marvin Lee. "The History of Nueces County to 1850." Master's thesis, University of Texas, 1933.

Nueces County Historical Society. *The History of Nueces County*. Austin: Jenkins Publishing, 1972.

Rodman, R. C. Rethinking Corpus Christi. *Names* 66, no. 3 (2018): 166–175.

Agua Dulce
Annaville
Banquete
Bishop
Bluntzer
Calallen
Chapman Ranch
Corpus Christi
Driscoll
Palo Alto
Petronila
Port Aransas
Rabb
Robstown
Violet

OCHILTREE

Ochiltree County Sesquicentennial Committee. *Wheatheart of the Plains*. N.p.: n.p., 1969.

Farnsworth
Huntoon
Notla
Ochiltree
Perryton
Twichell
Waka

OLDHAM

Oldham County Historical Commission. *Oldham County 1881–1981.* Dallas: Taylor, 1981.

Nolan, Frederick. *Tascosa: Its Life and Gaudy Times.* Lubbock, TX: Texas Tech University Press, 2007.

Robertson, Pauline D., and R. L. Robertson. *Cowman's Country: Fifty Frontier Ranches in the Texas Panhandle, 1876–1887.* Amarillo, TX: Paramount, 1981.

Adrian
Boys Ranch
Tascosa
Vega

ORANGE

Williams, Howard C. *Gateway to Texas: The History of Orange and Orange County.* Orange, TX: Heritage House Museum of Orange, 1988.

Bancroft
Bridge City
Connell
Mauriceville
Oilla
Orange
Orangefield
Texla
Vidor

PALO PINTO

Clarke, Mary Whatley. *The Palo Pinto Story.* Fort Worth: Manney, 1956.

Palo Pinto County Historical Association. *History of Palo Pinto County* (Word of Mouth Family History). Dallas: Taylor, 1978.

Brad
Graford
Metcalf Gap
Mineral Wells
Mingus
Oran
Palo Pinto
Salesville
Strawn

PANOLA

Panola County Historical Survey Committee. *Pioneer Panola County.* N.p.: The Committee, 1976.

Beckville
Buncombe
Deadwood
DeBerry
Fair Play
Furrh
Gary
Horton
Carthage
Clayton
Jumbo
Midyett
Snap
Tatum
Woods

PARKER

Holland, Gustavus Adolphus. *"The Double Log Cabin": Being a Brief Symposium of the Early History of Parker County, Together with Short Biographical Sketches of Early Settlers and Their Trials.* Weatherford, TX: Herald Publishing, 1931.

Parker County Historical Commission. *History of Parker County.* Weatherford, TX: The Commission, 1980.

Adell
Advance
Agnes
Aledo
Anneta
Authon
Azle
Baker
Bennett
Brock
Buckner
Cresson
Dennis
Dicey
Garner
Goshen
Millsap
Peaster
Poolville
Reno
Tin Top
Weatherford
Whitt

PARMER

Lewis, Nelson. *A History of Parmer County, Texas.* Quanah, TX: Nortex, 1974.

Black
Bovina
Farwell
Friona
Hub
Lariat
Lazbuddie
Rhea
Wilsey

PECOS

Daggett, Marsha Lea. *Pecos County History.* Canyon, TX: Staked Plains Press, 1984.

Hughes, Alton. *Pecos: A History of the Pioneer West*. Seagraves, TX: Pioneer, 1978.

POLK

Haynes, Emma R. *The History of Polk County, Texas*. Livingston, TX: Polk County Historical Commission, 1996.

Rothe, Aline Thompson. "The History of Education in Polk County, Texas." Master's thesis: University of Texas, 1934.

POTTER

Key, Della T. *In the Cattle Country: History of Potter County*. Austin: Eakin, 1980.

PRESIDIO

Gregg, John Ernest. "The History of Presidio County." Master's thesis, University of Texas, 1933.

Popik, Barry. *Marfa*. 2008. barrypopik.com/index.php/new_york_city/entry/marfa_summary.

RAINS

Tarpley, Fred. *Place Names of Northeast Texas*. Commerce: East Texas State University, Educational Research and Field Services, 1969.

RANDALL

Warwick, Clyde W. (Mrs.). *The Randall County Story, from 1541 to 1910*. Hereford, TX: Pioneer, 1969.

REAGAN

Werst, J. L. *The Reagan County Story*. Seagraves, TX: Pioneer, 1974.

REAL

Lewis, Grace Lorene. "A History of Real County, Texas." Master's thesis, University of Texas, 1956.

RED RIVER

Kerbow, Blewett Barnes. "The Early History of Red River County 1817–1865." Master's thesis, University of Texas, 1936.

Stroud, Martha S. *Gateway to Texas: History of*

Red River County. Austin: Nortex, 1997.
Tarpley, Fred. *Place Names of Northeast Texas*. Commerce: East Texas State University, Educational Research and Field Services, 1969.

REEVES

Hughes, Alton. *Pecos: A History of the Pioneer West*. Seagraves, TX: Pioneer, 1978.

REFUGIO

Huson, Hobart. *Refugio: A Comprehensive History of Refugio County from Aboriginal Times*. Woodsboro, TX: Rooke Foundation, 1953.
Moore, Robert Lee. "History of Refugio County." Master's thesis, University of Texas, 1937.

ROBERTS

Roberts County Historical Committee. *History of Miami and Roberts County*. Miami, TX: Roberts County Historical Committee, 1976.

ROBERTSON

Parker, Richard Denny. *Historical Recollections of Robertson County, Texas: With Biographical and Genealogical Notes on the Pioneers and Their Families*. Salado, TX: Anson Jones Press, 1995.

ROCKWALL

County Historical Foundation. *Rockwall County History*. Dallas: Taylor, 1984.

RUNNELS

Poe, Charlsie. *Runnels Is My County*. San Antonio: Naylor, 1970.
Self, Houston Bailey. "A History of Runnels County." Master's thesis, Texas Technological College, 1931.
Skinner, A. E. *Rowena Country*. N.p.: Nortex, 1973.

RUSK

Rusk County Historical Commission. *Rusk County History, Texas.* Henderson, TX: Rusk County Historical Commission, 1982.
Winfrey, Dorman H. "A History of Rusk County, Texas." Master's thesis, University of Texas, 1951.

SABINE

McDaniel, Robert Cecil. *Sabine County, Texas: The First One Hundred and Fifty Years (1836–1986).* Waco: Texian Press, 1987.
White, Edna McDaniel, and Blanche Finley Toole. *Sabine County Historical Sketches and Genealogical Records.* Beaumont: LaBelle Print Co., 1972.

SAN AUGUSTINE

Jones, Charla. *The Cradle of Texas: A Pictorial History of San Augustine County.* Austin: Eakin, 1997.

SAN JACINTO

San Jacinto Historical Commission. *Dim Trails and Blurred Footprints: A History of San Jacinto County, Texas.* Dallas: Taylor, 1982.

SAN PATRICIO

Guthrie, Keith. *The History of San Patricio County.* Austin: Eakin, 1986.

SAN SABA

Hamrick, Alma Ward. *The Call of the San Saba: A History of San Saba County.* San Saba: San Saba County Historical Society, 2011.
San Saba Historical Commission. *San Saba County History 1856–1983.* N.p.: n.p., 1983.

SCHLEICHER

Schleicher County Historical Society. *A History of Schleicher County*. San Angelo, TX: Anchor, 1985.

SCURRY

Scurry County Book Committee. *Footprints Across Scurry County*. Lubbock, TX: Specialty Publishing, 1984.

SHACKELFORD

Biggers, Don Hampton, and Joan Farmer. *Shackelford County Sketches*. Albany, TX: Clear Fork Press, 1974.

SHELBY

Shelby County Historical Commission. *History of Shelby County, Texas*. Dallas: Curtis Media, 1988.

SHERMAN

McDaniel, Marylou. *God, Grass and Grit*. Hereford, TX: Pioneer, 1971.

SMITH

Glover, Robert W. *Tyler & Smith County, Texas: An Historical Survey*. Tyler: American Bicentennial Committee of Tyler-Smith County, 1976.

Woldert, Albert. *A History of Tyler and Smith County, Texas*. San Antonio: Naylor, 1948.

SOMERVELL

Nunn, William Curtis. *Somervell: Story of a Texas County*. Ft. Worth, TX: Texas Christian University Press, 1975.

STARR

Lyndon B. Johnson School of Public Affairs. *Colonias in the Lower Rio Grande Valley of South Texas: A Summary Report*. Austin: LBJ School of Public Affairs Publications, 1977.

STEPHENS

Hartsfield, Loy William. "A History of Stephens County." Master's thesis, University of Texas, 1929.

STERLING

Daniels, Beverly. *Milling Around Sterling County: A History of Sterling County.* Canyon, TX: Staked Plains Press, 1976.

Watkins, Ira L. "The History of Sterling County." Master's thesis, Texas Technological College, 1939.

STONEWALL

Stonewall County Historical Commission. *A History of Stonewall County.* Aspermont, TX: Stonewall County Historical Commission, 1979.

SUTTON

Sutton County Historical Society. *Sutton County, 1887–1977.* Sonora, TX: Sutton County Historical Society, 1979.

SWISHER

Swisher County Historical Commission. *Windmilling: 101 Years of Swisher County, Texas History, 1876–1977.* Dallas: Taylor, 1978.

TARRANT

Roark, Carol, ed. *Fort Worth & Tarrant County, An Historical Guide.* Fort Worth: Texas Christian University Press, 2003.

Sergeant, George William. "Early History of Tarrant County." Master's thesis, University of Texas, 1953.

Young, Charles Hutchinson. *Grapevine Area History: Supplement 1979–1989.* Dallas: Taylor, 1989.

TAYLOR

Zachry, Juanita Daniel. *A History of Rural Taylor County.* Burnet, TX: Nortex, 1995.

TERRELL

Downie, Alice Evans. *Terrell County, Texas: Its Past, Its People.* San Angelo, TX: Anchor, 1978.

Dryden
Malvado
Sanderson

TERRY

Terry County Historical Commission, and Terry County Historical Survey Committee. *Early Settlers of Terry: A History of Terry County, Texas.* N.p.: n.p., 1985.

Brownfield
Gomez
Lahey
Lockettville
Tokio
Wellman

THROCKMORTON

Harvick, Mary Lou. *Throckmorton County History.* Lubbock, TX: Specialty Publishing, 1984.

Elbert
Lusk
Woodson

TITUS

Jurney, Richard Loyall. *History of Titus County, 1846 to 1960.* Dallas: Royal Publishing, 1961.

Argo
Blodgett
Cookville
Green Hill
Liberty Hill
Midway
Monticello
Mount Pleasant
Talco
Winfield

TOM GREEN

Bitner, Grace. "The History of Tom Green County, Texas." Master's thesis, University of Texas, 1931.

Green, William Elton. "Land Settlement in West Texas: Tom Green County, A Case Study, 1874–1903." PhD dissertation, Texas Tech University, 1981.

Carlsbad
Christoval
Harriet
Knickerbocker
Mereta
Orient
San Angelo
Tankersley
Vancourt
Veribest
Wall

TRAVIS

Barkley, Mary Starr. *History of Travis County and Austin, 1839–1899.* Austin: Steck, 1981.

Hardy, Aloise Walker. "A History of Travis County, 1832–1865." Master's thesis, University of Texas, 1938.

Austin
Barton Creek
Bee Cave
Colton
Creedmoor
Daffan
Del Valle
Dessau
Dunlap
Garfield
Littig
Lund
Maha
Manchaca
Manda
Manor
McNeil
Merrelltown
New Sweden
Pflugerville
Pilot Knob
Volente
Webberville

TRINITY

Hensley, Patricia Bartley, Joseph Woodrow Hensley, and Trinity County Book Committee. *Trinity County Beginnings.* Dallas: Curtis Media, 1986.

Apple Springs
Carlisle
Centralia
Chita
Friday
Friendship
Groveton
Helmic
Josserand
Nigton
Nogalus Prairie
Pennington
Saron
Sebastopol
Trevat
Trinity
Westville

TYLER

Moseley, Lou Ella. *Pioneer Days of Tyler County.* Fort Worth: Miran, 1975.

UPSHUR

Baird, G. H. *A Brief History of Upshur County.* Gilmer, TX: The Gilmer Mirror, 1946.
Loyd, Doyal T. *A History of Upshur County, Texas.* N.p.: Texian Press, 1970.

UPTON

Eagleton, N. Ethie. *On the Last Frontier: A History of Upton County, Texas.* El Paso: Texas Western Press, University of Texas, 1971.

UVALDE

Carmichael, Lois M. "The History of Uvalde County." Master's thesis, Southwest Texas State University, 1944.
El Progreso Club. *A Proud Heritage: A History of Uvalde County, Texas.* Uvalde, TX: El Progreso Club, 1975.

VAL VERDE

Escamilla, Romelia G., and Gwene Askew. *The Spirit of Val Verde.* Del Rio, TX: D. S. Zertuche, 1985.

VAN ZANDT

Hall, Margaret Elizabeth. *A History of Van Zandt County.* Austin: Jenkins Publishing Company, 1976.
Van Zandt County History Book Committee, and Van Zandt County Genealogical Society. *The History of Van Zandt County, Texas.* Dallas, TX: National ShareGraphics, 1991.

VICTORIA

Rose, Victor M., J. W. Petty, and Kate Stoner O'Connor. *History of Victoria County.* Victoria, TX: Book Mart, 1961.
Victoria County Genealogical Society. *The History and Heritage of Victoria County.* Austin: Nortex, 2000.

Anaqua
Bloomington
Coletoville
Dacosta
Fordtran
Inez
Kemper City
McFaddin
Mission Valley
Nursery
Placedo
Raisin
Telferner
Victoria
Wood Hi

WALKER

Crews, D'Anne McAdams. *Huntsville and Walker County, Texas, a Bicentennial History.* Huntsville, TX: Sam Houston State University Press, 1976.

Walker County Historical Commission, and Walker County Genealogical Society. *Walker County, Texas: A History.* Dallas: Curtis Media, 1986.

Bath
Crabbs Prairie
Dodge
Elmina
Hawthorne
Huntsville
Kittrell
New Waverly
Phelps
Riverside
San Jacinto

WALLER

Waller County Historical Survey Committee. *A History of Waller County, Texas.* N.p.: n.p., 1973.

White, Frank Edd. "A History of the Territory That Now Constitutes Waller County, Texas, from 1821 to 1884." Master's thesis, University of Texas, 1936.

Brookshire
Cardiff
Fetzer
Fields Store
Hegar
Hempstead
Howth
Katy
Monaville
Pattison
Waller

WARD

Texas Permian Historical Society. *Water, Oil, Sand and Sky: A History of Ward County, Texas.* Monahans, TX: Junior Chamber of Commerce, 1962.

Ward County Historical Commission. *Ward County 1887–1977.* N.p.: Taylor Publishing, 1977.

Barstow
Grandfalls
Monahans
Pyote
Royalty
Wickett

WASHINGTON

Dietrich, Wilfred O. *The Blazing Story of Washington County.* Wichita Falls, TX: Nortex, 1973.

Schmidt, Charles Frank. *History of Washington County.* San Antonio: Naylor, 1949.

Berlin
Brenham
Burton
Chappell Hill
Earlywine
Gay Hill
Independence
Klump
La Bahia
Latium
Muellersville
Rehburg
Washington
Wesley
Wiedeville
William Penn
Zionville

WEBB

Green, Stanley C. *The Rise and Fall of Rio Grande Settlements: A History of Webb County.* Laredo, TX: Border Studies Publishing, 1991.

Murillo, Hermelinda Aguirre. "A History of Webb County." Master's thesis, Southwest Texas State Teachers College, 1941.

Aguilares
Botines
Bruni
Callaghan
El Cenizo
Laredo
Las Tiendas
Los Huisaches
Los Nopalitos
Los Ojuelos

Minera
Mirando City
Nye
Oilton
Pescadito
Webb

WHARTON

Williams, Annie Lee. *A History of Wharton County, Texas, 1846–1961.* Austin: Von-Boeckmann-Jones, 1964.

Boling
Bonus
Burr
Danevang
Dinsmore
Don-Tol
East Bernard
Egypt
El Campo
Hillje
Hungerford
Iago
Lane City
Lissie
Louise
Mackay
New Taiton
Newgulf
Nottawa
Pierce
Sorrelle

WHEELER

Perkins, William Coy Perkins. "A History of Wheeler County, Texas." Master's thesis, University of Texas, 1938.

Allison
Benonine
Briscoe
Gageby
Kellerville
Lela
Mobeetie
Pakan
Shamrock
Twitty
Wheeler

WICHITA

Kelly, Louise. *Wichita County Beginnings.* Burnet, TX: Eakin, 1982.

Allendale
Bacon
Burkburnett
Clara
Electra
Haynesville
Iowa Park
Kadane Corner
Kamay
Thrift
Wichita Falls

WILBARGER

Wilbarger County Historical Commission. *Wilbarger County.* Vernon, TX: Wilbarger County Historical Commission, 1986.

Doans
Elliott
Grayback
Harrold
Lockett
Odell
Oklaunion
Tolbert
Vernon
White City

WILLACY

Allhands, J. L. *Gringo Builders.* N.p.: n.p., 1931.

Lasara
Lyford
Porfirio
Port Mansfield
Raymondville
San Perlita
Santa Monica
Sebastian
Willamar
Yturria

WILLIAMSON

Scarbrough, Clara Stearns. *Land of Good Water (Takachue Pouetsu): A Williamson County, Texas, History.* Georgetown, TX: Williamson County Sun Publishers, 1998.
Williamson County Genealogical Society, Jean Shroyer, and Hazel D. Hood. *Williamson County, Texas: Its History and Its People.* Austin: N.p.: Nortex, 1985.

Andice
Bagdad
Bartlett
Beyersville
Cedar Park
Circleville
Coupland
Florence
Frame Switch
Georgetown
Hare
Hoxie
Hutto
Jarrell
Jollyville
Jonah
Keelersville
Leander
Noack
Norman
Round Rock
Schwertner
Taylor
Theon

WILSON

Stadler, Louise. *Wilson County History.* Dallas, Tex: Taylor, 1990.

WINKLER

Wink Wednesday Study Club. *A History of Winkler County.* Wink, TX: Wink Bulletin, 1942.

Winkler County History Book Committee. *A History of Winkler County, 1887–1984: A Collection of Historical Sketches and Family Histories.* Lubbock: Specialty Publishing, 1984.

WISE

Gregg, Rosalie. *History of Wise County: A Link With the Past.* Austin: Nortex, 1975.

Moore, Mary Cates. *Centennial History of Wise County.* N.p.: Story Book Press, 1953.

WOOD

Hodson, Kay Barnes, and Herman F. Benthul. *Wood County, 1850–1900.* Marceline, MO: Walsworth Publishing, 1976.

YOAKUM

Yoakum County Historical Commission. *Yoakum County: From Sod to 1985.* Dallas: Taylor, 1986.

YOUNG

Crouch, Carrie Johnson. *Young County: History and Biography.* Rev. ed. Austin: State Historical Association, 1956.

ZAPATA

Fish, Jean Y. *Zapata County Roots Revisited.* San Antonio: Borderlands Press, 2004.

ZAVALA

Tate, R. C. "A History of Zavala County, Texas." Master's thesis, Southwest Texas State Teachers College, 1942.

Zavala County Historical Commission. *Now and Then in Zavala County: A History of Zavala County, Texas.* Crystal City, TX: Zavala County Historical Commission, 1985.